Managerial Economics

Managerial Economics

A European Text
Theories, Policies and Problems

GEORGE A. PETROCHILOS

"The customer is the most important
person in our business"
M. Gandhi

palgrave
macmillan

First published 2004 by
PALGRAVE MACMILLAN
Houndmills, Basingstoke, Hampshire RG21 6XS and
175 Fifth Avenue, New York, N.Y. 10010
Companies and representatives throughout the world

PALGRAVE MACMILLAN is the global academic imprint of the Palgrave
Macmillan division of St. Martin's Press, LLC and of Palgrave Macmillan Ltd.
Macmillan® is a registered trademark in the United States, United Kingdom
and other countries. Palgrave is a registered trademark in the European
Union and other countries.

ISBN 0–333–99423–X

This book is printed on paper suitable for recycling and made from fully
managed and sustained forest sources.

A catalogue record for this book is available from the British Library.

Library of Congress Cataloging-in-Publication Data
Petrochilos George A., 1937–
  Managerial economics : a European text : theory, policies,
and problems / George A. Petrochilos.
    p.cm.
  Includes bibliographical references and index.
  ISBN 0–333–99423–X (pbk)
    1. Managerial economics. I. Title.

HD30.22.P48 2003
330′.024′658—dc22   2003060862

10   9   8   7   6   5   4   3   2   1
13   12   11   10   09   08   07   06   05   04
Printed in China

To
Sophia – Athanasios – Panayiota
For their patience and help

Contents

Prolegomena

Managerial Economics is the application of economic theory to problems of decision making within the firm. In this respect, *Managerial Economics* helps bridge the gap between abstract economic analysis and everyday issues and problems facing management.

The present volume is the product of 17 years teaching of Managerial Economics to final year undergraduate students on various courses at Coventry University. It is mainly intended for students in the second or, preferably, third year of degree courses in Economics, Business Studies, Business Administration as well as students following MBA courses, although it could prove useful for a number of courses leading to professional qualifications too.

The book emphasises the role of economic analysis and quantitative techniques in managerial decision making and takes a problem-solving approach throughout. This approach shows through illustrative examples how mathematical and econometric methods, where applicable, can sharpen the conclusions of economic theory, and provide useful quantitative evidence to support those conclusions. There are also at the end of most chapters problems and exercises to consolidate the reader's understanding of the issues covered. Another pedagogical feature of the book is that at the end of various chapters there are special appendices discussing further certain points raised in the text and, in particular, giving illustrations from real-world situations to illuminate the analytical and theoretical discussion. The real-world cases are drawn from the experiences of various firms in a number of European countries. For student convenience and ease, each chapter is followed by appropriate bibliography, for further reading.

Approximately, half the chapters of the book, where aspects of optimisation are discussed, make use of elementary calculus, in addition to diagrammatic techniques and discursive argumentation. Despite the use of quantitative techniques, the focus is on economic principles and analysis and most of the quantitative tools required for the purposes of following some of the arguments are developed from first principles, within the book. However, it would be useful if readers have been exposed to a basic course in Mathematics and Statistics as well as Microeconomics, as is the case, certainly, with most Economics, Business Studies and related degree courses in British Universities and elsewhere, and we assume that this is the case with most readers of this book. It is expected that if there are students, mainly in MBA courses, who have not studied Economics and quantitative methods formally before, such students have sufficient alternative skills and knowledge, which will allow them, with the explanations offered on mathematical tools and econometrics and a little investment of their time, to follow the argument too and, thus, benefit from the discussion.

The structure of the book is as follows: We start by examining the relation of Managerial Economics to other areas of economics and other disciplines, such as Mathematics, Statistics and Operations Research and Econometrics and we go on to give a short review of the basic tools of optimisation, which will be used later in the book. We then move on to discuss the theories of the firm and of profits, and follow it up with an appendix on the innovation record and success of the Finnish firm Nokia. This is followed by demand analysis and sales forecasting. In the context of the latter, we provide a lengthy appendix on multiple regression analysis, and illustrate the discussion with two examples. Subsequently, we look at aspects of supply, such as production theory and costs. At the end of the chapter on production we examine, in an appendix, the fortunes of the Greek firm FAGE, and at the end of the chapter on costs there is an illustration of cost-cutting exercise at Corus (formerly British Steel). The next chapter introduces the usefulness of linear programming (LP), by means of a lengthy example, which helps to illustrate the simplex method. In addition, we provide in appendices a diagrammatic exposition of LP. The next chapter looks at aspects of marketing and advertising, and also it contains an illustration of the Marks & Spencer marketing philosophy and a case study on advertising on and inside taxis. Chapter 10 is a lengthy one as it provides a detailed analysis of pricing in theory and practice, by considering pricing problems under different market structures and particular settings and it concludes with an appendix on the steps to be taken in the pricing process. The next three chapters are concerned explicitly with dynamic changes and long-run, strategic decisions by the firm, as well as problems of risk and uncertainty. Thus, chapter 11 gives a detailed analysis of the problems of capital budgeting (internal growth) looking at appraisal techniques, risk and sources of finance. This is followed, in Chapter 12, by an explicit analysis of the problem of risk, uncertainty and decision theory, and an illustration, in an appendix, of how to reduce financial risk by means of future contracts. Aspects of external growth and size are treated in Chapter 13 through a consideration of mergers and acquisitions and joint-venture formation, particularly, international joint ventures. In the same chapter we also analyse the decision of firms to become multinational and consider, among others, the various theories of foreign direct investment, and provide an illustration of a cross-border merger, that is the VodafoneAirTouch–Mannesmann takeover. The penultimate chapter looks at the role of the public sector and public regulation, by examining the nature of public enterprises, privatised utilities and how such utilities are regulated. The same chapter gives a detailed exposition of competition policy (or antimonopoly legislation) in the US, UK and the EU. We highlight various aspects of competition policy in two appendices, which look into: who does what in British and EU competition policy; and merger control of German companies by the Bundeskartellamt and the European Commission. The final chapter represents a novelty in Managerial Economics textbooks, as it deals with the vexed question of ethics in business. Ethical questions have emerged as important issues in the business world worldwide in the last 30–35 years with specialist chairs in universities and specialist journals devoted to the subject, while organisations such OECD and the UN have prepared business codes on proper behaviour, to fight corruption and fraud.

We appreciate that in modularised and also semesterised courses it may not, and probably will not, be possible to deal with all aspects covered in this book. Clearly, the decision of what can be included and what can be left out will depend on what students have covered earlier in their studies, and only the teachers taking such classes can answer such questions, as they are the best judges in this case, and so the decision can be left safely to them. However, a course which looks at how economic analysis and quantitative methods can be profitably used to help management arrive at better business decisions must cover aspects of demand analysis and sales forecasting, production theory (single and multi-product firms), cost analysis, linear programming, marketing – advertising, pricing and output determination in theory and practice, capital budgeting, risk and uncertainty, growth, size of firms and the role of government. Depending on what students have already covered a syllabus can be constructed around the core material, which is provided by sales forecasting, multi-product firms, pricing in practice, capital budgeting, growth, size of firms and public regulation.

Acknowledgements

This book grew out of my teaching managerial economics to undergraduate and postgraduate courses at Coventry University for seventeen years, and other subjects for much longer. Naturally, during this period many debts have been incurred both to colleagues and former students, who over the years have helped with their criticisms and comments to sharpen the argument and clarify many points. I am grateful to various colleagues who either have read patiently parts of this book and have made perceptive and timely comments, or have provided me with helpful materials for the preparation of this text. Therefore, I am happy to take this opportunity to acknowledge their contribution and thank them for their help.

In particular, I thank Professor Emeritus Dr. Helga Grote, Manheim, Germany; Dr. A. Rovamo, international business coordinator, Ammattikorkeakoulu, Finland; Dr. C. Veloutsou, Department of Business and Management, University of Glasgow, UK; and Herr E. Stoll, Augsburg, Germany for preparing a number of illustrative cases that appear as appendices in the book.

Also, I want to express my gratitude to Dr. Ben Brobbey, Dr. Deb Ghosh, Mr. David Blight, Mr. Robert Evans, Mr. S. Hughes, Mr. Keith Redhead, Mr. Timothy Rodgers and Mr. S. Thandi all of Coventry University for their painstaking help at various stages in the preparation of the book. In fact, they have done such an excellent job that I am inclined to blame them for any mistakes that may be found! On second thoughts, however, I must absolve them of that, and accept that I alone am responsible for any errors and omissions that may remain.

Finally, a big thanks is due to Mr. Paul Jones of computing services and Mrs. Sandra Johnson, Mrs. Sally Sharman and Mrs. Iris Kaczkowski all of Coventry Business School for considerable technical support over the years with the preparation of the text for publication.

chapter one

Scope and Method of Managerial Economics

Learning outcomes

After studying this chapter you should know about:

- The nature of managerial economics

- Methods of managerial economics

- Its relation to microeconomics

- Its relation to macroeconomics

- Its relation to mathematics

- Its relation to statistics and operation research

- Its relation to econometrics

- Its relation to decision theory

1.1 WHAT IS MANAGERIAL ECONOMICS?

Managerial Economics is the application of economic theory to problems of decision making within the firm, so as the latter can achieve its aims and objectives in the most efficient manner. In this respect it helps in bridging the gap between abstract economic analysis and everyday practical issues and problems facing management. While Managerial Economics, sometimes also referred to as Business Economics, is directly applicable to business organisations, its methods and analysis are also relevant for managing non-profit bodies and public authorities.

Normally, in Economics we are faced with the problem of allocating scarce resource among competing ends. Thus, we are required to consider various trade-offs and choices between alternative courses of action. Managerial Economics is concerned with the allocation of the firm's (or for that matter any other manage-ment unit's) limited resources among that unit's activities, in a way that achieves the best possible result in terms of its objectives. This is referred to as the problem of optimisation. While for a variety of reasons optimal solutions may be unlikely to occur in practice and sub-optimisation may be the norm, nevertheless the con-cern of Managerial Economics on such solutions and, generally, sound decisions helps provide certain benchmarks against which one can judge actual perform-ance and take measures to improve such performance, particularly, if the latter falls significantly short of its benchmarks. Thus, Managerial Economics is goal-oriented.

In particular, Managerial Economics is called upon to answer questions regard-ing the making or buying of products; the type of products and services a firm should produce; the methods and techniques of production to be used; the kind and quantity of inputs to be employed in the productive process; the level of output to be produced; the price or prices to be charged; the timing for the replacement of plant and equipment; the choice between alternative machinery; the size and location of new plant including foreign locations and as mentioned earlier how capital should be allocated. These questions can best be answered when the firm has certain objectives or goals to achieve, so that the answers contribute to the achievement of the firm's objectives.

Whether the management unit is a business organisation geared to making profit, or a government agency or a non-profit body such as an hospital or an uni-versity, it faces up to a number of similar problems, namely, how best to use its existing physical and pecuniary resources to achieving its goals. In the case of a business firm this goal can be stated, for example, as profit or sales or growth max-imisation or something different. In the case of a hospital the goal to be achieved may be the maximum number of patients to be treated at an adequate standard and, similarly, in the case of an university the goal may be to educate the max-imum number of students at an approved standard. These goals have to be achieved subject to the various constraints operating in each particular case, which are, typ-ically, given in the form of physical and human capital resources of all kinds and the budget of the management unit. Consequently, a business firm will try to maximise, say, profit subject to technological and market information given by its limited available resources such as factories, buildings, machinery, materials, vari-ous kinds of labour, and their prices as well as the prices of the goods and services it will be producing and its budget. For a hospital the goal may be to maximise the number of patients treated to an 'adequate' standard (clearly, the 'adequate' will have to be defined beforehand) subject to utilising its existing resources in the form of buildings, beds, equipment, operating theatres, doctors, nurses, administrators and so on and its budget. Similarly, the goal of an university may be to educate the maximum number of qualifying candidates to an 'approved' standard (again the 'approved' will have to be pre-determined) subject to its limited resources of buildings, lecture theatres, laboratories, equipment, teaching staff, technical and administrative staff and so on and its budget. Alternatively, the goal may be stated as obtaining a given level of 'output' subject to the minimisation of the costs of producing that 'output'.

1.2   METHODOLOGICAL ISSUES IN MANAGERIAL ECONOMICS

The above are some of the very broad tasks that Managerial Economics is called to tackle and provide solutions to. And the solutions to these problems need to be optimal, or best, if resources are not to be misused or wasted. For this purpose Managerial Economics requires a sound analytical underpinning provided by economic theory and various quantitative methods and techniques provided by other disciplines, such as mathematics, econometrics, statistics, operations research (OR) and so on. If one is concerned with questions of optimisation, one needs to use and understand some of the basic optimisation methods available, and the idea of modelling, which is used to analyse and predict certain kinds of economic behaviour. Given that sound decision making requires strong supportive quantitative evidence, it becomes clear that the use of such techniques and methods is necessary.

In economic modelling we can use the deductive or inductive methods. The deductive method was developed by Aristotle in his Λογικά (Logic) in order to analyse real-world phenomena; he called it όργανον (organon–tool), since it was not a science in itself but an instrument in the use of scientists. Aristotle's method simply prevented scientists and philosophers to draw wrong conclusions from their premises. Essentially, the method took the form of rigorously correct deduction from one or more first principles, which are taken as self-evidently true. Yet, whereas this is how this method was applied during mediaeval times, Aristotle himself was not accepting first principles without examination and testing, which would make him the father of research too. The deductive method can be used both by natural and physical sciences as well as social sciences. Accordingly, in economics starting with the real world, we need to simplify the complexities of that world by means of theoretical abstraction. The result is a logical model that is suitable to explain the phenomena we observe. By logical argument (i.e., deduction) we arrive at logical or model conclusions, which can be transformed, by means of theoretical interpretation, into conclusions about the real world. Therefore, the model is used to arrive at conclusions or predictions about important aspects of economic behaviour. Consequently, in the deductive method, one moves from the general to the specific, since a hypothesis (theory) is proposed, which can consist of definitions and certain first principles, and then logical deduction is applied to develop predictions and, finally, test such predictions against the facts.

By contrast, the alternative inductive method was introduced by Francis Bacon in his book *Novum Organum* (New Organ), was improved by Isaac Newton, and was finalised by John Stuart Mill. The inductive method is the logical approach from the particular observations (such as experiments, measurements and so on) to the formulation of general statements or laws. According to the inductive method we start with the facts whose regularity helps to induce a theory, and which by logical deduction actually predicts the facts observed. In the inductive method one moves from the specific to the general, since the observation of particular phenomena – through for example, experiments – helps us to generalise, i.e., to formulate a general theory of law, which in turn can explain and predict such phenomena.

In terms of methodological positions we can distinguish one group of economists at one extreme of the spectrum, who since the times of John Stuart Mill (1806–73) reject testing and believe that economic theory is not susceptible to verification or refutation on empirical grounds. These people, called *praxeologists* or *extreme apriorists*, believe that the fundamental premises and axioms of economics are absolutely true; that the theorems and deductions from these axioms by the use of logic are true; that there is no need for empirical testing of either the theorems or the axioms and that the deduced theorems could not be tested, even if it were desirable to do so (Machlup, 1955).

At the other extreme of the spectrum of methodological positions there is a group of economists called *ultraempiricists*, who refuse to accept at any level of analysis propositions that are not independently verifiable (Machlup, 1955). They prefer to start with the facts, but this sacrifices the simplicity that is sought from the complexities of the real world; and they are deprived of model analysis, which could have enabled them to reach general conclusions.

Inevitably, a third middle-of-the-road methodological position has emerged that of *'logical positivism'* that has gained significant acceptance among economists. According to this position, the basic axioms and premises or assumptions of economic theory are not subject to empirical verification. However, the conclusions, or prediction and theorems of a model must be tested and verified against the real world. Thus, model predictions must be capable of being falsified by the real world. Proposed theories or models failing the falsification test are rejected, and only those theories whose predictions are in broad agreement with the real world can be acceptable as working hypotheses and should be open to constructive improvement, as and when additional information becomes available. It is this third position that is, largely, employed in Managerial Economics and the one adopted in this book.

1.3 RELATION OF MANAGERIAL ECONOMICS TO OTHER AREAS OF STUDY

The foregone discussion indicates that, in order for sound decision making in the area of Managerial Economics to take place, testing of various hypotheses is necessary but at the same time the hypotheses to be tested have to be formulated and specified by reference not only to the relevant economic theory but also the appropriate quantitative techniques. Thus, we expect a close connection between Managerial Economics on the one hand and microeconomics, macroeconomics, statistics, econometrics, OR and decision theory. In addition, Managerial Economics is related to other fields, among which we can include marketing, business administration, business policy, accounting and finance. Therefore, the managerial economist must be prepared to utilise concepts and methods from all these disciplines and areas of study to accomplish his task in helping achieve sound decisions within the management unit.

1.3.1 Relation to microeconomics

The bedrock of Managerial Economics is provided by microeconomic theory, which offers the bulk of concepts and analytical tools for the study and, particularly, the applications of the subject. Microeconomics encompasses the theories of markets and of the firm, that is, economic theory referring to economic agents such as consumers and producers, be they individuals or organisations.

In the present book we provide an overview of those concepts and tools that managerial economists will require in order to deal with the day-to-day business problems they are likely to face. However, since the intention of the book is to provide practical advice to the managerial economist or the business manager, the emphasis is on practical applications, and so only those theoretical issues are considered here that are thought to provide the necessary background for a better understanding of the issues involved. The book is not a repetition of microeconomic theory, which can be found in any text on microeconomics, and which most readers will be expected to have acquired earlier in their studies. Instead, the present book tries to emphasise applications of the subject to problems of decision making in various areas, such as, for example, sales and cost forecasting, linear programming, capital budgeting, risk analysis and so on.

1.3.2 Relation to macroeconomics

Economic agents whether they are individuals or large business enterprises and organisations do not operate in a vacuum. Instead, they operate within a macroeconomic environment provided largely by the economic and other policies of the governments of the countries of their domicile and/or operations. Consequently, the particular macroeconomic environment business organisations face represents some form of a constraint of which firms must be aware, and take cognisance of, since this economic environment underpins much of their activity. At the same time, it must also be recognised that the policies and activities of business organisations, in general, affect the overall economic environment, through their role in the determination of the circular flow of income or output.

For example, of primary concern to Managerial Economics are aspects of fiscal and monetary policy, which determine rates and levels of taxation, as well as interest rates that have an impact on the investment and saving plans of economic agents. These plans affect growth, which, in turn, determines levels of income and economic activity. When it comes to forecasting sales, business firms have to incorporate into their models macroeconomic variables, such as disposable national income, interest rates, inflation rates and so on that enter the modelling exercise as predetermined variables. Therefore, a managerial economist must be aware of the role and significance of the macroeconomic environment and how this environment is likely to affect the plans and policies of the business organisation. Thus, for a proper economic interpretation of results of the quantitative exercise a good understanding of macroeconomics is both desirable and necessary.

1.3.3   Relation to mathematics

By now it must be obvious that since Managerial Economics is concerned with the process of optimisation, the various quantitative methods provided by Mathematics are both useful and indispensable tools not only for the sharper understanding of the subject but also for its applications to everyday business issues, since they provide the necessary quantitative evidence to back up complementary discursive arguments in a debate. Quantitative methods help management in the provision of optimal solutions to a number of problems, and such solutions even when not attained in practice are, nevertheless, indicative to management of the direction of change required.

However, this book is not about mathematics or mathematical economics. Thus, mathematics is not used for its own sake and only basic mathematical techniques are used for illustrative purposes throughout. More complicated techniques are provided in the bibliography and are left for the interested readers to pursue at their own pace. However, the techniques used sharpen the focus and help in decision making within the firm. Therefore, the pay-offs from a little investment in such techniques are likely to be considerable. Besides, for most students of Managerial Economics such quantitative techniques are provided in other parts of their courses and, consequently, students are very likely to be familiar with them already. In the unlikely event that some readers may be unfamiliar with the basic techniques, there is an early chapter on aspects of optimisation, which, hopefully, will redress the deficiency.

This book has adopted a problem solving approach, where it has been deemed necessary and the argument proceeds through the use of examples. The appropriate and necessary quantitative techniques are developed from first principles early in the book and their use is illustrated by means of examples drawn from problems arising within the firm. In addition, the book emphasises an important element, namely, the economic interpretation of the solutions, which demonstrates that it is the economics that drives the mathematics, rather than the other way around.

1.3.4   Relation to Statistics and OR

Managerial Economics relies on Statistics in a number of ways. Statistics deals with the theory and methods of collecting, tabulating and analysing numerical data, which are necessary functions for the process of providing quantitative evidence and backing to management issues. At the heart of statistics lies the idea of *statistical inference*, by which we mean the process of inferring from data referring to a small part (*a sample*) a statement relative to the whole (*population*), and also provide a measure of the uncertainty surrounding the inference made. The process of *sampling* a small, well-stratified section of the potential consumer base to infer consumer preferences as regards, for example, new products is of major concern to management.

Given that in Economics in general and Managerial Economics in particular we cannot perform controlled experiments, *statistical inference* provides a powerful tool of quantitative analysis and the use of probability theory becomes central to the work of a practising managerial economist. In addition, most economic statements are conditional. For example, we expect a particular economic variable to move (change) in a particular direction provided certain other variable(s) related to the first variable are changed. While mathematical methods can establish the nature of the functional relationship between the variables, we are also interested in testing such hypothesis. Thus, hypothesis testing that is central to Managerial economics is another area that Statistics can provide significant help.

Also various methods of OR, such as stock control, queues, linear programming, transportation problems, scheduling, network analysis, theory of games and so on are of direct relevance and help to the managerial economist. For this reason some of these methods are described in some detail in the present book, e.g., linear programming and the theory of games.

1.3.5　Relation to Econometrics

Econometrics is derived from the Greek and literally means *measurement in economics*. More particularly econometrics is concerned with the application of statistical and mathematical techniques for the analysis of economic data. The chief role of econometrics is the specification, estimation and testing of economic models, and so it is used for the analysis, verification or refutation of economic models or theories. Therefore, it becomes evident that econometrics plays a crucial role in Managerial Economics, as regards, for example, the forecasting of sales, cost or any other function we are interested in.

Clearly, for a managerial economist interested in the values of the estimated parameters of functional relationships used in decision making and their economic interpretation, such as, e.g., elasticities, rates of change, multipliers and so on, a basic understanding of econometric methods, their assumptions and limitations is very useful if not indispensable.

Consequently, in the present book we provide a reasonably extensive treatment of the basic method of ordinary least squares (OLS) and its extensions used for the estimation of a number of econometric models through appropriate examples. In addition, we give in an appendix the basic assumptions upon which OLS is based. If such assumptions are satisfied, then the resulting estimated coefficients have certain desirable properties, and we can derive predicted values for our variables of interest and construct with a given probability, say 95%, a confidence interval around the estimated values. We can then state that with 95% probability, the confidence interval will contain the true, but unknown, population parameter value.

1.3.6　Relation to decision theory

Decision theory deals with the process of expectations formation under conditions of uncertainty and in addition it recognises that management may very well have a multiplicity of goals and objectives, some of which may be conflicting. On the other hand, neoclassical economic theory assumes conditions of certainty and perfect foresight and operates under a single objective, be it utility maximisation for the consumer, or profit maximisation for the firm. On the practical level it would appear that decision theory can make a very useful contribution to solving managerial problems, as its basic premises tend to be more in accord with the actual day-to-day management concerns. This should not be surprising. The task of Managerial Economics is to help understand the managerial process, and in this respect Managerial Economics follows an eclectic approach by borrowing ideas from different disciplines and fields of business administration and synthesising them in a way that produces the desired result.

Therefore, economic theory can be complemented by decision theory for the benefit of the business organisation. In this respect while in the bulk of the book the analysis is conducted along the simplifying assumptions of the neoclassical economic theory, in order to derive insights and optimum solutions, there is also a special chapter devoted to decision theory and a reasonably extended exposition of the basics of the theory of games, in which decisions are reached under conditions of uncertainty.

SUMMARY

In this very short introductory chapter we have discussed very briefly the scope and nature of Managerial Economics and have dealt with some basic methodological issues underlying economics in general. However, since Managerial Economics, has a significant empirical content some of the methodological issues raised are particularly pertinent to it, namely, those concerned with verification and testing of models. In addition, the chapter has considered the relationship of Managerial Economics to other areas of economic theory and other disciplines, such as microeconomics, macroeconomics, mathematics, statistics and OR, econometrics and decision theory.

BIBLIOGRAPHY

Ferguson, C.E. and Maurice, S.C. (1970), *Economic Analysis*, Richard D. Irwin, Inc.

Friedman, M. (1953), 'The Methodology of Positive Economics', in *Essays in Positive Economics*, University of Chicago Press.

Hutchinson, T.W. (1938), *The Significance and Basic Postulates of Economic Theory*, Macmillan.

Machlup, F. (1955), 'The Problem of Verification in Economics', *Southern Economic Journal*, **32**: 1–21.

Robbins, L. (1935), *An Essay on the Nature and Significance of Economic Science*, 2nd ed., Macmillan.

Samuelson, P.A. (1947), *Foundations of Economic Analysis*, Harvard University Press.

chapter two

The Tools of Optimisation

Learning outcomes

After studying this chapter you should know about:

- The concept of differentiation

- Functions of one variable

- Rules for differentiation

- Derivation of maximum and minimum values

- Functions of more than one variable – partial differentiation

- Optimisation of functions of several variables

- Constrained optimisation

- Lagrange multipliers

2.1 INTRODUCTION

As we pointed out in the opening chapter, the theme of managerial economics is the application of economic theory to problems of decision making within the firm. Such problems may have, for example, to do with the firm's pricing policy, its costs, level of advertising expenditure and so on. Whatever the case may be, we assume that the firm's management will respond in seeking to achieve the best solution possible. Indeed, an integral component of decision making is the quest for the best solution to the problem under consideration. This quest, in most instances, will mean an attempt to optimise a particular function derived from economic theory, which tries to model the particular problem, in a way that it is capable of getting a numerical answer as a solution. Economic models represent structural relationships between economic magnitudes, called variables. If we know the way the variables, entering the model, interact with one another, or the way one variable responds to changes in other variables, we can establish the mathematical form of the model, which makes it easy to derive the results on our variable of interest, when changes occur in the other variables. Inevitably, for reasons of comprehension, such models will concentrate on a few crucial variables and will represent an abstraction, a simplification of reality. Nevertheless, despite the fact that a model is not and, in the nature of things, cannot be a complete depiction of reality, it is based on economic theories which, typically, postulate a structural relation or correspondence between the variables of the model, on one hand, and various aspects of reality, on the other. This correspondence allows the model to represent a sector or sub-sector of reality in a simple way, abstracting from the complications of the real system, but because of the similarities with it, deriving satisfactory results, when used as a tool for decision making, thus justifying its use. Economic models then are judged on their ability to predict successfully, rather than on their realism.

In economic theory the concept of optimisation occupies a central role and a great deal of care and restrictive assumptions, notably those of certainty and full information, are required in order to achieve it. In managerial economics and, generally, in decision making we are concerned too with optimal solutions, in the form of maximum or minimum values, which will optimise our functions. This is not, necessarily, because managers wish to achieve or are capable of achieving such optimal solutions in the real world. In fact, in most instances they neither wish nor are they capable of doing so, because of multiple goals and/or incomplete information and uncertainty. Nevertheless, they wish to know, at least, the direction in which such solutions lie. Economic models, despite their limitations, imposed by the need to simplify in order to understand, do provide an improvement over alternative ways of decision making, based on crude rules of thumb or repetitions of past decisions, irrespective of circumstances.

At the heart of the optimisation process lies marginal analysis. Marginal analysis is concerned with changes at the margin, i.e., it tells us that if an independent variable, x, changed by one unit (preferably by an infinitesimal amount) by how much has the dependent variable, y, changed. In other words, the marginal concept has a precise meaning when the variation in x approaches zero. By contrast, the average concept between the two variables expresses the variation of y over the whole range of values of x, as y/x. Despite the fact that in managerial economics we are more concerned with incremental analysis – where the unit of change is the whole decision – rather than marginal analysis, a proper under-standing of the latter is essential for the purposes of sound decision making. This makes it important that we spend some time looking at the techniques and tools of marginal analysis, namely differential calculus.

2.2 THE CONCEPT OF DIFFERENTIATION, FUNCTIONS OF ONE VARIABLE

In calculus we are dealing with the analysis of movement and of change. Since economic relationships do involve change, this mathematical method is of direct importance for our purposes. In calculus we distinguish two main operations, dif-ferentiation and integration. The former is concerned with the problem of finding the rate of change of a function; the latter is concerned with the inverse problem of determining the function once its rate of change is known. We shall only present here some basic rules of differentiation, which will be sufficient to follow the argu-ment in the remainder of this book. We shall eschew complicated functions and shall not deal with integration either. The interested reader is advised, in any case, to consult any one of a great variety of books on Mathematics for Economists for a greater understanding of the issues involved.

We start by considering the concept of the derivative of a function. Given a function, such as $y = f(x)$, which can be represented graphically in the two-dimensional space of x and y as a curve, we define the derivative dy/dx at a point $A = (x, y)$ of this curve as the rate of change or the gradient of the curve (function) at that point, which is given by the gradient of a tangent to the curve at point (x, y). Given the point (x, y), the gradient may be approximated by taking another point $C = (x + \Delta x, y + \Delta y)$, as shown in Figure 2.1. The gradient of the curve between the two points is defined as:

$$\frac{y \text{ distance}}{x \text{ distance}} = \frac{(y + \Delta y) - (y)}{(x + \Delta x) - (x)} = \frac{\Delta y}{\Delta x} = \tan \hat{a}$$

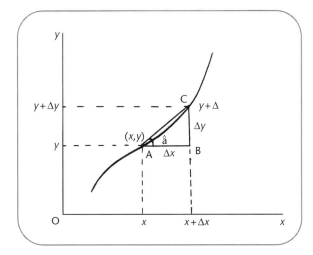

Figure 2.1 The derivative of a function

Alternatively, the same result is obtained by considering triangle ABC and taking the tangent of angle $\hat{a}$, which is given by the ratio $BC/AB = \Delta y/\Delta x$. We may now allow the second point, C, to come closer and closer to the initial point $A = (x, y)$, by making it $(x + \delta x, y + \delta y)$ and derive a better approximation of the gradient at point (x, y). In other words we make the change from the initial point smaller and smaller, i.e., δx can be made as small as possible. Taking now the limit of the above expression, as δx approaches zero, we get

$$\lim_{\Delta x \to 0} \frac{\Delta y}{\Delta x} = \frac{dy}{dx}$$

which is the derivative at point (x, y).

Other common notations for the derivative dy/dx of the function $f(x)$ we can use for our purposes are $f'(x)$ and y'.

As an example let us consider the function $y = x^2$ and try to find the derivative or gradient or slope at a point (x, y) on the curve.

$$y = x^2$$

$$y + \Delta y = (x + \Delta x)^2$$

$$\Delta y = (x + \Delta x)^2 - x^2$$

$$\Delta y = x^2 + 2\Delta xx + (\Delta x)^2 - x^2$$

$$\Delta y = 2\Delta xx + (\Delta x)^2$$

Dividing through by Δx we get

$$f'(x) = \frac{\Delta y}{\Delta x} = 2x + \Delta x$$

Therefore, the gradient at point (x, y) on the curve is given by:

$$\lim_{\Delta x \to 0} \frac{\Delta y}{\Delta x} = \lim_{\Delta x \to 0} (2x + \Delta x) = 2x$$

and hence $dy/dx = 2x$, which is the derivative at that point.

This process can be broken into a number of steps as follows: Starting with the function $y = f(x)$ we give increments to x and y to derive the expression

$$y + \Delta y = f(x + \Delta x)$$

re-arrange and substitute to get:

$$\Delta y = f(x + \Delta x) - f(x)$$

divide by Δx to obtain

$$\frac{\Delta y}{\Delta x} = \frac{f(x + \Delta x) - f(x)}{\Delta x}$$

finally, take the limit to get the derivative

$$y' = f'(x) = \frac{dy}{dx} = \lim_{\Delta x \to 0} \frac{\Delta y}{\Delta x} = \lim_{\Delta x \to 0} \frac{f(x + \Delta x) - f(x)}{\Delta x}$$

The preceding discussion demonstrates the general way of deriving the derivative at a point of a function. For example, in economics and business we are often confronted with the problem of finding the marginal values of particular relations, such as marginal revenue, marginal cost and so on. These concepts are defined as the rates of change of the relevant total relations, i.e., total revenue and total cost and are given by the derivatives of these total functions. In turn, this, allows us to find solutions to economic problems, for example, determining the maximum and minimum values of particular economic relationships of interest, such as the profit, revenue and cost functions. However, to avoid the tedious repetitions of deriving the derivative directly, rules have been devised for differentiating various types of functions. In what follows we provide the basic rules of differentiation and then use them to illustrate the process of maximisation and minimisation.

2.2.1   Rules for differentiation

For our purposes we shall concentrate only on polynomial and algebraic functions, ignoring logarithmic, exponential and trigonometric functions, for which the reader is advised to consult any of the reference books given at the end of this chapter. Derivatives of polynomial and algebraic functions are found by using the following rules:

1. *The derivative of a constant is zero*: By definition a constant is fixed, thus, it does not vary, and so if $y = c$, where $c = $ constant then, $y' = dy/dx = 0$.

    Example
    Let $y = 10$, then we get $y' = dy/dx = 0$.

2. *The power rule*: The derivative of a power function is given by the exponent multiplied by the constant and the independent variable raised to its initial power less one. That is,

    If $y = cx^n$ then we have $y' = dy/dx = ncx^{n-1}$

    Example
    Let $y = 10x^3$ then we derive $y' = dy/dx = 3(10)x^{3-1} = 30x^2$
    (a) Alternatively, the above can be expressed as follows. The derivative of a constant and a differentiable function is given by multiplying the constant by the derivative of the function. If $y = cv$, where $c = $ constant and $v = g(x)$, i.e., a differentiable function of x, then the derivative is given by: $y' = dy/dx = cv' = c(dv/dx)$.
    Example
    Let $y = 5x^4$ then $y' = dy/dx = 5(4)x^{4-1} = 20x^3$.
    (b) An extension of the power rule states that the derivative of the nth power of a differentiable function is given by n multiplied by the $(n-1)$th power of the function and the derivative of the function.

Thus, if $y = u^n$, where $u = f(x)$ is a differentiable function of x and n is any real number, then:

$$y' = \frac{dy}{dx} = nu^{n-1}\left(\frac{du}{dx}\right)$$

Example
Let $y = u^3$ where $u = (x^3 + 4)$, then

$$y' = \frac{dy}{dx} = 3(x^3 + 4)^2 3x^2 = 9x^2(x^3 + 4)^2$$

3. *The sums and differences rule*: The derivative of the sum (difference) of differentiable functions is the sum (difference) of their derivatives.

    That is, if $y = u + v + w$, where $u = f(x)$, $v = f(x)$ and $w = f(x)$ then the derivative of y is given by:

    $$y' = (dy/dx) = (u' + v' + w') = (du/dx) + (dv/dx) + (dw/dx)$$

    Example
    Let $y = 2x^4 - 3x^3 + 5x^2$ then $y' = dy/dx = 8x^3 - 9x^2 + 10x$.

4. *The product rule*: The derivative of the product of two differentiable functions is given by the first function multiplied by the derivative of the second function plus the second function multiplied by the derivative of the first function. That is, if we have $y = uv$, where $u = f(x)$ and also $v = g(x)$ then the derivative of y is given by:

    $$y' = uv' + vu' \quad \text{or} \quad dy/dx = u(dv/dx) + v(du/dx)$$

    Example
    If $y = (5x^3 - 2x^2)(3x^2 + 5x)$, where $u = (5x^3 - 2x^2)$ and $v = (3x^2 + 5x)$ then the derivative of y is:

    $$\begin{aligned} y' = dy/dx &= (5x^3 - 2x^2)(6x + 5) + (3x^2 + 5x)(15x^2 - 4x) \\ &= 30x^4 + 25x^3 - 12x^3 - 10x^2 + 45x^4 + 75x^3 - 12x^3 - 20x^2 \\ &= 75x^4 + 76x^3 - 30x^2. \end{aligned}$$

5. *Quotient rule*: The derivative of the quotient of two differentiable functions is given by the denominator multiplied by the derivative of the numerator minus the numerator multiplied by the derivative of the denominator and this sum is divided by the square of the denominator.
    That is, if $y = u/v$,   where $u = f(x)$ and $v = f(x)$ then

    $$y' = \frac{dy}{dx} = \frac{vu' - uv'}{v^2} = \frac{v(du/dx) - u(dv/dx)}{v^2}$$

Example
Let

$$y = \frac{x^3 - 2x^2 + 3}{2x^2 - 2x}$$

then the derivative is given by:

$$y' = \frac{dy}{dx} = \frac{(2x^2 - 2x)(3x^2 - 4x) - (x^3 - 2x^2 + 3)(4x - 2)}{(2x^2 - 2x)^2}$$

$$= \frac{6x^4 - 8x^3 - 6x^3 + 8x^2 - (4x^4 - 2x^3 - 8x^3 + 4x^2 + 12x - 6)}{(2x^2 - 2x)^2}$$

$$= \frac{2x^4 - 4x^3 + 4x^2 - 12x + 6}{4x^4 - 8x^3 + 4x^2} = \frac{2(x^4 - 2x^3 + 2x^2 - 6x + 3)}{2(2x^4 - 4x^3 + 2x^2)}$$

$$= \frac{x^4 - 2x^3 + 2x^2 - 6x + 3}{2x^4 - 4x^3 + 2x^2}$$

6. *Chain rule (or composite function)*: If y is a function of v and v is a function of x, then y is said to be a composite function or a function of a function; in this case the derivative of y with respect to x is given by the derivative of y with respect to v multiplied by the derivative of v with respect to x.
    That is, if $y = f(v)$ and $v = f(x)$ then $y' = dy/dx = (dy/dv)(dv/dx)$.

Example
Let $y = 3v^2$ and $v = x^2 + 1$ we get that $dy/dv = 6v$ and $dv/dx = 2x$
    Therefore,

$$y' = dy/dx = 6v2x \text{ and by substitution we have:}$$

$$= 6(x^2 + 1)2x = 12x(x^2 + 1) = 12x^3 + 12x.$$

2.2.2   Derivation of maximum and minimum values

The application of the above rules allows us to derive the minimum and maximum values of particular functions of interest, as follows: Given the function $y = f(x)$, by differentiating it and setting the first derivative equal to zero, i.e., $dy/dx = 0$, we obtain the so called turning point(s) of the function, as in points A and B in Figure 2.2. At points A and B, the rate of change of the function or its gradient or its derivative is equal to zero, having just become zero from a positive or negative value. For example, immediately to the left of point A the gradient is positive and immediately to the right of point A it turns into negative. The opposite happens at point B, where to the left of B the gradient is negative and to the right of B it turns into positive.

This allows us to establish at what values of x we derive the maximum and minimum values of the function, by considering how the gradient or derivative changes, which is tantamount to looking at the rate of change of the rate of change, which is given by differentiating again the first derivative dy/dx, and obtaining the second derivative, given by the expression d^2y/dx^2.

If the sign of the second derivative is negative, a local maximum is indicated, as at point A; if the sign is positive, a local minimum is derived, as at point B.

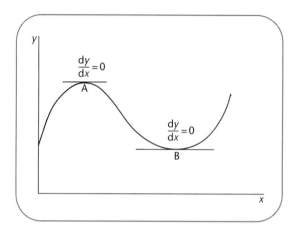

Figure 2.2 Maximum and minimum values of a function

This allows us to establish that the first-order condition for both a maximum and a minimum is to set the first derivative equal to zero and solve for the value of the independent variable; this is known as a necessary condition. The second-order condition for a maximum requires that the second-order derivative is negative, whilst for a minimum be positive; this is known as a sufficient condition.

Therefore, we can summarise the conditions for obtaining a maximum and a minimum of a function $y = f(x)$ as follows:

	Necessary condition		Sufficient condition
For a maximum	$\frac{dy}{dx} = 0$	and	$\frac{d^2y}{dx^2} < 0$
For a minimum	$\frac{dy}{dx} = 0$	and	$\frac{d^2y}{dx^2} > 0$

For example, we are told that the demand for a monopolist's product is given by the following linear function: $p = 160 - 4q$ and his total cost function is TC $= 500 + 40q$, where q is output. Assuming that the monopolist tries to maximise his profit, we have the following profit (Π) function:

$$\Pi = TR - TC = pq - TC = (160 - 4q)q - 500 - 40q = 160q - 4q^2 - 500 - 40q \quad (1)$$

Since we are interested in maximising the monopolist's profit, we proceed by differentiating the above profit function and by setting the first derivative equal to zero we obtain:

$$d\Pi/dq = 160 - 8q - 40 = 0 \quad (2)$$

which is our necessary condition for a maximum.

Solving relation (2) for the unknown value of output we get $q = 15$ and by substituting into the demand function we also derive $p = 100$. We have so far established that the profit function (1) has a turning point at output level $q = 15$.

To establish whether the solution $q = 15$ produces the maximum profit we now need evaluate the second-order derivative. We do this by differentiating relation (2) found earlier as follows:

$$d^2\Pi/dq^2 = -8 < 0 \tag{3}$$

which is our sufficient condition for a maximum. Since this is negative (-8) we confirm that producing 15 units of output is the optimal solution, which maximises profit.

Finally, we evaluate profit by substituting the values of $q = 15$ and $p = 100$ into our profit function (1) as follows:

$$\Pi = 160(15) - 4(15)^2 - 500 - 40(15) = 2400 - 900 - 500 - 600$$

$$= 2400 - 2000 = 400$$

Therefore, the maximum profit of the monopolist is 400 units.

2.3 FUNCTIONS OF MORE THAN ONE VARIABLE – PARTIAL DIFFERENTIATION

In many economic relations our variable of interest (dependent variable) may be expressed as a function of several other determining (or independent) variables in order to better describe the underlying conditions. For example, quantity demanded of a particular good can be expressed as a function of the price of the good, consumers' income, prices of other related goods, advertising, time and so on. Typically, we may write that variable z is a function of n variables as follows:

$$z = F(x_1, x_2, \ldots, x_n)$$

To proceed with differentiating such function, we need to know that the function is continuous at every point of the region of the plane of the independent variables. For example the function $z = f(x, y)$ is said to be continuous in the region of the xy-plane, if it is continuous at all points of this region. In the function $z = f(x, y)$ if x is held constant, then z becomes a function only of y and we can find its derivative with respect to y. Similarly, if y is held constant, we can find the derivative of z with respect to x. Such derivatives are called partial derivatives, and are derived easily, since only one of the independent variables varies at a time, whilst all the remaining variables are held constant. Partial derivatives have different notations, but for simplicity we shall use the following:

$$\delta z/\delta x, \quad \delta z/\delta y, \ldots \quad \text{or} \quad f_x, \ f_y$$

Generally, in a function involving several independent variables, we may compute a partial derivative with respect to each of these independent variables. As an example consider the function:

$$z = 3x^4 - 4x^2y + 6y^3$$

Differentiating first with respect to x and then with respect to y we get the following two expressions:

$$f_x = \delta z/\delta x = 12x^3 - 8xy \quad \text{and} \quad f_y = \delta z/\delta y = -4x^2 + 18y^2$$

2.3.1 Optimisation of functions of several variables

Turning to the optimisation process, we should bear in mind that the definitions of maxima and minima in the case of functions of several variables are similar to those discussed earlier for a function of one variable. For example, if we are interested in finding the maximum and minimum values of a function of two independent variables such as $z = f(x, y)$, we must: (1) compute the first-order partial derivatives with respect to these variables and set them equal to zero; the solution of the resulting relations will give us the values of the two variables for which the function has a local maximum or a local minimum, and: (2) determine the second-order partial derivatives and cross partial derivatives, denoted by

$$f_{11} = \delta^2 f/\delta x^2, \quad f_{22} = \delta^2 f/\delta y^2, \quad f_{12} = \delta^2 f/\delta x \delta y \quad \text{and} \quad f_{21} = \delta^2 f/\delta y \delta x$$

where f_{11} and f_{22} are the partial derivatives and f_{12} and f_{21} are the cross partial derivatives, and then investigate the sign of the resulting Hesssian determinant, given by the difference of the cross products of the following matrix:

$$\begin{vmatrix} f_{11} & f_{12} \\ f_{21} & f_{22} \end{vmatrix} = (f_{11}f_{22} - f_{12}f_{21})$$

It should be borne in mind that for a continuous function the cross partial derivatives are equal, thus $f_{12} = f_{21}$. Now the necessary conditions are that for both a maximum and a minimum the first-order partial derivatives be set equal to zero. The sufficient conditions require that all second-order partial derivatives be negative for a maximum and positive for a minimum. More formally, if the sign of the above determinant is positive and f_{11} and f_{22} are both negative we have a maximum, while if the sign of the determinant is positive and f_{11} and f_{22} are both positive we have a minimum. If the sign of the determinant is negative we have a saddle point, whereas if the sign of the determinant is zero the test fails and we need to examine the function near the critical points.

As an example, consider a firm which produces jointly two products X and Y, whose demand curves are given by the following relations: $p_x = 50 - 3x$; and $p_y = 40 - 4y$, and the joint cost of production is given by $C = x^2 + 3xy + 2y^2$, where x and y represent the quantities of the two products produced. We want to investigate for what values of x and y the profit of the firm is at a maximum.

The profit function is given by $\Pi = \text{TR} - \text{TC} = p_x x + p_y y - C$ and by substitution we obtain:

$$\Pi = 50x - 3x^2 + 40y - 4y^2 - x^2 - 3xy - 2y^2 \tag{1}$$

Partially differentiating (1) with respect to x and y and equating to zero yields the following two relations:

$$f_x = \delta\Pi/\delta x = 50 - 6x - 2x - 3y = 0 \tag{2}$$

$$f_y = \delta\Pi/\delta y = 40 - 8y - 3x - 4y = 0 \tag{3}$$

Relations (2) and (3) result in the system of equations

$8x + 3y = 50$

$3x + 12y = 40$

which has as a solution $x = 5.51724$ and $y = 1.954$

To find out whether the firm maximises its profit by producing these quantities, we evaluate the second-order partial derivatives as follows:

$$f_{xx} = \delta^2 \Pi / \delta x^2 = -6 - 2 = -8 < 0$$

$$f_{yy} = \delta^2 \Pi / \delta y^2 = -8 - 4 = -12 < 0 \quad \text{and}$$

$$f_{xy} = \delta^2 \Pi / \delta x \delta y = -3 \quad \text{and} \quad f_{yx} = \delta^2 \Pi / \delta y \delta x = -3$$

Clearly the conditions for a maximum are satisfied since the second-order partial derivatives have the required signs, i.e., they are negative and the determinant is positive, as it is clear from the following:

$$\begin{vmatrix} -8 & -3 \\ -3 & -12 \end{vmatrix} = [(-8)(-12) - (-3)(-3)] = (96 - 9) = 87$$

Therefore, it has been shown that the firm by producing 5.51724 units of x and 1.954 units of y achieves its profit maximisation position. This gives a total profit of 177.0115 units and it is obtained when the firm charges prices $P_x = 33.44929$ and $P_y = 32.194$. These calculations are left as an exercise for the reader.

2.3.2　Constrained optimisation – the reduction method

In many instances of economic activity, managers trying to optimise particular functions find that they are restrained in their efforts to do so by a number of constraints. This means that the values that the variables are allowed to take must satisfy certain side conditions. For example, in production theory managers try to maximise the level of output, while ensuring that they do not exceed a given level of expenditure. Or alternatively, they try to minimise the cost of production, subject to producing a given level of output. Similarly, managers may wish to maximise the total revenue of the firm, subject to satisfying a minimum profit constraint. In general, the constrained minimum or maximum values will differ from the unconstrained ones. Typically, the constrained maximum value a variable takes will be lower than the unconstrained one. In such cases we talk of constrained optimisation.

In particular instances the constraint equation can be incorporated, by substitution, into the function to be optimised and, therefore, the problem is reduced into one of finding the unconstrained maximum or minimum, by following the methods discussed earlier. This approach is known as the reduction method. For example, assume that a consumer's utility is given by the function $U = xy$, where x and y are quantities of two products X and Y, whose prices are €2 and €5 respectively. If the consumer's income is €100 per week what are the weekly quantities of X and Y that maximise his utility?

The constraint equation is written as $2x + 5y = 100$, from which we get that $2x = 100 - 5y$ or $x = 50 - 2.5y$. Therefore, substituting into the utility function, $U = xy$, we have:

$$U = xy = (50 - 2.5y)y = 50y - 2.5y^2 \tag{1}$$

Differentiating relation (1) with respect to y and setting the derivative equal to zero we obtain:

$$dU/dy = 50 - 5y = 0 \tag{2}$$

which results in $y = 10$.

Substituting this value into the expression for x, found earlier, we get:

$$x = 50 - 2.5y = 50 - 2.5(10) = 50 - 25 = 25.$$

To verify that the values of $x = 25$ and $y = 10$ are the optimal values which maximise the consumer's utility, we need to consider the second-order condition for maximisation, by differentiating relation (2) found earlier, as follows:
$d^2U/dy^2 = -5 < 0$. Therefore, since the sign of the second derivative is negative, the values $x = 25$ and $y = 10$ are indeed the utility maximising quantities of the two products.

2.3.3 The Lagrange multipliers method

However, the reduction method is not always feasible, particularly, when we have more than two independent variables and more than one constraints. In such cases, we shall use the method of Lagrange multipliers to tackle this sort of problem.

To approach the subject in general terms, assume that we want to maximise the function $V = f(x_1, x_2, \ldots, x_n)$ subject to the restriction that only those values of $x_1, x_2, \ldots, x_n$ satisfying the relation $g(x_1, x_2, \ldots, x_n) = 0$ are accepted. The Lagrange multipliers method involves forming the objective function Z as follows:

$$Z = f(x_1, x_2, \ldots, x_n) - \lambda g(x_1, x_2, \ldots, x_n)$$

which incorporates the original function V and the constraint. It is clear that in addition to the x variables, the function Z contains one extra variable, λ, which, at this stage is an unspecified Lagrange multiplier (different than zero), and whose meaning will become clear in the remainder of the book, when we have the opportunity to use this particular method. Partially differentiating Z, with respect to the x variables and λ and setting the partial derivatives equal to zero, enables us to solve for the point or points for which the function $V = f(x_1, x_2, \ldots, x_n)$ achieves a maximum or a minimum, subject to the given constraint $g(x_1, x_2, \ldots, x_n) = 0$. Also, it ensures that the constraint itself is satisfied. The second-order conditions require that the second-order partial derivatives be negative for a maximum and positive for a minimum, as above. However, if the function contains more than two independent variables the second-order conditions are varied slightly, requiring that for a maximum the sign of the principal minors of the bordered Hessian determinant (made up of the second-order partial derivatives and cross partial derivatives as above, but also bordered by the negative of the prices, coefficients, of the independent variables and a zero at the top left corner) alternate in sign starting with positive, whilst for a minimum they should all be negative. If this sounds a bit confusing we shall clarify it by looking at the following example.

A firm produces a product, Q, by means of two inputs x and y. The firm's production function is given by:

$$16q = 65 - 2(x - 5)^2 - 4(y - 4)^2$$

If the unit prices of the two inputs x and y are €16 and €8, respectively and the price of the product is €64 per unit, what is the profit maximising level of output, q, and the profit made, given that the firm has no other costs?

The profit function is formulated as

$$\Pi = TR - TC = 64q - 16x - 8y$$

i.e., the price of the product €64 multiplied by the quantity produced, q, gives us the revenue of the firm and since the only costs the firm incurs are the variable costs of using the two inputs x and y, multiplying these by their prices €16 and €8 respectively and subtracting these costs from the revenue gives us the profit function. Now to form the Lagrange objective function we rewrite the production function given earlier as:

$$16q - 65 + 2(x - 5)^2 + 4(y - 4)^2 = 0$$

place the whole expression on the left-hand side into brackets multiply it by our unspecified Lagrange multiplier, λ, and subtract it from the profit function found above. This gives us the following Lagrange expression:

$$Z = 64q - 16x - 8y - \lambda[16q - 65 + 2(x - 5)^2 + 4(y - 4)^2] \tag{1}$$

which can be written out for simplicity as:

$$Z = 64q - 16x - 8y - \lambda(16q - 65 + 2x^2 - 20x + 50 + 4y^2 - 32y + 64) \tag{2}$$

Partially differentiating (2) with respect to q, x, y and λ and equating to zero yields the following expressions:

$$\delta Z/\delta q = 64 - 16\lambda = 0 \tag{3}$$
$$\delta Z/\delta x = -16 - 4\lambda x + 20\lambda = 0 \tag{4}$$
$$\delta Z/\delta y = -8 - 8\lambda y + 32\lambda = 0 \tag{5}$$
$$\delta Z/\delta\lambda = -(16q - 65 + 2x^2 - 20x + 50 + 4y^2 - 32y + 64) = 0 \tag{6}$$

Notice that relation (6) merely restates our constraint given by the production function. From our partial differentiation we have that relation (3) implies that $\lambda = 4$ and substituting this value in turn into (4) and (5) gives the values of $x = 4$ and $y = 3.75$. Substituting these values into relation (6) we get that $q - 3.921975$. Finally, further substitution of these values into the profit function yields a profit of €157.

To consider whether this solution is optimal we need to investigate the second-order partial derivatives, which are computed as follows:

$$f_{qq} = \delta^2 Z/\delta q^2 = 0, \quad f_{xx} = \delta^2 Z/\delta x^2 = -4\lambda = -16, \quad f_{yy} = \delta^2 Z/\delta y^2 = -8\lambda = -32,$$
$$f_{qx} = \delta^2 Z/\delta q\delta x = 0, \quad f_{qy} = \delta^2 Z/\delta q\delta y = 0,$$
$$f_{xq} = \delta^2 Z/\delta x\delta q = 0, \quad f_{xy} = \delta^2 Z/\delta x\delta y = 0, \quad f_{yq} = \delta^2 Z/\delta y\delta q = 0,$$
$$f_{yx} = \delta^2 Z/\delta y\delta x = 0$$

The first three second-order partial derivatives are derived by differentiating again relations (3), (4) and (5) with respect to q, x and y, respectively. For the cross partial derivatives f_{qx} and f_{qy} we differentiate (3) first with respect to x and then with respect to y. For the cross partial derivatives f_{xq} and f_{xy} we differentiate (4) with respect to q and y respectively and, finally, for the cross partial derivatives f_{yq} and f_{yx} we differentiate (5) with respect to q and x respectively. Clearly, all these cross partial derivatives are zero.

Therefore, the bordered Hessian determinant is given as follows:

$$\begin{vmatrix} 0 & -p_q & -p_x & -p_y \\ -p_q & f_{qq} & f_{qx} & f_{qy} \\ -p_x & f_{xq} & f_{xx} & f_{xy} \\ -p_y & f_{yq} & f_{yx} & f_{yy} \end{vmatrix} = \begin{vmatrix} 0 & -64 & -16 & -8 \\ -64 & 0 & 0 & 0 \\ -16 & 0 & -16 & 0 \\ -8 & 0 & 0 & -32 \end{vmatrix}$$

According to Samuelson, we can define the principal minors of a determinant as sub-determinants formed by crossing out the same rows and columns, so that the elements of the main diagonal of the minor are contained in the elements of the main diagonal of the original matrix (Samuelson, 1965, p. 367).

A summary of the second-order conditions for both constrained and unconstrained optimisation is given in Table 2.1.

Therefore, since in our case we have one constraint, the principal minors of the above bordered Hessian determinant would be Δ_1 of order (3×3), and Δ_2 of order (4×4). The reason is that the smallest order of the quadratic form (matrix) we can have is (2×2) and when we border it, it becomes a (3×3) matrix. In terms of the sign we have that for $\Delta_1 (-1)^{3-1} = (-1)^2 = 1$, i.e., positive, while for Δ_2 it is $(-1)^{4-1} = (-1)^3 = (-1)$, i.e., negative. Thus, in our example we have:

$$\Delta_1 = \begin{vmatrix} 0 & -64 & -16 \\ -64 & 0 & 0 \\ -16 & 0 & -16 \end{vmatrix} \quad \Delta_2 = \begin{vmatrix} 0 & -64 & -16 & -8 \\ -64 & 0 & 0 & 0 \\ -16 & 0 & -16 & 0 \\ -8 & 0 & 0 & -32 \end{vmatrix}$$

As was mentioned above, for profit maximisation we require that the signs of the principal minors alternate starting with positive. In other words we require a positive value for Δ_1 and a negative sign for Δ_2.

Table 2.1 Second-order conditions in terms of signs of principal minors of dimension m of the Hessian matrix

| | Number of constraints | | |
	0	1	r
Maximisation	$(-1)^m$	$(-1)^{m-1}, m \geq 3$	$(-1)^{m-r}, m \geq 1 + 2r$
Minimisation	$(-1)^0 > 0$	$(-1)^1 < 0, m \geq 3$	$(-1)^r, m \geq 1 + 2r$

Checking for sign we obtain:

$$|\Delta_1| = \begin{vmatrix} 0 & -64 & -16 \\ -64 & 0 & 0 \\ -16 & 0 & -16 \end{vmatrix} = 64[(-64)(-16)] = 65536$$

which is positive and finally,

$$|\Delta_3| = \begin{vmatrix} 0 & -64 & -16 & -8 \\ -64 & 0 & 0 & 0 \\ -16 & 0 & -16 & 0 \\ -8 & 0 & 0 & -32 \end{vmatrix} = 64 \begin{vmatrix} -64 & 0 & 0 \\ -16 & -16 & 0 \\ -8 & 0 & -32 \end{vmatrix}$$

$$= 64\{-64[(-16)(-32)]\} = 64(-64)(512) = -2097152$$

which is negative, as required. Therefore, since the values of these determinants alternate in sign, starting with positive, the second-order conditions are satisfied and our earlier solution maximises profit and so it is optimal.

2.4   A NOTE ON DETERMINANTS

In the context of the earlier analysis we had cause to make use of the sign of the determinant. We provide here a very brief and rudimentary discussion of how to derive the value of a determinant. Again the reader is advised to consult the books given in the references for a thorough discussion of this subject. Given a square matrix A, i.e., a rectangular array of elements (such as, e.g., numbers) having the same number of rows and columns, we can represent some of its characteristics by a scalar, known as the determinant, denoted by $|A|$.

For example, the determinant of a 2×2 matrix is given by:

$$|A| = \begin{vmatrix} a & b \\ c & d \end{vmatrix} = (ad - cb)$$

which is the difference between the cross products of the elements, i e , the product of the elements on the main diagonal and the product of the elements on the other diagonal.

Example if $A = \begin{vmatrix} 2 & 1 \\ 3 & 5 \end{vmatrix}$

then $|A| = (2 \times 5) - (1 \times 3) = 10 - 3 = 7$.

For a 3×3 matrix, the determinant is found by expanding along the elements of the first row, which reduces it to three matrices of 2×2 and performing the indicated operations as shown below:

$$|A| = \begin{vmatrix} a & b & c \\ d & e & f \\ g & h & i \end{vmatrix} = a\begin{vmatrix} e & f \\ h & i \end{vmatrix} - b\begin{vmatrix} d & f \\ g & i \end{vmatrix} + c\begin{vmatrix} d & e \\ g & h \end{vmatrix}$$

$$= a(ei - fh) - b(di - fg) + c(dh - eg)$$

Example

Let $|A| = \begin{vmatrix} 2 & 4 & 6 \\ 3 & 2 & 3 \\ 1 & 4 & 9 \end{vmatrix}$

Expanding in terms of the elements of the first row we have:

$$|A| = 2\begin{vmatrix} 2 & 3 \\ 4 & 9 \end{vmatrix} - 4\begin{vmatrix} 3 & 3 \\ 1 & 9 \end{vmatrix} + 6\begin{vmatrix} 3 & 2 \\ 1 & 4 \end{vmatrix}$$

$$= 2(18 - 12) - 4(27 - 3) + 6(12 - 2)$$

$$= 2 \times 6 - 4 \times 24 + 6 \times 10 = 12 - 96 + 60 = -24$$

and similar arguments hold for higher order determinants, that is, we can go on expanding in terms of the elements of the first row until we reduce the given matrix to smaller 2×2 matrices and then proceed, as shown above.

This concludes our discussion on optimisation methods.

SUMMARY

In this chapter, we have provided only the basic mathematical material required for the reader to follow the discussion in the remainder of this book. Thus, in terms of calculus, only differentiation rules have been considered and only for very basic functions. No treatment of integration has been provided, as it is not, explicitly, the subject of this book. Also, only some elements of linear algebra have been discussed. However, additional material will be considered, as it becomes necessary, later in the book, particularly in Chapters 5 and 8. Nevertheless, if readers have not covered introductory mathematics for economics and business, they may need to supplement the discussion of this chapter by an appropriate text, among the ones listed in the bibliography.

BIBLIOGRAPHY

Allen, R.G.D. (1964), *Mathematical Analysis for Economists*, Macmillan.

Archibald, A.C. and Lipsey, R.G. (1967), *An Introduction to a Mathematical Treatment of Economics*, Weidenfeld & Nicholson.

Black, J. and Bradley, J.F. (1975), *Essential Mathematics for Economists*, John Wiley & Sons.

Chiang, A.C. (1984), *Fundamental Methods of Mathematical Economics*, 3rd ed., McGraw-Hill.

Dowling, E.T. (1992), *Introduction to Mathematical Economics*, 2nd ed., McGraw-Hill.

Draper, J.E and Klingman, J.S. (1972), *Mathematical Analysis – Business and Economic Applications*, 2nd ed., Harper & Row Publishers Inc.

Henderson, J.M. and Ouandt, R.E. (1980), *Microeconomic Theory, a Mathematical Approach*, 3rd ed. Appendix, McGraw-Hill.

Glaister, S. (1987), *Mathematical Methods for Economists*, revised ed., Blackwell.

Rosser, M. (1993), *Basic Mathematics for Economists*, Routledge.

Samuelson, P.A. (1945), *Foundations of Economic Analysis*, Appendix A, Atheneum.

Toumanoff, P. and Nourzad, F. (1994), *A Mathematical Approach to Economic Analysis*, West.

chapter three

Theories of the Firm and of Profits

Learning outcomes

After studying this chapter you should know about:

- The nature and theory of profits

- Functional, friction, innovation and technology profit theories

- Theories of the firm
  - Neoclassical theory and its appraisal
  - Managerial theories
    - Sales maximisation
    - Managers' utility maximisation
    - Marris' growth theory
  - Transaction costs
  - Principal–Agent
  - Evolutionary
  - Behavioural

- Appendix: NOKIA

3.1   INTRODUCTION

A firm is an organisation which controls and coordinates various factors of production, including knowledge, and transforms them into marketable goods and services, for the purpose of achieving its objectives. Such objectives may be characterised by considerable diversity, but a central place among them is reserved for the objective of making profits. Whatever other motives a firm may have, they can more easily be attained if the firm is profitable. Profits then become the litmus test of a firm's success or failure, for without them a firm cannot survive for long. Profits are used as a yardstick of an individual firm's performance in the market, and are necessary under any kind of economic system, since they ensure the firm's survival and provide the means of its expansion over time. In the context of the market economy, profits act as a signal or guide to the firm for the kind of goods and services to be produced and sold, and also help determine the derived demand for the various factors of production. Nevertheless, the concept of profits is not uncontroversial. It may mean, and usually does, different things to different people and the measurement of profits can cause problems. An economist's view of profits is different to that of an accountant's and, most significantly, to that of a tax collector.

3.2   THE NATURE AND THEORIES OF PROFITS

Profits are defined as the difference between sales revenue and costs of production. Yet, this apparent simple definition begs a number of questions, such as how do we define costs, why and when profits arise, and who gets them? In economic theory, wages represent income from direct labour; interest is income accruing to people from lending out their money to others; rent is the difference between the value produced by a factor of production and the payment required to induce that factor to work. Wages, interest and rent are perfectly straightforward, are recognised as costs of production – since without these expenses there cannot be production and thus sales and, therefore, precede profits in the priority of distributing the firm's revenue. This means that profits have an element of risk attached to them, since they accrue as a residual after the contractual obligations (costs of production) have been met. If contractual obligations are exactly equal to sales revenue, then the firm breaks even, but when such contractual costs of production exceed sales revenue, the firm makes losses.

Therefore, the central point is what to include as costs of production. In particular, are the remuneration (income) that owners of firms could get by working elsewhere; rent income on land and buildings, which the owners could get by leasing them to others; and interest that their capital could earn if lend out to others – instead of been invested in the firm – part of the costs of production? These are the familiar opportunity costs, discussed in Chapter 7, which are not included in the firm's books and its balance sheet and profit and loss account and, so, are excluded from the accounting concept of profits.

Typically, the accountant includes all explicit costs of production, which may be equated to mean the expenses on all hired factors, in order to arrive at accounting profit. Clearly, the greater the proportion of hired factors in the productive process is, the lower the accounting profit becomes. However the accountant excludes the 'earnings' of the 'own' or unhired factors, which are known as implicit costs. If these costs are deducted too, we arrive at economic profit.

If the economist does not include such items of expenditure in costs, his view of profit will not be different to that of the accountant, who looks at explicit, historical or past costs. However, to the extent that the economist is taking into consideration these opportunity costs, i.e., he imputes these implicit and future costs for the various factors as the relevant costs of production, economic profit is not the same as accounting profit. Indeed, from the economist's point of view, economic profits are of greater importance when considered for the future. It is the prospective or future profits, which guide the entrepreneur to use the scarce resources in their most lucrative line. For example, the value of the owner's time in running his firm is not included in the costs of production, although in modern large corporations, which have replaced the small undertakings, the functions of risk- and profit-taking are in the hands of hired management, whose remuneration is part of the costs of production. Also, if the economist wishes to deduct as a cost the interest on the owner's equity capital, he must choose which interest rate to use, and such a choice has different implications. If a 'riskless' interest rate, such as that on government bonds, is selected, then costing equity capital at that riskless rate means that what is left as economic profit is the premium return on capital for undertaking risks. But if equity capital is costed at an interest rate reflecting risk and uncertainty, then the remainder economic profit can be treated as a windfall.

Since in practice an interest cost on equity capital is not charged, it follows that what is reported as profit includes both interest return and rewards for risk-taking, as a result of which reported profits are exaggerated. Such profits tend to be a mixture of interest, possibly wages (of owners-managers) and rent, and economic profit. As if to complicate matters more, not only do we have the different perceptions between accountants and economists as to what exactly constitutes 'profit', but also disagreements between accountants themselves. For example, such disagreements arise on the methods of evaluating stocks. The method FIFO (first in first out) produces a different evaluation of profit from that of LIFO (last in first out) and, also, different depreciation methods, adopted by accountants, arrive at different concepts of profit.

We now turn to consider the various theories that have been put forward to explain economic, or 'abnormal', or above normal profit. Such theories can be classified in three major groups, according to the function profit performs, the factors it is based upon and so on. In early economic theory, under competitive conditions, profit was explained as reward for risk-taking and it gave rise to the functional or compensatory theories; later on the emergence of the large corporation and of monopolistic and oligopolistic market structures viewed profit as the result of friction and imperfections in the adjustment of the market to changes, giving rise to the friction and monopoly theories; and finally, a third group considers profit as reward for innovative activity under the technology and innovations theories.

3.2.1 Functional or compensatory theories

According to these theories, profit is seen as a reward for entrepreneurial services performed and risk undertaken. The entrepreneur brings together productive factors, some of which he owns and some of which he hires, for the purpose of producing marketable goods and services. In doing so, the entrepreneur organises, controls, coordinates and, generally, tries to combine such factors efficiently, and agrees to take the risk, i.e., to receive whatever residual is left over after the contractual payments have been made. Therefore, profit is a reward or a compensation for performing the crucial entrepreneurial function successfully; while losses are incurred for unsuccessful performance. Since most people dislike risky investments, a higher reward (profit) will be required as risk rises.

Here one must distinguish between risky and uncertain events. In the former, the probability distribution is known and we can establish an expected value (mean) and its variance, so that we can measure riskiness in terms of this variance. However, in the latter case of uncertain events we do not know the probability distribution, and so neither the expected value (mean) nor its variance can be calculated.

It is the case that quite a lot of entrepreneurial activity is subject to uncertainty, since dynamic changes in demand and supply factors, such as tastes, technology and so on, are not prone to actuarial calculations. While in modern industry considerable efforts can be made in negotiating a favourable environment for the firm, as the behavioural and organisational theories of the firm suggest, it still remains the case that such uncertainty cannot be eliminated. Therefore, this makes, e.g., the holding of specific purpose assets (like plants, machinery, buildings and so on) more uncertain than holding cash or its equivalent, although inflationary pressures may reduce the riskiness of holding goods and increase instead the riskiness of holding cash. Consequently, the functional approach views profit as the necessary compensation to induce the entrepreneur, in the face of this risk and uncertainty, to invest his capital and take his chances of making money.

However, while this compensatory approach was adequate in explaining profit in the context of the owner-managed small firm, it proved inadequate to do so in the context of the large corporation and the concomitant divorce of ownership from control. Here, ownership of capital equity excepted, all other coordinative and supervisory functions are at the hands of hired and salaried management. Even accepting that what such managers get is 'profit', one must allocate a share of the entrepreneurial function to passive shareholders, to justify the receipt by the latter of the residual profit. On the other hand, if we accept that dividends on common shares represent an interest cost of capital, one may just be able to make a case that such receipts are a reward to shareholders for risks undertaken in holding shares of the particular firm.

3.2.2   Friction and monopoly theories

We know that in the context of the perfectly competitive industry (or stationary economy), short-run 'abnormal' profits are possible. However, under the assumed smooth, frictionless, perfect knowledge and certainty world, the continuous competitive adjustment to changes in demand and supply together with profit maximisation will ensure that the industry will tend towards long-run equilibrium, in which all supernormal profits are competed away. In such equilibrium only normal profits are made, i.e., all resources receive as their remuneration a value equal to their opportunity cost, including the imputed wages, rent and interest of the owner-manager; leaving nothing as a residual profit, or economic profit.

However, what we observe in practice is that rigidities and frictions in the economy, some of which are economic and others social like customs, laws and traditions, prevent factor mobility and, thus, the quick competitive adjustment to changes in demand and supply. This is because factor mobility is not cost-less. Plants, buildings and other fixed capital take time to depreciate, and once they are installed they cannot easily and quickly move to alternative uses in search of higher rewards, if demand conditions alter or if technological change makes them less efficient. And even when such movement may be (or becomes) possible, imperfect knowledge regarding alternative opportunities often acts as a deterrent. All this means that economic surpluses do occur and are unlikely to be eliminated in the long-run, since in a dynamic setting we tend to move from dis-equilibrium to disequilibrium, due to the continuous emergence of new frictions and changes. For example, extraneous shocks of one kind or another (i.e., war crises), or patents and franchises issued to firms allow them to make monopoly profits for as long as such patents last. And while this monopoly advantage may be eroded by competitors, life does not remain still and new patents and fran-chises may be issued, thus, moving us further away from long-run equilibrium. Exclusive franchises in the areas of transportation, telecommunications, energy and so on. permit firms to make supernormal profits, as do patents and trade marks, which enhance and protect product differentiation. Generally, monopoly power, which is explained by entry barriers, economies of scale and product differ-entiation, allows the emergence and maintenance of economic profits over time. Therefore, it follows that profits cannot be explained merely by reference to the functional or compensatory theories; rather they arise from the rigidities and fric-tions as well as the imperfections of all kinds, operating on the demand and supply sides. Profit then is the result of imperfect competition in factor and goods mar-kets and disequilibrium situations, which tend to make the adjustment process a slow one.

Therefore, the friction and monopoly theories suggest that profits result and are likely to persist in all those situations in which, on the supply side, factors of production do not receive a reward equal to their marginal product and also, on the demand side, when price exceeds marginal cost (MC). This approach of explaining economic profit in terms of monopoly power and friction has also implications for industrial policy, or competition policy, a theme discussed in Chapter 13. There are many examples of firms, which receive either above or below 'normal' profits, defined as economic profits in which an adjustment is made for risks associated with the particular industry. For example, the risks associated with oil operations in the North Sea are considerably higher than operating a chain of foodstores in the High Street. The idea that economic profit arises because of frictions and imperfections in the markets is much broader, than we saw earlier under the com-pensatory theories focusing on profit as the reward for the entrepreneurial function of risk-taking.

3.2.3 Innovations and technology theories

The technology and innovations theories consider profit as the reward for under-taking the research and development activity and adapting the fruits of that inventing activity to industrial and commercial uses. The adaptation of such invention is called innovation. Technological change takes the form of know-how, which involves new skills and information. This confers an advantage on its owners, since technology is a proprietary right that has a scarcity value and is marketable. When such technology is adapted to business uses, it results in an improvement of existing products, product differentiation, new products altogether, new materials, new methods and techniques of production – which are more efficient and, thus, less costly than existing ones, new organisational and marketing methods and new markets.

The innovation theory derives from the work of Schumpeter (1934), which was initially put forward to explain business cycles and economic development, rather than profits. Nevertheless, profits are associated with a changing economy and dynamic development. When in a stationary economy, an innovating entrepreneur introduces new ways of performing a given task at lower cost, then clearly he stands to gain higher profits over his competitors by exploiting that particular advantage. This initial shock disturbs the system and in this way 'profit is the reward for disrupting the status quo' (Dean 1951). However, imitative responses soon set in, as other firms try to meet the 'challenge' by producing close substitutes of the original innovation. The result of this activity is that, eventually, all firms in the industry will be making lower profits; until a new idea comes along to disturb the system once again, and allow the innovating firm to earn economic profits and, in passing, to render obsolete the old product and/or methods of production/ organisation and so on. This process echoes the Schumpeterian thesis of the 'creative destruction of capitalism'. The economic system is, thus, regenerated by the innovative activity, which creates new products and new, more efficient methods and techniques of production/organisation to replace the old, less efficient and costlier ones.

Accordingly, the economy does not proceed in a smooth and orderly manner, as the static, competitive theory implied, but rather moves in waves of spurts and shocks. Therefore, the innovation theory of profits emphasises the dynamic aspects and various changes in the economy and the possession of asymmetrical information by entrepreneurs. In this respect, the innovation theory of profit is linked with the earlier monopoly theories, since it stresses the exploitation of particular, firm-specific proprietary rights. Such proprietary rights can be protected through patents, yielding further profits over time. However, in this latter case the profits have become monopoly revenue, which is not profit but rent. We can also view the innovation theory as part of a wider uncertainty theory of profits. For despite the research and development activity of most large firms, innovations cannot be predicted, and so adjustments cannot be prearranged and planned. This means that innovations, when they do occur, will be accompanied by economic profits, even if we lived in a competitive economy, since adjustments by competitors take time to initiate and realise. Thus, monopolistic and oligopolistic elements are not necessary for the innovations theory of profits.

Nevertheless, it is the case that most innovations in modern industry take place in monopolistic or oligopolistic market structures, which reinforces the Schumpeterian thesis that a degree of monopoly is required to produce technical change on which economic progress depends (Schumpeter 1952). This theme is revisited at the end of this chapter, in the context of the Evolutionary theory of the firm, where we are reviewing, briefly, Schumpeter's work. At this stage, having placed the various theories of profits in context, we proceed now to discuss the theories of the firm.

3.3 THEORIES OF THE FIRM

A theory of the firm represents a simplified and abstract description of reality, which helps us understand how firms operate. A theory (or a model or a hypothesis, since for our purposes these terms can be taken to be interchangeable) is based on a number of assumptions and definitions from which by logical deduction certain conclusions about entrepreneurial activity emerge. A theory must be a simplified abstraction of reality in order to be general and flexible enough to apply to various situations, in which the basic assumptions are fulfilled. A theory of the firm is primarily intended to predict changes in certain endogenous variables (i.e., those under the control of the firm, such as for example, prices, levels of output, advertising levels and so on) given changes to various exogenous variables (i.e., those outside the control of the firm, that is changes in cost, demand, tax conditions and so on). Also, a theory of the firm is useful in explaining how firms can allocate their resources in trying to achieve their objectives.

From the methodological point of view, the acid test of any theory is how well its predictions stand up to the evidence of the real world; i.e., we judge a theory on the basis of how successfully it can explain what is designed to do. It is possible that in drawing up a simplified model of the firm some of our assumptions may seem unrealistic. In actual fact we can never be sure of the accuracy of our assumptions. Nevertheless, according at least to one brand of positivism, this is no reason to abandon our theory as long as its predictions are not refuted by the evidence. As long as our theory passes the test of verification, i.e., it is not falsified by the evidence, it can be retained as a useful tool of analysis and prediction and can be improved upon constructively, by further research.

Also, it must be borne in mind that in economics we are dealing with stochastic models rather than deterministic ones. This means that economic models try to explain, analyse and predict the behaviour of a 'representative' or an 'average' member of a group of similar economic agents, be they consumers, firms and so on. It follows that the behaviour of any one individual firm may deviate from this 'representative' or 'average' behaviour, without this, necessarily, constituting a refutation of our theory. Failure of a general theory to account fully for the behaviour of any one individual firm does not represent sufficient ground for consigning it to the paper basket. At the same time, however, our theory should be tested and verified against a large number of cases, before it can be tentatively accepted as a working hypothesis.

It was pointed out at the beginning of this chapter that firms control and coordinate various factors of production and transform them into marketable goods and services, for the purpose of achieving their objectives. In doing so firms are confronted, on the one hand, by market information – in the form of prices of output and factors of production and, on the other hand, by technological information – in the form of the appropriate production function. These, taken in conjunction with the available financial means at the firm's disposal and whatever government regulations may be in force, represent constraints in its productive activities. However, in order to make the system work we need to assume something about what the firms try to achieve in engaging in production. Now depending on the central behavioural assumption made, regarding entrepreneurial motivation or objectives, different theories of the firm can emerge. We now turn to examine, briefly, some of the salient features of the alternative models of the firm proposed.

3.3.1 The profit maximisation theory of the firm and its appraisal

The main features of the profit maximisation model, or the neoclassical, or traditional theory of the firm are that the firm is owned and managed by a single individual, or a few individuals, so that the functions of ownership and management are performed by the same people and, thus, there is no conflict of interest, that the sole objective of the firm (or its owners) is profit maximisation, which results in the well known equilibrium condition of MR = MC (marginal cost) (see detailed analysis in Chapter 10). In addition, we assume a state of certainty and perfect knowledge and foresight, which means that the firm has full information regarding the present and future cost and demand conditions, thus, it can derive its MR and MC functions and equate them to find the point of maximum profits.

Frequently, the profit maximisation theory of the firm is considered in terms of the 'black box' conceptual framework. As mentioned above, information regarding factor and output markets together with financial and government regulation constraints, that is the demand and production conditions, enter the 'black box' and what emerges are outputs in the form of goods and/or services for sale and profit. In other words, it is inside the 'black box' that the transformation of inputs into outputs occurs. Also, the firm's share of the market and profit provide feedback, which can modify the content of the 'box'. Clearly, the content of the 'box' represents the firm's 'know-how' in the form of various blueprints or its secrets of transforming inputs into outputs, successfully. It is this 'know-how' that is the firm's source of 'competitive advantage', which in turn is the source of profits, and firms, naturally, have a very strong incentive to protect the secrets of their 'box'. When one considers that patents and copyrights are jealously guarded by firms and the lengths to which industrial espionage takes, the idea of the 'black box', as a source of competitive advantage is as relevant today as it ever was. We consider the concept of competitive advantage below, but we return now to some of the details of the neoclassical theory of the firm. Thus, the average cost curve is assumed to be U-shaped, so that a single optimum point can be found. A full analysis of the equilibria positions of this model under different market structures is presented in the first part of Chapter 10, but it will suffice for our purposes here to illustrate how profits can be maximised. However, before proceeding we must define the period of time during which such maximisation occurs. Certain decisions by the firm, such as expanding capacity, will affect future profits, and indeed this is the reason why investment within the firm takes place. The subject of capital budgeting is discussed in Chapter 11, but here we are assuming that the firm tries to maximise profits within a specific period, say a single period, and that the investment costs are given. This approach means that, following the discussion of Chapter 7, we can discuss profit maximisation, firstly, under the single period or short-run production and pricing decisions, and secondly, under the multi-period or long-run investment decision.

Profit maximisation in a single period is illustrated in Figure 3.1(b), where we have drawn the total revenue (TR) and the total cost (TC) functions (explained in Chapters 4 and 7), assuming the firm operates in a monopolistic market. Profit is defined as the difference between TR and TC, and when the vertical differences

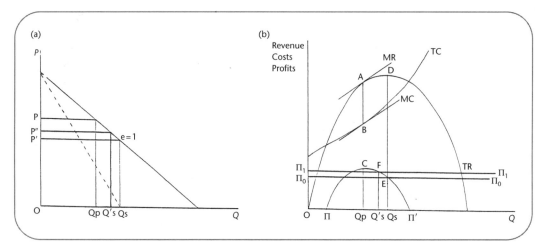

Figure 3.1 Single-period profit and sales maximisation

between the two functions are transferred to the bottom of the diagram they result in the profit function, given by the curve $\Pi\Pi'$.

Algebraically, the profit function is given by:

$$\Pi = TR - TC \tag{1}$$

Since all our relations in (1) are functions of output (Q) alone, differentiating (1) with respect to output and setting the derivative equal to zero results in:

$$\frac{d\Pi}{dQ} = \frac{d(TR)}{dQ} - \frac{d(TC)}{dQ} = 0 \tag{2}$$

or $d\Pi/dQ = MR - MC = 0$ giving finally

$$MR = MC \tag{3}$$

as the first-order condition (necessary condition) for profit maximisation, which can be solved for the profit maximising level of output. Notice that the second-order condition (sufficient condition) for profit maximisation is also satisfied, i.e., $d^2\Pi/dQ^2 < 0$, since MC rises faster than marginal revenue (MR). Substituting this value of output into the firm's demand function we derive the price at which it can be sold.

Diagrammatically, the profit maximising output is given by OQp, since at that level of output the vertical distance AB between the TR and TC functions is at its highest and is also equal to CQp. At output level OQp the tangents drawn at points A and B, representing MR and MC, respectively, are parallel to each other and, therefore, equal, as required. When the firm produces the profit maximising output OQp, it can find from its demand curve, shown in Figure 3.l(a), that it can charge a price of OP per unit. This discussion demonstrates the single-period profit maximising equilibrium of the firm.

However, the profit maximising theory of the firm has been criticised by various writers on a number of grounds, ranging from questions regarding the behavioural assumption of entrepreneurial activity to the assertion that the type of firm implied by the neoclassical theory is not easily found among actual business firms. The work of Hall & Hitch (discussed in Chapter 10) and Lester has demonstrated that businessmen utilise different concepts to those of the marginal analysis, while other critics have pointed out that actual firms cannot possibly have the kind of information required by the firm of the neoclassical theory. Therefore, a brief discussion of the criticisms leveled against the traditional theory is necessary, not only because it will provide us with a sharp insight into this theory but it will also give us a better understanding of the need for alternative models of the firm. We can summarise such criticisms under the following heading, suggested by Naylor and Vernon (1969):

1. *Goals*: The theory assumes that the firm maximises its profits in an 'objective rational' way, implying the existence of the 'economic man', i.e., someone omniscient and, thus, possessing full information on all relevant variables. Attacks on this assumption have been along the lines that profit is only one of many goals; that while the importance of profit is not denied, the assumption of maximising is replaced by profit sufficing; that uncertainty and imperfect information make the attainment of maximum profits impossible, and that imperfect information together with profit maximisation result in subjective rational behaviour rather than objective one, as the theory contends; that firms behave in a non-rational manner. Consequently, alternative business objectives are treated further on in this chapter.

2. *Perfect knowledge*: The theory assumes perfect knowledge of the firm's revenue, cost and production functions. However, this is not the case as information is not given and it is not costless. Instead, it must be searched for and discovered and the order in which the environment is searched determines the decisions to be made. Therefore, in Chapter 5 we discuss demand forecasting, and the method of least squares, examined there, can also be used to estimate cost functions.

3. *Complete certainty*: The assumption of complete certainty sidesteps some crucial aspects facing management, i.e., risk and uncertainty. We saw earlier that the crux of the entrepreneurial function is to undertake the risks of economic enterprise and assume the responsibility of making decisions under uncertainty, in the expectation of profit. We examine the problems of risk and uncertainty in Chapters 11 and 12.

4. *Decision-making process*: According to the neoclassical theory, firms decide what levels of outputs to produce and what factor inputs to buy on the basis of equating certain price ratios with the marginal rate of technical substitution and marginal rate of technical transformation. Certain studies have suggested that firms decide not on the basis of marginalist principles but rather by following a series of rules of thumb or heuristics. We cover some of these problems in Chapter 10.

5. *Organisation*: It has been argued that the firm of the neoclassical theory has few of the features of actual firms. It has no complex organisation, no control, no standard operating procedures, no budget, no controller. To certain critics it seemed implausible that a theory of an organisation (the

firm) can ignore the fact that it is an organisation itself. Other critics have suggested that organisation theory be integrated into the economic theory of the firm.

6. *Production process*: The neoclassical theory assumes a smooth, continuous, strictly concave, twice differentiable production function, which is determined by engineers and technologists and given to the economist. The firm's products and inputs are assumed perfectly divisible and, consequently, differential calculus is applied for the purpose of constrained optimisation, as shown in Chapter 6. However, the use of mathematical programming has been suggested as a more relevant optimisation method, and we cover this approach in Chapter 8.

7. *Static equilibrium*: The neoclassical theory of the firm is essentially a static one. The various functions (revenue, cost, production) remain unchanged and the firm's responses are examined in terms of comparative statics, i.e., given a change in an exogenous variable or parameter we try to trace out the effect on the endogenous variables after some time has passed to allow for adjustments to take place. However, this approach overlooks problems of growth, dynamic feedbacks, capital accumulation, capital budgeting and so on. Some of these problems are discussed in the remainder of this chapter and also in Chapters 11 and 12.

8. *Environment*: There are both a broad external environment within which the firm operates and a larger internal environment created by the firm. Both of these are ignored by the neoclassical theory. The external environment consists of attitudes and opinions related to the firm on the part of the government, other organisations and the public in general. The internal one has to do with the morale, self-discipline and attitudes towards the firm of all those closely connected with it.

The main proponent and defender of the neoclassical faith has been Friedman, who has argued that the critics have missed the point by concentrating their fire on the validity of the assumptions of the models. Friedman (1953) argues that the validity of a model does not depend on the validity of its assumptions, but rather on the ability of the model to predict the behaviour of the dependent (endogenous) variables, and he thinks that on this criterion the neoclassical model of the firm has been successful. Nevertheless, it is strange to state the assumptions of a model, proceed to exempt a subset of such assumptions from verification and then claim that the content of the theory is open to empirical refutation. Others have argued that the assumptions of the model are plausible, provided the cost and revenue functions are subjectively known to the firm, than objectively as the theory requires. Yet others content that although firms may not be able to use marginal analysis objectively in their decision-making processes, in the long run only those firms will survive, which make decisions consistent with neoclassical theory. Finally, to incorporate into the theory the changes proposed by the critics would, undoubtedly, make the models more 'realistic' but at the same time very difficult if not impossible to solve. Therefore, it may be better to remain with the neoclassical model, which is more flexible and easier to tackle.

3.4   MANAGERIAL THEORIES OF THE FIRM

The profit maximising theory of the firm is justified as long as firms are owned and run by an individual, or a few individuals – the entrepreneur, who, as we saw above, risks his capital, makes the decisions and earns his rewards. The entrepreneur is considered to be a rational 'economic man', i.e., an omniscient individual and thus capable of maximising his profits. Further, since there is no conflict between him and the firm, profit maximisation becomes also the sole objective of the firm. In addition, if we assume perfect competition (see discussion in Chapter 10), profit maximisation becomes also necessary for the long-term survival of the firm.

However, the development of the large public company has resulted in a separation of ownership from control of the firm, as was shown by the early work of Berle and Means (1932). Large companies are owned by a multitude of shareholders, each of whom is holding, typically, a relatively tiny number of shares, but run or controlled by experienced, salaried managers. Given the widely dispersed shareholding, individual shareholders, except perhaps a very tiny minority with relatively large holdings, play no role in company decisions. While this may be mitigated, somewhat, by the rise in recent years of the institutional shareholders, like insurance companies, pension funds and so on, it is still the case that the separation of ownership from control is very prevalent in industrially developed economies. This separation means that managers may develop their own distinct objectives such as salaries, pursuit of power, status, security, prestige and so on as opposed to the profit maximisation goal assumed to be desired by shareholders.

In addition, the monopolistic and/or oligopolistic structure of most of modern industry implies that large firms can extract monopoly profits through, e.g., the existence of various barriers to entry and, consequently, managers of such firms are not under the same kind of market pressure and discipline to maximise profit for the firm to survive, as under the framework of perfect competition. This means that there is an element of discretion in the hands of the managers, who may very well choose to exercise it in pursuit of alternative goals.

The managerial theories of the firm that have been put forward to challenge the neoclassical paradigm, all have in common the characteristics of the separation of ownership from control, the oligopolistic nature of modern industry and the existence of discretionary power, as demonstrated by the appearance of management or organisational slack.

3.4.1   Single-period sales maximisation model

Baumol (1958, 1959) proposed that, given the separation of ownership from control, firms try to maximise their revenue (sales) rather than their profits subject, however, to a minimum profit constraint. As long as firms make sufficient profits to satisfy the capital market and ensure the firm's standing, and keep their shareholders happy, and one may add, the managers in their positions, the latter are able to proceed with revenue maximisation, which will allow them to pursue their own objectives of higher salaries, perks, security, prestige and so on.

From the point of view of decision-making within the firm – which concerns us here, Baumol's model derives different predictions about the firm's behaviour, than that of profit maximisation. We saw earlier in Figure 3.l(b) that the profit maximising output is given by the equality of MR and MC as OQp, resulting in a price of OP per unit, as in Figure 3.l(a). If the profit constraint is not binding, i.e., if the minimum profit required is below Π_0 in Figure 3.l(b), then the sales maximising firm will produce the output level OQs, at which TR is at its highest, OsD, which is the same as the point of output at which MR is zero and price elasticity of demand is equal to one, as shown in Figure 3.1(a). It is obvious that the sales maximising output OQs is higher than the profit maximising output OQp. It is also obvious, from Figure 3.l(a), that this higher output can only be sold at the lower price OP' than the profit maximising one OP. When the profit constraint becomes operative, as in the case of Π_1 in Figure 3.1(b), then the firm will cut back its production to OQ's. While the constrained level of output is less than the unconstrained one, it is still greater than the profit maximising output, and the price OP'' at which it is sold will be lower than the profit maximising one, although, greater than the unconstrained one. This response will be retained as long as the minimum profit is set at a level lower than the maximum profit obtained at output level OQp.

Baumol felt that the profit constraint will be binding in all cases because of advertising expenditure or 'staff' expenditure (as in other managerial models of the firm), which can always increase the firm's physical sales, even though at a diminishing rate. This means that TR increases with advertising (or other similar expenditure, such as 'staff') albeit at a diminishing rate. Thus, there is no upper limit to TR as advertising increases, but the latter sooner or later will be restrained by the minimum profit constraint, which will determine the optimum level of advertising, as shown in Figure 3.2. In this figure we reproduce the firm's TR, TC and profit function and measure advertising on the horizontal axis. With a profit constraint of Π_0, the constrained sales maximising level of advertising is OAs, contrasting with the profit maximising level of advertising OAp. As long as the profit constraint is lower than maximum profit, the advertising expenditure of the sales maximiser will always be higher than that of the profit maximiser, resulting in a higher level of output and a lower price.

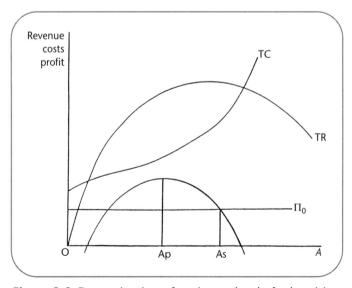

Figure 3.2 Determination of optimum level of advertising

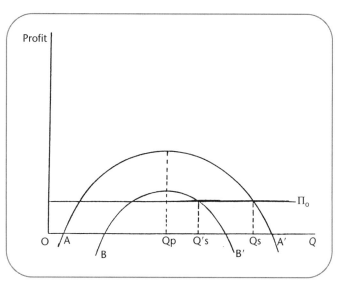

Figure 3.3 Effects of changes in fixed costs under profit and sales maximisation

Also, the two models of profit maximisation and sales maximisation predict different responses to output produced and prices charged, following a change in fixed costs. If there is an increase in fixed costs such, as for example, the imposition of a lump sum tax, the TC curve would shift upwards by the same amount at all output levels and, correspondingly, the profits curve would shift downwards, as shown in Figure 3.3. The original profits curve is given by AA' and the new one by BB'. It follows that the profit maximiser will be producing an output level of OQp before and after the change in fixed cost. Since the firm was maximising its profits before the change, it will continue to do so after the change, although it will be earning less profits now by the amount of the lump sum tax. Therefore, since there is no change in output its price also will remain the same. However, the sales maximiser, in trying to meet the minimum profit constraint of Π_0 will cut back its output from OQs before the change, to OQ's after the change and also raise its price.

Similar responses are observed if there is a change in the tax rate. If the corporation tax rate increases, it shifts the profits curve downwards but only for the profitable levels of output, as shown in Figure 3.4. In response to that sort of increase, the sales maximising firm reduces its output from OQs to OQ's (and raises its price) in order to meet its profit constraint. By contrast, the profit maximising firm will go on producing the same level of output OQp, and charge the same price, before and after the change in the corporation tax rate, since OQp results in the highest possible profits in both situations.

Finally, if there were a change in variable costs both the profit maximising and the sales maximising firm would react in a similar manner by cutting or raising output, depending on whether variable costs increased or decreased. This is illustrated in Figure 3.5, where for simplicity we draw the TC curves TC_1 and TC_2 as straight lines. In the original situation with costs given by TC_1, the profits function is shown as AA' and the profit maximising firm produces OQp, while the sales maximising firm, operating under a minimum profit constraint of Π_0, produces

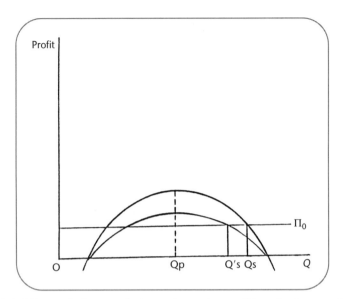

Figure 3.4 Effects of changes in tax rate under profit and sales maximisation

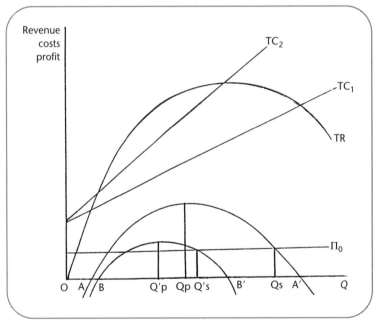

Figure 3.5 Effects of changes in variable costs under profit and sales maximisation

OQs. When the change in costs occurs, the profits function becomes BB′ and both types of firm reduce their output levels to OQ′p and OQ′s, respectively and also raise their prices. Similarly, if there were a shift in the demand curve, say an upward shift, both types of firm would react by raising output, since, *ceteris paribus*, the profits curve would shift upwards.

3.4.2　Algebraic comparison between profit and sales maximisation

We provide here a mathematical comparison between the profit maximisation and sales maximisation models. The variables used have the following meaning.

Q = Output
R = Total revenue = $R(Q, A)$
A = Advertising or 'staff' expenditure
C = Production cost = $C(Q)$
Π = Total profit = $(R - C - A)$
Π_0 = Minimum profit constraint
t = profits tax rate, $1 > t > 0$

3.4.2a　Profit maximiser

Here the objective is to maximise after tax profits, so the relevant profit function is:

$$\Pi = (1 - t)(R - C - A) = (1 - t)[R(Q, A) - C - A] \tag{1}$$

Partially differentiating (1) with respect to Q and A and setting the derivatives to zero gives:

$$\delta\Pi/\delta Q = (1 - t)(\delta R/\delta Q - \delta C/\delta Q) = 0 \tag{2}$$

$$\delta\Pi/\delta A = (1 - t)(\delta R/\delta A - 1) = 0 \tag{3}$$

Relations (2) and (3) are the first-order conditions (necessary conditions) for a profit maximum. If we divide through relations (2) and (3) by $(1 - t)$ and rearrange we obtain the following two conditions:

$$\delta R/\delta Q = \delta C/\delta Q$$

which is the familiar condition that for profit maximisation we require MR to be equal to MC, and

$$\delta R/\delta A = 1$$

stating that at the profit maximising output the change in TR brought about by a small increment in advertising (or any other 'staff' variable) is unity. The implication of this result is that the profit maximiser will go on increasing advertising expenditure for as long as such expenditure adds more to TR than it does to TCs and will stop when the last increment spent on advertising increases TR by exactly the same amount.

3.4.2b　Sales maximiser

In this case the objective is to maximise Total Revenue, R, subject to a minimum profit constraint $\Pi \geq \Pi_0$. Therefore, the Lagrange expression is formulated as follows (assuming that the constraint is satisfied as equality):

$$L(Q, A, \lambda) = R(Q, A) + \lambda\{(1 - t)[R(Q, A) - C - A] - \Pi_0\} \tag{4}$$

Partially differentiating (4) with respect to Q, A and λ and setting the partial derivatives to zero we obtain the following first-order conditions for revenue maximisation:

$$\delta L/\delta Q = \delta R/\delta Q + \lambda(1-t)\delta R/\delta Q - \lambda(1-t)\delta C/\delta Q = 0 \tag{5}$$

$$\delta L/\delta A = \delta R/\delta A + \lambda(1-t)\delta R/\delta A - \lambda(1-t) = 0 \tag{6}$$

$$\delta L/\delta \lambda = (1-t)[R(Q,A) - C - A] - \Pi_0 = 0 \tag{7}$$

Relation (5) can be written as:

$$\frac{\delta R}{\delta Q} = \frac{(1-t)\lambda}{1+(1-t)\lambda} \times \frac{\delta C}{\delta Q} \quad \text{where } 1 > t > 0 \text{ and } \lambda \geq 0 \tag{8}$$

If the minimum profit constraint is not binding, then $\lambda = 0$ and relation (8) simply reduces to $\delta R/\delta Q = 0$, which means that TR is maximised at the point where MR is zero, as found earlier. However, when the constraint is binding then $\lambda > 0$ and relation (8) gives us:

$$\frac{\delta R}{\delta Q} < \frac{\delta C}{\delta Q}$$

i.e., the sales maximiser will produce at the point where MC > MR, corresponding to an output level greater than that of the profit maximiser.

Similarly, relation (6) can be written as:

$$\frac{\delta R}{\delta A} = \frac{\lambda(1-t)}{1+\lambda(1-t)} \quad \text{where } 1 > t > 0 \text{ and } \lambda > 0 \quad \text{giving} \quad \delta R/\delta A < 1$$

i.e., in contrast with the profit maximiser, the sales maximiser will continue with advertising expenditure, or any other 'staff' expenditure, to a point where the increment in such expenditure adds less to TR than it does to TCs. Finally, relation (7) may be written as:

$$(1-t)[R(Q,A) - C - A] = \Pi_0$$

and as long as the equality in the relation holds, the after tax minimum profit constraint is satisfied; which is a behaviour entirely consistent with the sales maximising hypothesis.

3.4.3 Managers' utility maximisation hypothesis

Williamson (1963, 1964) has proposed an alternative model of business behaviour emphasising the well-being and self-seeking interest of the managers of firms. As in Baumol's case, Williamson's model is based on the separation of ownership from management and a monopolistic or oligopolistic environment. This structure allows managers to exercise their discretion in seeking to advance their own interests, in the form of maximising their utility, subject to a minimum profit constraint, imposed by the capital market, in order to provide sufficient dividends to shareholders and to show a reasonable rate of growth over time.

According to Williamson, managers are interested in salaries and other bonuses, security and professional excellence. The position and prestige of managers can be enhanced by their ability to direct additional expenditure on staff, S, on managerial emoluments or perquisites, M, and on discretionary investment, I_D. Salaries are, clearly, the primary factor affecting the well-being of managers, but not the only one. The number and quality of staff, S, reporting to a manager show the manager's importance and the larger the size of staff commanded the greater the monetary compensation of that manager is.

Also, the various emoluments or perquisites, M, that managers receive, in the form of luxurious offices, chauffer driven limousines, expense accounts and so on, which are beyond those strictly necessary for the running of the firm, are treated by Williamson as another element entering the managers' utility function. Finally, the extent to which managers can influence the new investment or discretionary investment, I_D, of the firm shows their power, since they are able to affect the future development of the firm. Therefore, the utility function that managers seek to maximise is given by:

$$U = U(S, M, I_D)$$

where S represents the excess expenditure on staff, known as management slack absorbed as staff expenditure (clearly, not all expenditure on staff is of this nature); M stands for the various emoluments, known as management slack absorbed as cost and, finally, I_D is the discretionary investment, which is beyond replacement investment, the latter covered by the minimum profit constraint.

Since we have more than two variables, it may be more appropriate to consider a mathematical presentation of the Williamson model.

The model

Williamson introduces four types of profits: maximum profits, actual profits, reported profits and minimum required profits. Maximum profits, Π^*, are the same as in the profit maximising firm. Actual profits, Π_A, are maximum profits less the excess expenditure on staff, so we have

$$\Pi_A = \Pi^* - S \tag{1}$$

Reported profits, Π_R, are actual profits less the amount of management slack absorbed as cost, M. Reported profits, Π_R, are the same as taxable profits, out of which the firm will pay taxes, dividends and also finance replacement investment, so we get:

$$\Pi_R = \Pi_A - M \tag{2}$$

Minimum required after tax profits, Π_0, are the lowest level of profits which are consistent with the managers retaining effective control of the firm. From these minimum profits Π_0, dividends are paid and replacement investment is financed, but not discretionary investment. If t is the tax rate and T represents taxes, then we have:

$$T = t\Pi_R \tag{3}$$

and the minimum profit constraint is given by:

$$\Pi_R > \Pi_0 + T \tag{4}$$

or

$$\Pi_R > \Pi_0/(1-t) \tag{5}$$

The amount of slack in the minimum profits constraint (4) represents the amount of discretionary investment, I_D, and so we get:

$$I_D = \Pi_R - \Pi_0 - T \tag{6}$$

Therefore, we have the managers' utility function:

$$U = U(S, M, I_D) \tag{7}$$

Managers' utility maximisation requires that we need to maximise function (7) subject to the minimum profit constraint given by relation (4), i.e., $\Pi_R > \Pi_0 + T$, which from relation (6) implies that $I_D > 0$. The other constraints are $S > 0$ and $M > 0$. We need now to find appropriate functions for M and I_D to incorporate them in (7), and we work as follows:

Let Q stand for output and also let

$$\rho = \Pi_R/\Pi_A \tag{8}$$

We have

$$TR = R = PQ \tag{9}$$

i.e., TR is given by the product of price (P) and output (Q) and define

$$P = P(Q, S, \varepsilon) \tag{10}$$

i.e., the demand function, as a function of output Q, staff expenditure S, and a shift parameter ε, such that:

$$\delta P/\delta Q < 0 \tag{11}$$
$$\delta P/\delta S > 0 \tag{12}$$
$$\delta P/\delta \varepsilon > 0 \tag{13}$$

These conditions tell us something about the demand function, i.e., how demand varies for small variations in Q, S and ε. Thus in (11) we have the usual inverse price–quantity relationship, and in (12) and (13) we hypothesise a positive relationship between demand and S and ε. In other words, additional expenditure on staff, S, increases the demand for the firm's products and so does an upward shift in demand, ε.

Total production costs are given by:

$$C = C(Q) \tag{14}$$

and so

$$\Pi_A = R - C - S \tag{15}$$

Using relation (8) above we get:

$$\Pi_A - \Pi_R = (1 - \Pi_R/\Pi_A)\Pi_A = (1 - \rho)\Pi_A \tag{16}$$

Now utilising relations (2), (15) and (16) we derive the following relation for management slack absorbed as cost, M:

$$M = \Pi_A - \Pi_R = (1 - \rho)(R - C - S) \tag{17}$$

From relations (3) and (6) we get:

$$I_D = \Pi_R - \Pi_0 - t\Pi_R = (1 - t)\Pi_R - \Pi_0 \tag{18}$$

and from relations (18), (8) and (15) we derive the following expression for discretionary investment, I_D:

$$I_D = (1 - t)\rho\Pi_A - \Pi_0 = \rho(1 - t)(R - C - S) - \Pi_0 \tag{19}$$

Finally, substituting relations (17) and (19) into relation (7) we derive the following expression for the managers' utility function:

$$U = U[S, (1 - \rho)(R - C - S), \rho(1 - t)(R - C - S) - \Pi_0] \tag{20}$$

Since the policy variables at the firm's disposal are the level of output Q, the staff expenditure S, and the proportion ρ of reported to actual profits, by differentiating expression (20) with respect to these policy variables Q, S and ρ, and setting the partial derivatives equal to zero, we obtain the following first-order conditions for utility maximisation:

$$\frac{\delta U}{\delta Q} = U_2(1 - \rho)\frac{\delta R}{\delta Q} - \frac{\delta C}{\delta Q} + U_3\rho(1 - t)\frac{\delta R}{\delta Q} - \frac{\delta C}{\delta Q} = 0 \tag{21}$$

$$\frac{\delta U}{\delta S} = U_1 + U_2(1 - \rho)\left(\frac{\delta R}{\delta S} - 1\right) + U_3\rho(1 - t)\left(\frac{\delta R}{\delta S} - 1\right) = 0 \tag{22}$$

$$\frac{\delta U}{d\rho} = U_2(-1)(R - C - S) + U_3(1 - t)(R - C - S) = 0 \tag{23}$$

where

$U_1 = \delta U/\delta S =$ marginal utility of staff expenditure

$U_2 = \delta U/\delta M =$ marginal utility of emoluments (management slack absorbed as cost)

$U_3 = \delta U/\delta I_D =$ marginal utility of discretionary investment

Relation (21) can be written as:

$$(\delta R/\delta Q - \delta C/\delta Q)[U_2(1 - \rho) + U_3\rho(1 - t)] = 0$$

which can only be satisfied if $\delta R/\delta Q = \delta C/\delta Q$ since the term in the bracket in the expression above is positive. This gives us the first-order condition for the utility maximising firm as:

$$\frac{\delta R}{\delta Q} = \frac{\delta C}{\delta Q} \qquad (24)$$

which equates MR to MC, as in the profit maximising firm.

Solving now relation (22) for $\delta R/\delta S$ we get:

$$\frac{\delta R}{\delta S}[U_2(1 - \rho) + U_3\rho(1 - t)] + U_1 - U_2(1 - \rho) - U_3\rho(1 - t) = 0 \qquad (25)$$

giving

$$\frac{\delta R}{\delta S} = \frac{-U_1 + U_2(1 - \rho) + U_3\rho(1 - t)}{U_2(1 - \rho) + U_3\rho(1 - t)} \qquad (26)$$

implying that

$$\delta R/\delta S < 1 \qquad (26a)$$

i.e., in equilibrium the utility maximising firm will employ staff beyond the point where the MC of staff is equal to its MR. In other words, the firm will employ more staff than a profit maximising one. This is an equivalent result to the treatment of advertising in the sales maximising model, showing advertising and 'staff' expenditure to be equivalent variables.

Finally, from (23) we obtain:

$$U_2 = U_3(1 - t) \qquad (27)$$

Therefore, relations (24), (26) and (27) determine the optimal values for the policy (or endogenous) variables Q, S and ρ. Notice that in (24) we obtain the same condition of the equality of MR to MC, as under profit maximisation. However, the optimal level of output, Q, is not the same in the two cases, since in the utility maximising firm the staff expenditure, S, is greater, as we see from (26a), resulting in higher output. From (27) we see that U_3 must be proportional to U_2, and the proportionality factor is $1/(1 - t)$. This shows that in the utility maximising firm some profit will be absorbed as emoluments (management slack absorbed as cost), the amount depending on the rate of tax, t. The higher t is the lower U_2/U_3 is, i.e., the smaller the marginal rate of substitution of emoluments for discretionary investment, and so more will be spent on emoluments and less on discretionary investment.

3.4.3a   Comparisons with profit maximisation

Under profit maximisation maximum profits are equal to actual profits and to reported profits and, thus,

$$\Pi^* = \Pi_A = \Pi_R \quad \text{so that} \quad \rho = 1 \tag{28}$$

and, therefore, the profits function is given by

$$\Pi^* = R - C - S \tag{29}$$

Differentiating (29) with respect to Q and S and setting the partial derivatives equal to zero we obtain the following:

$$\frac{\delta \Pi^*}{\delta Q} = \frac{\delta R}{\delta Q} - \frac{\delta C}{\delta Q} \tag{30}$$

$$\frac{\delta \Pi^*}{\delta S} = \frac{\delta R}{\delta S} - 1 \tag{31}$$

which can be rewritten to give us the following two relations:

$$\frac{\delta R}{\delta Q} = \frac{\delta C}{\delta Q} \tag{32}$$

$$\frac{\delta R}{\delta S} = 1 \tag{33}$$

Although (32) is the same as (24), the level of output, Q, is not the same in the two models, since $\delta R/\delta S$ is implicitly a function of S (staff expenditure) which is different in the two models. Also, relations (26) and (33) are different. As long as $U_1 > 0$ (which we expect it to be), relation (26), as we saw above, implies that $\delta R/\delta S < 1$, which contrasts with (33). Therefore, in the Williamson's model there are higher expenditures for staff, in much the same way that in Baumol's model there is higher level of advertising.

Table 3.1 summarises the comparative statics results of the utility and profit maximisation models by tracing out the changes in the policy variables output Q, staff expenditure S, and the profit proportion $\rho(\Pi_R/\Pi_A)$ induced by upward changes in a demand shift parameter ε, the tax rate t, and a lump sum tax T.

Table 3.1   Comparative statics results

| | Utility maximising firm | | | | Profit maximising firm | | |
| | Parameter | | | | | Parameter | | |
Variable	ε	t	T	Variable	ε	t	T
Q	+	+	−	Q	+	0	0
S	+	+	−	S	+	0	0
ρ	−	−	+				

In conclusion, it can be said that the only evidence for the utility maximising hypothesis is empirical observation based on field studies and statistical analyses. This model appears to be plausible on the basis of casual empiricism, however, it does not refute the profit maximising hypothesis, which seems to be very relevant particularly in the long run. Rather, it suggests that in certain types of market, where competition is weak, this type of business behaviour may have more empirical relevance than profit maximisation.

3.4.4 Theory of growth

A number of writers have emphasised the dynamic elements in the development of firms and have argued that growth is a necessary condition for the survival of the firm in the long run, in an uncertain and changing environment. They view growth and decline as complementary aspects of the competitive process of the economy. Baumol (1959) saw his sales maximisation theory, discussed above, as a basis for a theory of growth and, indeed, he developed a growth model, which in turn he used for the presentation of policy proposals. However, in what follows we present, briefly, the work of Marris (1964, 1971), as representative in the area of the theories of growth.

According to Downie (1958), Penrose (1959) and Marris, the firm is a multi-product firm as distinct from the single product firm of the traditional theory. The firm is considered as an administrative and social organisation capable of entering any field of activity, New products may be introduced and old ones dropped from production lines. Therefore, diversification is seen as the main vehicle of growth, particularly by Penrose and Marris. As long as the administrative structure of the firm can be adjusted and adapted to larger scales of operation, the firm can expand indefinitely. Firms are not limited to any market, industry or country, although, as a matter of deliberate choice they may specialise, if they perceive advantages in doing so. New assets and new personnel can always be recruited. Also, since the firm is not restricted to any one market, its growth is not limited by its existing market, and, thus, the demand side does not provide an upper limit to the size of the firm. However, there is an upper limit to its rate of growth, provided by various 'dynamic' constraints, such as financial, demand and managerial. Marris, utilising these three constraints, has formulated a rigorous theory of growth of the firm and developed, in passing, his theory of takeovers.

The model

The growth maximising hypothesis is concerned with the growth of assets, and, according to the hypothesis, the growth of assets may be financed in three non-exclusive ways.

1. By an increase in undistributed profits (i.e., by an increase in retentions).

2. By an increase in the amount of debt.

3. By an increase in the equity share issue.

Within the context of the theory of growth, the above three ways take the form of constraints on maximising behaviour. Now to illustrate Marris's theory of takeovers the following variables are defined:

A = total assets
D = total debt
b = 'gearing' ratio = leverage = debt ratio = D/A
S = number of equity shares issued
Ps = market price of shares
SPs = market valuation of firm
p = rate of return on assets
i = rate of interest on loan capital
U = undistributed profits
r = retention ratio = $U/$(total profits)

Ignoring taxes and denoting change by the Greek letter delta (Δ) we have three ways of financing a growth of assets, namely, through undistributed profits, through and increase in debt and, finally, through a change in the number of shares issued (e.g., by means of a rights issue), which will change the market price of shares and affect the market valuation. Therefore, we can represent these changes as follows:

$$\Delta A = U + \Delta D + \Delta SPs \qquad (1)$$

The total profits are given by (pA) out of which the firm must pay interest on debt, given by (iD). Therefore, after interest payments on debt have been made, the profit left is given by ($pA - iD$) and so relation (1) can be written as:

$$\Delta A = r(pA - iD) + \Delta D + \Delta SPs$$

Dividing the above relation through by A and substituting the value $b = D/A$ we get:

$$\frac{\Delta A}{A} = r(p - ib) + \frac{\Delta D}{A} + \frac{\Delta SPs}{A}$$

Substituting in the second term of the right-hand side of the above the value of $D = Ab$ and multiplying and dividing the last term by S, gives us the following:

$$\frac{\Delta A}{A} = r(p - ib) + \frac{\Delta Ab}{A} + \frac{\Delta S}{S} \times \frac{SPs}{A}$$

or

$$\frac{\Delta A}{A}(1 - b) = r(p - ib) + \frac{\Delta S}{S} \times \frac{SPs}{A}$$

Finally, solving for $\Delta A/A$ gives us the following expression:

$$\frac{\Delta A}{A} = r\frac{p - ib}{1 - b} + \frac{SPs}{A(1 - b)} \times \frac{\Delta S}{S} \qquad (2)$$

Now a key variable, the valuation ratio, is defined as the total market value of the firm divided by the value directly attributable to shareholders, i.e.,

$$V = \frac{SPs}{A - D}$$

In equation (2) the term SPs/$A(1 - b)$ can be written as SPs/$A(1 - D/A)$ which can be simplified as:

$$\frac{SPs}{A - D} = V \text{ which gives us the valuation ratio}$$

Therefore, by substituting the valuation ratio, V, into relation (2) we can finally derive the following:

$$\frac{\Delta A}{A} = r\frac{p - ib}{1 - b} + V\frac{\Delta S}{S} \tag{3}$$

From this final relation (3) we have that the balanced rate of growth of assets, $g = (\Delta A/A)$ depends on three classes of variables. First, there are a number of policy variables, which the firm can choose for itself. These are the gearing or leverage or debt ratio, b, the retention ratio, r, and the growth of share issue $\Delta S/S$. Marris considers that the main source of finance for growth is provided by retained profits. Clearly, the firm is conscious that, after a point, increased gearing (D/A) is associated with increased risk, and it needs to set an upper limit to the gearing ratio. Also, there is an upper limit to the retention ratio, set by the need to distribute dividends and keep the shareholders happy and also maintain the share price. Similar considerations apply to a share issue and, indeed, for prestige and other reasons this route of obtaining finance is not often, if at all, used by established firms. Second, the return on assets, r, can only be assumed with uncertainty. Third, the valuation ratio, V, and more particularly the rate of interest, i, depend mostly on external forces over which the firm has either very little or no control at all.

The gearing ratio, liquidity ratio and retention ratio form what Marris calls the financial security constraint, and, thus, the firm tries to maximise the balanced rate of growth subject to satisfying this constraint. Particular attention must be paid to the valuation ratio, as the firm grows. When $V = 1$, the market value of the firm is exactly equal to its net assets. But if the firm's actions in trying to achieve its growth objective were to reduce the valuation ratio, then there is a clear danger of takeover bids. That is, when $V < 1$, the market value (or the 'price' at which the firm can be taken over) is less than the value of its net assets, and represents a good bargain for a takeover raider. Therefore, as long as $V = 1$ or $V > 1$ the firm is safe, but when $V < 1$ the firm is unsafe; there is a danger of a takeover threat.

In Marris's theory, the managers' utility function is given by: $U = U(g, V)$, i.e., it depends on the growth rate, g, and the valuation rate, V; the latter acting as a constraint. The trade-off between the valuation ratio, V, and the growth rate, g, determines the shape of the managerial indifference curves, shown in Figure 3.7. The growth rate depends on the rate of profitability, p, and the rate of retention, r. The relationship between profitability and growth is shown in Figure 3.6. Growth in demand is provided by diversification and the supply of capital is met only by retaining internally generated funds. Initially, profitability increases, as growth rises, but after a critical rate is reached it diminishes because of the need to undertake higher expenditure in the form of advertising and R&D spending to achieve higher diversification rates. Therefore, the growth demand curve takes the form of an inverted U. The supply of capital relationship shows that the rate at which the firm can raise internal funds for future growth varies positively with the profit rate. However, the firm can choose different retention ratios and, thus, a different supply

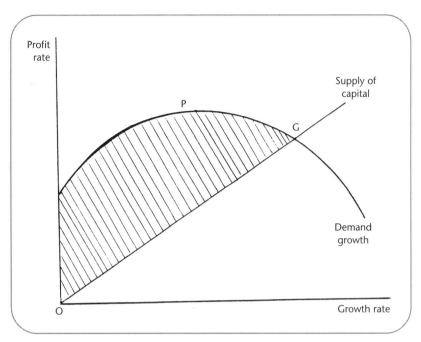

Figure 3.6 Relationship between profitability and growth

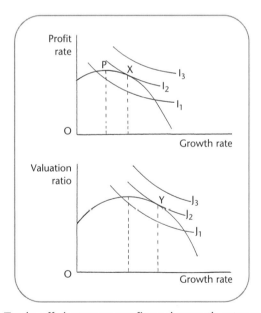

Figure 3.7 Trade-offs between profit and growth rates and between
valuation ratio and growth rate

of capital curve associated with each of those ratios. This means that the supply of
capital will pivot clockwise, and the shaded area in Figure 3.6 indicates the profit–
growth combinations available to the firm. The highest profit rate is attained at
point P, which is what the shareholders would like, but if managers are prepared

to pursue a higher growth rate, e.g., that given by point G, by accepting a lower valuation ratio and a higher threat of a takeover bid, the retention ratio rises, pivots the supply of capital curve to the right and equilibrium occurs at point G. However, if owners also like capital gains, which can be expected to arise with growth, then they may settle for a point right of P, such as X in Figure 3.7, corresponding to the point of their trade-off between dividends and capital gains, i.e., between profits and growth.

Managers trying to maximise the growth rate subject to a security constraint, in our case the minimum valuation ratio which will keep them in effective control of the firm, will choose point G in Figure 3.6, corresponding to point Y in Figure 3.7. In the top part of Figure 3.7, curves I_1, I_2 and I_3 represent the shareholder indifference curves between profit and growth, while in the bottom part, curves J_1, J_2 and J_3 are the managerial indifference curves between the valuation rate and growth. If there is a greater fear of a takeover bid, then the managerial indifference curves will be flatter and, in the limit, become horizontal, thus, indicating that equilibrium is attained at the shareholders' preferred point P.

3.5   THE TRANSACTION COSTS THEORY

In the last thirty years of so we have seen a proliferation of work in the related areas of transaction cost economics and the principal–agent problem. These areas are exploring significant facets of the firms and provide fascinating insights into the work of a modern enterprise, hitherto untouched by the earlier theories, and they have emanated, particularly, with dissatisfaction with the neoclassical theory considered above, which treats the firm as a 'black box' in the transformation of inputs into outputs. In particular, questions of firm organisation, of owning or leasing inputs and of various contractual relationships are very important in the operation of a firm. We can only provide a glimpse of these issues here, because of the limitations of a textbook analysis, but it is hoped that interested readers can consult the selected bibliography and the references contained therein for a better treatment and understanding of the issues involved. We start then with the transaction costs approach.

Under this approach, the main objective of the firm is the minimisation of the sum of external and internal transaction costs of its activities. Transaction costs have been defined by K. Arrow 'as the costs of running the economic system' and are distinct from production costs considered thus far (Williamson 1985). The firm can be considered as a 'Make-or-Buy' decision maker, which must evaluate carefully the costs and benefits of using the market. Accordingly, the firm may 'buy' all or part of its inputs from existing markets, or 'make' such inputs internally. However, producing such inputs in-house entails a greater or lesser degree of vertical integration, while buying from the market may expose the firm to opportunistic behaviour by suppliers and so on. It follows then that central to the transaction costs theory are the concepts of vertical integration and of contracts to deal with the problem of opportunism.

The starting point in the development of the transaction costs theory was the original question posed by Coase (1937) of 'why firms exist', and he argued that the establishment of a firm was necessary since 'the operation of a market costs something and by forming an organisation (a firm) ... certain marketing costs are saved'. These are transaction, contracting and coordinating costs of using the market, which can be avoided by vertical integration within the firm. Coase considered four main types of costs: the cost of discovering the correct price; the cost of arranging the contractual obligations of the parties in an exchange transaction; the risk of scheduling of goods and inputs and the taxes paid on exchange transactions. Clearly, the entrepreneur sidesteps these costs by using administrative or internal pricing between divisions (transfer pricing, discussed in Chapter 10), and controls the production and marketing of intermediate inputs (products) through vertically integrated operations. Consequently, according to Coase, firms exist precisely because they excel in the allocation of resources, and consumers can satisfy their needs through firms less expensively than through other means. In other words, firms exist because they are efficient. Coase's original ideas were examined further by a number of other researchers, notably Williamson (1975, 1985), who have explored the vertical integration (or vertical boundaries) of the firm, the significance of asset ownership and its effect on investments in assets specific to a particular relationship, the transaction costs of market exchange, problems related to market imperfections and so on.

3.5.1   Backward and forward integration (making versus buying)

The production of various products passes a number of stages or activities, which can be arranged in the form of a vertical chain from product design and the procurement of raw materials and other inputs to the distribution and sales to final consumers. For example, a typical vertical chain of production may involve raw inputs (such as mining to procure iron ore, coal, oil and so on); physical and human capital inputs (such as factories, transportation services to facilitate transport of raw materials to factories and products to markets, workers and administrative staff); various support inputs (such as accounting, marketing, legal departments and so on); distribution inputs (i.e., wholesalers, retailers and so on) to get the products to the final consumer. Equally, as products pass through the various stages of the vertical chain of production from raw materials to final products value is created. Porter (1985) calls this the value chain and separates the value-creating activities into five main or primary activities and four support or secondary activities. The former include inbound logistics, manufacturing activities, outbound logistics, marketing and sales and customer service, while the latter involve procurement, technology development, human resource management (HRM), and infrastructure activities, such as accounting, finance and so on.

As firms move to undertake activities closer to sources of supply they integrate backwards or upstream, whereas when they move to undertake activities closer to final consumer they integrate forwards or downstream. Firms may decide to involve themselves at various stages in the production process or have complete vertical integration. The oil industry is the closest example we have of a completely vertically integrated industry. Where exactly a firm finds itself operating on the vertical chain depends on an evaluation of the costs and benefits of using the market. It is this evaluation which defines the boundaries of the firm and establishes its position on the vertical chain of production.

The benefits associated with using the market have to do, primarily, with economies of scale and, thus, lower average costs that in-house departments producing only for exclusive needs cannot achieve, because of the limited size of the market occupied by the firm. In addition, market firms are under the discipline of the market and, therefore, they need to be efficient and innovative to survive. On the other hand, inefficiencies and lack of innovation of certain in-house depart- ments may be hidden by the overall success of the firm. Turning to the costs of using the market, it is observed that there are likely to be various transaction costs, originally identified by Coase, which can be avoided by undertaking these activit- ies in-house. In addition, sensitive information may be leaked when activities are performed by independent market firms rather than undertaken in-house, and, similarly, there may be coordination costs in the vertical chain of production, when activities are purchased from the market than performed in-house.

3.5.2   Contracts and market exchange

However, using the market requires that the conditions of the exchange are clearly spelled out. This is accomplished through a contract, which is an agreement defin- ing the conditions under which a particular exchange takes place. Contracts vary from very simple standard forms, for example a bus ticket allowing a passenger to travel for a given distance upon the payment of the fare, to very complicated ones, depending on the nature of the specific transaction. If contracts did not exist, it could be possible for one party to renege on an agreement, while the transaction was in progress and, therefore, injure the other party. Also, one party, by exploit- ing the weakness of the other party, once the latter had committed himself, could refuse to honour the initial agreement in the expectation of renegotiating it to his further advantage. Enforceable contracts, therefore, are necessary to protect one party of the exchange from the opportunistic behaviour of the other party, and in that respect they are said to promote economic efficiency.

However, opportunistic behaviour cannot be eliminated easily. It depends on the completeness of a contract and on existing legislation. A complete contract could specify all the rights and responsibilities of the parties concerned under all conceivable contingencies that could arise during a transaction, and it must be enforceable, which means that a third party, such as a judge or referee must arbit- rate on any problems arising during the transaction. Completeness of contracts is hampered by bounded rationality; difficulties in specifying and measuring per- formance and asymmetric information. Bounded rationality refers to the limited capacity of human intellect to process complex issues and pursue rational aims. On the other hand, when performance under a particular transaction is complex, it becomes very difficult to specify it exactly in a contract, and, thus, the rights and responsibilities of parties may be affected. Similar considerations apply in the case where performance cannot unequivocally be measured. But even when these problems are not present, a contract may still be incomplete, because the parties do not possess all the relevant information, in which case a state of asymmetric information is said to exist. Asymmetric information can take the forms of hidden information and hidden action. In the former case one of the parties to a transac- tion possesses information that the other party does not have and cannot acquire, consequently, the contract remains incomplete, in terms of key performance char- acteristics and/or important contingencies (Williamson 1975). This case of hidden information is known as the *adverse selection* problem. In the case of hidden action one of the parties can take actions, which are likely to affect performance but which actions cannot be observed or verified by the other party. This situation is referred to as the *moral hazard* problem. Again the contract will be incomplete in such a case. Both, *adverse selection* and *moral hazard* are concepts borrowed from the insurance literature. The former refers to the case of offering identical policy terms to various consumers with private knowledge of their risk characteristics, and has found application in any situation where one of the parties has private information, not available to the other party, about any intrinsic characteristic, likely to affect the performance of the transaction. In the latter case, it refers to the problems the insurer faces when policyholders can take actions that increase the risk of the insured event actually occurring, and which actions the insurer can neither monitor nor prevent. Thus, moral hazard is said to apply to those cases where parties in a contractual relationship can take actions which cannot be verified, and, therefore, cannot be contracted upon. Turning now to legislation as a way of completing contracts it is observed that contract law is written in broad terms, which makes it open to different interpretations when applied to specific transactions. Also, litigation can be a costly and long-drawn out affair often destroying the relationship between the two parties; thus limiting the usefulness of contract law as a way of completing contracts.

Transaction costs are also likely to occur in the cases where one of the parties has to undertake a specific investment to support the transaction. This is called a relationship-specific asset that cannot be easily re-deployed to alternative uses, without additional costs incurred. Therefore, when a transaction involves such specific assets, the parties cannot switch trading partners costlessly and are locked into a long-term relationship. This seems to have been the case with most of the Marks & Spencer suppliers, as explained in the Appendix to Chapter 9. In connection with the relationship-specific assets we have an important transformation occurring in the relationship between a buyer and a seller. At the beginning a buyer may have a number of sellers to choose from, which allows competitive bidding to occur. However, once a deal has been made and the specific investment has taken place, then the terms of the exchange are determined by bilateral negotiations between the two parties to the transaction. In effect, the relationship changes from a 'large numbers' bidding situation to a 'small numbers' bargaining situation, which Williamson (1985) has termed the fundamental transformation. Examples of the above can be found in the relationship between car assemblers and their component suppliers, whereas the relationship-specific investment may take the forms of site specificity; physical asset specificity; human asset specificity and dedicated assets (Williamson 1985). Under this situation, the buyer may still threaten to replace suppliers and the latter know that this can harm them, now that they have committed themselves to the transaction. Thus, the fundamental transformation can turn the relationship between buyer and seller into an acrimonious, distrustful and non-cooperative one, at the expense of production efficiencies and new production developments, which was one of the reasons why the market arrangement was preferred originally. In this respect, Marks & Spencer can claim, with some justification, that their close cooperation with their suppliers, regarding the design and quality of the merchandise to be produced, had enabled them to avoid, certainly until the late 1990s, when they decided to cancel contracts with their UK suppliers, the problems associated with the fundamental transformation.

Additionally, the asset specificity creates an asymmetry between the ex ante and ex post opportunity cost of the investment, which creates a difference between the rent and the quasi-rent of the seller. Typically, the ex post opportunity cost of the

investment will be lower, because since it is specific to the requirements of a particular customer, it will have few, if any, alternative uses without modifications,
which, even when possible, may be costly. Consequently, once the investment is
sunk, the relevant issue is the ex post opportunity cost, which must be added to
the variable costs of the order to give us the minimum revenue the seller requires
to prevent him from exiting the relationship. To illustrate these points consider
the following example.

Assume that a supplier is offered a long-term contract to produce a product for
a retailing firm. The estimated total variable costs of the contract are €50 00 000
per annum. The supplier needs to set up a plant specifically to process this order
and must commit funds of €200 00 000 for this purpose. On the basis of alternative
investment opportunities open to the supplier for his funds, the supplier estimates
that the minimum rate of return is 10% per annum. Therefore, on an annual basis
the supplier finds that the ex ante opportunity cost of his investment is €20 00 000
(€200 00 000 × 0.10). Therefore, the minimum revenue the supplier will require
to enter the contractual arrangement with the retailing firm will be given by the
sum of the total variable costs (€50 00 000) and the ex ante opportunity cost of the
investment (€20 00 000), which is €70 00 000 per annum. Assuming that there is
considerable competition for this type of product between suppliers, supernormal
profits or rents can be expected to be driven down to zero, thus, the supplier's total
annual revenue is €70 00 000 and, initially, both retailer and supplier are happy
with the arrangement. However, as mentioned above, the plant has been built for
the specific order in mind and has few alternative uses. Clearly, this affects the ex
post opportunity cost of the investment. We assume that the ex post annual opportunity cost of this plant, i.e., what it could earn in its next best use is only €8 00 000.
Consequently, the minimum annual revenue our supplier will demand in order to
prevent him from exiting the relationship will be €58 00 000 per annum, which is
the sum of the total annual variable cost and the ex post opportunity cost of the
investment. The retailing firm knowing this may wish to renegotiate the initial
contract downwards. Facing this opportunistic behaviour, the supplier will reject
anything less than €58 00 000 per annum, since he can earn more by discontinu-
ing his relationship with the retailing firm and utilising his resources elsewhere.
We can now establish the supplier's quasi-rent as the difference between the revenue the supplier would have received had the contract been executed according
to the original terms, i.e., €70 00 000 per annum, and the minimum revenue the
supplier must receive in order to be induced to remain in the relationship with the
retailing firm and not exit it, i.e., €58 00 000. Clearly this difference is €12 00 000
per annum. In this example we have zero rent but positive quasi-rent.

Allied to the earlier case we can have the holdup problem, when a supplier may
attempt to renegotiate a contract at the expense of a buyer who may be dependent on the supplier because the latter has already undertaken relationship-specific
investments, which other suppliers may not be prepared to undertake. Clearly,
here the boot is on the other foot but again we have opportunistic behaviour of
one party trying to exploit the vulnerability of the other party. The end result of the
holdup problem is that it increases the transaction costs because of more frequent
and more difficult negotiations; of investments to improve ex post bargaining
positions; of reduced investment in relationship-specific assets and of distrust.

The previous discussion explains why firms may consider vertical integration as
a way of economising on various transaction costs. Indeed, Williamson (1985) has

argued that the explanation for vertical integration is not so much based on techno-logical considerations of economies of scale, important though these may be, but rather on asset specificity and economising on transaction and governance costs. When asset specificity is low, market contracting is beneficial, since outside suppli-ers by aggregating orders can achieve economies of scale not available to any one individual firm and also governance costs of market procurement are negligible. However, as asset specificity increases this shifts the balance in favour of vertical integration. Nevertheless, vertically integrated firms too are faced with exchange costs, having to do with coordination of the various activities, agency and trans-action costs. Therefore, the problem of the firm is to balance technical efficiency and agency efficiency by minimising the sum of transaction and production costs.

The decision of a firm between making or buying a product can be considered in terms of Figure 3.8, reproduced from Williamson (1985), which measures cost as a function of asset specificity k. We let $\beta(k)$ represent the bureaucratic (transaction) cost of internal governance and $M(k)$ the governance cost of using the market, where k denotes an index of asset specificity. To start with, we assume that eco-nomies of scale and of scope are trivial and can be safely ignored. In this case what matters are governance cost differences. Williamson assumes $\beta(0) > M(0)$ but as k changes we get $M' > \beta'$, because markets have a comparative disability in terms of adaptability. We let the curve $\Delta G = \beta(k) - M(k)$, i.e., the curve ΔG shows differ-ences in exchange costs when the product is produced internally through vertically integrated activities and when it is bought from the market from an independent supplier. So, the curve ΔG reflects differences in agency efficiency between the two modes of organising exchange (Kantarelis 2000). Curve ΔG shows that market pro-curement is preferred where asset specificity is low because of the incentive and bureaucratic disabilities of internal organisation on the one hand and insignific-ance of the holdup problem on the other. But when asset specificity increases the

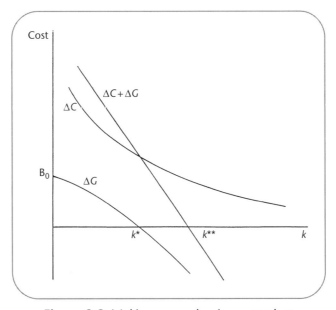

Figure 3.8 Making versus buying a product

transaction costs of market procurement are high and beyond a critical value k^* it pays the firm to integrate vertically in order to economise on market transaction costs.

However, when economies of scale and of scope are important we need, in addition, to consider differences in production costs as well. The curve ΔC in Figure 3.8 illustrates the differences between producing internally and procuring the same product in the market. Again ΔC is a function of asset specificity, i.e., $\Delta C = \beta(k) - M(k)$ and Williamson assumes that ΔC will be a decreasing function of k but remain positive throughout. The firm needs to minimise the sum of the production and governance (transaction) cost differences, given the optimal or specified index of asset specificity. The line $\Delta C + \Delta G$ is found by adding vertically curves ΔC and ΔG. The switchover value of k for which the sum $(\Delta C + \Delta G)$ becomes negative is given by k^{**}, which is higher than the value k^* found earlier. Thus, when asset specificity exceeds k^{**} it pays the firm to integrate vertically and produce the product internally. The analysis shows that the firm will never integrate for production reasons alone, since the curve ΔC is positive for all levels of asset specificity. Williamson (1985) and Kantarelis (2000) consider additional implications by introducing firm size (quantity) and organisation form effects, and interested readers are advised to consult the above and the useful bibliography contained therein and in Groenewegen (1996), as this is as far as we can take the transaction costs theory in the short confines of this discussion.

3.6 THE PRINCIPAL–AGENT THEORY

Agency theory has been developed to deal with the economic analysis of contractual relationships, mentioned above. Principal–agent problems exist whenever the actions of one individual have an effect on another individual. An agency relationship means that through a contract (explicit or implicit) one party, the principal(s), which could be the firm, engages another party, the agent (such as workers, dealers, managers and so on) to undertake certain tasks on behalf of the principal. Examples of agency relationships include, among others, those of employer–employee, insurer–insured and owner–manager. Consequently, a certain part of authority in decision-making is delegated from the principal to the agent and, crucially, the principal needs to devise a compensation schema to motivate the agent (the employee), so that the latter can act in the interests of the principal.

Thus, the compensation schema will include suitable incentives to induce the agent to behave in a particular way, given that the latter has a disutility for the particular action, whereas the principal does not. This is particularly so when the principal cannot, because of asymmetric information, observe the effort expended and/or the output produced by the agent. For example, a principal cannot observe the actions of his salesmen on the road, since he does not accompany them, and where effort may be observed output cannot be inferred, because of team work. Therefore, *moral hazard* problems, found above, are essentially *principal–agent* problems, whenever actions cannot be monitored perfectly. Linking this discussion with the earlier treatment of the managerial theories of the firm, we can consider the shareholders (owners) of the firm as principals and the managers as agents. If owners cannot monitor the actions of their managers completely, the latter can pursue their own objectives and their 'consumption' of perquisites constitutes 'X-inefficiency' according to Leibenstein (1966), and this leads to the firm exhibiting 'managerial slack' (Cyert and March, 1963).

It follows that an efficient compensation schema (a contract) must satisfy two constraints, namely, that it yields maximum expected payoff (profit) for the principal, and also that it is acceptable to the agent, who in a competitive environment, may be assumed to have alternative courses of action. Generally, the principal–agent approach has a mathematical flavour and focuses on the effects of preferences and asymmetric information. Typically, however outcomes are also affected by the state of nature (e.g., weather, good or bad luck and so on), which is represented by probabilities, observable only to the agent but not the principal. Therefore, the problem can be put as follows.

We start with a set of state of nature variables (N), known only to the agent. Also, we have a set of output variables (Q) known to both principal and agent and, finally, we have a set of input variables (I), denoting effort or actions, known only to the agent. Under these circumstances, a compensation schema is a payment from the principal to the agent, which is a function of only those variables known to both, principal and agent, i.e.,

$$Y = f(Q)$$

The agent chooses his effort, i.e., how hard or not to work, in order to maximise his expected utility, which is, thus, a function of his income and his actions and also the state of nature, that is:

$$\max EU(Y, I, N)$$

Output is a function of inputs and of the state of nature and is given by the following production function:

$$Q = Q(I, N)$$

The expected utility to the principal now depends on the agent's actions, the payments he offers to the agent (since these are costs which must be subtracted to produce the principal's residual income), and the state of nature. Thus:

$$EV = EV[f(Q), Q, I, N]$$

The principal's problem is to find f such that it maximises his utility: maxEV, while at the same time realising that the agent can affect f with his actions and, thus, the principal must offer the agent a compensation high enough to accept the job, i.e., $EU > \bar{U}$.

Alchian and Demsetz (1972) have argued that when monitoring is costly and/or ineffective, it pays the principal to offer the agent a profit-sharing schema in an attempt to induce more effort out of the agent and reduce slack (shirking).

Again, this is as far as we can take the discussion on this important area. Interested readers are advised to consult the bibliography at the end for further elaboration on these issues.

3.7   THE EVOLUTIONARY THEORY

The evolutionary theory of the firm emanates from the path-breaking work of J. Schumpeter. Following Marx, Schumpeter considers capitalist development as an evolutionary process, at the heart of which is the entrepreneur, who is looking always for new opportunities to exploit. In a remarkable chapter of his *Capitalism, Socialism and Democracy* (1952, originally published in 1942) he talks of the capacity of capitalism to regenerate and reinvent itself by destroying old technologies and products and replacing them by new, and more effective ones. He called this the 'creative destruction' of capitalism. Thus, the process of the perennial gale of capitalism results in new products, new techniques, new sources of supply and new types of organisation, all of which provide firms with their competitive advantage.

The source of these changes can be found in the R&D process of firms, which may also require a degree of monopoly power to sustain it. If monopoly profits are used to accelerate the process of product and technological innovation, restrictive practices may help encourage the process of creative destruction and bring about the dynamic effects of capitalism. The Schumpeterian thesis that a degree of monopoly power is required to produce technical change, on which economic progress depends, finds its echo in Galbraith too. Thus, '... a benign Providence ... has made the modern industry of a few large firms an excellent instrument for inducing technical change and that technical development has long since become the preserve of the scientist and the engineer. Most of the cheap and simple inventions have ... been made ... Because development is costly, it follows that it can be carried on only by a firm that has the resources which are associated with considerable size' (Galbraith 1963, pp. 100–1). While the empirical evidence between technical progress and size is somewhat equivocal, as explained in Chapter 13, in the sense that it suggests that technological change can be achieved without, necessarily, encouraging bigness, the above quotation has the merit of highlighting the association of R&D with oligopoly. It also illustrates the need and role of the entrepreneur, as someone who must organise and bring together the forces that will, eventually, result in the 'creative destruction'.

These forces are invention, entrepreneurship, investment, development, core capabilities, competitive advantage and diffusion (Kantarelis, 2000). These have been defined by Scherer and Ross (1990, p. 617) and Besanko *et al.* (1996, p. 441) as:

Invention: the act of insight by which a new and promising technical capability is worked out (at least mentally, and usually also physically) in its essential, most rudimentary form;

Entrepreneurship: involves deciding to go forward with the effort, organising it, obtaining financial support, and cultivating the market;

Investment: is the act of risking funds for the venture;

Development: is the lengthy sequence of detail-oriented technical activities, including trial-and-error testing, through which the original concept is modified and perfected until it is ready for commercial introduction;

Diffusion (or imitation): is the process by which an innovation comes into widespread use as one producer after another follows the pioneering firm's lead;

Core capabilities: are unique, tacit routines that the firm is involved in relative to its rivals; activities which are difficult to copy or imitate by reducing them to any simple formulas;

Competitive advantage: is the firm's capability 'to create more total value than its competitors. A firm that creates more total value can simultaneously earn higher profits and deliver higher net benefits to consumers than its competitors. The amount of value it creates depends on both its cost position and its differentiation position relative to its competitors'.

This dynamic efficiency results in competition which strikes at the roots of the problem by reducing costs significantly, than merely at the margins, as under static efficiency of the competitive model.

Thus, competitive advantage, entrepreneurial strategy and organisational structure become the major tenets of the evolutionary theory of the firm. These tenets by themselves are subjects of much extensive and deeper enquiry. Space does not permit us to develop these subjects here. The question of the multidivisional organisational structure, as opposed to the functional form, is touched upon in Chapter 10, whereas elements of strategic planning are covered in Chapter 13. However, as an illustration of strategic planning we provide at the end of this chapter a case study on the Finnish firm Nokia. Again interested readers are advised to consult the references and the bibliography therein.

3.8   THE BEHAVIOURAL THEORY

Another approach to the theory of the firm is provided by the behavioural theory, developed by Cyert and March (1963) and Simon (1959, 1976). They argue that uncertainty, insufficient information and the difficulty and complexity of decision-making make it impossible for the firm to maximise anything. Therefore, instead of maximisation they settle on the objective of 'satisficing', i.e., achieving a satisfactory performance on a number of goals, such as sales, profits and so on. The firm is seen as an organisation, a coalition of different groups of people, such as shareholders, managers, workers, suppliers and so on, each of whom has its own objectives and pushes hard for their adoption. Consequently, through a process of bargaining, compromise and side payments (in the form of either policy acceptances, or monetary) various objectives for the firm emerge, which might be contradictory or non-operational. Such compromise means that the objectives of the firm are usually in the form of minimum acceptable levels of attainment, rather than maximisation. Aspiration levels are fixed for each of the objectives and the firm tries to achieve them by concentrating on one goal at a time. If such goals are achieved, then they may be revised upwards. If not, the firm will search for a solution and, if no solution emerges, the goals will be revised downwards.

The behavioural theory has provided an insight into the process of goal formation and the stabilising role of the management slack in the various activities of the firm. However, from the managerial point of view of decision-making, there is very little that can be learned from this theory. Almost any kind of performance can be accepted and rationalised under the satisficing approach. Whilst it may provide a realistic picture of how a firm behaves, it does not explain anything about prices, outputs and so on. The theory does provide a simulation approach to the problems facing a complex modern multi-product firm but does not explain behaviour. The empirical evidence provides some support for this theory, but there are also indications that it may have been accepted simply because lack of information does not allow firms to profit maximise, despite the fact that they may wish to do so.

SUMMARY

This chapter has reviewed, briefly, the major theories of profits and of the firm. Accordingly, it has examined the nature, definition and measurement of profits leading to differences in their treatment between economists and accountants. It has provided explanations of profits in terms of the functional or compensatory theory, which views profit as a reward for entrepreneurial services and risk taking; in terms of friction and monopoly theory, which contends that profits arise as a result of market imperfections and in terms of the innovations and technology theories, which consider profit as the reward of undertaking R&D activity and adapting its fruits to industrial uses. In so far as theories of the firm are concerned, the chapter has discussed the neoclassical theory and a number of managerial theories, such as, sales maximisation, managers' utility maximisation and growth, in addition to looking, very briefly, at the evolutionary and behavioural theories. In passing, it has also looked at transaction costs and the principal–agent problem.

APPENDIX: NOKIA: FROM PULP VIA RUBBER AND CABLES TO HIGH TECH[1]

Nokia was established in 1865, at a time when Finland was a semi-independent part of the Imperial Russian Empire, by the Finnish mining engineer Fredrik Idestam as a wood-pulp mill, utilising the most advanced technology of its time. During the early 1920s the Finnish Rubber Works obtained majority control of both Nokia and another company, Finnish Cable Works (FCW), and started using Nokia as its brand name.

After the Second World War, Finland had to pay severe war reparations to the Soviet Union by 1952, and this opened the door to the Soviet Union for FCW. Exporting to the Soviet Union, the cable-business became the cash-cow of the three company coalition. The three companies finally merged in 1967 when OY NOKIA AB was formed. Following the merger, it was felt that the new company would have to diversify its portfolio of industries and a transition into electronics began. In 1967 electronics represented 3% of turnover and employing 460 people. The company was still best known for its toilet paper, car tyres and rubber boots.

Kari Kairamo, whom Nokia hired in 1970 as a senior vice president in charge of the international affairs, was the man to make Nokia an electronics company.

He once said: 'We must learn to become fast. If, for instance, one isn't fast enough in the most competitive segments of electronics, there just aren't any chances to succeed. We are gathering international experience at an accelerating pace. Our educational level is high. We can become fast'. Nokia began buying electronics companies across Europe, and by the mid 1980s electronics accounted for more than 40% of total sales, making Nokia Europe's third largest television manufacturer. However, the buying spree of electronics companies across Europe was financed by debt and by 1988 Nokia's accumulated huge debts made the position of Kari Kairamo, now the CEO of NOKIA, very difficult. The pressure proved to be too much for him to bear and he committed suicide.

Kairamo was followed by Simo Vuorilehto, who started restructuring the company. Diversification was abandoned in favour of *focusing*, which became the new key concept. This was the time of 'forced' *focusing*, as the company was practically on the verge of bankruptcy. Certain activities were streamlined and others divested. The entire company was restructured, traditional industries (rubber boots, tyres, cables) were sold, and only those activities considered strategic (such as consumer electronics, data communications, mobile phones and telecommunications) were left untouched. However, even these actions were not enough to reverse the financial position, which was getting worse. In 1992 Simo Vuorilehto was replaced by the current CEO Jorma Ollila, who was to carry out the 'forced' *focusing* strategy. Nokia decided to focus on mobile telecommunications, the new technology appearing at the time, and divest all of its non-core operations. In Ollila's vision the digital cellular business would drive revenues and boost profits, since Nokia was in a better position to exploit the new technology of the mobile phone, because of its focusing and flexibility, as compared with the large competitors Motorola, Siemens, Philips, Ericsson and Alcatel.

Clearly, the new technology of the digital cellular telecommunications represented an example of 'creative destruction', of the older forms of telecommunications, which were put aside. More importantly, it offered its creators (Nokia) an excellent opportunity to establish themselves in the industry, and acquire a significant share of the market, at the expense of much bigger competitors, who may have been either slow to react to the changes, or certainly they did not have the *focus* of Nokia, because of their many other activities.

In particular, Nokia was the first company to exploit the B-to-C market (i.e., the business to consumer market) to its full potential. At the early stages of the mobile phone market development ALL other companies, except Nokia, saw the market as an, essentially, business to business market and totally overlooked ordinary consumers as a target market for mobile phones. A contributory factor to this were the weight of the phones and their price, which were major handicaps at the time. However, as technology was progressing, handsets were getting smaller, lighter and cheaper and Nokia was the first company to target not only businessmen, but also ordinary consumers. This policy, in turn, gave them the chance to start mass production of the phones and penetrate the consumer market. For example, in 1993 the official sales target for the 2100 series was 400 000 units, but the firm sold 20 million units worldwide. The pricing policy helped penetration too. Because of the high price elasticity of demand for mobile phones, among ordinary consumers, Nokia's mass production allowed significant economies of scale, some of which were passed on to the final consumers as price reductions, which in turn, fuelled a high growth in sales.

Nordic countries had started to develop the Nordic Mobile Telephony (NMT) network in 1969, and by 1977 Equipment manufacturers had joined the process. Two years later the telecommunications arm of Nokia, Nokia–Mobira manufactured the first base stations for Finland PTT (i.e., Finland's state owned post and telecommunications company). The strategic objective of Nokia–Mobira was to ensure the long-term competitiveness of the Finnish radiophone industry. NMT was the first international system available, since the other 1G (i.e., first generation) systems that existed, e.g. in France, Germany, Italy and Japan, were local solutions not sold outside their home countries, before the breakthrough of GSM.

Mobira and the Finnish government tried to persuade other European countries to adopt the NMT technology. However hopes for a European NMT faded, when countries such as the UK, Germany, Italy and France adopted different standards. Nevertheless, Nokia did not give up, but started to promote the new GSM (Global System for Mobile Telephony) technology, which they had developed jointly with Ericsson. Success came when the European Commission, together with the European Telecommunications Standards Institute (ETSI), decided to adopt GSM as the single standard for EU's digital mobile telephones. The first GSM call was made on a Nokia phone using a Nokia network. Soon other countries and continents were to follow, so that by 2001 of the estimated 700 million mobile phone subscribers two-thirds were using GSM.

In the early 1980s Nokia entered the US market, and worked there in close cooperation with its US partner Tandy Corporation, selling mobile phones under the brand names of Radio Shack, Mobira and Technophone. From Tandy Corporation, Nokia learned the importance of not only monitoring manufacturing costs, but keeping them as low as possible while, simultaneously, charging a premium price, a policy they pursue even today.

Ever since the early 1970s the company has worked in close cooperation with the Finnish authorities. In the early 1980s the Finnish government saw electronics as a good long-term prospect for the country and as a way to decrease the reliance on the forest industry, which at the time was the backbone of the country's economy. The major players in electronics were to specialise in value-added products, and work together in order to optimize R&D expenditure and efforts. The government, in turn, facilitated this cooperative effort by establishing the National Technology Agency (TEKES) in 1983, whose role was, and still is, to support the R&D efforts of private companies. Technology was to provide the key for growth, according to Mr Martti Mäenpää, former director of TEKES. When TEKES was founded, Nokia was one of the first companies to benefit. With the new national technological cluster strategy, the domestic innovation system became a key priority. This effort boosted the national competitive advantage, placing Finland among the most competitive nations in the world. The proportion of R&D investments in Finland's GDP increased from 1.4% to 3.01% between 1994 and 1998, which was more than that of Germany, Japan or USA. In the year 2000, Nokia accounted for 4% of Finnish GDP, almost 25% of the value of Finnish exports and more than a third of the business sector R&D.

According to Nokia's CEO Jorma Ollila: 'Until the 1980s we were a Finnish company, in the 1980s a Nordic company and at the beginning of the 1990s an European company. Now we are a global company'. Of Finland's importance to Nokia he has said: 'The people, the atmosphere, the education and basic economic policies are right. Nokia's corporate culture, its underlying ethos and strength of its product development are all Finnish'. Already, as mentioned earlier, during the NMT phase Nokia realised that the mobile-phone market was a B-to-C market where a lot of attention had to be paid on design, features and image. In addition, Nokia grasped that a mobile phone was also a fashion accessory in the B-to-C market and tried hard to cultivate and exploit this idea and meet the needs that their marketing policies created. It was precisely this attention to detail that allowed Nokia to charge higher prices, a policy they continue to-day. This lead later to the successful creation of 'NOKIA – Connecting People' brand. This brand is one of the most easily recognised around the world and the consultancy Interbrand ranked it fifth most valuable brand in the world, behind Coca-Cola, Microsoft, International Business Machines and Intel. In that ranking, Nokia was the only non-American company in the top 10.

Nokia's technological development allows the company to-day to prosper by having a superior brand and the ability to launch new models 5–8 times a year. In terms of technological development, Nokia was the first in the world to launch the new phones featuring a camera, and the ability to send and receive pictures. Nokia's market share, estimated at 38% in the second quarter of 2002, makes Nokia the world's leading producer of mobile phones, and allows it the advantages of mass economies of scale, which are translated into wider profit margins. Thus, the profit margin of the cheapest Nokia phones is 15%, whereas the corresponding margins of its rivals in this segment of the market vary between 2% and 10%. Therefore, the combination of technological development, production efficiencies and marketing policies leave the company to-day in a healthy financial position.

Note

1. This material has been prepared by Dr Antti Rovamo of Ammattikorkeakoulu, Oulu, Finland.

BIBLIOGRAPHY

Alchian, A.A. and Demsetz, H. (1972), 'Production, Information Costs, and Economic Organisation', *American Economic Review*, **57**: 777–795.

Baumol, W.J. (1958), 'On the Theory of Oligopoly', *Economica*, **25**: 187–198.

—— (1959), *Business Behaviour, Value and Growth*, Macmillan.

Berle, A.A. and Means, S.C. (1932), *The Modern Corporation and Private Property*, Macmillan.

Besanko, D., Dranove, D. and Shanley, M. (1996), *Economics of Strategy*, Wiley.

Carroll, G.R. and Teece, D.J. (eds) (1999), *Firms, Markets and Hierarchies*, Oxford University Press.

Cyert, R.M. and March, J.G. (1963), *A Behavioural Theory of the Firm*, Prentice-Hall.

Dean, J. (1951), *Managerial Economics*, Prentice-Hall.

Downie, J. (1958), *The Competitive Process*, Duckworth.

Fama, E.F. (1980), 'Agency Problems and the Theory of the Firm', *Journal of Political Economy*, **88**: 288–307.

Friedman, M. (1953), *Essays in Positive Economics*, University of Chicago Press.

Galbraith, J.K. (1963), *American Capitalism*, Pelican.

Groenewegen, J. (ed.) (1996), *Transaction Cost Economics and Beyond*, Kluwer Academic Publishers.

Grossman, S.J. and Hart, O.D. (1983), 'An Analysis of the Principal–Agent Problem', *Econometrica*, **52**: 7–45.

Harris, M. and Raviv, A. (1978), 'Some Results on Incentive Contracts with Applications to Education and Employment, Health Insurance, and Law Enforcement', *American Economic Review*, **68**: 20–30.

—— (1979), 'Optimal Incentive Contracts with Imperfect Information', *Journal of Economic Theory*, **20**, 231–259.

Kantarelis, D. (2000), *Theories of the Firm*, McGraw-Hill.

Krepps, D.M. (1990), *A Course in Microeconomic Theory*, Harvester Wheatsheaf.

Leibenstein, H. (1966), 'Allocative Efficiency vs. X-inefficiency', *American Economic Review*, **56**: 392–415.

Macdonald, G.M. (1984), 'New Directions in the Economic Theory of Agency', *Canadian Journal of Economics*, **17**: 415–440.

Machlup, F. (1967), 'Theories of the Firm: Marginalist, Behavioral, Managerial', *American Economic Review*, **57**: 1–33.

Marris, R. (1964), *The Economic Theory of Managerial Capitalism*, Macmillan.

—— (1971), 'An Introduction to Theories of Corporate Growth', in Marris, R. and Wood, A. (eds), *The Corporate Economy*, Macmillan.

Naylor, T.H. and Vernon, J.M. (1969), *Microeconomics*, Harcourt, Brace & World Inc.

Penrose, E.T. (1959), *The Theory of Growth of the Firm*, Blackwell.

Porter, M.E. (1985), *Comparative Advantage: Creating and Sustaining Superior Performance*, The Free Press, Collier Macmillan Publishers.

Radice, H. (1971), 'Control type, profitability and growth in large firms', *Economic Journal*, **81**(3), September, 547–562.

Ross, S.A. (1973), 'The Economic Theory of Agency: The Principal's Problem', *American Economic Review*, **63**: 134–139.

Sawyer, M.C. (1979), *Theories of the Firm*, Weidenfeld & Nicholson.

Scherer, F.M. and Ross, D. (1990), *Industrial Market Structure and Economic Performance*, 3rd edn, Houghton Miflin Co.

Schumpeter, J.S. (1934), *The Theory of Economic Development*, Harvard University Press.

—— (1952), *Capitalism, Socialism and Democracy*, 5th edn, Unwin.

Simon, H.A. (1959) 'Theories of Decision-Making in Economics and Behavioral Science', *American Economic Review*, **49**: 253–283.

—— (1976), *Administrative Behavior*, 3rd edn, Macmillan.

Wildsmith, R.R. (1973), *Managerial Theories of the Firm*, Martin Robertson.

Williamson, O.E. (1963), 'Managerial Discretion and Business Behavior', *American Economic Review*, **53**: 1032–1057.

—— (1964), *The Economics of Discretionary Behavior: Managerial Objectives in a Theory of the Firm*, Prentice-Hall.

—— (1975), *Market and Hierarchies: Analysis and Antitrust Implications*, Free Press.

—— (1985), *The Economic Institutions of Capitalism*, Free Press.

chapter four

Demand Analysis

Learning outcomes

After studying this chapter you should know about:

- Cardinal and ordinal theories of demand

- Marginal and diminishing marginal utility

- Diminishing marginal rate of substitution

- Income and substitution effects

- Consumer equilibrium

- Revealed preference

- Bandwagon, snob and Veblen effects in demand

- Demand functions and demand curves

- Elasticities of demand:
  - own price
  - income
  - cross price and so on

- Factors affecting elasticity of demand

4.1 INTRODUCTION

The most central function of a modern market economy is exchange, i.e., the buying and selling of goods and services. Such exchange satisfies, on the one hand, the needs of consumers and provides, on the other, the sellers with their income or profit. Indeed, no matter how successfully the firm may have resolved other functions, such as for example production or R&D activity, it is when its products are actually purchased by final consumers that management is said to have succeeded in its role. Since profits are the difference between total revenue and total costs they are affected by the factors determining the demand for and supply of such goods and services. Consequently, an understanding of the principles underpinning consumer demand and cost of production becomes essential for business decision making. In this chapter we start by providing a conceptual framework for analysing consumer demand, which could be used at a later stage as a springboard for forecasting and measuring demand.

The role of demand analysis is to investigate and measure the factors which influence consumers' behaviour over time. The way in which such factors interact and affect the quantity demanded of a particular good is known as a demand function. Demand functions for goods and services are derived from the process of constrained maximisation of utility, which is discussed later. For the moment it suffices to emphasise that knowledge of the demand relationship could assist management in forecasting sales for its products and also in taking appropriate policy measures to influence sales, i.e., to manipulate demand.

Demand analysis, therefore, is important both for short-term and long-term managerial operations, since sales forecasts could help with preparing cash-flows and identifying the need for promotional activity, initiate changes in stocks held and production rates and also provide the firm with evidence, regarding the prospects of growth of demand, before expansion of capacity is undertaken.

4.2 THE THEORY OF DEMAND

In demand theory we start from the basic observation that people derive satisfaction or utility from the consumption of the various goods and services, and ask how consumers choose which goods and services and in what quantities to purchase with their income, given two sets of information. Taking the simple case in which there are two goods Q_1 and Q_2 there is first the objective information (or market or budget information) consisting of the prices p_1 and p_2 of the two goods and the income y of the consumer. Prices and income are usually fixed and given. The budget equation is written as $\Sigma p_i q_i = y$ and there will always be some budget constraint such that: $p_1 q_1 + p_2 q_2 = y$, which indicates the maximum quantities of the two goods the consumer can afford to buy. The second set of information is subjective and is given by the consumers' preferences, derived from his utility function. These two independent sets of information are linked together through the rationality postulate, which requires that the consumer behaves rationally. This means that he always chooses, among the various alternatives, the one which gives him the greatest satisfaction. In other words, the behavioural assumption underlying demand theory is that the consumer tries to maximise his utility. However, the consumer in pursuing this objective is inhibited by his limited income, which acts as a constraint. Consequently, the consumer's objective becomes the maximisation of his utility subject to his budget constraint.

4.2.1 Marshall's cardinal theory of demand

There are a number of different approaches to the problem of the equilibrium of the consumer. In Marshallian demand theory utility is assumed to be cardinal, i.e., measurable in some way, and the equilibrium of the consumer is arrived at by assuming that marginal utility (the satisfaction derived from consuming an extra unit of the good) is diminishing and that the utility of money (income) is constant. To maximise his utility the consumer allocates his income on different goods in such a way so as to get the same increment in utility from the marginal unit of his income, no matter on which goods he decides to spend it. This means that the marginal utilities of the various goods must be proportional to their prices, the proportionality factor being the constant marginal utility of income. This is achieved by equating the ratios of the marginal utility (MU) to the price (*P*) for all goods and setting them equal to a constant *k*, representing the marginal utility of income. Therefore, for a consumer confronted with goods A, B,...,Z the equilibrium condition for utility maximisation becomes:

$$MU_A/P_A = MU_B/P_B = \cdots MU_Z/P_Z = k$$

If this condition is not satisfied the consumer could increase his utility by switching some of his income from one good to another and purchasing more or less of particular goods. This will obviously affect the marginal utilities of the goods concerned – the numerators in our expression – and move the consumer closer to his objective. Only when this condition is satisfied for all goods, entering his utility function, has the consumer attained his objective of utility maximisation. From this basic relationship we can also derive the fundamental law of demand, i.e., the relationship between the quantity demanded of a good and its price. Starting from an initial equilibrium for, say, good A such as:

$$MU_A/P_A = k$$

We are interested in what happens to quantity demanded of A when its price changes. If price decreases, the ratio MU_A/P_A (arrived at by the initial equilibrium purchases of good A) becomes greater than *k*. Clearly, at the new lower price the consumer is no longer maximising his utility by purchasing the same quantity of A as before. To move towards his new equilibrium, he must buy more units of A which, because of the assumption of diminishing marginal utility, will decrease the marginal utility obtained from his extra purchases and thus, by reducing the numerator of the ratio MU_A/P_A, bring it back to equality with the constant marginal utility of income *k*. Therefore, other things being equal, a decrease in price brings about an increase in quantity demanded. Conversely, if the price of good A increases then the ratio MU_A/P_A becomes less than *k*. The new equilibrium will be attained when the consumer restricts his purchases of A, so that the marginal utility obtained from his restricted purchases increases. This will raise the numerator of the ratio MU_A/P_A and bring it back to equality with *k*. Consequently, other things being equal, an increase in price brings about a decrease in quantity demanded of the good and vice versa. This demonstrates the fundamental inverse relationship between quantity demanded and price, known as the law of demand.

4.2.2 The ordinal theory of demand

However, Marshall's theory is fraught with two difficulties. The first one is that it makes the notion of utility a measurable one and since utility is an abstract notion we do not have a suitable measure for it. The proposed util by neoclassical utility theorists is also an abstract and arbitrary tool and may not prove to be very helpful in practice. The second difficulty is that the assumption of the constant marginal utility of income can be interpreted to imply that consumer demand is independent of income. Marshall, however, did not mean by this assumption that the consumer's demand did not depend on his income; he merely neglected the income side. Nevertheless, this assumption – although an ingenious simplification – introduces an element of vagueness, which may not be harmless in all cases. Also a quantitative concept of utility is not necessary to explain market phenomena, thus rendering Marshall's cardinal theory of demand defective. Consequently, Hicks, in his ordinal theory of demand, disposed of the concepts of both marginal utility and diminishing marginal utility. Instead, he used the concepts of marginal rate of substitution and diminishing marginal rate of substitution. The former is the ratio of the marginal utilities of the two goods, and is defined as the quantity of the one good which will compensate the consumer for the loss of a marginal unit of the other good.

In reformulating demand theory Hicks starts from the assumption of a scale of preferences. All that is required is the preference map of the consumer. The latter has certain preferences among the various commodities. There are three possibilities of preference relations between any two possible collections of goods Qa and Qb. These are as follows:

Qa P Qb   which means that Qa is strictly preferred to Qb
Qb P Qa   which means that Qb is strictly preferred to Qa
Qa I Qb   which means that Qa is indifferent to Qb

This is an ordering way and denoting utility by U we have algebraically:

$$U(Qa) > U(Qb), \quad U(Qb) > U(Qa) \quad \text{and} \quad U(Qa) = U(Qb)$$

Therefore, collections of goods offering greater satisfaction will be placed on a higher indifference curve, collections of goods offering lower satisfaction will be placed on a lower indifference curve and, finally, collections between which the consumer is indifferent will be placed on the same indifference curve. Indifference curves, therefore, are geometric loci which have an important property, namely, that all points on such a curve represent combinations of goods which offer the consumer the same level of satisfaction.

Assume that the consumer has a given amount of income which he spends on two goods X and Y, whose prices are known and fixed. In Figure 4.1 we measure quantities of X and Y along the two axes. The curves labelled I_1, I_2 and I_3 are part of the indifference map of the consumer. The assumptions usually made about the indifference curves are as follows:

1. There exists an indifference curve through each point of the indifference map.

2. The indifference curves are continuous.

3. There is a normal range on an indifference curve in which there is no satiation in any direction. But we can allow some satiation far out.

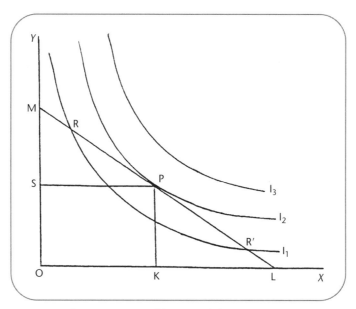

Figure 4.1 Equilibrium of the consumer

4. Indifference curves slope downwards from left to right, because if they did not then by moving along that curve one could get either more of both goods or more of the one good and the same amount of the other than before. But a collection which contains more of one good and not less of the other must always be preferred from the original one, and, on the principle of rationality, the consumer would not be indifferent between them.

5. Indifference curves are convex to the origin, and their slope reflects the diminishing marginal rate of substitution between the two goods (given by the ratio of the marginal utilities of the two goods). This must be so, since the more of, say, good X we acquire the less of Y we shall be prepared to give up for an additional unit of X. A diminishing marginal rate of substitution also ensures that we get a stable equilibrium.

6. Indifference curves do not intersect, because, if they did, we could have combinations of goods contradicting the principle of transitivity.

4.2.3 The equilibrium of the consumer

Returning to Figure 4.1, we observe that if the consumer spends all his income on either good he gets OM units of Y or OL units of X. Line ML is known as the price or budget line and shows the market opportunities open to the consumer. The slope of the line ML, given by the ratio OM/OL, is the inverse ratio of the prices of the two goods, i.e., P_X/P_Y. This market information is combined with the consumer's subjective information, i.e., his preferences given by his indifference curves and the behavioural assumption of utility maximisation, in order to arrive at his equilibrium. Starting off from any position, the consumer tries, by varying his purchases of X and Y and moving along ML, to maximise his total satisfaction (utility). This is achieved at point P, which is the point of tangency between the price line ML and the highest indifference curve he can reach. At P, the inverse price ratio $(-P_X/P_Y)$ is equal to the marginal rate of substitution (MU_X/MU_Y). The optimal quantities, therefore, of X and Y are OK and OS respectively. All other combinations of X and Y are either inferior or non feasible, given the consumer's income. For example, points like R and R' are not points of maximum utility and cannot be points of equilibrium, since they lie on a lower indifference curve. Notice that the equilibrium condition we have derived in this case is identical to that of Marshall's theory, since by ignoring the negative sign we get that $P_X/P_Y = MU_X/MU_Y$ which is the same as $MU_X/P_X = MU_Y/P_Y = k$.

4.2.4 The substitution and income effects

Moving from the equilibrium of the consumer to the derivation of the law of demand, it is necessary to consider what happens when the price of a good changes. If the price of a good falls, the consumer can buy the same bundle of goods as before the price change and still have some of his income unspent. So, the first effect of the price fall is to make the consumer feel that he had been given a rise in his income. Since we are assuming that the consumer must spend all his income – saving is considered as just another good – it is plausible to argue that the consumer will try to buy more of the goods he was already purchasing with this 'extra' income. Figure 4.2 shows how the consumer reacts to changes in his income while the prices of the goods remain fixed. The new budget lines M'L' and M"L" are parallel to the old one ML, since the price ratio has not changed. The higher incomes allow the consumer to reach higher indifference curves, and the new equilibrium positions are given by points P' and P". Joining points P, P', P" with the origin we get the curve ICC, which is known as the income-consumption curve, or Engel curve, and depicts the effect of income on consumption. This curve will normally slope upward and to the right, except in the case of inferior goods (see discussion

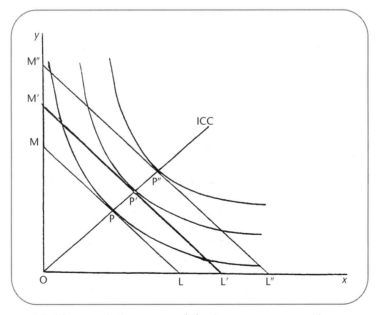

Figure 4.2 Changes in income and the income-consumption curve

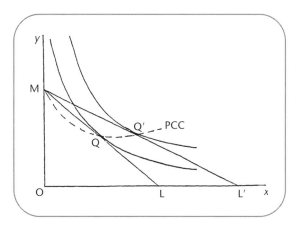

Figure 4.3 Changes in price and the price-consumption curve

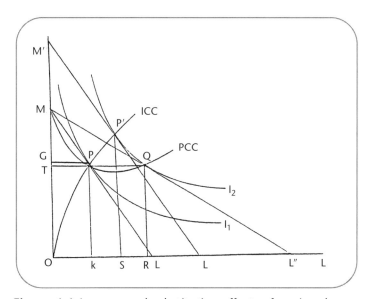

Figure 4.4 Income and substitution effects of a price change

below) when it will slope upward and to the left – if X is an inferior good – or after an upward stretch it will slope downward if Y is an inferior good.

Now if the income of the consumer and the price of Y remain fixed, while the price of X falls, the consumer, by spending all his income on X, can get OL′ units of X and his new budget line is given by ML′ in Figure 4.3. The new budget line touches a higher indifference curve at Q′. By joining points M, Q and Q′ we get the curve PCC, which is known as the price-consumption curve, or offer curve, and shows how consumption varies when the price of X falls, other things remaining constant.

Combination of Figures 4.2 and 4.3 yields Figure 4.4 from which we observe that the fall in the price of X has the following consequences. The new point of equilibrium is Q, at which the new price line ML″ touches the indifference curve I_2. At this point the consumer buys OR units of X and OT units of Y. Thus, he has increased his consumption of X by KR units and reduced his consumption of Y by GT units. Concentrating on the increase in X, we can say that the consumer has got this increase of KR units of X by moving along his price consumption curve PCC from P to Q. But this movement is equivalent also to the movement from P to P′ along the income-consumption curve ICC and then from P′ along the indifference curve I$_2$ to point Q. This second way of looking at the increase in the consumption of X provides us with a better insight in demand analysis. The fall in the price of X has provided the consumer with a relatively higher income than before. This will induce him to consume more, i.e., he will move along his ICC. But now that X is cheaper it pays him also to consume more X, by substituting more X for the relatively dearer Y. We have these two distinct effects of the fall in the price of X, namely, the income effect and the substitution effect, which explain the increase in the consumption of X. In terms of Figure 4.4 we can regard the amount KS as due to the income effect and the amount SR as due to the substitution effect. The substitution effect will in all cases be negative, i.e., a fall in the price of the good will induce the consumer to buy more of this good since it is now cheaper and vice versa. The income effect, however, is not as reliable. Normally we expect that the income effect will be positive, as in the present case, and reinforce the substitution effect. However, there exists a case in which the income effect is negative, when the good under consideration is an inferior good. But even in such cases the substitution effect will typically be stronger than the income effect and, therefore, a fall in the price of the good under consideration will still be accompanied by an increase in the quantity demanded. Only in exceptional circumstances will the negative income effect be stronger than the substitution effect and, thus, a fall in the price of the good will result in a reduction in its quantity demanded. This is known in the literature as a Giffen good. However, since not all consumers perceive the same good as a Giffen in all price ranges, it can be safely assumed that, once we aggregate the individual demand curves, the resulting market demand curve will be sloping downwards. Thus, the fundamental law of demand, asserting that quantity demanded of a good is inversely related to its price, has been demonstrated.

4.2.4a Equilibrium of the consumer

The same result can be derived algebraically, by setting up and solving the constrained utility maximisation problem as follows: Assume that a consumer has a monthly income of €2000, which he spends on two products a and b, whose prices are P_A = €4 and P_B = €5. Letting the quantities of a and b consumed be A and B, respectively, the budget constraint of this consumer is given by $2000 = 4A + 5B$. His utility function to be maximised is given by:

$$U = A^2 B^2 \tag{1}$$

To find the quantities of the two products purchased, we construct the Lagrangian expression:

$$L = A^2 B^2 + \lambda(2000 - 4A - 5B) \tag{2}$$

which is simply the utility function subject to the budget constraint, given by the expression inside the parenthesis and where λ is an unspecified Lagrange multiplier.

Differentiating expression (2) partially with respect to A, B and λ and setting the partial derivatives equal to zero gives:

$$\delta L/\delta A = 2AB^2 - 4\lambda = 0 \tag{3}$$

$$\delta L/\delta B = 2A^2B - 5\lambda = 0 \tag{4}$$

$$\delta L/\delta \lambda = 2000 - 4A - 5B = 0 \tag{5}$$

Dividing expression (3) by (4) and rearranging yields: $B/A = 4/5$ or $5B = 4A$. Substituting this expression into relation (5) and solving, we obtain $A = 250$ units and $B = 200$ units. The second order conditions require that the indifference curves are convex to the origin, or that the bordered Hessian determinant be positive.

4.2.5 Revealed preference and other developments

While the ordinal theory of demand represents a considerable advance in the theory of consumer, it nevertheless has its own limitations. The main one, is that it assumes axiomatically the existence and convexity of the indifference curves, instead of deriving them. Also, the strong assumption of rationality implies that the consumer is always capable of ordering his preferences in a precise manner, which may be questionable in practice. Finally, the concept of marginal utility is implied in the definition of the marginal rate of substitution. Consequently, in the development of consumer theory, Samuelson has proposed an alternative approach to consumer behaviour, which does not require the consumer's indifference map in order to establish his equilibrium. All we need to do is observe how the consumer reacts to changes in prices and incomes, provided his choices are consistent. That is, if a consumer prefers a collection of goods A to another collection B, then B cannot be preferred to A at the same time. Since A has been revealed to be preferred to B, B cannot, simultaneously, be revealed to be preferred to A! However, a further assumption is made which states that any collection of goods can be selected, if its price becomes attractive. Clearly, no indifference map is required to establish equilibrium, and although, the revealed preference approach can establish the consumer's indifference curves and their convexity – given enough observations, such information is redundant for the purposes of finding the law of demand.

To show how the law of demand is derived, consider Figure 4.5 where we assume that when the consumer faces the price line KK' he buys the collection of goods Y and X given by point A. If now the price of X falls, and concentrating only on the substitution effect, the new price line becomes LL'. The new equilibrium point must be a point like C and lie to the right of A. Points such as B which lie to the left of A on price line LL' contradict the revealed preference theory. The reason is that when the price line is KK' point A has been revealed to be preferred to point B. Now with the new price line LL' and with point A no more expensive than point B, if we chose the latter we would be inconsistent, since B would have been revealed to be preferred to A at the same time as A had been revealed to be preferred to B! But this is exactly what is ruled out by the revealed preference theory. Therefore, the new equilibrium must lie to he right of A and be given by a point like C, which involves the purchase of a larger quantity of the good X, whose

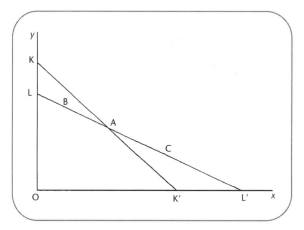

Figure 4.5 Revealed preference and the law of demand

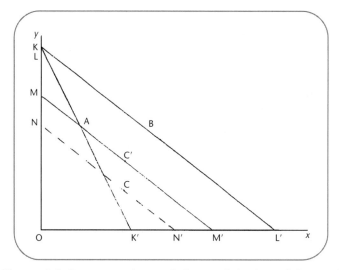

Figure 4.6 Compensating variation and the law of demand

price had fallen, thus, demonstrating the law of demand. The revealed preference theory is based on the assumption of consistency and of the strong ordering of the various alternative collections.

In the light of the revealed preference hypothesis, Hicks revised his demand theory, discussed in the preceding pages, in terms of the preference approach and consistency tests. But Hicks assumed weak ordering of the various collections in order to maintain indifference. The basic assumptions of income and substitution effects are maintained and the device of the compensating variation in income (or Samuelson's device of cost-difference) is used to separate the income from the substitution effect.

According to Hicks, the law of demand is derived as follows. A consumer is confronted with the initial price line KK', as in Figure 4.6, and chooses to buy the collection given by point A. Now if the price of good X falls we want to prove that the consumption of X will tend to rise. If the income of the consumer remained the same the new price line LL' will lie outside the old price line KK', and consistency theory decrees that any point on the price line LL', like a point B, will be shown to be preferred to the initial situation given by A. At this stage this is all we can say and we are not certain about the consumption of X in the new situation, which may increase, remain the same or fall. But in order to isolate the substitution from the income effect, following the price fall in X, assume an intermediate position C which will be taken by the consumer when his income is reduced, so far as to wipe out the gain in real income resulting from the fall in the price of X. This is called by Hicks the compensating variation in income. The new price line is given by NN', which is parallel to LL'. The consumer chooses on price line NN' a collection C which is indifferent to A. Consistency theory tells us that in order for A and C to be consistent choices, they must have one of the following positions: (a) both A and C lie on the cross of KK' and NN', (b) one must lie on the cross and the other outside the cross and (c) both A and C must lie outside the cross, as in Figure 4.6. These are the only possible cases, for points A and C to be indifferent. It then follows that, provided X is not an inferior good, its consumption will tend to increase between positions A and B. This approach has assumed weak ordering of collections, without which there cannot be indifferent positions.

Using, instead, Samuelson's cost-difference and strong ordering we can arrive at the same result. The cost-difference approach requires that, following the price fall in X, income be reduced by the difference between the cost of his previous consumption of X (given by point A), at the old price and the new one in a way that leaves the consumer able to purchase the collection given by A, if he so likes. The only difference is that the new intermediate price line MM' must, by definition, pass through point A, and, therefore, the new collection chosen, say by point C' must, for consistency, either coincide with or be to the right of A. Again, therefore, we have that the consumption of X will tend to increase, following a fall in its price.

4.3 SOME AWKWARD PROBLEMS, BANDWAGON, SNOB AND VEBLEN EFFECTS

In order to derive the market demand curve for a good, we add horizontally the quantity demanded by each individual consumer at each price. This requires the assumption that the individual demands are independent of each other i.e., that each consumer decides which goods and in what quantities to purchase on the basis of his tastes, income and prices and irrespective of what other consumers may be doing. If this assumption is fulfilled, then the market for a particular good is given by the summation of the individual demands.

Sometimes, however, a number of consumers may be influenced in their purchases of particular goods by the behaviour of other consumers. In a seminal article, Leibenstein (1950) has argued that this is the case when people want to be in vogue, by conforming to social consumption patterns or when, instead, they want to be different by preferring exclusiveness. In both instances, individual consumption ceases to be independent and becomes a function of the consumption of others. For example, if a good has become fashionable, more and more people are likely to buy it, in order to be seen to swim with the crowd; for such people conformity seems to be an important characteristic of their behaviour. In such cases, an individual demand is influenced by the market acceptance of that good. This is known as the bandwagon effect, and it influences the pattern of preferences of the consumer. In terms of the earlier analysis, it changes the marginal rate of substitution in favour of the good experiencing the bandwagon effect *vis à vis* the other good(s) contained in the consumer's basket. Since now the good under consideration is perceived by the individual consumer to provide higher levels of utility, it means that a smaller quantity of that good could provide the particular consumer with the same level of satisfaction as before. But as the pattern of tastes and preferences has changed, and assuming that prices and incomes remain unchanged, our consumer is no longer in equilibrium, since the new marginal rate of substitution is not equal to the price ratio. Therefore, the consumer will reallocate his income in favour of the good affected by the bandwagon effect, by purchasing more of that good and moving on to a higher indifference curve. The implication of the increased individual demand, brought about by the bandwagon effect, on the market demand is that the latter will be greater than the summation of the individual demands.

On the other hand, a different aspect of human nature, known as the snob effect, may be producing the opposite effect on market demand. The purchases of some people will decrease as the market demand of a particular good increases. Contrary to social conformity, such consumers value exclusiveness highly and are prepared to pay high prices to acquire a good, particularly when it first appears on the market. Such consumers see themselves as pioneers and trend setters, by adopting a product in its initial pioneering stage. However, as the good gains market acceptability and as more and more people purchase it, it is given up by the pioneers, who feel that their exclusiveness has been eroded by the masses and who move on seeking to offer their patronage to other novelties. Therefore, where the snob effect is present the market demand curve for a good will be less than the summation of the individual independent demands.

Both the bandwagon and the snob effects represent external influences on utility, that is, influences not connected with the qualities inherent in the good itself. Another 'oddity' in market demand is the Veblen effect. By Veblen effect we mean the phenomenon of conspicuous consumption, i.e., the tendency for the demand of a good to increase because its price is higher, rather than lower. This is because the utility derived from a good used for conspicuous consumption depends both on the qualities inherent in that good and on the price paid. The conspicuous consumption utility depends on the conspicuous price, which is the price that the consumer thinks other people think he paid for the good, and which is either the same as the market price or related to it. Therefore, when the price of that good falls, a number of consumers will stop purchasing it, since the reduced price will provide them with lower utility.

There may be situations where all these effects are present. In such cases, other things being equal, a price change will be accompanied by a price, a bandwagon, a snob and a Veblen effect, two of which will tend to increase the quantity demanded of the good in question and two will tend to decrease it. A price rise will result in negative price and bandwagon effects and in positive snob and Veblen effects, provided that the price effect outweighs the Veblen effect, that is, if the net result of the higher price decreases the quantity demanded. However, if the Veblen effect is stronger than the price effect, following a price rise, then the bandwagon effect will be positive and the snob effect negative. The opposite would be the case for a price fall. The implications of these effects on the derivation of the market demand curve of the good in question is to make such derivation a more complicated matter than the horizontal summation of the individual demands and also affect the price elasticity of demand for that good. The latter aspect is, clearly, of importance to firms, as it will be argued later in this chapter.

4.4   DEMAND FUNCTIONS

It was suggested earlier that demand functions are derived from the process of constrained utility maximisation. As an example consider a consumer who has an income given by Y and is confronted with two goods Q_1 and Q_2, their prices P_1 and P_2 and the utility function $U = Q_1Q_2 + 2Q_1 + 4Q_2$. Therefore, the Lagrange function to be maximised becomes:

$$L = Q_1Q_2 + 2Q_1 + 4Q_2 + \lambda(Y - P_1Q_1 - P_2Q_2) \tag{1}$$

Differentiating partially with respect to Q_1, Q_2 and λ and setting the partial derivatives to zero results in:

$$\delta L/\delta Q_1 = Q_2 + 2 - \lambda P_1 = 0 \tag{2}$$

$$\delta L/\delta Q_2 = Q_1 + 4 - \lambda P_2 = 0 \tag{3}$$

$$\delta L/\delta \lambda = Y - P_1Q_1 - P_2Q_2 = 0 \tag{4}$$

Dividing relation (2) by relation (3) and rearranging yields

$$\frac{Q_2 + 2}{Q_1 + 4} = \frac{P_1}{P_2}$$

which can be solved for Q_1 and Q_2 to give the following two relations:

$$Q_1 = \frac{P_2(Q_2 + 2) - 4P_1}{P_1} \quad \text{and} \quad Q_2 = \frac{P_1(Q_1 + 4) - 2P_2}{P_2}$$

Substituting these values into relation (4) we finally get:

$$Q_1 = \frac{Y - 2(2P_1 + P_2)}{2P_1} \quad \text{and} \quad Q_2 = \frac{Y - 2(2P_1 + P_2)}{2P_2}$$

which are the demand functions, expressing the quantity demanded of goods Q_1 and Q_2 in terms of the income of the consumer and the prices of the two goods. It is clear that if the original utility function incorporated additional variables, for example advertising, such variable(s) would be part of the demand functions.

Demand functions have two important properties, namely: (1) they are single-valued functions of prices and income and (2) they are homogeneous of degree zero with respect to prices and income. The latter property means that if prices and income change in the same direction and proportion nothing happens to the quantity demanded, since the price line remains the same. This behaviour implies that the consumer is free of 'money illusion'.

4.5 THE DEMAND CURVE

Generally, the market demand function for a good can be written as:

$$Q_D = f(P, P_O, Y, T, \ldots)$$

stating that the quantity demanded Q_D is a function of the price P of the good in question, the prices P_O of other relevant goods, the income Y of the consumer, tastes T and so on, although the exact specification of the function, i.e., the variables chosen and the way they interact, will depend on the particular good and be dictated by what economic theory has to say on the matter. If all other variables, except quantity and price, are held constant at predetermined levels, i.e., by assuming *ceteris paribus*, then the resulting relation becomes:

$$Q_D = f(P)$$

which is known as the demand curve. By specifying a linear relation, to keep matters simple, the above can be written as:

$$Q_D = a - bQ$$

where a is a constant (intercept) reflecting the combined effect of all other determinants of demand, which by assumption are held constant, showing the amount that would be demanded if price were set at zero; while b is a parameter or the slope of the demand curve, indicating the inverse influence of price on quantity demanded, i.e., it shows by how much quantity demanded would be affected by a unit's change in price. A demand curve is given in Figure 4.7 as AB.

If the price of the good changes this will be reflected by a movement along the demand curve AB. However, if any of the other determinants of demand

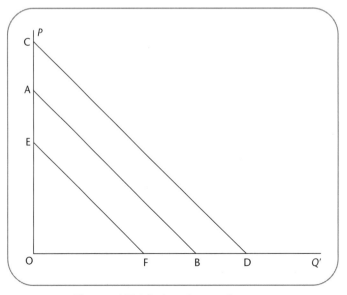

Figure 4.7 Market demand curves

(such as prices of substitute or complementary goods, incomes, tastes etc.) change, then this will be reflected by a shift of the demand curve to CD or EF, depending on whether the variation in the other determinants, on balance, raises or lowers demand.

4.5.1 The concept of elasticity

In formulating marketing policies, the firm (assumed to operate under non-competitive conditions) would wish to know the relative strength of each determinant in influencing the quantity demanded of its product(s). In particular, the firm would like to know how responsive demand is to variation in certain variables, commonly taken to be under its control, such as price, advertising expenditure, and so on. This information is provided by the various elasticities of demand. The concept of elasticity is quite general, and elasticities can be computed as the percentage change in some dependent variable brought about by a one percentage change in any independent variable. The use of percentages is important, since percentage changes are independent of the units of measurement of the variables and, thus, allow for the direct comparison of elasticities for different products.

4.5.2 The price elasticity of demand

The degree of responsiveness of quantity demanded of a particular good to variations in its price is known as the price elasticity of demand, and it is given by the percentage change in quantity demanded divided by a one percentage change in price. Since the value of price elasticity is negative, reflecting the inverse price-quantity relationship, it is often useful to multiply it by minus one (-1) so as to deal with positive values. The formula for the price elasticity of demand (η) is written as:

$$\eta = (-1)\frac{\% \text{ change in Q demanded}}{\% \text{ change in price}} = (-1)\frac{\Delta Q/Q}{\Delta P/P} = (-1)\frac{\Delta Q}{\Delta P} \times \frac{P}{Q}$$

If the demand curve is a straight line, the above formula measures the price elasticity at a particular point on the demand curve and this is known as the point price elasticity of demand. For example, if the demand curve is given by $Q_D = a - bP$, then $\Delta Q/\Delta P = -b$, and the price elasticity of demand at point (P_0, Q_0) is given simply by

$$\eta = b\frac{P_O}{Q_O}$$

If we take the demand curve to be $Q = 200 - 5P$ and we require the price elasticity at $P = 20$, we have $Q = 200 - 5 \times 20 = 100$ and therefore:

$$\eta = 5 \times \frac{20}{100} = 1$$

while at $P = 30$, we get $Q = 200 - 5 \times 30 = 50$, and the elasticity becomes:

$$\eta = 5 \times \frac{30}{50} = 1.5$$

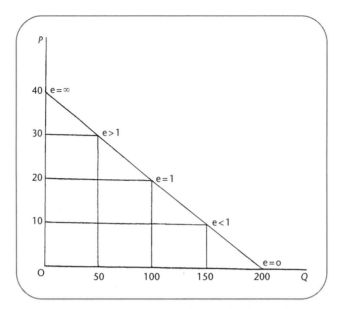

Figure 4.8 The elasticity–demand relationship

and finally at $P = 10$, quantity demanded is $Q = 200 - 5 \times 10 = 150$ and the elasticity is given by:

$$\eta = 5 \times \frac{10}{150} = 0.333$$

The above illustrates that even with a straight line demand curve the price elasticity of demand varies and its values range between infinity (∞), at the point where the demand curve meets the price axis ($P = 40, Q = 0$); and zero (0), at the point where the demand curve meets the quantity axis ($P = 0, Q = 200$) as substitution of these values into the formula reveals. In Figure 4.8 we plot the demand curve $Q = 200 - 5P$ and the results derived so far. As one moves up the demand curve, the price elasticity rises from a value of zero to a value of one at its midpoint and, finally, to a value of infinity. The lower segment, where $0 < \eta < 1$, gives the inelastic part of the demand curve, while the top segment, where $1 < \eta < \infty$, illustrates its elastic part. At the inelastic part of the demand curve, a given percentage change in price brings about a lower than percentage change in quantity demanded, while at the elastic part a given percentage change in price is followed by a greater than percentage change in quantity demanded. This has important implications on consumers' expenditure on the good in question, or the total revenue received by firms, which explains the significance of elasticity for decision making, as will become apparent later on. If, on the other hand, the demand curve is not a straight line, the formula for the point price elasticity of demand becomes:

$$\eta = (-1)\frac{dQ}{dP} \times \frac{P}{Q}$$

where dQ/dP represents the rate of change of quantity demanded with respect to price, i.e., it is the first derivative of the demand function with respect to price, and so its computation requires the use of calculus. So long as we are interested in very small price changes (infinitesimal) the use of the above formula for computing the price elasticity is uncontroversial.

However, this formula gives ambiguous results when it is used to compute elasticities over some range of prices, or over some range of the demand curve. In practice, this is more likely to occur either because the firm knows only a limited range of the demand for its product, or it wishes to concentrate on a particular range of prices. In such cases, using the point price elasticity of demand formula results in different values for the elasticity, depending on whether price was increased or decreased. For example, let the original position be given by: $P_1 = 30, Q_1 = 50$ and the new position, after the price change, be: $P_2 = 20$ and $Q_2 = 100$. Applying the formula gives:

$$\eta = (-1)\frac{\Delta Q}{\Delta P} \times \frac{P}{Q} = (-1)\frac{50}{-10} \times \frac{30}{50} = 3$$

However, by letting the initial position be: $P_1 = 20, Q_1 = 100$ and the new position be: $P_2 = 30, Q_2 = 50$, i.e., the same range of prices and quantities as before, the elasticity is calculated as follows:

$$\eta = (-1)\frac{\Delta Q}{\Delta P} \times \frac{P}{Q} = (-1)\frac{-50}{10} \times \frac{20}{100} = 1$$

To avoid this problem, which is due, mostly, to the large changes in price and quantity and to the direction of price change, we need to calculate an average measure of the price elasticity over the range of prices and quantities considered. This is known as the arc price elasticity of demand, whose value, thus, becomes independent of the direction of movement, and it is given by the formula:

$$\eta = (-1)\frac{\Delta Q}{\Delta P} \times \frac{(P_1 + P_2)/2}{(Q_1 + Q_2)/2} = (-1)\frac{\Delta Q}{\Delta P} \times \frac{P_1 + P_2}{Q_1 + Q_2}$$

Applying this formula to the earlier example, the arc price elasticity of demand is calculated as:

$$\eta = (-1)\frac{50}{-10} \times \frac{(30 + 20)/2}{(50 + 100)/2} = \frac{50}{10} \times \frac{50}{150} = 1.667$$

which lies between the two values of 3 and 1 found earlier.

Diagrammatically, the derivation of the point price elasticity of demand can be illustrated in Figure 4.9. Assume that we want to find the elasticity at point C. The formula gives:

$$\eta = (-1)\frac{\Delta Q}{\Delta P} \times \frac{P}{Q}$$

Since the demand curve is a straight line it has a constant slope given by $\Delta P/\Delta Q = OA/OB$ and, therefore, its reciprocal is also constant and it is given by $\Delta Q/\Delta P = OB/OA = GB/GC$. At point C, the price is $OE = GC$ and quantity demanded is given by $OG = EC$. Substituting these values into the point price elasticity of demand formula results in:

$$\eta = \frac{GB}{GC} \times \frac{GC}{OG} = \frac{GB}{OG} = \frac{GB}{EC}$$

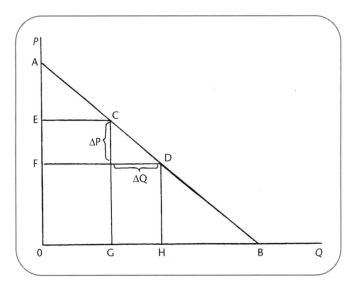

Figure 4.9 Derivation of point price elasticity of demand

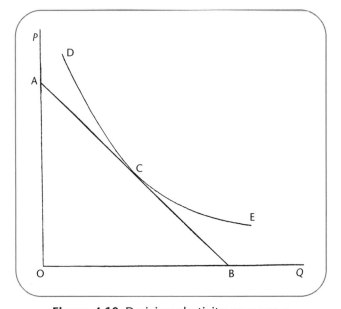

Figure 4.10 Deriving elasticity on a curve

but since the triangles CGB and AEC are similar, it follows that:

$$\eta = \frac{GB}{EC} = \frac{CG}{EA} = \frac{CB}{CA}$$

This final result is very useful since it enables us to find, diagrammatically, the price elasticity of demand at any point on the demand curve, even when the latter is non-linear. For example, assume that we want to find the price elasticity at point C on the demand curve DE on Figure 4.10. By drawing the tangent at point C and extending it to cut the two axes at A and B, the derivation of the price elasticity of demand at point C on the demand curve DE is equivalent to finding the elasticity at C on the curve AB in Figure 4.9, since both have the same slope at point C, and it is given by:

$$\eta = \frac{CB}{CA}$$

The above illustrates a general result, namely, that the price elasticity at any point on the demand curve is given by the ratio of the bottom segment of the tangent drawn to that point, divided by the top segment of that tangent.

4.5.3   Price elasticity, marginal & total revenue and optimal pricing policy

The degree of price elasticity has important implications on consumers' expenditure or the revenue received by firms, following changes in prices. As Figure 4.11 illustrates, at the elastic part of the demand curve a decrease in price from OP_1 to OP_2 results in raising total revenue ($P \times Q$) for the firm, since $OP_2BQ_2 > OP_1AQ_1$, while an increase in price, say from OP_2 to OP_1, decreases revenue. The reason is that, at the elastic part, a given proportionate change in the price of the good brings about a more than proportionate change in quantity demanded in the opposite direction, thus, revenue goes up or down depending on whether price falls or rises. On the other hand, at the inelastic part of the demand curve, a decrease in price from OP_3 to OP_4 reduces revenue, since $OP_4DQ_4 < OP_3CQ_3$, but a rise in price, say from OP_4 to OP_3 raises revenue. This is so because at the inelastic part a given proportionate change in price leads to a less than proportionate change in quantity in the opposite direction, thus, revenue goes up or down depending on whether price rises or falls. Finally, if the price elasticity of demand is unity, changes in price will leave the revenue received by firms unchanged, as Figure 4.12 shows, since $OP_1AC = OP_2BD$. This is the case because a given proportionate change in price is followed by the same proportionate change in quantity demanded in the opposite direction, therefore, leaving the product ($P \times Q$) unaltered.

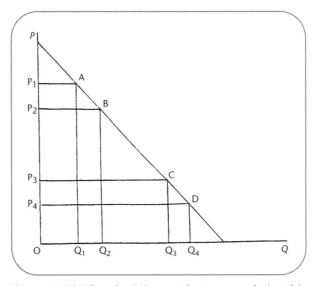

Figure 4.11 The elasticity–total revenue relationship

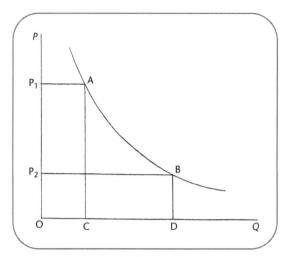

Figure 4.12 Rectangular hyperbola and total revenue

The foregoing discussion is clearly of significance to firms, because it indicates the range for optimal pricing policy as falling in the elastic part and explains the importance of deriving reliable estimates of price elasticities. Also, this analysis brings together price, marginal revenue and elasticity, which are linked through the formula:

$$MR = P\left(\frac{\eta - 1}{\eta}\right)$$

in which the negative sign of the price elasticity is ignored, whereas if one wanted to retain the negative sign of η then the formula becomes

$$MR = P\left(\frac{\eta + 1}{\eta}\right)$$

In either form the formula is a very handy tool at the hands of management, as it will be shown below, and is derived by noting that marginal revenue (MR) is the rate of change of total revenue (TR) and, thus, differentiating the function $TR = P \times Q$, with respect to Q, as follows:

$$MR = \frac{d(TR)}{dQ} = P \times \frac{dQ}{dQ} + Q \times \frac{dP}{dQ} = P + Q \times \frac{dP}{dQ}$$

By multiplying the final relationship through by the ratio P/P and rearranging we get the following:

$$MR = P\left(1 + \frac{Q}{P} \times \frac{dP}{dQ}\right) = P\left(1 + \frac{1}{\eta}\right) = P\left(\frac{\eta + 1}{\eta}\right)$$

The relationship between price, marginal revenue, total revenue and price elasticity can be illustrated by considering our earlier demand curve $Q = 200 - 5P$, deriving the appropriate figures entering Table 4.1 and then using them to obtain the graphical representations of the relationship of Figure 4.13.

It is obvious that maximum revenue of 2000 is obtained by the firm only when the price of the product is set at $P = 20$. At this price, marginal revenue is zero

Table 4.1 Relationship between price, total and marginal revenue

Quantity Q	Price P	Total revenue (TR)	Marginal revenue (MR)
200	0	0	
			875
175	5	875	
			625
150	10	1 500	
			375
125	15	1 875	
			125
100	20	2 000	
			−125
75	25	1 875	
			−375
50	30	1 500	
			−625
25	35	875	
			−875
0	40	0	

and price elasticity of demand is one. However, before getting the optimal pricing policy of the firm we require knowledge of its objectives, its cost structure and the price elasticity of demand for its product. Assuming the firm to be profit maximising and to know what the marginal cost of its product and its price elasticity of demand are, then application of the above formula will give us the optimal price. For example, if the marginal cost is given as MC = 20, we can calculate the profit maximising price for different values of price elasticity of demand, by substituting in our earlier formula, linking elasticity, price and marginal revenue MR = 20 (since for profit maximisation MR = MC). Indeed, for $\eta = 10$ we get:

$$P = \text{MR}\left(\frac{\eta}{\eta - 1}\right) = 20\left(\frac{10}{9}\right) = \frac{200}{9} = 22.223$$

while for $\eta = 5$ we obtain $P = 25$, for $\eta = 2$ we have $P = 40$, for $\eta = 1.5$ we derive $P = 60$, for $\eta = 1.1$ we get $P = 220$ and, finally, for $\eta = 1$ the price becomes infinite. These calculations are left to readers as an exercise. Thus, a general result emerges, namely, that for given MC, the optimal price is increased the lower the price elasticity becomes and vice versa, which shows that the optimal price will tend towards MC as elasticity increases and, finally, price will become equal to marginal cost ($P = \text{MC}$), when $\eta = \infty$, which is attained under conditions of perfect competition. It is also clear from the preceding discussion that the firm will always operate in the elastic part of its demand curve, since when, for example, $\eta = 0.5$ application of the above formula will result in a price of −40, a nonsensical result.

4.5.4 Other elasticities of demand

It was pointed out earlier that the concept of elasticity is a general one and, consequently, appropriate elasticities of demand can be computed with respect to

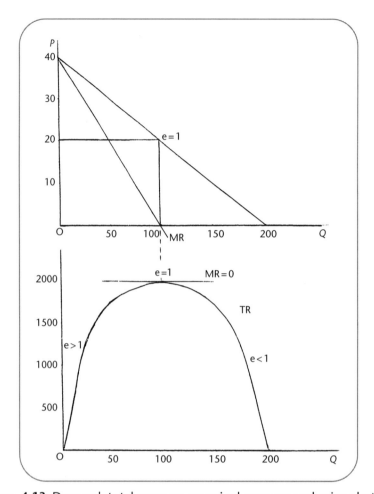

Figure 4.13 Demand, total revenue, marginal revenue and price elasticity

other demand determinants, such as income, prices of other relevant goods such as substitutes or complements, advertising expenditure, and so on.

The income elasticity of demand is defined as the percentage change in quantity demanded brought about by a one percentage change in income (Y), and the formula for the point income elasticity of demand is given by:

$$\eta_Y = \frac{dQ}{dY} \times \frac{Y}{Q}$$

whereas if it is desired to consider the income elasticity as an average measure over some income range, then the formula for the arc income elasticity of demand must be used, which is given by:

$$\eta_Y = \frac{\Delta Q}{\Delta Y} \times \frac{Y_1 + Y_2}{Q_1 + Q_2}$$

Knowledge of the values of income elasticities for different goods is very important, both from an analytical point of view and that of a business decision making.

For all normal goods, i.e., those whose consumption increases as income rises, the income elasticity of demand is positive; whereas inferior goods have negative income elasticities, meaning that as income rises, less of the good is demanded. Goods whose income elasticities lie between zero and unity are usually called necessities, while those whose income elasticities of demand exceed unity are termed as luxuries, although what constitutes a necessity or a luxury, at any one time and any one place, is very much a question of living standards. For example, what is considered as a necessity in some rich advanced countries may very well be a luxury in a third world country, or may have been considered as a luxury in the same advanced country at an earlier point in time. The relationship between income and expenditure on a specific good has a long history in economic enquiry and it goes back to the mid-nineteenth century, when Engel established, through empirical work, the famous 'Engel law' that the income elasticity of the demand for food was less than unity. This result has stood the test of time and has, since, been confirmed by other researchers.

From the point of view of the firm, the preceding discussion is useful since goods with income elasticities of demand less than unity imply that, for a given percentage growth in national income, the firm expects a less than proportionate rise in the demand for its goods. That is, if for good X, $\eta_Y = 0.7$ then a 1% rise in income increases demand for X by 0.7 of 1%. Clearly, in the context of a growing economy such goods do not provide the firm with considerable growth potential, although in periods of recession demand for such goods does not suffer too much. On the other hand, goods with income elasticities of demand greater than unity tend to get a bigger share of consumers' income (or expenditure) in periods of prosperity, but they also suffer considerable decreases in demand when incomes fall. Such information is clearly of vital importance to firms, when deciding on their product mix.

Another useful elasticity concept is the *cross price elasticity of demand*, which measures the degree of responsiveness of quantity demanded of good A (Q_A) brought about by a one percentage change in the price of good B (P_B). Again, we can distinguish between point and arc cross price elasticities of demand as follows:

Point cross price elasticity between A and B

$$\eta_{AB} = \frac{dQ_A}{dP_B} \times \frac{P_B}{Q_A}$$

Arc cross price elasticity between A and B

$$\eta_{AB} = \frac{dQ_A}{dP_B} \times \frac{P_{BI} + P_{B2}}{Q_A1 + Q_{A2}}$$

where the ones and twos in the subscripts refer to values before and after the change. The values of such elasticities can vary, theoretically, from minus infinity to plus infinity. Negative values denote that the two goods are considered as complementary to each other, whereas positive values show that the two goods are substitutes in the consumers' preferences. Again the strength of the elasticity is denoted by the absolute value, thus, if the cross price elasticity is less that one this denotes inelastic demand; while if the value of the cross price elasticity of demand is higher than one it shows elastic demand between the two goods.

Also, one can calculate the *advertising elasticity of demand* η_A, which shows the degree of responsiveness of quantity demanded of a particular good (Q) brought about by a one percentage change in advertising expenditure (A) as follows:

Point advertising elasticity of demand

$$\eta_A = \frac{dQ}{dA} \times \frac{A}{Q}$$

Arc advertising elasticity of demand

$$\eta_A = \frac{\Delta Q}{\Delta A} \times \frac{A_1 + A_2}{Q_1 + Q_2}$$

where A stands for advertising expenditure and subscripts denote values before and after the change. In general, as it was pointed out earlier, elasticities of demand can be computed as the rate of change of quantity demanded to changes in any one of the independent variables affecting such demand, weighed by the appropriate ratios of the values of such independent variables to the value of quantity demanded. In the next chapter we shall also consider an alternative method of establishing elasticities, by means of regression analysis.

4.5.5 Factors affecting elasticity

The main factors affecting elasticity of demand for various products are the availability or not of substitutes, the percentage of income spent on such products, the perception by consumers of products as necessary or not, the wider or narrower definition of products and the length of time.

The greater the availability of close substitutes, the greater the price elasticity of demand for a particular product, and vice versa. For example, apples can be very price sensitive because of the existence of many other fruits, which provide readily available substitutes. Thus, oranges, peaches, bananas, melons, grapes etc. provide the consumer with a plethora of other fruits at different periods and this ease of substitutability indicates that the demand for apples is likely to be elastic. Much effort of marketing and advertising is directed to emphasising particular attributes/characteristics of products, though product differentiation, in order to reduce the price elasticity and render them price insensitive.

On the other hand, the smaller the percentage of income spent on purchasing a particular product, the less sensitive consumers are to changes in its price and so elasticity tends to be low. For example, products like salt and matches come into this category. By contrast, cars, most household appliances etc., which require a considerable proportion of one's income, tend to have price elastic demands. People are more readily prepared to shop around when the product in question requires a large proportion of their income, rather than a very small one. In the first case such products tend to have elastic demands; in the latter case they have inelastic demands.

Also, the perception of consumers regarding the necessity or otherwise of products is important. For example, a certain amount of salt is considered a necessary purchase, irrespective of its price–at least for the range of prices normally considered and, therefore, its demand is price inelastic.

The wider the definition of a product, the less price elastic the demand for that product tends to be. Food, in general, has no close substitutes and, consequently, its demand is price inelastic. However, when we start distinguishing between different kinds of food, i.e., meat, fish, vegetables etc. and, in particular, different kinds of meat (such as beef, pork, lamb etc.), fish (like cod, plaice, mackerel etc.), vegetables (such as peas, beans, Brussels sprouts etc.) the price elasticity of demand for such varieties becomes much higher, because of the ability of consumers to substitute one with another.

Also, time plays an important role in determining price elasticities of demand. Other things remaining equal, one expects inelastic demands in the short run, because consumers do not react instantaneously to price changes, but as time passes they are able to adjust themselves to the new situations and, therefore, elasticities tend to rise. For example, when petrol prices rose significantly world-wide in the 1970s, demand was not curtailed drastically in the short run, because of the difficulty of consumers to turn immediately to suitable alternatives. However, as time passed, people were able to substitute different forms of energy in a number of previous petrol uses, and also to introduce – particularly in the motor car industry – petrol saving techniques, resulting in the raising of the price elasticity of demand for petrol in the long run.

Similarly, the magnitude of the other elasticities of demand we referred to above, such as income and cross price elasticities, are influenced mainly by the availability of substitutes.

SUMMARY

In this chapter we have reviewed the fundamentals of demand theory and sought to demonstrate the law of demand, i.e., the inverse relationship between price and quantity demanded of a product. Consequently, we have traced the developments in the theory of demand from Marshall's cardinal theory, to the ordinal theory of demand through the indifference curves analysis, to the revealed preference approach and Hicks' revision of demand theory. Additionally, we have looked at some awkward questions, such as bandwagon snob and Veblen effects arising in demand theory. In the second part we have looked at demand functions and from such functions we have derived demand curves, in order to develop and discuss, at some length, the various concepts of elasticity, which play an important role in managerial decisions.

PROBLEMS

1. A household has €420 available per week to spend on food and clothing. If the price of food is €20 per unit, and the household's utility function is given by:

$$U = 20 \log Q_F + \log Q_C$$

where Q_F and Q_C are the quantities of food and clothing consumed, what is the household's demand equation for clothing? Is this equation consistent with the law of demand? What can you say about the price elasticity of clothing?

2. A consumer spends €100 per week on tobacco and entertainment. The unit price of tobacco is €2 and the consumer's utility function is given by:

$$U = 2Q_T Q_E$$

where Q_T and Q_E are the quantities of tobacco and entertainment bought. What is the demand equation for entertainment? Find also the equations for average and marginal revenue and comment on your results.

3. A firm has estimated the demand function for its brand of toothpaste MOUTHFRESH to be given by:

$$\log Q = 200 - 1.2 \log P + 5 \log Y + 4 \log A + 1.5 \log P_C$$

where Q and P are the quantity and price of MOUTHFRESH respectively, Y is disposable income, A is the level of advertising undertaken by the firm and P_C is the price of an alternative brand of toothpaste, produced by a competitor firm.

(a) What are the price elasticity of MOUTHFRESH, the income elasticity, the advertising elasticity and the cross elasticity between the two brands of toothpaste?
(b) What knowledge does the firm derive from these elasticities about the demand for MOUTHFRESH?
(c) If the firm charges a price of €1.20 per unit of MOUTHFRESH, what is the marginal revenue of an additional unit of MOUTHFRESH?

4. The demand equation for a product A is given by: $Q = 2000 - 0.4P$.

(a) What are the equations for total revenue and marginal revenue?
(b) What is the point price elasticity of demand at $Q = 1000$? At the estimated point price elasticity, what is the marginal revenue, assuming price to be €20? Would the marginal revenue be different if price were €15?

5. The quantity demanded of a product X is determined by its price P, the price of a related product Z, P_Z, and the disposable income, Y, in the following way:

$$Q = 1000 - 0.5P + 20Y - 0.8P_Z$$

(a) Estimate the price elasticity of X when $Q = 900$, $Y = 50$ and $P_Z = 100$. If the firm contemplates a 10% reduction in price, in an attempt to raise revenue, would you advise it to proceed, other things being equal?
(b) Estimate the income elasticity of demand when: $Q = 1500, P = 2000$ and $P_Z = 120$. If outside information points to a 10% rise in disposable income in the following year, is the firm justified in expecting sales to rise, other things being equal?
(c) Estimate the cross price elasticity of demand between X and Z when $Q = 900, P = 2500$ and $Y = 62$. How would you describe the relationship between X and Z?

6. A consumer spends all his income on only two products. The following table gives some information about his budget and chosen consumption pattern in two different budgetary situations. You are also informed that the change from situation A to situation B is an undercompensated one.

(a) Fill in the missing figures.
(b) Which pieces of information are *not* needed in order to answer (a)?

	Income	Prices		Consumption	
	Y	P_1	P_2	Q_1	Q_2
Situations					
A	70	1	2	40	15
B	?	3	1	?	20

(Hint: An undercompensated budgetary change is one in which the new chosen position could also just be afforded in the initial situation, i.e., the new consumption point lies on the initial budget line, as well as on the new one).

BIBLIOGRAPHY

Baumol, W.J. (1977), *Economic Theory and Operations Analysis*, 4th edn., Prentice-Hall.
Henderson, J. and Quandt, R.E. (1990), *Microeconomic Theory*, 3rd edn., McGraw-Hill.
Hicks, J.R. (1946), *Value and Capital*, 2nd edn., Oxford University Press.
—— (1956), *A Revision of Demand Theory*, Oxford University Press.
Leibenstein, H. (1950), 'Bandwagon, Snob and Veblen Effects in the Theory of Consumers' Demand', *Quarterly Journal of Economics*, **64**.
Marshall, A. (1922), *Principles of Economics*, 8th edn., Macmillan.
Palda, K.S. (1969), *Economic Analysis for Marketing Decisions*, Prentice-Hall.
Samuelson, P.A. (1947), *Foundations of Economic Analysis*, Harvard University Press.
—— (1953), 'Consumption Theorems in Terms of Overcompensation Rather than Indifference Comparisons', *Economica*, **20**.

chapter five

Sales Forecasting

Learning outcomes

After studying this chapter you should know about:

- Trend projection and forecasting

- Economic and Business indicators

- Opinion polling and survey methods

- Model building – Econometric method

- Input–output analysis

- An overview on regression analysis

5.1   INTRODUCTION

In the present chapter we look more closely at sales forecasting and seek to provide some methods commonly used to derive forecasts, which are needed in planning quantities produced, stocks, prices, advertising outlays, product mix and cash flows. Successful forecasting is necessary for management as it helps to reduce avoidable risks and such forecasting is required for both short- and long-run managerial decisions. For example, good sales forecasting helps in budgeting cash flows, in stabilising production and employment, in controlling stocks of all kinds and in planning new capital expenditure for production and other facilities. Economic forecasting is also undertaken by governments to help them in a variety of decisions, as for example, with respect to raising taxes, appropriations, money and credit, supply, employment, balance of trade but also in planning new schools, hospitals, roads and other infrastructure projects. Forecasting methods vary in their degree of complexity, sophistication and cost, so choosing the right method is a problem in itself. Naturally, management requires forecasts to be accurate and available long in advance of the event they try to forecast, so that appropriate action can be taken in time. There is not much point in deriving a very accurate forecast if it becomes available too late in time to be of use. Correspondingly, in choosing a forecasting method consideration must be given to the results achieved by the method and its costs as well as the accuracy and the 'lead' of the forecast.

5.2   NAIVE METHODS OF FORECASTING – TREND PROJECTION

Naive methods of forecasting involve the extrapolation of the present situation into the future. We may start by assuming that there is an underlying structure in the time series we are trying to forecast. The simplest possible assumption regarding this structure is that the forecast value in the next period is the same as in the current period (i.e., there is no change), in which case we get the trivial solution $Y_{t+1} = Y_t$. Extending the analysis we can incorporate growth or a trend into the series as well as seasonal, cyclical and irregular effects. Generally, the observed value (O) of an economic variable, say sales of a good, is assumed to be influenced over time by trend (T), seasonal effects (S), cyclical variations (C) and irregular forces (I). Trend depicts the underlying growth or decline of the series, seasonal effects capture systematic influences on the economic variable of, perhaps, weather conditions, custom or institutional arrangements within a year (i.e., higher sales of ice cream during summer, or higher toy sales during Christmas, and so on), cyclical variations reflect the overall state of economic activity (business cycle) over a number of years, while irregular forces represent erratic influences, such as strikes, boycotts, wars and so on. If we can further assume that the trend represents a systematic growth component of the time series, while the other three influences (seasonal, cyclical and irregular forces) reflect divergences from the trend, then a way of forecasting future values of the variable under consideration is to isolate the trend of the series from the other influences. This can be achieved by, among others, the method of moving average (MA). This method is used to smooth out fluctuations in the time series and consists in replacing the values of the given series by the mean of that value plus some other values directly preceding it and immediately following it. If the chosen length of the MA equals that of the regular cycle in the series, we shall get a smooth curve. So, if we know that the cycle, from boom to boom or from recession to recession, is of a 4-year period we should select a 4-year period MA.

The great advantage of the MA method is its simplicity and flexibility in portraying long-run movements in the series. However, it fails to forecast turning points in the series and it misses out as many observations as the length of the chosen MA. Also, it suffers from certain methodological shortcomings. Since the method aims at averaging out the divergences from the trend, such divergences, that is, the seasonal, cyclical and irregular effects must be assumed to follow the same periodic fluctuations. But the cyclical and irregular influences do not have systematic periodic fluctuations and, therefore, applying the MA method to establish the trend can only be partially successful.

The MA method can also be used to isolate the seasonal variation from the more stable cyclical and irregular component. The causes of the seasonal variation have a relatively regular period pattern and by using a 12-month MA we tend to average out the seasonal divergences in the series.

5.2.1 Least squares trend projection

Another very popular and widely used method of projecting the trend is the method of least squares. Assume that we want to predict future sales of a good on the basis of time series of such sales, given in millions of euros, in Table 5.1, which also includes the 3- and 5-year MAs of sales.

Table 5.1 Sales, 3-year moving average MA(3) and 5-year moving average MA(5)

Year	Sales	MA(3)	MA(5)
1986	102	—	—
1987	104	103.3	—
1988	103	104.3	104.0
1989	106	104.7	105.0
1990	105	106.0	106.2
1991	107	107.3	108.0
1992	110	109.7	108.8
1993	112	110.7	109.4
1994	110	110.0	110.2
1995	108	109.7	111.0
1996	111	111.0	111.4
1997	114	113.0	112.6
1998	114	114.7	115.0
1999	116	116.7	—
2000	120	—	—

Projecting the trend requires that we make sales (Y) a function of time (t), by hypothesising: $Y = \alpha + \beta t + u$, where $1986 = 0, 1987 = 1$, and so on, and where u is an error term assumed to be normally and independently distributed with zero mean, as explained in the Appendix following this chapter, we derive the following predicting equation:

$$\hat{Y} = \underset{(116.65)}{101.8416} + \underset{(10.46)}{1.0893t} \quad \bar{R}^2 = 0.8856$$

which can be used to predict sales for any time, both within and outside the sample period, as it is illustrated in Figure 5.1. For example, this method predicts sales of €121.449 m for 2004. This is obtained as follows. The value of t for 2004 is 18, and therefore by substituting this value into the predicting equation we get:

$$\hat{Y} = 101.8416 + 1.0893 \times 18 = 101.8416 + 19.6074 = 121.449$$

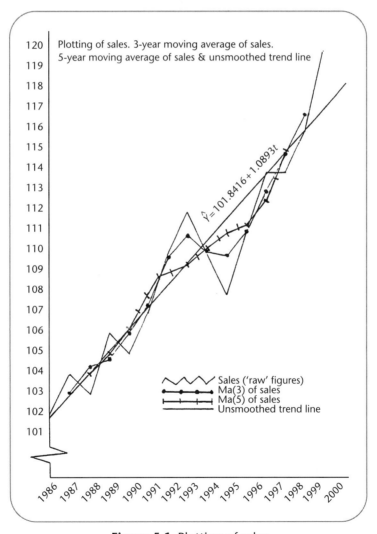

Figure 5.1 Plotting of sales

Table 5.2 Sales of good X with trend removed by subtraction and division

Time T	Sales Y	Estim. sales $\hat{Y}$	Residuals $Y - \hat{Y} = T + S + C + I - T$	Residuals $Y/\hat{Y} = TSCI/T$
1986	102	101.8416	0.1584	1.0016
1987	104	102.9309	1.0691	1.0103
1988	103	104.0202	−1.0202	0.9902
1989	106	105.1095	0.8905	1.0085
1990	105	106.1988	−1.1988	0.9887
1991	107	107.2881	−0.2881	0.9973
1992	110	108.3774	1.6226	1.0150
1993	112	109.4667	2.5333	1.0231
1994	110	110.5560	−0.5560	0.9950
1995	108	111.6453	−3.6453	0.9673
1996	111	112.7346	−1.7346	0.9846
1997	114	113.8239	0.1761	1.0015
1998	114	114.9132	−0.9132	0.9921
1999	116	116.0025	−0.0025	1.0000
2000	120	117.0918	2.9082	1.0248

In Figure 5.1 the origin has been shifted to 1986 and t is measured in years. Figure 5.1 also includes the plots of the two moving averages of sales, i.e., MA(3) and MA(5) given in Table 5.1.

As before, the disadvantage of this method is that it will not provide us with turning points in the series, although between such turning points the predicted values will tend to be accurate, particularly, if the cyclical changes develop slowly over time.

However, from the businessman's point of view it is the forecasting of the turning points that is important rather than the projection of the trend, since if the series continues in one direction no policy changes are implied; whereas if turning points are indicated policy changes can be initiated with respect, say, to production levels, stocks and so on. For this reason, attempts have also been made to refine this method in a way that it is capable of predicting also the turning points of the series. This has involved the cyclical or harmonic analysis of the residuals left, after removing the trend. The method consists in removing first the trend from the observed values and then the seasonal effect, by constructing the appropriate indices. One is then left with the cyclical and irregular factors, and to this residual series it is now possible to fit a cycle function, e.g. a sine function, to predict turning points.

Depending on the underlying assumptions made, regarding the way trend, seasonal, cyclical and irregular factors are interrelated in affecting the variable concerned – i.e., whether an additive form, such as: $O = T+S+C+I$ or a multiplicative one, like $O = TCSI$ is assumed – the trend can be eliminated either by subtracting it out from the observed values (i.e., $T + S + C + I - \hat{T}$) or by dividing it out ($TSCI/\hat{T}$), so as to leave us with the residual series involving seasonal, cyclical and irregular factors. Table 5.2 illustrates trend removal, assuming both an additive form and a multiplicative form, for the above example. In the next stage, assuming that we also have monthly data of the original series, we compute again through regression analysis the seasonal indices for the 4th and 5th columns of Table 5.2 and subtract it out or divide it out accordingly. This will leave us with a series involving only the cyclical and irregular factors, to which we may finally fit an appropriate function, such as for example a sine function, to derive the cycle, and thus obtain the desired turning points.

However, the residual method has been criticised because of its restrictive assumptions. The trend removal must precede that of the seasonal factors, but, clearly, the values of the series will be different if we changed the order of the removal. Also, the assumption that the various components of the series (trend, cyclical and so on) are affected by factors which are independent of each other, may not be tenable; trend and cycle may well depend on the same set of factors, in which case we cannot proceed with separating them. Also, the assumption that the trend is linear, or that the cycle has the same periodicity and amplitude may not necessarily be the case, as the above example illustrates with respect to the cycle. Similarly, the shorter the time period involved, the more probable it is that the irregular factors may outweigh in significance the regular movements of trend and cycle. It has also been shown that the use of the moving average method to remove the trend and seasonal effects from a series can induce cyclical effects into the series when no such cycles were present in the first place. So, while naive methods of forecasting may provide flexible and inexpensive tools for management, they suffer also from certain limitations, of which one must be aware.

5.3 TREND FORECASTING – THE USE OF SMOOTHING

The preceding discussion has demonstrated a number of shortcomings in the use of trend projection and simple moving averages. The latter do not quite satisfy the assumed steady growth or decline of the secular trend in the time series. Even with a relatively long moving average there will be oscillations indicating the existence of cyclical components in the series, in addition to the trend, as it is apparent in Figure 5.1 with the plots of the two moving average series. Also, a moving average terminates before the last available data, thus making projections more difficult. A way around this problem is to fit mathematical trend curves, including non-linear trends.

We may start by plotting the data to see if there is any special pattern. If the plot reveals an unusually erratic series we can smooth or filter the data by constructing a moving average. This has the effect of reducing the importance of sharp peaks and troughs, and the longer the length of the moving average the smoother the series becomes, as it is clear from Figure 5.1 where the MA(5) plot is much smoother than the MA(3) one. The plot then enables us to fit the series to a mathematical model. Most economic and business time series tend to exhibit smooth rates of growth, and therefore exponential trends may prove very useful.

In Figure 5.2 we depict a number of mathematical models. In Figure 5.2(a) we have the familiar linear model $Y = a + bt + u$, while in Figure 5.2(b) and (c) we

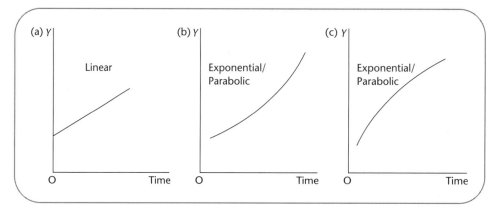

Figure 5.2 Different types of mathematical models

provide simple examples of exponential models. In Figure 5.2(b) the exponential model is given by the semi-logarithmic function: $\ln Y = a + bt + u$, or the same result may be depicted by the parabolic model $Y = a + bt + ct^2 + u$, where we expect $b < 0$. In Figure 5.2(c) the exponential model is given by $Y = \ln a + b \ln t + u$ and the parabolic by $Y = a + bt + ct^2 + u$, where we expect $c < 0$.

As an example we have used the series in Table 5.1 and their plots in Figure 5.2. The plots make it easier for us to choose the appropriate mathematical model(s). For illustrative purposes three models have been used; the linear, parabolic and cubic functions to which we have fitted the raw or un-smoothed series of sales, and the two moving average series of Table 5.1. The results are as follows, where figures in parantheses denote t-ratios.

'Raw' data, un-smoothed series of sales

Linear

$$\hat{Y} = \underset{(118.85)}{101.841667} + \underset{(10.46)}{1.089288t} \quad \bar{R}^2 = 0.8856 \quad \text{SEE} = 1.743145$$

$$\text{D–W} = 1.402$$

Parabolic

$$\hat{Y} = \underset{(86.71)}{102.697059} + \underset{(1.77)}{0.694499t} + \underset{(1.04)}{0.0282t^2} \quad \bar{R}^2 = 0.8863 \quad \text{SEE} = 1.73735$$

$$\text{D–W} = 1.479$$

Cubic

$$\hat{Y} = \underset{(75.99)}{101.484641} + \underset{(2.28)}{1.095576t} - \underset{(-1.41)}{0.204958t^2} + \underset{(1.63)}{0.011103t^3}$$

$$\bar{R}^2 = 0.902 \quad \text{SEE} = 1.628141$$

$$\text{D–W} = 1.677$$

Filtered or smoothed data: 3-year moving average of sales

Linear

$$\widehat{MA}(3) = 103.110989 + 1.03022t \quad R^2 = 0.9420 \quad SEE = 0.9928389$$
$$\underset{(198.14)}{} \quad \underset{(14.00)}{}$$
$$D\text{--}W = 0.891$$

Parabolic

$$\widehat{MA}(3) = 103.296703 + 0.928921t + 0.008442t^2$$
$$\underset{(138.296703)}{} \quad \underset{(3.23)}{} \quad \underset{(0.37)}{}$$
$$\bar{R}^2 = 0.9371 \quad SEE = 1.034425$$
$$D\text{--}W = 0.884$$

Cubic

$$\widehat{MA}(3) = 102.471703 + 1.966421t - 0.216558t^2 + 0.0125t^3$$
$$\underset{(131.71)}{} \quad \underset{(3.36)}{} \quad \underset{(-1.86)}{} \quad \underset{(1.97)}{}$$
$$\bar{R}^2 = 0.9511 \quad SEE = 0.9111827$$
$$D\text{--}W = 1.099$$

Filtered or smoothed data: 5-year moving average of sales

Linear

$$\widehat{MA}(5) = 104.309091 + 0.98545t \quad \bar{R}^2 = 0.97199 \quad SEE = 0.553994$$
$$\underset{(333.79)}{} \quad \underset{(18.66)}{}$$
$$D\text{--}W = 1.213$$

Parabolic

$$\widehat{MA}(5) = 104.204196 + 1.055385t - 0.006993t^2$$
$$\underset{(234.56)}{} \quad \underset{(5.11)}{} \quad \underset{(-0.35)}{}$$
$$\bar{R}^2 = 0.96897 \quad SEE = 0.583119$$
$$D\text{--}W = 1.269$$

Cubic

$$\widehat{MA}(5) = 103.634965 + 1.959829t - 0.244172t^2 + 0.015812t^3$$
$$\underset{(284.47)}{} \quad \underset{(5.91)}{} \quad \underset{(-3.07)}{} \quad \underset{(3.03)}{}$$
$$\bar{R}^2 = 0.9847 \quad SEE = 0.409828$$
$$D\text{--}W = 1.799$$

Since the dependent variable is measured in levels in all equations, the R^2s are comparable and the results suggest that the cubic model of the 5-year moving average provides the best fit. This model explains 98.47% of the variation in sales, is having the lowest standard error of estimate (SEE) and all its coefficients are significantly different than zero at the 95% level of significance, as shown by the t-ratios (values in parentheses) and the coefficients all have the expected signs. In addition, the Durbin–Watson (D–W) statistic indicates that this is the model least likely to suffer from autocorrelation, as explained in the Appendix. Using this equation we can now forecast the values of sales for 1999 and 2000 and check them against the actual values.

$$\hat{Y}_{t+1} = 103.634965 + 1.959829(11) - 0.244172(11)^2 + 0.015812(11)^3$$

$$= 116.694$$

$$\hat{Y}_{t+2} = 103.634965 + 1.959829(12) - 0.244172(12)^2 + 0.015812(12)^3$$

$$= 119.315$$

Since in the smoothing process we lost the last two observations of the sales series these provide us with an immediate check for our forecast figures. Thus, the 1999 forecast value is 116.694 as against the actual 116 and the forecast for 2000 is 119.315 compared with the actual value of 120. The foregoing has shown how single time series can be analysed and extrapolated in order to provide us with a forecast value. However, while this may be the simplest method it is neither the sole nor the most successful approach.

5.3.1 MA, AR & ARMA models: Box–Jenkins Analysis

Recent developments in time series analysis still start with plotting the data, smooth them and try to fit them to a mathematical model. However, since nearly all economic time series fall into one of three classes of models: MA, autoregressive (AR) and mixed autoregressive moving average (ARMA), the problem is one of fitting the series to one of these models. The method of doing this is known as Box–Jenkins analysis. A MA model is not the same as a MA filter discussed earlier but is a 'weighted sums' model. However, as this analysis goes far beyond the confines of this book, no discussion is given here and the interested reader is advised to consult instead the references given at the end of this chapter.

5.4 ECONOMIC OR BUSINESS INDICATORS (BAROMETRIC TECHNIQUES)

Economic or business indicators are sensitive indices or time series which act as barometers of economic conditions. Such series tend to move consistently in advance of other series we are interested in. Business forecasting has long sought such indices and it is said that the American steel industrialist Andrew Carnegie used to count the number of factory chimneys emitting smoke to tell which way business was going, and thus forecast the demand for steel. For an indicator to be used for forecasting purposes it must satisfy at least the following: (1) reflect the turning points of economic activity; (2) measure the amplitude of change; (3) measure the rate of growth or decline and (4) lead the series we are interested in forecasting.

The most comprehensive measure of aggregate economic activity is the gross national product (GNP), which is the total amount of final goods and services produced during the year, valued at market prices. Alternatively, it represents the total expenditure of government, businesses and individuals. The major advantage

may not be able to identify the factors correctly behind their purchasing decisions and also the importance of changes in such factors, whereas economic modelling, by seeking to specify demand functions for particular commodities or groups of commodities, may be better suited for forecasting such demand.

Economy-wide surveys have been more successful at forecasting the level of broad categories of inventory changes, capital expenditure and of total economic activity in general. Since in most countries the public sector accounts for anything between 30% and 55% of aggregate expenditure, knowledge of the state's budget for the following year can provide forecasters with some firm evidence of what the government is planning to do. Complementing this information with knowledge of sectoral investment plans can result in reasonably reliable estimates of total investment activity, which when added to a more stable total consumption expenditure can provide good forecasts of GNP.

In general, survey methods are used in conjunction with quantitative techniques of forecasting, as a supplement rather than supplanting them, hoping to show changes in consumer preferences – if and when occurring, and to capture those non-quantifiable psychological elements in economic conduct, left out of the quantitative analysis.

5.6   ECONOMETRIC METHOD–MODEL BUILDING

The model building or econometric method to forecasting involves the mulation and specification of economic relationship(s), the estimation of relationship(s) and the evaluation of the results. In trying to forecast demand commodity, we are involved in a number of steps. First, we have to choose, gu by economic theory, the appropriate variables used in the analysis by spe ing the economic relationship or relationships between the variables. This m s deciding on whether a single-equation model or a simultaneous-equations ;-tem depicts better the underlying economic structure we are interested in, an n the endogenous and predetermined variable(s) which will be used in the va us equations. Second, we seek to determine, on the basis of economic and/or sta ist-ical criteria, the mathematical formulation of the model, i.e., on whether a li ear formulation of the model is an appropriate one, or whether a log-linear or some other functional form might be preferred. Third, we decide on the appropriate estimating technique, which enables us to derive estimates of the coefficients of the structural relations, to be used in forecasting the future values of economic magnitudes or variables. Last, we evaluate our results with reference to a priori expectations regarding signs and magnitudes of the estimated coefficients and a number of diagnostic tests, which are designed to show whether or not the estimates obey certain desirable properties, before proceeding to use such estimates in any forecasting work.

The advantages of forecasting with an econometric model include not only that turning points in economic variables can be predicted but also the magnitudes of such changes. In addition, the reliability of the forecast can be tested by constructing confidence intervals, which enable us to say that the forecast value will lie within certain limits with given probability. Further, where a comparison between predicted and realised values showed wide discrepancies and thus poor predictive power of the model used, forecasters could introduce changes by, among

others, adding new variables to the model, which could lead to an improvement in forecasting.

As far as sales forecasting is concerned, management has the task of identifying those variables which are likely to be important determinants of sales and seek to influence those, among them, that are within its power. For example, the demand for a product may be affected by, among others, the price of the product and its quality as well as credit terms and promotional expenditure all of which to a larger or lesser extent can be varied at management's will. Of course, the demand for different products or groups of products will be affected by a different set of factors. In the case of consumer non-durable goods the following have been found to affect purchases: population and its characteristics, prices of own product and substitutes and discretionary income, i.e., disposable income plus transfer payments less fixed commitments. On the other hand, the demand for consumer durables is affected by the number of households, discretionary income, credit terms, prices of own product and substitutes, existing stock of such goods and average age of such stock (an important factor in relation to replacement demand).

Having identified the relevant variables entering the demand function, a relationship is hypothesised linking these variables, which provides us with an econometric model. For most forecasting purposes a single equation model will suffice. Such a model can be formulated either as a linear one or a log-linear one. The first is the simplest possible case and the estimated coefficients show the rates of change of the dependent variable with respect to the independent variables, whereas in the log-linear formulation the estimates are the relevant elasticities. For example, we may hypothesise that the demand (Q) for a commodity is determined by its price (P), an index of prices of other close substitutes (P_O), disposable income (Y) and advertising expenditure (A). This relationship can be formulated either as:

$$Q = b_0 + b_1 P + b_2 P_O + b_3 Y + b_4 A + u$$

or as:

$$\ln Q = \ln b_0 + b_1 \ln P + b_2 \ln P_O + b_3 \ln Y + b_4 \ln A + v$$

where u and v are stochastic terms, assumed to be normally and independently distributed with zero means and constant variances. Provided we have information on the relevant variables in the form of either time series or cross-section data, multiple regression techniques such as ordinary least squares (OLSs) can be applied to derive estimates of the coefficients b's. Once such estimates are available, forecasting future demand involves substituting the values of the estimates, together with values of the independent variables appearing on the right-hand side of the equation to give us a forecast value of Q. The estimated coefficients of our predicting equation will have certain desirable properties, such as unbiasedness and least variance, provided a number of assumptions underlying single-equation regression models are satisfied. A brief discussion of such assumptions, and the problems their breakdown gives rise to, is given in the appendix following this chapter and two examples of multiple regression analysis are provided as well.

5.6.1 Model building – The simultaneous-equations approach

Although in most cases a single-equation model will be adequate for our purposes, sometimes it is found that the interdependence of economic variables makes it necessary to set up a system of simultaneous equations to describe the structure of the economic relationships involved. To illustrate the problem, recall that in the example above we had assumed that the price of the commodity (P) was given from outside the model and, therefore, it was treated as an independent (exogenous) variable. However, this assumption is not often warranted, since quantities and prices are jointly determined variables in market systems. Also, since in equilibrium quantities bought and sold are equal we cannot treat our observations as reflecting either quantities demanded or quantities supplied. These points indicate that we require a system of separate relations for demand and supply to represent the market adequately of the commodity in question. Assuming a linear formulation we can write the system of equations as follows:

$$Q_D = a_0 + a_1 P + a_2 Y + a_3 P_O + a_4 A + u_1 \tag{1}$$

$$Q_S = b_0 + b_1 P + b_2 T + b_3 W + u_2 \tag{2}$$

$$Q_D = Q_S \tag{3}$$

The three relations reflect the structure of the market and they are known as the structural form of the model. Relations (1) and (2) are referred to as behavioural relations, since they show us the way the variables are interrelated in affecting the market. Relation (1) is the demand equation, where the meaning of the variables is as given above and relation (2) is the supply equation, which makes quantity supplied a function of the price (P) of the commodity, of a technological index (T) and of the wage rate (W). The stochastic terms u_1 and u_2 are also added to show that the relations are not exact. Relation (3) is the market clearing condition and as such it is an identity, since quantity bought equals quantity sold. The system of the three equations determines the three unknowns, i.e., the dependent or endogenous variables (Q_D, Q_S and P), and in that sense it is complete. In addition, we have another five variables (Y, P_O, A, T and W) given from outside the model and known as exogenous variables. Notice that it is the presence of these five exogenous variables, which enables us to uniquely identify the demand and supply relations, since they represent shift factors and appear only in one equation and not in both, and then proceed with their estimation. Such estimation is covered in introductory econometrics courses and is not given here. However, to illustrate how such a system of equations is used for forecasting purposes we utilise what is known as the reduced form of the model.

The reduced-form model expresses the endogenous variables as functions of the exogenous variables and disturbances alone, and it can be derived from the structural form by substitution. In our case, since $Q_D = Q_S$ we equate it to Q and get the two endogenous variables as P and Q. Equating (1) and (2) and solving for P gives:

$$P = \frac{a_0 - b_0}{b_1 - a_1} + \frac{a_2}{b_1 - a_1} Y + \frac{a_3}{b_1 - a_1} P_O + \frac{a_4}{b_1 - a_1} A - \frac{b_2}{b_1 - a_1} T$$

$$- \frac{b_3}{b_1 - a_1} W + \frac{u_1 - u_2}{b_1 - a_1} \tag{4}$$

Now putting (4) into (1) and rearranging results in:

$$Q = \frac{a_0 b_1 - a_1 b_0}{b_1 - a_1} + \frac{a_2 b_1}{b_1 - a_1} Y + \frac{a_3 b_1}{b_1 - a_1} P_O + \frac{a_4 b_1}{b_1 - a_1} A - \frac{a_1 b_2}{b_1 - a_1} T$$

$$- \frac{a_1 b_3}{b_1 - a_1} W + \frac{u_1 b_1 - a_1 u_2}{b_1 - a_1} \tag{5}$$

The system of relations (4) and (5) is known as the reduced form of the original structural model given by (1)–(3), and it provides us with a forecasting tool for price and quantity. So long as we have estimates of the structural coefficients a's and b's and values for the exogenous variables Y, P_O, A, T and W we are able to derive forecast values for the endogenous variables P and Q. The reduced-form coefficients, which are functions of the structural coefficients, measure the total effect, i.e., both direct and indirect, of a change in a predetermined variable on the endogenous variables, by taking into account the interdependency among the jointly determined endogenous variables. By contrast, structural coefficients measure only the direct effect of a change. Assuming that we are dealing with time series data, the reduced-form in our case can also be used to determine the time path of the response of an endogenous variable to an unsustained unit shock in one single period of an exogenous variable. This is so, because its coefficients, known as dynamic multipliers, describe the continuous effect of exogenous changes on the endogenous variables over the whole of the sample period. The first period's multipliers are known as impact multipliers, while the sum of all interim or dynamic multipliers gives a set of total multipliers of an economic system.

5.7 INPUT–OUTPUT ANALYSIS

The final forecasting method to be considered is the input–output analysis, developed by Leontief, which is an empirical approach to general equilibrium. Accordingly, the economy is divided into endogenous sectors or industries, producing outputs by using primary factors and their own outputs as inputs. In addition, there is an exogenous sector (which may consist of households, government and foreign trade) providing primary inputs (labour, entrepreneurship and so on) and consuming the output of the various endogenous industries, which is usually referred to as the final demand sector. The main feature of this analysis is the interrelationships between the various industries, which help explain how the change in the demand for an industry's output will bring about changes in the outputs of other industries. For example, the output of the steel industry is required as an input by the shipbuilding industry, the car industry, the construction industry and so on, in addition to the steel industry itself.

A number of assumptions considerably simplify the analysis. Consumer demands for goods and services are given exogenously, thus utility functions are ignored. The economy consists of various interacting industries (sectors), each of which produces a single good using only one process of production. The unit of production is the industry and the production function exhibits constant returns to scale and is characterised by fixed coefficients. The economy is assumed to be in long-run equilibrium and the costs of each industry, which include normal profits, are equal to its revenues. This means that the total output of an industry can be computed either by adding up the value of its inputs, including the primary factor, or by summing up the output that the industry delivers to itself (as an intra-industry input), to all other industries and to the final demand. The fixed production coefficients are found from the inter-industry flows table for some base year. To illustrate what is involved we assume that the economy consists of two industries agriculture and manufacture and for some base year the inter-industry flows are given as in Table 5.3.

Each industry's output can be measured either in physical units or in base year values, and it is measured across rows. Therefore, in the base year agriculture used 3000 euros worth of its own output as an input, it offered 5000 to manufacture and it delivered 2000 to final demand, giving a total of 10 000 units. Similarly, manufacture delivered 4000 euros worth of its output to agriculture, it kept for its own needs 6000 and shipped to final demand 10 000, a total of 20 000 units. On the other hand, reading down the columns we find that agriculture used as inputs 3000 units of its own output, 4000 of manufacture's output and 3000 of primary factor, while manufacture (column 2) used as inputs 5000 units of agriculture's output, 6000 units of its own output and 9000 units of primary factor. The fixed production coefficients are derived from the base year inter-industry flows table by dividing the elements of each column for each endogenous sector (industry) by the industry's total output. Therefore, Table 5.4 tabulates the input–output coefficients of our example as follows.

This information can now be utilised to show how input–output analysis can be used for forecasting purposes. Assume that we are given, from outside knowledge, that final demand for agriculture is expected to rise by 20%, or by 400 units. It follows then that agricultural output must rise by more than 400 units, since

Table 5.3 Inter-industry flows for base year

Industry	Agriculture	Manufacture	Final demands	Total output
Agriculture	3 000	5 000	2 000	10 000
Manufacture	4 000	6 000	10 000	20 000
Primary factor	3 000	9 000		

Table 5.4 Input–output coefficients for base year

Industry	Agriculture	Manufacture
Agriculture	0.3	0.25
Manufacture	0.4	0.3
Primary factor	0.3	0.45

the sector (agriculture) will require an extra $400 \times 0.3 = 120$ units as an additional input to meet the increased final demand of agriculture. However, since manufacture inputs are also required in the agriculture industry it follows that manufacture must also expand in order to help supply the additional 520 units required of agriculture. The increase in the output of manufacture is given by the additional agricultural output, i.e., 520 units multiplied by the relevant manufacture input coefficient contained in one unit of agricultural output, which is 0.4. Therefore, as a result of the projected increase by 20% in final demand for agriculture, the output of manufacturing must go up by $520 \times 0.4 = 208$ units.

The great advantage of this method is the explicit recognition of the inter-relationships between the various industries of the economy, which allow for the quantification of both direct and indirect effects on the outputs of particular industries when there are changes in the vector of final demands. However, there are also a number of shortcomings associated with the input–output analysis, which limit its usefulness for decision making within the firm. Such shortcomings have to do, in the first instance, with the forecast of the vector of final demands, which is given from outside the model, and whose accuracy or lack of it will be reflected in the input–output forecast values. Also, prices play a limited role in the analysis, since they only enter into the model in the form of the inter-industry flows (expressed in value terms) in the base year. But because of the lag between the base and the forecast year, prices will probably be different between the two time periods. Also, the lag between base and forecast years may tend to exaggerate the problems implied by the assumption of fixed coefficients. If the input–output tables are not updated regularly, and if there are considerable technological developments and/or changes in labour productivity, there will be considerable deviation between the actual values and the forecast ones, based on the fixed coefficients implied by the tables. Another drawback is that the input–output tables, constructed by most countries, may not be detailed enough for the forecasting purposes of individual firms. In such cases only firms operating in monopolistic or oligopolistic industries may find some use for such tables. In the US the 1977 input–output table provides a breakdown of the industrial sector into 537 different industries, which allows firms a greater scope of utilising it for their forecasting purposes, while in the UK economy the relevant 1984 input–output table involves 102 industries/products.

SUMMARY

In this chapter we have looked at some methods commonly used by management to help in forecasting sales. Such methods range from trend projection of any economic series (e.g., sales), to barometric techniques that make use of various economic and business indicators, to opinion polling and survey methods. All such methods rely on some knowledge of basic statistics. More sophisticated methods of forecasting make extensive use of econometrics and model building and we have sought to demonstrate how such methods work. We have also looked at input–output analysis, which can also be used to forecast sales. In two appendices to this chapter we provide the rudiments of multiple regression analysis and demonstrate the workings of such analysis through examples.

APPENDIX A: MULTIPLE REGRESSION ANALYSIS

5.A.1 Introduction

In discussing the econometric method of forecasting above we mentioned multiple regression analysis as the appropriate method of estimation of the parameter of the specified demand relation. In this appendix, we give a brief description of the method, its assumptions and the problem encountered when such assumptions break down.

5.A.2 Specification of the demand relation

Suppose that we are given that the demand for roses, D, is dependent on consumers' disposable income, Y, the price of roses, P, and the price of carnations, C. Therefore, we can write the function

$$D = f(Y, P, C) \tag{1}$$

Relation (1) is the specified demand relation, where variable D is called the dependent variable, while the ones appearing on the right-hand side are called the explanatory or independent variables. In the area of economic prognostication we assume that relations like (1) exist, and endeavour to establish whether they are stable, so that given information on the explanatory variables we can predict the value of the dependent variable, with reasonable accuracy. Typically, economic theory and the nature of the product will guide us in choosing the appropriate explanatory variables. Sometimes, particularly when we are dealing with time series the dependent variable, say Y, and one of the explanatory variables, say X, may be moving together in the same direction, reflecting an upward or downward trend. To avoid any spurious associations (or correlations) we may introduce a trend variable, T, into the body of the explanatory variables, and let it take values $1, 2, 3, \ldots, n$, which will have the effect that the coefficient of the explanatory variable X will now reflect the true association between Y and X, net of any linear trend. If we are dealing with prices, incomes and similar variables, which may be affected by inflation, we must deflate such variables by dividing nominal income, or nominal prices by the relevant consumer price indices, so as to run the regression in real terms. We may also express the variables in levels, logarithms, first differences and so on to suit our purposes, provided our results are interpretable in terms of economic theory.

5.A.2.1 Functional forms

The next stage is to decide on the appropriate functional form for (1). While a number of such forms may be available, in practice the linear and the logarithmic forms usually suggest themselves. The reasons have to do with the ease of calculations and the straightforward interpretation of the estimated regression parameters. For the above example, we may write (1) as follows:

$$D = a + bY + cP + dC + u \qquad (2)$$

for the linear functional form and

$$D = aY^b P^c C^d e^v \qquad (3)$$

for the multiplicative or logarithmic formulation, where u and v are error terms assumed to be normally and independently distributed with zero means and constant variances and e is the basis of natural logarithms. The purpose of the error terms is to make our relationships stochastic rather than deterministic, since economic relationships are not exact but, for a number of reasons, are subject to variation.

Relationship (2) states that quantity demanded, D, is given by some constant, a, plus the products bY, cP and dC. It could be said that the coefficient a shows what the quantity demanded of roses would be if Y, P and C were all set equal to zero. However, a more appropriate explanation of the constant term a is that it reflects the influences on the dependent variable D of all other factors, that is other than Y, P and C, which are currently excluded from the model. On the other hand, the coefficients b, c and d are the rates of change of D with respect to Y, P and C. This means that for every unit of change in consumers' disposable income Y, quantity demanded changes by b, for every unit change in the price of roses P, the quantity of roses demanded changes by c and for every unit change in C, the price of carnations, quantity demanded of roses changes by d. Whether D goes up or down as Y, P and C increase or decrease depends on the signs of the regression parameters b, c and d. A priori economic reasoning will enable us to form particular expectations as regards the signs of the coefficients and then test whether such expectations are verified by the evidence. Since the change in the dependent variable remains the same for a unit change in the independent variables, relation (2) is also called the constant change model.

On the other hand, the multiplicative formulation (3) can be written as the log-linear function given below, i.e.,

$$\ln D = \ln a + b \ln Y + c \ln P + d \ln C + v \qquad (4)$$

in other words it is linear in the logarithms and therefore linear regression can be performed on the logarithms of the original variables and the regression parameters

b, c and d can thus be estimated. Relation (3) is known as the constant elasticity model or the constant growth model, because the parameters b, c and d are the elasticities of quantity demanded D with respect to Y, P and C. To illustrate this point we differentiate (3) partially with respect, say, to Y (by ignoring the error term) to get:

$$\delta D / \delta Y = b a Y^{b-1} P^c P^d \tag{5}$$

The income elasticity of demand is given by $\eta_Y = (dD/dY)\,(Y/D)$ and by substituting (3) and (5) into it we derive:

$$\eta_Y = \frac{b a Y^{b-1} P^c C^d}{1} \times \frac{Y}{a Y^b P^c C^d} = \frac{b a Y^b P^c C^d}{a Y^b P^c C^d} = b$$

The same result can be shown for the own price elasticity c and the cross price elasticity d and shows that the exponent of the multiplicative relation (3) are indeed the elasticities. This property makes the log-linear function a very useful formulation in statistical estimation, although such formulations should be chosen to reflect, as far as possible, the underlying structure of the relationship being investigated. If economic theory cannot help or is equivocal in this respect, then statistical criteria can be used to differentiate and choose between alternative formulations.

5.A.3　Multiple regression – OLSs

Having shown that the multiplicative formulation can be reduced to a linear function in the logarithms of the original variables, we return to equation (2) to illustrate the application of regression analysis for the estimation of the parameters. Here we are concerned with linear regression models, i.e., models which are linear in the parameters a, b, c and d; they may or may not be linear in the variables, as in the case of equation (3). In other instances, variables may be expressed as $1/X, X_1/X_2, X^2, X^3$, and so on to reflect better the underlying economic theory, as for example in the case of the total cost function, which may be written as:

$$TC = a + bQ + cQ^2 + dQ^3 + u \tag{6}$$

Here equation (6) is linear in the parameters a, b, c and d, since such parameters appear with a power of one and are not the products or quotients of other parameters, such as bc or b/d; but non-linear in the variables, since Q appears also with a power, or index of 2 in Q^2 and 3 in Q^3. However, by defining variables $Z = Q^2$ and $W = Q^3$ we can transform (6) into: $C = a + bQ + cZ + dW + u$ and proceed by using the estimation method known as OLSs. In essence, this method consists in finding estimates of the unknown population coefficients (a, b, c and d), which minimise the sum of the squared residuals of the sample observations (Σe^2) from the line (or plane) of best fit. This is accomplished as follows: Since equation (2) expresses the unknown population relationship, we can estimate it on the basis of sample information on D, Y, P and C, by letting $\hat{a}, \hat{b}, \hat{c}$ and $\hat{d}$ be the estimates of the unknown coefficients a, b, c and d, and rewriting it as:

$$\hat{D} = \hat{a} + \hat{b}Y + \hat{c}P + \hat{d}C + e_i \tag{7}$$

or

$$e_i = D - \hat{D} \tag{7a}$$

where, e_i, are the residuals of the regression, which are taken to be the estimates of the unknown error terms, u_i, in (2). By squaring, summing up and rearranging equation (7) we get:

$$\Sigma e^2 = \Sigma(D - \hat{a} - \hat{b}Y - \hat{c}P - \hat{d}C)^2 \tag{8}$$

The sum of the squared residuals Σe^2 is minimised by differentiating equation (9) partially, with respect to $\hat{a}, \hat{b}, \hat{c}$ and $\hat{d}$ and setting the partial derivatives equal to zero. By simplifying and rearranging we obtain the system of the following normal equations:

$$\Sigma D = n\hat{a} + \hat{b}\Sigma Y + \hat{c}\Sigma P + \hat{d}\Sigma C \tag{9}$$

$$\Sigma YD = \hat{a}\Sigma Y + \hat{b}\Sigma Y^2 + \hat{c}\Sigma YP + \hat{d}\Sigma YC \tag{10}$$

$$\Sigma PD = \hat{a}\Sigma P + \hat{b}\Sigma PY + \hat{c}\Sigma P^2 + \hat{d}\Sigma PC \tag{11}$$

$$\Sigma CD = \hat{a}\Sigma C + \hat{b}\Sigma CY + \hat{c}\Sigma CP + \hat{d}\Sigma C^2 \tag{12}$$

which can be solved for $\hat{a}, \hat{b}, \hat{c}$ and $\hat{d}$, by means of the Cramer's rule. In practice, however, powerful computing regression packages are available, which can make light of the computational chores, and which not only provide the estimates of the parameters but also a whole array of diagnostic tests, to be discussed later in the examples. Such diagnostic tests help with the evaluation of the results and most packages will include the following.

The coefficient of correlation R and the coefficient of determination $\bar{R}^2$, adjusted for degrees of freedom. The latter shows the proportion of the variance in the dependent variable that is explained by the model, i.e., by the linear influence of the explanatory variables. The 't' ratios, which indicate whether the estimated coefficients are significantly different than zero or not, and thus provide evidence on the explanatory power of the variables to which such coefficients are attached. The D–W statistic, which shows whether there exists first-order serial correlation in the residuals. The extent to which there is multicollinearity present among the explanatory variables, evidenced by the simple correlation coefficients and so on. Also, another important consideration is whether the signs of the estimated coefficients agree with prior expectations, formed on the basis of economic theory.

The estimated parameters $\hat{a}, \hat{b}, \hat{c}$ and $\hat{d}$ are known as the OLS estimates and have some very useful and desirable properties, such as linearity, unbiasedness and least variance, provided some important assumptions are satisfied. Linearity is useful because of the ease of computations. On their own, neither unbiasedness nor least variance are very helpful, since an unbiased estimate may have a very large spread (variance) and an estimate with a very low or even zero variance may have an enormous bias. However, the combination of unbiasedness and least variance makes the estimates efficient and provides them with the smallest mean-square error, which is very important in the tests of significance and the construction of confidence intervals for the OLS estimates, and correspondingly the degree of reliance we can place upon them. Collectively, these are known as the BLUE properties, signifying that the OLS estimates are Best, Linear, Unbiased Estimates. This means that among the class of linear unbiased estimates, the OLS have the smallest variance, and, consequently, they are the most efficient ones.

5.A.3.1 Assumptions of OLS

However, for the OLS estimates to possess such desirable properties it is necessary that the following crucial assumptions are satisfied. In the general linear model:

$$Y_i = b_0 + b_1X_{1i} + b_2X_{2i} + \cdots + b_kX_{ki} + u_i$$

where i stands for the number of observations, it is assumed that the error term u_i is a normally and independently distributed random real variable with zero mean, $[E(u_i) = 0]$, and constant variance, $[E(u_i)^2 = \sigma^2]$. These assumptions are abbreviated as: $u \sim \text{NI}(0, \sigma^2)$. The assumption of the constant variance of the error term is also referred to as the homoscedastic variance, from the Greek, meaning same variance.

The value taken by the error term, u, in any one observation, i, is independent of the value it takes in any other observation, j, so that:

$$E(u_iu_j) = 0 \quad \text{for } i \neq j$$

This is the assumption of non-autocorrelation or serial independence of u's.

Further, the error term, u, is independent of any of the explanatory variables Xs such that:

$$E(u_iX_{1i}) = E(u_iX_{2i}) = \cdots = E(u_iX_{ki}) = 0$$

which is satisfied if the values of the various Xs are fixed numbers in repeated sampling.

The explanatory variables must not be perfectly linearly correlated, i.e., there must be absence of perfect multicollinearity between the explanatory variables.

In addition, the independent or explanatory variables must be measured without errors.

If we are dealing with macro-variables, such variables must be correctly aggregated.

The relationship under consideration must be identified, i.e., it must have a unique mathematical (statistical) form, in order to estimate it.

Finally, the relationship must be correctly specified, i.e., it must include all important variables and have the correct formulation.

5.A.3.2 Consequences of violations of the OLS assumptions

The violation of one or more of the above assumptions has a number of consequences on the properties of the OLS estimates. Generally, if such violations occur the OLS are no longer BLUE (best, linear, unbiased) and we need to have some means of detecting when such cases arise, before attempting remedial action, which in most instances may require the re-specification of the model and its re-estimation.

Normality

The OLS are still BLUE but the usual '*t*' and *F* tests of significance are only valid asymptotically, i.e., in large samples but not in small samples. Usually, in practice the researcher has available limited information, in the form of small samples, and the assumption of normality is crucial for the purposes of hypothesis testing and forecasting.

Randomness

The inclusion of the error term, *u*, in the model is justified by the need to account for the effect of a number of errors, caused by omitted variables, mathematical formulation of the model, errors of measurement in the dependent variable and so on, each of which is unimportant and unpredictable. However, if the errors exhibit a systematic pattern, because of, say, the wrong formulation of the model, or the exclusion of an important explanatory variable this affects the efficiency of the OLS estimates and one should try to re-specify the relationship, by including the missing variable(s) before re-estimation.

Zero mean $[E(u) = 0]$

This assumption is required to enable the estimation of a stochastic relationship. Its violation causes the constant term (the intercept) of the relationship to be biased, but if there are also different expected values for the error term in each observation, the OLS estimates of the slope coefficients may be biased as well as inconsistent, i.e., not only are they biased in small samples but also in large ones.

Constant variance, $\mathrm{var}(u) = E(u)^2 = \sigma^2 = constant$

When the assumption of homoscedastic error terms is violated, we have heteroscedastic disturbances, which means that the spread of the error term varies from one observation to another. In many economic applications the assumption of the constant variance of the random disturbances may not be satisfied for a number of reasons, such as for example error-learning behaviour, where people learn from experience and so the variance of their errors of behaviour becomes smaller; data collection techniques may be improving, thus causing a smaller variance of the errors of measurement over time; in cross-section studies the savings behaviour of low-income households will be affected differently than for high-income households, since the latter have more discretionary income and so they can have a more variable pattern of consumption expenditure (and thus savings), than low-income ones, whose savings pattern is more regular. The violation of the homoscedasticity assumption means that the OLS estimates, though still retaining the linearity and unbiasedness properties, are no longer best, i.e., they lose the least variance property, which affects tests of significance. There are a number of tests for the detection of heteroscedasticity, including the graphical representation of the squared residuals of the regression, to establish whether they exhibit a systematic pattern.

If such a pattern were to be found, then the remedy will typically involve a transformation of the original model. If the heteroscedastic variances are known, the remedy is to divide the original model by the standard deviation, σ_t, which has the effect of turning the variance of the transformed disturbances into a homoscedastic one, and then applying the method of OLS to the transformed data. This is known as the method of weighted least squares (WLS), which is a form of generalised least squares (GLS). The GLS estimates have lower variances and standard errors, as compared to the OLS estimates, and thus they are more efficient. If the heteroscedastic disturbances are not known, which is usually the case in practice, then some assumptions about the standard deviation of the error term, (σ_i), have to be made and transform the original model in a manner that the transformed model satisfies the assumption of homoscedasticity, so that OLS can be applied to the transformed model. For example, if as a result of the graphical representation of the squared residuals or on the basis of more formal tests, we think that the variance of the error term is proportional to the square of some explanatory variable X_i, i.e., $E(u_i)^2 = \sigma^2 X_i^2$, we can transform the original model by dividing through by X_i. This will turn the transformed error term into u_i/X_i and substituting from the above relationship will make the variance of the transformed error term homoscedastic, so that the application of OLS to the transformed model is justified. If heteroscadasticity were present, the standard errors of the estimated coefficients of the transformed model should be substantially lower than those of the original model and the transformation would have significantly reduced its effects. On the other hand, if there is, virtually, no difference in the standard errors of the original and the transformed models then heteroscedasticity were not present, and we could apply OLS to the original model. Therefore, as a general rule, it always pays to estimate models in their original form of levels and also in the ratio form. If, instead, it is believed that the variance of the error term is proportional to some explanatory variable X_i, the appropriate transformation is to divide the original model through by the square root of the variable X_i, before applying OLS to the transformed model. Also, another transformation is to run the regression in the natural logarithms rather than in the levels of the variables, thus reducing the difference between two values from a tenfold to a twofold one. For example, the number 100 is 10 times as large as 10, but $\ln 100 = 4.605$ is about twice as large as $\ln 10 = 2.3026$, and the differences become smaller for larger values.

5.A.3.3   Serial independence of u's – $E(u_iu_j) = 0$ for $i = / = j$

If the assumption of serial independence or non-autocorrelation of the u's is violated, then the OLS estimates, though still linear and unbiased, no longer have the correct values in any single sample. Also, the variance of the error term is likely to be seriously underestimated, leading to the underestimation of the variances of the OLS estimates, and so the usual 't' and F tests are no longer valid, and if applied may lead to wrong conclusions. If one of the explanatory variables (regressors) is a lagged value of the dependent variable, then in addition the estimates are biased. Finally, the predictions, based on OLS estimates will be inefficient, in the sense of having a larger variance, as compared with predictions derived from alternative methods. In practice, the assumption of serial independence of the error terms may be violated for a number of reasons, such as specification biases, resulting from omitted variables or using the incorrect functional form; omission of lagged values of independent variables, resulting in a systematic pattern on the error term of the influence of the lagged values; smoothing or manipulation of data, including interpolation or extrapolation, resulting in a systematic pattern which may not be present in the original 'raw' data.

Autocorrelation in the error term may be detected either by graphical methods – by plotting the error term against time or against its previous value; or by more formal diagnostic tests, such as the D–W statistic or its extensions, which are computed routinely by most computer regression packages. However, it should be noted that the D–W statistic is only intended to test for first-order autoregressive errors, and is not a reliable test for higher order autoregressive structures. Also, if one of the regressors is a lagged value of the dependent variable, the D–W statistic is biased towards the value of 2, which is the value we expect in the absence of autocorrelation and, therefore, misleads us into wrongly accepting that there is no autocorrelation in the residuals. For these reasons it may be better to employ the chi-squared test, (χ^2), found in a number of regression computer packages, which may be applied to an autoregressive structure of any order and allows one to choose between the alternative orders. If autocorrelation is detected, then the remedy, as in the case of heteroscedasticity above, lies in finding an appropriate transformation of the original model, which will result in a transformed model satisfying the assumption of serial independence of the error term, so that OLS can be applied to the transformed model. Again, this method is known as Generalised Least Squares (GLS) and the GLS estimates have narrower confidence intervals than OLS estimates, consequently, they are more efficient.

To illustrate the method of GLS, we require some assumption regarding the mechanism generating the error terms. The simplest one is a first-order autoregressive scheme, such as:

$$u_t = \rho u_{t-1} + e_t \quad \text{where } -1 < \rho < 1 \tag{1}$$

where ρ (rho) is the coefficient of autocorrelation and e_t is the stochastic disturbance, satisfying the OLS assumptions of zero mean, constant variance and zero covariance. Assuming that we have the model

$$Y_t = a + bX_t + u_t \tag{2}$$

in which u_t follows a first-order autoregressive scheme, as given above, then the transformation proceeds as follows: We lag expression (2) by one period, multiply it by ρ and subtract it from (2). In the resulting model

$$Y_t = a(1 - \rho) + bX_t - \rho bX_{t-1} + \rho Y_{t-1} + e_t \tag{3}$$

the error term e_t satisfies the standard OLS assumptions and thus by applying OLS to the transformed model (3) we can obtain the GLS estimates of a and b. In practice, since the value of ρ is likely to be unknown, we can experiment by using different values of ρ in the interval $-1 < \rho < 1$ and accepting that value that minimises the sum of the squared residuals.

5.A.3.4 Multicollinearity

In the general linear model we require that none of the explanatory variables is perfectly linearly correlated with any other explanatory variable (or any linear combination of other explanatory variables), so that each variable makes an 'independent' contribution in explaining the dependent variable. When this assumption is violated, i.e., when $X_2 = bX_3$ or $X_2 = a + bX_3$ or $X_2 = bX_3 + cX_4$, then we have the case of perfect multicollinearity. On the other hand, when all explanatory variables are uncorrelated with each other we have absence of multicollinearity, which is what is required by one of the basic assumptions of the general linear model. However, this is likely to be violated in practice, because most economic variables tend to vary at the same time. For example, in demand studies income and prices often rise together over time. In practice, we are likely to get cases in between these two extremes, which can be described by various degrees of inter-correlation between the explanatory variables. This means that the problem of multicollinearity is one of degree than of kind and it is a characteristic of the sample data rather than of the population. In the case of perfect multicollinearity, the OLS estimation procedure breaks down and so the estimates of the regression coefficients become indeterminate and their variances (and thus their standard errors) infinitely large. When two or more explanatory variables are not perfectly collinear, but are inter-correlated to some degree we can proceed with the estimation procedure but the estimated coefficients, though still unbiased, become imprecise and unstable, which renders the property of unbiasedness of little use. In cases of 'high' multicollinearity we get OLS estimates which have large variances and covariances, leading to large standard errors and, thus, to insignificant 't' ratios and wider confidence intervals. In such cases, the OLS estimates and their standard errors become very sensitive to small changes in the data. Of great importance here is when the degree of multicollinearity becomes 'high'. Since some multicollinearity is always present, the question arises at what point does it become 'harmful'? Unfortunately, there is no satisfactory answer to this question. One could say that multicollinearity is a serious problem when R^2 is high, but the 't' ratios for the regression coefficients are all 'insignificant'. But there may also be multicollinearity problems even with 'highly significant' 't' ratios. A simple diagnostic test of the extent of multicollinearity is provided by the correlation matrix, showing the correlation coefficients for pairs of 'independent' variables. A large correlation coefficient indicates that the two variables concerned are likely to cause problems and so provides a signal as to where efforts could be directed. However, low correlation coefficients may be deceptive and a more satisfactory approach could be the principal component analysis.

The remedies that have been suggested for the problem of multicollinearity are fraught with a number of difficulties and may be introducing additional complications. For example, in his 'general to specific' approach, Hendry suggests that the researcher is free to transform his data by differencing in a way that the data matrix becomes as orthogonal as possible, thus resolving the problem, provided that the results are interpretable in terms of economic theory. All that can be said is that the presence of high multicollinearity, more often than not, contributes to the unreliability of the estimated coefficients, in the form of higher variances and wider confidence intervals, but has no relevance for the results drawn from this unreliability. In other words, we cannot be sure that if multicollinearity were lower the estimated regression coefficients would be significant. Nevertheless, it has been suggested that if we are interested in forecasting the value of the dependent variable, rather than the estimation of the individual regression coefficients, we may disregard the problem of multicollinearity, provided we know that its pattern will continue during the period of prediction. We may get good predictions of the dependent variable even though we cannot disentangle the separate effects of the explanatory variables, so long as the latter continue to behave in the future in the same way as during the sample period. However, if this pattern were to change, then accurate forecasting requires also the knowledge of robust and accurate regression coefficients, which means knowledge of the separate effects of the explanatory variables on the dependent variable.

5.A.3.5 *Errors in variables*

The classical linear model assumes that all variables are measured without errors. However, if this assumption is violated we get the following results: If only the dependent variable contains measurement errors, whilst all other assumptions are satisfied, we obtain OLS estimates which are still unbiased but they have larger variances and standard errors leading to wider confidence intervals. However, if the explanatory variable is measured with errors, then the covariance between the explanatory variable and the error term is no longer zero, $[\text{Cov}(Xu) = 0]$ and this means that the OLS estimates are not only biased but also inconsistent, meaning that they remain biased even if the sample size increases to infinity.

5.A.3.6 *Model mis-specification*

The earlier case of measurement errors is a case of model mis-specification. Other cases of such mis-specification include the exclusion of relevant variable(s), the inclusion of irrelevant variable(s) and the use of the wrong functional form. In general, the consequences of including irrelevant variable(s) are less serious, in the sense that we still obtain unbiased and consistent estimates but their variances and standard errors are generally larger than those of the true model, thus rendering such estimates inefficient. However, if we omit a relevant variable, which may be correlated with other included variable(s), the estimated OLS regression coefficients are not only biased but also inconsistent, the variance of the error term is incorrectly estimated and the variances and standard errors of the coefficients are biased, thus the 't' tests and confidence intervals are likely to provide us with misleading conclusions about the significance of the estimated coefficients. Similarly, the use of the wrong functional form will also result in biased and inconsistent estimates. For example, if we wish to estimate a total cost function we may hypothesise that total cost is a function of output and experiment with a linear, a quadratic or a cubic functional form. Estimating the three different forms and plotting the residuals of each against output will reveal which form exhibits a pronounced pattern, which is an indication of a mis-fitted model. The D–W statistic may provide us with sufficient warning of the problem, and low values of the D–W statistic do not denote the existence of positive correlation in the residuals (first-order serial correlation), but model mis-specification. The solution, therefore, is not to use the GLS method, discussed earlier, but re-specify and re-estimate the model.

5.A.3.7 *Simultaneity*

One of the crucial assumptions of the general linear model is that the error term, u, should be independent of the various explanatory variables, Xs, so that

$Cov(Xu) = 0$. This assumption is also at the heart of the single-equation model we have been discussing, since it implies a unidirectional causation running from the Xs to the Y. In other words, the explanatory variables Xs are the cause of the variation in the dependent variable Y, which is the effect. However, many economic relationships are characterised by interdependence and so we find that one or more regressors are correlated with the error term. This occurs because the regressors in question are not truly predetermined, or exogenous or independent but are themselves determined within a more general model. To illustrate how such variables are jointly determined we consider the demand–supply model:

Demand $Q_D = a + bP + u$

Supply $Q_S = c + dP + v$

Equilibrium condition $Q_D = Q_S$

where Q_D = quantity demanded, Q_S = quantity supplied, P = price, u and v are errors and a, b, c and d are parameters, such that $b < 0$ and $d > 0$, so that we derive the equilibrium position in Figure 5.A.1(a).

If now the error term u changes (because it reflects the influence of omitted variables such as income, prices of other goods, tastes and so on) and shifts the demand curve upwards, a new equilibrium position is obtained, as in Figure 5.A.1b, which changes both P and Q. This shows that P and Q are jointly determined variables. The price–quantity relationship is one of interdependence (i.e., price affects quantity but also quantity affects price) and must be modelled accordingly; requiring two equations, where each variable appears as a dependent or endogenous, though each variable may appear in the other equation of the model as an explanatory variable. The consequences of applying OLS to estimate an equation which really belongs to a simultaneous-equations model is to derive biased and inconsistent estimates, i.e., estimates whose bias does not disappear by increasing the sample size. This is referred to as simultaneous-equations bias and means that we require alternative estimation methods.

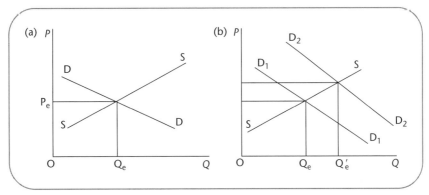

Figure 5.A.1 The identification problem. Stable demand and supply on the left. Stable supply, and shifting demand on the right

5.A.3.8 The Identification problem

However, before proceeding we must address the problem of identification, for without doing that we cannot proceed with estimation. To put it simply, the problem of identification revolves around the question on whether we are able to identify, or distinguish the various equations in a simultaneous-equations system, which is only possible if each equation has a unique mathematical or statistical form. For example, to continue with the earlier demand–supply system, if we had time series data on only P and Q how do we know that we are estimating the demand function, the supply function or any other function? In this case both the demand and supply equations have the same statistical form, i.e., they both contain P and Q and we cannot differentiate between the two, we cannot identify either equation and so we cannot proceed with estimation. The problem here is that we have omitted the shift factors, i.e., the other variables that cause the demand and supply to shift. Such factors include, on the demand side, the income of the consumers, wealth, prices of other goods, tastes and so on, while on the supply side, we may have weather, productivity, technological aspects, import restrictions, and so on. If we had knowledge of such factors and we were able to include them in our equations, then some variables will appear in one equation only and not in the other and so we would be able to identify both equations. To proceed with identification, we can examine either the structural form of the model or the reduced form of the model. More formally, there are two criteria for identification, the order and the rank. In terms of the structural form of the model, the order criterion states that for an equation to be identified, the total number of variables excluded from that equation but included in the other equations of the model must be at least as great as the number of equations of the system less one. This however, is only a necessary condition for identification. The rank criterion is a sufficient condition, and it states that in a system containing G equations any equation is identified, if and only if, it is possible to construct a non-zero determinant of order (G-1) from the coefficients of the variables excluded from that particular equation but included in the other equations of the model. The result of this exercise may be that particular equations will be found to be underidentified, in which case we cannot estimate them; others will be found to be exactly identified and, finally, others will be overidentified. For equations which are exactly identified we can apply consistent estimation methods such as indirect least squares, or two stages least squares, while for over identified equations we can use two stages least squares. As an illustration the earlier demand–supply model can be reformulated as follows:

$$Q_D = a + bP + cY + dP_O + u \tag{1}$$

$$Q_S = e + fP + gW + v \tag{2}$$

$$Q_D = Q_S \tag{3}$$

where P = price, Q_D = quantity demanded, Q_S = quantity supplied, Y = income, P_O = price of other goods, W = weather and a, b, c, d, e, f and g are parameters. The model is complete in the sense that it contains three equations and three endogenous variables, to be jointly determined by the system, i.e., P, Q_D and Q_S. It also contains three predetermined variables Y, P_O and W, which are given exogenously, that is, from outside the system. The total number of variables in the model both endogenous and predetermined is six. Applying the order criterion to the first equation we find that the number of excluded variables from equation (1) but included in the other equations is $6 - 4 = 2$. Since we have three equations it follows that $G - 1 = 3 - 1 = 2$, which means that the first equation satisfies the order criterion. Similarly, for equation (2) the number of variables excluded from that equation but included in the other equations is given by $6 - 3 = 3$, which is greater than $G - 1 = 3 - 1 = 2$, and so it follows that equation (2) also passes the order criterion. Assuming that both equations satisfy the rank criterion we can say that since in equation (1) the order criterion is satisfied as equality, equation (1) is exactly identified and we can use either indirect least squares or two stage least squares to estimate it. In equation (2) however, the order criterion is satisfied as inequality, which means that equation (2) is overidentified, and so the appropriate estimation method to use is two stages least squares.

APPENDIX B: MULTIPLE REGRESSION EXAMPLES

5.B.1 Introduction

In this section, we propose to give two applications of multiple regression analysis in order to illustrate its use in forecasting and also introduce, in passing, the use of dummy variables to account for seasonal effects. It is hoped that these examples, taken in conjunction with the earlier analysis, will help clarify any remaining doubts and problems. In the first case, following on from the discussion in the Appendix, we try to forecast weekly sales of roses for a florist; while in the second we want to establish a predicting equation of the demand for new cars for the Association of Automobile Manufacturers of Vretannia (AAM), a country very similar to Britain.

5.B.2 Forecasting sales of roses

In this example a florist wants to find a way of forecasting his weekly sales of roses and from experience he has found that such sales are related to the price he charges for roses, the price he charges for carnations and disposable income. Therefore, over a period of 20 consecutive weeks, he has recorded information regarding the sales of roses per week (in bunches) S, the price of roses (in euros per bunch) P, the price of carnations (in euros per bunch) P_C, and has also managed to find information on weekly household disposable income (in euros) Y. He has hypothesised that sales of roses is a linear function of the price of roses, the weekly household disposable income and the price of carnations, and he derives the following relation;

$$S = a + bP + cY + dP_C + u$$

OLS estimation, yields the following predicting equation and summary statistics:

$$\hat{S} = \underset{(0.8)}{100} - \underset{(-0.497)}{100P} + \underset{(6.93)}{0.5Y} + \underset{(1.02)}{100P_C}$$

$$\bar{R}^2 = 0.80847 \quad F_{(3,16)} = 27.733 \quad \text{D–W} = 1.40 \quad \text{SEE} = 13.6931$$

where figures in parentheses denote t-ratios (i.e., the ratios of the estimated coefficients divided by their standard errors).

5.B.3 Evaluation of results

The evaluation of the results requires consideration of a number of diagnostic statistics derived from the application of the regression package. To begin with, the value of the $\bar{R}^2$ denotes the coefficient of multiple determination, corrected for degrees of freedom, and illustrates that 80.85% of the variation in the dependent variable, i.e., sales of roses per week, is accounted for by the linear influence of the model. It gives, in other words, an overall impression of the ability of the variables included in the model to explain the variation in the dependent variable, and, *ceteris paribus*, when choosing among alternative models the one with the higher value of the coefficient of multiple determination (or alternatively, the lower standard error of estimate (SEE)) is preferred. Further confirmation of the significance of the model as a whole is provided by the estimated value of the F statistic, which is greater than the tabulated value $F_{(3,16)} = 5.29$, i.e., at (3, 16) degrees of freedom at the 1% significance level. Since the estimated value for the F statistic 27.73 is greater than the tabulated value of 5.29, we can conclude that the regression as a whole provides a significant explanation of the variation in the sales of roses.

The signs of the estimated parameters agree with a priori expectations drawn from economic theory, since the own price coefficient (P) is negative, and the income (Y) and price of substitute (P_C) coefficients are positive. The interpretation of the estimated parameters is as follows: The intercept term is not as crucial as the slope parameters, and it may be thought of showing the combined effect of all other factors which tend to influence sales of roses but which are currently omitted from the estimated equation. The coefficients of P, Y and P_C are the rates of change of S (sales) with respect to P, Y and P_C and are referred to as partial regression coefficients. For every change in the price of roses by €1, *ceteris paribus*, there is a change in sales of roses in the opposite direction by 100 bunches. Similarly, for every change in the price of carnations by €1, *ceteris paribus*, there is a change in sales in the same direction by 100 bunches, and for every change in weekly household disposable income by €1, *ceteris paribus*, there is a change in sales in the same direction by 0.5 bunch.

We can now test for the presence or absence of autocorrelation or serial correlation in the residuals by means of the D–W statistic. This statistic tests only for first-order autocorrelated disturbances and has also some other limitations, but for most purposes it is adequate in signalling whether or not autocorrelation is present in the residuals. There are upper (U) and lower (L) tabulated values for the number of explanatory variables and number of observations, which help us decide on the presence or absence of autocorrelation as follows, given the computed value d.

If $0 < d < d_L$ there is positive autocorrelation in the residuals

If $d_L < d < d_U$ the test is inconclusive

If $4 - d_L < d < 4$ there is negative autocorrelation in the residuals

If $4 - d_U < d < 4 - d_L$ the test is inconclusive

If $d_U < d < 4 - d_U$ there is no autocorrelation positive or negative

In our case, the tabulated values of the D–W statistic at the 5% level of significance for three explanatory variables and 20 observations are $d_L = 0.998$ and $d_U = 1.679$. Since the estimated value of $d = 1.4$ falls between the lower and upper limits, the test is inconclusive. However at the 1% level of significance, the tabulated values are $d_L = 0.773$ and $d_U = 1.411$, which means that we are very close to accepting that there may not be serious consequences to our estimates from first-order positive autocorrelation in the residuals.

Turning to discuss the significance of the estimated parameters, we note firstly from the table of the 't' Student's Distribution that the critical value of 't' for $v = n - k = 20 - 4 = 16$ degrees of freedom at the 5% level of significance is $t = 2.12$, while at the 1% level of significance we have $t = 2.921$. Inspection of our results reveals that only the income coefficient has a t-ratio (6.93) exceeding either of the tabulated values, and we conclude that it is significantly different than zero, which in other words means that income exerts a powerful influence in explaining sales. All other estimated coefficients have t-ratios well below the value of 2.12 and, thus, we are forced to accept the null hypothesis, i.e., that the two price coefficients and the constant term are not significantly different than zero. Ignoring the constant term, this implies that the price of roses and the price of carnations play no role in explaining the variation in the sales of roses. This may be a surprising result, requiring further investigation. However, a note of caution is needed first. In the face of insignificant regression coefficients, investigators are tempted to drop the relevant variables, to which such coefficients are attached, on the ground that they have poor explanatory power of the dependent variable. However, this may very well lead to model mis-specification and worsening of the situation. It may be that the underlying relation between the variables has not been picked up by the particular data set, or there may be other forces at work, which have masked such relation. In our case, the explanation may be provided by the presence of multicollinearity among the independent variables. Inspection of the table of simple correlation coefficients, between the explanatory variables, reveals

Table 5.B.1 Simple correlation coefficients for linear model

	Price of roses	Income	Price of carnations
Price of roses	1.000	0.000	0.996
Income	0.000	1.000	0.000
Price of carnations	0.996	0.000	1.000

that while income is uncorrelated with the two price variables (and it is thus an orthogonal variable), the two price variables are very strongly correlated, as evidenced by the value of $r = 0.996$. This indicates a high degree of multicollinearity among the two price variables, which has the effect of increasing the variances of the estimated price parameters and, thus, their standard errors, which correspondingly reduces their 't'-ratios, leading to the insignificance of the two price variables. As it was pointed out above, it would be wrong to drop one of the price variables in an effort to resolve the multicollinearity problem, if we believe, on economic grounds, that it should be included in the equation. One would be leaving the embrace of the Scylla of multicollinearity for the clutches of the Charybdis of mis-specification. The task is clearly one of obtaining additional and/or better data. Nevertheless, if we believe that the multicollinearity pattern between the two price variables were to continue in future, we could still use the estimating equation to derive a forecast of sales, since we are interested in the overall predictive ability of the model, evidenced by the coefficient of multiple determination, and not in the separate influences of the individual parameters. Therefore, if we were to hypothesise that the price of roses for the following week was set at €2.30p, the price of carnations was €3.10p and weekly household disposable income was €820, then the equation will forecast sales as follows:

$$\hat{S} = 100 - 100 \times 2.30 + 0.5 \times 820 + 100 \times 3.10$$
$$= 100 - 230 + 410 + 310 = 590$$

i.e., 590 bunches of roses. Having found this value, we can also construct a confidence interval for this forecast, by using the value of the SEE = 13.6931. At the 5% level of significance we have that our forecast value of 590 bunches will lie in the interval:

$$590 - 2.12 \times 13.6931 < \hat{S} = 590 < 590 + 2.12 \times 13.6931$$

or approximately $561 < 590 < 619$

This shows that we have a 95% probability that sales of roses for next week will lie in the interval of 561–619 bunches, with a best estimate of 590.

We can now find out whether sales of roses is elastic or inelastic with respect to the three explanatory variables used. Assuming that we wish to estimate the various elasticities at the means of sales, price of roses, income and price of carnations we have:

$$\bar{S} = 600 \quad \bar{P} = 2.0 \quad \bar{Y} = 600 \quad \bar{P}_C = 3.0$$

and therefore the price elasticity of demand is given by:

$$\eta = (-1)(dS/dP)(P/S) = (-1)(-100)(2/600) = (200/600) = 1/3$$

the income elasticity of demand is:

$$\eta_Y = (dS/dY)(Y/S) = 0.5(800/600) = 400/600 = 2/3$$

and the cross price elasticity of demand is found as:

$$\eta_{RC} = (dS/dP_C)(P_C/S) = 100(3/600) = 300/600 = 1/2$$

i.e., sales of roses is inelastic with respect to all three variables, taken at their means.

5.B.4 The log-linear formulation

At this stage we wish to experiment with the log-linear or constant elasticity formulation of the model to determine whether it has a higher predictive ability than the linear model. The sales relation is given by:

$$S = aP^b Y^c P_c^d e^v$$

which can be linearised by taking logs of both sides as follows:

$$\ln S = \ln a + b \ln P + c \ln Y + d \ln P_C + v$$

Performing the indicated regression in the logarithms of the variables yields the following predicting equation:

$$\ln \hat{S} = \underset{(2.564)}{1.64637} - \underset{(-0.405)}{0.259371 \ln P} + \underset{(6.945)}{0.663668 \ln Y} + \underset{(0.959)}{0.451226 \ln P_C}$$

$$\bar{R}^2 = 0.81505 \quad F_{(3,16)} = 28.91 \quad \text{D–W} = 1.32 \quad \text{SEE} = 0.022472205$$

With the exception that the constant term is now significant at the 5% level of significance and that the D–W statistic is somewhat lower than in the linear formulation, there is not much that can be added to the earlier discussion. However, it may be more appropriate to use this formulation than the linear one. In this second case the estimated parameters are the elasticities of sales with respect to the two price variables and income and can be compared directly with the earlier results.

5.B.4a Choosing between the two formulations

In choosing between the two formulations we note that the two $\bar{R}^2$s are not directly comparable, since in the linear case the variables are measured in levels and in the log-linear formulation in logarithms. Similarly, the SEE are not comparable, since in the linear formulation the SEE is expressed in levels and in the log-linear one it is expressed in percentages. Therefore, in order to achieve the comparison between the two we must convert the SEE of the log-linear formulation in levels and then choose the formulation with the lower standard error. This is achieved by multiplying the geometric mean of the dependent variable (sales) by the SEE of the log-linear formulation. This converts this standard error in levels and we can now compare it directly with that of the linear formulation and choose the formulation (and thus predicting equation) with the lower SEE.

In our case the geometric mean (g) is found from the computer printout of the log-linear formulation by summing up the logarithms of the actual observations of sales and dividing by 20 to arrive at a value of $D = (\Sigma D)/n = 6.39563535$, whose antilog is 599.2239192. Multiplying this by the SEE = 0.022472205 we derive the SEE of the log-linear formulation expressed in levels as 13.4659, which is lower than the SEE of the linear formulation (13.6931). This demonstrates that on the statistical criterion of the lower SE the log-linear formulation is preferred.

Using the predicting equation of the log-linear model to forecast sales for the following week, with the earlier values of $P = 2.30$, $Y = 820$ and $P_C = 3.10$ we obtain:

$$\ln \hat{S} = 1.64637 - 0.259371 \times \ln 2.3 + 0.663668 \times \ln 820 + 0.45122 \times \ln 3.1$$
$$= 1.64637 - 0.216032472 + 4.452750593 + 0.510518049 = 6.39360617$$

whose antilog is 598, and this gives the best forecast value of next week's sales of roses in bunches. Constructing also a 95% confidence interval for this forecast value we derive:

$$598 - 13.4659 \times 2.12 < \hat{S} = 598 < 598 + 13.4659 \times 2.12$$
$$598 - 28.5477 < 598 < 598 + 28.5477$$
$$569 < 598 < 627$$

As before, this result tells us that we have a 95% probability that next week's sales of roses will lie in the interval 569–627 with a best forecast value of 598.

5.B.5 Estimating the demand for new car registrations

In the second example, the AAM wants to establish a predicting equation of the demand for new cars. The Association's economists have hypothesised a function relating demand for new cars to disposable income, price of cars and price of petrol and have been able to collect quarterly data from 1990IV to 2000IV on new car registrations (in hundred thousands) D, on real disposable income Y, on price of cars relative to general level of prices X, and on price of petrol relative to general level of prices Z. The last three variables Y, X and Z are expressed as index numbers with base year 1995 = 100. A feature of the car market in Vretannia is that on 1 July every year new registration numbers come into operation, and therefore the economists of AAM expect to find a considerable seasonal effect in the demand for new cars.

In the first instance they hypothesise a linear relation, which when estimated by OLS produces the following predicting equation and summary statistics:

$$\hat{D} = \underset{(0.619)}{357.297573} + \underset{(5.147)}{4.190504Y} + \underset{(0.177)}{0.993008X} - \underset{(-2.836)}{3.920082Z}$$

$$\bar{R}^2 = 0.4148 \quad F_{(3,41)} = 11.396 \quad \text{D–W} = 1.684 \quad \text{SEE} = 84.4469$$

It is immediately clear that the forecasting power of this model is poor, since it explains only 41.4% of the variation in the demand for new car registrations. In addition, not only is the coefficient of the price of cars relative to the general price level insignificant it also has the 'wrong' sign. It is unlikely that using a different formulation of the same model will achieve a dramatic improvement in predictive power. Indeed, estimating the same model in its log-linear formulation provides only a marginal improvement of fit with a coefficient of multiple determination of 0.445, but all other problems remain the same. It would appear then that the original model is likely to be mis-specified.

5.B.6 The use of dummy variables

An inspection of the plot of the new car registrations, given by the continuous line in Figure 5.B.1, shows considerable seasonal variation with demand for new cars

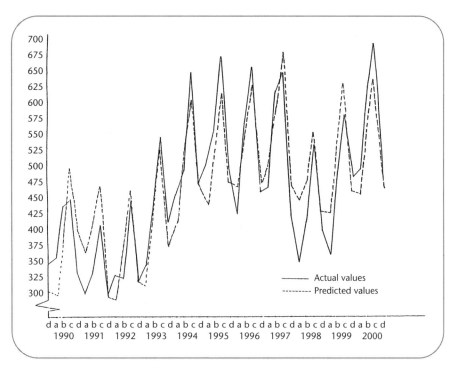

Figure 5.B.1 Predicting new car registrations

highest in the third quarter, when the new registrations come into operation. One can take account of this strong seasonal effect by introducing dummy variables S_1, S_3 and S_4 for the first, third and fourth quarters. These variables take the value of one (1) for the quarter they refer to and zero in all other quarters. When we re-run the regression for the re-specified model, we obtain the following results:

$$\hat{D} = 796.217327 + 4.053416Y - 3.221746X - 3.731596Z - 90.336421S_1$$
$$\quad\quad\;\;(2.17)\quad\quad\quad (8.173)\quad\quad\quad (-0.911)\quad\quad\quad (-4.405)\quad\quad\quad\quad (-4.029)$$

$$\quad\quad + 78.462252S_3 - 70.923641S_4$$
$$\quad\quad\quad\;\;(3.564)\quad\quad\quad\;(-3.301)$$

$$\bar{R}^2 = 0.78313 \quad F_{(6,38)} = 27.481 \quad \text{D–W} = 0.822 \quad \text{SEE} = 51.40850932$$

We notice that the re-specified model represents a considerable improvement over the earlier one, with over 78% of the variation in new car registrations explained by the linear influence of the variables included in the model. Also, the estimated value of $F = 24.481$ is much greater than the tabulated $F = 3.29$ value for $(6, 38)$ degrees of freedom at the 1% level of significance. Similarly, the standard error of estimate is much lower in the re-specified model at 51.41 than the value of 84.45 of the original model. As regards the signs and significance of the estimated coefficients, we note that, since the tabulated t value for 40 degrees of freedom at the 5% level of significance is 2.021 (and 2.704 at the 1% level), all estimated parameters are significantly different than zero, with the exception of the coefficient of the price of cars relative to the general price level. This implies that the role of price of cars is not as crucial a determinant in influencing sales in

Vretannia, where special factors such as, e.g., company car fleets, may be at work, which may very well cause sales to be relatively insensitive to the price of cars. However, the interesting feature of this re-specified model is that the estimated parameter of the price of cars relative to the general price level has now the 'correct' sign. Also, the coefficients of income and price of petrol relative to the general price level have the signs expected on a priori grounds. Considering the signs and significance of the dummy parameters, we find a strong positive seasonal effect on new car registrations in the third quarter and, equally, strong and negative influences on such registrations in the first and fourth quarters, much in line with what we expected on inspecting the plot on Figure 5.B.1. This figure also includes the estimated new car registrations from the re-specified model, given by the broken line. Nevertheless, whilst the estimated line may provide a reasonable approximation of the actual values within the sample period, the simulation is not tight enough to provide us with confidence on the forecast drawn from this model. In addition, the value of the D–W statistic at 0.922 indicates the presence of positive autocorrelation, since the tabulated lower limit at $k = 6$ and $n = 38$ is $d = 1.146$ at the 5% level of significance and $d = 0.966$ at the 1% level. This means that our estimated coefficients do not have the property of least variance and are not as efficient, as we may achieve by using GLS. Also, in the presence of autocorrelation we may have overestimated the coefficient of multiple determination and the usual t and F tests are no longer valid.

5.B.7 Generalised least squares

Therefore, it becomes necessary to correct for autocorrelation by utilising the Cochrane–Orcutt procedure, discussed earlier. This means setting up and estimating the transformed model, as explained in the Appendix to this chapter, preceding these examples. Consequently, the generalised difference equation to be estimated takes the following form:

$$D_t = a(1 - \rho) + b(Y_t - \rho Y_{t-1}) + c(X_t - \rho X_{t-1}) + d(Z_t - \rho Z_{t-1}) + e(S_{1t} - \rho S_{1t-1})$$
$$+ f(S_{3t} - \rho S_{3t-1}) + g(S_{4t} - \rho S_{4t-1}) + \rho D_{t-1}$$

We now proceed to estimate the generalised least squares estimates of the coefficients of the above equation, by incorporating the Cochrane–Orcutt iterative technique, and also correcting for possible heteroscedasticity, by estimating the White corrected standard errors of the coefficients. The resulting equation with the GLS estimates and summary statistics is as follows:

$$\hat{D} = \underset{(0.874)}{335.695762} + \underset{(4.808)}{4.350805Y} + \underset{(0.016)}{0.059262X} - \underset{(-3.312)}{2.896919Z} - \underset{(-5.986)}{85.439782S_1}$$

$$+ \underset{(6.638)}{80.049887S_3} - \underset{(-5.549)}{75.680173S_4}$$

$$\bar{R}^2 = 0.81334 \quad F_{(6,37)} = 32.228 \quad \text{D–W} = 1.902 \quad \text{SEE} = 40.9490630$$

$$\rho = \text{rho} = 0.57838$$

Here the constant term $335.695762 = a(1 - \rho)$. Since the value of ρ (rho) was found to be 0.57838 we have that $335.695762 = a(1 - 0.57838)$ from which we get that $a = 796.20455$, a value for our constant which compares very well with the earlier OLS value. This equation has the highest $\bar{R}^2$ and F statistics and the lowest SEE. The GLS estimates are more efficient than the earlier OLS and the only blemish is that the estimated parameter for the price of cars relative to the general price level is insignificant and reverts back to its 'wrong' sign. However the reduction in the SEE provides any forecast value with a much narrower confidence interval and, thus, improves our confidence in such forecasts.

Nevertheless we may still be able to improve the forecasting ability of this basic model by applying GLS to its log-linear formulation, to derive the following:

$$\ln \hat{D} = \underset{(0.709)}{2.691352} + \underset{(4.924)}{1.042699} \ln Y + \underset{(0.390)}{0.294192} \ln X - \underset{(-2.822)}{0.584673} \ln Z$$

$$- \underset{(-5.947)}{0.178718} \ln S_1 + \underset{(7.051)}{0.158586} \ln S_3 - \underset{(-6.103)}{0.162355} \ln S_4$$

$$\bar{R}^2 = 0.81592 \quad F_{(6,37)} = 32.765 \quad \text{D–W} = 2.0455 \quad \text{SEE} = 0.084297093$$

$$\rho = \text{rho} = 0.60564$$

The geometric mean of the dependent variable is $g = 449.5393137$; (it is found by dividing the sum of the logarithms of the dependent variable by n and taking its antilog). Therefore, the SEE of the log-linear model is converted in levels as: $449.5393137 \times 0.084297093 = 37.89486$. Since this value is less than the SEE $= 40.94906$ of the linear formulation found earlier, the log-linear formulation is preferred, and this then becomes our final predicting equation for new car registrations. Notice that the income elasticity of demand for new cars in Vretannia is 1.043, which is lower than similar elasticities computed for the demand for cars in the US, which have varied between 1.2 and 2.536 (Nemmers 1967, p. 111).

5.B.8   Epilogue

Naturally, the quest for a more accurate predicting equation for new car registrations does not stop here. Even with the final generalised difference equation the model explains 81.59% of the variation in the dependent variable leaving 18.41% of the variation unexplained. This is a large proportion, and extensions of the work to try to reduce the unexplained variation may involve re-specification of the model by incorporating variables such as credit terms, interest rate, average scrappage age, replacement pressure and so on, which have been found, amongst others, to be important determinants of the demand for new cars, in studies conducted in the US. Other considerations may focus on the exogeneity of the regressors used in the model, since for forecasting purposes we require regressors (explanatory variables), which are at least weakly exogenous. This means that we cannot treat the price of new cars as a truly exogenous variable, because it is affected by demand, and this in turn means that the estimated regression coefficient of price of cars relative to the general level of prices is subject to simultaneity bias. Therefore, it follows that we need a simultaneous-equations model, in which both demand for new car registrations and price of new cars are endogenous variables, to be determined simultaneously. Of course, similar comments apply also to our earlier attempt to estimate a predicting equation for roses. However, as this goes beyond the confines of this book it is not attempted here, and it only remains to be said that if interested readers have had their appetites whetted by the preceding discussion, they can proceed, by consulting the relevant literature, and construct more appropriate models of a simultaneous-equation nature, discussed in the appendix to this chapter.

PROBLEMS

1. A florist has observed the following information on prices (in cents) and quantities of carnations (in bunches) sold in his shop over a period of 12 consecutive weeks:

   P: 100 90 80   70 70   70 70   65   60   60   55   50
   Q: 55 70 90 100 90 105 80 110 125 115 130 130

   (a) Estimate a linear demand curve for carnations which is given by: $Q = a + bP + u$.
   (b) What is the quantity demanded of carnations at a price of 75c?
   (c) What is the price elasticity of demand for carnations at the mean price?
   (d) Assume that the current price of carnations is 55c and the florist contemplates reducing it in order to increase sales. Advise the florist on his pricing policy.
   (e) What is the price at which demand for carnations disappears? How many bunches could be given away, if carnations were a free good (i.e., if price were set at zero)?

2. The following table shows the average annual household disposable income in €s, the price index of durables and the expenditure on durables in €s of a 'representative' household in Aetolia.

Year	Expenditure on durables (€s)	Household disposable income (€s)	Price index
1985	1 850	22 000	102
1986	1 900	22 500	100
1987	2 000	23 000	95
1988	2 150	23 550	100
1989	2 100	25 000	102
1990	2 150	25 100	95
1991	2 200	25 400	95
1992	2 400	27 750	94
1993	2 000	27 550	110
1994	2 050	24 950	110
1995	1 950	24 050	112
1996	2 350	28 550	115
1997	2 050	25 350	120
1998	2 400	29 650	127
1999	2 500	30 100	130
2000	2 500	30 000	128

(a) Derive an estimating equation for expenditure on durables for Aetolia.
(b) How much of the variation in the expenditure on durables is explained by the linear influence of household disposable income and prices?
(c) What is the income elasticity of demand for durables at the mean values of expenditure and income?
(d) If the government of Aetolia expects average household disposable income to grow at 3% per annum for the next three years and price to remain constant at their current levels, what is your forecast for the expenditure on durables at the end of 2003?

3. The Association of Clothing Manufacturers of Arcadia wishes to estimate a demand function of expenditure on clothing. It has collected the following information on expenditure on clothing in billion €s (Y), the price index of clothing (P) and total expenditure in billion €s (E) for the last 19 years.

Expenditure on clothing (bil. €s)	Price index of clothing	Total expenditure (bil. €s)
8	95	45
9	98	52
10	98	55
12	95	60
14	96	65
18	98	80
16	102	75
20	100	90
22	98	95
26	105	110
27	110	115
25	115	110
28	120	120
30	118	130
31	120	135
33	125	140
34	127	145
36	125	150
41	120	170

(a) Derive an estimating equation for expenditure on clothing for Arcadia, given by the linear form: $Y = a + bP + cE + u$.
(b) Also derive an estimating equation given by the constant elasticity form: $Y = aP^b E^c e^v$.
(c) Give an economic interpretation of the coefficients b and c in the two equations.
(d) Find the $\bar{R}^2$s and the SEE in the two estimating equations and evaluate your results. Which estimating equation do you choose on economic and/or statistical criteria?

4. The following table provides information on average annual household income in €s and average household expenditure on food in €s for Frygia for the past 13 years, during which the country has seen unprecedented growth. The government of Frygia expects the high rate of growth to continue and estimates that the average household income for the following year to be around €20 000. The Federation of Food Manufacturers has asked you to provide them with a forecast of household expenditure on food for the next year.

Average household income in €s (X)	Average expenditure on food in €s (Y)
310	187
630	285
870	357
1 120	415
1 360	466
1 830	510
2 220	543
2 710	601
3 400	677
4 400	753
6 870	831
11 440	1 010
17 290	1 715

(a) To help you choose the appropriate functional form to use, plot average expenditure on food on average household income. What pattern emerges?
(b) Estimate a predicting equation of expenditure on food on income given by the linear form: $Y = a + bX + u$. Estimate also the parabolic function given by: $Y = a + bX + cX^2 + u$.
(c) Which functional form fits the data best and why?
(d) Which 'law' is demonstrated by this example? Explain.
(e) Which is the maximum household expenditure? At what level of household income is this maximum achieved? What are the implications of your findings for the Federation of Food Manufacturers of Frygia.

5. The COSMOS PLC is a large multinational enterprise contemplating entry into Paionia, a developing country, but only if the economy of that country has reached a minimum of GNP of €150 billion. COSMOS PLC after considerable research effort have established the following information:
They expect consumption expenditure in Paionia in the current year to be €5 billion plus 80% of disposable income, while investment expenditure is expected to be €2 billion plus 70% of last year's profits, which were €12 billion. The government of Paionia has announced that its expenditure of all kinds in

the current year to be €40 billion and a uniform tax rate of 20% will be levied on all income. Further, Paionia in the last five years has averaged a small surplus in its balance of payments of €1 billion, and expects a similar sum in the current year.

Formulate a model for the Paionia economy and use it to forecast the values of consumption, investment, tax receipts, disposable income and gross national income. Would you advise COMSOS PLC to invest in Paionia?

BIBLIOGRAPHY

Box, G.E.P. and Jenkins, G.M. (1976), *Time Series Analysis: Forecasting and Control*, revised edn, Holden-Day.

Gilbert, C.L. (1986), 'Professor Hendry's Econometric Methodology', *Oxford Bulletin of Economics & Statistics*, **48** (August) 283–307.

Granger, C.W.J. and Newbold, P. (1986), *Forecasting Economic Time Series*, 2nd edn, Academic Press.

Gujarati, D.N. (1988), *Basic Econometrics*, 2nd edn, McGraw-Hill.

Kmenta, J. (1971), *Elements of Econometrics*, Macmillan.

Koutsoyiannis, A. (1977), *Theory of Econometrics*, 2nd edn, Macmillan.

Maddalla, G.S. (1977), *Econometrics*, McGraw-Hill.

Nemmers, E.E. (1967), *Managerial Economics*, John Wiley & Sons.

Pappas, J.L. and Hirschey, M. (1990), *Managerial Economics*, 6th edn, Dryden Press.

chapter six

Production Theory

Learning outcomes

After you have finished studying this chapter you should know about:

■ The law of variable returns

■ Total, average and marginal products

■ Production functions

■ Isoquants

■ Input substitution

■ Elasticity of substitution

■ Output maximisation

■ Cost minimisation

■ Interpretation of Lagrange multipliers

■ Profit maximisation

■ Returns to scale

6.1   INTRODUCTION

Goods and services are produced in units known as firms. Such units can extend from the very simple one-person, one-product or service undertaking to huge multinational concerns, employing hundreds of thousands of people, operating in many countries of the world and producing thousands of products and/or services. However, despite such tremendous discrepancies both sets of firms share a number of basic common features. A firm is a technical unit which utilises various factors of production, known as resources or inputs to produce outputs in the form of goods or services. This process of transformation of inputs into outputs adds value and is achieved by means of various productive processes or activities, which are part of the firm's production function. Having produced and sold the outputs the difference between the proceeds of the sale and the costs of production represents the income of the firm.

The role of production theory is to provide us with an understanding of how firms organise their transformation activities to solve a number of management problems such as, for example, given information regarding prices of inputs and the firm's weekly budget, how much output should be produced? If such prices and expenditure change, how do they affect the optimal quantities? What is the best input mix to produce a given output? And many others. Such questions are answered by means of two sets of information and the firm's objectives. First, the firm possesses technological information, embodied in the production function, which relates inputs and outputs; second, the firm is faced with market information regarding prices of inputs, outputs and of total expenditure, and last the firm's goals or objectives bring the two sets of information together, in order to achieve the firm's equilibrium position. Production theory could apply equally well to different sizes of firms, involved in many different activities, such as agriculture, manufacturing, transportation, distribution and many other forms of service provision, and this general applicability makes it a very useful tool for decision making.

6.2   THE LAW OF VARIABLE RETURNS: TOTAL, AVERAGE AND MARGINAL PRODUCTS

The law of variable returns underlies most of production theory, by stating what happens to output as we vary the usage of one input while holding all other inputs constant. It states that at the beginning as we increase the use of one factor of production, say labour, from very low quantities by x%, while keeping all other inputs constant, output rises by more than x% and we refer to this as the stage of increasing returns to our factor. Clearly, in such a case we have an incentive to use more of the factor, assuming that its price remains constant, but after a while we find that further percentage increase in the use of the factor brings forward an equiproportionate rise in output, thus reaching the stage of constant returns to our factor. If we were to apply more of our variable factor to the other fixed factors of production we shall find that output changes by less than the proportionate rise in the variable factor. This last case is known as the stage of diminishing returns to our factor. The explanation of the workings of the law of variable returns to a factor is to be found in the specialisation of tasks that an increased usage of a factor affords. In terms of our earlier example, as the quantity of the variable factor, labour, is increased from very low levels, this allows greater specialisation of the workers, who can perform with great dexterity and competence specific tasks, thus, labour productivity rises. However, at very high levels of labour usage, with the other factors remaining constant, there is congestion and/or frequent breakdowns of machinery, and so labour productivity falls.

To illustrate the law of variable returns to a factor of production we anticipate the discussion of the next section and assume that the firm utilises two inputs, capital (K) and labour (L) to produce a single product. Its production function, established by its engineers and technologists, is given by:

$$Q = 10K^2L^2 - 0.2K^3L^3 \qquad (1)$$

The prices of the two factors are $P_K = €100$ and $P_L = €5$ per unit. The firm has fixed the amount of capital at $K = 10$ units, and therefore by substituting this value into the latter relation (1) the latter can be rewritten as:

$$Q = 1000L^2 - 200L^3 \qquad (2)$$

giving total output as a function of the variable input L alone. The average productivity (AP) of labour is derived by dividing relation (2) by L, and the marginal productivity (MP) of labour is found by differentiating (2) with respect to L, giving:

$$AP = Q/L = 1000L - 200L^2 \text{ and } MP = dQ/dL = 2000L - 600L^2$$

Therefore, by varying the amount of the variable factor labour (L), the total, average and marginal products are found and are given in Table 6.1. It is clear that total output increases, reaching its highest value at a labour usage of around 3333 units, while average and marginal products are at first rising, as we increase labour usage, and then decline in accordance with the law of variable proportions.

Figures 6.1 and 6.2 reproduce the information of Table 6.1 in a diagrammatic form and show that as labour usage rises, total, average and marginal products all increase at first. However, marginal product increases faster, reaches its maximum point earlier and turns to cut the average product curve at its maximum point and becomes zero at the point where the total product reaches its maximum. This is essentially a short-run analysis, since we have assumed that only one factor is variable and all others are fixed at predetermined levels, but it will suffice at the moment. We shall consider later what happens when we allow all factors to vary.

6.3 THE PRODUCTION FUNCTION

At the heart of production theory is the production function, which is a technological relation between inputs and outputs encompassing technical efficiency. This means that of the various combinations of inputs available to produce a particular output only the most efficient are incorporated in the production function, i.e., those that provide us with the maximum output for given inputs, or alternatively the minimum combination of inputs necessary to produce a given output. In other words, the production function differs from technology, since the latter includes all physical possibilities between inputs and outputs. It follows that all points of the production function are equally efficient from the technical point of view, since they represent the best utilisation of inputs; to find the most appropriate

Table 6.1 Total, average and marginal products of labour

Quantity of L (000s)	Units of output Q	Average product AP = Q/L	Marginal product MP = dQ/dL
0.1	9.8	98	194
0.2	38.4	192	376
0.3	84.6	282	546
0.4	147.2	368	704
0.5	225.0	450	850
0.6	316.8	528	984
0.7	421.4	602	1 106
0.8	537.6	672	1 216
0.9	664.2	738	1 314
1.0	800.0	800	1 400
1.1	943.8	858	1 474
1.2	1094.4	912	1 536
1.3	1250.6	962	1 586
1.4	1411.2	1 008	1 624
1.5	1575.0	1 050	1 650
1.6	1740.8	1 088	1 664
1.7	1907.4	1 122	1 666
1.8	2073.6	1 152	1 656
1.9	2238.2	1 178	1 634
2.0	2400.0	1 200	1 600
2.1	2557.8	1 218	1 554
2.2	2710.4	1 232	1 496
2.3	2856.6	1 242	1 426
2.4	2995.2	1 248	1 344
2.5	3125.0	1 250	1 250
2.6	3244.8	1 248	1 144
2.7	3353.4	1 242	1 026
2.8	3449.6	1 232	896
2.9	3532.2	1 218	754
3.0	3600.0	1 200	600
3.1	3651.8	1 178	434
3.2	3686.4	1 152	256
3.3	3702.6	1 122	66
3.3333	3703.703	1110.89	0
3.35	3703.425	1105.5	−33.5
3.4	3699.2	1088	−136

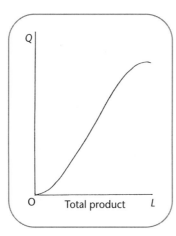

Figure 6.1 Total product

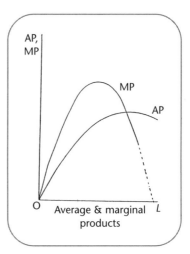

Figure 6.2 Average and marginal products

combination for the production of a particular product we require information about prices of inputs and outputs, as will be shown later.

To illustrate what is involved, we assume that a single-product firm utilises variable quantities of two inputs K and L to produce a product Q. The production function states the quantity of output q as a function of the quantities of K and L, and it can be expressed as:

$$Q = f(K, L) \tag{3}$$

To proceed we must specify, f, the shape of the production function, i.e., how the two resources interact in producing Q. At the theoretical level, we can start by assuming that the function is continuous and defined for all non-negative values of inputs and outputs, as negative values are clearly meaningless in the present context. This means that the firm is able to substitute freely one resource for another and that such input substitutability is perfect, giving us a whole continuum of production possibilities, which is known as the case of the variable coefficients of production. Alternatively, we can assume that there is only one way the two resources can be utilised to produce Q, thus obtaining the case of fixed coefficients of production. Between the two extreme cases of perfect and of zero substitutability, we may have situations of partial substitutability. At the practical level, it means digging into the nature of the production process itself, and exploring the possibilities of different technically efficient combinations of the two resources, which is an engineering task, before we can arrive at our production function.

6.3.1 From the production function to isoquants

We shall be considering both cases but for the purposes of establishing certain common results, we begin by assuming that the production function is smooth, continuous, twice differentiable, which is known as the neoclassical production function of economic theory.

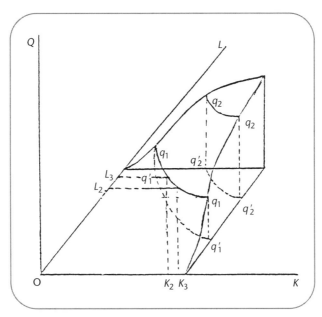

Figure 6.3 Production surface, production contours q_1q_1, q_2q_2 corresponding to isoquants $q_1'q_1'$ and $q_2'q_2'$

In this case, we can utilise a two-dimensional diagram measuring on the two axes quantities of the two inputs and introducing the concept of an isoquant, or curve of equal quantity. An isoquant is the geometric locus of all combinations of the two inputs K and L yielding a specified level of output. Isoquants are contours of the production surface and their derivation is shown in Figure 6.3. Using the given production function $Q = f(K, L)$ we form a three-dimensional diagram, the height of which measures quantity of output and the other two diamensions measure quantities of the two inputs. For example, if input combinations K_2L_3 and K_3L_2 produce the same quantity of output, then by passing a plane at that height of output (q_1q_1) we get the contour q_1q_1, as shown on the diagram. Therefore, contours are derived by drawing planes at different heights of the production surface parallel to the input plane LOK. Another higher contour q_2q_2 is also shown, indicating a higher level of output. When these contours are transferred on the 'floor' of the diagram, i.e., the input plane, they produce the broken curves $q_1'q_1'$ and $q_2'q_2'$, which represent the isoquants. A family of such isoquant is shown in Figure 6.4, having been derived from a continuous production function and displaying diminishing substitutability between the factors of production.

Isoquants look very similar to the indifference curves of demand theory but the former show levels of output which are easily measurable, while the same cannot be said of the latter; resulting from the fact that the production function is objective while the utility function is subjective. Isoquants display a number of like properties to those of indifference curves, namely: (1) they slope downwards from left to right; (2) they do not intersect; (3) isoquants lying higher on the two-dimensional diagram correspond to higher levels of output and those lying lower to lower levels of output and (4) they are convex to the origin, implying that the marginal rate of technical substitution of one input for the other diminishes.

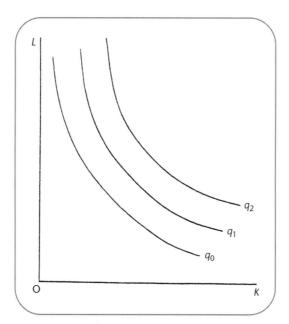

Figure 6.4 Isoquants for continuous production functions

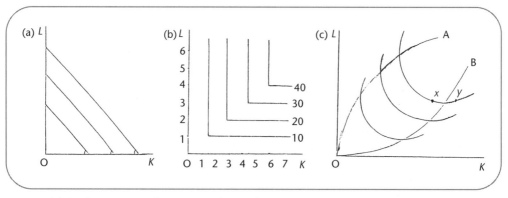

Figure 6.5 (a) Perfect input substitution; (b) perfect input complementarity; (c) imperfect input substitution

6.3.2 Input substitution

The shape of the isoquants depends on the degree of substitutability between inputs, but they all tend to obey the above properties. In the case where the one input is a perfect substitute of the other, the production process can utilise either of the inputs or any combination of such inputs to produce a given quantity of a product or service, and the isoquants are given by downward sloping straight lines, as in Figure 6.5(a), showing that the rate at which one factor can substitute for the other remains the same. On the other hand, where there is only one way of combining the two inputs in order to produce a good, implying no substitutability at all between the inputs, the isoquants take the shape of right angles convex to the origin, as shown in Figure 6.5(b). Finally, where inputs can be substituted one for another but such substitutability is not perfect, it means that the ability of one input to substitute another, and vice versa, diminishes, as more of that input is used in the production process, and the isoquants take their more familiar shape, as shown in Figure 6.5(c).

The marginal rate of technical substitution (MRTS) between the two inputs K and L is defined as the negative of the slope of the tangent to any point on the isoquant, and it is given by:

$$\text{MRTS} = -\mathrm{d}L/\mathrm{d}K \tag{4}$$

To derive an expression for the marginal rate of technical substitution we take the total differential of the production function and have:

$$\mathrm{d}Q = F_1\mathrm{d}K + F_2\mathrm{d}L \tag{5}$$

where F_1 and F_2 are the partial derivatives of the production function with respect to K and L, in other words the marginal products of K and L. Since movements along the same isoquant leave the level of output unchanged, $\mathrm{d}Q = 0$ and therefore we have:

$$F_1\mathrm{d}K + F_2\mathrm{d}L = 0 \tag{6}$$

giving

$$\text{MRTS} = \frac{\mathrm{d}L}{\mathrm{d}K} = \frac{F_1}{F_2} \tag{7}$$

This shows that the marginal rate of technical substitution between any two inputs at a point on an isoquant is equal to the ratio of the two marginal products of the inputs at that point.

However, as we showed in Table 6.1 the marginal product of one factor may become negative, if too much of that factor is used. In such a case, if the marginal product of one factor is negative and the marginal product of the other factor is positive the marginal rate of technical substitution becomes negative, as it is at point Y in Figure 6.5(c). The producer gets the same level of output at X as at Y, but by moving from Y to X he uses less of both inputs K and L. Point X is preferred, since the producer will have to pay for the inputs and even in the case where one of the inputs may have been amortised (say, the use of a machine), again the opportunity cost of using that machine time is not zero, if it could be used to produce something else. It follows then that the producer will never operate on the positive sloping sections of the isoquants, since it is uneconomic, and instead he will be confined within the ridge lines OA and OB, which define the economic region of his operations.

6.3.3 Elasticity of substitution

When the relative prices of factors of production change, the producer has an incentive to substitute one factor for another, by using more of the factor whose price has fallen, in order to maintain the equilibrium condition between the factor-price ratio and the marginal rate of technical substitution (MRTS). With convex isoquants, as we move from left to right the MRTS and the input ratio L/K both diminish. The extent of substitution of factors of production is measured by the elasticity of substitution, which is defined as the proportionate rate of change of the input ratio divided by the proportionate rate of change of the MRTS, and it is given by the following formula:

$$s = \frac{d(L/K)/(L/K)}{d(F_1/F_2)/(F_1/F_2)} = \frac{d\ln(L/K)}{d\ln(F_1/F_2)} \tag{8}$$

The value of the elasticity of substitution, s, can vary between 0 and ∞, and the larger the s, the greater the incentive of management to substitute the relatively cheaper input for the more expensive one.

6.4 OPTIMUM BEHAVIOUR: MAXIMUM OUTPUT, MINIMUM COST

So far we have only looked at the technological information, incorporated in the production function. We can now bring in the market information by assuming that the firm buys its inputs in perfect markets, i.e., the prices of K and L are given, say, by r and w and are constant. Therefore, the firm's total cost (TC) of production is given by:

$$TC = rK + wL + B \tag{9}$$

where r and w are the prices and K and L the quantities of the two inputs and B stands for the fixed costs of production. If the firm has a given weekly or monthly budget of x euros it follows that its total costs cannot exceed that amount per week or month, say TC′, consequently, the above relation can be written as:

$$TC' = rK + wL + B \tag{10}$$

The firm can clearly buy different combinations of inputs for this specified expenditure of TC′ and this leads to the idea of the isocost line, or line of equal cost. We define the isocost line as the locus of all input combinations that can be bought for a given amount of expenditure. To construct the isocost line we solve the above for K and L, resulting in the following two relations:

$$K = \frac{TC' - B}{r} - \frac{w}{r} \times L \tag{11}$$

and

$$L = \frac{TC - B}{w} - \frac{r}{w} \times K \tag{12}$$

If the firm were spending all of its expenditure buying either of the two inputs, it could buy quantities of K and L given by the intercepts of the two relations shown above, i.e., $K = (TC' - B)/r$ and $L = (TC' - B)/w$, which in Figure 6.6 are indicated by points K_1 and L_1. Joining these two points results in the isocost line K_1L_1, giving different combinations of the two inputs corresponding to total

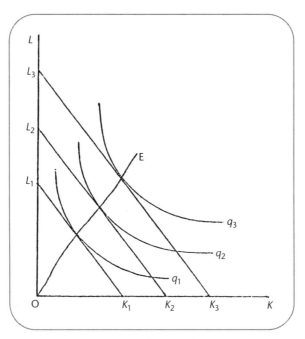

Figure 6.6 Output maximising and cost minimising input combinations

expenditure TC'. The slope of the isocost line is given by the inverse of the input price ratio $(-r/w)$. If the firm could increase its expenditure, it could clearly buy more variable inputs K and L, and so long as input prices remain constant, this can be shown by higher isocost lines corresponding to higher levels of expenditure. Such isocost lines are also shown in Figure 6.6 as L_2K_2 and L_3K_3. By combining now market and technological information and introducing the objective of output maximisation for a given outlay, we can see where the firm will operate. Clearly, the firm will try to produce as much output for any given expenditure as possible. This is a problem of constrained maximisation, and the Lagrangian expression, M, maximising output subject to the expenditure constraint is formulated as follows:

$$M = f(K, L) + \lambda(TC' - rK - wL - B) \tag{13}$$

where λ is an unspecified Lagrange multiplier. Differentiating (13) partially with respect to K, L and λ and setting the partial derivatives equal to zero gives:

$$\delta M/\delta K = F_1 - \lambda r = 0 \tag{14}$$

$$\delta M/\delta L = F_2 - \lambda w = 0 \tag{15}$$

$$\delta M/\delta \lambda = TC' - rK - wL = 0 \tag{16}$$

Rearranging the first two equation and dividing (14) by (15) results in the following:

$$F_1/F_2 = r/w \tag{17}$$

i.e., in equilibrium the firm must equate the ratio of the marginal products of the two inputs to the ratio of their prices. This is the first-order condition for output maximisation. Now, utilising also relation (7) we find that:

$$\text{MRTS} = F_1/F_2 = r/w \tag{18}$$

which states that in equilibrium, the marginal rate of technical substitution must be equal to the inputs price ratio. This merely states that, in terms of Figure 6.6, equilibrium is achieved at the tangency point between the relevant isocost line, corresponding to the given outlay, and the highest isoquant that isocost line can touch. This is so because at that point the slope of the isocost line, given by the inverse of the input price ratio, is the same as the slope of the isoquant, i.e., the marginal rate of technical substitution. The second-order conditions for output maximisation require that the isoquants are convex from the origin, as shown in the diagrams.

Alternatively, the firm may have as its objective to minimise its costs of production, subject to producing a given amount of output Q'. In this case, the constrained minimisation problem is formulated as follows:

$$V = rK + wL + B + \mu[Q' - f(K, L)] \tag{19}$$

Where again μ is an unspecified Lagrange multiplier. Differentiating partially with respect to K, L and μ and equating the partial derivatives to zero yields:

$$\delta V/\delta K = r - \mu F_1 = 0 \tag{20}$$

$$\delta V/\delta L = w - \mu F_2 = 0 \tag{21}$$

$$\delta V/\delta \mu = Q' - f(K, L) = 0 \tag{22}$$

Again by rearranging the first two equations and dividing (20) by (21) we obtain:

$$r/w = F_1/F_2 \tag{23}$$

which states that for cost minimisation the firm must operate at the point where it equates the inputs price ratio to the ratio of the marginal products of the two inputs, and by making use of relation (5) we have that in equilibrium

$$\text{MRTS} = F_1/F_2 - r/w \tag{24}$$

This, clearly, is the same condition found earlier. In terms of Figure 6.6 the firm tries to find the lowest isocost line touching the relevant isoquant, whose output is required. Again, the second order conditions for cost minimisation require that the isoquants are convex to the origin. Therefore, points of tangency between isocost lines and isoquants are equilibrium points, solving both problems of constrained output maximisation and constrained cost minimisation. Joining such points results in the line OE in Figure 6.6, called the expansion path, and showing how a firm will expand its output if it could vary its expenditure, other things remaining equal.

Relations (14) and (15) can be solved for λ to give $F_1/r = \lambda = F_2/w$, which specifies λ as the marginal product of cost and shows that in equilibrium, the firm will be purchasing inputs up to the point where the last euro produces the same increase in output irrespective of the factor of production it is spent on. Similarly, relations (20) and (21) can be solved for μ to give us: $r/F_1 = \mu = w/F_2$, which is the reciprocal of λ found above, and specifies μ as the marginal cost with respect to product. Therefore, the unspecifed Lagrange multipliers λ and μ have a clear economic interpretation in that they are the shadow prices of cost and output in relations (14) and (20), respectively, showing how output changes for small variation in costs (λ), and how cost changes for small variation in output (μ). In other words, λ is the derivative of output with respect to cost, and μ is the derivative of cost with respect to output, which is our familiar marginal cost (MC) concept.

Example

By way of illustrating some of the points raised above, we assume that a firm's production function is given by: $Q = K^{0.3}L^{0.5}$, its monthly budget by €38400 and the prices of the two inputs are $P_K = 60$ and $P_L = 20$. We require to maximise output.

The Lagrangian expression to be maximised is formulated as follows:

$$M = K^{0.3}L^{0.5} + \mu(38400 - 60K - 20L) \tag{25}$$

Differentiating partially with respect to K, L and μ, and setting the partial derivatives equal to zero we obtain the first-order conditions, as follows:

$$\delta M/\delta K = 0.3K^{-0.7}L^{0.5} - 60\mu = 0 \tag{26}$$

$$\delta M/\delta L = 0.5K^{0.3}L^{-0.5} - 20\mu = 0 \tag{27}$$

$$\delta M/\delta \mu = 38400 - 60K - 20L = 0 \tag{28}$$

Dividing expression (26) by expression (27) we obtain

$$\frac{0.3K^{-0.7}L^{0.5}}{0.5K^{0.3}L^{-0.5}} = \frac{60}{20} = 3$$

which simplifies into

$$0.6K^{-1}L^1 = 3 \text{ or } 0.6L/K = 3 \text{ or } L = 5K \tag{29}$$

Substituting (29) into (28) we get: $38400 - 60K - 100K = 0$, from which we solve for $K = 240$ and using (29) we also get that $L = 5K = 5 \times 240 = 1200$.

Therefore, output is maximised when the firm buys 240 units of K and 1200 units of L, which yield a monthly output of

$$Q = 240^{0.3}1200^{0.5} = 179.33 \text{ units}$$

The value of μ, i.e., the marginal cost with respect to output for the optimal values of K and L is calculated as follows:

$$\mu = \frac{P_K}{MP_K} = \frac{60}{0.3K^{-0.7}L^{0.5}} = \frac{60}{0.3 \times 240^{-0.7} \times 1200^{0.5}}$$

$$= \frac{60}{0.224163034} = 267.6623$$

Notice that the same value for marginal cost is achieved if we worked, instead, with the price and marginal product of the other factor, L.

$$\mu = \frac{P_L}{\mathrm{MP_L}} = \frac{20}{0.5K^{0.3}L^{-0.5}} = \frac{20}{0.5 \times 240^{0.3} \times 1200^{-0.5}}$$

$$= \frac{20}{0.074721013} = 267.6623$$

thus, confirming relations (20) and (21).

(*Note on derivation:* To derive the value $1200^{-0.5}$, enter 1200 on a calculator, then enter 0.5 followed by the $+/-$ sign to turn the exponent into a negative number and finally press the $=$ sign to find the value 0.028867513).

6.4.1 Profit maximisation

However, if expenditure and output can be varied it is more usual to state the equilibrium of the firm in terms of a different objective, rather than constrained output maximisation or cost minimisation. The firm is more likely to be concerned with the revenues and profits associated with any production decisions and the neoclassical theory assumes that the prime and sole objective of the firm is profit maximisation. Further, it assumes that the firm is faced with a smooth, continuous, twice differentiable production function. Also, in order to develop the equilibrium rules, it may be easier at this stage to assume that the firm operates in perfect input and product markets, i.e., it buys its factors of production and sells its product at known constant prices. In this case, the profit (Π) of the firm is the difference between total revenue and total cost and the profit function is given by:

$$\Pi = \mathrm{TR} - \mathrm{TC} \tag{30}$$

Ignoring other costs, such as marketing and so on, or treating them as fixed costs and incorporating them into B, we get by substitution the following:

$$\Pi = pf(K, L) - rK - wL - B \tag{31}$$

where p is the price at which the firm's product (Q) is sold in the market. The first order conditions for profit maximisation require that we set the partial derivatives of Π with respect to K and L equal to zero and solve, thus, getting:

$$\delta\Pi/\delta K = pF_1 - r = 0 \tag{32}$$
$$\delta\Pi/\delta L = pF_2 - w = 0 \tag{33}$$

which result in:

$$pF_1 = r \text{ and } pF_2 = w \tag{34}$$

Since F_1 and F_2 are the physical marginal products of the two inputs K and L, respectively, it follows that by multiplying them by the price, p, of the product we get the marginal revenue productivity of the two inputs, i.e., by how much

Since returns to scale have clearly their implications on costs, a fuller analysis of their sources is postponed until we have discussed costs, but suffice it to note here that they have mainly to do with the effects of greater specialisation, which can be achieved by increasing the size of the firm at the plant level.

SUMMARY

This chapter has provided a discussion of the law of variable proportions, which underpins production and cost theories. Also, it has given an analysis of production theory, based on the neoclassical production function. It has looked at total average and marginal products, isoquants, input substitution and elasticity of substitution. It has also considered the equilibrium of the firm and established the conditions for such equilibrium, under output maximisation, cost minimisation and profit maximisation. In addition, it has provided an economic interpretation to Lagrange multipliers and looked at returns to scale.

PROBLEMS

1. A firm can produce a single product by means of the following production function:

$$Q = X^{0.3} Y^{0.5}$$

where Q is the level of output and X and Y are quantities of two inputs, which can be bought in perfect markets at unit prices of $P_X = €6$ and $P_Y = €2$. If the firm has a weekly budget of €3840, determine the optimal quantities of X and Y and the optimal weekly output, Q.

2. A firm's production function is given by:

$$Q = 10K^{0.7}L^{0.1}$$

where Q is the level of output, and K and L are quantities of capital and labour, which can be bought in perfect markets at unit prices of €28 and €10, respectively. Given that the firm can spend €4000 per week, find the optimal quantities of capital and labour and then determine the optimal weekly output.

3. If the production function is given by:

$$Q = 10K^{0.6}L^{0.4}$$

determine the marginal products of capital and labour and estimate the effect on output of an additional unit of capital and labour at the point $K = 10$ and $L = 30$.

4. If the equation for a production isoquant is given by:

$$10K^{0.6}L^{0.4} = 2000$$

determine the MRTS between K and L, and evaluate it at the point $K = 53$, $L = 27$.

5. For the following production functions, determine the degree of homogeneity and the nature of returns to scale:

(i) $Q = K^2 + 4KL + 5L^2$

(ii) $Q = K^3 - KL^2 + 2L^3 + K^2L$

(iii) $Q = \dfrac{K^2}{2L^2}$

APPENDIX: FAGE – FROM A SMALL CORNER SHOP TO THE INTERNATIONAL MARKET[1]

Yoghurt is a semi-fluid milk food with smooth texture. There are many types of plain and flavoured yoghurt, made from the milk of various animals, such as cows, sheep or goats. Although its precise origin is unknown, it has been very popular in various countries of Asia, North and Central Europe and some African countries for many centuries and is now known and consumed in almost all parts of the world. Yoghurt consumption witnessed a strong and continuous growth in most European countries in the period 1995–99, stronger than that of ice scream, various chilled desserts and other milk and dairy products. Changes in the life style, and the fact that health concerns increasingly influence the eating habits, certainly favour this particular product. According to the BMRD International's Target Group Index, yoghurt in 2000 was used by more than 80% of the households, and is increasingly popular to younger and more affluent customer groups (Keynote 2001, pp. 56–8).

One of the yoghurt types with constantly increasing popularity is the strained (Greek) yoghurt. In 1999 Greece, together with Belgium/Luxembourg and the Republic of Ireland, was classified as the fourth largest supplier of yoghurt in UK, accounting for 3% of the yoghurt imports. Greek yoghurt is made, typically, from cow's milk and has a richer taste and a thicker velvety texture than most other types of yoghurts, although many Greek local small firms produce yoghurts made from sheep's milk or a mixture of cow's and sheep's milk, with even thicker texture. In the yoghurt market, a relatively small by world standards Greek company, Fage, appears to be developing a strong position in the international arena.

The Fage story began in 1920 in Athens, where the founder of the company opened a little corner shop selling various dairy products. Among these, the most popular proved to be a particular type of yoghurt, the strained yoghurt variety. In the 1920s, yoghurt was considered as a traditional part of the Greek diet, but old-fashioned. By 1954 the two sons of the founder, Ioannis and Kyriakos Filippou, had already established a distribution network, which allowed them to sell their yoghurt in the wider Athens area. Following their original success, they build a small yoghurt manufacturing unit in 1964, which was replaced by a bigger and better establishment in 1974. The demand for their products was constantly on the rise, helped by the fact that Greeks are one of the world's highest per capita consumers of yoghurt, and in 1975 they introduced the first branded Fage yoghurt in the Greek market.

Fage accelerated its efforts to change the positioning of yoghurt as a product in the customers' minds. It invested highly in product innovations and marketing communications, developing the product's taste consistency and securing a longer self life. Branding supported the company's growth, secured its future and extended its product life cycle. The company managed to modernise its product image and to build strong brand awareness in the Greek market. In 2002, its product range included traditional types of yoghurt, as well as products which are perceived as more innovative in the country, such as fruit and cereal combination yoghurts. The majority of the Greeks are familiar with its most popular yoghurt brand names, namely, Total and Ageladitsa targeting the mass market. The rest of its yoghurt brands (Silouet, Junior and Fruyo) are targeting more specific customer segments, such as the weight-conscious, children or the novelty market, and are well known to these segments. Fage is the market leader in the Greek market. In 2001 its market share in sealed yoghurt was 58%.

Although yoghurt is Fage's most popular product, the company extended its brand portfolio and it now produces various other dairy products. The development of new innovative products appears to be the strategy currently employed by most of the major European competitors and Fage is very innovative. In 2002, it had 30 product lines and marketed 125 products under 50 brand names, including milk (since 1993), cheese (since 1991) and more recently dairy desserts and delicatessen products.

After securing its position in the Greek market, Fage has successfully introduced its products in the international arena. The brand Total was the first strained yoghurt to be launched in Europe. In 2001 the brand was sold by approximately 25000 retail outlets in 22 countries, through independent sales representatives and distributors. The product was very well received and adopted by the consumers in most of these countries, helped also by the fact that every year in excess of 11 million tourists visit Greece and have the chance to purchase and taste the product there. As a response, many competitors responded by introducing 'Greek Style' yoghurts. However Fage managed to develop a positioning allowing it to differentiate its brands from those offered by the other international players. In 2001 Total was the market leader in branded strained yoghurts in the UK and had a notable market share in other European countries.

Although the various types of plain and flavoured Total yoghurt are the most popular products in the export markets, other Fage products are also exported. Taking advantage of the demand for some of the most popular types of Greek cheeses and the legislation relating to the Protected Designation of Origin (PDO) status of the European Union, Fage is exporting, in addition, its cheese products, with Feta on the top of the list.

Fage is basing its positioning heavily on its country of origin, and associates its name and products with Greece. Based on this strategy, the company develops a competitive position that is difficult to imitate. None of the major international competitors in the dairy industry could imply that they are selling authentic Greek products. Although other Greek companies have entered the international market, mostly with cheese products, Fage is now more exposed and experienced and it can rely on its already established reputation.

The company is clearly attempting to develop further its international image and to communicate with its current and potential customers in the various countries it operates. For example, the decision to become one of the main sponsors of the Athens 2004 Olympics, indicates the company's dedication and single mindedness to maintain and enforce its position in the consumer's minds as an important international player in the dairy industry and support its Greek positioning.

Following the international trends, Fage is constantly improving its targeting. Some of the more specific smaller groups of customers (i.e., market niches) are perceived by the company as very important for its future development. For example, the children's yoghurt segment is perceived as one of the key areas for future development.

Note

1.   This item was contributed by Dr C. Veloutsou, Department of Business and Management, University of Glasgow, Scotland.

Bibliography

Euromonitor (2001), European Market for Ice Cream, Yoghurt and Chilled Desserts
Fage (2001), Annual Report
Fage www.fage.gr
Keynote (2001), Milk & Dairy Products Market Report

BIBLIOGRAPHY

Baumol, W.J (1977), *Economic Theory and Operations Analysis*, 4th edn, Prentice-Hall.
Henderson, J. and Ouandt, R.E. (1980), *Microeconomic Theory*, 3rd edn, McGraw-Hill.
McElroy, F.W. (1969), 'Returns to Scale, Euler's Theorem, and the Form of Production Functions', *Econometrica*, **37**(2): 275–279.
Pappas, J.L. and Hirschey, N. (1990), *Managerial Economics*, 6th edn, The Dryden Press.
Walters, A.A. (1963), 'Production and Cost Functions: An Econometric Survey', *Econometrica*, **31**(1–2): 1–66.

chapter seven

Cost Analysis

Learning outcomes

After studying this chapter you should know about:

- Opportunity cost

- Direct–indirect costs, explicit–implicit costs

- Incremental–sunk costs, fixed–variable costs

- Short- and long-run costs

- Cost functions and cost curves

- Long-run costs and plant size

- Economies/diseconomies of scale and cost elasticity

- Minimum efficient scale (size) MES

- Learning or Experience curve

- Economies of scope

- Breakeven analysis

7.1 INTRODUCTION

Economic theory suggests that the cost of production is one of the most significant determinants of the quantities and prices of goods and services. Costs determine the firm's supply of its output, which by interacting with demand enables firms to arrive at their equilibrium position, given their objectives. However, it is also the case that practically every managerial decision involves a comparison between costs and benefits. For example, introducing a new product (or abandoning an existing one) requires a comparison of the costs and benefits associated with the introduction (or abandonment) of the product. Similarly, buying a new machine, or building a new warehouse requires a comparison of costs and benefits of the project. The same is also true of deciding to increase the rate of output by hiring more variable inputs, or of deciding to use subcontracting instead of own facilities, or to rent out such facilities. It follows that cost analysis is a very versatile and useful tool at the hands of management, but there are various concepts of costs and different approaches towards it by economists and accountants, consequently, an understanding of the nature of costs is essential in decision making.

7.2 THE NATURE OF COSTS – THE CONCEPT OF OPPORTUNITY COST

A central concept in economics is that of opportunity cost. Opportunity cost merely expresses the foregone opportunities in using a resource in a particular way and considers what that resource would have earned in its best alternative use. For example, if a person buys a car for €10 000, its opportunity cost is what that sum of money would have earned in its next best opportunity. If a firm commits €50 000 building a warehouse, its opportunity cost is what that amount would have earned for the firm in its next best opportunity. In other words, one thinks of alternative uses or opportunities open to individuals, firms etc. for their resources, and of the various such opportunities we pick the one where the resources earn the highest value, in order to express what we have foregone by using the resources in the way we have.

In decision making, the concept of opportunity cost plays a crucial role in helping allocate scarce resources. To illustrate what is involved, suppose that a plumber, employed by a firm and earning currently €30 000 per year, decides to set up his own business. He invests €5000 of his savings to buy his tools, which can be resold at any time for the same amount of money. In addition, he uses one room of his house, which could be rented out for €500 per month, as office and storeroom for his business. Assume that he is indifferent, from the psychic point of view, as between being self-employed or working for somebody else and that the only thing that prompted him to become self-employed was the prospect of higher rewards, and also that tax rates are such that his tax position will not be affected by his decision. At the end of his first year in self-employment his gross receipts are €50 000 and his expenses for various materials total €15 000, he reckons that since he made €35 000, which is more than the €30 000 he was earning before, his decision to work for himself was justified. Further, he expects that current conditions will be repeated in the future and looks forward to earning an extra €5000 per year from self-employment as compared to working for somebody else. Is he right to congratulate himself?

Our plumber has only looked at what his labour would have earned him elsewhere (€30 000) but has omitted to look at the cost of the other resources he is using, namely, his €5000 tied up in his business and the alternative use of the room in his house. His €5000 deposited with a building society or a bank would have earned him interest. If the rate of interest on such accounts is 5% per annum, he would have earned €250 in a year, which he foregoes by having his €5000 tied up in his business. Also, renting out the room of his house, currently used for his business, would have earned him another €6000 pounds per year. It follows that the true cost, in terms of alternative opportunities, of the resources tied up in his business are: the wages/salary he would have earned elsewhere (€30 000), the interest (€250) and the rent (€6000), i.e., a total of €36 250, which must be compared with the €35 000 his own business has netted him. Clearly, the plumber is worse off by €1250 per year working for himself, rather than for somebody else and he should reconsider his decision.

However, while the above example illustrates that the use of the opportunity cost concept provides a better yardstick of profitability, nevertheless, the profit and loss account drawn up by the plumber (or his accountant), for the purposes of submitting his tax return will show, correctly, that his business' income for the year was €35 000. What matters for the tax authorities are the actual historical receipts and costs, which determine profit or loss on which tax is levied. These become the relevant magnitudes for the particular task of tax liability. However, from the point of view of the plumber's (or managerial) decision to proceed or not with self employment, the relevant costs are the opportunity costs, as shown. This demonstrates that the relevant costs, defined as the costs having a bearing on a particular decision, may differ according to the task or decision, and it is such relevant costs that must be identified and used in the decision.

Other cost concepts, used extensively in managerial decisions, which we shall consider, briefly, are direct and indirect costs, explicit and implicit costs, incremental and sunk costs and short- and long-run costs.

7.2.1 Direct and indirect costs

The basis of the distinction between direct and indirect costs is the ability or not of management to identify and trace costs to a specific product, group of products, activity, operation and so on. Where costs can be, thus, ascertained and charged to specific lines of products or operations they are called direct. On the other hand, indirect costs are costs which cannot be identified and traced to a specific product, group of products, activity or operation. Such indirect costs are overheads of all kinds (although some overheads may be direct to some departments), which are still charged to individual products or operations on the grounds that they are related to the volume of operations. Examples of such indirect costs include depreciation charges, as well as gas and electricity bills, which are affected by the level of output. In the case of a multiple product firm, the joint costs of producing a package, consisting of different products, cannot be traced to the individual products and, therefore, such joint costs are allocated in the same way as the indirect costs. Clearly, the task of ascertaining and charging costs to individual products is more pronounced in multiple product firms, but for the purposes of pricing policy what is important is the ability to relate costs to groups of products, connected on the supply and/or demand side, rather than to tracing exactly such costs to the individual products.

7.2.2 Explicit and implicit costs

Explicit costs are actual costs incurred in the production of goods and services, that is, expenses for the payment of factors of production, such as wages, salaries, rents and rentals for buildings and machinery, interest on loans, dividends, raw materials, advertising and so on. These are cash costs entering the firm's books and recognised as legitimate expenses by the tax authorities, for the assessment of the firm's tax liability. Explicit costs are straightforward accounting costs, easy to comprehend, and they are taken into account in decision making in estimating incremental costs. However, there may also be costs for which no actual payment has been made, consequently, they are not entering the firm's books, and so they tend to be ignored in decision making. Such non-cash costs are called implicit costs and are as important in decision making as the explicit ones, however, they can only be established by reference to their opportunity cost. For example, where the entrepreneur or the firm is using owned facilities for which no payment is made, i.e., a shop or a building for which no rent is paid, the implicit cost of the resource is the rent it would command if it were decided to rent it out to other parties. In the earlier example of the plumber, the implicit cost of using the room in his house as an office/storeroom for his business is its opportunity cost, that is the rent the room would fetch if it were rented out, i.e., €6000 per year. Similarly, there is the implicit cost of the plumber's services for which he is not charging his business, that is, what he would have earned by working elsewhere, i.e., €30 000 per year. It is obvious that, where a particular decision involves explicit as well as implicit costs, both have to be taken into consideration in evaluating such decision. Otherwise, by ignoring implicit costs, we are failing to consider foregone opportunities of resources, which leads to incorrect decisions.

7.2.3 Incremental and sunk costs

Incremental costs are the extra costs a firm incurs as a result of accepting a particular decision. They are differential costs as between accepting the decision or doing without it, i.e., they involve a change in cost brought about by a change in business activity. This may involve accepting a new order, building a new warehouse, buying a machine, increasing the level of output, and so on. In this sense, the incremental cost is similar to the marginal cost (MC) of the marginal analysis. However, while MC refers to the extra cost incurred as a result of an infinitesimal change in a particular variable, say output, incremental costs are the *total extra* costs associated with the decision, and as such they are much broader in nature than MCs. This means that *all* costs affected by the decision must be considered, including future costs.

Estimating the incremental cost of a decision is not always easy. For example, assume that a firm has currently spare capacity and it is offered an order priced at €5000. The direct cost of labour and materials of this order is €4000, but a full allocation of overheads results in a price of €6000. Clearly, the firm has an incentive to accept the order, since the price offered (5000) covers the relevant incremental costs (4000) and makes some contribution towards overheads and profit and since there do not seem to be currently any other alternatives open to the firm to fill in the slack. The overheads are not affected by accepting or rejecting the order, and so they should be ignored. However, if the firm expects a recovery soon and a regular stream of orders priced at 6000, which includes the fully allocated overheads charge, or even at a higher price, the acceptance of the earlier order at 5000 may force the firm to reject more profitable future orders, because of lack of capacity and, thus, forego the opportunities to add to its profits. In this case, future costs become important and are part of the relevant costs to be considered. It follows then that in order to arrive at the incremental costs of the decision, all such relevant costs affected by the decision, both current and future, should be taken into account.

On the other hand, costs which are invariant with respect to the decision are called sunk costs. Sunk costs will have to be met irrespective of the change in activity and are irrelevant as far as the decision is concerned, thus, they should be ignored.

7.2.4   Fixed and variable costs

A distinction usually made in economics is between fixed and variable costs. Fixed or constant costs are invariant with respect to output. They are incurred by the firm irrespective of the level of production. Examples of fixed costs include rents on buildings, rates, interest on loan capital, rentals on leased machinery and equipment, depreciation charges (when measured as a function of time than output) and certain administrative expenses, such as office lighting and salaries of personnel, which is retained even when productive activity is curtailed or even stopped temporarily, for purposes of maintenance and/or security of buildings and so on. Fixed costs are sometimes interchangeably referred to by economists as overheads, although in accounting practice overheads are similar to indirect costs, and they may include not only fixed but also some costs that are variable.

By contrast, costs that are a function of output are called variable costs. The cost function, of which more below, showing the relationship between cost and output, is derived from the relevant production function, the expansion path and the prices of the inputs. Variable costs include the value of materials and other supplies used in the productive process, as well as energy, labour, depreciation charges (when measured as a function of output rather than time) and so on. Such costs may vary proportionally with the level of output, less than or more than proportionally, depending on the stages of production, which in turn depends on the law of variable proportions, discussed earlier.

However, some of the fixed costs mentioned above may be fixed within prescribed levels of output, and when the limits are reached, such costs also tend to vary. For example, the number of skeleton staff, required to maintain a ship that has been laid up as a result of a depression, may have to be dismissed altogether if it were decided to send the ship to the breaking yard, because the depression is expected to last much longer. Also, the number of foremen required by a firm may change only once a prescribed level of output is reached, i.e., such changes occur in a discontinuous manner. Labour costs associated with these changes, which are fixed within prescribed ranges of output, but vary outside these ranges, are called semi-variable costs.

7.2.5 Short- and long-run costs

Fixed and variable costs are connected with another cost distinction, namely, short- and long-run costs. In economics, short-run is that period of time within which at least one factor of production remains fixed. Long-run, on the other hand, is defined as that period of time which is long enough for all factors of production to become variable. The short-run implies that the firm is constrained in its expansion by previous capital budgeting decisions, and other long-term commitments, which have fixed its plant capacity. In such a case, increased variable factors of production may be combined with a fixed amount of machines to produce more output, but the number of shifts or the amount of overtime undertaken and, generally, the use of variable inputs is limited by the existing plant capacity. Therefore, short-run costs vary with the degree of plant utilisation or the level of output. During the short-run the firm incurs fixed costs and also variable costs; the latter being a function of output. Since in the short-run a given stock of resources (capital equipment) produces, in combination with variable factors, a flow of output, the short-run costs of such output may vary proportionally with output, less than or more than proportionally, depending on the law of variable proportions and input prices.

The length of the short-run cannot be given on *a priori* considerations. It depends on the nature of the production process and the degree of resource specialisation. In some cases, like a barber's shop or an advertising agency using rented accommodation, the short-run may be a matter of months, i.e., the time it takes for their leases to expire and free them from their past commitments. In other cases, like shipbuilding, where the firm has committed itself to large investment in fixed capital, the short-run will, typically, extend over the lifetime of that capital equipment. Generally, the longer it takes to amortise existing fixed capital equipment, the longer the short-run becomes, since amortisation is the way fixed resources become variable. Also, the more specialised the resources used, the longer the short-run is, because the firm cannot easily dispose of such specialised factors, on account of their limited alternative uses.

Long-run costs, on the other hand, are a function of output level and plant size. It follows then that as the firm is contemplating changing its plant size (moving from one short-run position to another), all costs become variable. In the short-run the firm's problem is the optimum utilisation of its existing plant size. In the long-run the problem becomes one of selecting the most appropriate plant size, in order to minimise the cost of production entailed by the conditions prevailing at that time. Therefore, the long-run costs would be showing the minimum cost of producing each output level, if the firm were allowed to vary the size of its plant.

7.3 COST FUNCTIONS AND COST CURVES

The cost function, expressing cost as a function of output, can be derived from knowledge of the production function, the expansion path and the prices of the inputs. In general we can write the short-run cost function as follows:

$$C = f(Q) + B \qquad (1)$$

where B is the fixed cost to be paid irrespective of the level of production, while the part $f(Q)$ gives the total variable cost. To find the cost function, we choose one point on the expansion path. Such a point corresponds to particular levels of inputs, which we can substitute in the production function to obtain the level of output. By multiplying the quantities of inputs required to produce that level of output by their prices we derive the total variable cost of the output and, finally, by adding the fixed costs we arrive at the total cost (TC) of production.

By way of illustration we utilise the information of Table 6.1. It is recalled that the postulated production function was given by:

$$Q = 10K^2L^2 - 0.2K^3L^3$$

where K and L were the quantities of capital and labour used, and their prices were €1000 per machine and €5 for the wage rate. In a short-run analysis, the amount of capital used was fixed at 10 machines, i.e., $K = 10$, which meant that the production function could be rewritten as:

$$Q = 1000L^2 - 200L^3$$

giving output as a function of the variable input, labour, alone. In terms of costs, the firm incurred in the short-run fixed costs of €10 000 (10×1000), i.e., the cost of capital, which is fixed at $K = 10$. Additionally, since the wage rate was €5, variable costs of €5 per man were also incurred. Since, for the purposes of Table 6.1 the unit of labour was taken to be 1000 men, the price per unit of labour was €5000. Therefore, in terms of the example illustrated in Table 6.1, the TC function can be written as:

$$TC = 10\,000 + 5000L$$

This information allows us to construct Table 7.1, with the various cost concepts derived as follows:

Average fixed cost = (fixed cost)/output = FC/Q

Average variable cost = (variable cost)/output = VC/Q

Average total cost = (total cost)/output = TC/Q

Marginal cost = d(TC)/dQ = $\dfrac{\text{Price of labour}}{\text{Marginal product of labour}}$

according to the discussion of Section 6.4.

Table 7.1 Total, average fixed, average variable, average and marginal costs

L (000s)	Fixed cost	Variable costs	Total costs	AV/GE Fixed cost	AV/GE VAR/LE cost	AV/GE Total cost	Marginal cost
0.1	10 000	500	10 500	1020.408	51.020	1071.429	25.7732
0.2	10 000	1 000	11 000	260.417	26.042	286.458	13.2979
0.3	10 000	1 500	11 500	118.203	17.730	135.934	9.1575
0.4	10 000	2 000	12 000	67.935	13.587	81.522	7.1023
0.5	10 000	2 500	12 500	44.444	11.111	55.556	5.8824
0.6	10 000	3 000	13 000	31.566	9.470	41.035	5.0813
0.7	10 000	3 500	13 500	23.730	8.306	32.036	4.5208
0.8	10 000	4 000	14 000	18.601	7.440	26.042	4.1118
0.9	10 000	4 500	14 500	15.056	6.775	21.831	3.8052
1.0	10 000	5 000	15 000	12.500	6.250	18.750	3.5714
1.1	10 000	5 500	15 500	10.595	5.828	16.423	3.3921
1.2	10 000	6 000	16 000	9.137	5.482	14.620	3.2552
1.3	10 000	6 500	16 500	7.996	5.198	13.194	3.1526
1.4	10 000	7 000	17 000	7.086	4.960	12.046	3.0788
1.5	10 000	7 500	17 500	6.349	4.762	11.111	3.0303
1.6	10 000	8 000	18 000	5.744	4.596	10.340	3.0048
1.7	10 000	8 500	18 500	5.243	4.456	9.699	3.0012
1.8	10 000	9 000	19 000	4.823	4.340	9.163	3.0193
1.9	10 000	9 500	19 500	4.468	4.244	8.712	3.0600
2.0	10 000	10 000	20 000	4.167	4.167	8.333	3.1250
2.1	10 000	10 500	20 500	3.910	4.105	8.015	3.2175
2.2	10 000	11 000	21 000	3.689	4.058	7.748	3.3422
2.3	10 000	11 500	21 500	3.501	4.026	7.526	3.5063
2.4	10 000	12 000	22 000	3.340	4.010	7.350	3.7202
2.5	10 000	12 500	22 500	3.200	4.000	7.200	4.0000*
2.6	10 000	13 000	23 000	3.080	4.010	7.090	4.3706
2.7	10 000	13 500	23 500	2.980	4.030	7.010	4.8733
2.8	10 000	14 000	24 000	2.900	4.060	6.960	5.5804
2.9	10 000	14 500	24 500	2.830	4.110	6.940	6.6313
3.0	10 000	15 000	25 000	2.780	4.170	6.950	8.3333
3.1	10 000	15 500	25 500	2.740	4.240	6.980	11.5207
3.2	10 000	16 000	26 000	2.710	4.340	7.050	19.5313
3.3	10 000	16 500	26 500	2.700	4.460	7.160	75.7576
3.333	10 000	16 665	26 665	2.700	4.500	7.200	Infinite

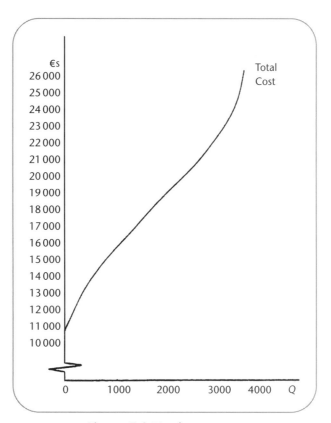

Figure 7.1 Total cost curve

The above information can be illustrated in Figures 7.1 and 7.2, by drawing the curves for the average fixed cost (AFC) of production, the average variable cost (AVC), the average total cost (ATC or AC), which is simply the sum of the AVC and AFC at each level of output and, finally, the MC. Clearly, there is a close correspondence between the information of Tables 6.1 and 7.1. Since the variable factor, L, is bought at a constant price of €5 per unit, it follows that the stage of increasing returns to the factor L corresponds to decreasing unit costs, while at the stage of diminishing returns we have increasing unit costs. Particularly, what happens to the MC of production (last column of Table 7.1 and Figure 7.2) is the direct consequence of the movement of the marginal product of labour (L), dQ/dL, given in Table 6.1 and illustrated in Figure 6.2.

It is the operation of the law of variable proportions which explains the 'U' shape of the AVC, AC and MC curves. However, despite the fact that we have presented the various cost curves of Figure 7.2 with a smooth 'U' shape, the law of variable proportions allows for the case of a long horizontal section in the MC curve. Indeed, this is the case of constant returns, which corresponds to constant MC. It is perfectly possible that for some range of output, the marginal product of the variable factor remains constant and so does the MC; therefore the MC curve will have a long horizontal section, will coincide with the AVC curve and look like the one shown in Figure 7.3. Indeed, empirical research provides evidence that unit costs decline at first as output increases, reach a minimum at point A

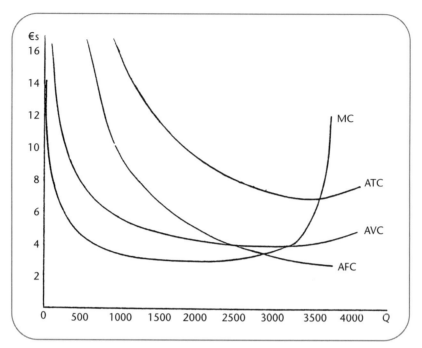

Figure 7.2 Average fixed cost, average variable cost, average total cost and marginal cost curves

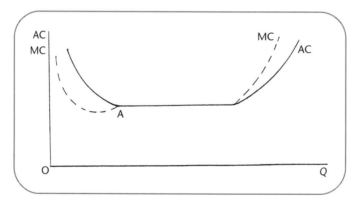

Figure 7.3 L-shaped average cost curves

and then remain constant over larger ranges of output, before start rising as we are approaching the plant capacity, as indicated in Figure 7.3. This is the result of economies or returns to scale, which is discussed below.

7.3.1 Long-run costs and plant size

The preceding analysis has been a short-run one, since one factor of production has been held constant. However, as we noted earlier, in the long-run when the firm is able to vary all factors of production, the problem becomes one of choosing the right plant size, i.e., the one which minimises the cost of production. It follows then that long-run costs are a function of output and plant size. An example of this

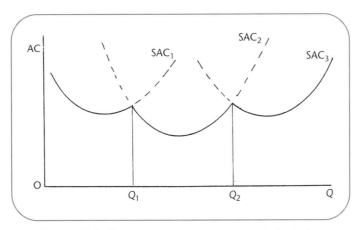

Figure 7.4 Short-run average costs and plant size

is provided in the context of the competitive equilibrium of the firm in Chapter 10, which illustrates that while in the short-run the TC function $TC = 0.03q^3 - 0.9q^2 + 10q + 5$ with an equilibrium output of $q = 22$ yields average cost of production of €4.95, by varying the size of plant in the long-run to accommodate the changed conditions, the TC function becomes $TC = 0.03q^3 - 0.95q^2 + 11q$. This function has an equilibrium output of $q = 20$ and yields unit cost of €4, demonstrating that in the long-run the objective of the firm is to produce at minimum cost.

In the long-run, since the firm is able to vary all its inputs, the problem becomes one of choosing the plant size which minimises the cost of production. The point at which unit cost is minimised is referred to as the efficient capacity of the plant in question. However, once the firm has committed itself to a plant size and built it, a new short-run starts. To begin with, assume that a firm has the option of three plant sizes A, B and C, whose average cost curves are given by SAC_1, SAC_2 and SAC_3, as shown in Figure 7.4. Plant size A involves relatively low capital expenditure, and if the firm expects its output not to exceed Q_1, then it has an incentive to build and operate plant size A, since unit costs are lowest. However, such costs rise when its capacity is reached and for levels of output between Q_1 and Q_2 plant size B is the most appropriate one; while for output levels beyond Q_2, unit costs will be lowest with plant size C. Plant sizes B and C use, progressively, more capital than does A. So, in this case the long-run average cost (LAC) curve can be approximated by the lowest portions of the three SAC curves, i.e., the continuous line in Figure 7.4. This illustrates the discrete case, where plants are available in specific sizes only.

However, if one could envisage that for each output level the firm could build the plant of the appropriate size to minimise the cost of production, we could have a whole continuum of plant sizes each with their SAC curve, and the corresponding LAC curve will be a much smoother curve still having the 'U' shape and providing an 'envelope' to the various SAC curves. Each point of the LAC curve would be tangential to a SAC curve and the LAC curve will show the minimum possible unit cost for the different output levels. This is demonstrated in Figure 7.5, illustrating the continuous case and showing the LAC curve as having a much flatter 'U' shape than the SAC curves. In practice, due to the indivisibilities, the firm is likely to be limited in its choice of plant sizes and, thus, the discrete case of Figure 7.4 may

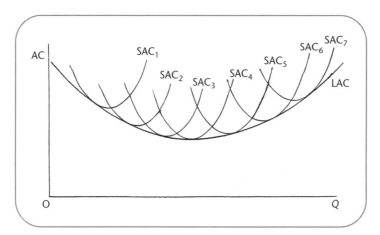

Figure 7.5 Long- and short-run cost curves

reflect better the range of choices available, than the continuous case of Figure 7.5. Nevertheless, the principles involved are essentially the same. The shape of the LAC curve depends on the availability of economies of scale, or returns to scale, which allow unit costs to decline at first as output increases, and then rise when diseconomies of scale set in. Therefore, we need to examine how such economies and diseconomies arise.

7.3.2　Economies and diseconomies of scale and the cost elasticity

In introducing the question of economies of scale we may recall the discussion of the last section of Chapter 6, which illustrated how output changes when *all* inputs are changed by some given proportion. Here, we are concerned with the behaviour of costs as output rises, and a useful concept in this context is the cost elasticity, which is a measure of the responsiveness of costs to changes in output. More specifically, the cost elasticity, e, is defined as the percentage change in TC brought about by one percentage change in output (Q), i.e.,

$$e = \frac{\delta(TC)/TC}{\delta Q/Q} = \frac{\delta(TC)}{\delta Q} \times \frac{Q}{TC}$$

Assuming fixed input prices, for a given increase in output, say by 10%, if $e < 1$, costs increase by less than 10% and this case corresponds to increasing returns to scale. If $e = 1$, costs and output increase at the same rate, which indicates constant returns to scale and, finally, if $e > 1$, costs increase faster than output, corresponding to decreasing returns to scale. This illustrates that the concept of cost elasticity with respect to output and the output elasticity with respect to inputs (encountered in Chapter 6), are linked through the relations of cost and production functions.

However, in the long-run, largely because of technological changes, firms do not normally change all their inputs in the same proportion as they expand output. Also, the nature of the inputs may be changed as output increases and, in addition, input prices may also change. This means that economies of scale, can be 'real', when input proportions change and 'pecuniar', when input prices change. Economies of scale are responsible for the fall in unit costs to reach a minimum, like point A in Figure 7.3, as a result of producing a larger level of output. Such economies can be 'internal' to the firm, as well as 'external'. The former, which are the most important ones, include among others, labour, plant or technical/engineering, marketing, purchasing and managerial economies and occur as a result of specific managerial decisions inside the firm, to change its own organisation; while the latter arise where the increase in the size of a particular industry causes the costs of the firms making up the industry to fall.

Labour economies of scale are brought about by division of labour and specialisation, although the extent of such division is clearly limited by the size of the market, since in a small firm workers are doing several tasks, which limits their dexterity as compared with workers of larger firms who can specialise in one task, and perform it more efficiently. Also, larger firms tend to be more capital intensive, which increases labour productivity further. Technical/engineering or plant economies arise mostly as a result of the indivisible nature of various types of capital equipment, which allows the utilisation of processes with better price-performance ratios. For example, a 300 000 tons tanker costs much less than three 100 000 tons tankers and its running costs in terms of fuel and crew are also lower. Also, the large volume of production enables the firm to introduce automated processes, like robotics, which involve high initial costs, as compared with alternative production processes, but the former are more cost effective, because their higher productive efficiency allows the spreading of such set-up costs over a larger output, thus, causing unit costs to fall. However, unless the firm has the demand to justify such high initial costs, it would be better advised to use alternative processes, which will be more cost effective for the sort of production run anticipated. For example, a car manufacturer expecting to sell around 5000 units a year will have little use of an automated plant, whose efficient capacity is 500 000 units a year, but whose cost is prohibitive for the demand conditions facing the firm.

Economies in marketing result from the basic consideration that, within wide ranges, the cost of marketing does not vary proportionally with the level of output. A large firm operating nationally and/or internationally can advertise through television, thus, reaching, potentially, the whole population. Also, it could replicate, with suitable adjustments, the same advertising message for other markets, therefore, reducing significantly the unit cost of the advertising expenditure. However, for a small firm, operating in a small local market, such form of advertising is ruled out by its cost and the alternatives may very well result in a higher cost per unit. Also, larger firms producing more than one product, particularly when such products are related on the demand side, find that it is not 20 times as difficult to sell 20 different products than it is to sell one, because of complementarities and brand loyalty.

Purchasing economies arise from bulk buying of various inputs, enabling the large firm to acquire significant discounts from its suppliers, which are not available to the small firm. This extends also to the capital market, where the large firm is able to derive better terms for its credit, as compared with small firms, in the form of lower interest rates, easier repayment schedules and so on. In other words, the quasi monopsonistic power of the large firm provides it with a significant cost advantage, which contributes to the lowering of unit costs at higher levels of output.

Managerial economies result from the ability of the managerial team to organise, within broad limits, a large level of output equally efficiently as a small one, without management costs varying directly in proportion to output. In all these instances of economies of scale the effect is a fall in unit costs as output rises. This is similar to the fall in AFCs as output increases in the case of the short-run. The difference in the long-run is that all factors of production are variable, but they can be more efficiently combined at higher levels of output than lower ones, because of the indivisible nature of such factors. It is not possible to divide factors into small units. In much the same way that a plant which is used at below capacity is producing less efficiently, a manager asked to produce half the current output can only do so less economically, since we cannot chop the manager in half.

Nevertheless, at very high levels of output not only are economies of scale exhausted but they are reversed into diseconomies. A larger output will have to be sold over a wider area, thus, transportation costs will tend to rise dispropor-tionately. Also, input prices may have to rise as output expands, because the firm may have difficulty in securing the extra inputs it needs, and it may have to offer a higher price to coax them away from their current occupations. The larger the firm, the more difficult the problems of its coordination and control become. It is not possible for the firm to go on increasing its output at constant unit cost, because it cannot always add to its managerial team new members, who are equally effi-cient. While education and training do have an impact, they require time and, clearly, the supply of management is not perfectly elastic. Indeed, management seems to be the bottleneck factor which causes eventually unit costs to rise.

7.3.3   Minimum efficient scale and empirical evidence on costs

The verification of the traditional theory of costs, analysed in the previous sections, requires consideration of the empirical evidence. The available evidence on costs includes various forms such as statistical cost studies, econometric estimates of cost curves, interviews and survey data. There are clearly problems of estimation and interpretation, making the results of the various studies less than conclusive, but most of the evidence tends to refute the U-shaped average cost curve of the traditional theory, which implies that diseconomies of scale are not observed in the real world, at least for the ranges of output contemplated. Rather, the evidence suggests that in the short-run total variable costs rise in proportion to output, which means that AVC and MC are constant and equal to each other, while in the long-run the average cost falls initially, as output expands, reaches a minimum, and thereafter remains constant as the scale of operations increases. This means that the evidence accepts the presence of economies of scale in practice but not of diseconomies, implying that the LAC curve is L-shaped rather than U-shaped.

The level of output at which LAC is first minimised is known as the minimum efficient scale (MES), and plays an important role both in the theory of industrial organisation and in decision making within the firm. From the point of view of the firm, MES shows the minimum scale or size of output required to reap the full economies of scale. If MES is small in relation to the market, the firm will have no difficulty in setting up a plant of the efficient size to compete on equal terms with other efficient firms. Also, since the efficient output is not very large, only modest marketing efforts may be required to sell it. However, the higher the MES is in relation to the total market, the more difficult it becomes for the firm to compete

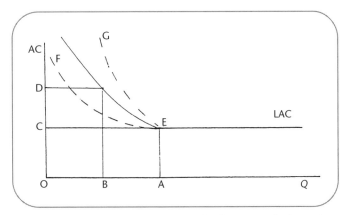

Figure 7.6 Cost disadvantage of sub-optimal plant size

efficiently, because, firstly, the initial cost of setting up the MES plant may be very high and, secondly and more importantly, the market may not be able to absorb this output, at the projected price, particularly in the case of a newly established firm. From the point of view of industrial organisation theory, a small MES is indicative of a less concentrated market, populated by a relatively large number of small efficient firms; whereas a high MES illustrates the case of a concentrated market, which allows only for a few large efficient firms. In other words, MES becomes an important barrier to entry facing new firms.

To overcome the difficulty of disposing of a large output necessitated by a large MES, firms may consider building a plant of sub-optimal size to produce half the output of the efficient scale, in which case a cost disadvantage is incurred. Figure 7.6 illustrates some of the points raised so far. The MES is given by output OA, but if the firm were to build a sub-optimal plant to produce OB, which is half of OA, it will incur a cost penalty per unit given by CD. Such cost penalties will be lower with a flatter LAC, like the portion FE than with a steeper one, like GE. Researchers have been interested both in the measurement of economies of scale and the MES and also the cost penalties of building and operating sub-optimal plants. Following the pioneering work of Bain (1956), in the context of US manufacturing, they have approached the problem by using technical information about the production processes involved, estimating physical input requirements, converting these into costs and considering the behaviour of costs as output changes. It should be stressed that such costs concentrate on raw materials, direct labour and capital inputs but exclude indirect costs, such as the expenses of the administration or the sales force and so on. So, whilst cost curves derived in this way can provide useful guidance for decision making, they do not necessarily give a complete picture of costs for the firm.

Pratten (1971), has undertaken a study on economies of scale in the UK manufacturing industry and Table 7.2 gives his findings for selected industries. Pratten's work shows that in some industries the MES was a significant proportion of the UK market, and the cost penalty of sub-optimal plants may appear high, thus, implying certain courses of action in terms, say, of merger activity, which could lead to economies of scale, but at the same time help increase concentration. However, changes in technology and, most importantly, the creation of the single market in the European Union necessitate a reconsideration of these findings.

Table 7.2 Economies of scale in UK manufacturing industry

Industry	MES in absolute terms	MES as % of UK output in 1969	% increase in costs at 50% of MES (value added per unit)
Oil	10 million tons per annum (m.t.p.a)	10	27
Chemicals			
Ethylene	300 000 tons p.a.	25	30
Sulphuric acid	1 m.t.p.a.	30	19
Dyes	>UK output for individual dyes	100	44
Synthetic fibres			
(a) Polymer	80 000 tons p.a.	33	23
(b) Filament yarn	40 000 tons p.a.	16	11
Beer	at least 1 million barrels p.a.	3	55
Bread	A throughput of 30 sacks of flour	1	30
Soap-detergents	per hour 70 000 tons p.a.	20	20
Cement	2 m.t.p.a.	10	17
Bricks	>25 million bricks p.a.	0.5	30
Steel via blast and LD furnaces	9 m.t.p.a.	33	12–17
Rolled steel products including wide strip	4 m.t.p.a.	80	13
Motor cars			
(a) One model	500 000 cars p.a.	25	10
(b) Range of models	1 million cars p.a.	50	13
Aircraft (one type)	>50 aircraft	>100	>25
Bicycles (range of models)	<100 000 bicycles p.a.	4	Small
Diesel engines			
(a) Range 1–100 h.p.	100 000 units p.a.	10	10
(b) Large marine ones	Annual output at least 100 000 h.p.	10	15
Turbo generators			
(a) One design	4 p.a	100	100
(b) Range of designs	>6 000 M.W. p.a.	50	50
Domestic electric appliances	>0.5 million units p.a.	20	12
Books (one title, hardback)	10 000 copies	100	50

Source: Pratten C.F. (1971), pp. 269–277.

Indeed, the European Commission has estimated that of the industries it surveyed in the run up to the Single Market, 89% had levels of MES less than l0% of the EU market, and 75% had less than 5%. Also, the cost disadvantage of operating sub-optimal plants was modest for most sectors. These findings suggest that most sectors can support at least 20 efficient producers and possibly more. Also, evidence provided by Geroski (1991) suggests that a large number of firms exist in UK industries where MES is high. Given that the distribution of plant sizes is large, it is inconceivable that this range of plant sizes would exist in the presence of large economies of scale and high cost disadvantage of operating sub-optimal plants. This may very well imply that the quest for economies of scale may have been overstated. In addition, continuing changes in technology mean that the MES is likely to fall. For example, the changes brought about in publishing by the revolution in information technology, means that the MES in books publishing has most certainly fallen.

The above discussion has certain implications about the structure of industries. The shape of the LAC, in conjunction with demand for the product, will determine the size of the firm (plant). So long as the efficient output can be sold profitably, firms will tend to grow to achieve that size. However, many firms in the UK operate beyond the MES output, which tends to imply that objectives other than cost minimisation may be at work, such as for example the desire to acquire monopoly power. We examine again some of these issues in the chapter on growth and merger policy.

7.3.4   The learning or experience curve

A related but distinct concept to economies of scale is provided by the learning or experience curve. It shows the relation between unit costs of production and cumulative increases in output. It is based on the idea that the efficiency of labour increases with practice and this causes unit costs to fall as output increases. Productivity of labour increases through the repetitive nature of many productive processes, to the extent that fewer resources are required to produce the next, say, 1000 units of the product as the previous 1000 units; since people learn from their experience and correct mistakes, cut out unnecessary waste and, generally, become more efficient.

We can measure the learning effect by considering the percentage fall in unit costs as output doubles over time. However, we must be careful here because we may also be getting the familiar economies of scale effect and also input prices may be changing. In so far, as the latter is concerned, we can overcome the problem by considering constant input prices between the two periods. In the case of economies of scale we move down along the same LRAC curve as output increases, but the learning effect is denoted by a downward shift of the LRAC. In Figure 7.7 the learning effect causes the unit cost curve to shift from $LRAC_1$ to $LRAC_2$ between periods 1 and 2. It is similar to the effect that a technological breakthrough might have on costs, and it shows that the experience gained by the workforce in period 1 in producing output OQ_1 at a unit cost OZ enables them to produce the same level of output in period 2 at a unit cost OY, giving a reduction per unit of ZY, due entirely to their increased knowledge, and representing the learning-curve effect. However, as the firm expands output in the second period to

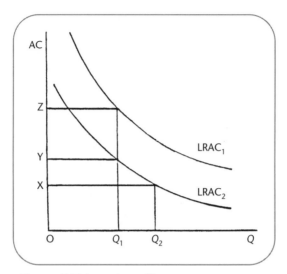

Figure 7.7 Learning effect on average costs

OQ_2, unit costs fall to OX, which incorporates also the economics of scale effect, given by XY.

The preceding analysis implies that the learning curve looks something like Figure 7.8, where at the beginning, and starting from low levels of output, learning and experience has a considerable effect in reducing unit costs, as improvements are spotted early on and adopted in the production process. However, as cumulated output increases to large levels, further improvements are less obvious and less significant. Nevertheless, a large firm producing a large level of output has a distinct cost advantage over smaller firms producing much smaller quantities, since the former can more easily adopt processes of quality control, monitoring performance, spotting and correcting faults all of which enable the workforce to learn and improve its productivity, by working through much higher volumes of output and, thus, derive also rewards for increased efficiency. Typically, the learning curve as drawn in Figure 7.8 is characterised by a constant percentage fall in unit costs as cumulative output increases.

In terms of Figure 7.8, we can measure the learning effect as the constant percentage fall in unit costs from OZ to OY when output doubles from OQ to O2Q over time. Assuming that OZ = €100 and OY = €80, this is given as:

$$\text{Learning rate} = \left(1 - \frac{OY}{OZ}\right) \times 100 = (1 - 80/100) \times 100 = (1 - 0.8) \times 100 = 20\%$$

This means that each time output doubles, unit costs fall by 20% and, therefore, the learning curve of Figure 7.8 can be called an *eighty per cent* learning curve. Learning effects of well over 20% have been experienced in practice by many firms, particularly in the areas of technologically advanced products, such as electronics, and this knowledge has been very useful to management. It has enabled management to derive more accurate forecasts of future movements in unit costs as output expanded, incorporate such cost savings – due to learning – into its future pricing policies, and coupled with possible elastic demand for the product, obtain not only increases in market size but also market share too.

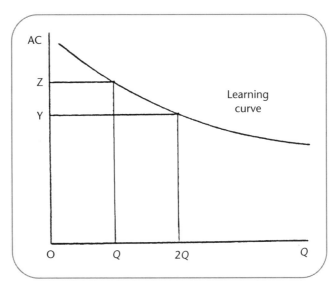

Figure 7.8 Learning curve

Knowledge of the constant learning rate allows us to utilise a mathematical formula to derive the learning curve giving us the unit cost reduction as we double output. The formula giving the learning curve is as follows:

$$C_X = AX^n$$

where

C_X = cost of producing the xth unit of output

A = cost of producing the Ath unit of output (usually the first)

X = Number of units of product

$n = \log S / \log 2$ and

S is the slope parameter of the learning curve.

In our case a constant rate of decline of 20% implies an 'eighty per cent' learning curve, i.e., $S = 0.8$. Assuming the unit cost for the first unit to be $A = €10\,000$, by utilising the above formula, we can estimate the unit cost for the 2nd, 4th, 8th, 16th, 32nd, 64th and so on units, as we double output, and construct the Table 7.3.

For example, to derive the cost for the 64th unit we substitute in the formula and get:

$$C_{64} = 10\,000 \times 64^{\log 0.8 / \log 2} = 10\,000 \times 64^{-0.322}$$

$$= \frac{10\,000}{64^{0.322}} = \frac{10\,000}{3.8158382} = 2621$$

Table 7.3 Derivation of the 80% learning curve

Units of output	Cost per unit
1	10 000
2	8 000
4	6 400
8	5 120
16	4 096
32	3 276
64	2 621
128	2 097
256	1 677
512	1 342

and similarly for the other values. It becomes apparent that the reduction in unit costs in the table follows the hypothesised constant 20% decline. For example, moving from the 32nd to the 64th unit we get: $3276 \times 0.2 = 655$ and so $3276 - 655 = 2621$, which confirms the figure in the table for the 64th unit. Thus, having constructed the learning curve, management may even consider underpricing the product in an effort to boost volume sales and derive the learning and experience benefits of higher production runs quickly, which in turn will reduce costs and so raise profits.

7.3.5 Economies of scope

By economies of scope we mean the reduction in unit costs resulting from the joint production of goods or services, rather than producing each product separately. Therefore, economies of scope arise in multiple product firms and indeed, help explain why firms have diversified into multiple product lines, because of the complementary nature of many goods and services. These complementarities necessitate that one looks at both direct and indirect effects for evaluating the profitability of any product line, as explained in the incremental approach.

Complementarities may exist in the production, distribution and marketing operations of many firms. Knowledge and expertise acquired in a particular product line may be easily and profitably translated into another line, through diversification. For example, a soft drinks manufacturer may diversify into food products, like Schweppes and Pepsi Co., and use their extensive distribution networks and marketing facilities to market both lines. Similarly, banks and other financial institutions may find that although personal current accounts are not as profitable as various other lines of financial services into which they have diversified (such as insurance, buying and selling shares, bonds and so on), nevertheless, such personal current account holders provide the banks with an easy target of prospective customers for other, more profitable, financial services. In other words, as explained in the chapter on pricing joint products, certain products, displaying strong complementarities, may be deliberately used as 'loss leaders' in an effort to maximise the firm's profits from its overall operations.

In summary, the concept of economies of scope is linked with economies of scale, since it involves diversification which will utilise certain existing facilities and capabilities. Also, it illustrates the areas of potential profitable new lines into which the firm may diversify.

7.4 COST–VOLUME–PROFIT ANALYSIS (BREAKEVEN ANALYSIS)

The cost–volume–profit analysis or breakeven analysis depicts the relationship between total revenue, total cost and profit as output varies. The exact nature of the relationship depends on the assumptions made regarding the revenue and cost functions. In the simple case of constant price and constant average variable (and marginal) cost, the total revenue and TC functions are both linear, as shown in Figure 7.9. Breakeven analysis is a useful tool for managerial decisions, as it shows the profitable and unprofitable output ranges.

For example, assume that a firm produces a product at a constant AVC of €4, but it also incurs fixed costs of €10 000. Demand conditions are such that the firm can sell all the output it can produce at a price of €12 per unit. Given these conditions, the firm wishes to know at what level of output it breaks even. The TC function is $TC = 10\,000 + 4Q$ and the total revenue function is $TR = 12Q$. Algebraically, the breakeven point, defined as the output at which total revenue is

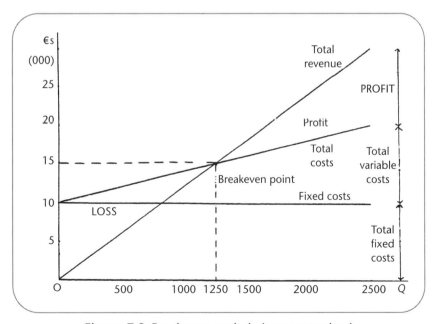

Figure 7.9 Breakeven analysis (constant prices)

equal to TC, is given by:

$$TR = TC$$
$$12Q = 10\,000 + 4Q$$
$$8Q = 10\,000$$

and so

$$Q = 10\,000/8 = 1250$$

Diagrammatically, the situation is illustrated in Figure 7.9 and as expected the breakeven point is given at the output level of 1250 units. Before this quantity is reached, the firm is making losses, after this quantity is passed, the firm moves into the profitable range of its operations. This suggests that in the case of constant price and AVC, the breakeven quantity can be determined as follows.

Given P = price of product, Q = quantity produced and sold, FC = fixed costs and B = AVC, we obtain TR = $P \times Q$ and TC = FC + $B \times Q$. Equating TR and TQ and solving for Q we get:

$$P \times Q = FC + B \times Q \quad \text{or} \quad P \times Q - B \times Q = FC \quad \text{or} \quad (P - B)Q = FC$$

and therefore

$$Q = FC/(P - B) \tag{2}$$

However, while this formula gives us the level of output at which the firm covers exactly its TCs, the breakeven analysis fails to tell us the quantity which maximises profits. As it is obvious from Figure 7.9, with linear functions the firm has an incentive to go on producing higher and higher levels of output. The profit function has no finite maximum, as it is not bounded from above. Continuing the earlier example, the profit function is written as:

$$\Pi = TR - TC = 12Q - 10\,000 - 4Q \quad \text{and so} \quad d\Pi/dO = 12 - 4 = 8$$

However, for a maximum we require $dP/dQ = 0$ and $d^2\Pi/dQ^2 < 0$ and as $d\Pi/dQ = 8$ neither the first nor the second-order conditions are satisfied, thus the profit function has no maximum.

Also, in the case where demand conditions are such that the firm can affect the price of the product, the demand function will be downward sloping and given by: $P = a - bQ$, resulting in a total revenue function of TR = $P \times Q = aQ - bO \times O = aQ - bQ^2$. If this is combined with a linear TC, or non-linear TC function (like a quadratic or cubic function), then we can derive a non-linear breakeven chart, which will indicate the ranges of profitable and unprofitable operations for the firm. This case is illustrated in Figure 7.10, showing that between output levels 0 to Q_1 and after Q_2 the firm incurs losses, while between Q_1 to Q_2 we have the range of profitable operations. Quantity Q_1 gives us the lower breakeven output, while Q_2 provides us with the upper breakeven point. Here it is also possible to establish the profit maximising level of output, as the one in which the vertical distance between the total revenue (TR) and TC curves in Figure 7.10 is the greatest, which is attained where MR = MC.

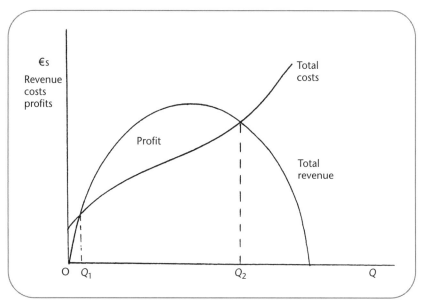

Figure 7.10 Breakeven analysis (linear demand)

Similarly, knowledge of the exact TR ard TC functions allows the algebraic derivation of the breakeven points, by setting up the profit function, equating it to zero and solving for Q.

SUMMARY

This chapter has provided a detailed discussion of various cost concepts, such as opportunity cost, direct and indirect costs, explicit and implicit costs and short-and long-run costs. It has looked at cost functions and cost curves and their derivation and considered economies and diseconomies of scale, the concept of minimum efficient size and the cost elasticity. In addition it has explained the learning or experience curve, economies of scope and breakeven analysis.

PROBLEMS

1. A firm buys and installs a piece of specialised machinery costing €20 000, in the expectation of high sales of the product made by the machine. The machine has no other use than its present one and its scrap value is negligible. Its estimated useful life is 5 years. However, due to a change in economic conditions

at the end of the first year the accounts show that the running costs of the machine are €3000, and the revenue brought in by the machine's operations amounts to €5500. The economic conditions are now forecast to remain the same for the future. In addition, the firm's accountant insists that the firm should also count as cost €4000 per year, as depreciation charge to recover the initial outlay. Clearly, if this advice were adopted, it would mean that a loss was incurred and the firm would be better off by stopping production altogether. Your advice has been sought on this matter. What advice would you give to the firm's management?

2. The accounts of a transport firm show that it pays out in 1 year labour costs of €360 000 and other operating costs of €280 000. It owns its own premises for storing goods and garaging its lorries, and has also used €80 000 of its own capital to help finance its operations during the preceding year. Its revenue for the year is €700 000; and the amount of €80 000 is retained for further financing. The firm also uses its own fleet of eight lorries, costing on average €25 000 each. The firm anticipates that the same figures are expected in future years. What do you think is the best course of action for the firm?

3. It has been estimated that the total annual cost of operating a hospital can be approximated by the relationship: $TC = 15\,000\,000 + 0.000135X^2$, where X is the number of patient days (taken to be a measure of output). Derive an expression for the relationship between the cost per patient day and the number of patient days. Also, estimate how big must a hospital be – in terms of patient days – in order to minimise the cost per patient day?

4. In the real world do you think that the shape of the (LAC) curve depends solely on the nature of the returns to scale exhibited by a firm's production function?

5. You have been given some sketchy information regarding the cost structure of your firm, as it appears in the following table, and you have been asked to complete the table by inserting the missing figures.

Q	TC	TFC	TVC	ATC	AFC	AVC	MC
0	100	—	—	x	x	x	x
1	—	—	—	130	—	—	—
2	—	—	40	—	—	—	—
3	—	—	—	48.34	—	—	—
4	—	—	—	—	—	—	3
5	—	—	50	—	—	—	—
6	—	—	—	28.67	—	—	—
7	—	—	—	—	—	15	—
8	—	—	160	—	—	—	—
9	—	—	—	—	—	30	—
10	—	—	—	—	—	—	180

6. A firm produces a toy which it sells to a few wholesalers. The weekly normal output (defined approximately as 80% of full capacity), is 250 units at a TC

of €4375. The firm has estimated that its full capacity output per week is 310 toys at a TC of €4825, which it can easily achieve.

(a) What is the average cost of normal output?
(b) What is the AVC?
(c) How much is the fixed cost?
(d) What is the AFC of normal output?

Currently the firm is negotiating with a foreign dealer the possibility of either of the following two contracts, on a trial basis of a month. The foreign dealer has offered to buy and market under a different brand name: Either: 50 units per week at a price of €12 per toy, or: 100 units per week at a price of €10 per toy. Should the firm accept either offer?

7. You have been told that a firm's TC function is given by:

$$TC = 2q^3 - 3q^2 - 12q$$

Find the equations for the MC and average cost functions. At what level of output is the average cost at its minimum? Do you expect to find such functions representing cost conditions in business? (Hint: Plot the functions to answer the last part.)

8. For each of the following general types of TC functions, find the MC, AVC, and average TC functions and the respective cost elasticities with respect to output. Plot the various cost functions and comment on the nature of returns exhibited by each category of cost function.

(a) $TC = a + bQ$ (Linear)
(b) $TC = a + bQ + cQ^2$ (Quadratic I)
(c) $TC = a + bQ - cQ^2$ (Quadratic II)
(d) $TC = a + bQ - cQ^2 + dQ^3$ (Cubic)

9. The number of units of a commodity that a firm produces is the product of the numbers of units of the two variable factors it uses. The firm buys the two inputs at fixed per unit prices of €16 and €4 respectively, and fixed costs are €100.

(a) Derive the TC function for the firm.
(b) If the selling price for the commodity is €4 per unit, what is the minimum quantity the firm would be prepared to produce to remain in business in (i) the short-run, (ii) long-run approximately?
(c) The firm can choose between a government order for 900 units at a price of €4 per unit and selling in the open market, where demand, Q, at any price P, is given by:

$$P = 50 + \frac{16}{\sqrt{Q}} - 0.25Q$$

APPENDIX: A CASE STUDY OF COST CUTTING AT BRITISH STEEL/CORUS

At the beginning of the 1980s the loss-making British Steel Corporation had registered its biggest annual loss of €1.8 billion. Yet, at the end of that decade the company had been privatised, was the fourth largest steel maker in the world with an output of 14.2 million tonnes, and was considered as one of the most profitable and efficient steel producers worldwide, with pre-tax profits of €733 m. in 1989–90 and €254 m. in 1990–91. This remarkable metamorphosis in performance was achieved by a combination of managerial decisions aimed at streamlining the company's operations. Major contributions to the streamlining efforts were made by a very large reduction in the workforce, the closure of a large number of old inefficient plants, some of which reminded one of nineteenth century steel-making processes rather than end of the twentieth, never mind the twenty-first, the concentration of bulk steel making in only four big integrated works and considerable investment activity to modernise such plants.

More specifically, during the 1980s the number of workers at British Steel declined from 166 400 to around 56 100 at the end of 1991, of which 51 600 in the UK and the rest overseas. This represented a massive 66.3% reduction in the labour force. Steel plants were also closed throughout the country, including two in South Wales, two in the Midlands, two in the North West, as well as works in Yorkshire, the North East and Scotland.

Bulk production of steel was concentrated in four major integrated plants at Scunthorpe, Redcar (Teeside), Llanwern (near Newport) and Port Talbot, following the announcement of the closure of the Ravenscraig works near Glasgow. Also, steel analysts expected that British Steel may have had to close yet another plant, either the one at Teeside or Scunthorpe, to achieve greater cost reductions. At the same time considerable investment in the remaining plants was undertaken. This is best exemplified at the changes in the hot strip mill at Port Talbot, which rolls billets of steel into sheet steel. Ten years earlier this cavern of a building, almost a mile long, would have had 100 or more men working in it. Following the changes and the investment, the process was controlled by a handful of men from a computerised control room. In addition, apart from investment in new plant, British Steel was spending on workforce training. In 1989–90 spending on labour training was nearly 1% of a turnover of €5113 million.

The effect of all these changes was a tremendous increase in productivity and profitability, as shown in the following tables:

Pre-tax cost of producing a tonne of cold-rolled coil, in $	
Taiwan	446
British Steel	470
South Korea	484
Brazil	486
Australia	487
Canada	507
France	508
America	510
West Germany	534
Japan	536

Pre-tax profit per tonne, in $	
British Steel	85
Japan	44
France	32
West Germany	9
America	4

The figures are based on representative plants in each country and apply to October 1990.
Source: Paine Weber, as quoted in Andrew Lorenz: Forging Steel's Future, *The Sunday Times*, 14 October 1990.

The results of the aforementioned exercise in cost cutting and the turnaround in performance led to the privatisation of British Steel, though many had argued that the desire to privatise the company forced through the closure programme and cutbacks in the workforce. Nevertheless, the senior management of the company believed that the main effect of privatisation was to liberate the company of political interference on closure and investment decisions. In addition, the management of the company considered that their freedom of political interference was their main advantage vis à vis the main competitors of British steel worlwide, since the latter were mainly either state-owned or quasi-state-owned.

However, that good performance of British Steel was short-lived. The collapse of the Iron Curtain in 1989, and the eventual opening up of the markets of Eastern Europe, provided additional competition and cheap imports of steel started flooding the markets, particularly the US and Western Europe. For example steel imports into the UK, from outside the EU, rose from 0.64 m.t. in 1991 to 2.2 m.t. in 2000 and 2.58 m.t. in 2001. British Steel, as a privatised company, struggled in the 1990s and saw the price of its shares (priced at 125p at privatisation) collapse, with shareholders receiving either little or no dividends at all. The basic reasons were sluggish demand for steel and considerable overcapacity worldwide. This, taken together with cheap imports from East Asia and Eastern Europe, lead to depressed prices for steel, although not everyone was affected equally. Certain lean companies, for example Nucor of the US, with new technologies, such as mini mills, and more flexible, lower cost (because of non-unionisation) workforce, were able to withstand the pressure of reduced demand much better. However, for most integrated steelmakers, i.e., those using blast furnaces, iron ore and coked coal to produce steel, the answer to the problem of overcapacity was consolidation, in an effort to close down inefficient plants, concentrate production in the most efficient plants and, thus, reduce costs.

Consequently, in 1999 British Steel merged with the Dutch company Koninklijke Hoogevens NV to form Corus Group. Profitability, however, did not improve and the company continued making losses throughout this period, culminating in a €385 mil. loss for 2001, when again no dividend was declared. In an effort to streamline their operations, additional restructuring measures were taken in 2001 as part of cost reduction. Accordingly, 'the Group reduced its UK flat products capacity by some 3 m.t. with the closure by the end of June (2001) of iron and steelmaking activities at Llanwern, together with finishing facilities at other works' (Corus Group Report to 30/6/2001). Additional productivity improvements were undertaken in other businesses, including the Dutch plant at IJmuiden, where it was anticipated that the plant would be operating at an annual rate of output of around 1 m.t. by early 2002. Clearly, the closure of the plant at Llanwern resulted in significant job losses. Also, Corus disposed of its 51% subsidiary investment in Avesta Sheffield. As a result of these restructuring measures, at the end of December 2001 the number of employees at Corus Group was down to 52 700 as compared with 64 900 at 31 December 2000, showing a loss of 12 200 jobs.

Whilst in the aftermath of these measures the share price of Corus recovered somewhat the recovery did not last and the company faced the ignominy of dropping out of the FTSE 100 towards the end of 2002 and by March 2003 it was staring insolvency in the face. In addition, serious disagreements arose between the Dutch and British partners, with the former accusing the latter that, instead of a 'marriage of equals', the British had taken control and draining the Dutch operations of the company of funds to finance the inefficient British part. The basic underlying feature was one of inefficiency, since the price of steel in the international market at $330–350 per tonne was allowing competitors to Corus such as ThyssenKrupp and Arcelor to be profitable, while Corus was losing more than a million pounds a day. As a result more cuts have been announced by the management, in order to reverse the situation.

BIBLIOGRAPHY

Bain, J.S. (1956), *Barriers to New Competition*, Cambridge, MA.

EEC (1988), 'The Economics of 1992', *European Economy*, No. 35, March.

Geroski, P.A. (1991), 'European Industrial Policy and Industrial Policy in Europe', *Oxford Review of Economic Policy*, **5**(2), 20–36.

Hay, D.A. and Morris, D.J. (1991), *Industrial Economics and Organisation: Theory and Evidence*, 2nd ed., Oxford University Press.

Henderson, J. and Quandt, R.E. (1980), *Microeconomic Theory*, 3rd ed., McGraw-Hill.

Johnston, J. (1960), *Statistical Cost Analysis*, McGraw-Hill.

Keat, P. and Young, P.K.Y. (1992), *Managerial Economics*, Macmillan.

Koutsoyiannis, A. (1979), *Modern Microeconomics*, 2nd ed., Macmillan.

Pappas, J.L. and Hirschey, M. (1990), *Managerial Economics*, The Dryden Press.

Pratten, C.F., (1971), *Economies of Scale in Manufacturing Industry*, Department of Economics, University of Cambridge, Occasional Papers: No. 28, Cambridge University Press.

Varian, H.R. (1993), *Intermediate Microeconomics*, 3rd ed., Norton.

Linear Programming

8.1 INTRODUCTION

Programming, linear or non-linear, is a practical mathematical technique designed to optimise (maximise or minimise) an objective function subject to a number of constraints. Where both the objective function and the constraints are linear, we speak of linear programming (LP), and this is the subject of the present chapter. So far, we have tackled optimisation problems subject to constraints by means of the classical optimisation technique of Lagrange multipliers. Thus, we have considered, for example, how a consumer maximises his or her utility subject to their budget constraint, or how a producer maximises his output subject to a given level of expenditure. In the Lagrange multipliers method, the objective function $F = F(X_1, X_2, \ldots, X_n)$ is optimised subject to the constraint(s) $H_i(X_1, X_2, \ldots, X_n)$, where, typically, the constraint(s) is (are) satisfied as equalities, and where we assume that the objective function and the constraint(s) are differentiable. Therefore, the need for an additional optimisation technique requires some justification.

8.2 RATIONALE FOR LINEAR PROGRAMMING (LP)

There are three main reasons which provide the justification for (LP). First, economic variables are, normally, assumed to be non-negative. There is no meaning in saying that we produce minus 5 tonnes of coal; we either produce something or not, in which case output will be positive or zero. However, with the Lagrangian method we may very well obtain negative values satisfying the first and second optimality conditions.

Second, if the objective function $F=F(X_1, X_2, \ldots, X_n)$ – where the Xs represent the variables – is linear, then the partial derivatives $\delta F/\delta X_1, \delta F/\delta X_2, \ldots, \delta F/\delta X_n$ are constants and the necessary conditions for a maximum or a minimum cannot be satisfied. A linear function has no finite maximum or minimum, as we showed in the previous chapter in the case of the breakeven analysis, unless the variables are further constrained by certain conditions, including non-negativity conditions.

Third, one or more of the constraints take the form of inequalities, rather than equalities, as in the Lagrangian method. For example, in a production problem, the firm may be trying to maximise its profit or its revenue function subject to particular technical, financial constraints and the availability of resources. There is no reason to expect that the firm will need to use up exactly all the available resources. It is perfectly possible, and more natural to assume, that for a variety of reasons, one or more of the resources are not fully utilised, in which case the firm will be left with some resources to spare. Therefore, the constraint can take the form of a weak inequality, that is, $H_i(X_1, X_2, \ldots, X_n) \leq C_i$. If we disregard the inequalities and treat them as equalities, we can proceed with the Lagrangian method, but it may turn out that there are no feasible solutions when all the inequality constraints are replaced by equations, and, therefore, the Lagrangian method breaks down.

Economic problems characterised by non-negativity requirements, linearities and inequalities are very common in practice; consequently, LP provides a versatile and useful tool of tackling them. For example, in production theory, the objective function to be maximised may be profit or revenue, while the constraints may denote how inputs are utilised to produce various outputs according to the available technology. The assumption of linearity implies that we have fixed coefficients of production and, thus, constant returns to scale. We shall consider first the algebraic approach to LP, by introducing the Simplex method, we shall follow it up by the diagrammatic approach and, finally, we shall reconsider production theory in the light of the LP analysis.

Despite the fact that there are computer programmes designed to make light of the tedious computations and arrive at solutions, nevertheless, it is instructive to consider in some detail the workings of the Simplex method, because of the important economic insights, ramifications and interpretations it provides. A little time spent to master the essentials of the Simplex method will go a long way in reinforcing the understanding, say, of production theory provided by marginal analysis. Besides, the Simplex method provides a partial answer to the so-called Black Box treatment of the marginal analysis, and it is much closer to what businesses do in everyday life.

8.3 THE SIMPLEX METHOD – AN EXAMPLE

The Simplex method is essentially an iterative procedure, which searches systematically for an optimal solution to an LP problem, from a set of finite basic and feasible solutions, known as corner solutions. We shall consider these problems later on in the diagrammatic approach, but in this section we can set out the problem by means of an example from production theory, by following Vandermeulen (1971).

Example

Assume that a company can produce four products X_1, X_2, X_3, and X_4 by utilising two different resources K and L (these can be times of different machines, raw materials or anything else, but for the purposes of this example, it suffices to consider such resources generally). The technological conditions are such that to produce one unit of X_1 requires 6 units of K and 4 units of L. Similarly, one unit of X_2 needs 2 units of K and 2 units of L, one unit of X_3 requires 2 units of K and 4 units of L, and, finally, one unit of X_4 requires 6 units of K and 2 units of L. The processes of production are independent of each other and display constant returns to scale. The company has available 360 units of K and 320 units of L per week, and it has estimated that on the basis of current prices and costs, the unit profits per product are €20 for X_1, €8 for X_2, €10 for X_3 and €12 for X_4. It is required to determine the best weekly output mix in order to maximise the firm's profits.

Denoting by lower case letters x_1, x_2, x_3 and x_4 the quantities of the four products produced, the above can be formulated as an LP problem as follows:

$$\text{Maximise } P = 20x_1 + 8x_2 + 10x_3 + 12x_4 \tag{1}$$

$$\text{subject to} \quad 6x_1 + 2x_2 + 2x_3 + 6x_4 \leq 360, \ K \text{ constraint} \tag{2}$$

$$4x_1 + 2x_2 + 4x_3 + 2x_4 \leq 320, \ L \text{ constraint} \tag{3}$$

$$x_1, x_2, x_3, x_4 \geq 0, \ \text{Non-negativity constraint} \tag{4}$$

Expression (1) is the objective function to be maximised, which is the profit function of the firm. It tells us simply that the total profit is derived by multiplying the quantities of the four products produced by their unit profits and summing up. Expressions (2) and (3) denote the constraints, reflecting the technological conditions of production. Considering the LHS of (2) we find the total requirements (or demand) we make on resource K. Since we need respectively 6 units of K for one unit of X_1, 2 for X_2, 2 for X_3 and 6 for X_4, multiplying these coefficients by the quantities produced of the four products and summing up we arrive at the total requirements of input K. Clearly, such requirements cannot exceed the available supplies, that is, the 360 units of K, given by the RHS of (2). This explains the weak inequality, that is, the equal or less than sign $\leq$ in (2). The firm can use up to 360 units of K per week but no more. Similar considerations apply for expression (3). Therefore, (2) is the so-called K constraint, since it refers to resource K, and relation (3) gives us the L constraint. Finally, expression (4) reflects the non-negativity conditions.

In introducing the Simplex method, it is necessary to consider first a number of useful definitions.

Basic solution: A solution is basic if the number of non-zero variables (in our case products) appearing in it does not exceed the number of constraints.

Feasible solution: Any basic solution that satisfies the constraints.

Optimal solution: A basic and feasible solution that optimises the objective function.

For a solution to exist, the constraints must be consistent with each other. If there exist inconsistent constraints, there is no solution to the LP problem.

8.3.1 Stage 1

The above imply that since in our problem we have two constraints and four potential products, the Simplex method requires that we start considering various pairs of basic solutions like (x_1, x_2), (x_1, x_3), (x_1, x_4), (x_2, x_3), (x_2, x_4) and so on. But we may find it easier to transform the inequalities (2) and (3) into equalities by adding non-negative slack variables S_1 and S_2 respectively, which can absorb any discrepancy between the RHS and LHS of the two constraints, so we get:

$$6x_1 + 2x_2 + 2x_3 + 6x_4 + S_1 = 360 \tag{5}$$

$$4x_1 + 2x_2 + 4x_3 + 2x_4 + S_2 = 320 \tag{6}$$

$$x_1, x_2, x_3, x_4, S_1, S_2 \geq 0 \tag{7}$$

This step has enabled us to begin the Simplex method, since we have, according to the rules, our fist basic solution consisting of $x_1 = x_2 = x_3 = x_4 = 0$ and $S_1 = 360$ and $S_2 = 320$. This solution interprets the slack variables as the amounts of the original resources and tells us that nothing has been produced yet, and the firm has all its resources intact. The solution is feasible, since it does not violate the constraints (5)–(7), but it is not optimal. We can tabulate these findings in the following table, and the interpretation of this table is as follows: The first column indicates the variables in the current basis, that is, S_1 and S_2, while the last column, labelled b_i, shows the values (outputs) of the variables in the basis. As we said earlier $S_1 = 360$ and $S_2 = 320$. The first two rows (8) and (9) repeat the technological information of the constraints (5) and (6). The final row, P, repeats the unit coefficients of the objective function and shows at the right corner, under the column of b_i, the value of the objective function, that is, the net profits after each iteration. Clearly, the value of the objective function remains at zero, since no Xs have been produced so far, as it can be verified by (10) later. Nevertheless, it could be argued that such a solution *could be optimal*, if each of the four products required variable inputs, whose value per unit of product exceeded the selling price, thus, resulting in negative unit profits. Clearly, in such a situation the firm would have no incentive to produce. Returning now to our problem, the initial basis has produced the following table:

	x_1	x_2	x_3	x_4	S_1	S_2	b_i	
S_1	6	2	2	6	1	0	360	(8)
S_2	4	2	4	2	0	1	320	(9)
P(max)	20	8	10	12	0	0	0	(10)

In this case the row of the objective function (10) reveals that the unit profits for all four potential products are positive. This indicates that profit could be increased from zero by producing some quantity of any of the four products. The requirement of the basic solution means that we can try to improve the solution by excluding S_1 or S_2 and introducing one of the X variables. Any of the Xs will enable us to proceed, but we may find it a useful shortcut to introduce the variable with the highest profitability, X_1, on the grounds that it may achieve faster our objective of profit maximisation. However, it should be remembered that any variable can also be dropped from the basis, including the one that we had brought in earlier, if it is not consistent with constrained optimisation, of which more later. Therefore, we choose variable x_1, which is called the entering variable. However, if x_1 is to enter the basis, then either S_1 or S_2 must depart, to make room for x_1, so that the solution remains basic. To find out which of the Ss must be dropped, we ask: 'How much of x_1 can we produce?'. Clearly, this depends on the production coefficients of x_1 (6 and 4), shown under the column of x_1 and the availability of inputs, given under column b_i.

From the first constraint, denoting the K input, we have:

$$6x_1 = 360 \quad \text{or} \quad x_1 = 360/6 = 60$$

and from the second constraint, denoting the L input we get:

$$4x_1 = 320 \quad \text{or} \quad x_1 = 320/4 = 80$$

The figures just derived tell us that we have sufficient units of the K resource to produce 60 units of x_1, and also sufficient units of the L resource to produce 80 units of x_1. However, since both resources are required to produce one unit of x_1, it means that the 60 units, corresponding to the K constraint, provide an effective ceiling to the production of x_1. It follows that by producing 60 units of x_1 the first resource is fully exhausted, whilst we are still left with some quantity of the second resource. This analysis indicates that the variable S_1, which was identified earlier as the quantity of the first input, must be dropped from the basis to allow x_1 to enter. As the production of x_1 increases, the excess capacity of S_1 is driven to zero, while the excess capacity of the second input, S_2, is still positive. We are now ready to proceed with the introduction of x_1 into the basis. However, before doing so we must digress a little to introduce the essentials of the Simplex method.

8.3.1a   Digression

In systems of linear equations there are two types of algebraic operations which allow us to transform the equations without affecting the solution. The first one permits us to multiply an equation in the system by any constant number $k \neq 0$, whilst the second one allows us to multiply an equation in the system by any constant number $k \neq 0$ and add it to another equation. Systematic use of this process leads to the elimination of variables from equations, until there is only one variable in each equation, which gives us the solution. Application of these rules reduces a system of linear equations to a triangular form, that is, a system in which each variable has a coefficient of one along the diagonal running from the top left corner to the bottom right. Below the diagonal all variables are eliminated (or are present with zero coefficients), forming a triangle. As an example of this process, consider the following system:

$$2x + y + 4z = 4 \tag{1}$$

$$x + 2.5y + z = 5 \tag{2}$$

$$4x + 5y + 10z = 16 \tag{3}$$

We wish to eliminate first the variable x from equations (2) and (3). We start by multiplying (1) by 0.5 so as to leave variable x with a coefficient of one, and get:

$$x + 0.5y + 2z = 2 \tag{4}$$

We now multiply equation (4) by -1 and add the resulting equation $-x-0.5y-2z = -2$ to equation (2), so that the new equation becomes:

$$2y - z = 3 \tag{5}$$

Having eliminated x from equation (2) we proceed by multiplying equation (4) by -4 and adding the resulting equation $-4x - 2y - 8z = -8$ to equation (3), deriving, thus, the new equation:

$$3y + 2z = 8 \tag{6}$$

The new system of equations becomes:

$$x + 0.5y + 2z = 2 \tag{4}$$

$$2y - z = 3 \tag{5}$$

$$3y + 2z = 8 \tag{6}$$

In the next stage we multiply (5) by 0.5 to get:

$$y - 0.5z = 1.5 \tag{7}$$

and then multiply (7) by -3 and add the resulting equation $-3y + 1.5z = -4.5$ to equation (6) to get the new equation

$$3.5z = 3.5 \text{ or } z = 1 \tag{8}$$

This has transformed the original system into the triangular or diagonal form given by the following:

$$x + 0.5y + 2z = 2 \tag{4}$$
$$y - 0.5z = 1.5 \tag{7}$$
$$z = 1 \tag{8}$$

The reader can verify that by substituting (8) into (7) we get $y = 2$ and substitution of the values of y and z into (4) yields $x = -1$. These values of x, y and z represent the solution to the system.

However, as in LP we are likely to have more variables than equations, we must choose a subset of variables equal in number to the number of equations, known as the square subset, in order to reduce it to the triangular or diagonal form. This is the logic behind the earlier requirement of the basic solution, in which the number of non-zero variables entering the solution is equal to the number of constraints (equations). We found earlier that the slack variables S_1 and S_2 represented a first basis. The Simplex method involves shifting from one basis to another in its quest for the optimum solution. The process of shifting from one basis to another is called pivoting or pivot operation. The pivot is the non-zero coefficient of the new variable entering the basis. Pivoting allows us to eliminate variables and, therefore, a succession of pivot operations reduces the system to diagonal form, leading to the solution. In terms of relations (8) and (9) of our table above, we have the first basic solution of $S_1 = 360$ and $S_2 = 320$, obtained by looking at the square subset of variables S_1 and S_2 in equations (8) and (9), which are expressed in diagonal form. It should be added that the term diagonal form is appropriate for the constraints alone in the case of the LP. However, when we include the objective function we have one more equation than the number of basic variables and the term used to describe the system as a whole is known as the canonical form. To show any LP in its canonical form we should: (1) express the constraints as equalities than inequalities; (2) reduce the constraints to diagonal form, with respect to a subset of variables that forms a basis and (3) eliminate the basic variables from the objective function row.

8.3.2 Stage 2

We are now returning to the introduction of x_1 into the basis. Since, as we have seen, S_1 must depart to make room for x_1, the new x_1 row will be derived from the old S_1 row in such a way so as to get a unit coefficient in the position (x_1x_1). This simply means that the coefficient 6 in bold in (8) in our earlier first table is our pivot, must be transformed into 1. This is achieved by multiplying (8) by 1/6 in order to derive (11). Clearly, for this procedure to be effective, we require a positive coefficient in the column of the entering variable, in order not to violate the non-negativity conditions. If this is not the case, then this is a signal for a check to be made either in the formulation of the programme or for errors in the computations. Algebraically, at least one coefficient, say a_{21} (in our case 4), can be negative. This means that the second input is actually an output of the first productive process, a joint product with x_1. By shifting the term $-a_{21}x_1$ to the RHS of the constraint it becomes positive, showing that increases in the x_1 increase rather than decrease the supply of the second input (Vandermeulen, 1971, p. 36). To derive the new row for S_2 we multiply (11) by -4 and add the resulting row to (9). Clearly, in the new row (12) for S_2, the coefficient for x_1 is 0, as required. Similarly, by multiplying (11) by -20 and adding the resulting row to (10) we get the new row (13) for the objective function. Therefore, at the end of this iteration, the second table looks as follows:

	x_1	x_2	x_3	x_4	S_1	S_2	b_i	
x_1	1	1/3	1/3	1	1/6	0	60	(11)
S_2	0	2/3	8/3	-2	$-2/3$	1	80	(12)
$P-Z$	0	4/3	10/3	-8	$-10/3$	0	-1200	(13)

Row (11) reveals that x_1 has entered the basis with a value of 60, that is, we are producing 60 units of x_1, and as we saw earlier, the production of 60 units of x_1 leads to the exhaustion of the first resource K. However, we still have some spare capacity of the second resource L. Since each unit of x_1 requires 4 units of resource L, it follows that the production of 60 units of x_1 uses up 240 of the second resource leaving 80 units of that input as unused capacity, that is,

$$S_2 = 320 - 4x60 = 80$$

This is exactly the information conveyed by row (12). Also, since we have produced 60 units of x_1, we expect profits to be $60 \times 20 = 1200$. Row (13) confirms that the value of the objective function has risen from 0 to 1200. Concentrating for the moment on the objective function, we see that the elimination of the coefficient of x_1 from (10) has added the term $-[c_1(b_1/a_{11})]$, or $-20(60)$ to the RHS of expression (13). (Please refer to Appendix A for the slight change in symbols). The term $b_1/a_{11} = 60$ shows the amount of x_1 produced at this iteration, and multiplying it by $c_1 = 20$ gives us the profit obtained by this particular basic and feasible solution. But in any such solution, the non-basic variables are all zero (i.e., the products are not produced) and the basic variables appear with zero coefficients in the objective function row, because of their elimination; therefore the LHS is zero. So we have: $0 = P - Z$, or $P = Z$, which is the profit obtained from our particular basic and feasible solution, which in our case is $Z = 1200$. Therefore, we should ignore the minus sign in front of 1200, as it is a product of the computations. If an optimal solution to a LP exists, the Simplex method will arrive at such a solution when all the figures in the objective function row have been turned into either zeros or negative.

8.3.3   Stage 3

We now recognise that since there is unused capacity of the second resource, there is also scope for introducing another product. If a product can be produced without using the first resource, its production will not reduce the quantity of the first product and it will increase profits directly. However, when a second product can only be produced by making use of both resources, as in our case, then its production must entail a cutback in the production of the first product, in order to release the necessary units of the first input for use in the production of the second product. This means that the gain in profits from the production of the new product must be balanced against the loss in profits from the cutback in production of the old product. Given that prices are constant, the relevant information is the rate at which the first product must change in relation to the production of the second product, which is given by the relative requirements for the first input. So, if we decide to produce the second product and the first resource continues to be fully utilised, the following condition: $a_{11}\Delta x_1 + a_{12}\Delta x_2 = 0$ must be satisfied. (Note: This notation is explained in Appendix A at the end of this chapter). Since a_{11} and a_{12} are the production coefficients, stating the amount of the first resource required to produce a unit of the first and second products, respectively, x_1 and x_2, it follows that the increased use of the first input, necessitated by the production of the second product x_2 and shown by: $a_{12}\Delta x_2$ must be balanced by a decrease in its use by the first product, which is given by $a_{11}\Delta x_1$. Therefore, the rate is shown as:

$$\frac{\Delta x_1}{\Delta x_2} = \frac{a_{12}}{a_{11}}$$

which states that for each unit of x_2, the production of x_1 must be reduced by a_{12}/a_{11}, with a concomitant loss in profits given by $c_1(a_{12}/a_{11})$. However, since a unit of x_2 has now been produced, it adds to profits an amount of c_2, and so the net change in profits is given by the expression: $c_2 - c_1(a_{12}/a_{11})$. Clearly, only when this expression is positive, is it worth to introduce the second product. We saw earlier that in order to eliminate $c_1 = 20$ from the row of the objective function, i.e., row (10), we multiplied (8) by $1/a_{11} = 1/6$, then by $(-c_1)$ or (-20), and added it to the objective function row (10). But these pivot operations are the same ones, which are required to convert the coefficient of x_2 into the expression for the net change in profits given above. This shows a general property of the Simplex method, namely, that when a system has been reduced to its canonical form, with respect to a given basis, each coefficient in the row of the objective function shows the net change in the objective function brought about by increasing the relevant variable by one unit.

The preceding discussion illustrates that profits can be increased further by introducing into the basis either x_2 or x_3, whose coefficients in (13) are both positive. Since the coefficient of x_3 is greater than that of x_2, i.e., $10/3 > 4/3$ we decide to bring into the basis x_3, which must replace either x_1 or S_2. To decide which one must leave the basis, we compute the ratios $(1/3)x_1 = 60$ giving $x_1 = 3(60) = 180$ and $(8/3)S_2 = 80$ giving $S_2 = 3(80)/8 = 30$, and drop the variable corresponding to the least one, since this ratio shows the effective or binding production limit imposed by input availabilities. Therefore, row (12), which is the row of the departing variable, is the relevant one from which we shall compute the new row for x_3. It means that the coefficient $8/3$ in bold in (12) is our pivot, which must be transformed into 1, in order to give us our canonical form. This is achieved by multiplying (12) by 3/8 and deriving row (15) for x_3. The new row (15) is now used to obtain row (14) as follows: We multiply (15) by $-1/3$ and add it to row (11). Similarly, to derive the objective function row we multiply (15) by $-10/3$ and add it to (13), thus, getting (16). At the end of this iteration, the results are summarised in the following table, which shows the new basic and feasible solution to be $x_1 = 50$, $x_3 = 30$, yielding a value for the objective function of $Z = 1300$ of total profits, i.e., $20(50) + 10(30) = 1300$.

	x_1	x_2	x_3	x_4	S_1	S_2	b_i	
x_1	1	1/4	0	5/4	1/4	$-1/8$	50	(14)
x_3	0	1/4	1	$-3/4$	$-1/4$	3/8	30	(15)
$P - Z$	0	1/2	0	$-11/2$	$-5/2$	$-5/4$	-1300	(16)

8.3.4 Stage 4

We notice that in this latest basic and feasible solution the constants, b_i, give us the output levels only of the two products x_1 and x_3. When this happens we have a change in the meaning of capacity. Originally, capacity was given in terms of the quantities of the available inputs, i.e., 360 units of capital and 320 units of labour per week. However, in this latest basic and feasible solution, capacity is redefined as the output levels of x_1 and x_3 that fully utilise these two inputs. This is also the practice in industry, where the capacities of particular plants are expressed in terms of outputs. This change in the meaning of capacity does not affect the application of the Simplex method, but alters the economic interpretation.

In the present context, we observe that in (16) the coefficient of x_2 is 1/2, implying that our solution given by (14)–(16) is not optimal. It means that each unit of x_2 produced increases profit by 1/2, and so we have the incentive to increase the output of x_2 to the highest possible level. The fact that we have no spare or excess capacity of inputs, since they are currently fully utilised in the production of x_1 and x_2, in no way represents a constraint. The inputs required for the production of x_2 can and must be diverted from x_1 and x_3, and the ceiling in the production of x_2 occurs when the diversion of inputs forces one of the current outputs, i.e., x_1 or x_2 to zero.

We saw in the first stage that, when products were entered into the basis to take up the excess capacity of inputs, the a_{ij} coefficients in the main body of the table (matrix) measure the input requirements per unit of output. But with two outputs in the current basis, the $\tilde{a}_{ij}$ (barred) coefficients do not have the same interpretation; now they show the rate at which the variables in the basis change with respect to x_2. (This change in interpretation is denoted by the change in notation, i.e., the barred coefficients). As x_2 increases, the total use of the inputs remains fixed. Therefore, to find what changes are induced in x_1 and x_3 by a change in x_2, we have:

$$\Delta x_1 + \tilde{a}_{12}\Delta x_2 = 0 \text{ and } \Delta x_3 + \tilde{a}_{22}\Delta x_2 = 0$$

or $\Delta x_1 + (1/4)\Delta x_2 = 0 \text{ and } \Delta x_3 + (1/4)\Delta x_2 = 0$

giving:

$$\frac{\Delta x_1}{\Delta x_2} = -\tilde{a}_{12} = -\frac{1}{4} \text{ and } \frac{\Delta x_3}{\Delta x_2} = -\tilde{a}_{22} = -\frac{1}{4}$$

Therefore, these rates of change tell us by how much x_1 and x_3 must change in order to release enough resources to produce one unit of x_2. On the rule of the minimal positive ratio (otherwise the solution will not be feasible), which we have been using so far, variable x_3 must be dropped, since $(1/4)x_1 = 50$ and $(1/4)x_3 = 30$ imply $x_1 = 200$ and $x_3 = 120$. Therefore row (15), i.e., the row of the departing variable, will be used to derive the row of the entering variable x_2. Clearly, the coefficient in bold $\mathbf{1/4}$ is our pivot. The new row (18) is derived simply by multiplying (15) by 4, giving us row (18) in its canonical form. Now row (18) can be used to obtain the canonical form for x_1 and the objective function. First, row (18) is multiplied by $-1/4$ and added to row (14) to give us row (17), which is the canonical form for variable x_1. Second, row (18) is multiplied by $-1/2$ and added to row (16) to obtain the new objective function row (19) in its canonical form. At the end of this iteration, the new basic and feasible solution is $x_1 = 20$ and $x_2 = 120$, giving a value for the objective function of 1360, i.e., $20(20) + 8(120) = 1360$, and the computations and results are summarised in the following table:

	x_1	x_2	x_3	x_4	S_1	S_2	b_i	
x_1	1	0	-1	2	1/2	$-1/2$	20	(17)
x_2	0	1	4	-3	-1	3/2	120	(18)
$P-Z$	0	0	-2	-4	-2	-2	-1360	(19)

Since the coefficients of the objective function row (19), showing the net change in its value from the introduction of one unit of the relevant variable in the basis, are either zero or negative, it follows that the solution $x_1 = 20$ and $x_2 = 120$ is not only basic and feasible, but also optimal. For example, introducing either x_3 or x_4 will result in a reduction in profits, since for every unit of x_3 produced, the net change in the value of the objective function is -2, while for every unit of x_4 produced, the net change is -4.

To confirm that we have obtained a feasible solution, we substitute the values of $x_1 = 20$ and $x_2 = 120$ into the constraints (2) and (3) above and get:

Feasibility check

$$6(20) + 2(120) = 120 + 240 = 360$$
$$4(20) + 2(120) = 80 + 240 = 320$$

Since the constraints are satisfied, our basic solution is also feasible. Furthermore, because the two constraints are satisfied as equalities, it means that in producing 20 units of x_1 and 120 units of x_2, we have fully utilised the two inputs and no spare capacity remains. This is to be expected, since in the basic solution the Ss appear with zero coefficients.

8.4 THE ISSUE OF DUALITY – OPTIMALITY CHECK

Confirmation, however, that our solution is also optimal requires the use of the so-called duality theorem. This states that the maximum value of the objective function of the primal, is equal to the minimum value of the objective function of the dual. This in turn requires that we discuss, briefly, the issue of the dual.

Allied to any LP, which we may call it the primary programme or the primal, there is another programme which is the mirror image of the primal, called the dual. To illustrate the derivation of the dual, we take the case of our earlier example and rewrite the LP in the following slightly different form:

Subject to $6x_1 + 2x_2 + 2x_3 + 6x_4 \leq 360$

$$4x_1 + 2x_2 + 4x_3 + 2x_4 \leq 320$$

Maximise $20x_1 + 8x_2 + 10x_3 + 12x_4$

$$x_1, x_2, x_3, x_4 \geq 0$$

To obtain the dual from the primal, we interchange columns with rows, the coefficients of the objective function with the constant terms b_i, the variables from, say, xs to ys, the inequality signs from $\leq$ to $\geq$ and the objective from maximisation to minimisation. In summary form, the interchanges are as follows:

Primal LP		Dual LP
Maximisation	:	Minimisation
x variables	:	y variables
Objective function coefficients	:	Constant terms, b_i
Column coefficients	:	Row coefficients
Therefore, the dual programme can be written as:		
Subject to $6y_1 + 4y_2 \geq 20$	(20)	
$2y_1 + 2y_2 \geq 8$	(21)	Constraints
$2y_1 + 4y_2 \geq 10$	(22)	
$6y_1 + 2y_2 \geq 12$	(23)	
Minimise $360y_1 + 320y_2$	(24)	Objective function
$y_1, y_2 \geq 0$		

The dual has been generated from its primal by turning everything round and introducing new variables, ys, as required. The easiest way to achieve this is to consider the original tabled data (of the primal programme) in terms of its columns than its rows. Therefore, in the dual the constraints (rows) relate to the columns of the primal programme. A new variable is required for each of the original primal constraints, in our example, two, which we call y_1 and y_2. If a constraint in the primal programme is of the form of a weak inequality, as both constraints are in our example, then the associated dual variable is required to be non-negative. The coefficients of the primal's objective function become the constant terms of the dual's constraints and, correspondingly, the constants in the primal's constraints become the coefficients of the dual's objective function. The inequality signs in the dual's constraints are the opposite of those in the primal's constraints. Finally, the primal's maximising objective is changed in the dual to a minimising one.

The result of all these interchanges is given above. We shall provide, presently, an economic interpretation of the dual but we need say, first, a few words about its solution. We saw earlier that the Simplex method provided us with the solution of the primal programme as $x_1 = 20, x_2 = 120$ and a value of the objective function of $P = €1360$. If we knew what the values of y_1 and y_2 were, then we could substitute these values into the dual's objective function and establish, according to the duality theorem, mentioned above, whether or not the solution to the primal was optimal. Such a solution for the dual does, indeed, exist in our case and the Simplex method has already provided it! One of the great advantages of the Simplex method is that it is providing solutions to *both* the primal and the dual programmes. The solution of the dual, i.e., the values for y_1, y_2 and objective function can be read off the final row (19), as the coefficients for S_1, S_2 and b_i, i.e., 2, 2 and 1360 (ignoring the negative signs). Substituting the values of y_1 and y_2 into (24) we get:

Optimality check

$$360(2) + 320(2) = 720 + 640 = 1360 \tag{9}$$

which is the same as the value of the objective function of the primal and confirms that our solution to the primal is optimal.

8.4.1 The economic interpretation of the dual

In a standard primal programme which is a production problem, as given above, the task is to determine the profit maximising outputs, subject to the constraints provided by the limitational factors of production. Even when such factors have been completely amortised, so that the firm does not have to pay for them, such factors are entirely responsible for providing the firm with its profits. Therefore, if we wanted to allocate or to impute the firm's profits to the scarce factors of production, we need to determine some sort of accounting values, or shadow prices for each of the inputs, in such a way that the sum of values for all the inputs going into the production of any product is exactly equal to the unit profit of that product.

Considering the constraints (20)–(23) we see that the constants on the RHS, such as 20, 8, 10 and 12, are the unit profits for the four products x_1, x_2, x_3 and x_4 expressed in € money terms. Consequently, the LHS of the constraints (20)–(23) must also be expressed in terms of € per unit of the relevant product. Concentrating for the moment on constraint (20), we observe that the coefficient 6 is the number of units of capital required per unit of product x_1, and hence it must be multiplied by a number of € per unit of capital. This establishes the unit of measurement of y_1, and shows that this variable is some sort of price of capital. For this reason, it is usually, called the resource's shadow price. Similarly, the coefficient 4 in (20) represents the number of units of labour required to produce a unit of product x_1, and it is multiplied by a number of € per unit of labour. Therefore, y_2 is the shadow price of labour. Clearly, similar considerations apply for the LHS of constraints (21)–(23). Since in all constraints the constants represent the units of capital and labour required to produce one unit of x_1, x_2, x_3 and x_4, the variables y_1 and y_2 represent the shadow prices of the two resources. This establishes the general result that the LHS of each constraint shows the shadow cost or opportunity cost to the firm of the limitational factors per unit of the corresponding product. In addition, the constraints tell us that the shadow cost must not be less than the net revenue, i.e., that shadow profits must not be positive. This last point has already been demonstrated by the Simplex method, which requires that the coefficients in the objective function row (19) are negative or, in the case of the basic variables, are zero. For example, in constraint (20), the LHS illustrates that the opportunity cost to the firm of the resources required for one unit of x_1 is:

$$6(2) + 4(2) = 12 + 8 = 20$$

which is exactly equal to the RHS constant, which we know it to be the unit profit of x_1. It might also appear that we could satisfy relations (20)–(23) as strict inequalities, by choosing values for y_1 and y_2 high enough to achieve this. However, we are not allowed to choose any values we like, because we are required also to minimise the value of the objective function (24). We notice that since the coefficients of the objective function of the dual are the total amounts of capital and labour available to the firm, the function measures the total shadow cost or opportunity cost of all the resources used in the production process. We saw in the solution of the primal, that the usage of the resources available to the firm has resulted in a profit of €1360. We have also seen that the value of the objective function of the dual, showing the opportunity cost of the resources, is €1360 too. This shows that in the optimal solution, the values y_1 and y_2 can be used to impute the firm's total profit to the scarce resources, even in the case where such resources have been completely amortised. Since it is the availability of these resources which is responsible for generating the outputs and profit, that profit is 'owed' in some sense to the scarce factors of production and must be imputed to them. Summarising, we can say that the objective function of the dual gives us the total valuation to the firm of all the factors under its disposal. But this has to be the very minimum valuation of the firm's factors, which completely accounts for all the profits of each of the outputs produced (Baumol 1977).

Substituting the values of y_1 and y_2 in the dual we obtain:

Minimise $360(2) + 320(2) = 720 + 640 = 1360$ (24′)

Subject to $6(2) + 4(2) = 12 + 8 = 20 = 20$ (20′)

$2(2) + 2(2) = 4 + 4 = 8 = 8$ (21′)

$2(2) + 4(2) = 4 + 8 = 12 > 10$ (22′)

$6(2) + 2(2) = 12 + 4 = 16 > 12$ (23′)

Clearly, the solution $y_1 = 2$ and $y_2 = 2$ is basic, feasible and optimal. We notice that the first two constraints (20′) and (21′), corresponding to products x_1 and x_2 – which are actually produced–are satisfied as equalities, whilst constraints (22′) and (23′), corresponding to products x_3 and x_4 – which are not produced – are satisfied as inequalities. The interpretation and implications of these equalities and inequalities are considered below, once we have discussed the issue of competitiveness and complementarity.

8.4.2 Competitive and complementary products

Having found the optimal solution, we may ask what changes in x_1 and x_2 would occur, as a result of a decision to produce either one unit of x_3 or x_4 on the assumption that their unit profit coefficients changed sufficiently to warrant their production? Again, since both inputs are fully utilised by the production of x_1 and x_2, the relevant information is conveyed by the rates of change given by the $\tilde{a}_{ij}$ (barred) coefficients in the final row (19) of the final table under the x_3 and x_4 columns.

Thus, for x_3 we have:

$$\Delta x_1 + \tilde{a}_{13}\Delta x_3 = 0 \text{ or } \Delta x_1 - 1\Delta x_3 = 0 \text{ or } (\Delta x_1)/(\Delta x_3) = 1$$
$$\text{and} \quad \Delta x_2 + \tilde{a}_{23}\Delta x_3 = 0 \text{ or } \Delta x_2 + 4\Delta x_3 = 0 \text{ or } (\Delta x_2)/(\Delta x_3) = -4$$

Similarly, for x_4 we get:

$$\Delta x_1 + \tilde{a}_{14}\Delta x_4 = 0 \text{ or } \Delta x_1 + 2\Delta x_4 = 0 \text{ or } (\Delta x_1)/(\Delta x_4) = -2$$
$$\text{and} \quad \Delta x_2 + \tilde{a}_{24}\Delta x_4 = 0 \text{ or } \Delta x_2 - 3\Delta x_4 = 0 \text{ or } (\Delta x_2)/(\Delta x_4) = 3$$

These results are interesting because they reveal the relationship between the various products. We see that the rate of change of x_1 with respect to x_3 is positive, given by 1, implying that increases in x_3 increase rather than decrease production of x_1. (Indeed, this can be verified by the earlier basic and feasible solution $x_1 = 50$ and $x_3 = 30$). This means that in order to introduce x_3, the required inputs can be secured from the decrease in the production of x_2; the rate of change of x_2 with respect to x_3 is negative, given by -4. The reason is provided by the input requirements of the various products. For example, from the original information, the input requirements for x_1 (6, 4) are almost in inverse order of size with those for x_3 (2, 4). This means that x_1 and x_3 blend well together, or in other words, they *complement* each other in the use of inputs. This leads to an important result. When an $\tilde{a}_{ij}$ (barred) coefficient is negative and the corresponding rate of change is positive, the two products are *complementary* in the use of inputs, or complements with each other. When, instead, an $\tilde{a}_{ij}$ (barred) coefficient is positive and the corresponding rate of change is negative, the two products are *competitive* in the use of inputs or substitutes for each other. However, since the coefficients vary with the basis, the relationship of complementing or competing in the use of inputs is relative to the specific basis, and it may change if a new variable were introduced into the basis. In our example, with respect to the optimal solution (basis), we have the following rates of change and relationships:

- Between x_1 and x_3 (1)   i.e., x_1 and x_3 are complements in the use of inputs
- Between x_2 and x_3 (-4)   i.e., x_2 and x_3 are substitutes in the use of inputs
- Between x_1 and x_4 (-2)   i.e., x_1 and x_4 are substitutes in the use of inputs and
- Between x_2 and x_4 (4)   i.e., x_2 and x_4 are complements in the use of inputs

8.4.3 Opportunity cost again

We saw that for the third product, x_3, we have two choices: either produce a unit of x_3 or continue to utilise the resources to produce the first two products x_1 and x_2. But for each product there is a cost, even if there are no variable costs and we do not have to pay for fixed inputs because, say, of amortisation. This cost is the familiar opportunity cost. For x_3, the opportunity cost is the most lucrative alternative, i.e., producing x_1 and x_2.

If we divert inputs from producing one unit of x_3 to produce instead x_1 and x_2, we gain in profit an amount equal to $(c_1 a_{13} + c_2 a_{23})$. This is the amount the firm foregoes by producing one unit of x_3. Clearly it is only worth producing a particular product, such as x_3, only if its unit profit exceeds its opportunity cost per unit, i.e.,

$$\check{c}_3 = c_3 - (c_1 \tilde{a}_{13} + c_2 \tilde{a}_{23})$$

In our case, substituting the relevant figures for product x_3 we have:

$$\check{c}_3 = 10 - [20(-1) + 8(4)] = 10 - (-20 + 32) = 10 - (12) = -2$$

which is exactly the information we get in the objective function row (19) as the coefficient of x_3. Similarly, for x_4 we have:

$$\check{c}_4 = c_4 - (c_1 \tilde{a}_{14} + c_2 \tilde{a}_{24}) \text{ giving:}$$
$$\check{c}_4 = 12 - [20(2) + 8(-3)] = 12 - (40 - 24) = 12 - (16) = -4$$

Therefore, it follows that the unit profit coefficients of x_3 and x_4 must increase to at least 12 and 16, respectively, before we consider bringing them into the basis.

However, we could have approached this issue in a different way by asking what effect do new activities or changes in the technological coefficients a_{ij} have on the optimal solution? Is it worthwhile to bring them into the basis? The easiest way to check is to consider whether the associated dual constraint is satisfied by the current values of the dual. In the context of our example, x_3 and x_4 may be taken to be the new activities. Letting their unit profits be c_3 and c_4, the question is at what values of c_3 and c_4 is it profitable to produce x_3 and x_4? From (20)–(24) the associated dual constraint for x_3 is:

$$2y_1 + 4y_2 \geq c_3 \text{ or } 2(2) + 4(2) = 4 + 8 = 12$$

Therefore, if $c_3 \geq 12$ it pays to introduce x_3. Similarly, for x_4 the associated dual constraint is:

$$6y_1 + 2y_2 \geq c_4 \text{ or } 6(2) + 2(2) = 12 + 4 = 16$$

i.e., provided $c_4 \geq 16$ it pays to introduce x_4.

This discussion leads to the same conclusions reached above and demonstrates once again the economic importance of the dual. In the following appendices we provide some important theorems and a diagrammatic approach to linear programming and, also, take a fresh look at production theory, in the light of this analytical method.

SUMMARY

The chapter has looked at an alternative optimisation technique to marginal analysis, that of linear programming. It has offered a rationale for this technique and considered, in detail, the workings of the Simplex method, in the context of production theory. It has provided an explanation of the dual programme and an economic interpretation of its solution. In the appendices that follow we present, without proofs, the basic theorems and a diagrammatic exposition of linear programming, in the context of a two-resources five-products economy, to draw its similarities with marginal analysis.

PROBLEMS

1. A firm can produce two products, A and B. Profits are €40 per unit of A and €160 per unit of B. The production of one unit of A requires one unit of labour and two units of capital, while the production of one unit of B requires 2 units of labour and 20 units of capital. The production processes are independent of each other and display constant returns to scale. The firm has available 30 units of labour and 60 units of capital per week. How many units of each product should the firm produce per week in order to maximise its profits?

2. The services of three machines A, B and C are required in the production of two products I and II. One unit of product I needs 2 hours on machine A, 1 hour on machine B and 6 hours on machine C, whilst one unit of product II, requires, respectively, 2 hours, 5 hours and 2 hours on machines A, B and C. The producer has available 48 hours on machine A, 88 hours on machine B and 120 hours on machine C. The unit profit on product I is €6 and on product II is €9. How many units of each product should be produced in order to maximise profits. Give both, the graphical and Simplex method solutions.

3. A toy company manufactures two types of doll, a basic model, doll A, and a deluxe model, doll B. Each doll of type B takes twice as long to produce as one of type A, and the company has time to make a maximum of 4000 per week, if it produces only the basic model. The supply of plastic is sufficient to make 3000 dolls per week of both types. The company estimates that it makes a profit of €3 on doll A and €5 on doll B. Given that the firm wants to maximise its weekly profits.
   (a) Formulate and solve the above linear programme.
   (b) Write down its dual.
   (c) Investigate if your solution to (a) is optimal.
   (d) Give an economic interpretation of the dual.

4. A farmer can produce oats and corn, which can be sold on perfect markets at prices of €1800 and €1700 per tonne, respectively. Each tonne of oats requires the services of 6 men and 4 acres of land, whilst each tonne of corn needs the services of 5 men and 11 acres of land. The production processes are independent of each other, perfectly divisible and display constant returns to scale. The farmer has available 95 acres of land and can hire 85 equally skilled men. The cost of other inputs, such as seeds, fertilisers, tractors and the like is €600 per tonne of oats and €500 per tonne of corn.

   (a) What is the optimal solution?
   (b) Suppose that by raising the wage rate from €170 to €190 the farmer can obtain 10 additional and equally skilled men. *Ceteris paribus*, will the farmer hire them?

5. A firm produces three products A, B and C which involve lathe work grinding and assembling. The lathe, grinding and assembling time required for one unit of A are 2, 1 and 1 hours, respectively. Similarly, they are 3, 1 and 3 hours for one unit of B and 1, 3 and 1 hours for one unit of C. The unit profits of A, B and C are €4, €4 and €8, respectively. The production processes exhibit constant returns to scale and are independent of each other. Assuming that there are available 600 hours of lathe time, 600 hours of grinder time and 480 hours of assembly time, how many units of each product should be produced to maximise profits?

   If the firm is prepared to pay 30c per hour, instead of the current rate of 20c per hour for lathe time, it can obtain an additional 50 units of lathe time. *Ceteris paribus*, will the firm buy this extra time? Also, the firm is offered the opportunity of an extra 50 hours of assembling time at 5c per hour, instead of the current rate of 15c. What should the firm do?

6. A firm has available three fixed inputs W, X and Z and can produce five potential products (A, B, C, D and E). The following table gives the technological conditions, representing the amount of each input required to produce one unit of each output.

Input	Output				
	A	B	C	D	E
W	3	2	2	6	8
X	2	2	1	4	4
Z	3	4	3	6	4

   The unit profit coefficients for the outputs are as follows: $A = 4$, $B = 4$, $C = 3$, $D = 6$ and $E = 4$, while the available supplies of the inputs are: $W = 120$, $X = 80$ and $Z = 160$. Set up as a linear programming problem and find the optimal solution.

   (a) In the optimal solution classify the outputs not produced as relative complements or relative substitutes of the outputs in the basis. Explain the meaning of the distinction.

(b) Set up the dual of this programme and comment on its economic significance.

7. A farm can produce four different crops, wheat, barley, oats and corn, which can be sold on perfect markets at prices of €2000, €3000, €4600 and €600 per unit, respectively. Each process of production is independent of the others, is perfectly divisible, displays constant returns to scale, and requires a constant minimum amount of each input per unit of output. The farm consists of 20 500 acres of homogeneous land and has contracted to hire the services of 1300 equally skilled men. These two resources cannot be augmented. There are two different ways of producing wheat. One requires the services of 7 men and 90 acres of land per daily unit output, while the other uses 6 men and 115 acres. Each unit of output of barley requires 40 men and 180 acres; a unit of oats needs 18 men and 135 acres, and a unit of corn requires 1 man and 28 acres. The unit costs of other inputs (such as fertilisers and the like) for these five processes are, respectively, €1500, €1500, €1000, €3600 and €500.

(a) The objective of the farm is to maximise its short-run profits. What is the maximum.

(b) Which processes are used and how much of the products are produced in order to achieve maximum profit? Is the solution unique?

(c) What are the 'shadow prices' of the limitational resources?

(d) Now consider alternative limits to the amounts of labour and land available. Is there any process, which would never be worth using no matter what the resource limitations were? Explain.

(e) Given the original limitations, suppose that a neighbouring farm offers our farm the services of 10 extra skilled men in return for the use of 200 of the 20 500 acres. Is the offer worth accepting?

(f) Given the original limitations again, consider a technical improvement in oats production such that 12.5% more output can be obtained from any given combination of inputs. At the same time the price of oats falls to €4200 per unit. How can the shadow prices found in (c) be used to determine whether or not it is worthwhile producing oats in the new circumstances?

(N.B. No more mathematics than simple arithmetic and geometry is needed to answer this question).

9. The following problems can be solved either graphically or using the Simplex method.

(a) Maximise $4X + 3W$

Subject to $X + 3.5W \leq 9$

$2X + W \leq 8$

$X + W \leq 6$

$X, W \geq 0$

(b) Maximise $4X + 6$

Subject to $0.5X + W \leq 4$

$2X + W \leq 8$

$4X - 2W \leq 2$

$X, W \geq 0$

(c) Maximise $4X + W$

Subject to $X + 2W \leq 5$

$3X + 2W \leq 4$

$X, W \geq 0$

(d) Maximise $3X + 7W + 6Z$

Subject to $2X + 2W + 2Z \leq 8$

$X + W \leq 3$

$X, W, Z \geq 0$

APPENDIX A

8.A.1   Introduction

In the course of the discussion of Chapter 8, it was felt necessary, at various stages, to resort to the general notation of linear programming. Therefore, in this appendix we look at the general algebraic representation of linear programming and provide, largely without proofs, some very useful theorems of this mathematical technique. It is hoped that the discussion of this appendix will help reinforce the results of the earlier analysis and provide a firmer underpinning of the workings of linear programming.

As discussed earlier, linear programming is a constrained maximum or minimum extension. We try to programme something, like production, allocation of specific tasks to individuals, scheduling arrangements of various kinds and so on, in order to achieve some objective, such as maximising profit, revenue, performance and the like or minimising cost, subject to a number of constraints. The first point to be made is that we require this programme to be linear; everything in the mathematical schema is a linear function of something else. Linear programmes are the easiest type of programming to handle. We could also have non-linear programmes, integer programmes, as well as programmes under uncertainty and parametric programmes. The later refer to comparative statics, i.e., we alter some parameters of the original programme, find the two solutions corresponding to the original and new programmes and compare the effects of the change in parameters on the dependent variable (objective function).

8.A.2   General notation

We could define linear programming as the process of optimising (maximising or minimising) a linear function of a set of variables (called the objective function), subject to a set of linear constraints on those variables. Typically, to make programmes meaningful, only non-negative values of the variables are allowed, and also, typically, the constraints take the form of weak inequalities, i.e., they are of the *equal or greater than* ($\geq$) and *equal or less than* ($\leq$) variety. Therefore, we have two types of constraints to consider. First, there are technical, financial or other constraints of the type:

$$x_1 + 2x_2 + x_3 \leq b_j \tag{1}$$

or

$$y_1 + 3y_2 + 2y_3 \geq c_i \tag{2}$$

and second, we have the non-negativity constraints (conditions):

$$x_1, x_2, x_3, y_1, y_2, y_3, b_j, c_i \geq 0 \tag{3}$$

To turn the inequalities into equalities, we add (or subtract) non-negative variables, called slack (or surplus) variables, which will absorb any slack (or surplus). For example, in (1) we add the slack variable S_1, and in (2) we subtract the surplus variable S_2, so that the constraints become:

$$x_1 + 2x_2 + x_3 + S_1 = b_j \tag{4}$$

and

$$y_1 + 3y_2 + 2y_3 - S_2 = c_i \tag{5}$$

As we showed in the earlier discussion of Chapter 8, in constraints of the type (1), the slack variables (Ss) help provide us with an initial basis. Unfortunately, in constraints of type (2), the surplus variables (Ss) cannot do likewise, because they violate the non-negativity conditions. Therefore, in the case of constraints of type (2), we need in addition to the surplus variables, to insert non-negative *artificial* variables, A_i, which will help generate the first basic and feasible solution. Consequently, the constraint (5) is written as follows:

$$y_1 + 3y_2 + 2y_3 - S_2 + A_1 = c_i \tag{6}$$

On the other hand, to turn a given equality into an inequality implies that we have two forms, i.e., ($\geq$) and ($\leq$), so that the equal ($=$) sign lies in-between these two. For example, the equality $2x + 3w = b$ implies the two forms:

$$2x + 3w \geq b \quad \text{and} \quad 2x + 3w \leq b$$

which in diagrammatic terms is shown in Figure 8.A.1. Solutions of $2x + 3w = b$ lie on the straight line AB; solutions of $2x + 3w < b$ are found inside the area AOB and, finally, those of $2x + 3w > b$ lie outside the area AOB.

In general terms, a linear programme can be written as follows:

Maximise $\quad F = c_1 x_1 + c_2 x_2 + \cdots + c_n$

Subject to $\qquad a_{11} x_1 + a_{12} x_2 + \cdots + a_{1n} x_n \leq b_1$

$\qquad\qquad a_{21} x_1 + a_{22} x_2 + \cdots + a_{2n} x_n \leq b_2$

$\qquad\qquad \cdots$

$\qquad\qquad a_{m1} x_1 + a_{m2} x_2 + \cdots + a_{mn} x_n \leq b_m$

$\qquad\qquad\quad x_1, x_2, \cdots, x_n \geq 0$

with $i = 1, 2, \ldots, n$ variables and $j = 1, 2, \ldots, m$ constraints.

In the above, assuming that it is a standard production programme, the xs are the variables, such as quantities of different products; the $c_i s$ represent parameters, such as profit or revenue per unit of product; and the $b_i s$ are given constants, such

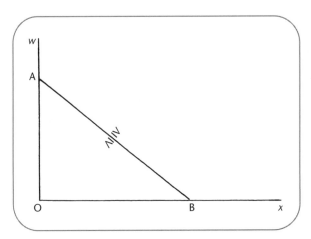

Figure 8.A.1 Boundaries of solutions

as available supplies of resources. If we take the above to be the primal programme, then we can easily find its dual programme. The dual is a distorted mirror image of the original one, and it is formulated as follows:

$$\text{Minimise} \quad G = b_1 y_1 + b_2 y_2 + \cdots + b_m x_m$$

$$\text{Subject to} \qquad a_{11} y_1 + a_{21} y_2 + \cdots + a_{m1} y_m \geq c_1$$

$$a_{12} y_1 + a_{22} y_2 + \cdots + a_{m2} y_m \geq c_2$$

$$\cdots$$

$$a_{1n} y_1 + a_{2n} y_2 + \cdots + a_{mn} y_m \geq c_n$$

$$y_1, y_2, \cdots, y_m \geq 0$$

where : $c' = (c_1, c_2, \ldots, c_n)$ $y' = (y_1, y_2, \ldots, y_m)$

$$A = \begin{vmatrix} a_{11} & a_{12} & \ldots & a_{1n} \\ a_{21} & a_{22} & \ldots & a_{2n} \\ \cdots \\ a_{m1} & a_{m2} & \ldots & a_{mn} \end{vmatrix} \quad x = \begin{pmatrix} x_1 \\ x_2 \\ \cdots \\ x_n \end{pmatrix} \quad b = \begin{pmatrix} b_1 \\ b_2 \\ \cdots \\ b_n \end{pmatrix}$$

Therefore, in matrix notation, the two programmes can be written as follows:

Primal programme		Dual programme	
Maximise	$F = c'x$	Minimise	$G = y'b$
Subject to	$Ax \leq b$	Subject to	$y'A \geq c'$
	$x \geq 0$		$y \geq 0$

A quick inspection of the two programmes reveals that in the dual the vector y' replaces vector x of the primal, the vectors c' and b are interchanged, the maximisation process in the primal becomes a minimisation process in the dual and the *less than or equal* sign ($\leq$) in the primal becomes now a *greater than or equal* sign ($\geq$) in the dual.

8.A.3   Some useful theorems of linear programming

We now provide a number of theorems on linear programming without proofs:

1. Each linear programme (primal) has a dual, which is another linear programme.

2. The dual of the dual is the primal.

3. If the primal has a solution, so has the dual (and vice versa).

4. The optimal value of the primal is equal to the optimal value of the dual. That is, the maximum value of the primary objective function is equal to the minimum value of the dual's objective function. (This is the so-called duality theorem, which provides confirmation of the optimality of the solution).

5. Considering any one of the original xs, say x_j, we may say that if $x_j > 0$, then the corresponding constraint in the dual is satisfied as equality. Similarly, if $x_j = 0$, then the corresponding constraint in the dual is satisfied as inequality. (The meaning of this theorem is that in the first case the opportunity cost of the resources per unit of product is equal to the unit profit, so that the product is produced – as with x_1 and x_2 in our example in Chapter 8. In the second case, the opportunity cost of the resources per unit of product exceeds the unit profit, and it is not profitable to produce the product – as was with x_3 and x_4 in our example in Chapter 8).

6. If the ith constraint of the primal is satisfied as a strict inequality, then the corresponding variable in the dual is zero, i.e., $y_i = 0$. Then the ith constraint is said to be a definitely ineffective one, and vice versa. (The meaning of this theorem is that if there is excess capacity of a particular input, its shadow price is zero, whereas if a primal constraint is satisfied as equality, the corresponding dual variable is positive.)

7. If a shadow price in the dual is positive, then the corresponding constraint in the original primary programme is effective (binding).

8. The number of variables that enter positively into an optimal solution need never exceed the number of fully utilised constraints. That is, if we had 6 variables and 4 constraints, we do not have to consider solutions involving more than 4 variables. (This theorem is the basis of the Simplex method, in the sense that it tells us in advance the sort of solutions that we must expect.)

By theorems (5) and (6), if we take any one primary variable and its corresponding dual constraint, then both strict inequalities cannot hold. Therefore, in general if $x > 0$ and $y'A > c'$, then by post-multiplying the second by x, we get: $y'Ax = c'x$. They can both be satisfied as equalities, but not as inequalities. Also, by the same argument, if we take $Ax < b$ and $y' > 0$ and premultiply the first by the second, we derive $y'Ax = y'b$. Combination of our earlier results yields the following:

$$G = y'b = y'Ax = c'x = F$$

which states that the optimal values of the two programmes are the same.

When we consider the above, in the light of the solution of the example in Chapter 8, we observe that our solution provides confirmation of all the theorems.

APPENDIX B

8.B.1 A diagrammatic exposition of LP

In this appendix we provide a diagrammatic exposition of the linear programming approach. When in a particular linear programme the number of variables or the number of constraints is two, it is possible to utilise the two-dimensional space and provide a geometric solution to the problem. This is a much easier task, since no elaborate techniques are required to achieve it. This has the merit of showing the similarities of LP with marginal analysis, particularly in the context of isoquants. Again, we proceed with the help of a general example.

Example

Consider the following simple production task facing a firm, which can produce two products, F and M. The net profits are €69 per unit of product F and €50 per unit of product M; these are determined by market forces. The production of one unit of F requires 5 units of labour and 3 units of capital, while the production of one unit of M requires inputs of 2 units of labour and 4 units of capital. The production functions are independent of each other and exhibit constant returns to scale. The amounts of resources available per week are 44 units of labour and 46 units of capital. The firm needs to know how many units of each product to produce in order to maximise its weekly profits.

Clearly, the above economic problem is an example of a linear programming problem. Because of its simplicity, no elaborate techniques are needed in order to solve it. Neither are many of the important theorems of LP theory, mentioned in the previous Appendix A, necessary in order to examine it. However, it is useful to discuss it in some detail, in order to illustrate in a simple way what are, in general, rather abstract and complicated arguments.

8.B.2 The output space

The objective function or total profit from both products is obtained as: $69F + 50M$, in which F and M are the, as yet, unknown levels of outputs. The total usage of input of labour is the usage in each product (or activity) added together, i.e., $5F + 2M$, and this must not exceed the total supplies available, i.e., 44. Similarly, the total usage of input of capital is the usage in each activity added together, i.e., $3F + 4M$, and this must not exceed the available supplies per week, i.e., 46. Finally, it makes no economic sense to consider negative outputs (or inputs for that matter). The programme, therefore, is formulated as follows:

$$\text{Maximise} \quad 69F + 50M \tag{1}$$

$$\text{Subject to} \quad 5F + 2M \leq 44 \tag{2}$$

$$3F + 4M \leq 46 \tag{3}$$

$$F, M \geq 0 \tag{4}$$

Since the problem contains only two unknowns, F and M, it is easy to solve it geometrically, which at the same time has advantages over a purely algebraic

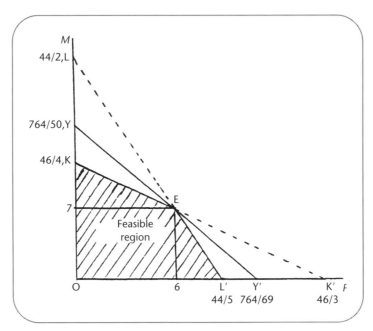

Figure 8.B.1 The solution of the primal – the output space

computation. In the output space of Figure 8.B.1, the line LL′ is the graph of the equation of the labour constraint, i.e., (2). The slope of the labour line is given by the negative ratio of the labour coefficients, −5/2, and so the line slopes downwards. The firm has just enough labour to produce any one of the output combinations, which give the coordinates of points along this line; it does not have enough labour to produce output mixes represented by points northeast of the line, and it has more than enough labour to produce output mixes to the southeast of the line. An analogous interpretation applies to the line KK′, whose slope is −3/4, pertaining to the capital constraint (3). The two constraint lines LL′ and KK′ intersect at point E, because the ratio of the resources lies between the corresponding ratios of input–output coefficients in the two activities. The solution of the two equalities in (2) and (3) gives the coordinates of point E, as $F = 6$ and $M = 7$. Therefore, the firm can produce 6 units of F and 7 units of M per week.

Since both constraints must be satisfied (in order to have a feasible solution), the firm can only choose a product mix represented by a point on or below *both* constraint lines. Finally, the non-negativity constraint (4) shows that the firm cannot produce west of the vertical axis or south of the horizontal axis; it is constrained to produce within the positive quadrant MOF. Consequently, the set of feasible outputs, i.e., the set of alternative production possibilities, is the set of coordinates of points 'on' (i.e., on the border or in the interior) of the polyhedron OKEL′O. The set of feasible points in a linear programming problem is always a convex polyhedron, like OKEL′O.

Fixing a value for the objective function (1) yields a linear equation, which is plotting into a straight line in the two-dimensional output space with slope −69/50, i.e., in-between the slopes of the constraint lines. This is called an isoprofit line. For example, YY′ is the isoprofit line for a weekly profit of €764. A higher (or lower) value leads to an isoprofit line parallel to YY' but proportionately further from (or nearer to) the origin.

Since YY' touches the polyhedron OKEL'O at point E, it is visually apparent that the resources, technology and unit profits make it possible to get a total weekly profit of €764, by producing 6 units of F and 7 units of M per week, using up in the productive processes all of the two resources to do so. This is easily verified by the arithmetic. It is also visually obvious that no greater profit is feasible, since any higher isoprofit line lies wholly outside the feasible output set. This is, therefore, the solution to the constrained profit maximisation problem.

8.B.3 The input space

Figure 8.B.2 presents a useful alternative geometric solution, this time in the two-dimensional input space. The production of product F requires capital and labour in the ratio 3/5 if neither input is wasted, and output is proportional to inputs used in this ratio. Thus, the output of F may be measured along the ray OF, whose slope is 3/5. For example, point C represents 30 units of labour and 18 units of capital, yielding an output of 6 units of F, according to the original requirements of the problem (i.e., for one unit of F, we require 5 units of labour and 3 units of capital). Because of the assumption of constant returns to scale, doubling these inputs means doubling the distance along the ray OF from the origin and yields double the output of product F, and similarly for any other proportion. The ray OM shows the analogous picture for activity M. For example, its slope is the capital/labour ratio in the production of M, i.e., 4 : 2 or 2, and, consequently, point A represents an output of 7 units of M, for inputs of 14 units of labour and 28 units of capital.

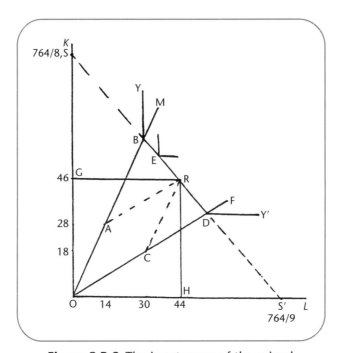

Figure 8.B.2 The input space of the primal

Now consider a given combination of outputs, say 6 units of *F* and 7 units of *M*. Adding the corresponding inputs of labour together, 30 + 14, gives us the total usage of labour, which is 44. Similarly, the two capital inputs, 18 and 28, amount to 46. These totals map into the point R in Figure 8.B.2. Geometrically, the total point, like R, is found by adding the separate points vectorially by 'completing the parallelogram'. In our case, the parallelogram is OARCO. This is achieved by drawing from point C a line parallel to ray OM, and from point A a line parallel to ray OF. These lines meet at point R to complete the parallelogram. We can use the same process of finding the total usages of each input for any combination of output levels. Since the output levels have to be non-negative, the individual output points must lie somewhere along the rays OM and OF and their total point, i.e., the fourth corner of the parallelogram, lies 'on' the 'output cone' MOF. If one of the outputs is zero, the total point simply coincides with the other point, and so it lies on the appropriate ray. Given a point on the cone, there is one and only one way of forming a parallelogram from it, the origin and the two rays. The two points on the rays, determined in this way, then show the allocation of the total usages of inputs between the two activities, i.e., the two products *F* and *M*.

An alternative way of looking at the inputs space, which will also allow us to derive the production indifference curves, is to consider products *F* and *M* as two different activities by which a given product is turned out by utilising different combinations of inputs, and look at the quantities of the two inputs required to produce, say, 10, 20, 30 and so on units of this product. In such a case, we know from the input requirements and the assumption of constant returns to scale, that activity F needs 50 units of labour and 30 units of capital to produce 10 units of our product; by extension it requires 100 units of labour and 60 units of capital to produce 20 units of the product etc. Similarly, activity M requires 20 units of labour and 40 units of capital to turn out 10 units of the product; by extension it needs 40 units of labour and 80 units of capital to produce 20 units of the product and so on. In Figure 8.B.3 point W represents 10 units of the product, produced by activity M and point X represents 20 units of the product, produced by the same activity, given by the ray OM. As before, the slope of the ray OM is given by 4/2, i.e., 2, which

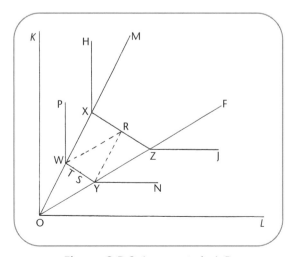

Figure 8.B.3 Isoquants in L.P.

is the capital/labour inputs ratio of activity M. Also, point Y represents 10 units of the product, produced by activity F and point Z shows 20 units of the product, turned out by the same activity, given by the ray OF. The slope of the ray OF is given by 3/5, which is the capital/labour inputs ratio of activity F. Therefore, the production indifference curve (or isoquant), involving the production of 10 units of the product, must pass through points W and Y, the production indifference curve (or isoquant), involving 20 units of the product, must pass through the points X and Z and so on. But also part of the 10 units isoquant is the section WY, part of the 20 units isoquant is the section XZ and so on. Despite the fact that no other activities are present, and so no other rays pass between OM and OF, points between these two rays can be thought of as if they were utilising the two activities in different proportions or intensities to produce our product simultaneously. For example, a point like S, which is a midpoint between W and Y, indicates that 10 units of the product are produced; half by process OM and half by process OF. Similarly, point T, which is located 3/4 of the way along WY towards W, will represent the production of 10 units of the product by means of the two processes but in the ratio 3/4 for process OM and 1/4 for process OF. The remainder of the production indifference curve can now be constructed easily and so, PWYN is the 10 units isoquant, HXZJ is the 20 units isoquant and so on. If one could conceive of a greater number of processes, the isoquants will become smoother and smoother, and as we go on increasing the number of processes (i.e., the substitutability of the factors of production) the isoquants will be approaching the shape of those of the marginal analysis, considered in Chapter 6.

The next step is to construct isoprofit curves in this space, just as in the output space of Figure 8.B.1. Point D in Figure 8.B.2 corresponds to point Y′ in Figure 8.B.1. The output of product F is 764/69 and the coordinates, 5(764/69) and 3(764/69), show the inputs required. Total profit is €764. If no product M is produced, then this point D lies on the €764 isoprofit curve. In a precisely analogous manner, so does point B, representing 764/50 units of product M and no F. Now suppose that, as we argued above, half the output of the first product of F is produced together with half the output of the second product, M. This combination yields an allocation point C for product F, halfway between O and D and an allocation point A for product M, halfway between O and B. By elementary geometry, it is clear that the two points C and A add vectorially to a point halfway between D and B. Total profit is again €764, since there is half of this profit coming from product F and half from product M. Therefore, this new point also belongs to the €764 isoprofit curve. The same is true for any other proportion summing to unity. For example, 1/4 of the D output of product F and 3/4 of the B output of product M result in the same total profit and yield a total usage point 1/4 of the way from B towards D.

For all such points, the inputs must be fully used, and used efficiently in order to result in €764 of profit. Clearly, the same result could be obtained by having more labour or more capital, or both, and either not using the inputs fully, or using them inefficiently. For example, any point in the northeast area bounded by the right-angled lines with point E at the corner could generate €764 of profit by using only the inputs of point E and wasting the rest. Therefore, the actual €764 curve, is properly defined as the southern or western boundary of all input combinations capable of yielding €764 of profit. Consequently, the curve is completed by adding the horizontal stretch DY′ and the vertical stretch BY. A point along DY′, e.g., represents an input combination in which only product F is produced and some labour is not used. With more processes or products, there may be more line segments making up the isoprofit curve. However, in all cases the efficiency idea, expounded above, together with the linearity properties ensure that an isoprofit curve is continuous, consists of straight line segments, nowhere slopes upwards, and is weakly convex to the origin.

For each different (non-negative) level of profit there is a different isoprofit curve. Each one is a radial projection of any other. The associated level of profit is proportional to the distance from the origin in any fixed north-easterly direction. Consequently, there is an isoprofit curve through each point in input space.

The given resources, i.e., 44 units of labour and 46 units of capital, plot into point R, in Figure 8.B.2. Therefore, the feasible region consists of points in the rectangle OGRH, formed by the origin, the two axes and the resources point. The objective of the firm is to maximise profits, i.e., to choose a point in the feasible region which lies on the highest isoprofit curve. Clearly, in this example, the optimum is at R itself, since the €764 isoprofit curve can be reached at this point, and every other point in the rectangular feasible area OGRH lies on a lower isoprofit curve. Notice that the usual first order condition for constrained maximisation, namely, that the optimum isoprofit curve must touch but not cut the feasible area, is seen to be satisfied. The usual second-order condition, that it touch it 'from above', is automatically satisfied in any linear programming problem, because of the convexity of the isoprofit curves and the rectangularity of the feasible area in the input space. The optimum point is then found from the parallelogram subtended from the resources point R. In our case, the allocation points are C and A, yielding outputs of 6 units of product *F* and 7 units of product *M*, as found earlier in Figure 8.B.1.

8.B.4   The dual

In the discussion of Chapter 8 we suggested that it is often useful and convenient to formulate a new problem, called the 'dual', associated with the original problem, called the 'primal' for contrast. In our example, the dual is:

$$\text{Minimise} \quad 44W + 46R \tag{5}$$

$$\text{Subject to} \quad 5W + 3R \geq 69 \tag{6}$$

$$2W + 4R \geq 50 \tag{7}$$

$$W, R \geq 0 \tag{8}$$

As discussed in Chapter 8, a dual is always generated from its primal by turning everything round and introducing new variables as needed, in our case W and R. As the derivation of the dual and its economic interpretation were explained in detail earlier in Chapter 8, we shall not repeat it here, but readers may wish to refresh their memory by looking up the relevant section. Suffice only to remind readers that the two variables W and R are the 'shadow prices' of the two resources L and K. Here, we are concerned with the diagrammatic representation of the dual.

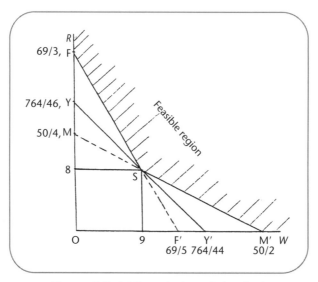

Figure 8.B.4 The solution of the dual

Since the dual is also a linear programming problem, it can be solved by the same general methods. In our example, the same geometric methods suffice, since the new problem is of the same simple dimensions (i.e., only two variables).

The counterpart to Figure 8.B.1 is Figure 8.B.4 and it is drawn from the statements of the problem, i.e., (5)–(8), just as Figure 8.B.1 is drawn from the statements of the primal (1)–(4). However, this time there is an important difference. The feasible region is *on* or *above* the constraint lines, because of the reversal of the inequality signs. The lines are FF' and MM', together with the axes, and so the feasible region is bounded by RFSM'W, as indicated by the shaded sides. Notice that the feasible set is again a convex polyhedron. The contours of the dual's objective function may be called iso-shadow cost lines. There is one through each point in the space, they are all parallel to each other with slope $-44/46$, and the cost is proportional to the distance from the origin in any fixed direction. The objective is to reach the lowest total shadow cost which is feasible. The optimum isocost line is, therefore, YY', representing a total shadow cost of €764, since it can be reached by choosing point S and every other point lies on a higher isocost line. It is a matter of simple arithmetic to check that the solution is to assign a shadow price of €9 to labour and of €8 to capital.

Just as Figure 8.B.2 provides an alternative geometric approach to Figure 8.B.1 for the primal, so can Figure 8.B.5 serve the same role instead of Figure 8.B.4 for the dual. In the space of unit net profits P_F and P_M or unit shadow costs of product F and product M, the slope of the ray OW is $2:5$, the ratio of labour coefficients in the two activities (industries). As an example, consider point V. Its coordinates are 45 and 18. This represents a shadow price of labour of €9, since the labour coefficients multiplied by this 'price' yield the values 45 and 18, which are, thus, simply the unit shadow labour costs of the respective products. Similarly, the slope of ray OR is the ratio of capital coefficients, and is the locus of unit shadow capital costs of the products, as the shadow price of capital is varied. The sum of the separate unit shadow factor costs for each product is the product's unit

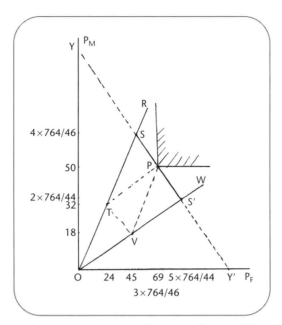

Figure 8.B.5 Iso-shadow cost lines in L.P.

shadow cost of production. Geometrically, each pair of points on the rays sum up vectorially, by the parallelogram technique, to a point representing unit shadow costs of production. Conversely, any unit shadow production cost point in the cone can be split up into the associated unit labour and capital costs. For example, unit shadow labour cost point V and unit shadow capital cost point T correspond to unit shadow production cost point P, as is easily checked by comparing their respective coordinates.

Next consider the objective function to be minimised (5). Point P in Figure 8.B.5 represents a total shadow cost of resources of €764, since P is associated with V and T, which represent shadow prices of €9 and €8, and these values for W and R in (5) yield a total of €764. Similarly, any other point along the line segment SS′ represents the same total shadow cost. For instance, point S itself has coordinates of 3(764/46) and 4(764/46). Dividing by the respective capital coefficients 3 and 4 yields a shadow price of capital of 764/46. Since the firm has available 46 units of capital per week, the total shadow capital cost is €764. But point S represents a positive price for capital and a zero price for labour, and hence €764 is the total cost. Such calculations show that SS′ is the €764 iso-shadow cost line for the cone SOS′ of Figure 8.B.5. Linearity and homogeneity show that there is an iso-shadow cost line through each point of the cone, they are all parallel to each other, and the cost is in proportion to their distances from the origin in any fixed direction.

Finally, the given unit profits €69 and €50 plot into point P. The constraints of the dual state that only points on the two rays adding up vectorially to points neither south nor west of P are allowed; the shaded area indicates the feasible region near P. Consistent with these requirements, it is required to reach the lowest iso-shadow cost line. Clearly, the optimum is at P itself, on iso-shadow cost line SS′, since no lower iso-shadow cost line meets the feasible region at all. As we have already seen, point P represents shadow price of €9 for W and €8 for R, confirming the results already found from Figure 8.B.4.

BIBLIOGRAPHY

Baumol, W. (1977), *Economic Theory and Operations Analysis*, 4th edn, Prentice-Hall.

Dorfman, R. (1953),'Mathematical or Linear Programming: A Non-Mathematical Exposition', *American Economic Review*, **XLIII**, December, 797–825. Reprinted in Archibald A. (ed.), *Theory of the Firm*, Penguin, 1971, pp. 387–421.

Dorfman, R., Samuelson, P. and Solow, R. (1958), *Linear Programming and Economic Analysis*, McGraw-Hill.

Vandermeulen, D. (1971), *Linear Economic Theory*, Prentice-Hall.

Wu Yuan-li and Ching-wen Kwang (1960), 'An Analytical and Graphical Comparison of Marginal Analysis and Mathematical Programming in the Theory of the Firm', in Boulding, K.E. and Spivey, A.W. (eds), *Linear Programming and the Theory of the Firm*, Macmillan.

chapter nine

Marketing – Advertising[1]

Learning outcomes

After studying this chapter you should know about:

- The marketing concept

- Market analysis

- Marketing mix

- Design and development

- Product life cycle hypothesis

- Distribution

- Promotion and promotional mix

- Rational methods to determining advertising budget

- Optimal advertising determination (marginal approach)

- The Dorfman–Steiner theorem

- Practical methods to determining advertising budget

- Percentage-of-sales approach

- All-you-can-afford approach

- Return-on-investment approach

- Objective-and-task approach

- Competitive parity approach

- Advertising and market structure

9.1 INTRODUCTION – THE MARKETING CONCEPT

In Chapter 4 under Demand Analysis, we pointed out that exchange represents the most important function of a market economy and stressed that no matter how well a company may have resolved other matters, it is only when its products are actually bought by final consumers that it has succeeded in its tasks. A central role in this is played by marketing. The process of marketing is initiated by human needs, which are a state of deprivation leading to human wants. The latter are human needs shaped by culture and individual personality. When wants are backed up by purchasing power, they are translated into demands for goods and services to satisfy such wants and, thus, eliminate the original state of deprivation. This in turn, leads to exchange of desired goods and services for money between two parties. This arrangement is known as transaction, and transaction requires some sort of market, defined as a set of actual or potential buyers and sellers of a product or service, who are able to communicate to each other their demands and supplies.

Before applying a marketing approach and the marketing strategy, the firm's objectives should be determined. Objectives must be selective and operational and in most instances they will be multiple. Naturally, making money, i.e., profits, will also help achieve the firm's (other?) objectives. Certain companies consider profitability as their main purpose and end, i.e., the main if not the only objective; others look at it as a measurement of how well the firm discharges its functions. However, it is important that objectives are formulated clearly, so that the marketing process has a target to aim at.

The strategies and tactics, which could facilitate the marketing process and the organisational objectives, are very much related to the firms' environment. This is because customers' requirements for the satisfaction of their needs and wants are influenced by market conditions. Therefore, different marketing tactics will be employed in different market structures, and firms have to adjust the contact with the market. This has been recognised in the literature. Thus, Moutinho *et al.* (2002), suggest that firms should be prepared for possible environmental changes, and suggest the use of scenario planning as a method to predict and prepare for alternative futures. Also, others have examined how changes in the context will influence the firm's approach in various marketing fields. For example, Laing *et al.* (2002) have analysed the influence of various environmental conditions on services marketing, Morgan and Hunt (2002) on marketing strategy and Veloutsou *et al.* (2002) on relationship marketing.

In a competitive environment, firms can successfully sell their products and services only when their offers satisfy their prospective customers' needs and wants in a way that is perceived as superior to the alternative competitive propositions and, thus, they are selected by the customers. In such a context, marketing refers to the process by which consumer wants are identified, analysed and anticipated by firms, which subsequently respond by developing and producing appropriate products, promoting and selling them in order to meet such demands more appropriately than competitors, while at the same time satisfying organisational objectives. It is clearly the job of firms to correctly identify such wants and seek to satisfy them, which provides the firms with their *raison d' être*. In other words, this merely tries to answer the basic question of any management, which is: 'What is our business and what are we in business for?'

The customer, market and competitor focus are the key elements of the modern marketing concept. Therefore, firms should examine their market structure and develop appropriate marketing tactics to contact the market. These two topics will be examined in this chapter.

9.2 MARKET ANALYSIS

Market analysis has the purpose of investigating, analysing and evaluating information on consumer demand for the products/services that firms are prepared to supply. Such information is derived by researching and analysing the firm's environment, which is made up by consumer demands, alternative product/services meeting such demands and the conduct of competitors supplying them and how the market is likely to develop, particularly, in the medium and longer term. The latter aspect is crucial in terms of growth, potential rivals and capital expenditure, assuming that expansion of capacity may also be required, as in most cases it is, to accommodate the introduction of new products. In this context, it may be found that pilot runs are the appropriate means to gauge opinion, test market responses and obtain consumer feedback. Only when the results of such pilot runs are favourable, should the firm commit itself to full-scale production, with possible modifications based on customer feedback, and the requisite expansion of capacity.

Various techniques of market research are available to test the marketability of new products, and the earlier analysis of Chapter 5 on Sales Forecasting is pertinent here. Of special importance in the present context, is the discussion of Section 5.5 on opinion polling and survey methods, and the doubts expressed there about the efficacy of such techniques. Specialist market research organisations are entrusted with testing consumer acceptance of, or resistance to, new products, by conducting tightly controlled experiments. As we pointed out in Section 5.5, survey techniques have been developed mostly for new products/services. These involve the design of questionnaires, the subsequent sampling of well-chosen, small, representative and stratified cross-sections of the population and the evaluation of the answers.

Nevertheless, it has to be emphasised that such techniques are fraught with dangers and there are no safe ways of guaranteeing the success of new products. The evidence suggests that, even among well-managed firms, only a small fraction of new products put out on the market, in the post-Second World War period of development of such products, turned out to be successful as money-makers.

9.3 THE MARKETING MIX

The way marketing has just been defined makes it clear that it is a multidimensional process involving various components; it is a mixture of important elements that must be attended sequentially than merely promotional activity, as it is sometimes made out to be. It includes all the marketing strategies and tactics aiming at the satisfaction of customers' needs and wants in a competitive manner. A number of new trends have been recognised in the marketing literature, such as the relationship marketing approach discussed by various scholars, including Grönroos. However, the most widely used and traditional tool associated with marketing, is the Marketing Mix. Most agree that the marketing mix consists of four main elements, known as the four Ps. These are the Product, Price, Place and Promotion. The role of other elements, such as the People, Physical evidence and Process for the support of services has also been appreciated, but their discussion and analysis is beyond the scope of this text. Interested readers are advised to consult the specialist literature, such as, for example, Palmer (2001).

The aim of the activities associated with the marketing mix, is to change the position and shape of the demand curve for the firm's products by making it more inelastic at various price ranges and also shifting it to the right. This process simply implies a greater degree of product differentiation, which aims at conferring greater monopoly power on the successful firm. Nevertheless, many firms decide, consciously, to opt for the opposite to product differentiation marketing policy, namely, that of imitation. The objective of the latter is to provide the imitating firms with the opportunity to exploit high elasticity of demand with lower prices, than the more successful branded products. In such cases, the advertising campaigns of the imitating firms may be stressing the similarities of their products to those of their competitors, rather than their differences, while at the same time emphasising the lower prices. This indeed, is occasionally, the case in the car industry, where products have achieved a high degree of standardisation.

We shall consider, briefly, these various elements of the marketing mix in turn. Also, given the importance of advertising budgets and their relevance to the economic thought, we shall consider in a separate section how such budgets are determined.

9.4 PRODUCT

The physical products (goods) and the services are the main elements that any supplier offers to the market. It is important at this point to clarify what exactly is offered by the firms to the customers, in marketing terms. Most of the offers are a combination of physical products and services. The degree that the offer is tangible or intangible differs depending on the nature of the offer.

A specific core benefit is associated with every offer. It is for this reason that the customer is going to make the purchase. For example, a customer buys a house to obtain shelter. However, customers require and purchase much more than the core benefit. Other elements which are offered instantly, such as the product design, the packaging and promises for future additional features linked with the transaction, for example, warranties and the after sales service, as well as the perceived quality of all the components of the total offer, are of paramount importance. These are the elements that will be considered during the evaluation of alternative options when a buying decision is made and will be the basis of differentiation between competitive offers.

After sales service has been recognised to be of considerable significance to the marketing process. It aims at satisfying consumer concerns about product dependability and at fostering and establishing a long-term relationship between company and products, on the one hand, and the final consumer, on the other. Only when customers are satisfied with the products they have bought, is the transaction really completed. Indeed, as Drucker has remarked, the transaction is completed when the product sold is consumed, not just when it leaves the seller's premise. A satisfied customer, of course, makes common sense both because he is likely to consider buying, in the future, the same product as a replacement and, more importantly, he can pass on the message of the product's good qualities to his friends, associates and the like by word of mouth. This is the best form of advertising and it is free!

After sales service is usually associated with consumer durable goods. While its importance in that area needs no special emphasis, after sales service applies equally well to all other products, if it happens that the customers find out, after they have bought the product, that they are not satisfied with them, for whatever reasons. An obvious reason for dissatisfaction may be that the product turns out to be defective, in some way. No amount of quality control can guarantee 100% satisfaction at all times, particularly, when the customer has changed her/his mind. A policy of refunding and exchanging goods, without questions asked, is clearly intended at demonstrating to the customer not only goodwill and good sense at public relations, but also that the products are, indeed, dependable and the company can be trusted.

Quality is a function of cost and after a point there are diminishing returns. Low and medium levels of quality may be achieved at relatively low or moderate cost, but at high levels – as quality approaches perfection – cost becomes prohibitively high. Consequently, at one end of the spectrum, products of very high quality close to perfection have a prohibitive cost, making them available to only a few customers who are rich enough to afford them. Clearly, this policy is not feasible for mass consumption products. However, in the case of mass consumption products, firms have a choice between operating a policy of low or medium quality products involving low or medium cost, or alternatively, adopting a policy of high quality products for high cost. If a low cost policy were adopted, low prices may very well accompany it, to penetrate large sections of the market. However, if the firm decided to opt for a high quality product, it may also organise its production and marketing processes in such a way to achieve cost minimisation, through economies of large scale production, and then pass on such economies to consumers, thus, offering a quality product at a reasonable price, which enables firms to acquire a large clientele for the large production runs.

Turning to the question of the brand name, we find that different views have been proposed in the literature regarding this term, which have been summarised by de Chernatony and Dall'Olmo Riley (1998). Nevertheless, it is generally agreed that the brand name is the main communication cue used by firms to distinguish their offer. Every brand name signals certain promises in relation to the real and imaginary offer features. Customers expect to obtain similar utility from the offers carrying the same brand name. Therefore, a brand name could be an asset, since it could reduce the required effort to make the offers' specific features known to the customers.

Successful brand names have become powerful selling focal points, enabling firms to sell a whole range of products and services, sometimes even seemingly incompatible ones, for example, food and clothing, or banking services, air travel and soft drinks under a well-known company label. Such a brand name makes it also easier and, most importantly, cost effective to advertise the whole range of products/services associated with the company label. In certain instances, a successful brand name has replaced in the minds of the customers even the generic name of the product, to the extent that customers may, unconsciously, equate demand for the product as demand for the brand. Clearly, this brand loyalty implies a lowering of price elasticity of demand for the goods in question and confers some power on the successful firms, since it shows that goods may carry some price premium, without affecting demand adversely.

The marketing literature has mostly two concerns in relation to the product. The first is the need for and the practices used to develop new products. The second is the management of the product portfolio over time. Some of the key issues related to these concerns will be discussed in the following sections.

9.4.1 Design and development

In a dynamic economy characterised by monopolistic/oligopolistic structures, new product development is an important component of competitive behaviour. Research and development is expected to lead to product improvement. The flow of innovation, in the form of new products, new forms of production methods and new distribution and selling techniques, tends to create new substitutes for old products. This is the Schumpeterian thesis of the 'creative destruction of capitalism', which includes the destruction of old products and forms of production and their replacement by new, more efficient ones. Product research is the main source of new product proposals, and once proposals for certain products have been accepted, such products should be launched in a way that maximises their chances of success. In this respect, an important element of the marketing process is the design and qualitative development of products. It is a fallacy to think that qualitative development could and should be confined only to up-market products. Whilst market segmentation and product differentiation are used as weapons of competitive rivalry, the ability to produce and market well-designed products of quality materials for mass consumption at prices that are within the reach of large sections of consumers, can prove to be very profitable, particularly, where price elasticity of demand is high. This value-for-money aspect, or consumers' surplus of traditional theory, is the result of meticulous design, choice of new raw materials and production techniques and processes, quality control, production engineering and so on.

This was very much the marketing policy of Henry Ford, with whose name it is associated, with the innovations he introduced in the automobile market. It has been argued that rather than looking at Henry Ford as a production genius we should consider him as a marketing genius. 'We think that Ford was able to cut his selling price and therefore sell millions of $500 cars because his invention of the assembly line had reduced his costs. Actually, he invented the assembly line because he had concluded that at $500 he could sell millions of cars. In other words, mass production was the result not the cause of his low prices' (Levitt 1960). Even in today's post-Fordism, and to some, post-industrial society, this quotation remains both relevant and powerful. We still consume all the products of the industrial era and many more besides. The assembly line is still in use today, producing even products of the new economy, although because of the change in the relevant production coefficients more of the work is undertaken by robotics.

9.4.2 The product life cycle hypothesis

One of the most important concepts in marketing is the product life cycle (PLC). It is a versatile tool of analysis and provides insights into the product's competitive dynamics. It has been used in, among others, marketing, international trade and

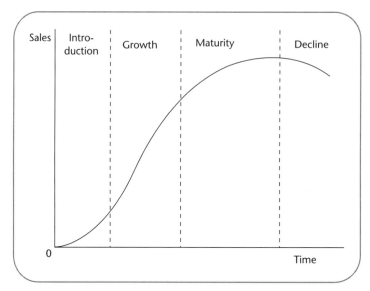

Figure 9.1 The product growth curve

foreign direct investment to illustrate the development of products over their life-time. Following the pioneering work of Dean (1951) in this area, the hypothesis contends that products go through the stages of introduction, exponential growth, maturity and decline in their lives, and that the growth curve of their sales follows the pattern exhibited in Figure 9.1.

This cycle has been described by Dean as the cycle of competitive degeneration through which all products of lasting distinctiveness pass.

> The invention of a new marketable specialty is usually followed by a period of patent protection when markets are still hesitant and unexplored and when product design is fluid. Then comes a period of rapid expansion of sales as market acceptance is gained. Next, the product becomes a target of competitive encroachment. New competitors enter the field, and innovations narrow the gap of distinctiveness between the product and its substitutes. The seller's zone of pricing discretion narrows as his distinctive 'specialty' fades into a pedestrian 'commodity' that is so little differentiated from other products that the seller has limited independence in pricing, even if rivals are few (Dean 1951, p. 411).

The problem of pricing products over their life cycle is considered in Chapter 10 under Section 10.3 and the reader is referred to that discussion.

Figure 9.1 shows sales as a function of time; at the introduction stage, sales rise very slowly, the new product faces resistance from the existing products it tries to replace and it takes time, effort and money for the new product to be established. This is a critical zone, as most new products fail at this stage. If the product is successful, it goes though the next stage of exponential growth, when demand rises and the size of the market expands, as the reputation of the product increases and repeat purchases grow. During the maturity stage, sales tend to stabilise and there are few opportunities for new customers. Nevertheless, this stage tends to provide the firm with the bulk of its sales over its life cycle. Eventually, the product enters the final stage of its life; decline, when sales fall due to competition from new products.

The PLC hypothesis makes certain assumptions. More specifically, it is based on the following:

1. Products have a limited life.

2. Profits rise and fall at different stages of the life cycle.

3. Product sales and profits pass through distinct stages, each posing different challenges to the producer.

4. Products require different strategies in each stage of the life cycle.

However, these assumptions are not always valid. Doyle (1995) has identified six problems associated with the concept, which limit its contribution to the development of marketing strategy. He suggests that the PLC:

1. is an undefined concept. It could be linked with the customers' requirements, the solutions provided, the technology, the product or a brand. For each one of these bases of analysis its length will vary, while some products' life does not reach an end;

2. could follow various patterns and shapes;

3. has unpredictable turning points, while the time frame where the transition through the various stages could happen is not specific;

4. has unclear implications. Depending on the specific environmental conditions, profits could be different than what was expected;

5. is not necessarily exogenous, since the firm's actions are often influencing the development of sales;

6. is too product-oriented. It has been argued that the concept is more a production than a marketing concept.

In addition to the above, continuous research and development can affect the growth curve of sales, as illustrated in Figure 9.2, where a firm tries to extend the maturity stage by product development. Changes and improvements could be related to real or/and imaginary product features and elements of the marketing mix, or other marketing tactics. These practices aim at promoting more frequent usage of the product by current users, developing more varied usage of the product among current users and creating new users for the product by expanding the market.

The extension of the PLC may prove to be quite long and rewarding, but at the end decline will set in. Therefore, the company must be prepared for this eventuality and must have established, through its research and development programmes, the new generation of products to replace the old ones.

The life cycle hypothesis can be used to answer a number of interesting questions, such as, for example: (1) can we predict the shape of the growth curve and the duration of each stage of the cycle?; (2) given a product, how do we find what stage it currently occupies?; (3) how can we affect the growth curve through

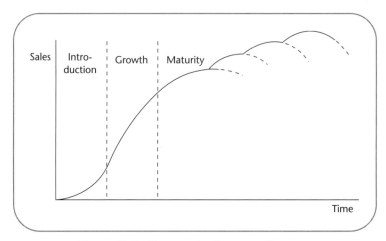

Figure 9.2 Changes in the growth curve

innovating activity and the profit performance of products, currently occupying a particular stage? Answers to these questions and many more can be obtained by consulting the specialist marketing literature and are not pursued here. The interested reader is referred to such literature and the books by Kotler, Porter, and Baker and Hart, given in the references, are a good starting point, although any tentative conclusions must be tempered by Doyle's suggestions.

9.5 PROMOTION

As mentioned earlier, the task of management is to ensure that a particular product that gets produced is actually purchased. The market should learn of its existence and the special characteristics or attributes that differentiate it from alternative products. Therefore, every firm must consider ways to communicate with its present and potential customers. The activities associated with the firm's communication with the public are a part of the marketing mix, known as promotion.

Many different tools could be used for the promotion, often called 'promotional mix' or 'communicational mix'. The most important of these tools are Advertising, Sales Promotion, Public Relations and Personal Selling. They all work together, to achieve various communication objectives. The importance of each individual tool varies, depending on the internal and external situation. The marketing literature discusses the various communicational tools and their interrelationship extensively, since communications have always been one of the significant subjects of analysis. Clearly marketing scholars give extensive coverage and emphasis to each of the elements of the communicational mix and their integration. However, of the various communicational tools, economists choose mostly to focus on advertising, its role and its effectiveness. Therefore, only issues related to advertising will be discussed in this chapter. Readers who wish to pursue the communication issue more deeply, so as to get a better understanding of some of the marketing communications concerns, can start by consulting the specialist literature, such as for example, Belch and Belch (2001), De Pelsmacker *et al.* (2001) and Shimp (2000).

9.6   ADVERTISING

Currently, advertising expenditure in the UK represents, approximately, 2.25% of the total consumers' expenditure, or 1.65% of gross national product, at factor cost. This is a large sum of money, and it enables a lively industry of advertising to thrive. The size of advertising budgets and their role in enhancing sales, makes advertising one of the key components of the marketing mix of firms. Together with the other elements of the marketing and the promotional mix, advertising aims at manipulating demand and promoting the firm's goods.

We can measure the responsiveness of sales to advertising, by estimating the advertising elasticity of demand, keeping other elements of the marketing mix (such as price, quality etc.) constant. In this connection, there is a difference between: (1) advertising elasticity of demand for the whole industry, which is the responsiveness of industry's sales to advertising; and (2) share elasticity, showing the responsiveness of a firm's market share to changes in its share of the industry's advertising. Advertising elasticity is expected to vary over the product's life cycle and, similarly, share elasticity may also change with the stage of the product's development. Of course, this presupposes that we have a clear idea not only of our revenue and cost functions, but also of the way advertising is affecting sales. This knowledge is hardly known, with any kind of precision and, in addition, the effectiveness of a firm's advertising is also circumscribed by the rivals' reactions to it. This interdependence points to the necessity of the firm making certain assumptions about the likely response of its rivals to its advertising actions, since the different reactions can lead to different outcomes, and it may be dangerous for the firm to assume no response by its rivals; an all too frequent occurrence by many management teams!

Typically, we distinguish two elements in advertising; the informational aspect and the persuasive one. The former aims at shifting the demand curve for the firm's product to the right, by providing information and increasing the awareness of the public about the existence and, in particular, the characteristics of the product, while the latter attempts to create product differentiation, by inducing brand loyalty and, thus, reducing price elasticity of demand. From a public policy standpoint, informational advertising is welcome, since it is, clearly, enhancing welfare by helping consumers to make more rational choices. However, persuasive advertising is frowned upon as increasing product differentiation, erecting barriers to entry and, thus, raising monopoly power. Nevertheless, it has also been argued that while the advertising effort of any individual firm is designed, clearly, to increase brand loyalty for the firm's product(s) and, thus, market imperfection, the attempts by rivals to differentiate their products have tended to cancel each other out, so that the overall effect of advertising in an industry is to reduce, somewhat, other elements of imperfection, for example, those resulting from ignorance and inconvenience. We discuss such issues, briefly, in the section on Advertising and Market Structure below. However, for the present we turn our attention to the important question of how the advertising budgets are determined.

9.6.1   Methods for determining the advertising budget rationally

A major postulate of neoclassical economics is that both organisations and individuals make rational decisions. Therefore, the literature suggests that the same rationality postulate could be applied for the determination of the advertising budget. In the following two sections we pursue some of these views and, in particular, we present and discuss the optimal advertising determination and the Dorfman–Steiner theorem.

9.6.1a   Optimal advertising determination

Given the large sums of money spent by firms on advertising every year, the question arises whether there are any principles designed to help us in the determination of optimal advertising outlays. Other questions in this area relate to how advertising expenditure should vary over time, particularly with changes in the business cycle, how such expenditures should be distributed between the firm's various products, regions etc.

Monopolistic and oligopolistic markets, with their emphasis on non-price competition, have made advertising a legitimate area of economic analysis. Advertising expenditure becomes an area of concern in much the same way as production costs do. However, advertising costs are differentiated, normally, from the firm's production costs. The latter, as we have seen, are a function of output, and they are the result of sales. By contrast, advertising costs are not, necessarily, functionally related to output and they represent a cause, not a result of sales. Nevertheless, we would like to know what prescriptions, if any, can economic theory offer to the determination of such selling costs.

The response of static marginal analysis to the problem of advertising is summarised in Figure 9.3, which, in part, repeats the discussion of Chapter 3. In our context, sales revenue is a function of advertising, and its S-shape is derived as follows: We assume that a certain amount of sales can be accomplished without advertising, but, as we increase advertising from zero, sales rise only very slowly, demonstrating the fact that since advertising is very low it has not reached large numbers of potential customers. However, once a critical threshold of advertising has been passed, the sales curve moves into its exponential phase, where sales increase very rapidly. This stage of increasing returns to advertising is explained by economies of specialisation, in that large advertising spending may make it feasible for the firm to use expert services and more economical media, with national coverage, to put its message across, which tends to reduce the average cost per contact., However, more important than economies of specialisation are economies of repetition; these by hammering the same message, time and time again, can overcome inertia for the existing consumer pattern, and scepticism about the firm's product by attrition. Eventually, though, diminishing returns set in, because most custom has already been tapped, and additional customers can only be attracted away from rival products at ever increasing advertising levels. In Figure 9.3, on the cost side, the total cost curve is inclusive of both production and advertising costs.

The profit maximising firm will increase advertising up to the point where the change in sales brought about by a small increment in advertising is unity (i.e., $\delta S / \delta A = 1$). This means that the profit maximiser will go on spending on advertising for as long as such expenditure increases sales by more than it does costs, and will stop when the last euro spent on advertising raises sales by exactly one euro. Therefore, the profit maximising firm's equilibrium is given by point Ap, implying an optimal advertising level of OAp, in Figure 9.3. The analysis of Chapter 3 has also shown that for a sales maximising firm, the equilibrium condition is given as

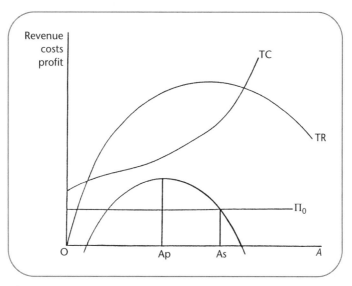

Figure 9.3 Determination of optimum level of advertising

$\delta S/\delta A < 1$ and, thus, if the firm operates under a profit constraint Π_0, equilibrium is reached at point As, which denotes an optimal level of advertising of OAs for that firm.

9.6.1b The Dorfman–Steiner theorem

The Dorfman–Steiner theorem is an application of the marginalist approach to advertising and it states that for a firm which can vary both the level of its advertising, A, and the price of its product, P, profit maximisation occurs where $\eta = \mu$, i.e., where the price elasticity of demand, η, equals the marginal sales effect of advertising, μ, i.e., the change in sales due to an infinitesimal change in advertising.

We assume that the firm has constant unit costs, so that AC = MC, and that the price, P, and advertising, A, are independent variables so that $\delta P/\delta A = 0$. We further assume that $\delta Q/\delta P < 0$ (i.e., the usual inverse price–quantity relationship) and that $\delta Q/\delta A > 0$ (i.e., advertising exerts a positive effect on the demand function, by shifting it to the right). Therefore, given the demand and total cost functions as: $Q = f(P,A)$ and $C = C(Q)$, respectively, the profit function can be written as:

$$\Pi = TR - TC - A = P \times f(P, A) - C(Q) - A = 0 \tag{1}$$

Differentiating relation (1) partially with respect to advertising, A, and price, P, slightly manipulating and setting the partial derivatives equal to zero, we obtain:

$$\frac{\delta \Pi}{\delta A} = P\frac{\delta Q}{\delta A} + Q\frac{\delta P}{\delta A} - \frac{\delta C}{\delta Q} \times \frac{\delta Q}{\delta A} - 1 = 0 \tag{2}$$

and

$$\frac{\delta \Pi}{\delta P} = P\frac{\delta Q}{\delta P} + Q\frac{\delta P}{\delta P} - \frac{\delta C}{\delta Q} \times \frac{\delta Q}{\delta P} = 0 \qquad (3)$$

Since by assumption $\delta P/\delta A = 0$, relation (2) can be re-written as follows:

$$\frac{\delta \Pi}{\delta A} = P\frac{\delta Q}{\delta A} - \frac{\delta C}{\delta Q} \times \frac{\delta Q}{\delta A} - 1 = 0 \qquad (4)$$

Since $\delta C/\delta Q = $ MC, by factorising relation (4) we obtain:

$$\frac{\delta Q}{\delta A}(P - \text{MC}) = 1 \qquad (5)$$

Multiplying now relation (5) through by the advertising to sales ratio, (A/PQ), and remembering that AC = MC we obtain:

$$\left(\frac{\delta Q}{\delta A} \times \frac{A}{PQ}\right)(P - AC) = \frac{A}{PQ} \text{ or } \left(\frac{\delta Q}{\delta A} \times \frac{A}{Q}\right)\left(\frac{P - AC}{P}\right) = \frac{A}{PQ} \qquad (6)$$

Considering now relation (6) we observe that the term in the first parenthesis is e, i.e., the advertising elasticity of demand, whilst the term in the second parenthesis is the mark-up over average cost, which is known as the Lerner index, measuring the extent of monopoly power. This relation can be re-written as follows:

$$e\left(\frac{P - AC}{P}\right) = \frac{A}{PQ} \qquad (7)$$

Relation (7) states that the higher the firm's advertising elasticity of demand, the higher the advertising expenditure should be. Similarly, the greater the mark-up, or the monopoly power, the greater the advertising must be.

We now multiply relation (3) through by the ratio (P/Q) to obtain:

$$P\left(\frac{P}{Q} \times \frac{\delta Q}{\delta P}\right) + Q\frac{P}{Q} - \left(\frac{P}{Q} \times \frac{\delta Q}{\delta P}\right)\frac{\delta C}{\delta Q} = 0 \qquad (8)$$

However, from the discussion of Chapter 4 we know that the price elasticity of demand is given by:

$$\eta = (-1)\frac{P}{Q} \times \frac{\delta Q}{\delta P}$$

Therefore, by substituting the symbol η into relation (8) and simplifying, we obtain the following:

$$P(-\eta) + P - \text{MC}(-\eta) = 0 \text{ or } (-\eta)(P - \text{MC}) = -P \qquad (9)$$

since AC = MC from our earlier assumption. Dividing relation (9) through, first by $(-P)$ and then by η, we get:

$$\frac{P - AC}{P} = \frac{1}{\eta} \qquad (10)$$

Direct substitution of relation (10) into (7) yields the following:

$$e\frac{1}{\eta} = \frac{A}{PQ} \quad \text{or} \quad \frac{e}{\eta} = \frac{A}{S}, \quad \text{where sales } S = PQ \tag{11}$$

Relation (11) states that the ratio of advertising elasticity of demand to price elasticity of demand (e/η) must, for profit maximisation, be equal to the advertising to sales ratio (A/S).

The final aspect of the Dorfman–Steiner theorem, i.e., that the firm will operate at the point where the price elasticity of demand, η, equals the marginal sales effect of advertising, μ, is derived by multiplying relation (11) by P, and simplifying as follows:

$$P\frac{A}{Q} \times \frac{\delta Q}{\delta A} \times \frac{1}{\eta} = \frac{PA}{PQ} = \frac{A}{Q}$$

Dividing the above expression through by the ratio (A/Q) we get:

$$P\frac{\delta Q}{\delta A} \times \frac{1}{\eta} = 1$$

which when multiplied by η, finally gives us the relation we require, namely:

$$\mu = P\frac{\delta Q}{\delta A} = \eta \tag{12}$$

This is a neat and elegant result, but in common with other aspects of the marginal approach, it has been criticised, and we turn now to consider such criticisms.

9.6.1c *Problems when attempting to determine advertising budgets rationally*

Both static models, presented above, suffer from a number of shortcomings. Their problems have been widely considered and discussed even in the marketing literature. It is believed that it is unrealistic to claim that an advertising campaign can, with any certainty, be classified as successful, while it is very difficult – if not impossible – to directly quantify its results. The limitations are of such importance that Beerli and Santana (1999) suggest that advertising objectives and evaluation of results should not be confused with commercial objectives and sales. Instead, they should be based on the response to the advertising message itself and elements such as attitude, recall or knowledge. When it is attempted to associate sales volume and advertising budget, in addition to our imprecise knowledge of revenue and cost functions and of our inability to specify exactly the sales–advertising relationship referred to above, some of the most important criticisms are as follows:

1. Sales are a function not only of advertising, but also of other tactics employed by the firm and the elements of the marketing mix and the promotional mix, such as pricing, product improvement, distribution channels, other selling activities and so on.

2. Various customer and exposure-related aspects could influence the effectiveness of advertising. Some of these aspects can be specific and measurable.

For example, Bhargava and Donthu (1999) suggest that a mediating factor to the sales response of outdoor advertising, is the location of exposure. Other aspects can be very subjective or case specific. For example, Mehta (2000) argues that the general attitude towards advertising appears to influence the way that people react to a particular advertisement.

3. The environmental conditions, including the macro and micro environment, are not taken into account. For example, the models fail to account for the reactions of rivals, i.e., of oligopolistic interdependence.

4. In practice, advertising takes place in discrete sums of money and it should be treated as an indivisibility, rather than the smooth, continuous variation implied by the static model.

5. Not all advertisements and advertising campaigns are the same. Different media and creativity are used in every advertising campaign. Both those elements require monetary and time resources for their development and will influence the customers' response to the advertising stimuli. For example, Costley et al. (2001) argue that the presentation medium clearly affects the recall of the original information presented and, therefore, the advertising effectiveness.

6. The effects of advertising are both short-and long-run (time lag effects). To further complicate the situation, Berkowotz et al. (2001) have also suggested that different media have different time lag effects, and that this should be considered when allocating the media budget. If the delayed or long-run effect is likely to be significant, then the static model is not appropriate to describe the sales–advertising relationship, and advertising should be considered as an investment project.

7. Although approximations of the sales–advertising relationship can be obtained, by using multiple regression analysis, and the results utilised for the purposes of establishing optimal advertising budgets, not all influential factors are easily identified and might change over time.

Despite attempts by economists such as Chamberlin, Buchanan, Boulding and others to improve the basic model and make marginal analysis the main tool of determining advertising outlays, a number of problems still remain, which limit its applications to the business world. Nevertheless, the marginal approach provides a useful guide about advertising expenditure and a logical framework against which a number of practical methods, which have been proposed to help with the determination of such expenditures, can be contrasted and analysed. It is to such methods that we turn our attention now.

9.6.2 Practical methods to determining advertising budgets

Given the difficulties encountered with the marginal approach to advertising budget determination, J. Dean has considered a number of alternative, practical, rule-of-thumb methods to such determination, which have been used extensively by firms. These rules-of-thumb are as follows:

- The percentage of sales

- All you can afford
- Return on investment
- Objective and task
- Competitive parity.

In what follows we examine each one of these practical methods, briefly. It should be mentioned also that this analysis draws, mainly, on Dean's pioneering work in this area.

9.6.2a   The percentage-of-sales approach

This is a mechanistic method, which advises us to determine an advertising budget as a percentage of past or anticipated sales. The percentage can be either fixed or variable, although no instruction is given as to what this percentage should be. In practice, it may be found that the percentage is usually chosen on the basis of what the company had been spending in the past, which does not mean that it is, necessarily, the right one. The method also suffers from a number of conceptual shortcomings. Advertising is used to increase future sales, rather than be dependent on past sales. This method, however, implies that advertising is the result of sales, instead of one of its causes. The amount spent to shift the demand curve should depend on how much the extra demand is worth, but the level of existing sales does not tell us anything about the cost or the worth of getting extra sales. Similarly, if the advertising outlay is a percentage of expected sales, the criterion becomes indefensible, so long as such sales depend also on factors other than current advertising, such as past advertising, level of disposable income and other components of the marketing mix.

Dean argues that the explanation for the widespread use of this method is to be found in the desire of management for certainty and the illusion of control, derived from relating advertising in a systematic way to revenue. Also, it allows the cyclical timing of advertising spending to vary with the ability to pay. Another reason of the popularity of the method is that if all firms in an industry were using this method and adopted the same percentage of sales, the advertising expenditure of such competitors would be roughly proportional to their market shares. This would tend to restrain advertising and, thus, have a stabilising effect.

9.6.2b   All-you-can-afford approach

This rule advises us to spend on advertising all that the company can afford, which in practice means a predetermined share of the profits, or an amount depended on liquid resources and borrowed funds. This method has the merit of setting a ceiling to advertising budgets, which, in the case of uncertainty about the effects of advertising, can protect the firm from possible gambles. Given that there is a time lag between advertising spending and sales results, a firm must ensure that it does not overextend itself, particularly when the time lag is long. The ceiling of what a firm can afford also involves the availability of outside funds.

However, there is no relation between the firm's liquidity and the prospects and opportunities offered by its advertising outlay, and this makes the all-you-can-afford rule unsatisfactory. If a firm expects that the returns of a particular advertising campaign far exceed its cost, then management would be failing in its tasks and responsibilities by restricting its advertising to what can be afforded, instead of borrowing funds to finance the profitable advertising budget. Also, but rather less frequently, the opposite may be the case; the limit of what can be afforded goes beyond the point at which the extra returns from advertising equal their cost. In this instance, the rule suggests spending money simply because it is available, irrespective of its return.

Nevertheless, given that excess earnings tend to have low utility for management, spending on advertising could well result in higher returns for the firm, ensuring its survival in the long run, because of the delayed and cumulative effects of advertising, despite less satisfactory returns in the short run. This would point to spending anything above a reasonable rate of return on advertising, in an attempt to consolidate and increase the firm's net worth over time.

9.6.2c   Return-on-investment approach

The principle underlying this method is that advertising has short-run and lon-run effects. Apart from affecting sales immediately, advertising also has a cumulative, delayed effect, which builds future goodwill for the firm. This is known as the dynamic response of sales to advertising and considers how a particular advertising campaign can affect future sales. We can consider various ways of this response over time, namely, that the effect on sales will decline at a constant rate, or at a rapidly declining rate, or it will increase first and decline later. Therefore, this realisation leads us to consider advertising as a capital expenditure budgeting problem, rather than a current expense one. It follows then that, to the extent that there is an institutional or cumulative element, advertising must compete for scarce funds in the same way as any other kind of investment; that is, on the basis of the prospective rate of return, present value or any other criterion of capital budgeting appraisal, as it will be discussed in the chapter on Capital Budgeting. Borrowing from the econometrics literature, advertising could be modelled as a distributed lag equation to deal with some of these issues.

However, it is very difficult, if not impossible, to disentangle the separate effects of any advertising campaign. Even cases of institutional advertising, such as, e.g., supporting the arts, which, clearly, aim at building goodwill, are not completely divorced from short-run considerations. In addition, there is considerable inter-action between the short-run and long-run effects, since the existing reservoir of goodwill affects the efficiency of advertising campaigns aimed at immediate sales. These problems, together with the difficulty of measuring the effect of advertising accumulation upon long-run sales volume and the possibility of eventual price premia, and also estimating the dissipation of goodwill – resulting from compet-itors' advertising and the need to take measures to protect it – make it almost impossible to find the rate of return on advertising investments.

Nevertheless, whilst the foregone discussion seems to rule out the rate of return as a single criterion for deciding on advertising budgets, it does not invalidate the approach as such. The rate-of-return approach is the correct conceptual framework to analyse this kind of expenditure, which also has elements of long-run nature.

9.6.2d   Objectives-and-task approach

Under this approach, the advertising budget is the sum of money which is required to achieve certain predetermined objectives of the firm. Therefore, the firm must first establish the objectives it wishes to achieve; second, it must work out the means or the tasks of attaining the objectives; and, finally, it must estimate the cost of realising these tasks. The aggregate of the separate costs of the various tasks is the advertising budget. For example, the firm may wish to capture a given share in a particular region for its product. The means or tasks of achieving this can be an advertising campaign consisting of a number of inserts in a local paper. It should be easy then to cost the inserts and compare the cost with the extra value accruing to the firm from achieving this particular objective.

Clearly, the main problem here is that the objectives must be stated in a way that their value is measurable, so that a comparison can be made with the cost of achieving them. This will bring the method much nearer to the marginal equivalency rule of revenue and costs. Otherwise the objective-and-task rule may justify any advertising expenditure, since it assumes that advertising is always worth the cost. Often the high marginal productivity of advertising may provide the advertiser with ex post justification, but it does not clarify the issues involved. The valuing and costing of objectives enables the firm to either expand or contract advertising plans in order to bring them in line. It follows then that this approach also allows objectives to be reshaped in the light of the cost of achieving them and vice versa.

9.6.2e   Competitive parity approach

According to this rule, the company should spend on advertising the same percentage of sales, profits, market share or some other variable, as its rivals do in the same industry. This rule is defensive in nature and is supposed to ensure security, which may explain its popularity.

However, what other firms are spending on advertising is not a guide to what a firm should spend in order to equate the additional benefits with the extra cost. Similarly, basing one's advertising budget on, say, the industry's average advertising to sales ratio, assumes that one's objectives are identical to those of the other firms in the industry, and that such firms know what they are doing. Given the differences in outlook and also differences in the advertising to sales ratios of the various competitors, the industry average tends to be meaningless.

Competitors' advertising affects the productivity of a firm's advertising, and also its optimum spending. But this optimum advertising spending is not determined by parity to the competitors' expenditure. The reason is that firms have different objectives, competitive maturity and marketing methods, which render the competitors' advertising to sales ratio of no value to any individual firm. Also, it must be remembered that advertising is only one of the components of the marketing mix, so that a firm may react to a rival's increased advertising by a strategy of lower prices or higher quality and so on.

Of the five practical methods of setting advertising budgets reviewed here, only the return-to-investment approach is conceptually sound, although difficult to implement. The remaining ones cannot be easily defended on analytical and economic grounds and owe their popularity to the difficulty of deriving the marginal revenue and costs of the advertising effort. Yet, they may lead to advertising expenditure well in excess of its optimal level, as the statement of the late Lord Leverhulme suggested, namely, that 'probably half of every advertising appropriation is wasted, but nobody knows which half'. However, there may be enough information available to enable us to use economic analysis to approximate the advertising–sales relationship, and proceed to estimate it by econometric techniques as a distributed lag model; thus, reaching a better decision on the amount of advertising, rather than considering rules of thumb, which, although simple, tend to be irrelevant.

9.6.3 Advertising and market structure – the evidence

One of the most awkward questions in economic theory is the relationship between advertising and concentration. A long time ago Kaldor (1950) argued that advertising promoted concentration of economic power, while Telser (1964) found that there was no empirical evidence of a relationship between advertising and market structure. However, Comanor and Wilson (1967) provided support for a statistically significant positive relation between advertising and profit rate, which they take it to be an indicator of market power, and also Mann *et al.* (1967) found that advertising as a proportion of sales increases with concentration. Similarly, Guth (1971) found that advertising has a statistically significant and quantitatively important impact upon the size distribution of firms in an industry, while Ornstein (1976) has provided support for both sides of the controversy by reversing the causation and trying to explain advertising in terms of concentration and sales.

In addition, it has been argued that concentration alone is not a proper measure of monopoly power, which is also affected by barriers of entry, economies of scale and other factors. This means that correlations between advertising and concentration provide a poor test of the effect of advertising on competition. In surveying the relevant literature, Comanor and Wilson (1979) found that in some industries heavy advertising contributed to high levels of market power and suggested that if this power were to be reduced, without restricting the flow of information to consumers provided by advertising, it could promote social welfare. However, they concluded that policies to curb excessive advertising 'require the assessment of the value to consumers of the information lost by reducing the volume of advertising, as compared with the value to consumers of the lower prices that would likely accompany a reduction in monopoly power', but this was very difficult, since it would require knowledge of consumers' response to advertising.

The difficulty in establishing unequivocal causality between advertising and concentration, may be the result of model (miss)specification. Since in the studies mentioned above the relationship is specified as a single-equation model, while a simultaneous-equations approach may be more appropriate, a number of authors have considered the relationship in the framework of a system of equations. Some of these have utilised a two-equations model (Cable 1972; Comanor and Wilson 1974; and Schmalensee 1972), while others have argued for a three-equations model (Greer 1971; and Strickland and Weiss 1976). In the Strickland and Weiss work, which incorporates ideas of earlier studies, a three-equations model is proposed in which advertising, concentration and the price-cost margins are the endogenous variables. Regarding the advertising–concentration relationship, it is argued that the effect of concentration on advertising takes the form of an inverted

U, meaning that advertising rises with concentration at first, but it falls at very high levels of concentration, either because of collusion between oligopolists to avoid mutually offsetting and wasteful advertising, or because of the case of pure monopoly. On the other hand, the effect of advertising on concentration is expected to be positive. The findings of this study show that the regression coefficients are statistically significant and take the expected signs, i.e., in the advertising equation, the coefficient of concentration (C) is positive, and that of C^2 is negative, so that an inverted-U relation is derived. Similarly, in the concentration equation, the coefficient of advertising is positive.

As if to underline the complexity of the issues involved, Sawyer (1982) argues that most of the structure–performance relationships – particularly those of advertising and profitability – which have been estimated, are subject to serious flaws, because they have not been derived from a single, coherent view of the firm's behaviour. This means that the independent variables entering the structure–performance relationships have been derived from appeals to these alternative and conflicting approaches of firm motivation. Sawyer argues that the use of a coherent approach indicates that the relevant equations are likely to be highly non-linear, and that simultaneous-equations estimation is neither required nor appropriate, and he concludes, that in some cases single-equation estimation is adequate, and in other cases reduced form equations are needed.

9.7 PLACE

Developing an appropriate product and making it known to the target group of customers (target market) can help any company to achieve its objectives. However, the product cannot be purchased unless it is available to the market. Therefore, the firm must consider distribution channels as part of the marketing mix.

Before taking any decision related to distribution, certain issues should be addressed first. The characteristics of the product, the customers, the competition and the firm and its objectives should be carefully considered. They might be very influential when making distribution-related decisions. More specifically, the two main areas that should be considered are the availability and the suitability of certain distribution channels, as well as the physical distribution.

The major channels available should be first determined and evaluated. This process is a very important one, since companies today are competing as networks of companies and the final choice could even be a source of competitive advantage. The type and the number of the existing intermediaries and distribution channels must be identified. There are many different options. The degree of match with the producer and each possible channel should be evaluated, using both economic and control criteria. Economic criteria include mostly the examination of the sales and cost associated with each one of the alternative channels. Control criteria are related to the relative power of the various distributors and the producer in each alternative distribution channel and their ability to influence or lead the channel members. The final choice should be re-examined regularly, to reassure that the selected channel remains the optimal one over time.

The second area that should be considered is physical distribution. It includes the transportation of the products from the point of production to the point of sale, in a manner which meets both organisational and customer needs. Physical distribution involves several activities. These include sales forecasting, order processing, warehousing, inventory levels determination and transportation. All these activities and decisions are cost related, and should be carefully evaluated as factors influencing the variable cost of the firm.

The interested reader is referred to marketing literature to further study the issues related to distribution. The book by Kotler, given in the references, is a good starting point.

9.8　PRICE

Setting the right price for a product is one of the core concerns in economics and the subject is covered in the next chapter. In addition to all the considerations related to pricing discussed there, such as the cost and the competitive actions, marketing emphasises the importance of customers' perceptions in relation to the product and the overall organisational and marketing objectives when setting the price. The price should reflect the customers' subjective evaluation of the quality of the product, as it is formed by the other elements of the marketing mix and the competitive actions. In addition, different pricing strategies could be in place for different stages of the product's life cycle, as explained in Chapter 10. Since we provide a reasonably extensive discussion of pricing in both theory and practice in the next chapter, we defer discussion until then.

SUMMARY

This chapter has provided a very brief discussion of some of the salient features of marketing and advertising, that are, typically, the concern of management. At the danger of doing the discipline an injustice, because of the very selective inclusion of material and the brevity of its treatment, we have considered the marketing concept, market analysis and marketing mix. Under product, we have looked at design and development, as well as the product life hypothesis. Under promotion and advertising, we have focused on various methods determining advertising budgets and have explored the relationship between advertising and market structure and have concluded by examining, briefly, the aspects of place and price.

APPENDIX A: THE MARKS & SPENCER MARKETING PHILOSOPHY[1]

As an illustration of a management and marketing philosophy, which has been put into practice very successfully, we shall consider the case of the retailing firm of Marks & Spencer, and their brand name, St. Michael. It has long been recognised that retailers exercise, by dint of their direct contact with customers, considerable power, much greater than that of producers. In that respect, Marks & Spencer are clearly no exception but, in addition, they have, over the years, initiated marketing policies and undertaken functions and activities, which have revolutionised retailing, propelled the firm to the top of British retailing and established themselves as one of the most efficiently managed companies in Britain.

They have achieved this status by setting out, clearly, their objectives, which can be summarised in the triptych: *quality-value for money-human relations*. These have helped mould the following set of fundamental principles for the firm's operations:

1. to offer customers a selective range of high-quality, well-designed and attractive merchandise at reasonable prices under the brand name St. Michael;

2. to encourage suppliers to use the most modern and efficient production techniques;

3. to work with suppliers to ensure the highest standards of quality control;

4. to provide friendly, helpful service and greater shopping comfort and convenience to customers;

5. to improve the efficiency of the business, by simplifying operating procedures; and

6. to foster good human relations with customers, suppliers and staff and in the communities they trade.

It is apparent that profitability is not stated as one of their major goals. This is not to say that the company is not interested in profits! On the contrary, they are highly profit conscious and, with the exception of the late 1990s and the early stages of the new millennium, they have been very profitable; after all without profit, none of their other objectives can be attained. However, they view profit not as a goal but a need; profit is the result of doing things right, rather than the purpose of business activity. The distinction is important, since it demonstrates the philosophy of the company to do things right and, thus, earn its rewards. Of course so long as this is achieved, and the capital market and the shareholders remain happy, the company can also afford to have this 'social face', and satisfy its other stakeholders. If things are not going well, as undoubtedly they had been in recent years, the company needs to rethink its strategy. Nevertheless, that short-run hiccup in profitability in no way casts doubt in the value of the Marks & Spencer overall marketing philosophy, to which we now turn.

The original company, popularised as the Penny Bazaar, was started by a Polish Jewish immigrant, Michael Marks, in 1884 in Leeds, after he had been a travelling peddler in the Yorkshire countryside for 2 years. Marks, for his own convenience, established the innovation of displaying, openly, all the merchandise for inspection, and priced most articles at one penny. This enabled, his mostly illiterate working-class customers to browse freely, select for themselves what they wanted and, generally, shop at ease, without been pestered. This element of operational simplicity was an important innovation, and the simple ideas of self-selection and self-service were to become cardinal principles in retailing, in the second half of the twentieth century, despite the fact that they had been introduced, unwittingly, more than 70 years earlier in a market bazaar. However, the adoption of a fixed price policy meant that Marks had to search, incessantly, for merchandise of as high quality as possible, that could be sold for a penny. Inevitably, he had to accept very low profit margins, and make up for this by achieving a large turnover. This pricing policy became the forerunner of the major dual preoccupations of the new company, which was established, originally, as a partnership in 1894 between Marks and Spencer, and later as a limited liability company, achieving an increasing turnover at low profit margins and sourcing for and creating products of high quality, to be sold at, relatively, low prices.

After the death of the founders, the firm passed in the hands of the Marks family, and, in the interwar years (1918–39), a new price limit of 5 shillings (i.e., a quarter of a pound sterling) was introduced. Apart from its simplicity and the lowering of the cost of decision making, the policy also meant that the firm could not be the passive recipient of what the manufacturers had to offer. They had to be proactive in persuading the manufacturers to produce the goods their customers wanted, at prices which were within their reach. This led to a new marketing philosophy, which is still fundamental to the firm today. On the one hand, where products were within the price reach, attempts were made to improve their quality in order to satisfy increasing standards of taste. On the other, where good quality products existed but were outside the price range, they tried to find ways, with their suppliers, to reduce the cost of production, without loss of quality. Therefore, product improvement and product creation of high quality, but at reasonable prices, became the firm's credo.

The company realised early on the significance and complementarities of large scale retailing and large scale production, but it had to convince its suppliers that it was to their benefit to cooperate with this particular policy.

> The task which the firm had consciously set itself was to create a chain of stores which would be equipped to handle so large a flow of goods across its counters that, because of the very large orders the firm could place with its suppliers, it could obtain all the benefits of the most modern and efficient methods of production. From this point of view, the company's store development and merchandising policies were interconnected and mutually complementary; it would be true to say that they were merely different aspects of what was essentially one and the same problem. Only large-scale production could achieve the economies which would ensure supplies of merchandise in the quantity, of the quality, and at the price which Marks & Spencer required; only large scale retailing, through a chain of stores commanding very large selling areas, could give manufacturers an assurance of orders of a scale which would justify them in introducing the most modern and efficient machinery and techniques (Rees 1973, pp. 97–98).

To this end, the firm decided that all its stores would sell, exclusively, only one brand of merchandise – St. Michael (registered in 1928). All the products are either designed by the company or jointly designed with the supplier and are produced against precise and exacting specifications furnished by the company to ensure high and consistent quality. To achieve this, the company employs a large number of technologists who work closely with the manufacturers, advising on and monitoring on choice of raw materials, choice of production processes and techniques, quality control, production engineering and the like. Of particular significance in this context, was the special relationship of the firm with its suppliers. In essence it involved Marks & Spencer buying considerable capacity of suppliers' plants for their exclusive use, and through long-term contracts they encouraged suppliers to invest in modern capital equipment. This, indeed, is the specific relationship issue, discussed under transaction economics in Chapter 3. However, that specific relationship was ruptured in the 1990s, when the company's management, in trying to reverse a severe fall in profitability, among other measures, decided to limit its commitments to domestic suppliers. The latter, naturally, complained that this abrupt ending of long-standing contractual obligations left them exposed, given the commitments they had already undertaken themselves.

Drucker, considering the business of Marks & Spencer calls it social revolution because 'Marks & Spencer redefined its business as the subversion of the class structure of nineteenth century England by making available to the working and lower-middle-classes, upper-class goods of better than upper-class quality, and yet at prices the working and lower-middle class customer could well afford' (1974, p. 96).

The earlier discussion of the PLC characterises, practically, all of the Marks & Spencer merchandise. Typically, at the introduction stage, most of the new of refined products go through pilot runs to test the market, and get customer response. This occurs through display and sales at selected stores. Only when customer feedback is promising do they proceed with possible modifications and full launching of the product in all stores. An important difference from the earlier discussion is that the firm, with some exceptions regarding informative advertising, does not advertise its merchandise in the usual way. It relies on the best advertisement there is, i.e., word of mouth of satisfied customers. With one of the best distribution channels in the country, that is a chain of over 260 of its own stores, selling exclusively its own brand products, along with a product buying team which conducts its own market research and pre-launching planning, it can avoid many costly mistakes. Furthermore, Marks & Spencer start with many advantages as compared with many manufacturers, who have no direct access to customers to test the market. At the growth stage, their relationships with their suppliers enable them to regulate the flow of merchandise in the required manner, since what they are buying from suppliers is productive capacity, rather than products. At the maturity stage, the buying team is concerned with product development, which will extend the product's life. Finally, at the decline stage, Marks & Spencer are ruthless in phasing out 'slow-moving' products. They check the products every fortnight to identify the slow selling ones and take appropriate action. Also, they operate the counter footage, expecting every foot of counter space to pay for the various costs, including overheads, and also contribute to profit. They have no blind spots on counters, and those products which do not contribute to sales and profit are eliminated.

In addition to the team of technologists, working to improve existing products and develop new ones and, thus, contribute to technical efficiency, Marks & Spencer are also famous for their drive against bureaucracy. In other words, quality control affects not only the merchandise but every aspect of the firm's operations.

Finally, and perhaps most importantly, we need to consider the special relationship between the company and those coming into contact with it, employees, suppliers and customers. We have touched upon the last two categories, but regarding employees it is the good human relations policy of the firm that seems to motivate them above all. The firm seems to spend more on personnel work than other similar companies, by providing career-long training and development for its staff, to allow success and growth with the company and to enable all staff to contribute to the full extent of their ability. This may very well explain the higher productivity of the staff, demonstrated by the higher sales and profit per employee earned by the firm, than other retailers over a long period of time.

APPENDIX B: ADVERTISING ON AND INSIDE TAXIS[2]

The development of an advertising plan involves a number of important decisions. The objectives and the budget of advertising campaigns should first be determined. When these have been established, the message and the media mix that will be used are the next choices to be made. Finally, as in any other management process, the results of the advertising campaign should be evaluated.

Media selection is of major importance for the effectiveness of advertising. To maximise the impact, almost every advertising campaign makes use of one primary medium and one or more secondary media. Resources should be allocated to a set of different media, including TV, radio, cinema, magazines, newspapers, outdoors and the internet.

In this context, the choice of a particular medium is of critical importance. Different media have relative strengths and weaknesses in relation to the contents of the advertising message. Some media are most effectively used to put simple messages across to a vast audience, while others are more effective at targeting specific groups of customers. For example, the contact with outdoor advertising cannot easily be avoided, but people do not, normally, have time to read the messages. Therefore, outdoor advertising messages must be built on a strong, creative and compelling concept, which is easily and instantly interpreted. Generally, its copy should be minimal and the best campaigns include short, catchy phrases that, initially, catch an audience's attention and then remain memorable in their mind.

Although outdoor advertising is probably the oldest form of recorded advertising in history and can be traced back to ancient Egypt and ancient Greece, through inscriptions and graffiti, it is always popular and there is evidence that many companies increase their expenditure in outdoor media. Further, the development of innovative media continues to keep the profile of outdoor advertising fresh. Nowadays, one could advertise on the floor tiles of supermarkets, on petrol pumps or even on humans. Vehicles could be used to carry advertising messages, proposing a mode of communication called 'transit advertising'. In addition to posters in subway stations, train stations and bus shelters, names and signs are often painted and messages often written inside or on the sides of lorries, buses and taxis.

Transit advertising has been one of the fastest growing areas of the outdoor advertising market. Many companies spend more on it, while in the UK it is accounting for more than one-third of all outdoor spending. Its development is such that at present a number of companies operate in the market producing campaigns explicitly for transit media and offering innovative ideas on transit advertising, while, due to its increased usage, the need for its regulation is rapidly emerging. In addition, transit advertising is somewhat different from traditional outdoor advertising, due to the mobility factor.

The taxi as a medium can be categorised under the umbrella of transit media. It involves the creative use of the traditional black cabs and consists in their partial or total transformation. It is a medium of such growing interest that some advertisers value it so highly, that they even develop loyalty programs between their brand, which is advertised on the cabs, and the taxi drivers. Although it is not used as a primary advertising medium, its usage seems to increase over time. Companies offering advertising services tailored to black cabs, appear to grow very quickly, since the turnover of some of them rises by more than 40% a year.

Taxi advertising can take several forms and intensities and can be placed outside or inside the car. When a black cab is totally transformed, it conveys a corporate brand representation. The taxi is painted with the advertiser's colours and logo, in various potential intensities. Advertisers could choose to apply colour graphics along the full width of the double doors of the taxi, along the full width of the taxi or even completely cover the vehicle. In 2002, there were many taxis in various major cities in the UK transformed in such a way that they supported the image of various brands, including the mineral water Evian, the travel agent Thomas Cook, Henderson Global Investors and the corporate brand of the products under the umbrella Easy (easyEverything). This form of taxi advertising resembles the traditional outdoor advertising, with the main difference that it is mobile. The contact with this form of taxi advertising cannot be avoided by those living in the area that taxis operate, while it can be encountered in various places where outdoor advertisement is very expensive or even not allowed. In addition to placing a message outside a taxi and transmit it in the street, as a sort of traditional billboard, it could send messages during its journey when the audience cannot avoid them. Advertisements are placed inside taxis, on the seats or even on the taxi receipts. Clearly, such messages only reach those that use taxis.

Although most of the characteristics of taxi advertising are common to many transit advertising media, taxis are somewhat different, or even unique. While other vehicles, such as buses and trains follow pre-specified routes, taxis travel in various places. This characteristic influences the reach and frequency of the advertising message and can be beneficial or problematic, depending on the campaign's objectives. In addition, one could argue that those using taxis for their travelling are likely to have a different profile and more disposable income than those using public transport. Based on this view, it has been suggested that advertising inside taxi cabs, is one of the best ways to reach busy business executives and decision makers, who are enjoying a rare moment of peace between meetings or when they are travelling to and from an airport.

Questions

1. How suitable is taxi advertising for products in each one of the different stages of their product life cycle?
2. What are the problems that one would have to overcome when attempting to determine the optimum spending on taxi advertising?

Notes

1. This section draws heavily on the works by Rees, G. (1973), *St. Michael: A History of Marks & Spencer*, revised edn, Pan, and Tse, K.K. (1985), *Marks & Spencer: Anatomy of Britain's most Efficiently Managed Company*, Pergamon Press.
2. This case study was prepared by Dr C. Veloutsou, Department of Business and Management, University of Glasgow, Scotland.

Bibliography

Beale, C. (1999), 'Lack of Marketing means Outdoor is Left Out in the Cold', *Campaign*, 23 July, 22.

Campaign (1999), 'The Outdoor Advertising Association/Council of Outdoor Specialist Award', *Campaign*, 19 November, 11.

Cuterman, J. (2001), 'Outdoor Interactive: Targeted Ads Atop Taxicabs to be The Next Big Idea in Outdoor Advertising, *American Demographics*, August, 32–34.

Freeman, L. and Fahey, A. (1990), 'Package Goods Ride with Transit', *Advertising Age*, 23 April, 28.

Fry, A. (2000), 'Take a Cab to get Seen Around Town', *Marketing*, 17th February, 31.

Gorman, M. (1997), Media Choice: Transport', *Marketing*, 2 October, 11.

Hemsley, S. (1999), 'Moving Message', *Marketing Week*, 23 September, 41–43.

Marketing (1994), 'Ads on the Move Grab their Share', *Marketing*, 4th August, 25.

Siebert, T.W. (1999), 'Bus Ads Caught in Cross Fire: What's Commercial and What's Political on Transportation?', *Adweek*, 8th February, 3. http://www.taximedia.com/

NOTE

1. I wish to thank Dr C. Veloutsou, Department of Business and Management, University of Glasgow, Glasgow, Scotland for helping me prepare this chapter.

BIBLIOGRAPHY

Baker, M. and Hart, S. (1998), *Product Strategy and Management*, Prentice-Hall.

Beerli, A. and Martin Santana, J. (1999), 'Design and Validation of an Instrument for Measuring Advertising Effectiveness in the Printed Media', *Journal of Current Issues and Research in Advertising*, **21**(2), Fall, 11–30.

Belch, G. and Belch, M. (2001), *Advertising and Promotion: An Integrated Marketing Communications Perspective*, 5th ed, McGraw Hill.

Berkowotz, D., Allaway, A. and D'Souza, G. (2001), 'The Impact of Different Lag Effects on the Allocation of Advertising Budgets across Media', *Journal of Advertising Research*, March–April, 27–36.

Bhargava, M. and Donthu, N. (1999), 'Sales Response to Outdoor Advertising', *Journal of Advertising Research*, July–August, 7–18.

Cable, J. (1972), 'Market Structure, Advertising Policy and Inter-Market Differences in Advertising Intensity', in Cowling, K. (ed.), *Market Structure and Corporate Behaviour*, Grays Mills.

Comanor, W.S. and Wilson, T.A. (1967), 'Advertising, Market Structure and Performance', *Review of Economics and Statistics, **49***, 423–440.

—— (1974), *Advertising and Market Power*, Harvard University Press.

—— (1979), 'The Effect of Advertising on Competition: A Survey', *Journal of Economic Literature*, **18**, 453–476.

Costley, C., Das, S. and Brucks, M. (2001), 'Presentation Medium and Spontaneous Imaging Effects on Consumer Memory', *Journal of Consumer Psychology*, **6**(3), 211–231.

Dean, J. (1951), *Managerial Economics*, Prentice-Hall.

de Chernatony, L. and Dall'Olmo Riley, F. (1998), 'Defining a "Brand": Beyond the Literature with Experts' Interpretations', *Journal of Marketing Management*, **14**, 417–443.

De Pelsmacker, P., Geuens, M. and Van den Bergh, J. (2001), *Marketing Communications*, Prentice-Hall – Financial Times.

Doyle, P. (1995), 'Product Life Cycle Management', in Baker, M. (ed.), *The Companion Encyclopaedia of Marketing*, chapter 28, Routledge.

Drucker, P. (1974), *Management: Tasks, Responsibilities, Practices*, Heineman.

Greer, C. (1971), 'Advertising and Market Concentration', *Southern Economic Journal*, **38**, 19–32.

Grönroos, C. (1994), 'From Marketing Mix to Relationship Marketing: Towards a Paradigm Shift in Marketing', *Management Decision*, **32**(2), 4–20.

Guth, L.A. (1971), 'Advertising and Market Structure Revisited', *Journal of Industrial Economics*, **19**, 179–198.

Kaldor, N. (1950), 'The Economic Aspects of Advertising', *Review of Economic Studies*, **18**, 1–27.

Kotler, P. 2002, *Marketing Management*, 11th ed., Prentice Hall.

Koutsoyiannis, A. (1982), *Non-Price Decisions*, Macmillan.

Laing, A., Lewis, B., Foxall, G. and Hogg, G. (2002), 'Predicting a Diverse Future: Directions and Issues in the Marketing of Services', *European Journal of Marketing*, **36**(4), 479–494.

Levitt, T. (1960), 'Marketing Myopia', *Harvard Business Review*, **38**(4), July–August.

Mann, H.M. *et al.* (1967), 'Advertising and Concentration', *Journal of Industrial Economics*, **15**, 81–84.

Mehta, A. (2000), 'Advertising Attitudes and Advertising Effectiveness', *Journal of Advertising Research*, May–June, 67–72.

Morgan, R. and Hunt, S. (2002), 'Determining Marketing Strategy: A Cybernetic Systems Approach to Scenario Planning', *European Journal of Marketing*, **36**(4), 450–478.

Moutinho, L., Davies, F. and Hutcheson, G. (2002), 'Exploring Key Neo-Marketing Directions Through the Use of an Academic "Think-tank": A Methodological Framework', *European Journal of Marketing*, **36**(4), 417–432.

Ornstein, S.I. (1976), 'The Advertising–Concentration Controversy', *Southern Economic Journal*, **43**, 892–902.

Palmer, A. (2001) *Principles of Services Marketing*, 3rd edn, McGraw Hill.

Porter, M.E. (1980), *Competitive Strategy: Techniques for Analysing Industries and Competitors*, The Free Press.

Reekie, W.D. and Crook, J.N. (1987), *Managerial Economics*, 3rd ed, Philip Alan.

Sawyer, M.C., 'On the Specification of Structure–Performance Relationships', *European Economic Review*, **17**, 295–306.

Schmalensee, R. (1972), *The Economics of Advertising*, North-Holland.

Shimp, T. (2000), *Advertising Promotion: Supplemental Aspects of Integrated Marketing Communications*, 4th edn, Dryden press.

Strickland, A.D. and Weiss, L.W. (1976), 'Advertising, Concentration and Price–Cost Margins', *Journal of Political Economy*, **84**, 1109–1121.

Telser, L.G. (1964), 'Advertising and Competition', *Journal of Political Economy*, **72**, 537–562.

Veloutsou, C., Saren, M. and Tzokas, N. (2002), 'Relationship Marketing: What if …?' *European Journal of Marketing*, **36**(4), 443–449.

chapter ten

Pricing in Theory and Practice

Learning outcomes

After studying this chapter you should know about:

- Price and output determination under various market structures

- Perfect competition, monopoly, monopolistic competition, oligopoly

- Discriminating monopolist, cartels, price leadership, game theory

- Pricing practices

- Full cost, going rate, incremental approach, life cycle

- Pricing new products

- Multiple product pricing

- Transfer pricing under different conditions

10.1   INTRODUCTION

Pricing policy together with the product and investment policies of the firm are the main instruments at the disposal of management for the attainment of the firm's objectives. In the context of the structure – conduct – performance approach, such policies represent the behaviour of firms, which lead to particular levels of performance. Pricing, therefore, is a means towards specific ends rather than an end in itself. If, for example, the objective of the firm is profit maximisation, this results in the well-known rule of producing at the level of output where $MR = MC$ and then reading off the demand curve the price which will maximise profits. This in turn requires some knowledge of the market supplied by the firm, i.e., knowledge of its industrial structure. It follows then that in order to obtain pricing rules, it is necessary to discuss both the objectives of the firm and the nature of the industry within which firms find themselves operating. We can distinguish two approaches to pricing: (1) the prescriptive approach, according to which specific pricing rules are derived in order to achieve a given objective and (2) the descriptive approach, which provides a description of how firms actually set their prices, in particular situations, to achieve specific objectives again. Both approaches will be considered in this chapter and the question whether there is a difference between the two will be addressed at the end.

10.2   MARKET STRUCTURES

By market structure we mean important characteristics of a market which influence the conduct of firms supplying that market and which in turn affect their performance. The main features of market structure characterising an industry are the level of concentration, the degree of product differentiation and the presence or absence of barriers to entry of new firms into the industry. Market concentration has to do both with the number and the relative importance of firms supplying a market, product differentiation deals with the type of products produced, i.e., whether such products are standardised or differentiated and, barriers to entry is concerned with the existence or not of various obstacles, and their degree, in the attempts by newcomers to enter a market. A by-product of significant product differentiation is that it can supplant price competition by various elements of non-price competition.

The main feature of concentration is whether the supply of a particular market is dominated by a few large firms. Such concentration can be measured by means of the concentration ratio, which tells us what percentage of the industry's sales, value added (or any other appropriate size variable) is controlled by the largest x firms in the industry. Whilst it may be wrong, without any other discussion and evidence, to equate high concentration with increased monopoly power, particularly as regards policy issues, nevertheless high concentration ratios are useful first indicators of the degree of competition in an industry. By product differentiation we mean the various distinguishing features which enable products of one producer to be different from those of another producer in the same industry. These may include trade marks, brand names, stylistic features, differences in shape, colour and the like, which enable consumers to distinguish the various alternative products. Product differentiation is the result of the R&D activity of firms and of considerable promotional activity in the form, for example, of advertising, marketing. The main result of product differentiation is to make the demand curve for the differentiated product more inelastic, as compared to that of a standardised product, thus allowing the producer a greater control over the price of the product. While concentration and product differentiation tell us something about the nature of existing actual rivalry in particular markets, barriers to entry tell us something about potential competition, since they refer to the conditions of entry into such markets. Such entry may vary in particular industries from a very easy to a blockaded one. Leaving aside the reasons for such barriers and concentrating instead on their effects, we may say that industries with 'low' barriers will not permit a price well above a competitive price (i.e. one that is arrived at by equating average revenue to average cost) without attracting new entrants, while industries with 'high' entry barriers will allow price to be set at or near the one which maximises short-run profits (i.e. the one at which MR = MC) without attracting new rivals. The absence or presence, and in varying degrees, of these features in particular industries will result in less concentrated and more concentrated markets and in order to analyse the former we can use the models of perfect competition and monopolistic competition, whereas for the analysis of the latter, the models of oligopoly and monopoly are more relevant.

10.2.1 Perfect competition

The combination of a very large number of knowledgeable producers, each acting independently to maximise his profits by producing a standardised product and having no control over its price and no patents or other protection against potential rivals, with a large number of equally knowledgeable consumers, each acting independently and trying to maximise his utility, results in the market structure known as perfect competition. The price of the product is set by the market forces of demand and supply, and firms are forced to accept that price or leave the market. The demand curve facing each firm is perfectly elastic, resulting in AR = MR, because of the assumption of product homogeneity, and firms in such a market are price takers.

The short-run equilibrium of the firm under these conditions is illustrated in Figure 10.1(b). The market price is set in Figure 10.1(a) and we start with an initial equilibrium of price and quantity given by P_1 and Q_1. Price P_1 is then accepted by a typical firm in Figure 10.1(b) and the profit maximisation output is given by Q_1, since at that output MR = MC. Notice that while the vertical axes in Figure 10.1(a) and (b) are drawn on the same scale, the scales of the horizontal axes in the two diagrams differ significantly with the scale of Figure 10.1(a) being a great many times larger than that of Figure 10.1(b). At this price and quantity combination, the firm makes supernormal profits given by the area P_1ABC.

As an example consider the case of a small dressmaker, who can sell as many garments of a particular type to a large department store at €15 each. The dressmaker has estimated that his weekly total costs are given by:

$$TC = 0.03q^3 - 0.9q^2 + 10q + 5 \qquad (1)$$

where q is the number of garments produced per week. How many garments should be produced to maximise profits?

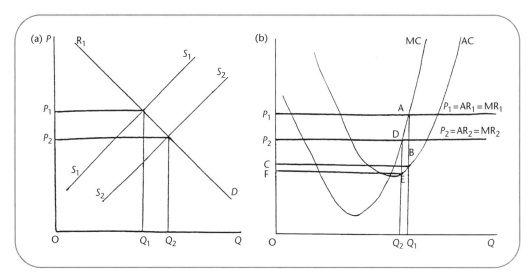

Figure 10.1 Short-run equilibrium (a) Market; (b) For perfectly competitive firm

The rule for maximum profits is to set the marginal cost equal to price and solve for output. Differentiating the total cost function (1) to derive the marginal cost, setting MC equal to price 15 and rearranging, we derive the following quadratic equation:

$$0.09q^2 - 1.8q + 10 = 15 \quad \text{or} \quad 0.09q^2 - 1.8q - 5 = 0 \tag{2}$$

which has roots of $q = 22.47$ and $q = -2.47$. Negative solutions are clearly meaningless in this context, as we cannot have negative outputs, and so profits will be maximised if the dressmaker produces approximately 22 garments per week. It can be verified that the rate of change of marginal cost is positive at $q = 22$, since

$$\frac{d^2(TC)}{dq^2} = 0.18q - 1.8 = 0.18 \times 22 - 1.8 = 3.96 - 1.8 = 2.16 > 0$$

which confirms that at the point of equilibrium, marginal cost is rising, as required. The weekly profits of the dressmaker are then calculated as:

$$\Pi = TR - TC = pq - (0.03q^3 - 0.9q^2 + 10q + 5) = 765.6 - 544.44 = 221.16$$

Clearly, such profits attract newcomers into the industry, whose output increases the total supply and in our geometric terms pushes the market supply to S_2S_2 and, assuming demand conditions remain the same, a new market equilibrium is arrived at price P_2 and Q_2. The firm, in turn, has to adjust its equilibrium to the new price, by restricting its output to Q_2, at which it maximises its profits. The new supernormal profits earned by the firm are lower than before and are given by the rectangle P_2DEF. These profits attract new entrants into the industry and, with each successive round, market supply is increased bringing down the market price and forcing firms to accept these lower prices, or force them out of the market altogether if they are inefficient. The process continues so long as

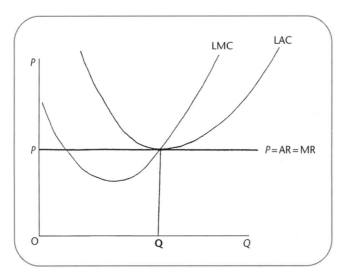

Figure 10.2 Long-run equilibrium for the perfectly competitive firm

there are firms making supernormal profits until in the end all such profits have been competed away. When this happens not only firms but also the industry as a whole are said to be in long-run equilibrium. Each firm in the industry is producing where $P = AR = MR = LMC = LAC$ and makes only normal profits, i.e., it earns the opportunity cost of capital, which is the same for all firms and is included in its LAC. The long-run equilibrium of the firm is shown in Figure 10.2. The quest for maximum profits has resulted in zero supernormal profits and all remaining firms in the industry, being equally efficient, are sharing the market and earning the same rate of return! However, the curves in Figure 10.2 are the long-run AC and MC ones. Whilst the LAC is the envelope of the short-run AC curves, the LMC curve represents the rate of change of the long-run total cost, when all costs are variable. This means that while in the short run the firm has a fixed plant, given by its fixed costs, and its management is concerned with the optimum utilisation of that plant, in the long-run the firm is free to vary the size of its plant, according to prevailing market conditions. Fixed resources become variable through depreciation and the firm must decide on its 'size of plant', thus, our dressmaker from the earlier example must decide on the number of sewing machines, the amount of space needed and so on. There is an optimum plant size associated with every level of output, which minimises the total costs of production, and the long-run MC curve can be defined as the geometric locus of those points on the short-run MC curves, which correspond to the optimum plant size for each level of output. Therefore, in the long run total cost is a function of output and size of plant, s. To illustrate, various short-run cost curves can be derived from:

$$TC = 0.03q^3 - 0.9q^2 + (11 - s)q + 5s^2 \tag{3}$$

where s stands for plant size. If $s = 1$, we are back to the original short-run cost function of our dressmaker, as the reader can verify by substitution. Now by differentiating (3) partially with respect to s, and equating to zero we get an expression for s, as follows: $-q + 10s = 0$, or $s = 0.1q$. Substituting this value into (3) and simplifying the algebra results in a new total cost function given by:

$$TC = 0.03q^3 - 0.95q^2 + 11q \tag{4}$$

which shows that in the long run fixed costs are zero, as expected. If now the dressmaker is offered a price of €10 per garment, his new equilibrium will be found by finding his long-run MC and equating it to €10. Thus, by differentiating (4) with respect to q and setting the derivative equal to 10, we obtain:

$d(TC)/dq = 0.09q^2 - 1.9q + 11 = 10$. Simplifying the above, we get the quadratic expression $0.09q^2 - 1.9q + 1 = 0$, which gives the following roots: $q_1 = 20.57$ and $q_2 = 0.539$. At $q_1 = 20$, the rate of change of marginal cost is found to be:

$d^2(TC)/dq^2 = 0.18q - 1.9 = 0.18 \times 20 - 1.9 = 3.6 - 1.9 = 1.7 > 0$, thus marginal cost is rising, showing that the solution is optimal. Therefore, the dressmaker produces 20 garments per week. His profits in this situation are given as:

$$\Pi = TR - TC = 10 \times 20 - (0.03 \times 20^3 - 0.95 \times 20^2 + 11 \times 20)$$
$$= 200 - 240 + 380 - 220$$
$$= 580 - 460 = 120$$

Thus, the dressmaker has reduced his output to 20 units per week, which together with the price cut, means that his profits are now lower than before. Also, the implication of the aforementioned changes is that he must build a plant of optimum size $s = 0.909 = (20/22 = 0.909)$. Clearly, since supernormal profits have not been eliminated, there is still scope for more firms to enter the market increase output and lead to another round of price reductions. This will require again a reappraisal of the optimum plant size until prices have fallen to their minimum long-run average cost for all firms in the industry, before such industry is to be in long run equilibrium. In practice, continuous technological changes and other adjustments too may very well mean that such equilibrium is never attained.

10.2.2 Monopoly

By contrast, in the case of monopoly there is only one firm producing a unique product, i.e., one which has no close substitutes and entry into this market is blocked, as a result either of legal franchises or ownership of exclusive patents, technical know-how or materials required in the production process, which allow the firm to exercise absolute control over such inputs. In this case, the demand curve facing the monopolist is the whole market demand curve, sloping downwards in the usual manner, and it provides the monopolist with considerable control over the price of the product, so that he is considered a price maker. However, even here the monopolist can control either the price or the quantity of the product, not both. Therefore, assuming that the monopolist wishes to maximise his profits, he will produce the output level at which $MR = MC$. His equilibrium is illustrated in Figure 10.3. Accordingly, the monopolist produces OQ_e and charges a price of OP_e. Consequently, his supernormal profits are given by the area P_eBCA.

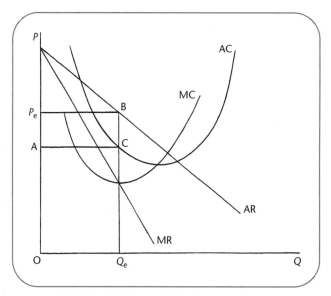

Figure 10.3 Equilibrium of the firm under monopoly

We can illustrate some of the points mentioned above by means of the following example. A monopolist faces a demand curve for his unique product given by: $P = 1820 - 4q$, and produces at an average cost of $AC = 20 + 8q$. Assuming that he wishes to maximise his short run profits, we need to form his profit function as follows:

$$\Pi = TR - TC = (1820 - 4q)q - (20 + 8q)q = 1820q - 4q^2 - 20q - 8q^2$$
$$= 1800q - 12q^2$$

Maximum profits are derived by differentiating the above expression with respect to q, setting the derivative equal to zero and solving the resulting equation for the optimum level of output. Thus, $d\Pi/dq = 1800 - 24q = 0$ from which we get $q = 75$ and substituting this value into the price equation we derive the price at which this output can be sold as: $p = 1820 - 4(75) = 1820 - 300 = 1520$. Thus, the monopolist produces 75 units and sells them at a price of 1520. To verify that this solution is optimal, we need to examine the sign of the second derivative of the profit function above, which is found to be: $d^2\Pi/dq^2 = -24 < 0$. Since this is negative, it follows that the solution $q = 75$ and $p = 1520$ does indeed result in maximum profits, which are given as: $\Pi = 1800(75) - 12(75)^2 = 67500$.

If, instead of using the rule $MR = MC$, the monopolist had set price equal to MC, then the solution would have been: $1820 - 4q = 20 + 16q$, which can be solved for $q = 90$, $p = 1460$ and $\Pi = 64800$, i.e., a higher output, which can be sold at a lower price to yield lower profits than before. (The calculations are left to the reader, as an exercise.)

A managerial problem that occurs frequently is the response of the firm to an imposition of taxes by governments. Three cases can be considered: those of (1) a lump sum tax, (2) a profit tax and (3) a sales tax of x euros (or cents) per unit of product. The responses of the firm in the first two cases are the same. If the firm were maximising profits before the imposition of either the lump sum or the profit tax, it will continue to do so after the imposition, by producing the same level of output and charging the same price. Clearly, the firm cannot avoid the imposition of a lump sum tax, T, but while this will reduce the firm's profit by T, it will not necessitate a change in the firm's determination of output and price, since the profit function can be written as:

$$\Pi = TR - TC - T$$

where TR and TC are functions of output as before and T is a constant, which vanishes upon differentiation, thus leaving the same marginal condition for profit maximisation, that is, MR = MC as before.

Similarly, if the government imposes a $t\%$ corporation tax, it means that the company has to pay to the government a proportion $t\%$ of its profits as tax. In the previous example of the monopolist, assume that the government imposes now a 40% corporation tax. The firm's profit function is now:

$$\Pi = (1 - t)(TR - TC) = (1 - 0.4)(1820q - 4q^2 - 20q - 8q^2) = 0.6(1800q - 12q^2)$$

Differentiating the above with respect to q, equating to zero and solving for q we have: $d\Pi/dq = 0.6(1800 - 24q) = 0$, or $1080 = 14.4q$ which gives $q = 75$. Substituting this into the price equation yields $p = 1520$, i.e., the same answer as before. However, the profit function is evaluated now as:

$$\Pi = 0.6[1800(75) - 12\,(75)(75)] = 40500$$

i.e., a reduction of the original profit of 67 500 by 40% ($67500 \times 0.4 = 27000$).

However, if the government were to impose a tax of €300 per unit of product sold, then for the firm this will be similar to an increase in costs by $300q$ and so the profit function can be written as:

$$\Pi = TR - TC - xq = (1820q - 4q^2 - 20q - 8q^2 - 300q)$$

and setting $d\Pi/dq = 0$ we get $d\Pi/dq = 1500 - 24q = 0$, which yields $q = 62.5$ and $p = 1570$. Thus, profit becomes:

$$\Pi = 1500(75) - 12(75)(75) = 46875.$$

Therefore, output is reduced by 12.5 units, price goes up by 50 and profits are reduced by 20625 ($67500 - 46575$) as compared to the pre-tax case, as a result of the imposition of a sales tax, which yields to the government $300(62.5) = €18750$. Notice here that if the government had simply imposed a lump sum tax on the company of €18750, it would have received the same tax revenue *but* the company would have been better off, since its profits would have been: ($67500 - 18750$) = 48750, and also the consumers would have been better off, since the company would be producing its 75 units and charging a price of €1520, as compared with $q = 62.5$ and $p = €1570$, found above.

Since entry into this market is blocked, the monopolist is able to carry on producing the same output in the long run and enjoy supernormal profits. Therefore, so long as we retain the strict assumptions about the blockaded entry, the short- and long-run equilibria positions of the monopolist can remain the same. In practice, however, this is unlikely to be the case because the dynamic changes occurring in both supply and demand conditions will eventually erode the monopolist's position.

10.2.2a Price discrimination

A special case arises where a monopolist produces in one plant but serves two separate markets A and B with different demand curves. Assuming again that the monopolist wishes to maximise his profits, the optimal rule is to produce the level of output at which his marginal cost (MC) is equal to the combined marginal revenue (MR_{A+B}), and distribute the product between the two markets in such a way that the last unit of output sold in either market adds the same amount to his revenue. In Figure 10.4(c) we construct the combined MR_{A+B} curve by adding horizontally the market revenues of the two markets MR_A and MR_B. Thus, the equality of MC with the combined MR_{A+B} determines the profit maximising output OM. This output is then distributed between the two markets as indicated in Figure 10.4(a) and (b), so as to get $OM = OM_A + OM_B$ by equating MC with the two marginal revenues and charging different prices OP_A and OP_B in the two markets. It is clear that price is higher in market B with the relatively more inelastic demand. Profit maximisation in this case requires that the monopolist practises price discrimination.

This can be demonstrated by considering a firm which produces a unique product in a single large plant but services both a home market and an overseas market. The demand curve of the home market is given by: $P_H = 260 - 3Q_H$ and that of the overseas market by $P_O = 180 - 4Q_O$. The total cost function of the firm is given by $TC = 3000 + 20Q$, where $Q = Q_H + Q_O$. Profit maximisation requires that the firm equates the MC to the marginal revenues of the two markets. These MRs are obtained by finding first, from the demand curves, the total revenues in the

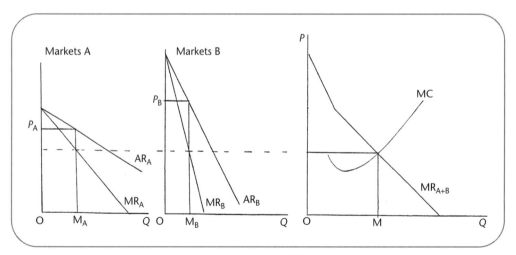

Figure 10.4 Equilibrium for the price discriminating monopolist (a) Market A; (b) Market B; (c) Markets A + B

two markets and then differentiating these total revenue functions with respect to output, as follows:

$$TR_H = (260 - 3Q_H)Q_H = 260Q_H - 3Q_H^2 \text{ and}$$

$$MR_H = d(TR_H)/dQ_H = 260 - 6Q_H \text{ and}$$

$$TR_O = (180 - 4Q_O)Q_O = 180Q_O - 4Q_O^2 \text{ and}$$

$$MR_O = d(TR_O/dQ_O) = 180 - 8Q_O$$

Therefore, since MC = 20 we have for the home market the following relationship: $260 - 6Q_H = 20$, from which we get $Q_H = 40$. For the overseas market we have: $180 - 8Q_O = 20$, which gives $Q_O = 20$.

Thus, the firm produces $Q = Q_H + Q_O = 40 + 20 = 60$ units and allocates 40 units to the home and 20 units to the overseas markets.

Substituting these values into the price equations for the two markets we get:

$$P_H = 260 - 3(40) = 140 \text{ and } P_O = 180 - 4(20) = 100$$

Since $MR = P(1 - 1/\eta)$, these prices imply that the price elasticities in the two markets are: $\eta_H = 1.1667$ and $\eta_O = 1.25$, as the reader can verify. As expected the market with the more inelastic demand, that is the home market, is charged a higher price. Finally, the profit of the firm is given by:

$$\Pi = TR - TC = (260 - 3Q_H)Q_H + (180 - 4Q_O)Q_O - (3000 + 20(Q_H + Q_O))$$

$$= (260 - 3 \times 40)40 + (180 - 4 \times 20)20 - [3000 + 20(40 + 20)]$$

$$= 7600 - 4200 = 3400$$

However, if the firm had decided instead to charge the same price in both markets, then its demand function would have been given by adding the two separate demands. For this, we need to solve the two demand functions for Q and then add them together as follows:

$$Q = Q_H + Q_O = 260/3 - p/3 + 180/4 - p/4 = 1580/12 - 7p/12,$$

which can be written as: $p = 1580/7 - 12Q/7$

The next step is to derive the total revenue function by multiplying the price equation obtained earlier by Q, which will give us $TR = 1580Q/7 - 12Q^2/7$. Therefore, for profit maximisation we need to set MR = MC and so we obtain:

$1580/7 - 24Q/7 = 20$, which yields $Q = 60$, i.e., the same total output as under price discrimination. Substituting this value into the price equation gives: $P = 1580/7 - 12(60)/7 = 122.857$. Finally, profits are now calculated as:

$\Pi = TR - TC = 122.857(60) - 3000 - 20(60) = 3171.42$, which shows that price discrimination is more profitable.

Clearly, for the monopolist to be able to do so, two conditions must be fulfilled. The first is that the price elasticity of demand is different in the two markets and the second that the markets are sufficiently isolated, so that no resale from the lower-price market to the higher-price market occurs. In practice, transportation costs and other obstacles to trade often allow producers to charge differential prices.

10.2.3   Monopolistic competition

In the case of monopolistic competition, the market is characterised by a relatively easy access so that a large number of sellers are competing by producing considerably differentiated products. This element of product differentiation allows producers some control over the price of the product, but this remains within rather narrow limits because of the availability of close substitutes. In addition, there is considerable non-price competition with the emphasis on advertising and other promotional activities for the creation of brand loyalty, for when such activities prove successful, products can carry significant price premia, despite the existence of close substitutes.

To derive the equilibrium of the monopolistically competitive firm in the short run, we assume again profit maximisation and proceed in the usual fashion to construct the revenue and cost curves and find the profit maximising output by equating MR = MC. Figure 10.5(a) illustrates this case and the diagram looks almost identical to that of the monopoly situation, except that the demand curve refers to the differentiated product of each individual seller, and the scale of the horizontal axis is a great many times smaller than the corresponding one of the monopoly case. At the profit maximising output Q the firm is making super-normal profits, given by the area PABC. These encourage outsiders to enter the market, since entry is relatively easy to achieve. The newcomers into the industry, competing for the custom of the existing firms, have the effect of reducing the demand for the previously established firms. Therefore, such firms find that the demand curves for their products shift to the left. Equilibrium of the firm is again obtained at the MR = MC output, but such output is lower than before and so are profits.

This process of entry by outsiders, increasing industry output and reducing the demand for the output of existing firms, and consequently their profits, continues

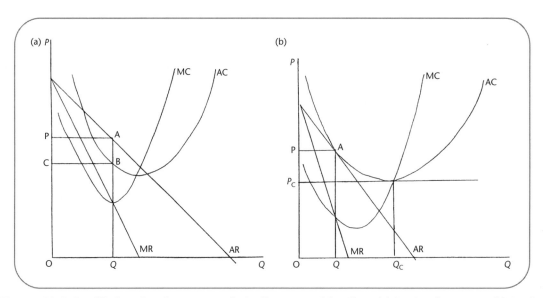

Figure 10.5 Equilibrium for the monopolistically competitive firm (a) In the short run; (b) In the long run

for as long as there are firms making supernormal profits. In the end, when demand has shifted to the left sufficiently for all such profits to have been competed away, the monopolistically competitive firm finds its equilibrium again at the level of output Q, at which MR = MC, as shown in Figure 10.5(b). At this level of output, since supernormal profits have been eliminated, the firm also equates AR with AC. However, as these two pairs of equalities are not also equal to each other, it means that output Q is not produced at minimum cost. This result could be contrasted to the long-run perfectly competitive equilibrium, which could be accomplished at the price and output configuration P_C and O_C. Monopolistic competition, therefore, involves considerable under-utilisation of capacity.

However, in practice, it is unlikely that supernormal profits under monopolistic competition are competed away. The long run may never arrive. Even when products are identical, customers may still perceive them as different, conditions of sale may differ in many ways, customers may have definite preferences about the available brands of a commodity and, more importantly, the R&D process of firms will be coming up with either new products altogether or even finer degrees of product differentiation, which could be cemented in consumer preferences by promotional activity. All this will have the effect of making the demand curve for the differentiated products more inelastic, in which case even price increases may lead to increased profits.

10.2.4 Oligopolistic competition

Under oligopoly, the market is dominated by a few large firms, which produce and sell either a standardised or a differentiated product, where price competition has been supplanted by various forms of non-price competition, mainly product differentiation, and where potential entrants face significant barriers. The main feature of oligopoly, which sets this market structure apart from the ones considered so far, is the considerable mutual interdependence of producers. This interdependence arises from the fewness of producers, the similarity of the products and the consequent power over a market, which such small numbers of producers entails. It follows that oligopolists have considerable control over the price of the product, but such control is also circumscribed by their mutual interdependence. This interdependence increases oligopolistic uncertainty and one way of avoiding such uncertainty, or restricting it, may be sought in collusive agreements among oligopolists, which clearly enhance their market power.

Collusive agreements may take the forms of gentlemen's agreements, formal cartels or price leadership arrangements, which will usually fix a price and firms, except the leader, view themselves as price takers. However, collusive agreements may be aiming at issues other than price fixing, such as, for example, sharing markets. The extent to which such arrangements may take place, if at all, depends on the number of firms, type of product and, particularly, government legislation that, typically, in industrial countries prohibits these arrangements as restrictive practices. Price competition is, normally, avoided between oligopolists because there is a danger that it may degenerate into a price war and eventually to a cut-throat competition. In contrast to the other forms of market structure, equilibrium of the profit maximising firm under oligopoly cannot be established independently of the actions of the other firms in the industry. Additional assumptions are required as regards the way oligopolists react to their rivals' actions with reference to, for example, pricing and product policies, pointing to different approaches to establishing equilibrium under oligopoly, depending on the assumptions made. This means that we do not have a general theory of oligopoly, but several. We shall consider only a few of these approaches and their implications on oligopolistic behaviour.

10.2.4a The kinked demand model – price stickiness

This model does not purport to show how equilibrium is reached but rather to illustrate that once a price has been chosen it will tend to remain stable. This is due to a kink in the relevant demand curve that results from a particular assumption regarding the behaviour of the oligopolists. Assume that a price P_E has, somehow, been arrived at. An oligopolist starting from this price, at point K, ponders that if he were to lower his price, in order to get more custom, his rivals will follow his move and lower their prices too, fearful that if they do not they will lose out. On the other hand, if he were to increase his price his rivals will be more than willing to let him do so while keeping theirs at the same level. The implications of these actions and reactions (behaviour) are that for price increases the demand curve is more elastic than for price decreases, and they are shown in Figure 10.6. Therefore, the relevant demand curve for price increases is the portion KD_1, while for price decreases the relevant demand curve is given by the portion KD_2. This means that the demand curve becomes D_1KD_2, having a kink at point K and, consequently, the marginal revenue is given by D_1LMN, which has a discontinuous segment LM directly below K. If the marginal cost curve passes through this discontinuous segment, the equilibrium output and price are given by Q_E and P_E, but it is clear that the same equilibrium is consistent with a great variety of cost conditions

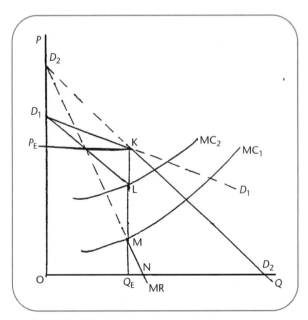

Figure 10.6 Equilibrium under the kinked demand model

between MC_1 and MC_2. Prices, therefore, under the kinked demand model tend to be stable over a range of cost changes.

This observed price stability may be the result of unconscious or even tacit collusion between oligopolists, brought about by fear, not to rock the boat, by initiating price cuts that may lead to price wars. Nevertheless, under conditions of upward demand pressure or of inflation, oligopolists are able to raise their prices, justifying, usually, such raises on increased input prices. To reduce oligopolistic interdependence, firms have established various non-price competitive strategies taking, normally, the form of product differentiation. The latter, as explained earlier, aim at not only reducing the own-price elasticity of demand but also at lowering the cross-price elasticity of demand, thus providing producers with an element of independent action in their pricing policies, by reducing somewhat uncertainty.

However, alternative ways of reducing oligopolistic uncertainty have been cartels and price leadership arrangements. These are restrictive practices, which are frowned upon by antimonopoly legislations in industrialised countries, but as they do occur, they provide legitimate areas of study.

10.2.4b   Cartels

Cartels represent overt agreements between two or more producers to joint maximisation of profits for the industry as a whole and then sharing these profits on the basis of some objective criterion, usually, of production quotas. Where such agreements are possible, and the producers can exercise control over the market, they can act as a monopoly and produce where the market marginal revenue equals the market marginal cost, thus establishing an equilibrium price and quantity for the industry as a whole. All firms in the cartel agreement can sell at that equilibrium price, but their individual outputs will be found by equating the equilibrium marginal revenue with their individual marginal costs.

The equilibrium is shown in Figure 10.7. For simplicity assume that there are two firms A and B participating in the cartel agreement, with the cost conditions given in Figure 10.7(a) and (b). The analysis can be easily extended to cover more participants. Figure 10.7(c) gives the market demand curve for the product in question with its marginal revenue, and the industry marginal cost curve ΣMC, which

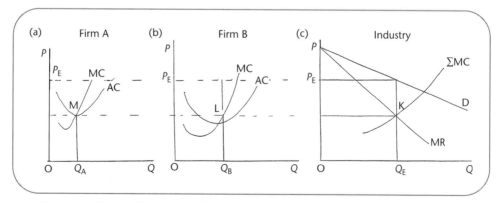

Figure 10.7 Equilibrium for firms and industry under cartel conditions

is simply the horizontal summation of the individual marginal cost curves, given in Figure 10.7(a) and (b). Point K determines the equilibrium output Q_E and price P_E. The two firms both charge a price P_E, and their outputs are determined by equating the market marginal revenue with their respective marginal costs at points L and M, giving outputs Q_B and Q_A for firms B and A, such that $OQ_A + OQ_B = OQ_E$. It is obvious that the more efficient firm, B, produces more.

Conceptually, the case of a cartel is similar to that of a monopolist operating a number of different plants to supply a single market. Profit maximisation occurs where the monopolist equates the MC of each of his plants to the common MR. In the same manner, oligopolists realising their mutual interdependence may agree that the best course of action is to collude in order to maximise the industry's profit and then share it in some agreed way. The case of the *OPEC* cartel, of which more below, follows similar lines, in the sense that once a price is agreed, then individual countries, the oil exporting producers have to stick to their predetermined quotas, for example, Q_A and Q_B given in Figure 10.7.

We can illustrate some of these points by means of the following example. Assume that there are three firms, each producing a similar product. Because of interdependence, the total demand curve is given by: $P = 1000 - 2(Q_1 + Q_2 + Q_3)$, where Q_1, Q_2 and Q_3 are the quantities produced by each. Therefore, we have $Q = Q_1 + Q_2 + Q_3$. If the average cost functions of the three producers are $AC_1 = 100 + 4Q_1$, $AC_2 = 200 + 3Q_2$ and $AC_3 = 400 + 2Q_3$, we need to establish the industry's output, price, profits and their distribution to the three producers.

The industry's profits function is given by the following expression:

$$\Pi = TR - TC = 1000(Q_1 + Q_2 + Q_3) - 2(Q_1 + Q_2 + Q_3)^2$$
$$- 100Q_1 - 4Q_1^2 - 200Q_2 - 3Q_2^2 - 400Q_3 - 2Q_3^2$$

Setting the partial derivatives with respect to Q_1, Q_2 and Q_3 equal to zero and rearranging gives the following system of simultaneous equations:

$$12Q_1 + 4Q_2 + 4Q_3 = 900$$
$$4Q_1 + 10Q_2 + 4Q_3 = 800$$
$$4Q_1 + 4Q_2 + 8Q_3 = 600$$

This can be solved by using Cramer' rule or substitution to give the solution: $Q_1 = 50$, $Q_2 = 50$ and $Q_3 = 25$.

Therefore, price is $P = 1000 - 2(50 + 50 + 25) = 750$ and total profit is found to be €50 000. At the equilibrium solution, the marginal costs of the three firms are all equal to each other (at 500 each) and the profits of the three firms are evaluated as €22 500 for the first, €20 000 for the second and €7500 for the third firm, i.e., a total of €50 000, as readers can verify.

In practice, cartels tend to be rather unstable arrangements prone to collapse, mainly because of reasons of greed. Cartels may even require governmental or inter-governmental support for their survival, as in the case of the formerly powerful International Air Transport Association (IATA), a cartel of, mostly, international nationalised air carriers. IATA used to regulate, strictly, international air travel between any two points (outside US), for example, Britain and Germany, allowing the markets to be shared, normally, by the two national carriers of those countries, i.e., British Airways and Lufthansa, both charging similar, if not identical prices. This cosy arrangement came to a close in the 1990s, with the considerable de-regulation in the air travel industry, which introduced competition and the privatisation of many nationalised airlines. Currently, the best example of an existing cartel is the Organisation of Petroleum Exporting Countries (OPEC), consisting of the most influential oil producing countries in the world. Its scope is the regulation of the industry, by the setting of a common price to yield a joint profit which is to be distributed among the various producers according to strict (?) quotas. Therein, however, lie the seeds of instability as the quotas cannot be policed. Each producer has an incentive to increase, somewhat, their production hoping that the others will stick to their quotas. If that happened then there is a chance that the culprit may get away and enjoy the fruits of his cheating. More often, however, others will act or react in a similar manner, thus, increasing production and bringing price down, unless some other producer(s) decided to decrease their production accordingly to maintain the agreed price. This had happened on a number of occasions with OPEC, when agreed quotas had been violated, only for Saudi Arabia, the biggest oil producer and exporter in the world, to intervene to cut its own production in order to maintain the price. But when Saudi Arabia decided to follow the same practice, production increased significantly and world prices for crude oil collapsed to the sheer pleasure of consumers.

10.2.4c Price leadership

Price leadership models are attempts by oligopolists to reduce uncertainty through cooperation. Such cooperation need not be overt, since in such a case it becomes simply price fixing and market sharing, frowned upon by anti monopoly legislation and agencies. More usually it takes the form of tacit arrangements in which one firm becomes the leader of the market, either through its size (dominant position in the market), lower costs or knowledge and ability to correctly evaluate industry trends about price setting and price changing (barometric price leader). The successful leader is the one who sets a price at which all firms make some profit!

As an illustration of price leadership we consider the case of the dominant firm model, which may be applicable in situations of undifferentiated oligopoly. In this case the dominant firm sets a price which maximises its profit, but allows the other firms in the industry to sell as much as they like at the established price. This means, effectively, that the other firms in the industry (followers) face a fixed price in much the same way as under perfect competition, while the leader acts as a monopolist and price setter. In Figure 10.8 the market demand for the product is given by D_M, the marginal cost of the leading firm is MC_1 and the curve $\sum MC_F$ is the horizontal summation of the marginal cost curves of the followers, or their supply curve. The followers operate by equating their marginal cost to price and, therefore, they could supply the total demand for the market at a price OP_2 (given by the intersection of the market demand D_M and the followers' supply curve $\sum MC_F$), leaving nothing for the leading firm. However, at all prices below OP_2, the leading firm can have a positive demand, given by the horizontal distance between the market demand D_M and the total supply curve of the followers $\sum MC_F$. For example, at price OP_0 this distance is FE and so the demand for the leading firm at OP_0 is given by $P_0D = FE$, and similarly for all other prices. Thus, having found the leading firm's demand

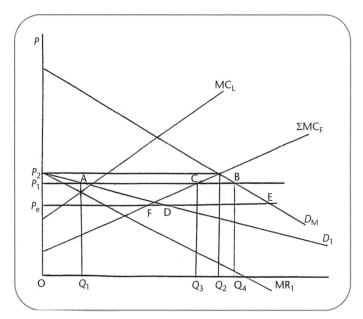

Figure 10.8 Oligopolistic leadership equilibrium

curve D_1, its marginal revenue curve MR_1 can be constructed and the leading firm can then proceed to maximise its profits by producing, where $MR_1 = MC_1$, an output OQ_1 at a price of OP_1. At a price of OP_1 the total market demand is OQ_4 and it is met by the leading firm supplying $OQ_1 = Q_3Q_4$ units, while the followers are supplying, collectively, the remainder Q_1Q_4 units.

10.2.5 The theory of games

The theory of games, developed by von Neumann and Morgenstern, is an ingenious way of tackling decision making under conditions of social conflict and uncertainty. It is designed to analyse and explain decision making in cases where the outcome depends also on choices made by one's rivals, by accepting that the pursuit of individual maximum gain may have to be circumscribed in the interests of either safeguarding particular positions or avoiding making things worse. Since uncertainty, caused by rivals' interdependence, is a feature of oligopolistic markets, Clausewitz's work 'Principles of War', which contains both parallels between military and business strategy, but also a method of a general approach to the problem, may be closer to describing oligopolistic interdependence and warfare, than the traditional theory of value. Similarly, the work of von Neumann and Morgenstern in 'The Theory of Games' (1944), starting from the recognition of the inadequacy of classical optimisation techniques to deal with the problem of oligopolistic interdependence, and emphasising the element of strategy in oligopolistic environments – in the same way as in games – was originally hailed as providing a general theory of oligopoly. This approach can also be used to explain choices involving risks, by maximising the expected utility of payoffs of uncertain outcomes. The expected utility is an index, a measure of utility, which is cardinal in its properties and can be used to rank various risky alternatives, such as gambles, lotteries and the like. The introduction of the word utility was unfortunate, in the sense that it led to much misunderstanding and controversy as to whether utility is cardinal or not. The theory of games did not prove that utility is cardinal in the traditional neoclassical sense, but the way of measuring utility is cardinal.

The expected utility hypothesis contends that the subject, for example, player, firm, consumer will choose in a way to maximise the mathematical expectation of utility. If the utility function is given by:

$$U = U(A, B, \ldots, Z, p_A, p_B, \ldots, p_Z)$$

where $A, B, \ldots, Z$ represent bundles of goods and $p_A, p_B, \ldots, p_Z$ are the respective probabilities, then the expected utility is given by the expression:

$$E(U) = p_A U(A) + p_B U(B) + \cdots + p_Z U(Z)$$

i.e., it is the sum of the individual utilities weighted by their respective probabilities.

In the theory of games we must have alternatives or strategies to choose from. For example, a firm trying to capture a bigger share of the market may employ price cuts, more advertising or even introduce a new brand. By game we mean a set of specific rules and conventions for playing; play refers to a particular realisation of the rules; move is a point in the play at which one of the players picks out an alternative from a set of strategies, and choice is the alternative or strategy picked out.

Games are classified according to their outcome, number of players, number of moves or possibilities and cooperation. According to the outcome we have zero-sum games, where the winnings are exactly matched by losses, so as to leave their sum at zero, constant-sum games, where the outcome is a constant number (thus zero-sum games are a special case of constant-sum ones), non-zero (or non-constant) sum games, where all players may win, or lose, or some win and some lose but the winnings are not matched by the losses. This class of games is extremely important in economics, since the economic process usually changes the variables under consideration (wealth, incomes, profits). According to the number of players we may have one-person game (which is a rather trivial case), two-person game, three-person and in general n-person games, whereas on the basis of number of moves we may distinguish finite games, which have a finite number of moves or possibilities, and infinite games, where the number of moves at the disposal of the players is infinite. Also, we may have cooperative and non-cooperative games, depending on whether or not collusion among players is allowed. In addition, we may have games of strategy (such as bridge, chess and the like) and games of pure chance (such as roulette, dice and the like). However, despite the wide variety of games, we shall restrict ourselves to the competitive finite two-person zero-sum game, i.e., to cases of duopoly or bilateral monopoly, for which the behavioural assumptions of the theory provide specific equilibrium solutions for the players, and for which we do have various practical applications of the theory. For this class of games the solution was given by von Neumann and Morgenstern. For other classes of games John Nash has offered a general formulation, known as the *Nash equilibrium*, through which such games can be approached and solved.

Nash equilibrium occurs when each player's strategy choice is the best reply to the strategies chosen by the other players.

10.2.5a   Two-person zero-sum game, minimax = maximin = saddle point

In this case, the gain of one player equals the loss of the other player and the game can be applied to duopolistic markets or those of bilateral monopoly. Since both players have a set of strategies, the payoffs of the interaction of the various strategies can be arranged in the form of a matrix, with the rows indicating the strategies open to the first player (row player) and the columns giving the strategies open to the second player (column player). The elements of the matrix represent the payoffs of the game to the row player (the maximiser), with the payoffs to the column player indicated by the same figure with an opposite sign. For example, if the row player possesses $i = m$ strategies and the column player $j = n$ strategies, the matrix of the payoffs is given by:

	C_1	C_2	...	C_n
R_1	a_{11}	a_{12}	...	a_{1n}
R_2	a_{21}	a_{22}	...	a_{2n}
R_m	a_{m1}	a_{m2}	...	a_{mn}

where a_{ij} is the value of the game to the row player if he employs his ith strategy and the column player employs his jth. Correspondingly, the value of the game to the column player is given by $-a_{ij}$. A strategy is called pure if the player is always picking out the same alternative, mixed if the player is employing different alternatives in a certain combination and completely mixed if the player is using all the alternatives open to him in a certain combination. Furthermore, a strategy is called optimal if it leads to the value of the game, V, which is the final outcome of the game. Therefore, in a game the various payoffs are given and the problem is to derive the maximum or minimum value of the game, depending on which player we are looking at.

The behavioural assumption underlying the theory of games, as formulated by von Neumann and Morgenstern, is that we play the game prudently, or safely, i.e., we try to avoid making things worse than they could have otherwise been. This means that we play, in some sense, pessimistically. This is achieved by using the concepts of maximin and minimax. From the given matrix of the payoffs, we choose the minimum values of each row and then pick out the maximum of these values. This value is called the maximin, it is the maximum of the row minima, and it is the value the row player should choose, according to the theory. Similarly, we take the maximum values of each column and of these we pick out the minimum value, giving us the minimax, which is the value the column player should choose.

To illustrate some of these points, assume that two duopolists are battling for control over a market. The first has at his disposal two strategies, R_1 and R_2, whereas the second player can use four counter strategies, C_1, C_2, C_3 and C_4. The matrix of the payoffs, representing changes in profits in million euros, are given in the following table:

	C_1	C_2	C_3	C_4	Row minima
R_1	8	35	15	5	5
R_2	10	−20	−10	−8	−20
Column maxima	10	35	15	5	5

The decision problem for the duopolists is to select their optimal strategies, in a way that they maximise their returns (or minimise their losses), but without exposing themselves to the risk of a smaller return or a bigger loss if their rival suddenly changed his strategy(ies). In essence, this means that each player tries to discover that strategy which maximises his gains (or minimises his losses), given his rival's best possible counter strategy. Inspection of the table reveals that the best outcome for the first player is given by the element (35), which can be obtained when the first player plays his first strategy, R_1, and the second player plays his second strategy, C_2. Similarly, the best result for the second (column) player is given by the element (−20), which is obtained when the raw player plays his second strategy and the column player his second, i.e., R_2 and C_2. So, while the first player has an incentive to play his first strategy in the hope of enticing the column player to employ his second strategy, the column player will avoid playing his second strategy (despite the fact that it promises a profit of −20 if the row player played his second strategy), because he is afraid of losing 35 if the row player, suddenly, changed his mind and employed his first strategy. In other words, the column player's second strategy is a very high-risk strategy, because it exposes him to a considerable loss. The behavioural assumptions of the game allow for the equilibrium value to be determined by obtaining the row minima, given in the last column of the table, and the column maxima, given in the last row of the table. Finally, we choose the maximum of the row minima, i.e., the maximin, (5) in our case and the minimum of the column maxima, i.e., the minimax, which is again (5). This gives the equilibrium value of the game that is obtained when the row player plays his first strategy and the column player plays his fourth strategy. In this case, where maximin = minimax, the value (5) is known as a saddle point, because like a saddle, it is a maximum in one direction and a minimum in the other direction.

Notice that in the above example the column player will *never* play his first strategy, because he is bound to lose more than if he had played his fourth strategy, irrespective of what strategy the row player employs. This means that C_4 dominates C_1 and this case is referred to as pure dominance; therefore, the column player can delete his first strategy, by striking out the first column. This will leave us with the following shortened table of payoffs:

	C_2	C_3	C_4
R_1	35	15	5
R_2	−20	−10	−8

By a similar argument the row player will *never* play his second strategy, since he can always win more by employing his first strategy, irrespective of the strategy employed by the column player. Therefore, strategy R_1 is said to dominate R_2 and so the row player will eliminate his second strategy from further consideration, leaving us with the following shortened table of payoffs:

	C_2	C_3	C_4
R_1	35	15	5

It is obvious that the only way the column player can minimise his losses, and thus restrict the winnings of his rival, is to ignore his second and third strategies and only employ his fourth strategy, which indeed dominates the other two. So, in the case where minimax = saddle = maximin, the equilibrium value of the game is given by the saddle point, and it is arrived at by the two duopolists employing pure strategies.

10.2.5b Mixed strategies

However, where this condition is not satisfied, the maximin and minimax can only help in establishing the limits within which the value of the game is to be found. In such cases it can be shown that a solution to a two-person zero-sum game exists if we allow mixed strategies, i.e., if the two players are allowed to mix their strategies in a probabilistic way. To illustrate this case, consider the following.

Two large firms are battling for control of a market. Firm A has the options of either cutting price or increasing advertising expenditure. Firm B has the same options, but in addition it can offer a new product, which is slightly higher in price. When firm A decides in favour of a price cut and firm B opts for a price cut there is no change at all in the sales of either firm, but if firm B chooses to spend more on advertising, firm A loses €3 million, whereas if firm B decides to introduce the new product firm A gains €1 million. When, instead, firm A chooses to increase its advertising expenditure and firm B opts for a price cut, firm A gains €3 million, but if both firms decide to increase their advertising expenditure they manage to counteract each other's efforts and there is no change at all in their sales, and finally, if firm B chooses to introduce the new product, firm A loses €3 million. What should the two firms do and what will the final outcome be?

The matrix of the payoffs of this game is given as follows, with firm A as the maximiser (row player) and firm B as the minimiser (column player):

			Firm B			
			C_1 Cut price	C_2 Advertise more	C_3 New product	Row minima
Firm A	R_1	Cut price	0	−3	1	− 3
	R_2	Advertise more	3	0	−3	− 3
		Column maxima	3	0	1	− 3 \ 0

It is apparent from this table of the payoffs that no saddle point exists, since minimax, which is zero, 0, is greater than maximin, which is −3. However, by

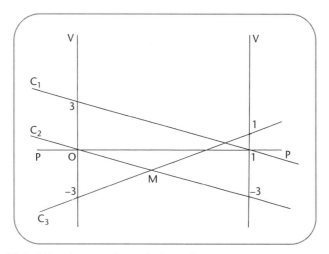

Figure 10.9 Mixed strategies solution of a two-person, zero-sum game

letting firm A play its first strategy with probability p and its second strategy with probability $(1 - p)$, we can find the outcomes of the game (E) to firm A, when firm B plays its first, second and third strategies. These outcomes, giving the expected value of the game to firm A for the different strategies of firm B are as follows:

$$0p + 3(1 - p) \geq V \text{ against firm B's first strategy}$$

$$-3p + 0(1 - p) \geq V \text{ against firm B's second strategy}$$

$$1p - 3(1 - p) \geq V \text{ against firm B's third strategy}$$

When, as in this case, the resulting matrix of the payoffs is one of $2 \times n$ or $m \times 2$, we can represent the solution diagrammatically, as follows. The expressions of the LHSs of the above relations are plotted in Figure 10.9 for the various feasible values of p, measured along the horizontal axis.

The highest point on the lower boundary of these curves is M, which is the intersection of lines C_2 and C_3. Therefore, by equating these we get:

$$-3p + 0(1 - p) = 1p - 3(1 - p)$$

which gives $p = 3/7$ and $(1 - p) = 4/7$. By substituting these values into the three expressions above, we get the outcomes of the game as follows:

$$0(3/7) + 3(4/7) = 12/7$$

$$-3(3/7) + 0(4/7) = -9/7$$

$$1(3/7) - 3(4/7) = -9/7$$

Despite the fact that firm A stands to win 12/7, if firm B plays its first strategy, firm B, by playing carefully can keep the mathematical expectation of its payments down to the value of $-9/7$, which is actually a gain for firm B. Playing carefully here means that firm B avoids its first strategy and mixes its second and third strategies with appropriate probabilities. In this case, inspection of the original table of the payoffs reveals that firm B will never employ its first strategy of cutting price, since by employing its second and third strategies with, say, probabilities 2/3 and 1/3, respectively, it can achieve a combined result of $-5/3$ (when firm A employs its first strategy of cutting price), and also a combined result of -1 (when firm A uses its second strategy of increased advertising). Since this column vector of $(-5/3 - 1)$ is far better than the vector of the first strategy $(0\,3)$, the game is said to have convex or mixed dominance, and therefore, firm B will ignore its dominated strategy, since it can do better by employing a mixture of its second and third strategies. This will leave the two firms with the following shortened table of payoffs:

	C_2	C_3
R_1	-3	1
R_2	0	-3

Now if firm A employs its first strategy with probability p and its second strategy with probability $(1-p)$, then the expected value of the game to firm A, when firm B employs its second strategy is given by:

$$E_1 = -3p + 0(1-p)$$

Similarly, if now firm B decides to employ its third strategy, the expected value of the game to firm A is given by:

$$E_2 = 1p - 3(1-p)$$

By equating these two expected values, we have

$$-3p + 0(1-p) = 1p - 3(1-p)$$

which gives $p = 3/7$ and $(1-p) = 4/7$, exactly the same values we found earlier. Now, in order to find firm B's probabilities, we let it play its second strategy with probability q and its third strategy with probability $(1-q)$. This produces the following outcomes for firm B:

$$3q + 1(1-q) \leq V \text{ against firm A's first strategy}$$

$$0q - 3(1-q) \leq V \text{ against firm A's second strategy}$$

By equating we get: $3q + 1(1-q) = 0q - 3(1-q)$ which is solved to give $q = 4/7$ and $(1-q) = 3/7$, and upon substitution in the two relations above, results in the following expected values of the game for firm B:

$$E_2 = -3(4/7) + 1(3/7) = -9/7$$
$$E_3 = 0(4/7) - 3(3/7) = -9/7$$

To summarise, the solution is for firm A to mix its strategies of cutting price and advertise more with probabilities 3/7 and 4/7, respectively, whereas for firm B the solution is to ignore its first strategy of cutting price (i.e., employ it with probability zero) and mix its other two strategies of advertising more and launching a new product with probabilities 4/7 and 3/7, respectively. The value (outcome) of the game is that firm B wins €9/7 million.

10.2.5c   Relationship between game theory and linear programming

In cases where we are unable to reduce the matrix of the payoffs into one of $2 \times n$ or $m \times 2$, so that we may employ the diagrammatic technique for the solution of the game, we can transform the game into a linear programme and use the Simplex method, discussed earlier in the chapter on Linear Programming, to obtain the solution.

To illustrate the derivation, assume that the matrix of the payoffs, in millions of euros, for two firms – a large one and a small one – fighting for control over a market is given as:

| | | Small firm's strategies | | |
		C_1	C_2	C_3
	R_1	4	−2	5
Large firm's strategies	R_2	1	4	0
	R_3	1	3	4

In this case, it may be easier to approach the problem from the small firm's point of view (i.e., the column player). The objective of the small firm is to minimise the value of the game V, and so the objective function can be written as

Minimise V

Since mixed strategies are allowed, we assume that the small firm mixes its strategies with probabilities q_1, q_2 and q_3. This means that when the large firm employs in turn, its first, second and third strategies, the outcomes of the game to the small firm are given respectively by:

$E_1 = 4q_1 - 2q_2 + 5q_3 \leq V$

$E_2 = q_1 + 4q_2 + 0q_3 \leq V$

$E_3 = q_1 + 3q_2 + 4q_3 \leq V$

The small firm as a minimiser tries to keep the value of the game (the expressions on the LHS) less or equal to the minimax. In addition, we have that the probabilities must sum up to 1 and also that they must be non-negative. These are additional constraints, which must be incorporated into the programme. Therefore, the given game is formulated as a linear programme as follows:

$$\text{Minimise } V$$

$$\text{subject to} \quad 4q_1 - 2q_2 + 5q_3 \leq V$$

$$q_1 + 4q_2 + 0q_3 \leq V$$

$$q_1 + 3q_2 + 4q_3 \leq V$$

$$q_1 + q_2 + q_3 = 1$$

$$q_1, q_2, q_3 \geq 0$$

Since the minimisation of V is equivalent to maximising $1/V$, we can divide the constraints through by V and define the following new variables:

$$y_1 = q_1/V, \quad y_2 = q_2/V, \quad y_3 = q_3/V$$

and because from our fourth constraint the sum of the probabilities is equal to one, we get that:

$$y_1 + y_2 + y_3 = \frac{q_1 + q_2 + q_3}{V} = \frac{1}{V}$$

which allows us to formulate the programme as follows:

$$\text{Minimise } V = \text{Maximise } 1/V = \text{Maximise } y_1 + y_2 + y_3$$

subject to
$$4y_1 - 2y_2 + 5y_3 \leq 1$$
$$y_1 + 4y_2 + 0y_3 \leq 1$$
$$y_1 + 3y_2 + 4y_3 \leq 1$$
$$y_1, y_2, y_3 \geq 0$$

When this linear programme is solved by means of the Simplex method, it yields the solution $y_1 = 19/67$, $y_2 = 12/67$, $y_3 = 3/67$ and $1/V = y_1 + y_2 + y_3 = 34/67$ and corresponding shadow prices as: $s_1 = 11/67$, $s_2 = 20/67$ and $s_3 = 3/67$.

These results imply that the value of the game is $V = 67/34$ and the probabilities of the small firm are given as:

$$q_1 = y_1 V = (19/67)(67/34) = 19/34, q_2 = y_2 V = (12/67)(67/34) = 12/34 \text{ and}$$
$$q_3 = y_3 V = (3/67)(67/34) = 3/34,$$

while the probabilities of the large firm can be computed by making use of the shadow prices as follows:

$$p_1 = s_1 V = (11/67)(67/34) = 11/34, p_2 = s_2 V = (20/67)(67/34) = 20/34 \text{ and}$$
$$p_3 = s_3 V = (3/67)(67/34) = 3/34.$$

Inspection reveals that each set of probabilities sums up to one, as required, and the value of the game, if these probabilities are used to mix the strategies, is a gain for the large firm of €(67/34) or €1.676 millions.

10.2.5d   Two-person non-zero-sum games

This class of games is extremely important because it demonstrates that the pursuit of atomistic self-interest may produce an inferior result than at least one of the alternatives. This is often referred to as the case of the 'prisoner's dilemma', which illustrates that cooperation can lead to a more favourable outcome for the players. For example, two firms A and B fighting for control over a market can employ two strategies, i.e., increase price and advertise more. The table below gives the combined matrix of payoffs, where figures in the bottom left of each square are the outcomes of the game to firm A, and figures in the top right give the outcomes of the game to firm B.

		Firm B	
		Increase price	Advertise more
Firm A	Increase price	15 15	20 −10
	Advertise more	−10 20	−3 −3

It is obvious that the best result for both firms is to increase their prices at the same time, rather than engage in wasteful advertising. However, this is a risky strategy undertaken in isolation and it indicates that some cooperation is necessary if maximum profits are required, because if a firm increases its price while the other firm advertises more, the firm raising its price will incur a considerable loss, while the more advertising minded firm stands to make a considerable gain. This illustrates the fact that in such cases there is a considerable incentive for both firms to collude in order to maximise their joint profits, since a collusive agreement results in a better outcome. Also, the incentive to double-cross one's 'partner' is present, since each firm stands to win more by cheating on the agreement, although if both firms tried to double-cross each other, they both end up losing. Whether, of course, collusive agreements can take place is another matter; in fact in most industrialised countries such behaviour is prohibited; nevertheless, the theory suggests that cooperation can lead to more satisfactory results than the pursuit of self-interest. Given that the theory of games is powerful and flexible and can be applied to a wide range of situations, like wage bargaining, pricing of goods, personal relations as well as international relations and military confrontation, the above suggests possible ways of preventing unhappy outcomes for all, which are the results of selfish behaviour.

10.3 PRICING PRACTICES

10.3.1 Introduction

The preceding discussion on pricing has assumed that firms, producing a single product, try to maximise their short-run profits and, consequently, it has focused on the marginalist principles, i.e., on the firm's marginal revenue and marginal cost, necessary for the determination of the optimal price, to achieve that objective. Generally, the discussion has shown that the type of competitive pressures in the market affect pricing decisions, and in the case of oligopoly, it has emphasised the element of increased uncertainty brought about by interdependence, and considered some approaches to reduce such uncertainty. However, if the objective of the firm is not to maximise profits, what are the implications about pricing rules?

Indeed, the development of the joint stock company and the large corporation, with the concomitant separation of ownership from control has resulted in the rise of the managerial class and a conflict of interest between the owners (shareholders) and the professional managers running the firm. This led to the emergence of a number of theories of the firm based on managerial objectives and reviewed briefly in Chapter 3, in which while profit may play some role, it is neither the exclusive nor primary motive, as under the neoclassical theory of the firm. Since managerial salaries and other emoluments depend on the firm's growth record, such theories have focused on the need to maximise sales or market share (Baumol), or maximise growth (Marris), or maximise managers' utility (Williamson) even at the expense of profits. So long as a minimum profit constraint is satisfied, i.e., so long as shareholders feel reasonably satisfied with the return on their capital, managers are free to pursue their own objectives. It must be pointed out that under the managerial theories of the firm, while profit maximisation is jettisoned in favour of some other objective, the aspect of maximisation is retained, implying that sufficient information is available at the hands of management regarding demand, cost and other functions for it to apply classical optimisation techniques, such as Lagrange multipliers to maximise sales or growth or utility.

In addition to these theories, another group of researchers lead by Simon and Cyert & March have developed the behavioural theory of the firm, briefly discussed in Chapter 3. It is recalled that according to this theory, the firm is viewed as a 'coalition' of managers, shareholders, workers, salesmen and the like, all of whom have their own objectives, which they try to have adopted by the firm. Through a process of compromise and side payments (either in the form of policy acceptances or monetary rewards), various objectives emerge but, because of the compromises involved, they are often in the form of minimum acceptable levels of attainment rather than maximum ones. The emphasis, therefore, is in trying to 'satisfice' a number of goals, treating them one at a time, rather than to maximise anything. It follows then that the resulting prices under these alternative theories of the firm will be different than the ones emerging under profit maximisation. The empirical evidence tends to support the 'satisficing' approach, but there are also indications that it has been adopted mainly because of lack of adequate information, leading to inability to pursue profit maximisation (Hague 1971).

Indeed, if information about marginal costs and revenues cannot be obtained, i.e., if firms are uncertain about their cost and demand functions, how can they set prices? Other factors that play a role in price determination are the type of product (whether consumer or capital good), the stage the product has reached in its life cycle (new, existing or mature product), the nature of the product (single, joint, or multiple), the state of capacity (utilising existing spare capacity or requiring new one) and so on. These considerations lead, naturally, to the question of how actually firms set their prices. This question, originally asked over 60 years ago by Hall and Hitch (1939), initiated considerable and almost continuous research into business pricing practices, which has revealed that most firms do not necessarily take into account marginal conditions when setting their prices. Therefore, on the face of this evidence, there seems to be a conflict between theory and practice which needs to be resolved, once we have looked at some pricing practices.

10.3.2 Full-cost pricing

In a seminal work by Hall and Hitch (1939) on the pricing procedures of 38 UK firms, it was found that entrepreneurs were interested in objectives other than profit maximisation and were using a pricing policy known as full-cost pricing. Subsequent studies on both sides of the Atlantic reaffirmed this finding, although some have also lent support for the profit maximising paradigm, while at the same time considerable research was also directed towards the objectives of the firm, resulting in the alternative theories of the firm mentioned earlier. Full-cost pricing, also referred to as cost-plus or average cost pricing or as absorption costing, is based on the idea that the 'correct' price must cover all the costs incurred plus the profit which will yield the target return on capital employed. This means that the firm takes into account variable and fixed production costs, as well as variable and fixed selling and administrative costs plus a mark-up for profit. Fixed costs, such as rent, rates, depreciation, debenture costs and the like are incurred irrespective of the level of output and for a firm to survive in the long run, such costs must be met. Assuming that budgeted sales equal actual sales, it is clear that the method will ensure that total costs are covered.

At its simplest, the method involves finding the cost of materials and direct labour and then adding a percentage of these direct costs to cover overheads (say 100%), another percentage to cover administrative and selling expenses (say 30%) and, finally, a mark-up for profit (say 20%) and dividing the total by the level of output to arrive at the price of the product. However, in more elaborate versions of this method, a differential allocation of overheads and selling expenses may be required according to the product. This pricing practice has been criticised on the grounds that it ignores the demand side and the forces of competition and also that it may be based on the wrong conception of cost. We consider the aspect of competition later, but as far as costs are concerned, such costs may be actual (i.e., historical costs), expected costs (which represent predicted costs at current prices and output rates) or standard costs (i.e., hypothetical or estimated costs at some normal rate of output, such as, e.g., 70% or 80% of capacity). However, such costs are neither definite nor unequivocal and when used as a basis for pricing may lead to 'wrong', i.e., non-optimal prices charged. In particular, if selling prices are computed as a fixed percentage of their cost, different prices may result for the same handling and conversion of bought-in materials by companies, with disproportionally high prices for products requiring expensive materials and lower prices for products made by less expensive materials, although the handling and conversion of such materials into final products, i.e., the value added, was the same in both cases. For pricing purposes incremental or future costs may be more relevant than average or past costs, used by the full-cost approach. This raises the question of why firms seem to prefer such a pricing method over the marginalist approach.

It has been argued that full-cost pricing is a simple and inexpensive rule of thumb, which cuts the cost of decision making, particularly when firms are uncertain about the shape of the demand curves for their products, and so it may not be antithetical to profit maximisation. Prices based on full costs are considered more stable and fair to consumers and competitors and less inconvenient to salesmen, than prices based on marginal magnitudes. Full-cost pricing may also lead to long-run profit maximisation, since in the long-run prices tend to equal the cost of production. Indeed, it can be shown that if the mark-up is not fixed by convention, but related to market conditions, full-cost pricing leads to the same result as marginalist pricing.

We define the mark-up, K, as follows:

$$K = \frac{\text{Price} - \text{Average cost}}{\text{Average cost}} = \frac{P - C}{C}$$

which gives:

Price = Average cost $(1 + \text{Mark-up})$, i.e., $P = C(1 + K)$ (1)

We found in Chapter 4 (Section 4.5.3) that: $P = MR(\eta/(\eta + 1))$ and therefore for profit maximisation, substituting $MC = MR$ in above

we get: $P = MC\left(\dfrac{\eta}{\eta + 1}\right)$.   (2)

Assuming constant costs gives us $MC = AC$, which is also the case in long-run equilibrium under the neoclassical theory, and therefore relation (1) becomes

$$P = MC(1 + K)$$ (3)

Equating the RHS of (2) and (3) results in:

$MC(\eta/(\eta + 1)) = MC(1 + K)$ giving $K = (\eta/(\eta + 1)) - 1$ and finally $K = -1/(\eta + 1)$

The above expression shows that the mark-up, K, is inversely related to the price elasticity of demand, η, varying from ∞ at $\eta = -1$, to 0 at $\eta = -\infty$. For more normal values of price elasticity of demand, one obtains, for example, the following values for the mark-up. If $\eta = -1.2$, K is calculated as 5 or 500%, whereas when $\eta = -1.5$, $K = 2$ or 200%, for $\eta = -2$, $K = 1$ or 100%, for $\eta = -3$, $K = 0.5$ or 50% and so on. Therefore, provided the mark-up is flexible and reflects market conditions, full-cost pricing can arrive at the same result as that of marginal analysis.

However, the evidence does not suggest that firms, with perhaps a few exceptions, are trying to relate the mark-up to the price elasticity of demand for their products. The reason is that in an uncertain market, where knowledge is incomplete, the high costs of information regarding estimates of demand may deter management from departing from full costs as a basis for pricing and applying a mark-up which may be considered 'fair' or 'normal' in the industry. Nevertheless, while the above reasons may explain the widespread use of this practice, they do not necessarily justify it as the logical approach to pricing. It does not help in the identification and allocation of costs and there are also problems in relating the mark-up to cover overheads to the unknown future volume of sales. For if one expects a recession, the formula suggests raising the mark-up and price, which may not be the right policy under the circumstances. Management should consider first whether estimates of demand and incremental costs could be derived, without too much expense, before utilising a pricing rule of thumb that ignores demand and may give a false precision to existing cost estimates.

10.3.3 Going-rate pricing

Another rule of thumb usually followed in practice is the going-rate pricing. This involves monitoring the prices charged by the industry for similar products and setting one's prices accordingly. Whereas in full-cost pricing the emphasis is on costs, in going-rate pricing it is on the market. This may seem to imply that the prices charged are the competitive ones and the producers are, somehow, 'price takers', as in the case of perfect competition, since they follow the market. In fact, most instances of going-rate pricing are simply cases of price leadership and followership, discussed earlier. The market leader sets the price and the rest of the industry follow, ensuring that costly price rivalry is avoided in oligopolistic settings. While this may stabilise prices, it is not the same as a competitive price, since firms have some power to set their own prices but they choose not to exercise it. They may prefer to adopt the policy of others and follow what they consider to be a safe course, rather than try to be price makers and be prepared to take the consequences of their action.

10.3.4   Incremental approach in pricing

It has been suggested that a way of bridging the abstraction of the traditional theory of prices with the inflexibility of the rules of thumb, such as the full-cost approach, may be provided by the incremental approach in pricing. Incrementalism is the real life equivalent to marginalism. Instead of dealing with infinitesimal changes to quantities, revenues and costs, brought about by, say, changes in product or factor prices, incremental reasoning requires that we consider the impact of a particular decision on revenues, costs or profits. In other words the unit of change is the decision facing the firm.

So long as the decision raises revenues by more than it raises costs, or lowers costs by more than it lowers revenues, net profits are increased and so the decision (project) should be accepted by the firm. Conversely, so long as the decision raises costs by more than it raises revenues or lowers revenues by more than it lowers costs, net profits are reduced and so the decision should be rejected by the firm. The focusing of the incremental approach to changes in total magnitudes implies that the total impact must be considered. So, if the firm considers, say, the introduction of a new product, the incremental approach requires an evaluation not only of the revenues and costs of the new product itself, but also of the changes in revenues and costs to existing products, resulting from the addition of the new product to the product line. Therefore, complementarity and substitutability relations must be considered and an evaluation of how the revenues and costs of existing products are affected by the decision must be carried out. Indeed, this may show that even when a product may be unprofitable on its own, particularly in the short run, it may have such strong complementary relations, by blending nicely with existing products, that total profits increase, and so its introduction is justified. This approach then is similar to a systems analysis. Therefore, incrementalism involves knowledge of market pressure in the form of estimates of elasticities, both own and cross. Also, the incremental approach considers both the short and long run. Carrying on with the earlier example of introducing a new product, where the new product is utilising existing spare capacity, it should not be charged with overheads, since its introduction does not affect them. However, in the long run, when new capacity is required, such fixed costs must be considered, which is similar to the treatment of fixed costs in the neoclassical theory, where capacity costs become variable in the long run and are, thus, included in price considerations. While this discussion shows that incrementalism is not necessarily an easy method to apply, as compared to marginalism, it is nevertheless more relevant and closer to businessmen's thinking. Clearly, when a pricing decision is involved, we are concerned with its impact on the changes in total revenue and cost and disregard the allocation of overheads, in much the same way as the traditional theory of pricing ignores fixed costs.

To illustrate what is involved, it is better to proceed through an example. Assume that a firm has spare capacity and is offered an order by a customer. The variable costs of the order are €6000 and the firm estimates that a full allocation of overheads plus a profit mark-up will require a total mark-up of 100% on the variable costs, which means that the firm evaluates the order at €12 000. However, the firm has been offered only €10 000. On the full-cost basis, the order does not cover the firm's estimated costs and, therefore, it should be rejected. However, the incremental costs of the order amount only to €6000, leaving €4000 as net contribution to overheads and profits. Since the firm has spare capacity the opportunity cost of using the existing equipment is zero, and so long as the offer price covers the variable costs of the order and leaves a net contribution to profits, the order should be accepted. Otherwise, the firm will fail to exploit the opportunity of adding to its profits. Nevertheless, one must be careful here. If it is likely to have repeat orders, this will inevitably become part of the firm's normal production activity and will also involve wear and tear of machinery and equipment. Clearly, in this case fixed costs become important and must be included in the calculations, which means that prices must be raised. Also, if other customers, who were being charged for similar orders on the basis of full-cost, became aware of the firm's new pricing policy, they may object and demand similar treatment, which may leave the firm in a very awkward position. This shows that the incremental approach has to be used cautiously lest it disturbs customer goodwill, by considering both the short- and the long-run views. The important thing to remember is that the incremental approach is the appropriate tool for sound decision making, whereas full costs are relevant for determining the profit and loss account and the net worth of the firm.

10.3.4a   Entry deterrence pricing

Often we observe that a monopolist, in setting prices, does not follow the MR = MC rule and does not try to maximise his short-term profits, despite the fact that currently his firm is the only one in the market. In such cases we need to consider the issue of barriers to entry. As concentration reflects the number of actual rivals of a firm, the condition of entry into a market tells us something about potential competition. We start by assuming a situation of certainty, where potential entrants have identical information and complete certainty with the incumbent firm. A monopolist controlling patents that protect him from rivals actual or potential, or who has particular franchises offering the same protection can, probably, charge the price that maximises his short-term profits and still feel confident that he will retain his market in isolation in the long run. Here entry is blockaded, because of patents or other franchises. Another monopolist, however, who has no actual rivals may feel that, because he does not control patents to protect him, charging a price to cover his average costs may be his best policy to keep potential entrants, having the same technology, at bay. This monopolist is afraid that, if he tried to maximise his short-term profits by setting price according to the MR = MC rule, will invite rivals into his market. Therefore, he opts for a quieter life by charging a competitive price, $P = AC$, producing a higher, than monopoly, output and earning normal profits that do not attract rivals. We refer to this as entry deterrence pricing. This monopolist has no actual long-run monopoly power. Entry into his market is easy.

The blockaded and easy entry allow us to look at the barriers to entry as a feature of market performance. In blockaded entry, the barriers are very high, thus allowing the monopolist to reap high profits, both in the short and long run. In the easy entry, however, any price higher than that yielding normal profits attracts rivals. Therefore, in principle, the market's barriers are measured by the highest price, which will just fail to tempt new firms into the market.

Diagrammatically, the story can be presented in Figure 10.10, where for simplicity we assume constant average costs, thus AC = MC. Clearly, 'low' barriers to entry will not permit a price much above the competitive price P_C arrived at by equating AR = AC, since rivals will be tempted into the market. On the other hand, 'high' barriers to entry will permit a price at or near the monopoly price P_M found by setting MR = MC. In-between 'low' and 'high' barriers, we can locate 'moderate' barriers allowing price yielding profits above the normal competitive level, but not the short-term maximum profits, and still protecting the incumbent monopolist from potential entrants.

However, if we now assume that a potential entrant has incomplete information and only knows the incumbent's costs probabilistically, the decision to enter hinges upon the entrant's beliefs regarding this probability. In addition, the incumbent monopolist knows that the potential entrant is uncertain regarding the incumbent's costs and can use it to his advantage. If the potential entrant did decide to enter, then the problem becomes one of post-entry duopoly competition of the Cournot type, where the two firms simultaneously and independently choose to supply the market in the periods following entry. This could be approached via a decision tree, in the spirit of sequential equilibrium and it is of the form of a Cournot subgame. However, as this goes beyond the scope

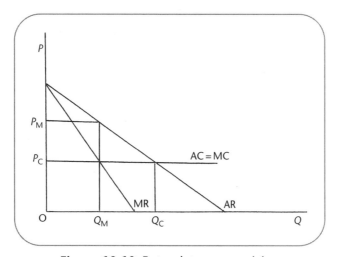

Figure 10.10 Entry deterrence pricing

of this book, interested readers may consult the appropriate literature on games given in the Bibliography, including Kreps (1990, pp. 468–480).

10.3.5 Pricing over the life cycle of products

According to the life cycle hypothesis, products go through the stages of initiation, exponential growth, slowdown and decline, corresponding to the processes of introduction, spread, maturity and senescence. We discussed the life cycle hypothesis in Section 9.4.2, and in this section we concentrate on the pricing policy during the various stages or phases of a product's life. Following the pioneering work of Dean (1951) in this area, we assume that new products, when first put on the market, have a given protected distinctiveness, i.e., at the beginning they start as innovations and command elements of monopoly power, guarded by industrial secrets, such as patents. At this initial stage, such products are likely to be price insensitive. However, as time goes on and market acceptance of the products increases, demand grows and it sets in imitative responses among competitors, who try to emulate the success of the pioneers by producing similar products. Clearly, the introduction of substitutes reduces the distinctiveness of the original product until it becomes a mature commodity. An indication of the loss of distinctiveness is provided by the cross price elasticity of demand, which had been very low at the beginning, but now, with the emergence of competing products, it rises. The process by which distinctiveness disappears has been termed by Dean (1951) as the 'cycle of competitive degeneration', which echoes the Schumpeterian thesis of the 'creative destruction of capitalism'. At a later stage such products, having passed through the maturity and saturation phases, are displaced by new products in the market, and their sales decline. This process has been apparent in many manufactured products, which at the beginning of their lives appeared as novelties, representing a drastic departure from existing goods, e.g., ball-point pens, transistors and mobile phones, but with the emergence of competing products they have matured and become pedestrian. The recognition, therefore, that products go through various changes in their life cycles means that pricing must be adjusted over the various phases of the cycle to reflect such changes.

10.3.5a Pricing new products

The problem starts when a firm hits upon an idea, through mainly its R&D programme, and develops a product that is a radical change from accepted ways of performing a service. Since the new product is protected by various proprietary rights, control of scarce resources or other barriers, this protection, together with promotional expenditure, enhances the significant product differentiation and offers the firm considerable control over price. However, the process of fixing the price of the new product involves a number of steps such as:

1. *Estimating demand*: Clearly, this is a more difficult question than for established products and what the firm must find out is whether the new product will be accepted by the market, assuming it is priced competitively; the range of these competitive prices and sales volume achieved at various prices, which means deriving some rough estimates of price elasticities and the

possibility of retaliation from producers of displaced products, if any. In answering these questions, opinion polling techniques can be of some use, although they must be complemented with information derived from other sources.

2. *Deciding on market targets*: Having established some demand estimates for the new product, the firm must decide on market targets, such as the share of the market it expects to capture to recoup its initial investment, whether the new product blends or not with its existing products (for complementary sales), what production methods to follow (economies of scale may be relevant here), promotional expenditure plans and distribution networks.

3. *Designing promotional strategy*: Since the firm is facing the problem of considerable initial promotional expenditure in order to create a market for the new product, it must find the right blend of price and promotional activity to recoup its initial high costs, while it is still enjoying the novelty advantages and the protection, and also to ensure long-run profitability.

4. *Choosing distribution networks*: Different distribution channels may have different distribution costs (in the form of despatching and receiving orders, storing and handling) that must be taken into consideration when setting prices. In addition to these physical distribution costs there are promotional costs by the retailers (display and shelve space, local advertising and the like) that must be taken into account for retailers' profit margins. Whether, for example, a policy of high distributors' margins, coupled with high promotion outlays and high prices is better than a policy of low prices in order to achieve expansion of the market, is a question that must be answered in each specific case. Clearly, the distribution network and marketing effort chosen will have implications on the final price that consumers have to pay and on which the success of the product in the market will depend.

Usually, the choice of pricing new products is between (1) an initial high price to skim the cream of the market and (2) a low initial price to penetrate the market. Skimming pricing may be appropriate for products that are very different from existing ones, and for which the novelty appeal ensures low price elasticity of demand. In such cases, high initial prices are unlikely to deter pioneering buying by the trend setters. In addition, such high prices tend to segment the market into sections of different elasticities that can be exploited by successive reductions in price. Also, high initial skimming prices are safer in an uncertain market, when the elasticity of demand cannot be easily established, and the product has not yet been accepted. In the exploratory stage, a high initial price can act as a refusal price, in the sense that the product will not be marketed, unless it can cover all its costs very quickly.

By contrast, the firm can use low initial prices for the new product in order to penetrate quickly mass markets. This is a riskier policy than skimming pricing, where prices are only lowered gradually in response to competition, and requires market research at the development stage. It appears that factors conducive to penetration pricing to expand the market are high price elasticity in the short run, cost savings resulting from economies of scale, product acceptability by the mass of consumers and the threat of potential competition, so that a big share of the market must be captured quickly. Most of these factors have, probably, been at work in the case of Nokia's mobile phones, discussed in Chapter 3.

10.3.5b   Pricing in maturity

The choice of pricing new products will have implications on the speed with which products can proceed from the initiation stage to the expansion and maturity stages that will provide the firm with most of the revenues and profits. In the case of pricing a mature product, the firm needs to establish when such maturity is approaching. In most cases of pricing mature products, we are also dealing with oligopolistic markets, which as we show earlier circumscribe the freedom of oligopolists to act independently. Maturity will be approaching when the once unique product starts losing much of its appeal due to the imitators, who enter the market and produce similar products. Dean suggests that the symptoms of product degeneration are likely to be: (1) weakening of preferences for the leading brand, evidenced by higher cross-price elasticities; (2) reduced physical variation in the competing products, leading to standardisation; (3) market saturation, usually indicated by an increase in the ratio of replacement sales to new sales; (4) increase in the own-label competitors, such as main retailing chains and (5) stabilisation of production methods, as cost reductions resulting from innovation are fully achieved. Once maturity has been reached, the product will not be able to carry a price premium, and so real prices will have to be reduced. However, such price reductions must be carefully linked to costs and price elasticity of demand, since in oligopolistic settings price wars are to be avoided, and efforts must be directed towards different forms of competition, such as product improvement and market segmentation. Such non-price competitive efforts mean further refinement, stylistic changes, after sales service and the like, which can segment the market and allow the firm to prolong the life of the product, as discussed under Section 9.4.2, extracting further profits.

Pricing, therefore, has to be adapted over the various stages of the cycle to reflect the changes in the market conditions for the product (substitutes, consumer preferences and the like), but it is also apparent that the stage the product has reached is, among others, the result of past pricing decisions.

10.3.6   Multiple product pricing

The pricing decisions we have been discussing so far have implicitly assumed that the firm produces a single product. However, with very few exceptions, firms produce a whole line of products and, therefore, they face the problem of multiple-product price and output determination. The main new element here is the appearance of interdependence, in the form of demand and/or supply interrelationships among the various products. On the demand side, products may be substitutes (competitive) or complements and, thus, the successful promotion of one will be affecting the sales of the other. On the supply side, we may have again complementarity and substitutability relations, in terms of resource utilisation by the various products and also joint production, as for example, in the case of crude oil refining. These interrelationships must be taken into consideration when fixing outputs and prices, since they affect the firm's overall profitability, by properly adjusting the marginal rules.

10.3.6a *Products related on demand*

The demand relationship between the products of a firm's line may be one of competition (substitutability), as with the case of a firm's confectionery brands or of complementarity, as with razors and blades. Clearly, changes in the price of one product will be affecting not only the revenues and profits of that product but also those of the other products as well. This means that the demand function for any product i, where $i = 1, \ldots, n$, can be written as:

$$q_i = f(p_1, p_2, \ldots, p_n) \tag{1}$$

For simplicity, we assume that there are no interrelationships on the supply side, and so the cost function is given by:

$$C = c(q_1, q_2, \ldots, q_n) \tag{2}$$

Thus, the profit function becomes:

$$\Pi = p_1 q_1 + p_2 q_2 + \cdots + p_n q_n - c(q_1, q_2, \ldots, q_n) \tag{3}$$

To maximise profits, the firm must set the partial derivatives of (3) with respect to various products qs equal to zero and solve, thus, obtaining the following:

$$p_1 + q_1 \frac{p_1}{\delta q_1} + q_2 \frac{\delta p_2}{\delta q_1} + \cdots + q_n \frac{\delta p_n}{\delta q_1} = \frac{\delta c}{\delta q_1}$$

$$p_2 + q_1 \frac{\delta p_1}{\delta q_2} + q_2 \frac{\delta p_2}{\delta q_2} + \cdots + q_n \frac{\delta p_n}{\delta q_2} = \frac{\delta c}{\delta q_2} \tag{4}$$

$$\ldots$$

$$p_n + q_1 \frac{\delta p_1}{\delta q_n} + q_2 \frac{\delta p_2}{\delta q_n} + \cdots + q_n \frac{\delta p_n}{\delta q_n} = \frac{\delta c}{\delta q_n}$$

because of the assumed interrelationships on the demand side. The various $\delta p_i / \delta q_j$ are the cross-partial derivatives and when they are multiplied by the various qs, they produce the cross-marginal revenue terms appearing on the LHS of the above expressions. If the products are complementary to each other, the cross-partial derivatives will be positive and the price of the product in question will be lower than when products are substitutes to each other and the cross-partial derivatives are negative. To show this let us assume that we have only two products q_1 and q_2 and solve equation one of (4). This gives us:

$$p_1 = \frac{\delta c}{\delta q_1} + q_1 \frac{\delta p_1}{\delta q_1} \pm q_2 \frac{\delta p_2}{\delta q_1}$$

the term $(\delta p_1 / \delta q_1)$ is always negative because of the inverse demand relationship and therefore it is transferred to the RHS as positive. The term $(\delta p_2 / \delta q_1)$ will be positive or negative, depending on whether the two products are complementary or substitutes to each other, and so it is transferred to the RHS with opposite sign. This means that the cross-marginal revenue between the two products will increase or reduce the excess amount over the marginal cost of production $(\delta c / \delta q_1)$, charged by the producer, depending on whether the products are substitutes or complements. It follows then that the optimal pricing rule will have to be adjusted, so that the price charged reflects the substitutability and/or complementarity relationships.

In the case where the complementarity relationship is so strong that:

$$q_1 \frac{\delta p_1}{\delta q_1} < q_2 \frac{\delta p_2}{\delta q_2}$$

this leads to $P_1 < MC_1$, i.e., the product will be sold below its marginal cost, in an effort to maximise profits from the whole product line. In practice, this discussion provides the rationale for 'loss leaders'.

10.3.6b   Products related on production

Interrelationships on the production side arise mainly as a result of the nature of certain products, which can only be produced jointly, as in the case of hides and meat production (or different cuts of meat), or are by-products of others, e.g., in oil refining, as well as of technological considerations. In such cases, since the products are produced as a result of the same operation, the joint cost of production cannot be easily allocated to the separate products. In other words, we are producing a whole package consisting of various products and the joint or composite cost function can be written as:

$$C = C(q_1, q_2, \ldots, q_n)$$

Typically, the total cost of producing the package will be lower than the sum of producing the various products separately. In the present context, we can distinguish two cases: (1) joint products with fixed proportions and (2) joint products with variable proportions.

In a situation where two joint products are always produced in the same ratio, say $1:1$, each unit of the package will consist of one unit of the first product and one unit of the second, and we talk of fixed proportions. To illustrate this case, assume for simplicity that we have two products, whose demand curves D_1 and D_2 and marginal revenue curves MR_1 and MR_2 are given as in Figure 10.11(a). Since the horizontal axis measures the quantity of the package (i.e., both products 1 and 2), an increase by one unit of the quantity will result in added revenues by both products and, therefore, we must add vertically the marginal revenues of the two products in order to derive the combined MR_{1+2}, which must be equated with the joint MC of production, for profit maximisation. The intersection of the combined marginal revenue curve MR_{1+2} with the MC curve determines the optimum output of the package, which results in product 1 priced at P_1 and product 2 priced at P_2.

As an algebraic example, assume that a firm produces two products Y and Z in fixed proportions $1:1$. The total cost of production is given by:

$$TC = 5000 + 100Q + 2Q^2$$

If the demand functions for the two products are $P_Y = 900 - 2Q_Y$ and $P_Z = 600 - 3Q_Z$, what must be the quantities and prices of Y and Z to maximise profits?

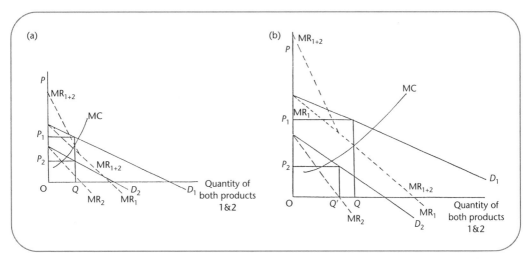

Figure 10.11 Pricing of joint products with fixed proportions

Clearly, since each unit Q of the package contains one unit of Q_Y and one unit of Q_Z, it means that $Q = Q_Y = Q_Z$, and therefore the profit function can be written as:

$$\Pi = \text{TR} - \text{TC} = P_Y \times Q_Y + P_Z \times Q_Z - \text{TC}$$
$$= 900Q - 2Q^2 + 600Q - 3Q^2 - 5000 - 100Q - 2Q^2$$

which gives:

$$d\Pi/dQ = 1400 - 14Q = 0 \text{ and so } Q = 100$$

Substituting into the price equations we derive: $P_Y = 900 - 2 \times 100 = 700$ and $P_Z = 600 - 3 \times 100 = 300$. The marginal revenues of the two products at $Q = 100$ are: $\text{MR}_Y = 900 - 4Q_Y = 900 - 4 \times 100 = 500 > 0$ and $\text{MR}_Z = 600 - 6Q_Z = 600 - 6 \times 100 = 0$. Since both marginal revenues are non-negative, they imply that profits are indeed maximised when the firm produces a package of 100 units, containing 100 units of each product. Profits are evaluated as:

$$\Pi = 900(100) - 2(100)(100) + 600(100) - 3(100)(100)$$
$$- 5000 - 100(100) - 2(100)(100) = 65\,000$$

However, if the two products are not produced and sold in the ratio $1:1$ then we must adjust the demand function accordingly. For example, if in the above case each unit of the package contained three units of Z and one unit of Y, the demand curve for Z must be expressed as $P_Z = 3(600 - 3Q_Z)$ and then proceed to find the marginal revenues, since the rule requires that we compare the marginal cost of the composite (package) good with its marginal revenue. The latter is found by adding the values of the relevant marginal revenues of the units of the two products produced, contained in the package.

Nevertheless, it is possible that the MR_2 becomes negative before the combined MR_{1+2} curve cuts the joint MC curve, as it happens in Figure 10.11(b). If now the firm tried to sell all the units of product 2, contained in the optimal package Q, it will depress the price of product 2 to the point where $MR_2 < 0$, and this will result in the marginal units sold at a loss. In this case, the optimal output/pricing policy is for the firm to produce the output package Q, charge a price P_1 for product 1 and a price P_2 for product 2. The derivation of price P_1 is straightforward. Price P_2 is obtained, simply, by selling product 2 up to the point where its MR_2 becomes zero, i.e., the units of product 2 contained in the output package Q', and then reading off the demand curve D_2 the price P_2, corresponding to output Q'. In this case, profit maximisation requires that part of the production of product 2, given by $Q - Q'$, be destroyed, otherwise P_2 will be depressed and the firm will fail to maximise profits. In the algebraic example above, all the units of Z are sold, since at $Q_Z = 100$, the marginal revenue is zero. Had more than 100 units of the composite product been produced, the excess over 100 units for Z should have been withdrawn from the market.

When products can be produced in variable proportions, we cannot construct a single marginal cost curve for the package of the products but rather have to consider, given the input prices, various marginal cost relationships for each product as we vary the production of that product while holding the production of the other(s) constant. In the case of two joint products X and Y we can then construct production possibility curves (PPC), showing the configurations of X and Y that can be produced from given quantities of variable inputs. This means that the PPCs can be considered as isocost curves. An increased quantity of product X can then be achieved either by employing the same given inputs and moving along the same production PPC, thus reducing the quantity of product Y (substitution effect), or using more variable inputs, i.e., moving on to a higher PPC (scale effect). By bringing in prices of the two products X and Y we can construct isorevenue curves (loci of all output configurations of X and Y representing equal revenue). As usual, optimal solutions require tangency points between a PPC and an isorevenue curve. At such tangency points, the slope of the isorevenue curve (given by the price ratio of the two products) is equal to the marginal rate of transformation between the two products (given by the ratio of the marginal products). Starting from an equilibrium position, if the prices of the products were changing, this will affect the slope of the isorevenue curve and a new equilibrium will be sought. For example, an increase in the price of product X will lead to a rise in its production, since the firm will have an incentive: (1) to cut back on the production of Y, thus releasing resources to be used in X, and (2) to hire more inputs for such production. The first (substitution effect) is shown by moving along the same PPC, while the second (scale effect) by moving on to a higher PPC. In terms of Figure 10.12, we can start with the initial isorevenue curves 1, 2 and 3 and derive equilibrium at C. An increase in the price of X will result in the new isorevenue curves 1', 2' and 3'. This increase brings about a scale effect, since the firm can hire more variable inputs, and a substitution effect, since it can sacrifice some of product Y. Both effects will tend to increase the production of X. For example, at point A, isorevenues 1' and 2 meet and the firm can get the same revenue by producing and selling the output configuration given by B, instead that of C. The quantity of Y has gone down and that of X has increased (substitution effect), but since we now operate on a lower PPC, fewer resources are required to earn the same revenue as before. However, the increase in the price of X means that the firm may now move on to a higher PPC and establish a new equilibrium at point D (scale

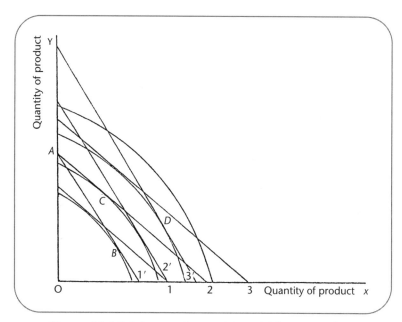

Figure 10.12 Joint products with variable proportions

effect), by buying more variable inputs and producing more X, assuming there are no budget constraints and demand remains buoyant. Again the equilibrium will be established at that tangency point between a PPC and an isorevenue curve, where the difference between total revenue and total cost is the greatest. Whether the quantity of Y produced, subsequent to an increase in the price of X, decreases or increases depends on the shape of the PPC, i.e., on whether the products are competitive or complements in the use of inputs.

What emerges from this brief discussion is that when we are faced with products related either on the demand or the production side, we must try to evaluate the contribution to overheads and profits of each product, under different assumptions about price, before we can establish the most profitable output configurations of such products. Marginal costs and marginal revenues must be adjusted appropriately to reflect the substitutability and complementarity relationships between the various products. Palda (1969) suggests that the multiple-product approach can be used in the following situations, where the cross-partial derivatives, indicative of the substitutability and complementarity relationship have been taken into account in adjusting the MR and MC for the ith product.

Applicability of multiple-product theory	
Situation	**Equilibrium condition**
Products related on both sides	$adjMR_i = adjMC_i$
Products related only on demand	$adjMR_i = MC_i$
Products related only on production	$MR_i = adjMC_i$
Products unrelated	$MR_i = MC_i$

10.3.7　Transfer pricing

Large, vertically integrated firms are often organised, internally, along the lines of what is known as the multidivisional form, i.e., they are split into different divisions, dealing with separate functions, like production, marketing and so on. Such internal organisation may be necessary for the more effective management and control of the firm's operations, and the divisions are, usually, granted considerable autonomy for their day-to-day decisions and can be viewed as separate profit centres. Nevertheless, they have to serve the firm's overall objectives of profitability laid down by the general office, which is responsible for the coordination of the separate divisions' functions. This divisionalisation, however, creates the problem of transfer pricing, i.e., what prices should be charged for goods transferred within the firm from one division to another. This is a crucial managerial problem, since prices diverging from values and costs will lead to wrong decisions, which will affect the firm's overall profits, even if one division's paper profits may be augmented as a result. The optimal pricing rule is that intra-firm transfers should take place at the market price (opportunity cost) of the product, assuming an external market for that product exists, or, in the absence of an external market, at the marginal cost of production. In what follows we refer to the transferring division as the T division, and the manufacturing of the final product division and facing the final market as the M division.

10.3.7a　Transfer pricing with no external market

It is often the case, particularly in the more R&D intensive industries, that firms produce unique intermediate products (resulting from their R&D), which they then use in the manufacture of well differentiated or even exclusive products. For example, a pharmaceutical firm produces at its laboratories (which we may call it the transferring division) a specialised and unique ingredient, which is then used by the manufacturing division for the manufacture of a medicine, for which the said ingredient is a necessary component. Since the firm has decided to exploit to the full the fruits of its R&D effort, by using the ingredient in producing the medicine itself, there is no external market for the specialised ingredient but only for the final product, i.e., only for the medicine.

　In this case, the optimal transfer price, P_T, which leads to overall profit maximisation, is to set it equal to the marginal cost of the transferring division (T), i.e.,

$$P_T = MC_T$$

and let the manufacturing division (call it M) buy from the transferring division all those units of the ingredient which promise to make a contribution to profitability. This is achieved as follows.

　Knowledge of the demand for the final product (D_M) allows the derivation of the marginal revenue for the final product (MR_M). Since the manufacturing division knows the marginal costs of processing the ingredient and turning it into a final product, as well as distributing it, it can calculate the net marginal revenue for the final product, by subtracting these costs from MR_M. This net marginal revenue for the final product becomes, in effect, the demand curve facing the transferring division. Therefore, by equating the net marginal revenue for the final

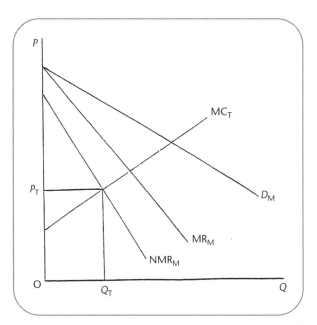

Figure 10.13 Transfer pricing with no external market

product (NMR_M) with the marginal cost of the transferring division (MC_T), we obtain output Q and the transfer price P_T, as illustrated in Figure 10.13. This, clearly, is the optimum position, since both divisions operate at a point of output at which they equate their respective MRs to their MCs. The transferring division has an incentive to expand output so long as its MR (given by P_T) is above MC_T, thus adding to profits. Also, the manufacturing division has an incentive to go on buying from the transferring division so long as the price they have to pay to the transferring division, P_T (which is some sort of net marginal cost to them), is below NMR_M. Expansion for both divisions stops where $NMR_M = MC_T$, i.e., at output Q. What this means is that the firm will be adding to its profits so long as the price of the final product exceeds the sum of the marginal costs of the transferring and manufacturing divisions.

To illustrate the equilibrium of the firm through an example under these conditions, consider VULCAN Ltd. which operates two divisions, the Foundry and the Engineering Tools. The latter produces and sells a patented tool for which it requires a special casting from the Foundry. The demand equation for the tool is: $P = 20 - 0.0035Q_M$. It is estimated that the processing and finishing costs of the casting by the Engineering Tools division are €5 per unit. The total costs of producing the castings in the Foundry are given as:

$$TC = 500 + 0.0015Q_C^2$$

We need to find how many units of the patented tool should be produced and at what price should they be sold. Also, we need to find the transfer price of the casting from the Foundry division to the Engineering Tools division.

Since the only demand for castings comes from the Engineering Tools division, the Foundry can only produce and sell to them, and it means that we can replace

Q_M and O_C with Q. It follows that overall profit for VULCAN Ltd. is maximised when the Foundry charges the Engineering Tools a transfer price equal to the MC of casting. This is found by differentiating the total cost function, given above, as:

$$MC_C = 0.003Q$$

The Engineering Tools in order to maximise their profits, will, in turn, be producing where they equate their MR to MC. To find their MC, they must add to their processing and finishing costs of €5 per unit, the transfer price charged to them by the foundry. Therefore, their MC is

$$MC_M = 0.003Q + 5$$

Next, we need to find the MR of the Engineering Tools division, which is found by multiplying the demand equation, given above, to derive the total revenue function as $TR = 20Q - 0.0035Q^2$ and then differentiating the latter with respect to Q. Thus, we derive $MR = d(TR)/dQ = 20 - 0.007Q$. By equating this to their MC established above, we get:

$$20 - 0.007Q = 0.003Q + 5$$

from which we get $0.01Q = 15$ and, finally, $Q = 1500$. Therefore, the Foundry will charge the Engineering Tools a transfer price of $P_T = 0.003(1500) = 4.5$. In turn, the patented tool will be offered to the market at a price of:

$$P = 20 - 0.0035(1500) = 14.75$$

Finally, the profits of VULCAN are calculated as follows:

$$\Pi = TR - TC = 20(1500) - 0.0035(1500)(1500)$$
$$- 500 - 0.0015(1500)(1500) - 5(1500) = 10\,750.$$

Thus, the Foundry division produces 1500 castings of the tool and sells them to the Engineering Tools division at €4.50 each. The latter, after applying their processing and finishing touches, sells the finished product in the market by charging €14.75 per unit, and the total profit made is €10 750. The analysis can also be extended to cover the case where the manufacturing division could use the same ingredient to produce a number of different final products. The optimal pricing rule, i.e., $P_T = MC_T$ advises that only those products should be adopted, whose prices exceed the sum of the marginal costs of the transferring and manufacturing divisions, because they add to profits, while products whose prices fall short of the sum of the marginal costs of the two divisions should be rejected.

However, in the context of divisional autonomy and emphasis on separate profit centres, there may be a potential for resentment, since, quite rightly, the transfer price does not include any allowances for overheads or fixed costs of the transferring division. It would appear then that the transferring division could not cover its full costs at that price. This argument is similar to the earlier full cost versus incremental cost discussion. While this may be resented by the transferring division, it has to be remembered that what is important is the firm's overall profitability rather than any full cost allocations, which could lead to wrong decisions and lowering of profits. As we saw, the firm's overall profits are maximised when the transfer price equals the marginal cost of the transferred intermediate product. The general office of the multidivisional firm could find alternative ways of ensuring that such fixed costs are covered, by making, for example, the manufacturing division contribute towards the transferring division's overheads, through a lump sum payment for the right to use the intermediate product, irrespective of the number of units purchased from the transferring division.

10.3.7b   *Transfer pricing with a competitive external market for the intermediate product and an imperfect market for the final product*

In the case where the transferring division T could also sell the intermediate product on to an external competitive market, the optimal transfer pricing rule will require that intra-firm transactions are priced at the market price. Here again the firm's overall profitability requires that both divisions operate at the point where their respective MRs and MCs are equal. Two cases can be illustrated: (1) where division T's output cannot cover the needs of division M, and the latter has to resort to the external competitive market to make up the shortfall, and (2) where division T produces more than division M can absorb, and the surplus is sold on to the external market. The first case is shown in Figure 10.14(a), which repeats the same information as the earlier Figure 10.13, but also incorporates the competitive demand for output Q_T with a transfer price of P_T, with all units of the intermediate product up to point A adding to profits. However, for division M, equilibrium is at Q_M, since at this output $NMR_M = P_T = D_T$. Up to point B the division M adds to profits since $NMR_T > D_T$, whereas beyond point B the inequality is reversed. Division M buys OQ_T units of the intermediate product from division T and the remainder $Q_M - Q_T$ from the external market, since it is cheaper. If division M were buying instead all their output from division T, total profits will be reduced by the

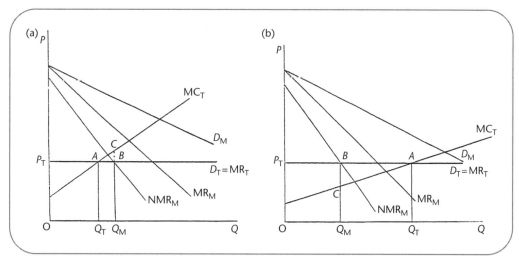

Figure 10.14 Transfer pricing with a competitive external market for intermediate product (a) shortage and (b) excess

Managerial Economics

amount given by the triangle ABC. Figure 10.14(b) illustrates the case where division T produces more than division M requires, and sells the excess to the external market. Again, for division T equilibrium is at $MR_T = MC_T$, i.e., at output Q_T with a transfer price of P_T, whereas for division M equilibrium is at $NMR_M = P_T$, i.e., at output Q_M. If division T's output were restricted to satisfying only the needs of the manufacturing division, then the firm would have failed to add to profits the area given by the triangle ABC. We can demonstrate the above by the following example:

Consider Agroindustries Ltd., which operates an agricultural division producing fruits and vegetables and a manufacturing division concerned with the processing and canning of the products of the agricultural division. The latter can sell its products either to external markets or to the manufacturing division. Among others, the agricultural division produces tomatoes, which can be sold (and bought) in an external market at €1.50 per kilogram. The total costs for the tomatoes production have been estimated as:

$$TC = 4000 + 0.00005Q_T^2$$

The cost of the manufacturing division of processing and canning of tomatoes into high quality concentrated tomato paste is €0.75 per kilogram. The demand curve for that particular tomato paste is given by:

$$P = 3 - 0.00025Q_M$$

Assuming that 1 kg of tomatoes produces 1 kg of tomato paste, what is the quantity of tomatoes produced by the agricultural division and where is it sold? How much tomato paste is produced by the manufacturing division and at what price is it offered for sale? What are the profits of Agroindustries Ltd. of the combined operations of tomatoes and tomato paste?

Since there is an external competitive market, the transfer price between the agricultural and manufacturing divisions for tomatoes is the price prevailing in the market, i.e., €1.5 per kilogram. Therefore, the agricultural division will be maximising its profits when it equates this price, which is its effective MR, to its MC which is $d(TC)/dQ_T = 0.0001Q_T$. This gives us the following equation:

$$1.5 = 0.0001Q_T$$

i.e., $Q_T = 15\,000$ kg of tomatoes. Thus, the agricultural division will be producing 15 000 kg of tomatoes, and we can now calculate the profits of the agricultural division as follows:

$$\Pi = TR - TC = 1.5(15\,000) - 4000 - 0.00005(15\,000)(15\,000) = 6250.$$

On the other hand, the manufacturing division will be in equilibrium when it equates its MC to its MR. Since the cost of processing and canning is €0.75 per kilogram, by adding to this the transfer price of €1.50 we obtain the marginal cost to the manufacturing division of a kilogram of tomato paste. This cost is, clearly, €2.25 and it is now equated to the manufacturing division's MR, which is $MR_M = 3 - 0.0005Q_M$, in order to find the manufacturing division's equilibrium output. Thus, we obtain: $2.25 = 3 - 0.0005Q_M$ or $Q_M = 1500$ kg of tomato paste. By substituting this value in the price equation of tomato paste, we can derive the price of tomato paste as:

$$P = 3 - 0.00025(1500) = 2.625$$

The profits of the manufacturing division are then estimated as:

$$\Pi = TR - TC = 3(1500) - 0.00025(1500)(1500) - 2.25(1500) = 562.5$$

Consequently, the total profit for Agroindustries Ltd. of the combined operations of tomatoes and tomato paste production is given as: €6250 + €562.5 = €6512.5. Finally, the agricultural division sells 1500 kg of tomatoes to the manufacturing division for its needs, and the remainder 13 500 kg to the external market.

Again, if the intermediate product could be used internally to produce different final products, all of which had imperfect final demands, while the intermediate product could also be sold on to a competitive external market, the transfer price would be set at the market price as before. To allocate the intermediate product to the internally produced final products, we must estimate the net marginal revenues of these products, sum them up and equate the aggregate NMRs to the transfer price P_T (the net marginal cost to the manufacturing division), which will give us the total requirements of the intermediate product and then equate the transfer price (MC) to the separate NMRs to derive how much of the intermediate product should be purchased internally for the different final products.

10.3.7c Transfer pricing with imperfect external markets for both the intermediate and final products

When the intermediate product can be sold in an imperfect external market, then again the transfer price should be set equal to the marginal cost of producing the intermediate product. To establish how the intermediate product is to be allocated between the external market and intra-firm use(s), we must sum up the net marginal revenue(s) of the final product(s) that the intermediate product can help produce inside the firm and add to that total the market marginal revenue of the intermediate product and, finally, equate this aggregate marginal revenue to the marginal cost of producing the intermediate product, MC_T. In Figure 10.15(a), we show the demand for the final product(s) that can be produced by means of the intermediate product and the net marginal revenue, NMR_F. Figure 10.15(b) shows the market demand for the intermediate product D_T, from which we can find MR_T. Finally, in Figure 10.15(c) we sum NMR_F and MR_T to derive the aggregate marginal revenue, $\sum NMRs$ which intersects with the marginal cost curve of the intermediate product, MC_T, to determine the equilibrium output Q_T and the transfer price P_T. The total output Q_T is then allocated between the two uses as Q_F and Q_M, just as in the case of the discriminating monopolist, where $Q_F + Q_M = Q_T$. From (b) we read off the demand curve the price P_M, at which the intermediate product sells in the open market, whereas in (a) we see that the transfer price is equal to the marginal cost of the intermediate product. This is the combination of prices and quantities which will maximise the firm's overall profits.

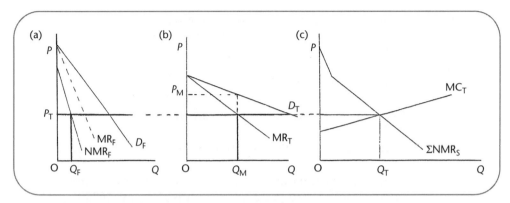

Figure 10.15 Transfer pricing with imperfect markets for both

10.3.8 Concluding remarks

The above discussion has emphasised both the theoretical foundations of pricing and some pricing policies adopted in practice, to achieve particular objectives. Since pricing is not an end in itself but a means towards achieving the firm's particular targets, the question arises as to what extent such pricing practices, merely, follow rules of thumb or are consistent with marginal analysis. The original study by Hall and Hitch (1939), referred to earlier, initiated a considerable and wide ranging debate, at the heart of which was whether marginalism constituted a relevant approach for decision making, and whether profit maximisation was a universally adopted objective by firms.

In an classic article, Rothschild (1947) argues that in oligopolistic settings another motive, equally important to maximum profits, is the desire for secure profits, and, what is more important, under oligopoly the desire for security coexists with the power to act on this desire. This means that there is a struggle for position, in which price plays a pivotal role and has to be seen as a dynamic phenomenon. The price charged must allow the oligopolist to maintain his position both against existing or potential competitors, and *vis-à-vis* customers. 'This means that in "normal" periods the price must not be so low that it provokes retaliations from the competitors, nor so high that it encourages new entrants, and it must be within the range which will maintain the goodwill of the customers – i.e., will maintain a protection against aggressive policies of the rivals' (Rothschild 1947). Accordingly, Rothschild finds that the full-cost principle is a perfectly logical outcome in the market surveyed by Hall and Hitch, once security considerations are recognised, because the oligopolist will make his costs the basis for his pricing. To these costs a profit margin will be added, which will depend on the strength of the oligopolist's position. This also explains why price rigidity becomes an essential aspect of 'normal' oligopolistic strategy. At the same time, however, there are additional elements which tend to reduce price rigidity, such as changes in quality, credit and discount arrangements, salesmanship and the like and also the conflicting interests of the various departments within the firm (such as sales, costing, legal, technical, advertising and others), which imply that the quoted price will be the result of a variety of conflicting tendencies within the firm. Security requires both a powerful position (obtained through increased size), and plentiful resources. In addition, consumers have to be 'conditioned' against rivals' inroads through advertising, and also raw materials and other supply sources must be safeguarded through vertical integration or at least by interlocking directorates and shareholdings. The security motive also leads the major oligopolists to seek and exploit political power by spending considerable sums in the various lobbies. This is an area as yet unexplored by theorists, which is surprising, since '... the gap that divides selling expenditure from political activities is methodologically much smaller than the one that divides the former from production costs proper' (Rothschild 1947). At the final stage, the oligopolistic struggle manifests itself in expansion abroad, through foreign direct investment. Therefore, a full explanation of oligopoly behaviour and price requires the consideration of both economic factors and these 'non-economic' elements. However, this implies that the result may not be quite as precise as value theory has suggested, but '... it is better to be vaguely right than precisely wrong'.

Returning to the Hall and Hitch thesis and leaving aside alternative paradigms to the theory of the firm, a number of writers have questioned the validity of the Hall and Hitch study and its relevance, by arguing that the full-cost approach merely meant that entrepreneurs did not use 'economic' jargon, but had formulated instead their own rules in terms which they understood to maximise profits. For example, they (entrepreneurs) had recognised that policies, such as high prices, appropriate for short-run profit maximisation could adversely influence sales and profits in the long-run, and by being 'fair' to consumers they were, in fact, maximising long-run profits. Besides, it was argued that full-cost pricing was not necessarily antithetical to profit maximisation, if the mark-up was related to price elasticity of demand, as was shown above. This body of opinion were dismissive of studies which asked entrepreneurs what they were doing, on the grounds that they were not always likely to get to the truth of the matter and/or the results might be difficult to interpret, so the results of such studies should be ignored.

If this approach smacks of complacency and academic arrogance, it did not prevent many other similar studies, which mainly took the form of a combination of personal interviews and questionnaires. These have been referred to as 'micro' studies and have tended to be rather inconclusive. Earley (1956), in a study of 'excellently managed' large firms, found that their managers distrusted full-cost principles and instead adhered to marginalist ones, by aiming to achieve higher profits at the early stages in the life of a product, varying their profit margins in accordance with elasticity of demand, splitting their costs into variable and fixed and trying to allocate the latter to relevant lines of products, as a result of having adopted sophisticated accounting and costing methods.

On the other hand, in a study of the Brookings Institution, Kaplan *et al.* (1958) surveying the pricing policies of large US corporations found a great variety of such policies, such as pricing to achieve: (1) a target return on investment; (2) stabilisation of prices and margins; (3) pricing to maintain or improve market share; (4) pricing with respect to product differentiation and (5) pricing to meet competition and follow it (i.e., cases of price leadership/followership). Also, they found that pricing was influenced greatly by a number of factors such as the character of the product and its place in the product mix, pricing objectives, price and non-price competition, advertising, anti-trust considerations, leadership and so on, and concluded that big business were unable '...to fit their price policies into a common category'. Additional support for the non-marginalist approach was provided by the work of Barback (1964), who found that of the British firms he studied neither thought in a marginalist way nor behaved in such a way, and although there was a desire to increase profits there was no attempt to maximise them over time because of the existence of other objectives. Hague in some earlier studies on pricing policies in Britain found that prices were based on average cost (1949), and in the case of the British rayon industry, Courtaulds had used in 1933, price decreases (made possible through cost saving resulting from technical progress) as part of their business strategy (1957). However, the same author found in another study (1971) that the information available to firms, as a result of the sophistication of their accounting procedures, made a significant difference to the policies adopted. Large firms with advanced accounting systems had the necessary information and did maximise their profits. However, firms with less sophisticated accounting techniques pointed out that, although they would like to maximise profits, they did not have the requisite information on which to base their decisions and instead resorted to some rule of thumb as a second best procedure.

Another group of studies, referred to as 'macro' ones, rely not on interviews and questionnaires but on the analysis of published data; they are essentially econometric studies trying to establish whether firms behave in a way consistent with profit maximisation. Despite the fact that they tend to arrive at conflicting results, they have the advantage over the 'micro' studies, since they are more objective. They can be classified as: (1) time series studies, investigating the relationship between market structure, prices and profits, with the expectation that prices would be more stable over time under rules of thumb than under marginalism, and that profits would be higher as concentration increases, if marginalist rules were adopted; (2) studies showing the effect of different market structures on changes in prices and profits over the business cycle, with the expectation that prices will tend to vary more under marginalist conditions, since under the full-cost regime prices vary only with changes in costs and not with changes in demand and, finally, (3) studies concerned with movements over time in industrial prices, particularly in periods of inflation. By and large the 'macro' studies support the profit maximisation hypothesis, while the 'micro' ones tend to refute it.

In addition to the various pricing practices referred to above, there are many others which claim to simplify the pricing problem but which, despite their use, are not necessarily better than the ones they try to supplant. We are not, therefore, trying to provide an exhaustive treatment of such practices here. Suffice to mention only two of these: odd-number prices, such as, for example, €2.99 instead of €3, because it is claimed consumers are influenced by price reductions below a round figure, or the exact opposite policy of round-number pricing, such as €5 or €3.50 to enhance the quality reputation, instead of €4.99 or €3.49, which may give the impression of cut-rate products. Odd-number prices ending at €0.95 or €0.99 are much in evidence in practice and are reminiscent of the pricing policies of the behavioural theory of the firm, suggested by Cyert and March (1963). These pricing practices can also be connected to the tendency by consumers of judging quality by price, which results in a different pricing strategy, known as prestige pricing. According to this approach, when the price is low, the product or service is perceived by consumers as of lower quality compared with other similar products or services. On the other hand, when a good is priced higher than other similar goods, it may be perceived by consumers as qualitatively superior to its rivals, i.e., as possessing greater prestige, and so a price rise may result in an increased demand. Consequently, the prestige approach to pricing postulates a direct relationship between price and quantity demanded, which is reminiscent of the 'Veblen effect', discussed in Chapter 4.

In conclusion, however, it should be emphasised that perhaps there has been an overstressing of the importance of price setting. It should be mentioned that since price is only one of the tools at management's disposal for achieving its objectives, other policies, like investment and product policies, deserve no less attention than that which has been devoted to pricing. For it is the overall effect of such policies on the performance of firms that matters. In this sense, considering the firm's marketing mix in terms of the quality of the product, its promotion and its price may be a more fruitful way of understanding how firms are tackling this complex problem.

QUESTIONS AND PROBLEMS

1. The demand, Q, for a monopolist's product at any price, P, is given by: $P = 200 - Q$ and his total cost function is $C = 10 + 2Q^2$.

   (a) What are the profit maximising values of price and output and what is the level of profit (i) before and (ii) after, the imposition of a tax of 20 per unit of output?

   (b) If the firm is, instead, a marginal cost pricer, what would price, output and profit be, before the tax and after it? (Note: the tax would be added on to the pre-tax marginal cost).

   (c) Now assume that the firm prices at average variable cost +50% (market demand conditions being satisfied). What are the values of price, output and profit in this situation, before and after the tax? (Note: the tax is added on to AVC before the mark-up 50% is added).

   (d) Compare and comment upon profits, prices and outputs in (a), (b) and (c).

   (e) In (b) and (c) would the firm have been better advised to 'pass on' the tax by raising the pre-tax price by the amount of the tax? Comment in the light of the observed behaviour of firms.

2. The market demand for a product X is given by: $P = c - dQ$. A monopolist produces X at an average cost $(aQ + b)$ for output Q and sells it to a merchant at a price M, which maximises his profits. The merchant is a monopolist too with constant distribution costs and maximises his profits by selling on the market at price P. Show that the optimal amount of X produced and sold is:

$$Q = \frac{c - b}{2(a + 2d)}$$

Find also the optimal values of M and P.

3. A dairy firm produces milk, which it can sell either for fluid consumption or for the production of cheese. The demand for milk for fluid consumption is given by: $P_F = 100 - 4Q_F$, while the demand for milk for cheese consumption is given by: $P_T = 120 - 8Q_T$. The firm's total costs of production are: $C = 100 + 10(Q_F + Q_T)$.

   (a) What are the profit maximising prices and quantities in each market, and the overall profit?

   (b) What are the elasticities of demand in the two markets at the profit maximising prices? Comment.

   (c) If the dairy firm decided to charge the same price in each market, what this should be in order to maximise profits? Compare the profit made here with that under (a).

4. A profit maximising firm produces a product in a single plant at a total cost of

$$TC = 2000 + 10Q - 0.02Q^2 + 0.001Q^3$$

   and can sell it in two separate markets. If the demand curves for the product in the two markets are given as $P_1 = 400 - 1.6Q_1$ for the first, and $P_2 = 400 - 3Q_2$ for the second, what quantity should be offered in each market and at what price? Estimate also the price elasticities at the profit maximising levels and discuss your results.

5. A profit maximising monopolist can vary the quality of the single product he produces. The best price he can charge is governed by the relation: $P = 16 - 2x/y$, where x is output, P is the price and y measures the quality of the product, which is continuously variable between $y = 1$ and $y = 10$. The firm's total production costs, are given by: $C = 7 + 4x + 3y^2$.

   Find the firm's optimal output, price, quality and profit.

6. Agora Ltd. is a monopolist producing a single product, whose demand function is given by:

$$P = 18 - Q - 50/A, \quad \text{where } P > 0$$

   where, P is price, Q is output and A is advertising expenditure. In the short run, the total costs of production, C, are given by:

$$C = 6 + Q + 2Q^2, \quad \text{where } Q > 0$$

   Show that in the short run Agora's optimal advertising expenditure is 10, and find the optimal values of output, price and profit.

7. The demand curve of a monopolist's product is given by: $Q = 1220 - 4P$. The monopolist has estimated that his long-run cost function is given by:

$$TC = Q^2 + 20Q - 15sQ + 50s^2$$

   where Q is quantity produced and s is the plant size. What are the profit maximising values of Q and s and the profit made?

8. The market for a particular product is shared by two duopolists, *A* and *B*. The demand for the first duopolist's product is given by:

$$Q_A = 1000 - 2P_A + P_B$$

while the demand for duopolist *B*'s output is given by:

$$Q_B = 800 - 2P_B + P_A$$

where Q_A and Q_B measure the outputs and P_A and P_B the respective prices of the two duopolists. Firm *A*'s total costs are given by:

$$C_A = 10 + 2Q_A + Q_A^2$$

and firm *B*'s total costs are given by:

$$C_B = 20 + 2Q_B + Q_B^2$$

Each firm tries to maximise its own profit, working on the assumption that its behaviour has no influence on the price charged by the other duopolist. At what prices are both firms in equilibrium simultaneously? Can such an equilibrium position be sustained?

9. Consider three towns, *A* 10 km west of *B*, *B* 10 km west of *C*. A large firm and a small firm manufacture a similar product. Each wishes to build a plant in one of the towns in order to supply all three towns. Each firm knows that the other firm is contemplating such action. Of the total demand for the product 20% comes from *A*, 30% from *B* and 50% from *C*. If the large firm is nearer to a town, it will capture 80% of that town's business. If both firms are equally distant, the large firm will get 60% of the business. If the small firm is nearer, the large firm will obtain 40% of the business. Which is the best safe location for each firm, assuming that each firm is interested in maximising its share of the total market? Explain.

10. A contractor is going to build a number of houses for Coventry Corporation. Four types of houses have been considered; semi-detached, detached, terraced and cottage; and the Coventry Corporation Housing Committee will choose two of these types for the contractor to build. The contractor has the opportunity to buy materials in bulk, thus, saving considerable money, but he must order in advance of the Committee's decision and can order only one type of material. If the Committee chooses semi-detached and detached, the contractor will make an (extra) profit (in thousands of euros) of 125, 120, 60, and 50 if he orders semi-detached, detached, terraced and cottage materials, respectively. If the Committee chooses semi-detached and terraced, he will make 90, 40, 80 and 75, respectively; if the Committee chooses semi-detached and cottage, he will make 150, 30, 75, and 100, respectively; if the Committee chooses detached and terraced, the contractor will make 70, 70, 75 and 65, respectively; if the Committee chooses detached and cottage, he will make 90, 80, 80 and 120, respectively; while, finally, if the Committee chooses terraced and cottage, the contractor stands to make 80, 40, 130 and 80, respectively.

How should the contractor order his materials so as to maximise his minimum expected extra profit, and what will this extra profit be?

11.　An oil company produces jointly two types of petrol from refining crude oil; a high octane type A and a low octane type B. The demand, per litre, for type A petrol is given by: $Q_A = 400 - 2P_A$ and that for type B petrol by $Q_B = 1300 - 10P_B$. The two types of petrol are produced in the ratio $1:1$ and the total costs of production are given by:

$$TC = 2000 + 10Q + Q^2$$

What quantities of the two types are produced and at what prices are they sold to maximise profit? What is the profit? If now you were told that the refining process produces two units of type B for every one unit of type A petrol, everything else remaining the same, how would your answer differ?

12.　The Kent Apples Ltd. operates its own orchards for the production of apples which can be used for the production of apple juice, or of cider or, finally, sold to the external fruit market. The company is split between the Orchard division, concerned with the production of apples; the Cannery division, concerned with the production and canning of apple juice; and the Cider division, concerned with cider production. The total cost function of producing apples is given by:

$$TC = 50\,000 + 0.0005Q^2$$

where Q is expressed in 100 kg. Apples can be sold to (or bought from) the external market at €40 per 100 kg. The processing costs of the Cannery division for producing apple juice are €50 per 100 lit and the demand equation for apple juice is given by: $P_J = 1000 - 5Q_J$ for 100 lit of juice. Also, the processing costs of producing 100 lit of cider are €70 and the demand equation for cider is: $P_C = 1500 - 3Q_C$ per 100 lit. Assuming that 1 kg of apples produces either 1 lit of apple juice or 1 lit of cider, find the quantity of apples produced, where it is sold, what quantities of apple juice and cider are produced and at what prices are they sold and the total profit of Kent Apples Ltd. of the combined operations of apples, apple juice and cider.

13.　FARMA Medicines is divisionalised between the Laboratory division, producing a special chemical ingredient and the Medicines division, which utilises the special ingredient to produce a patented medicine. The Laboratory division produces the ingredient at a total cost of

$$TC = 5000 + 0.03Q^2$$

and can only sell it internally to the Medicines division. The latter incurs processing costs of €10 per unit of medicine and estimates the demand equation for the medicine to be: $P = 200 - 0.02Q$. If one unit of the ingredient is required to produce one unit of the final product, what quantity of the final product should be produced and at what price should it be sold to the market? What price should the Laboratory division charge for the ingredient and what is the profit of FARMA Medicines.

APPENDIX: STEPS IN THE PRICING PROCESS

The preceding discussion has demonstrated that the setting of prices in practice is a complex process, requiring, particularly, in the context of a multiple product firm, a number of important steps regarding, e.g., the firm's objectives; the estimation of demand and cost conditions for the product in question; the interrelationships with other substitute and/or complementary own products; the effect of competitor products; the possible reaction of competitors; the time period involved; the practice and structure of rebates, discounts and credits; government policies; the state of capacity of plant(s) and so on.

A number of writers, starting with Dean's pioneering work (1951), have considered in detail the pricing process and produced a checking list of steps to be followed in arriving at individual prices. In the case of pioneering pricing, i.e., that of pricing an altogether new product, Dean suggests that the firm should set about: (1) estimating the demand, by finding out something about the preferences of consumers, the relevant price range which makes the product a 'good value' for the consumers, probable sales from several possible prices and the possibility of retaliation from displaced competitor products; (2) deciding on market targets; (3) designing its promotional strategy and (4) choosing the channels of distribution.

A similar multi-stage approach to pricing has been suggested by Oxenfeldt (1960), who proposed that in setting prices, the following six sequential stages should be observed: (1) selecting market targets, concerned with the identification of the market the firm wishes to reach given its objectives, capabilities and resources; (2) choosing a brand image, establishing the reputation of the firm for high quality or mass-produced products and directing its marketing efforts to build such image; (3) composing the marketing mix, dealing with the coordination of all marketing and promotional activities with the pricing decision; (4) selecting a pricing policy, within which individual prices can be determined, e.g., follow the price leader or use a predetermined markup on full-cost and so on; (5) determining a pricing strategy, which is consistent with the firm's objectives, and (6) setting specific prices. This multi-stage approach is considered useful in organising the various pieces of information required in arriving at a price, and the sequence of the stages is important, because each step is calculated to simplify the next stage and to reduce the probability of error.

In an extensive field work on pricing in business, Hague (1971) has considered the pricing practices of a number of firms in the UK and established the various stages involved in setting their prices. This has enabled him to produce a comprehensive pricing check list, under the major headings of: (1) preliminary work, dealing with terminology, product specification, objectives of the firm and whether the decision will set the price of all or part of the output; (2) pricing objectives, covering the time span, profit, market and other objectives and consistency of the various objectives among themselves; (3) information required for the pricing decision, including information on pricing objectives listed under (2), external information on the total market, on competitors' products and prices and on government policies, and internal information on costs, revenues and profits; (4) availability of information, involving its sources if information is not currently available, reliability of such information and priorities of acquiring it, given its cost; (5) pricing decision, dealing with effects of alternative prices on costs, sales, market share, competitors reactions and objectives, choosing the best alternative but, if none contributes to firm's objectives, reconsidering product specification and design, recording the decision made and its assumptions; and, finally, (6) reviewing the results of the pricing decision and initiating remedial action if results are unsatisfactory, reviewing pricing objectives in the light of results and reviewing procedures for pricing decisions.

The suggested price check list, which follows in the next section is based on the three works mentioned above as well as on those by Oxenfeldt (1961) and Haynes (1962).

A suggested price check list

The purpose of a price check list is to seek and then organise the information necessary for pricing and also split the complicated pricing process into a number of successive simpler steps. Thus, we have:

1. Specifying the product and its relationship with other products in the firm's product line.

2. Setting the objectives (market share, profit and the like) that pricing can be expected to achieve over a period of time.

3. Estimating the demand function and finding elasticities of demand with respect to its crucial determinants.

4. Identifying the role of suppliers and retailers in determining prices (rebates, discounts, price maintenance and the like).

5. Taking account of the role of government, in the form of taxes, money and credit controls, purchasing power of the state, i.e., procurements (if applicable), restrictive practices and/or other relevant legislation.

6. Establishing the reaction of existing competitors and potential rivals to different prices.

7. Deriving information on alternative production methods and their costs, on own and rivals' costs (also on distribution, selling and promotional spending), and on alternative volume–cost relationships.

8. Setting alternative prices and finding out their effects on revenues, production volumes, profits, plant and labour usage by taking account of possible complementarities/substitutabilities on other products in the firm's product line.

9. Establishing the reaction of existing and potential rivals to such alternative prices.

10. Investing in new facilities according to estimated volumes, revenue and profits in the future at projected optimum prices.

11. Identifying the impact of alternative prices on the firm's objectives, such as profits, market share, market growth and the like.

12. Choosing amongst the alternatives, the price that makes the greatest contribution to the firm's objectives.

13. Reconsidering product specification, design, revenues, costs, profits and objectives if none of the alternatives considered contributes significantly to the firm's objectives.

14. Reviewing the pricing decision(s) in the light of results and initiating action to meet changing demand and cost conditions.

15. Evaluating the impact of price changes on the 'image' of the firm and on customer goodwill.

16. Identifying the different stages of the life cycle of the product and devising appropriate price strategies to take account of different demand conditions.

17. Avoiding overestimation of the role of pricing, for it is only one element in the marketing mix and alone it may not lead to profitable outcomes.

BIBLIOGRAPHY

Bain, J. (1956), *Barriers to New Competition*, Cambridge, Mass.

Barback, R.H. (1964), *The Pricing of Manufactures*, Macmillan.

Binmore, K. (1992), *Fun and Games: A Text on Game Theory*, D.C. Heath & Co.

Cyert, R.M. and March, J.C. (1963), *A Behavioral Theory of the Firm*, Prentice-Hall.

Dean, J. (1951), *Managerial Economics*, Prentice-Hall.

Demsetz, H. (1982), 'Barriers to Entry', *American Economic Review*, March, 47–57.

Earley, J.S. (1956), 'Marginal Policies of Excellently Managed Companies', *American Economic Review*, March.

Hague, D.C. (1949), 'Economic Theory and Business Behaviour', *Review of Economic Studies*.

—— (1957), *The Economics of Man-made Fibres*, Duckworth.

—— (1971), *Pricing in Business*, George Allen & Unwin.

Hall, R.L. and Hitch, C.J. (1939), 'Price Theory and Business Behaviour', *Oxford Economic Papers*, May, 12–45.

Haynes, W.W. (1962), *Pricing Decision in Small Business*, University of Kentucky Press.

Haynes, W.W. and Henry, W.R. (1979), *Managerial Economics*, 4th ed., Business Publications.

Horowitz, I. (1970), *Decision Making and the Theory of the Firm*, Holt-Rinehart-Winston.

Kaplan, A.D.H., Dirlam, J.B. and Lanzilotti, R.F. (1958), *Pricing in Big Business*, The Brookings Institution, Washington DC.

Kreps, D.M. (1990), *A Course in Microeconomic Theory*, Princeton University Press.

Luce, R.D. and Raiffa, H. (1957), *Games & Decisions*, John Wiley & Sons.

MacDonald, G. and Slivinski, A. (1987), 'The Simple Analytics of Competitive Equilibrium with Multiproduct Firms', *American Economic Review*, 77, December, 941–953.

von Neumann, J. and Morgenstern, O. (1953), *The Theory of Games and Economic Behavior*, 3rd ed., John Wiley & Sons.

Oxenfeldt, A.R. (1960), 'Multi-Stage Approach to Pricing', *Harvard Business Review*, July–August, 125–133.

—— (1961), *Pricing for Marketing Executives*, Wadsworth Publishing Co.

Palda, K.S. (1969), *Economic Analysis for Marketing Decisions*, Prentice-Hall.

Pappas, J.L. and Hirschey, M. (1990), *Managerial Economics*, 6th edn, The Dryden Press.

Rasmusen, E. (1991), *Games and Information: An Introduction to Game Theory*, Blackwell.

Reekie, W.D. and Crook, J.N. (1992), *Managerial Economics*, 4th edn., Philip Allan.

Rothschild, K.W. (1947), 'Price Theory & Oligopoly', *The Economic Journal*, LVII, 299–320.

Scherer, F.M. and Ross, D. (1990), *Industrial Market Structure and Economic Performance*, 3rd ed., Houghton Miflin Co.

Silberston, A. (1970), 'Price Behaviour of Firms', *The Economic Journal*, 80, 511–592.

Stigler, G.J. (1968), 'Price and Non-Price Competition', *Journal of Political Economy,* February, 149–154.

Varian H.R. (1993), *Intermediate Microeconomics: A Modern Approach,* 3rd ed., W.W. Norton & Co.

chapter eleven

Capital Budgeting

Learning outcomes

After studying this chapter you should know about:

- Discounting, compounding

- Time preference

- Internal rate of return

- Present value

- Investment appraisal methods
  - ☐ Payback
  - ☐ Discounting Cash Flow Techniques

    Net Present Value (NPV) criterion
    Internal Rate of Return (IRR) criterion

  - * Conflict between NPV and IRR criteria
  - ☐ Imperfect capital market and capital rationing

- Risk and capital budgeting:
  - □ The Finite-horizon and the risk-adjusted discount rate

- Sources of finance
  - □ Retained profits, issuing of bonds, issuing of new shares

- Financial policy and the cost of capital
  - □ Dividend Valuation Model
  - □ Capital Asset Pricing Model (CAPM)

11.1 INTRODUCTION

By capital budgeting we mean the various procedures of investment decision making of firms, i.e., the body of economic analysis which tries to answer questions about the capital projects the firm should invest in, the amount of capital expenditure undertaken by the firm, and how this expenditure should be financed. The crucial point about capital budgeting is how to arrive at correct decisions, when time is involved, and it is so irrespective of whether the investment decision refers to individuals, firms or countries. In other words, it is a question of resource allocation over time. If in other areas of economic enquiry we were able, at least initially, to ignore time, and consider static models and their properties as a way of analysing the behaviour of individuals, firms and so on, in capital budgeting time enters explicitly into the analysis and is of paramount importance. Capital budgeting then is the dynamic process par excellence, in which managers base their present decisions partly on what they believe now and partly on what they anticipate to happen in future. Clearly, if the expectations about the future change, they influence present decisions in a different manner. This, inevitably, leads to the biggest headache management faces, i.e., risk and uncertainty, and the discussion of Chapter 12 is very relevant here. Nevertheless, we shall firstly consider the problem by assuming a state of certainty and perfect foresight, in order to develop appraisal methods for optimum solutions. Subsequently, we shall extend the analysis by introducing the problems of risk and imperfect knowledge and modify our decision criteria to take account of these.

However, before proceeding we need to consider firstly the ideas of compounding and discounting, which play a crucial role in capital budgeting and, thus, develop the algebraic tools necessary for the ensuing analysis.

11.2 THE TIME VALUE OF MONEY – COMPOUNDING AND DISCOUNTING

The concept of the time value of money is one of the most fundamental ideas in economics. The idea that money has a time dimension simply means that 1€ to day is worth more than 1€ tomorrow, and this is the case under conditions of complete certainty, perfect foresight and absence of inflation. It follows then that in order to compare money due or accruing at different points in time, we must either compound or discount such values and decide on the basis of such compounded or discounted values. For example, consider that you are given the choice between a gift of €100 to day and a gift of €100 in a year's time. Despite assurances that the €100 will be paid in a year's time, you would be right to choose the €100 now. The reason is that €100 received now can be put in a bank or building society, and assuming an interest rate of 5%, it will grow to be €105 in a year's time. This is more than the €100 you would have received, had you chosen instead to delay the receipt of €100 by one year.

To illustrate the issues involved, we start by assuming that we can deposit now with a bank an amount of €V at an interest rate of d%. It follows that in a year's time our initial deposit, assuming no taxes on interest, will be worth:

$$V_1 = V_0(1 + d)$$

where subscripts denote periods, i.e., V_0 is the sum initially deposited with the bank. If at the end of the year we decide to leave the money in the bank for another year, the value of our deposit at the end of the second year will grow to be:

$$V_2 = V_1(1+d) = V_0(1+d)^2$$

provided the interest rate remains the same. In general, leaving the initial sum of money in the bank for n periods at a constant interest rate of $d\%$, its value at the end of n periods will be given by:

$$V_n = V_0(1+d)^n \tag{1}$$

Relation (1) is the compounding interest formula. It shows how the initially deposited sum and the interest earned in each year are compounded to give us the compounded value V after n years. Looking now at the reverse process, we may ask, what is the present value of a sum of money €V accruing after n years, at a constant compounding rate of $d\%$? The answer is provided by solving relation (1) above for V_0 and is given by:

$$V_0 = \frac{V_n}{(1+d)^n} = V_0 D^n \tag{2}$$

Relation (2) gives us the discounted or present value of a sum of money accruing in the future, and it denotes the discounting process, which plays an essential part in capital budgeting. In the above expression, D, is the discount factor and we may find it easier in the following discussion to use expression (3).

$$D = \frac{1}{(1+d)} \tag{3}$$

Let us now assume that a particular investment project is associated with the following expected future income stream:

$$(V_0 = R_0 - C_0), \quad (V_1 = R_1 - C_1), \quad (V_2 = R_2 - C_2), \dots, (V_n = R_n - C_n)$$

where the Rs and Cs are the respective revenues and costs associated with the project over its lifetime, and the Vs are the net returns of the project. Since the stream of Vs represents the stream of surpluses of revenues over costs of the investment project, we may wish to find its capitalised or discounted or net present value (NPV). Assuming the interest rate to be $d\%$, and to remain constant during the period under consideration, we have:

$$NPV = V_0 + V_1 D + V_2 D^2 + V_3 D^3 + \cdots + V_n D^n = \sum_{t=0}^{n} V_t D^t \tag{4}$$

where $t = 0, 1, 2, \dots, n$ denotes time, with 0 standing for the present. Relation (4) is the general formula for discounting purposes.

If we are given an annuity or a constant stream of income of V euros per year to perpetuity, its present value, assuming a constant interest rate of $d\%$, is calculated as follows:

$$\text{NPV} = \sum_{t=1}^{\infty} VD^t = V \sum_{t=1}^{\infty} D^t = V\left[D(1 + D^2 + D^3 + \cdots)\right]$$

$$= V\left(\frac{D}{1-D}\right) = V\frac{1}{d} = \frac{V}{d} \tag{5}$$

Relation (5) implies that an annuity or a stream of income of €100 per year in perpetuity at an interest rate of 10% has a present value of €1000, whereas at an interest rate of 5% its present value becomes €2000, and at an interest rate of 20% it is only €500.

We have just seen the case of a constant stream of future income. We can now consider the case that the Vs are growing at a proportional rate g% every year, so that: $V_t = V_0(1+g)^t$. Provided that $g > -1$ the formula becomes:

$$\text{NPV} = \frac{V_0(1+g)}{(1+d)} + \frac{V_0(1+g)^2}{(1+d)^2} + \cdots + \frac{V_0(1+g)^t}{(1+d)^t} \tag{6}$$

By letting now $(1+g)/(1+d) = 1/(1+\gamma)$ and substituting in (6) we get, after summing up:

$$\text{NVP} = V \sum_{t=1}^{n} \frac{1}{(1+\gamma)^t} \tag{7}$$

This expression has a finite solution if and only if $-1 < 1/(1+\gamma) < 1$, which implies that $g < d$. If $g = d$, then $1 + g = 1 + d$ and, consequently, $\gamma = 0$. In this case NPV $= V_0 + V_1 + V_2 + \cdots$, which is infinitely high and no solution exists.

So far the analysis has been conducted in real terms, i.e., we had been assuming an absence of inflationary pressures. Consider now the case where the underlying conditions remain constant with respect to the various net returns (i.e., there is no growth) but there is inflation. This means that while the net returns are constant in real terms, they are not observed, and instead we observe their monetary values. This means that our formula (4) has to change to accommodate the inflationary pressures. To distinguish this case from the earlier ones, we let the inflation rate to be f% per annum and the money rate of interest to be r% per annum and denote the monetary net returns as S_t and the real ones as S_t^*. This necessitates the following changes to formula (4). First of all with a money rate of interest of r% we have:

$$\text{NPV} = \sum_{t=0}^{n} S_t \frac{1}{(1+r)^t} \tag{8}$$

With an inflation rate of f% per annum we define:

$$S_t^*(1+f) = S_t \tag{9}$$

from which we derive the following formula, which is useful for deflationary purposes:

$$S_t^* = \frac{S_t}{(1+f)^t}$$

By substituting relation (9) into (8) we get:

$$\text{NPV} = \sum_{t=0}^{n} S_t^* \frac{(1+f)^t}{(1+r)^t} \tag{10}$$

We now define the real rate of interest, ρ, to be:

$$\rho = \frac{1+r}{1+f} - 1$$

from which we get that $(1+f)/(1+r) = 1/(1+\rho)$. Finally, by substituting this last relation in expression (10) we derive the following formula:

$$\text{NPV} = \sum_{t=0}^{n} \frac{S_t^*}{(1+\rho)^t} \tag{11}$$

which is expressed in real terms, and must be employed in all those cases in which inflation is present, since we are interested in the real values of the variables, not the monetary ones.

As an illustration of the preceding discussion, consider the effect of changes in the inflation rate on the present value, by means of the following simple example. We expect to receive in a year's time €110 and wish to find its present value, assuming that the money rate of interest is 20% and the inflation rate is 10%. Therefore we have:

$$S^* = \frac{S}{1+f} = \frac{110}{1.1} = 100$$

The real rate of interest is given by:

$$\rho = \frac{1+r}{1+f} - 1 = \frac{1.2}{1.1} - 1 = 0.0909$$

and therefore we find that

$$\text{NPV} = \frac{100}{1.0909} = €91.667$$

Now assume that the inflation rate falls to 5% while all else remains the same as before. In this case, we have:

$$S^* = \frac{110}{1.05} = 104.7619$$

However, the real rate of interest is now:

$$\rho = \frac{1.2}{1.05} - 1 = 0.1428571$$

consequently, the NPV is now estimated as:

$$\text{NPV} = \frac{104.7619}{1.1429571} = €91.667$$

i.e., exactly the same result as before, which shows that changes in the inflation rate leave the present value unaffected, since we are working in real terms.

Equipped with these tools we turn now to a brief discussion of some important underlying economic principles involved in capital budgeting theory, which will help us, among others, in the derivation of optimal appraisal methods.

11.3   THE MICRO-FOUNDATIONS OF CAPITAL BUDGETING: A DIGRESSION

In order to get a better insight into the process of capital budgeting, we digress for a while to consider some important issues from utility theory. Since the object of capital budgeting is the provision of increased returns over time and the maximisation of utility resulting from such an increased income, the role of utility theory is of relevance in this context.

In capital budgeting we have to specify the horizon which is to be taken into account for our decision. We may have a short horizon, a multiperiod horizon or an infinitely long one. For convenience, we start our analysis with a two period horizon and examine the behaviour of an individual consumer. The results can then be extended to longer horizons without difficulty. In Figure 11.1 we measure on the horizontal axis income and consumption in the current period (i.e., now), Y_0 and C_0 and on the vertical axis income and consumption in the next period, Y_1 and C_1. Allowing for intra-temporal substitution (i.e., within one period) as well as inter-temporal (i.e., between different periods), we want to examine the income stream and consumption stream open to the individual. Assume for the moment that the income stream is given by endowment. This gives us a point on Figure 11.1, such as point A, which implies a current income of Y_0' and income of Y_1' in the next period. The opportunities for consumption depend on the capital environment,

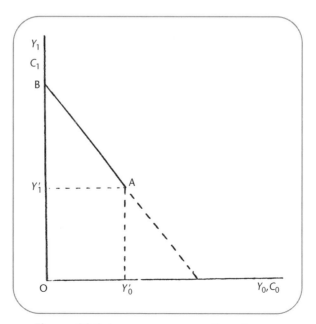

Figure 11.1 Income, consumption streams

and in some cases they are given by the income point, when goods are perishable and cannot be stored. But if goods can be stored, the consumer can substitute present consumption for future consumption. In this case, and if the goods are perfectly divisible and storage presents no problems, the consumer's consumption opportunities can be depicted along the line AB. The final consumption point lies somewhere along the line, showing that the consumer can consume less to day for the sake of higher consumption next year.

Therefore, current consumption is not dependent on current income but rather on current resources, which means income in the current period, income in the next period and the rate of interest. This means that an individual can use the capital market to borrow or lend out money to achieve a better consumption point. Assuming a perfect capital market, i.e., one in which we have a single interest rate and one can borrow or lend out as much as they wish, and starting again with the endowment point A, the consumer is able to move in either direction, as shown in Figure 11.2. To increase his current income and current consumption opportunities, the consumer borrows money, thus moving towards the horizontal axis, repaying the loan out of next year's income; in the opposite case he lends money out by moving up the line BC, thus reducing his current income and consumption. Therefore, the line BC acts as a budget constraint and provides the consumption opportunities open to our individual. Since we have assumed a perfect capital market, the line BC is a straight line with slope $1 + \rho$, where ρ is the externally given objective real interest rate.

However, in the case of an imperfect capital market, the lending rate, l, is less than the borrowing rate, b, consequently, the consumption opportunity line is no longer a straight line as before. So long as we can borrow or lend out as much as we please at the going borrowing and lending rates, the corresponding opportunity line is shown as BAC, in Figure 11.3. The slope of the upper section AB is given by

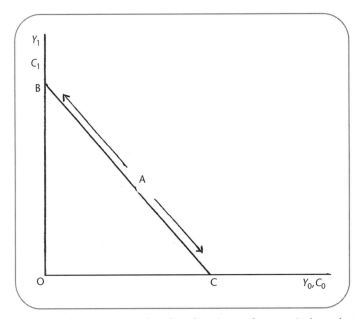

Figure 11.2 Borrowing–lending line in perfect capital market

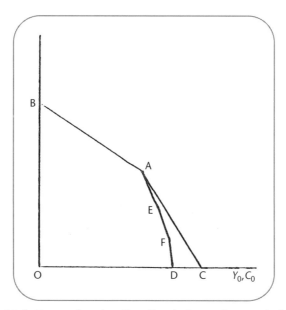

Figure 11.3 Borrowing–lending line in imperfect capital market

$1 + l$, where l is the lending rate, and the slope of the section AC is given by $1 + b$, where b is the borrowing rate. Nevertheless, this may not happen at all times. What is more likely to happen is that in imperfect capital markets one may borrow only finite amounts of money at any going rate and one can only secure larger amounts at greater borrowing rates. Consequently, the opportunity line becomes BAEFD, i.e., we get more kinks than before, reflecting the successively higher borrowing rates. (This analysis ignores the problem of capital rationing, which we discuss below).

11.3.1 The consumption point, time preference

The consumer's purpose is to find out the various streams of future income, resulting from different interest rates and which will provide him with the opportunity lines for consumption. The latter will provide the consumer with a set of feasible solutions out of which he will try to maximise his utility.

For this purpose, we require the consumer's subjective rate of interest between consumption in the current period and consumption in the next period. That is, we require the consumer's time preference rate. This information is provided by the time preference map or the time preference indifference curves relating the current year's and next year's consumption, which in effect means that we allow for inter-temporal substitution. The marginal rate of time preference, t, between any two periods and any two goods is estimated as the corresponding marginal rate of substitution (MRS) minus one, i.e., $t = \text{MRS} - 1$, and it is the premium we require from future consumption to compensate us for the loss of one unit of current consumption. In Figure 11.4 we have incorporated the information of the perfect capital market and the consumer's time preference indifference curves. Starting again from our endowment income point A, the consumer maximises his utility at the tangency point C, at which the slope of the opportunity line $1 + \rho$ is

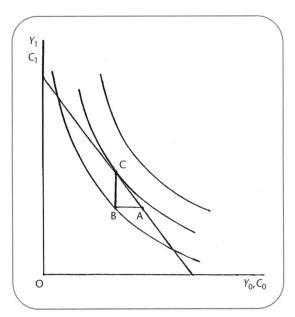

Figure 11.4 Borrowing, lending and time preference indifference curves

equal to the slope of the highest indifference curve we can attain, which is given by the MRS, or by its equivalent, $1 + t$. The consumer achieves his equilibrium by moving from point A to C, i.e., by lending out some of his money on the capital market. The resulting triangle ABC is known as the saving triangle. At point C, the first order condition for utility maximisation is satisfied, since:

$$1 + \rho = 1 + t \quad \text{implying} \quad \rho = t$$

i.e., in equilibrium the real market rate of interest equals the consumer's subjective rate of interest or his time preference rate.

11.3.2 Internal rate of return and present value

Until this point we have considered our individual as trying to maximise his utility over time, subject to his income stream and the market rate of interest, in other words, he is trying to exploit the external opportunities offered by the capital market. We can now extend the analysis by considering also internal investment opportunities arising, say, within the firm. This extension necessitates that we look at both, the profitability of various investment projects, and the present value. This profitability is measured by the internal rate of return of the projects. The internal rate of return (IRP) is defined as that rate, which when used for discounting purposes, will make the NPV of a stream of future income equal to zero. This is equivalent to Keynes' marginal efficiency of investment, and it is easily estimated, as will be shown below. Our interest in the present values of the income streams of the various investment projects arises from the fact that maximisation of the present value leads to maximisation of utility.

As a way of linking the earlier algebraic discussion with the diagrammatic exposition, consider Figure 11.5, in which we have again the two-period model,

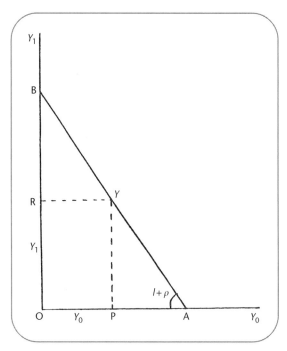

Figure 11.5 Present value of a stream of income

measuring current income on the horizontal axis and next year's income on the vertical axis. Assuming the real market rate of interest to be ρ, we can draw the budget line AB and pick an income point like Y on it, from which we can draw the perpendiculars on the two axes. This allows us to find the income stream, which is given by Y_0 (OP) and Y_1 (OR). To find the present value of this stream of income, only the second term requires discounting, since Y_0 is current income. Since the slope of the budget line is given by $1 + \rho$, we get from triangle APY that $(1 + \rho) = PY/AP$ and, therefore, $AP = PY(1 + \rho)$. However, $Y_1 = OR = PY$ and by substitution we get that $AP = Y_1/(1 + \rho)$. This last result shows that the present value of the income stream denoted by point Y, is given by the distance OA, which is not surprising. In fact, any income point chosen arbitrarily on the budget line will produce a different income stream but the same present value, OA. Similarly, the compounded value of any income stream, chosen by points along AB, is given by distance OB, the proof of which is left to the reader, as an exercise.

Suppose that now we are interested in both the income and consumption points, given a number of alternatives, which result in different income streams. The objective is utility maximisation, subject to any given constraints, and the way of doing so is by maximising the present value of the income stream. Therefore, the maximisation of present value is not an end in itself, it is the means towards the end, which is the maximisation of utility. This means that of all the opportunities for earnings facing the firm, we choose the one with the maximum present value.

To show this we assume that the firm is faced with a whole continuum of possible independent investment projects. We proceed by finding their IRR and rank these various investment projects in terms of their profitability, starting with the most profitable, the second most profitable and so on until the least profitable.

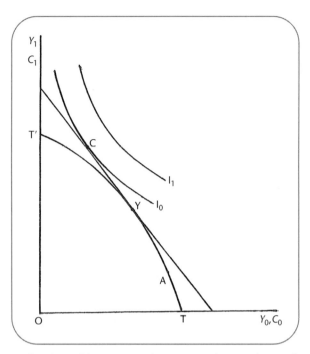

Figure 11.6 Determination of income and consumption under perfect capital market

We present this diagrammatically in Figure 11.6, where the transformation curve TT' defines the set of alternative income streams associated with the various investment projects, i.e., the transformation curve shows the internal opportunities open to the firm. The slope of the transformation curve is defined as the marginal rate of transformation (MRT), and the IRR, e, is given by the MRT minus one, $e = \text{MRT} - 1$, providing us with the internal rate of our possibilities in real terms.

However, the firm is also faced with external opportunities given, as before, in the form of the borrowing–lending line or budget line. It is crucial for the purpose of the maximisation of present value that we operate in a perfect capital market, as shown in Figure 11.6, where the slope of the budget line is given by $1 + \rho$. Starting from any initial point on the budget line, equilibrium is attained at point C, by either borrowing or lending out money. This is the equilibrium consumption point, since it satisfies an important condition, namely that at point C we have:

$$e = \rho = t$$

i.e., the IRR is equal to the, externally, given objective market rate of interest and also equal to the subjective time preference rate. It is clear from Figure 11.6 that at point C we have $t = \rho$, as shown earlier. However, at point Y, which is our income point, the slope of the transformation curve, $1 + e$, is equal to the slope of the borrowing–lending line, $1 + \rho$, which means that at point Y we have that the IRR, e, is equal to the external market rate of interest, ρ, but since we operate in a perfect capital market ρ remains the same throughout and, therefore, we get the equality $e = \rho = t$.

Figure 11.6 can also be used for yet another important purpose. It can provide the rationale of a criterion of appraisal. The criterion advises us that among alternative sets of investment we choose that set which maximises the present value of the resulting income stream, discounted at the external rate of interest. Ambiguities as to what external rate of interest we should use are resolved by discounting at the opportunity cost rate. This means that we only invest in internal opportunities if the IRR, e, is greater than the external rate of interest, ρ. Therefore, starting from any point on the transformation curve, such as A, we have that the slope of the transformation curve is MRT $= 1 + e$, which is greater (because it is steeper) than the slope of the borrowing–lending line, $1 + \rho$. Therefore, starting from a position where $e > \rho$ we have an incentive to invest, and to carry on investing, by moving up the transformation curve, to the point where $e = \rho$, which in Figure 11.6 is given by point Y. However, beyond Y the internal opportunities become worse than the external opportunities and we do not have any inducement for further investment, since to the left of Y the slope of the borrowing–lending line becomes steeper and therefore $e < \rho$. In other words, the external opportunities are better than the internal ones to the left of Y. If by any chance we had started from a point on the transformation curve to the left of Y, the inducement would be to dis-invest.

The IRR, e, has been derived in real terms. If we need to express this rate in monetary terms, we can do it by using the formula:

$$(1 + e)(1 + f) = (1 + i)$$

where i is now the internal monetary rate of return, since, f, is, as before, the rate of inflation.

11.4 INVESTMENT APPRAISAL METHODS

The preceding discussion has touched upon one of the most important questions in capital budgeting, namely, that of appraising investment proposals. The investment policies of firms in plant and equipment raise questions as to the right types, amounts, and timing of installation and replacement. The answers are crucial, because they determine the firm's whole future size, growth, location and industrial classification. Yet, most firms use methods, which generally lead to wrong decisions.

In this section, we shall consider a number of appraisal criteria, which fall into two broad categories: (a) the naive criteria or rules of thumb and (b) the discounting cash flow (DCF) techniques. The various methods discussed can be equally applied to various kinds of investment, like net investment, replacement, scrapping etc. Also, all investment criteria require that we have, somehow, estimated the entire stream of expected future receipts and expenses associated with the project. In this respect only the marginal contribution of the project should be taken into consideration. For example, where a project is part of a system and affects the profitability of the entire system, such effects should be taken into account. In other words, if a machine can contribute €20 000 annually to the firm's profits, but at the same time its operation reduces the contribution of another machine by €5000, the net marginal contribution of the machine is €15 000, and this is the relevant figure to be taken into consideration. The estimation of the stream of future income is the most difficult part of capital budgeting, and it is more than likely that such estimates can be based, at best, on guesswork. Whilst the assumption of certainty allows us to proceed with the development of optimal appraisal criteria, it should be firmly kept in mind that the derivation of the stream of future income is the most crucial aspect in capital budgeting, and that efforts should be directed towards improving such forecasts.

We may find it useful to classify the various types of investment projects into two broad categories: (a) projects independent and (b) projects mutually exclusive. In the first case the undertaking of a particular project does not prevent the firm from undertaking any other project or all of them, subject to whatever capital limitations may be in operation. In the second case, however, once a choice has been made it renders the other alternative projects superfluous, since the firm has satisfied its needs. Another distinction that we can make is in terms of: (a) capital rationing and (b) no capital rationing. In the first case the firm is prevented from undertaking certain projects, because its capital is limited; however, in instances of mutually exclusive projects for the problem of choice to arise we assume that there is sufficient capital to undertake either of two projects.

11.4.1 Rules of thumb – the payback (or payout) period

This is a simple and crude method of investment appraisal but one which is widely used. It is defined as the time period required for an investment project to generate sufficient funds to recoup its initial cost. As an illustration are given the future income streams of the following two projects, expressed in thousands of euros.

Project	Initial capital	End of 1st year	End of 2nd year	End of 3rd year	End of 4th year
A	−200	100	100	30	30
B	−200	50	100	100	100

The payback period of project A is two years and that of project B is 2 years and 6 months (on the assumption that receipts are evenly distributed throughout the year). Accordingly, if the two projects are mutually exclusive, the criterion advises us to choose the project with the shortest payback period. Sometimes, a cut-off period is chosen beyond which the investment project is rejected, if it has not paid off its initial cost. The payback method appears attractive because of its simplicity and can be useful in industries, which are subject to rapid technological change, so that capital equipment becomes obsolete before the end of its physical life. It is also claimed by proponents of this rule of thumb that since it considers cash receipts it helps to assess a firm's future cash flows, particularly, when the firm faces liquidity problems. However, the method fails to measure long-term profitability, since it ignores receipts accruing after the payback period. Also, because the method often uses the receipts gross of tax, the claim that it can be used as a measure of profitability is nonsensical.

Additionally, the method ignores the time pattern of receipts and is unable to distinguish between projects having the same payback periods, but different earning streams. It is essentially a myopic rule, which assigns probabilities of one to the receipts up to the cut-off period and zero probabilities to the ones accruing after that period. Whilst management's telescopic faculties of looking into the future are clearly not perfect, nevertheless, this asymmetric treatment of uncertainty is not warranted, since it can lead, more often than not, to the wrong decisions.

However, the major weakness of the payback rule is that it ignores completely the aspect that money has a time dimension. Consequently, the criterion treats receipts accruing at different points in time as equivalent, which as we have already seen is wrong.

Considering our earlier example, it is clear that the rule leads to the wrong decision, since project B is more profitable. In fact, this is ironic because the payback period sometimes is defended on the grounds that is a 'dynamic' criterion, since projects are accepted if they are paid off quickly, but this argument does not allow for the fact that highly profitable projects do not pay off at the initial stage but can provide larger gains later on.

11.4.2 Discounting cash flow methods

A crucial factor ignored by the payback method is that money has a time value. Therefore, investment appraisal techniques must take into account this element and use discounting methods to arrive at present values, along the lines we have already discussed, in order to make meaningful comparisons between alternative projects. As we saw in Section 11.2 the present value of a future sum of money depends on two factors: how far in the future the sum is due and the rate of discount. The farther away in future the sum is or the higher the discount rate is, the lower the present value of the sum will be.

Utilising the discounting concept, we are able to derive some sort of 'exchange rate' for future income streams over different periods, by means of their present values, thus, enabling us to compare such future cash flows safely. There are three major methods of investment appraisal making use of the discounting process. They are the NPV, the IRR and the annual capital charge (ACC). However, the ACC is mainly applied when the investment is associated with a constant stream of future income, and it is used mostly by public utilities and property companies. Because of its limited applicability we shall not consider it, but concentrate, instead, on the NPV and the IRR methods.

11.4.2a The net present value criterion

This criterion advises us that in our choices of projects we should favour those with the higher NPV, the latter, as we know, is given by the present value of the stream of receipts minus the present value of the stream of costs. If the problem is one of accepting or rejecting a particular investment proposal, the NPV criterion advises us to invest in the project as long as its NPV is positive, and reject the investment proposal if its NPV is negative. The reason is that when the stream of future income is discounted at the cost of capital, a concept which we shall discuss later, and gives us a positive NPV, the project can cover both interest charges and depreciation charges, and, thus, the positive NPV represents a clear profit, which increases the wealth of the firm. Obviously, in the case of a negative present value the criterion tells us that we shall incur a loss in our internal investment opportunity, thus, we should not invest, but consider, instead, exploiting the external opportunities by lending any money in the capital market.

To illustrate the workings of the NPV criterion consider an investment project with an initial capital cost of €15 000, which promises to pay €4000 net returns at the end of each of the next 5 years and then stop, leaving no scrap value, and assuming that the firm's cost of capital is 10%. Since the discount rate is l0% it means that the discount factor D is given by $D = 1/1.1 = 0.9091$. Now using formula (4) from Section 11.2, we have:

$$\begin{aligned} \text{NPV} &= -15000 + 4000(0.9091) + 4000(0.9091)^2 + 4000(0.9091)^3 \\ &\quad + 4000(0.9091)^4 + 4000(0.9091)^5 \\ &= -15000 + 3636.4 + 3305.8 + 3005.2 + 2732.0 + 2483.6 \\ &= -15000 + 15163.0 = 163.0 \end{aligned}$$

Therefore, the NPV is €163.0 and the criterion advises us that the project is profitable and we should accept it. Assuming that the cash flows are risk free, the NPV of €163.0 represents an immediate increase in the 'wealth' of the firm. This result means that the firm can, in effect, borrow €15 163, use €15 000 for the investment project, distribute €163 to its shareholders, and at the end of 5 years the project's proceeds pay off the loan.

The NPV method is quite versatile and can also accommodate real-life complications in the form, say, of investment grants, capital allowances, cash flows arising in the middle of the year and inflation. Lastly, the use of appropriate tables giving the discount factors for a great variety of interest rates and periods, and more importantly, the use of appropriate computer programmes have made the actual calculations a very easy task.

11.4.2b   The internal rate of return criterion

The IRR rule tells us that in our choices of projects we should prefer those with a higher IRR, provided such rates are higher than the firm's cost of capital. The IRR, as we have seen, is defined as the rate of discount which would make the NPV of the project's flow of net returns equal to zero. In other words, it is in effect the rate of discount, which would make the present value of the stream of annual net returns equal to the initial capital expenditure of the project.

To find the IRR we solve formula (4) for the discount rate. However, in most cases, the discount rate which will reduce the NPV of the project to zero can be found by trial and error: if at the discount rate used the NPV is positive, the rate is too low; if a negative value is obtained for the NPV then the rate is too high. In practice, it should be possible to arrive at the IRR by carrying out two trial discount rates, chosen in such a way so that the one yields a positive and the other a negative NPV and then use interpolation to determine the true IRR.

As an illustration consider again the earlier example of the previous section. There we found that discounting the stream of future income at l0% the NPV turned out to be €163. This means that this rate is too low to be the IRR, but we can use it as one of our two trial discount rates. We now use 12% as our second discount rate. Therefore, the discount factor is $D = 1/1.12 = 0.89286$, and the

NPV is calculated as follows:

$$NPV = -15000 + 4000(0.89286) + 4000(0.89286)^2 + 4000(0.89286)^3$$
$$+ 4000(0.89286)^4 + 4000(0.89286)^5$$
$$= -15000 + 3571.4 + 3188.8 + 2847.1 + 2542.1 + 2269.7$$
$$= -15000 + 14419.1 = -590.9$$

Clearly, the chosen rate of discount 12% is too high, resulting in a negative NPV. However, the IRR can now be found through interpolation, as follows:

The difference of two percentage points in the rate of discount between 10% and 12% results in a difference in the present value of $163 + 590.9 = 743.9$ euros. We ask, therefore, by how much the 10% discount rate must increase for the NPV to be reduced by 163 euros, thus, giving us a NPV of zero. Using a well-known arithmetic rule, this is calculated, approximately, as: $2 \times 163 = 326 : 743.9 = 0.438$. Therefore, the rate of discount, which reduces the NPV of the stream of income to zero is 10.438%, and this is our IRR. (It must be pointed out that this calculation is only an approximation, since the present value function is not a straight line.)

As long as the external rate of interest is less than the estimated IRR of 10.438%, the criterion advises to invest in the project. The IRR shows the annual rate of return on the capital outstanding on the investment. Consequently, in common with the NPV criterion, the IRR will be higher if the bulk of the future income is received earlier, rather than later in the life of the project, reflecting the fact that the project would have recovered more capital in its initial stages, so that the remaining flows represent a higher rate of return.

Comparing this result with the earlier decision under the NPV criterion, we find that both criteria find the project profitable and advise us to accept it. This is not surprising, since the discount rate used under the NPV approach was l0%, which is lower than the IRR. This is a standard result between the two DCF methods and the correspondence of the two methods is shown in Figure 11.7, which depicts the present value of the project as an inverse function of the rate of discount, and the capital outlay of the project as a straight line drawn at the level of €15 000. The intersection of the present value curve with the initial capital outlay line determines the IRR. As long as the discount rate is less than 10.438%, the present value function lies above the capital outlay line, and so the NPV is positive. At rates of discount above 10.438%, the NPV becomes negative, and again the two methods will agree in rejecting the project. Notice that the same result could have been arrived at by using, instead, the NPV curve, which results after subtracting from the present value curve the initial outlay of €15 000, thus, the IRR will be determined at the point of intersection of the NPV curve with the horizontal axis. That is, this is achieved by a vertical shift downwards of the present value curve by €15 000.

11.4.3 The conflict between the NPV and IRR criteria

We have seen that in the case of accept/reject investment decisions, i.e., where we are merely interested in the profitability of individual or independent investment projects, the two criteria of the NPV and the IRR lead to the same conclusions, consequently, we could use either. Actually, in most cases the project with the largest

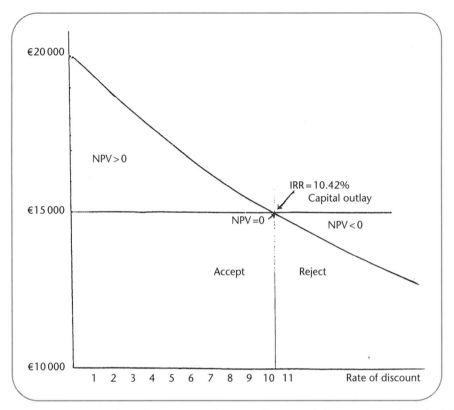

Figure 11.7 Present value of income and expenditure and the accept–reject decision

NPV is also the project with the highest IRR, and either criterion will select the right project; so this would point to the conclusion that the two methods are equivalent to each other. However, this is not always the case and the conclusion that the two criteria are equivalent is not justified. There are two main areas of conflict between the two methods, firstly, choosing between mutually exclusive or alternative projects and, secondly, deciding on the profitability of projects with multiple IRR. In such cases we tend to get conflicting answers from the two methods, as is shown below.

Consider the case illustrated in Figure 11.8 where we draw the NPV curves of two mutually exclusive projects A and B. The curve AA' represents the NPV curve of project A, and the curve BB' shows the NPV curve of project B as functions of the rate of discount. The IRR criterion tells us to choose the project with the highest IRR, provided it is higher than the external rate of interest. Clearly, project B has the highest IRR since B' > A'. Therefore, according to the IRR criterion we should choose project B, as long as the rate of discount is less than B'. On the other hand, the NPV criterion tells us to discount the two projects at the appropriate rate of discount and choose the project with the highest NPV. It is obvious from the diagram that while the IRR method always chooses project B, the NPV method discriminates between the two, as the rate of discount varies. In other words, if the rate of discount is between 0 and C and above E, the NPV method also chooses project B, since its NPV at such rates exceeds that of project A. However, when

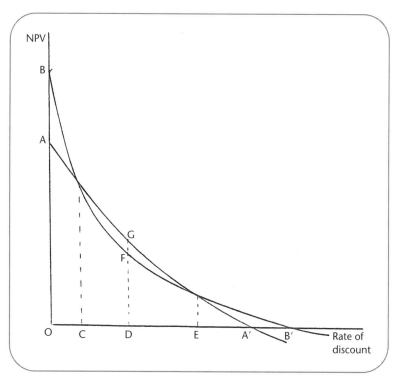

Figure 11.8 Conflict between NPV and IRR

the rate of discount is between C and E, the NPV method chooses project A, since at such rates project A has the higher NPV. For example, at discount rate D, the NPV of A exceeds that of B by FG euros. Clearly, this is a serious clash between the two criteria, and the better criterion is the NPV. The reason is that, given the choice between the maximisation of the rate of return and the maximisation of the present value, the rational thing to do is maximise the present value, which leads to utility maximisation, our ultimate objective, as suggested earlier.

The other area of conflict arises whenever we get dual or even multiple IRR. To see how these may come about, we need to consider both algebraic and economic aspects. From the algebraic point of view, the IRR is the solution of the polynomial:

$$0 = V_0 + V_1 D + V_2 D^2 + \cdots + V_n D^n$$

where $D = 1/(1 + d)$, with d giving us the IRR. Clearly, this is a polynomial of the nth degree and so we expect n roots. Nevertheless, the kind of solution we get depends on the pattern of sign changes of the coefficients (Vs) of the above polynomial, which as we have already seen are simply the returns over costs of the investment project over time.

In the standard case of future income streams we have been considering so far, we have assumed that the capital outlay (denoted by a negative sign) was incurred in the present and was followed by positive net returns, giving us the following pattern of the signs of coefficients:

$- + + + + +$

Since there is only one change in the pattern of signs (i.e., moving from negative to positive), it implies that the polynomial has only one positive root, the rest are negative or complex. It is this positive root that enables us to calculate the IRR. Negative roots, resulting in negative rates, are clearly meaningless, while complex roots are responsible for introducing cyclical variations in the present value function. Even by slightly varying the pattern, by assuming that costs arise in the early part of a project's life, as is shown below:

$$- - - - - + + + + +$$

again results in only one sign change, and we still get one positive root and one positive, and unique, IRR.

However, there may be occasions in which negative Vs (net returns) appear in the middle or at the end of the stream of future income. For example, in most extractive industries, terminal costs may have to be incurred at the end of the useful life, say, of a mine in order to secure it. This means that the sign pattern becomes:

$$- + + + + + + + -$$

Here we have two sign changes (the first from negative to positive, at the beginning, and the second from positive to negative, at the end), and, thus, there are two positive roots to the polynomial, resulting in two IRR, as shown in Figure 11.9.

Now we have two rates at which the NPV curve becomes zero, and so two IRR as A and B. If the rate of discount is C, the IRR criterion advises us both to accept and reject the project, depending on whether we take B or A to be the IRR! This sort of ambiguity is avoided by using the NPV method. At a rate of discount C, the NPV is positive, so we should invest in the project, as indeed we should do if the rate of discount is between A and B. On the other hand, for rates of discount between 0 and A and above B, the NPV rule advises us to reject the project. These are clear, unequivocal answers to the question on whether or not to invest in the

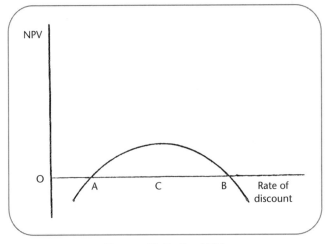

Figure 11.9 Dual IRR

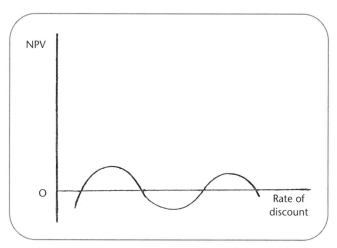

Figure 11.10 Multiple IRR

project, which the IRR criterion, despite a lot of refinements aimed at correcting its shortcomings, cannot match.

It is also possible to envisage patterns of sign changes like the following:

$$- + + - + -$$

which will generate multiple rates of return, as shown in Figure 11.10, and make the task of deciding, on the basis of the IRR rule, meaningless. On the other hand, no such problems arise with the NPV method. Given any discount rate, the method evaluates the present value that the firm must assign to the project, and, in the case of alternative projects it chooses the one which makes the largest contribution to the firm's wealth. In the case of accept/reject it advises to do so on the basis of whether the NPV is positive or negative, at the chosen discount rate.

The foregone discussion shows that the IRR criterion is nonsensical under classical conditions. It is indeed difficult to account for its popularity. It leads to ambiguities (in the form of multiple rates), it can result in wrong decisions in the case of mutually exclusive projects, and of course it involves more troublesome calculations than the NPV rule. The idea of the IRR may be legitimately used to describe the equilibrium situation in a standard model, but not to find it. Thus, the IRR equals the rate of interest at the margin of worthwhile investment in a perfect capital market, but nothing can be said about the IRR of return of intra-marginal investment.

In conclusion, despite attempts to correct the shortcomings of the IRR criterion and improve its performance, such problems still remain and make the NPV rule the only rational way to investment appraisal, subject to the limitations discussed in Section 11.4.3b.

11.4.3a Example

As an illustration of the workings of the NPV rule consider the following problem. A profit maximising firm is faced with two mutually exclusive capital projects:
(a) The first involves buying machine A, at an immediate cost of €1 880 000 and

promises an expected net surplus of receipts over costs of €2 790 000 in the following year; (b) The second involves buying a different machine B, with an initial cost of €800 000 and an expected net surplus of €1 800 000 2 years later. The firm is able to borrow or lend in the capital market any amount it likes for a year at a time, at the ruling rate of interest, which is expected to remain constant, for the period under consideration. We assume that the firm's horizon is not longer than the lifetime of any particular project it has in mind. What are the values of the market rate of interest for which it is worth buying (i) machine A, (ii) machine B and (iii) neither machine?

Solution

Letting the interest rate (or discount rate) be $d\%$, the discount factor becomes $D = 1/(1 + d)$, and the NPVs of the two machines are given by the following expressions (for convenience we have divided through by 1000):

$$NPV_A = -1880 + 2790D \quad \text{and} \quad NPV_B = -800 + 1800D^2$$

Clearly, machine A is preferred, is indifferent or is not preferred to machine B according to whether the following expression holds:

$$NPV_A - NPV_B \gtreqless 0 \tag{1}$$

i.e., if this difference is positive for particular interest rates machine A is preferred; if the difference is negative machine B is preferred and if the difference is zero, we are indifferent between the two machines, since they have the same NPVs. We now form relation (1) and solve it as an equality, which will give us the interest rates (or discount rates) for which the two machines have the same NPVs. Thus we have:

$$-1880 + 2790D - (-800 + 1800D^2) = 0 \text{ from which we derive:}$$

$$-1800D^2 + 2790D - 1080 = 0 \text{ and multiplying by } (-1) \text{ we get:}$$

$$1800D^2 - 2790D + 1080 = 0 \text{ Dividing through by 90 yields the following}$$

simple quadratic equation:

$$20D^2 - 31D + 12 = 0 \tag{2}$$

Solving (2) we find the interest rates for which the firm is indifferent between the two machines:

$$D = \frac{31 \pm \sqrt{31^2 - 4 \times 20 \times 12}}{2 \times 20} = \frac{31 \pm \sqrt{961 - 960}}{40} = \frac{31 \pm \sqrt{1}}{40} = \frac{31 \pm 1}{40}$$

giving values of $D_1 = 3/4$, implying $d_1 = 1/3$ or 33.3% and $D_2 = 4/5$, implying $d_2 = 1/4$ or 25%.

Notice that for very low interest rates, the quadratic equation (2) is positive, and so machine B is preferred at such rates (remembering that we had multiplied by −1). Therefore, at interest rates 25% and 33.3% the NPVs of the two machines are identical, and so we are indifferent between the two. However, we have just seen that at low interest rates the quadratic is positive, thus, machine B is preferred outside the range of interest rates of 25%–33.3% and machine A is preferred inside the range of 25%–33.3%. To complete the range of interest rates we need the IRR of project B, which is given by:

$$800 = 1800D^2 \text{ from which we get: } 8 = 18D^2 \text{ or } 4 = 9D^2 \text{ giving}$$

$$D^2 = \frac{4}{9} \text{ or } D = \pm\sqrt{4/9} \text{ yielding } D = \pm 2/3$$

Ignoring the negative root, the positive root $D = 2/3$ implies a value of d =1/2 or 50%. Therefore, the IRR is 50%, consequently, we can summarise our findings as follows:

- Between interest rates 0–25% machine B is preferred.

- Between interest rates 25–33.33% machine A is preferred.

- Between interest rates 33.3–50% machine B is preferred

- Neither machine is preferred for interest rates above 50%.

If, in addition, we wanted to consider the solution diagrammatically, we also need to find the IRR of machine A to draw the NPV curve of that machine, which is given by:

$$1880 = 2790D \text{ thus } D = 0.6738, \text{ yielding a value of } d \approx 48.4\%.$$

This information enables us now to draw Figure 11.11. The figure shows that the present value line for project A is drawn as a straight line as expected, since the

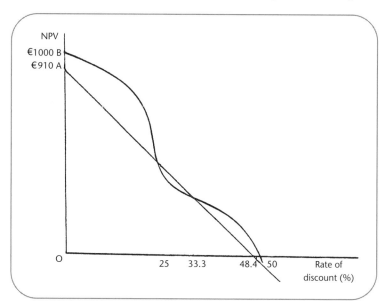

Figure 11.11 NPV curves of two mutually exclusive projects

present value function for that project is a linear function. This cuts the vertical axis at €910, which is the present value at zero discount rate, and the horizontal axis at a rate of discount 48.4%. The curve for the present value of project B cuts the vertical axis at €1000 and the horizontal axis at a discount rate of 50%, and lies above the present value line of project A for rates of discount between 0 and 25% and 33.3% and 50% and below it for rates of discount between 25% and 33.3%.

This example provides us also with the opportunity to examine how the firm could use the capital market to finance the purchase of either machine. Suppose that the interest rate is now 1/6. We know from the preceding discussion that at this interest rate machine B is preferred. (Nevertheless, it is suggested that you find the NPVs of the two projects to convince yourselves). Yet, it is instructive to consider the problem in some greater detail, in order to get valuable insights. Any financial arrangements open to the firm for one machine, are obviously available for the other too. So it should be possible to start with the income stream of machine B, and by allowing borrowing or lending for a year at a time, as necessary, at the interest rate of 1/6 to try to emulate the income stream of machine A and be left with something to spare. However, the opposite will not be possible.

Starting with machine B, in the current year the firm spends only €800 as against €1880 for machine A. Therefore, to emulate the first term of machine A's income stream, the firm lends out €1080 at an interest rate of 1/6, and so we have −€1080 − €800 = −€1880, which has emulated the first term. In a year's time the firm receives back €1080 × 7/6 = €1260. The firm now borrows from the market €1530, and so it is able to emulate the second term of machine A's income stream, since €1260 + €1530 = €2790, and also emulate machine B's second term of 0. In a year's time, the firm must repay the loan, which has grown to be €1530 × 7/6 = €1785, out of the proceeds of machine B, leaving the firm with a net profit of €1800 − €1785 = €15 out of these proceedings.

Now starting with machine A, the firm borrows in the current year €1080, in order to emulate machine B's first term as follows, +€1080 − €1880 = −€800. The loan, which grows to be €1080 × 7/6 = €1260, is repaid in a year's time out of the proceeds of machine A, leaving the firm with €2790 − €1260 = €1530. Now, the firm lends out this sum of €1530 for a year, at the end of which it grows to be €1530 × 7/6 = €1785. However, this falls short by €15 of the required €1800 to emulate the last term of machine B.

This exercise shows that, given our assumptions about the capital market and an absence of transaction costs, at the given interest rate 1/6 machine B is preferred to machine A.

11.4.4 Profitability index

However, the NPV rule of investment appraisal is not without its problems. Surprisingly, one of its alleged shortcomings in some parts of the literature, namely, that it is an 'amount of net return' criterion rather than a rate or yield; consequently, businessmen have difficulty in comparing it directly with the cost of capital, is not one. Apart from slurring businessmen, one can easily divide the NPV by the initial cost of investment, thus, expressing it as percentage of the capital expenditure. For example, in the problem of the earlier section, the NPVs of the two machines at a rate of discount of 1/6 are calculated as $\text{NPV}_A = 511.43$ and $\text{NPV}_B = 522.45$, which expressed as percentages of the initial cost of capital of the two projects give us, respectively, 27.2% for machine A over 1 year, and 65.3% for machine B over 2 years.

A variant of the NPV method has been developed to deal with this particular problem. This is the profitability index (PI), or the benefit/cost ratio, and is defined as the ratio of the present value of the stream of future income divided by the initial outlay, thus:

$$PI = \frac{\sum_{t=1}^{n} V_t D^t}{V_0}$$

where V_0 is the initial cost of the project. This criterion tells us to accept projects as long as PI > 1 and reject them when PI < 1. These statements are equivalent to NPV > 0 and NPV < 0, respectively, so the two criteria lead to the same accept/reject decisions. Considering again the example given above, we find that the present values of the two projects A and B at the discount rate of 1/6 are €2391.43 and €1322.45, resulting in the following profitability indices:

$$PI_A = 2391.43/1880 = 1.272037 \text{ and } B = 1322.45/800 = 1.65306$$

Nevertheless, for projects of unequal size the NPV and PI criteria can give different rankings, so we must be careful in the choice and evaluation. In fact, when projects are independent but capital is rationed, it is necessary to work out the profitability indices of the various projects, rank them in order of their PIs, and then proceed down the list until capital is exhausted. Ranking them according to the amount of net return (i.e., according to the NPVs) is likely to lead us astray, that is, to prevent maximisation of the t o t a l surplus over cost, achievable in the given circumstances. For example, consider the following case, giving five projects, with their initial capital outlays and present values expressed in thousand euros, which have been ranked according to their NPVs:

Project	Initial cost	Net present value
A	2500	260
B	2500	250
C	2000	240
D	2000	220
C	1000	200

If we had €5 000 000 capital available, and proceeded down this list until it was exhausted, we would carry out projects A and B. But we could, obviously, obtain a greater total NPV (i.e., a greater total surplus of benefits over costs) by undertaking projects C, D and E. The proper choice will not be indicated unless we re-rank the projects according to their profitability indices, as follows:

Project	Initial cost	Present value of returns	Profitability index
E	1000	1200	1.20
C	2000	2240	1.12
D	2000	2220	1.11
A	2500	2760	1.104
B	2500	2750	1.10

Now if we proceed down this list until our capital of €5 000 000 were exhausted, we shall make the right choice, by maximising the total surplus over costs under the given circumstances.

It is also possible to get different rankings between the NPV and PI rules for mutually exclusive projects of unequal size. The NPV criterion ranks projects in absolute terms (according to the amounts of their NPVs), while the PI criterion ranks them in relative terms. If the firm has large resources and the objective of maximising wealth, the NPV method is better. However, for a firm with limited resources, the PI rule may be more appropriate, since it evaluates projects in terms of their relative efficiency, i.e., in terms of their present values per euro of initial investment, thus, avoiding a bias towards larger projects. This tends to lead to better combinations of projects, producing higher benefits over costs, as we saw earlier.

11.4.5 Imperfect capital market and capital rationing

The main difficulty with the NPV criterion is the assumption of a perfect capital market, which allows us to use the external market rate of interest as a rate of discount. The market, of course, is not perfect and, in practice, we have a multiplicity of interest rates, with higher borrowing than lending rates, so it may not be obvious what rate to use for discounting purposes. Nevertheless, depending on the circumstances in particular cases with respect to cash flow and profitability of the firm, we may be able to work out some rate. For example, if the firm can use its own funds to finance the investment, the lending rate may be more appropriate to use, as it is a better measure of the firm's opportunity cost of capital. Whilst, this may be overcome and a rate can be established and used for discounting purposes, the next problem is almost intractable. The amount of capital a firm can borrow from the market, usually, is limited, and if capital rationing is effective, i.e., if the firm is forced to choose between two mutually exclusive projects on the basis of capital limitation, then no unambiguous answer can be given as to the cost of capital.

Under capital rationing there is no well-defined interest rate. The firm would like to borrow more capital at the current interest rate, than it is actually allowed to, thus, the marginal value to the firm of extra capital exceeds the current rate, but the firm is effectively barred from taking advantage of it. In some cases, the criterion of the NPV may be inappropriate. For instance, if the borrowing rate exceeds 3.33% and the lending rate is less than 3.33%, there is no sure method using the objective data alone of correctly choosing between alternatives: $A = -1\,000\,000, 1\,100\,000$ and $B = -4\,000\,000, 4\,200\,000$. While from the firm's point of view these may be dismissed as academic exercises of little relevance, one should also be aware of certain limitations of the proposed criteria.

The fundamental question is this: of the alternative projects available to the firm, is there one which is unequivocally at least as good as any other? As we saw in the earlier exercise, project B is unequivocally at least as good as project A if it is possible, by the permitted borrowing and lending rates, to start from B and give the decision maker at least as much profit in every period and more in some period as he would have in A; while it is not possible to start from A and get more profit in some period(s) and no less in any period than in B. In this case, the projects can be ordered in terms of preference, according to the economist's maxims about rationality. Otherwise, they cannot be ranked, simply, from a knowledge of the objective factors alone, and further information, usually, of the form of the decision maker's subjective time preference rate may be required to resolve the issue. With a perfect capital market, any set of alternatives is accurately ordered by the NPV criterion, which is why it is correct to use the discounting theory in these circumstances. However, it may be invalid under other conditions.

A way out may be to use a programming approach to the problem of capital budgeting, which can incorporate elements of indivisibility of investment programmes, interdependence of such projects as well as capital rationing. The objective function of the programme becomes the maximisation of the sum of the NPVs of all investment projects considered, subject to a number of constraints. In this respect, capital rationing is seen as just one of the constraints facing the firm. The question of indivisibility means that we can only consider the relevant variables (i.e., number of the indivisible projects) to take integer values, since there is no meaning in fractions of a machine, and this can give us another of the constraints. Also, the element of interdependence means that sometimes the firm needs to consider combinations of investment projects, which are complementary to each other. Again, the programming technique is well suited to accommodate such issues.

We have seen that given the relevant information, the theory of the NPV leads to rational decisions. The big practical problem is to get accurate data, which is required irrespective of the appraisal rule employed. Moreover, the firm, typically, will not have single-valued expectations, so it would be necessary to form the 'certainty equivalents' of the expectations spectra, a theme we discuss in Chapter 12. Finally, the criterion of the NPV assumes that the firm is only interested in profit maximisation, but different decision rules, generally, emerge if there are other objectives.

11.5   RISK AND CAPITAL BUDGETING

So far the analysis has proceeded on the assumption of perfect knowledge and certainty, which has enabled us to estimate a project's net returns over its lifetime as single-valued expectations, and in addition allowed the development of appraisal criteria, without the complication of imperfect foresight. However, the problems associated with such imperfect foresight have always been lurking in the background, and in this section we discuss, briefly, methods which have been proposed to deal with the issue of risk in capital budgeting.

Since the problem has to do with the actual values of the future income stream of the proposed investment project, the analysis of Chapter 12 is very pertinent in the present context. Therefore, to avoid repetition, the reader is referred to that discussion, and we only consider here some additional methods, not covered elsewhere.

11.5.1 The finite-horizon method

This is a crude, rule of thump, which lays down a terminal date for the investment project, and, thus, its stream of future income. The method tells us to take into consideration the cash flow up to that date and ignore everything that accrues after such date. This is similar to the payback approach, and often the two methods are described as first cousins. The logic behind the finite-horizon approach is that predictions beyond the terminal date are so fraught with uncertainty and unreliability, that it is better to ignore them altogether. Baumol (1977) refers to the case of the US Federal government having frequently adopted a 50-year horizon for a number of public investment projects. The implication of this rule is that such projects will simply disappear from the face of the earth exactly 50 years after their construction.

This is again a very myopic view, particularly for many public investment projects, which by their very nature are having considerable long-term effects. Projects like afforestation, dams, bridges and so on, tend to deliver most of their returns over much longer periods, since their conservation effects take time to materialise, yet on a strict application of the finite-horizon method such long-term effects are to be ignored, thus, rendering some of these projects 'unprofitable' and so causing their cancellation. In other words, there is an in-built bias against longer investment projects in this method.

Similar considerations apply also for private firms, where long-term investments are essential, since they provide a framework for the future development of the company. Therefore, they should be evaluated over their whole lifetimes rather than their initial stages. While one may have some sympathy with the basic idea that our abilities at forecasting over longer periods of time are limited, the adoption of such a rule is unwarranted, since it forces us to abandon what little we can predict about the distant future with some confidence.

11.5.2 The risk-adjusted discount rate method

This approach advises us to increase the interest rate, $d\%$, to be used in the discounting of the future income stream by a risk premium $\delta\%$. For example, if the interest rate is 8% and we decide that the risk premium for the investment project under consideration is 2%, the discount rate, which will be used in the discounting process, becomes 10%. The effect of this increase in the discount rate is to discount more heavily the future cash flow and, therefore, impose more stringent conditions to be met before a project can qualify as profitable. In effect, the method is a defensive measure by reducing our expected returns.

This can be seen by considering our discount factor D, which as long as the interest rate is positive is less than one. This discount factor, when adjusted for risk can be denoted by D', becomes lower than the corresponding unadjusted figure D, i.e., $D' = 1/(1 + d + \delta) < D = 1/(1 + d)$. This means that, other things being equal, the higher the risk premium is the lower our evaluation of the expected returns becomes. We can see this by looking again at the discounting formula:

$$NPV = V_0 + V_1 D' + V_2 D^{2'} + V D^{3'} + \cdots + V_n D^{3'}$$

Since $D' < 1$, higher and higher powers of this risk-adjusted discount factor will yield successively lower and lower figures, which, when multiplied by the respective Vs will result in a lower NPV than if the adjustment had not taken place. This is a straightforward method of direct operational applicability, which tends to account for all terms of the future income stream, no matter how distant they are. This is a great improvement over the earlier finite-horizon approach, since it allows such distant flows to make their contribution to the project's NPV. This method is much sounder from the analytical point of view.

However, the difficulty with the risk-adjusted discount rate method is that we do not know what the risk premium is, consequently, such risk premia are, for all practical purposes, determined subjectively by management. For example, the management may have established from experience that mildly risky projects should carry a risk premium of 1–2%; moderately risky projects should be charged an additional 3–4%, and highly risky projects should be charged a risk premium of over 5%. Nevertheless, the subjectivity involved in deriving the risk premium is consistent, also, with the discussion of Chapter 12 on the question of risk-aversion of the investor. In addition, this could provide flexibility for the investor, by allowing the risk premium to vary over time, whereas the choice of a unique and objective risk premium, were it be possible, would imply that the riskiness of the project was invariant to the passage of time, an assumption which may not be warranted.

11.6 SOURCES OF FINANCE

For an investment programme to be implemented, the company must have first acquired the necessary capital. In this section we consider, briefly, some of the main sources of corporate finance. Such considerations are important not only because finance is a crucial aspect of the managerial function in its own right, but also because the financial mix, chosen by management, affects the firm's cost of capital, which is necessary for the capital budgeting procedure. The sources of finance are divided into two broad categories: (a) internal and (b) external. Internal finance is provided by retained profits (or plowback), depreciation charges and tax provisions. External finance takes the form of long-term capital, which can be either equity capital or bond financing and short-term capital, which includes, principally, bank credit.

11.6.1 Retained profits

Internal funds have for years provided the bulk of finance for corporate investment. In the UK during the period 1950–72 internal funds accounted for an average of 76% of total funds raised, of which about 40% was retained profits, according to the Diamond Report (1971). Also, the Bullock Report (1977) arrived at similar conclusions, and more recent information tends to confirm these figures, with only about 6–6.5% of total funds coming from equity capital. Similar and even higher proportions of internal funding are also observed in US corporations, as well as European ones. In addition, this method of financing is open to all firms, irrespective of size and whether or not their shares are quoted in the Stock Exchange, as is the case with alternative methods. Therefore, the question arises as to the reasons for the preponderance of this method of financing.

The availability of retained profits depends on the past profitability of the firm as well as its policy. There is a widespread belief in the business community that retained profits show the prosperity, efficiency and prudence of management. Also, and more importantly, retained profits provide the company with considerable freedom of action and ensure its independence, since management is certain of the funds it has retained, while the same degree of certainty cannot be attached to efforts in organising external finance, through the issuing of new shares or bonds. In addition, the firm avoids heavy transaction costs involved in the marketing of new issues or borrowing. Shareholders, too, may prefer this method of finance because it transforms current income (i.e., what they would have got in the form of dividend earnings) into capital gains, by increasing the value of their shares. The reason of such preference lies in the differential tax treatment of income (i.e., dividends) and capital gains (i.e., the positive gain realised when a share is sold above the price paid for its acquisition). Since, typically, income tax is higher than capital gains tax, big shareholders prefer to take their earnings in the form of capital gains and, thus, be taxed at a lower rate than have dividends, which not only are taxed at a higher rate but may put rich shareholders on to a higher income bracket, thus raising their tax liability even more. These are powerful reasons for preferring retained profits, as a method of financing new investment projects.

11.6.2 The selling of bonds

A firm can also raise loan capital in the money market to finance its investment programme by selling bonds. A bond is a promise to pay the bondholder the face value of the bond upon its maturity (which is the expiry date of the loan) plus interest. To the firm the interest payments on its outstanding bonds represent costs, and so such interest payments are not subject to corporate taxation; while dividends, which are the corresponding payment on its shares, are considered as income and, thus, they are taxable. In addition, the firm has a legal obligation to pay bondholders interest, whereas no such obligation exists to shareholders to declare a dividend.

This differential treatment means that bonds are less risky than shares and this explains why interest on bonds is usually less than the yield of the shares (i.e., the percentage rate of return on an investment) of the company. The implication of this is that the selling of bonds is an inexpensive way of getting finance, and this differential between yield and interest on bonds provides shareholders with the opportunity to engage in trading on the equity or in leverage. This means that the greater the proportion of bond funds that finance an investment project, the higher the return available to current shareholders. That is, if an investment project offers a return of 10%, the interest on a bond is 5% and that on other forms of finance is 7%, the net return to the shareholders is 5% when the whole of the investment is financed by bonds, but it is 4% when it is financed in equal proportions by bonds and other forms of finance.

However, because bondholders accept fewer risks than shareholders, there is a greater danger to the latter and to the firm, caused by increased uncertainty, which is higher the greater the number of bonds outstanding. This uncertainty arises because interest payments on bonds are contractual obligations, and if the firm cannot meet them for whatever reasons – like poor profitability, can put its existence in jeopardy. The implication of this is that the price of the shares of a highly indebted company tend to be very volatile, following the business cycle, i.e., rising sharply in periods of recovery and boom and falling sharply in periods of recession. In addition, there are considerable transaction costs involved in placing the bonds, and the firm may be open to the vagaries of the capital market. For these reasons, a prudent management may dislike high amounts of debt.

11.6.3   The issuing of new shares

The last method of finance to be discussed involves the issuing of new shares to increase the equity capital of the firm. As compared with bond financing, by this method the firm can limit the speculativeness of its shares, and avoid the contractual interest payments, since it does not have to declare a dividend every year. However, while shareholders may be prepared to take the long-term view and accept a policy of no dividend for a while, the company must have a clear policy of growth and future dividends and persuade its shareholders to hold on to their shares and not try to dispose of them in large quantities, thus, bringing down the price of the shares and the value of the firm.

The disadvantage from the issue of new shares to the firm are that the latter incurs heavy transaction costs and is also forced by law to disclose considerable information about its operations to the public (and to its competitors). These are powerful deterrents, and, in addition, the payment of corporation tax on dividends, make the issue of new shares an expensive method of finance. Perhaps this explains why only 6–6.5% on the average of the total funds raised in the UK come from this source. Also, the timing of the new share issue may cause problems between new and old shareholders if there is volatility in the capital market, so that in a 'high' market a new shareholder pays a much higher price for the same amount of a future dividend; thus, the old shareholders benefit because they get finance inexpensively. But if the market, subsequently, falls, there is resentment among new shareholders. The opposite can happen when the market is 'abnormally low', so that new shareholders gain. For these reasons, sometimes, the firm resorts to a 'rights issue', which means that the new shares are offered to existing shareholders, thus, keeping transaction costs down and also minimising disclosure, since current shareholders do not need the same amount of persuasion as new ones do.

11.7   FINANCIAL POLICY AND THE COST OF CAPITAL

The preceding discussion has indicated that management has at its disposal a variety of financing methods, and it is now pertinent to ask what effects, if any, such methods, individually or in combination, have on the firm's capitalised value and its cost of capital. According to the traditional or orthodox view of financial policy, careful consideration must be given to the competing needs of the firm and its shareholders for retained profits and dividends, respectively, and also to the mix between debt and equity finance, since they affect both the value of the firm and its cost of capital. Indeed, the traditional view contends that an optimal financial policy, i.e., one which maximises the firm's market value while at the same time minimising its cost of capital, can be worked out by varying the financial structure of the firm, i.e., the debt to equity ratio (D/E), known as leverage.

However, it has been argued by Modigliani and Miller (1958, 1961) that in a frictionless world in which there are no imperfections of any kind, transaction costs and taxes, there is nothing to choose between the different methods of finance, thus, there is no optimal financial policy, consequently, both the value of the firm and its cost of capital remain constant. While these are interesting hypotheses offering important insights into the workings of the financial markets, their simplifying assumptions of a frictionless world make them of very little value for practical purposes, since they imply that a financial policy can always be found by tossing a coin, and such a policy can be as good as any other.

The major point is that the effect of taxes and of transaction costs are very important. Shareholders, particularly big ones, tend to prefer profit retention to dividends, because they pay lower tax on their capital gains as compared with the higher income tax on their dividends. Also, such shareholders incur transaction costs if they wished to reinvest their dividends, whilst they avoid such costs when the firm reinvests retained profits automatically. The firm, too, by retaining profits avoids transaction costs that it will, otherwise, incur if it tried to raise funds in the capital market to replace the dividends. Interestingly enough, the same imperfections explain why some shareholders may prefer dividends than profit retention. Some may wish to see their commitment in the firm's capital held constant than increasing. For small shareholders it is less expensive, when their tax rate is low, to receive dividends than go through the process of selling some of their shares to supplement their income and incur, relatively, heavy transaction costs. For these reasons, we do not pursue the Modigliani–Miller thesis further, but refer interested readers to the references given at the end.

The earlier discussion indicated that modest amounts of debt may be beneficial to the firm and its shareholders, since debt financing is relatively inexpensive as compared with equity financing, because of the differential risks involved. This enables us to estimate a firm's cost of capital as the weighted average of the current cost from all sources. For our purposes we assume that the sources of finance are equity and debt, so we need to evaluate separately the costs of these two different sources, before combining them to derive the firm's overall or average cost of capital.

11.7.1 The equity cost of capital

We can consider the derivation of the firm's cost of equity capital by means of: (a) The dividend valuation model and (b) the capital asset pricing model (CAPM).

11.7.1a The dividend valuation model

This model argues that from the individual shareholder's point of view, his wealth is given as the present value of his expected returns, i.e., the dividends, D, and the capital gains of his holdings, discounted at the firm's rate of return K_E. Assuming for simplicity that there is no growth so that the dividend, D, remains the same, and the shareholder is prepared to keep his shares in perpetuity, the market price of the share, P, will be equal to the present value of the stream of income, i.e., of Ds in perpetuity, discounted at K_E, which was found in Section 1.2 to be given by relation (5), so that

$$P = \frac{D}{K_E} \text{ which implies } K_E = \frac{D}{P}$$

which states that the return, and, thus, the cost of equity capital is given by the dividend to share price ratio. However, if the dividend per share, D, grows at a constant annual rate of $g\%$, in perpetuity, the present value of this stream – recalling relations (6) and (7) of Section 1.2 – , which is equal to the market price per share is:

$$P = \frac{D}{K_E - g} \text{ from which we get } Ke = \frac{D}{P} + g$$

as the firm's cost of equity capital, which is the same as above augmented by the growth rate.

11.7.1b   Capital asset pricing model

This model contends that the rate of return required by shareholders is made up of a risk-free rate, R_F, plus a premium compensating the shareholder for accepting the inherent risk of holding the particular share. Clearly, such risk premia vary from firm to firm, depending on the nature of their activities. Normally, and this theme is also discussed in Chapter 12, higher returns are associated with higher risks, and so for one to be persuaded to invest in a particular risky venture there must be the compensation of a higher expected return.

However, in contrast to that discussion, where we are interested in the total variability of returns, in the CAPM model we need to consider the variability of the returns of a particular share relative to the variability of the returns of the shares of all other companies. Therefore, the required rate of return of the share of a given company becomes a function of the volatility of its returns relative to the returns of the overall market, as measured by a broad market index. This volatility is known as the β coefficient, which is estimated by simple regression analysis. In this analysis we assume a linear relationship between the dependent variable, which is the returns of the share of the company under consideration and the independent variable, which is the returns for the overall market index. Therefore, we have the model: $R = \alpha + \beta I + u$, where R represents the returns of the company, I is the overall market index, and u is the stochastic error term satisfying the classical assumptions.

If $\beta = 1$, it shows that the share's volatility is the same as that for the market as a whole. If $\beta < 1$, the returns of our share are less volatile than the market's volatility, and thus the share is less risky, while if $\beta > 1$, the returns of the share are more volatile than the market's volatility, and so the share is riskier.

Therefore, the CAPM model evaluates the returns on a firm's equity capital and, thus, its cost of equity capital as follows:

$$K_E = R_F + \beta(K_M - R_F)$$

where R_F is the risk free return, normally taken to be the interest rate on long-term Treasury bonds or equivalent long-term interest rates in other countries, K_M is the rate of return on the market as a whole and β is the estimated β coefficient from running the regression. For example, if for a particular company β has been estimated as 0.75, the long-term interest rate is 3% and the rate of return of a market portfolio is 8%, the company's rate of return is estimated as:

$$K_E = 3 + 0.75(8 - 3) = 3 + 0.75 \times 5 = 3 + 3.75 = 6.75\%$$

The above two methods of estimating the firm's cost of equity capital, have been criticised on the ground of difficulties in obtaining the required data for such estimations. In addition, the CAPM model suffers, as all regression models do, from the assumption that past behaviour will continue in the future, by trying to forecast the rate of return on past data, thus, ignoring the point that new investment opportunities have to do with expected future returns, than past ones. Also, the stability of the estimated β coefficient has been questioned in many studies, further casting doubts on this method.

11.7.2   The cost of debt (bonds)

The cost of debt is the interest rate that must be paid to investors to persuade them to lend the company their capital. However, since interest payments on bond finance are considered as cost and, thus, are tax deductible, the actual cost to the company is the after-tax cost. This means that if the interest rate on the bond is K_D, and the corporation tax rate is $t\%$, the cost of debt, K_I, is given by:

$$K_I = K_D(1 - t)$$

For example, if a firm issues €10 million of 12% first mortgage bonds at par, and the corporation tax rate is 40%, the after-tax cost of debt to the company is:

$$K_I = 12(1 - 0.4) = 12 \times 0.6 = 7.2\%.$$

11.7.3   The firm's overall cost of capital

Having established the separate components, the firm's overall cost of capital is estimated as the weighted average of these separate equity and debt costs, weighted by the relevant proportions of equity and debt in the overall market value of the company. Therefore, letting E stand for the market value of the equity capital, I denoting the market value of debt and V be the total market value of the firm (i.e., $= D + I$, we have that the overall cost of capital, K_O, is given by:

$$K_O = K_E \left(\frac{E}{V} \right) + K_I \left(\frac{I}{V} \right)$$

11.7.4 Optimal financial policy

As was pointed out earlier, the equity cost of capital K_E, is expected to be higher than the cost of debt, K_I. If the capital structure of the company contains only equity capital, its overall (average) cost of capital coincides with the equity cost of capital. But as the firm starts introducing debt into its capital structure, the average or overall cost of capital, K_O, decreases, since the cost of debt, K_I, is lower than K_E, and goes on decreasing up to a range (or a point) of optimal leverage (D/E). As a consequence of that development the value of the company increases over this range of leverage. This is shown in Figures 11.12 and 11.13, where the cost of capital is a function of leverage, and the value of the company is a function of leverage, respectively.

As we move from zero debt up to an optimal range of leverage Y–Z, the average cost of capital falls and the value of the company rises. This is why it was argued earlier that modest amounts of debt are beneficial to the company. However, increased leverage brings, eventually, financial uncertainty, which causes both the cost of equity and the cost of debt to rise, thus, pushing up the overall cost of capital and causing the value of the company to decline.

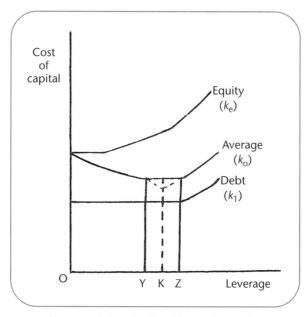

Figure 11.12 Optimal financial policy

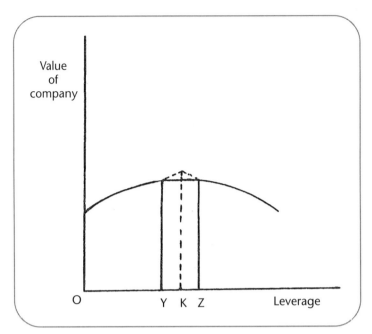

Figure 11.13 Optimal financial policy

It is not clear whether the minimum overall cost and the maximum value are achieved over a range *Y–Z* in Figures 11.12 and 11.13 or at a point such as *K*. However, this range (or point) of optimal leverage will differ from industry to industry and between firms within the same industry, depending on the variability of the firm's cash flows, which in turn depends on the characteristics of the specific firm and the industry it operates. This means that firms and industries characterised by low uncertainty will be able to use higher leverage ratios than those operating in areas of greater risk.

SUMMARY

This chapter has looked at the fundamentals of capital budgeting and, in particular, at compounding, discounting, time preference, present value and IRR. Also, it has examined the various investment appraisal methods and compared and contrasted them and, in addition, it has suggested ways of treating risk. The chapter concluded by considering the various sources of finance as well as the financial policy and the cost of capital of the firm.

PROBLEMS

1. If the interest rates are 5%, 10%, 15% and 20%, find the corresponding discount factors, D, for 5 years and tabulate them in the following table:

Year	Discount factors: Interest			
	5%	10%	15%	20%
1	—	—	—	—
2	—	—	—	—
3	—	—	—	—
4	—	—	—	—
5	—	—	—	—

   What happens to the discount factors as you increase the interest rates and lengthen the horizon?

2. The following stream of income gives the net returns of a particular investment project in thousands of euros:

Initial capital	End of 1st year	End of 2nd year	End of 3rd year	End of 4th year
−10000	3000	2000	5000	4000

   If the rate of interest is 8%, find the NPV of this project. Find also its IRR and its PI, and comment on whether or not we should invest in this project.

3. A firm is faced with three mutually exclusive projects, which have the following income streams, in thousands of euros:

Initial capital	End of 1st year	End of 2nd year	End of 3rd year
−2000	1000	1400	1000
−1200	800	1600	—
−1800	700	500	2000

   (a) Find the payback period of each project.
   (b) Estimate their IRR.
   (c) At an interest rate of 10% calculate their NPVs and
   (d) Their PIs.
   (e) Rank the three projects according to the four criteria above and comment on your results.

4. A firm is considering buying either of two machines for its operations. Machine A has an initial cost of €1500 and promises to yield a net surplus of €50 by the end of the first year and a net surplus of €3300 by the end of the second

year, when it is scrapped. The alternative machine B involves an initial outlay of €4000 and promises to generate a net surplus of €5800 by the end of the first year, when it, too, is scrapped. Neither machine leaves any scrap value. The firm looks no further ahead than the lifetime of whatever machine it contemplates. It is always free to borrow or lend for a year at a time in any quantity at the ruling rate of interest, which is expected to remain constant. At what rates of interest, if any, is it optimal to choose: (a) machine A; (b) machine B and (c) neither machine?

5. Two investment projects A and B have the following expected future net annual income streams:

```
A:  1000   6000   2000   -1000   7000   5000
B:  1000   6000   5000   -1000   2680   5000
```

If either project is chosen, the firm plans to replace it by a precisely similar project each time it finishes:
(a) At what constant rate of discount per period is the total present value the same for each indefinitely repeated project?
(b) If the above rate of discount is less than the actual rate at which funds can be borrowed, but more than the rate at which money can be lent out, what can you say about the relative desirability of the two projects?

Hint: For the second part of this question try to use the emulation procedure illustrated in the example given in the text, by using the rate found in (a), but taking into consideration the conditions given in (b).

6. The cost of equity capital of a particular company has been found to be 12%. The company intends financing a specific investment project costing €20 million by using a mixture of debt and equity in the proportions 60 : 40. The company issues €12 million of first mortgage bonds at a par. If the company is taxed at 45%, find its overall cost of capital.

BIBLIOGRAPHY

Baumol, W.J. (1977), *Economic Theory and Operations Analysis*, 4th edn, Prentice-Hall.
Bierman, H. and Seymour, S. (1984), *The Capital Budgeting Decision*, 4th edn, Macmillan.
Bromwich, M. (1976), *The Economics of Capital Budgeting*, Penguin.
Hirschleifer, J. (1958), 'On the Theory of Optimal Investment Decision', *Journal of Political Economy*, Vol. LXVI, August, 329–352; reprinted in Archer, S.H. and D'Ambrosio, C.D. (eds) (1967), *The Theory of Business Finance*, A Book of Readings, Macmillan.
Johnson, M.B. (1971), *Household Behaviour*, Penguin.
Lorie, J.H. and Savage, L.J. (1955), 'Three Problems in Rationing Capital', *Journal of Business*, XXVIII, October, 229–239; reprinted in Solomon, E. (1959), op. cit.
Modigliani, F. and Miller, M.H. (1958), 'The Cost of Capital, Corporation Finance and the Theory of Investment', *American Economic Review*, **49**: 655–659; reprinted in Archer, S.H. and D'Ambrosio, C.D. (1967), op. cit.
Modigliani, F. and Miller, M.H. (1961), 'Dividend Policy, Growth and the Valuation of Shares', *Journal of Business*, **34**: 411–433; reprinted in Archer & D'Ambrosio (1967), op. cit.

Report of the Commission of Inquiry into the *Distribution of Income and Wealth* (the Diamond Report), No. 2, HMSO, 1971.

Report of the Commission of Inquiry on *Industrial Democracy* (the Bullock Report), HMSO, 1977.

Shackle, G.L.S. (1970), *Expectations, Enterprise and Profit,* Allen & Unwin.

Solomon, E. (ed.) (1959), *The Management of Corporate Capital*, The Free Press.

chapter twelve

Risk and Uncertainty – Decision Theory

12.1 INTRODUCTION

Managerial economics tries to bridge the gap between the abstract economic theory and business practice for the purpose of sound decision making. To understand the nature of decisions, we need an appropriate analytical tool or framework of analysis. Typically, when we are confronted with a problem, we start by trying to identify it properly, and proceed to consider alternative courses of action to solving the problem. Subsequently, we have to evaluate the various alternatives by using cost–benefit analysis and choose the best alternative, on the basis, of some predetermined criteria. The next stage involves the optimisation of the chosen alternative, i.e., the solving for the best solution and, finally, we have the task of implementing the decision.

Most of the discussion thus far, with few exceptions, has been conducted on the understanding that the firm has been deciding on various aspects of its policies under conditions of full information and complete certainty. For example, the firm knew exactly what the demand and supply conditions were and, therefore, it could find the appropriate marginal revenue and cost and use them to establish its output and price determination, on the assumption it wished to maximise its profits. However, it is a fact of life that, practically, all business decisions are taken within the context of risk and uncertainty and that consideration provides the justification for the discussion of this chapter. The subject matter of decision theory is the evaluation of alternative courses of action and the choice of the best alternative, under conditions of uncertainty. Following Knight's distinction between risk and uncertainty, we define risk as the state under which the probabilities of the alternative outcomes are known or can be estimated. Uncertainty, on the other hand, refers to situations where the probabilities of the outcomes are unknown. By contrast, a state of certainty exists when the probability of outcomes is one.

Decision theory has been developed with a view to helping under conditions of uncertainty, in a variety of ways. Among others, it may help us to understand the problem with greater clarity, to assign probabilities to outcomes, to take a consistent approach to particular problems and to determine the sensitivity of outcomes to changes in underlying conditions and/or assumptions. Decision theory is essentially concerned with how expectations are formed under uncertainty. From our point of view, we are concerned with how businessmen are making decisions in an uncertain world. It is natural to expect that they have mostly approached the problem in a personal and subjective way, and so decisions have depended on the personality and experience of the decision maker. Nevertheless, a plethora of analytical, quantitative methods have also been developed for the analysis of uncertainty and for providing assistance in the process of decision making. Bayesian statistics, decision trees, games theory, queuing theory, Monte Carlo studies, Markov processes and the like have all been put forward to supplement the 'unquantifiable' factors in tackling uncertainty. As this is a book on managerial economics, the emphasis will be on economic analysis than statistical theory. Nevertheless, we shall attempt a very brief discussion of some of the analytical tools referred to above.

12.2 THE PROBLEM OF RISK – EXPECTED VALUE

When the probabilities of outcomes of particular events are known or can be computed in an objective way, we talk of risk. Such objective probabilities may be found either by an a priori manner deductively, on the basis of assumed principles, for example, deriving the probability of obtaining heads from the toss of a fair or unbiased coin as 0.5 or 50%; or derive the probability a posteriori, i.e., on the basis of past evidence and the assumption that we expect such evidence to continue in the future. Insurance actuarial work involves the calculation of risk by means of a posteriori probabilities.

A significant part of decision theory has been borrowed from the work of von Neumann and Morgenstern on the 'Theory of Games' (1944). The latter has been presented in some detail in Chapter 10, and for our purposes here it suffices to note that the concepts of strategy, the payoff matrix, the expected utility (value) and the minimax principle are present in decision theory. However, whereas in games theory (as in the case of two person, zero-sum game) there is a rival player consciously striving to oppose the first player from achieving his/her objective, in decision theory there is not an opponent as such and the role of the second player is taken by nature. Therefore, the payoff matrix of various outcomes depends, first, on the different strategies adopted by the firm (first player) and, second, on the state of nature, such as, for example, expectations of a rising, stable or falling market.

Under conditions of risk, the main decision criterion is expected value, which is given by the following expression:

$$E(V) = p_1 V_1 + p_2 V_2 + \cdots + p_n V_n = \sum_{i=1}^{n} p_i V_i, \ i = 1, \ldots, n$$

where V_i is the value of the ith payoff and p_i its probability.

Having found the expected values of the different strategies, the decision criterion tells us to choose the strategy with the highest expected value, thus the decision criterion is known as the maximisation of expected value. The expected value of a given strategy is the weighted mean of the values of the outcomes multiplied by their respective probabilities which act as weights. It represents a summary measure, or the average value of all possible outcomes under the specified conditions.

To illustrate, assume that a firm has to decide on whether to introduce a new product in the market or to carry on with its existing lines. How profitable the proposed project will be depends on whether the market for the new product rises in the future, stays reasonably stable or declines. In a rising market, it is anticipated that the project will have a positive net present value of €100 millions, in a stable market €25 millions and in a falling market it will lose €50 millions. On the other hand, if the new product is not introduced and the amount of its original outlay is diverted to the firm's existing lines, these will produce additional surpluses of €50, €20 and €10 millions, for the three states of the market, respectively. We present these possibilities in Table 12.1.

Further, we assume that the firm has some idea of the probabilities of the state of the market and has estimated, on the basis of past experience, that there is a 50% chance of a rising market, a 30% chance of a stable market and a 20% chance of a falling market. It is now easy to estimate the expected value of each course of action. Thus, the expected value of introducing the new product is:

$$E(V_1) = 0.5 \times 100 + 0.3 \times 25 + 0.2 \times (-50) = €47.5 \text{ millions}$$

Table 12.1   States of nature

Strategies		Rising market	Stable market	Falling market
S_1	Introduce new product	100	25	−50
S_2	Carry on with existing lines	50	20	10

and the expected value of continuing with the existing lines is:

$$E(Y_2) = 0.5 \times 50 + 0.3 \times 20 + 0.2 \times 10 = €33 \text{ millions}$$

Therefore, in this case we choose to introduce the new product, since the expected value of that course of action exceeds that of the alternative.

12.2.1   Measuring risk

Carrying on with the above example we notice that in neither strategy do we have the values of €47.5 millions and €33 millions. In other words, there are no circumstances yielding the above returns. This, of course, merely illustrates the fact that these figures represent the expected values or means, as discussed above. However, since we decided to introduce the new product we are now aware that the returns of this particular strategy can vary from €100 millions profit to a €50 millions loss. Clearly, this variation in possible returns is very important to the firm, since the big possible loss may imply serious debt or cash flow problems. The question then arises on whether we can take account of such variations.

A way of measuring the dispersion of returns of the two projects is to calculate the standard deviation, which is a measurement of the variation of the expected payoffs of the two strategies. The standard deviation is, thus, a measurement of risk. The higher the standard deviation, the greater the variation of possible payoffs and, thus, the greater the risk.

The standard deviation is given by the following formula:

$$\sigma = \sqrt{\sum_{i=1}^{n} (V_i - \mu)^2 p_i}$$

where μ is the mean, or the expected value of the payoffs, and it has been found earlier to be €47.5 millions for the strategy of introducing a new product and €33 millions for the strategy of carrying on with the existing lines. To find the standard deviation of each strategy we subtract each possible payoff from the respective mean, square the resulting value and multiply it by its respective probability and, finally, we sum up and take the square root. Applying these steps to the figures for the first strategy (project) of the firm, we construct the table overleaf and when we take the square root of 3431.25 we find that the standard deviation of introducing the new product is €58.576 millions. Similarly, we find that the standard deviation of carrying on with the existing lines is €17.349 millions; the calculations for the second strategy's standard deviation are left for the reader as an exercise.

Calculating the standard deviation

V_i	μ	$(V_i - \mu)$	$(V_i - \mu)^2$	p_i	$(V_i - \mu)^2 p_i$
100	47.5	52.5	2756.25	0.5	1378.125
25	47.5	−22.5	506.25	0.3	151.875
−50	47.5	−97.5	9506.25	0.2	1901.250
			Total		3431.250

On the evidence of these figures, we could conclude that introducing the new product is almost 3.4 times riskier than carrying on with the existing lines. However, since the expected values of the two projects are different, this is not a valid comparison. The above figures measure absolute risk than relative one. Only when the two distributions of payoffs have the same mean are we entitled to compare them directly by their standard deviations. A different way to measure relative risk, as distinct from the absolute risk we found earlier, is to consider the coefficient of variation. This is simply given by dividing the standard deviation by the expected value, or mean, of each strategy and multiplying the ratio by 100. Thus:

Coefficient of variation $C = (\sigma/\mu)100$

Therefore, for the first strategy we have:

$$C = \frac{56.576}{47.5} \times 100 = 123.316$$

and for the second strategy we get:

$$C = \frac{17.34}{33} \times 100 = 52.57$$

The computation of the coefficients of variation for the two strategies (projects) leads to the same conclusion, regarding the riskiness of the two projects, reached earlier on the basis of the standard deviation; introducing the new product is riskier than carrying on with the existing lines. This may not always happen when the expected values of the projects under consideration differ significantly. A higher standard deviation means greater absolute risk. The coefficient of variation indicates the relative risk, i.e., the risk per euro of expected value.

12.2.2   Risk-earnings trade-off and certainty equivalent

As we have just seen, the introduction of a new product is associated with a high expected value, but it is also very risky. Carrying on with the existing lines is far less risky, but it has a low expected value. This illustrates a fundamental relationship between risk and earnings of various assets. Higher earnings are associated with higher risks and lower earnings with lower risks. Which course of action is attractive to the decision maker will ultimately depend on the latter's attitude to risk.

We can demonstrate this by means of Figures 12.1 and 12.2, which incorporate the curve AB, representing different attainable risk-earnings combinations, and

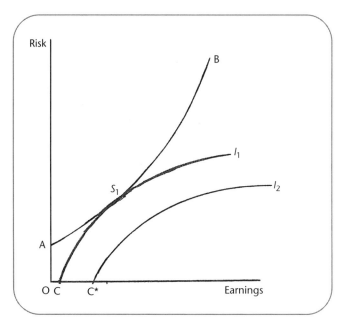

Figure 12.1 Risk-earnings trade-off and 'risk-averter'

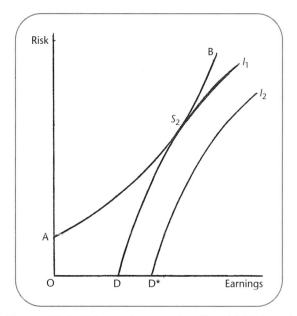

Figure 12.2 Risk-earnings trade-off and 'risk-lover'

indifference curves of two decision makers. Higher indifference curves, like those labelled I_2, are drawn closer to the horizontal axis, as they are more desirable, showing more earnings for less risk. Clearly, curve AB provides the objective or market information regarding the trade-off between risk and earnings, while the indifference curves indicate the subjective preferences of the investor between risk and earnings. As usual, equilibrium occurs at a tangency point between curve AB and the highest indifference curve.

Figure 12.1 shows an indifference map for a 'risk-averter', one who prefers low risk and low earnings, and who finds his equilibrium at point S_1. In terms of our earlier example, he chooses the second project, i.e., carrying on with existing lines. By contrast, Figure 12.2 shows an indifference map for a 'risk-lover', i.e., one who is prepared to accept high risks for high earnings, and in terms of our example, he chooses to introduce the new product.

On Figure 12.3 we plot the information of our example. On the vertical axis we measure risk, in terms of the standard deviation and on the horizontal axis we measure the expected values of the payoffs. Points S_1 and S_2 correspond to the two sets of expected values and standard deviations for the two projects. Such points clearly lie on the risk-earnings possibility curve AB open to the firm. By superimposing the indifference curves of the two decision makers of Figures 12.1 and 12.2, we may conclude that S_1 will be chosen by a 'risk-averter', while S_2 will be preferred by a 'risk-lover'. The indifference curves of the 'risk-averter' in Figure 12.1 are drawn on the assumption of diminishing marginal utility of money, implying that the decision maker requires a large amount of potential returns to compensate for a small increase in risk. Conversely, Figure 12.2 implies an increasing marginal utility of money for the decision maker, i.e., the latter is prepared to accept much higher risks for a small return. von Neumann and Morgenstern have shown that an index of expected utility can be constructed in a way that has cardinal properties and then it can be used to rank various risky alternatives, as discussed in Chapters 10 earlier. If this were adopted, the decision would be re-cast in terms of utility rather than money and the decision techniques applied, such that we maximised expected utility. In this context, it is also worth referring to the approach proposed by Shackle for dealing with risk and uncertainty. Shackle argues that

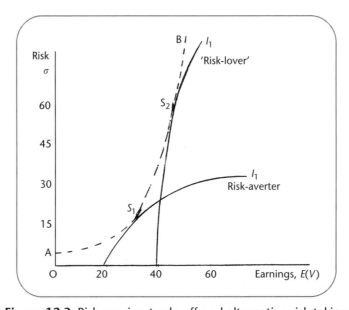

Figure 12.3 Risk-earning trade-off and alternative risk taking

people characterise the risk involved in any decision by means of two represent-ative outcomes, such as a potential gain or a potential loss, which he calls *focal gain* and *focal loss*. He also introduces the concept of *potential surprise* to show how much people would be surprised if outcome A transpired than B. So, if A and B have an equal probability of occurring, then we should not be surprised if either outcome did occur. This means that both have zero potential surprise, despite the fact that on an actuarial basis they should be heavily discounted. Making also use of the investor's indifference map, Shackle arrives at the *certainty equivalent* of any risky decision, such as an investment. Accordingly, the certainty equivalent of a project X is defined as another project X* which is completely riskless and the investor is indifferent between X and X*. Using the information on Figures 12.1 and 12.2, point C represents the certainty equivalent of any combination of risk and earnings lying on indifference curve I_1 and point C* is the certainty equivalent of any combination of risk and earnings lying on the higher indifference curve I_2, in Figure 12.1. Similarly, in Figure 12.2 points D and D* represent certainty equi-valents of combinations of risk and earnings lying on the indifference curves I_1 and I_2, respectively.

12.2.3   Decision trees

Decision trees are graphic ways of representing sequential decisions and their expected results, made under various sets of circumstances and conditions of risk. A decision tree starts with the first or earliest decision and develops through a series of decisions and actions in time. If the decision maker is faced with various possible courses of action, the tree branches out to show all these various alternatives and their associated probabilities, until at the end all possible outcomes and payoffs are shown.

The decision tree approach makes use of the so-called rollback technique. This requires that we start from the extreme right hand tips of the branches of the tree and work backwards, towards the initial decision point by following two rules. The first is that when we are confronted with a probabilistic event, we calculate its expected values by using the payoffs and probabilities associated with that event. The second requires that when we reach a decision point, we select the course of action with the highest expected value and ignore the other course of action.

We can demonstrate a decision tree by looking again at our earlier example of the introduction of a new product. The various steps are depicted in Figure 12.4. The starting decision is whether the firm should spend an amount of money to introduce a new product in the market, or to spend the same amount on its existing range of products. A decision is denoted by a square. If it is decided to introduce the new product, the firm must take into account three different states of the market, namely, that it may be faced by a rising, stable or falling market. This situation regarding the market environment is exogenous, i.e., the firm cannot control it, and is denoted by a circle. Branching out of the circle we have the three possibilities of the state of the market as rising, stable and falling, and their associated probabilities, which the firm has been able to determine on the basis of past information. Since we also know the possible payoffs, we are able to calculate the expected value of the decision to introduce the new product as €47.5 millions $[100 \times 0.5 + 25 \times 0.3 + (-50) \times 0.2]$, and insert the resulting value in the top circle.

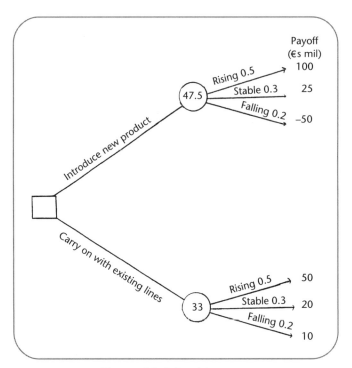

Figure 12.4 Decision tree

The alternative strategy of the firm is to spend the same amount of money on its existing range of products, and is shown on the lower part of the decision tree. Here too, we have the exogenous environment of the market over which the firm cannot exercise any control, denoted by a circle. Again, branching out of the circle we have the three states of the market: a rising, stable and falling market with their associated probabilities. Knowledge of the possible payoffs and the probabilities enables us to calculate the expected value of this alternative as €33 millions ($50 \times 0.5 + 20 \times 0.3 + 10 \times 0.2$) and insert it in the lower circle. Since the decision criterion is the maximisation of the expected value of the given alternatives, the firm should introduce the new product.

In practice, decision trees are, typically, more complex than the one presented above, with additional sequential or multi-period decision points and states of nature. The firm may seek the opportunity to improve the knowledge of the likely future state of the market, through, for example, market research or econometric analysis. The result of such studies may very well be the revision of the relevant probabilities.

To illustrate these points, consider an extension of the earlier decision tree. The firm is considering commissioning a market research report, and it knows from past experience how reliable such reports are. For example, when in the past the outcome was one of a rising market, this had been preceded 70% of the time by a 'rise' forecast, 20% of the time by a 'stable' one and 10% of the time by a 'fall' forecast. Similarly, in the case of a resulting stable market, the corresponding figures were 20%, 60% and 20%, respectively, whilst for a falling market, the figures were 10%, 10% and 80%, respectively. We can now summarise this information in Table 12.2.

Table 12.2   Probabilities of success of research report forecast

Outcomes	State of nature		
	Rising market	Stable market	Falling market
Rising market	0.7	0.2	0.1
Stable market	0.2	0.6	0.2
Falling market	0.1	0.1	0.8

Notice that the rows add up to one, as expected. Adding down the columns is meaningless.

We can now use this information together with the earlier knowledge that a rising market occurs 50% of the time, a stable market 30% and a falling market 20%, to determine the total success percentages (or joint probabilities) of a 'rise', 'stable' and 'fall' forecast and actual outcomes. Since a rising market occurs 50% of the time and on those occasions it is preceded 70% of the time by a 'rise' forecast, we can estimate that a 'rise' forecast is followed by an actual rise $0.5 \times 0.7 = 0.35$ of the time. Similarly, a 'rise' forecast is followed by a stable outturn $0.3 \times 0.2 = 0.06$ of the time and, finally, a 'rise' forecast is followed by an actual fall in the market $0.2 \times 0.1 = 0.02$ of the time. Clearly, adding these figures we find that, in total, 'rise' forecasts are obtained 0.43 of the time. That is, pre-multiplying the row vector (0.5 0.3 0.2) to the first column vector {0.7 0.2 0.1} of the (3 × 3) 'state of nature' matrix produces the column vector of the intermediate joint probabilities {0.35 + 0.06 + 0.02} for a rising market, which add up to 0.43, giving the marginal probability for a 'rise' forecast. Similarly, for 'stable' forecasts we pre-multiply the row vector (0.5 0.3 0.2) to the second column vector for a 'stable' market {0.2 0.6 0.1} of the 'state of nature' matrix to obtain the intermediate joint probabilities column vector {0.10 + 0.18 + 0.02}, which add up to 0.30 as the marginal probability, suggesting that 'stable' forecasts are obtained 0.30 of the time. Finally, for 'fall' forecasts, we pre-multiply the row vector (0.5 0.3 0.2) to the third column vector {0.1 0.2 0.8} of the 'state of nature' matrix' for a 'fall' market to derive the intermediate joint probabilities column vector {0.05 0.06 0.16} which sum up to 0.27 as the marginal probability, suggesting that 'fall' forecasts are obtained 0.27 of the time. The marginal probabilities add up to one. Therefore, these joint and marginal probabilities are calculated by pre-multipying the row vector (0.5 0.3 0.2) to the matrix of the outcomes found earlier. Since we pre-multiply a (1 × 3) row vector to a (3 × 3) matrix, the resulting matrix of marginal probabilities is another (1 × 3) row vector, as follows:

					Joint probabilities				Marginal probabilities		
	0.7	0.2	0.1		0.35	0.10	0.05				
(0.5 0.3 0.2)	0.2	0.6	0.2	=	0.06	0.18	0.06	=	(0.43	0.30	0.27)
	0.1	0.1	0.8		0.02	0.02	0.16				
									Rise	Stable	Fall

Table 12.3 Conditional probabilities

Outcomes	Report forecasts		
	Rising market	Stable market	Falling market
Rising market	0.814	0.333	0.185
Stable market	0.140	0.600	0.222
Falling market	0.046	0.067	0.593
Total	1.000	1.000	1.000

The new information, which we have derived by undertaking the research report, makes it now possible to improve our knowledge of the likely future state of the market, by reasoning as follows. As a 'rise' forecast is obtained 0.43 of the *total* time, and is followed by a rise 0.35 of the *total* time, the chances of a 'rise' forecast being followed by an actual rise in the market are $0.35/0.43 = 0.814$. Similarly, the chances of it being followed by a stable outturn are given by $0.06/0.43 = 0.140$ and by a falling outturn are $0.02/0.43 = 0.046$. In other words, these chances known as conditional probabilities are obtained by dividing the joint probabilities by the marginal ones. Repeating this exercise for 'stable' and 'fall' forecasts we are able to establish Table 12.3, giving the conditional probabilities of the state of nature forecasts and outcomes.

We can incorporate these conditional probabilities into the decision tree, shown in Figure 12.5, where there is now another decision to be taken before the product decision, i.e., whether or not to spend money on a research report. As it is shown, the extra information from the research report raises the expected value to €54.3 millions, as compared with €47.5 millions without the report. Clearly, as long as the report costs less than €6.8 millions, it is worth undertaking.

Also, when a decision tree involves multi-period points, it is possible to consider the feedback of earlier periods on to the next ones, as the decision tree branches out into the future. In our example of the introduction of the new product, we could have considered that its success in the second period was attributed to its success in the first period, its success in the third period was affected by its success in the second period and so on. This means that we could have derived the appropriate conditional probabilities and incorporated them into the decision tree, for a fuller sequential analysis of the development of the product over time.

12.3 COPING WITH UNCERTAINTY

We saw earlier that a state of uncertainty is said to exist when the outcomes of particular courses of action are not even known on a probabilistic basis. However, despite the fact that objective probabilities are not available, the decision maker

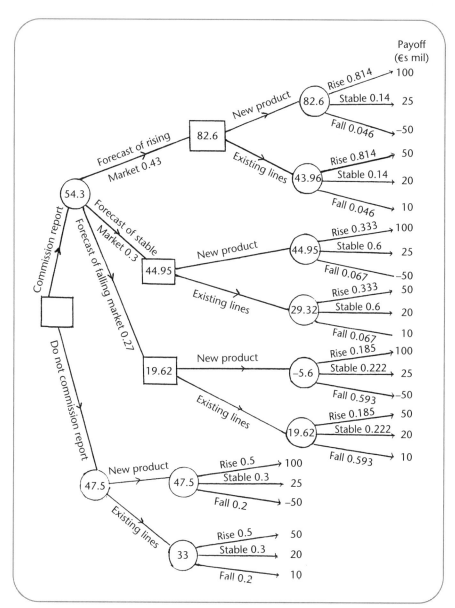

Figure 12.5 Decision tree of the market research report

may have enough background information, regarding the problem under consideration, to enable him to assign subjective probabilities to various outcomes. If this is the case the problem reduces to one of risk, and expected values can be estimated for the various outcomes to determine the optimal strategy, as shown earlier. In the opposite case where no estimates of subjective probabilities can be assigned, it is clearly impossible to insure against uncertainty or incorporate it into the firm's future incremental costs or forecasts. This is especially the case where decisions are unique or 'one-off'. Nevertheless, even in such cases given that the decision maker has to take a decision than do nothing, there are certain approaches and decision

Table 12.4 Payoffs

Strategies	State of the market			
	Rise	Stable	Fall	Row minima
A	500	100	−50	−50
B	300	250	0	0
C	100	70	50	50
		Maximin		50

criteria available, which are used by businessmen to reduce uncertainty. Such approaches range from reference to some higher authority – if possible – or the use of rules of thumb, diversification of activities, attempts by the firm to control the environment, hedging, flexible investments through to acquisition of additional information and the modification of goals. As some of these issues are touched upon elsewhere, we concentrate here only on certain decision criteria that have been put forward to cope with uncertainty.

To illustrate the application of these decision criteria, consider a firm which must decide between three strategies, namely, on whether: (**a**) to introduce a new product representing a drastic departure from its existing product with new packaging at a much higher price to replace the existing product; (**b**) to moderately change the ingredients of the existing product with a new packaging and a moderate increase in price or (**c**) to change the existing product slightly but advertise it as new with a small increase in price. The firm estimates that the various payoffs (in thousands of euros) will be affected by three states of the market, namely, on whether the market rises (R), remains stable (S) or falls (F) and are given in Table 12.4, where we also derive the row minima (in the last column) and the maximum value of those minima, known as maximin.

Given the above information, the firm can use: (1) the Wald decision criterion or the maximin; (2) the maximax; (3) the Hurwicz alpha criterion; (4) the Savage criterion or the minimax regret and (5) the Laplace or Bayes criterion. In what follows we try to explain in turn these various criteria.

12.3.1 The Wald or maximin criterion

The Wald decision criterion, also called the maximin, advises us to select the minimum payoff of each strategy and of these minima select the maximum value, i.e., the maximum of the row minima, called the maximin, and thus the strategy to which the maximin belongs. This is a very pessimistic criterion, which suggests that we should look at the worst possible outcome under each strategy and then choose the strategy with the best minimum payoff. In our case the maximin is 50, and it suggests that we select strategy C, i.e., that we go for minimal changes in our existing product.

Whilst one can argue the merits of conservatism, this criterion is unnecessarily restrictive and ignores completely all other elements in the payoff matrix. As we have seen in Chapter 10, von Neumann and Morgenstern have shown that this may indeed be the optimal policy, when we are faced with an opponent (such as a competing firm) trying hard to harm us. However, in this case this pessimism is not very justified, since the nature of the market cannot be likened to a rival trying actively and consciously to compete with us. Nevertheless, for small firms this conservative approach may be the only policy, if they do not want to jeopardise their market position and, ultimately, their survival. Since small firms probably have all their assets invested in one product, they must be careful not to endanger them, by trying policies which offer high rewards but which can also go disastrously wrong.

12.3.2   The maximax

In complete contrast to the maximin, the next criterion, the maximax, advises us to be bold and go for the strategy offering the highest reward, in the hope that nature and luck can be favourable. In our case, the highest reward is 500, corresponding to strategy A. Now it may be that he who dares wins because luck may favour the daring, but this criterion is very optimistic, touching on recklessness, and will typically be avoided by most managements, which tend to be conservative in their outlook. The criterion may very well appeal to a gambler, who is attracted by the glitter of the first prize, despite the obvious dangers. Like the maximin rule, the maximax criterion ignores all other intermediate values and the implication is that one who follows it is prepared to give up a big advantage in the lesser payoffs for a small difference in the highest prize. In terms of the earlier discussion this will appeal to a 'risk lover', a gambler. This decision criterion is not seriously proposed in the literature, but rather described in order to be contrasted with the pessimism of the maximin rule.

12.3.3   The Hurwicz alpha criterion

As a compromise between the minimax and the maximax, Hurwicz has proposed that we use as a decision criterion a weighted average of the maximum and minimum payoffs of each strategy, and pick the strategy with the highest weighted average. The weights are a coefficient of optimism, α, which is applied to the maximum value and its counterpart $(1 - \alpha)$, applied to the minimum value. Clearly, the coefficient of optimism will depend on the psychology of the decision maker, on his attitude towards risk. If $\alpha = 1$ we are back in the case of complete optimism of the maximax, while if $\alpha = 0$ we are in the case of complete pessimism, or the minimax. The Hurwicz criterion is designed to consider the best and worst payoffs of each strategy and force the decision maker to assign subjective probabilities to both. However, this criterion too neglects the intermediate, less extreme payoffs of the various strategies. In our example, assuming a coefficient of optimism $\alpha = 0.75$ and $(1 - \alpha) = 0.25$ we have the following outcomes:

Strategy A: $0.75 \times 500 + 0.25(-50) = 375 - 12.5 = 362.5$

Strategy B: $0.75 \times 300 + 0.25(0) = 225 + 0 = 225$

Strategy C: $0.75 \times 100 + 0.25 \times 50 = 75 + 12.5 = 87.5$

Hence, the Hurwicz criterion will select strategy A, i.e., the introduction of the revolutionary product. If, instead, we were to reverse the weights and set $\alpha = 0.25$ and $(1 - \alpha) = 0.75$, we derive the following:

Strategy A: $0.25 \times 500 + 0.75(-50) = 125 - 37.5 = 87.5$

Strategy B: $0.25 \times 300 + 0.75(0) = 75 + 0 = 75$

Strategy C: $0.25 \times 100 + 0.75 \times 50 = 25 + 37.5 = 62.5$

that is, again the criterion indicates strategy A. Clearly, in the case of a small firm adopting strategy A, it can be very serious, if it transpired that the market fell. And while medium- and large-sized firms may consider this approach as a 'one-off' case, since they may be able to absorb any losses from other more profitable operations, fully utilising this decision rule for all of their projects could well result in substantial losses for such medium and large firms, as to make it unwarranted.

12.3.4 The Savage criterion or minimax regret

The Savage criterion considers the opportunity cost of making incorrect decisions, which we come to regret. It is designed to protect the decision maker from making costly mistakes, when he has decided on a course of action (strategy) but a different state of nature (less favourable) has transpired. The Savage criterion tries to minimise the regret before actually selecting the strategy.

From the original matrix of payoffs, we compute a new matrix showing the regrets (costs of our mistakes). These regrets can be measured by the difference between the highest payoff the decision maker could have received, under each state of the market, and the payoffs he may actually receive under that state of the market and his different strategies. Thus, continuing our example, and starting with state of nature R, i.e., a rise in the market, the investor's regrets can be found as follows: Reading down the column R, we find that the highest payoff for that state of nature is 500. If the decision maker had chosen strategy A and R occurred, then he would experience no regret at all, since he would have received the highest value; thus we can assign a zero in the regret matrix in that position. But if he had chosen B and R occurred, he would experience regret given by 200 ($= 500 - 300$). Similarly, if he had chosen strategy C and R occurred, the cost of his mistake would be 400 ($= 500 - 100$). In similar manner we can compute the regrets for the other states of nature and strategies, by remembering that the highest payoff for a stable market (S) is 250 from which we need to subtract the elements of the second column, and for a falling market (F) the highest payoff is 50. Therefore, we can now tabulate our findings as in Table 12.5.

Savage suggests that the decision maker can guard against experiencing high regrets by selecting the strategy which minimises the maximum regrets, i.e., by selecting the strategy involving the minimax of the regret matrix. This is obtained by taking the row maxima of the regret matrix and selecting the minimum value of these maxima. In our case, this is clearly 150 and it corresponds to strategy A. Again, in our example this criterion too has tended towards optimism. Generally, depending on the figures of the payoff matrix, this decision criterion will tend to select either a strategy emphasising optimism or a strategy favouring pessimism.

Table 12.5   Regret matrix

Strategies	State of market			
	R	S	F	Row maxima
A	0	150	100	150
B	200	0	50	200
C	400	180	0	400
		Minimax		150

12.3.5   The Laplace or Bayes criterion

The Laplace or Bayes criterion has a much longer history than the other criteria and assumes that the various states of nature all have an equal probability of occurring. This criterion revolves around the principle of insufficient reason, i.e., if there is no reason for something to happen, it will not happen. When this principle of insufficient reason is used with probabilities, it is associated with Bayes. His hypothesis simply states that if we know of no reason for probabilities to be different, we should consider them to be equal. Therefore, in the absence of any other information, we assign equal probabilities to the various states of nature, estimate the expected outcome of each strategy and select the strategy with the highest expected outcome. Unlike all other criteria we have considered, the Bayes criterion takes into account all possible payoffs. In our example, by assigning equal probabilities of 1/3 to each of the three states of nature, we derive the following expected outcomes:

Strategy A: $1/3 \times 500 + 1/3 \times 100 + 1/3(-50) = 183.33$

Strategy B: $1/3 \times 300 + 1/3 \times 250 + 1/3(0) = 183.33$

Strategy C: $1/3 \times 100 + 1/3 \times 70 + 1/3 \times 50 = 73.36$

For the first time, strategy B comes also into the reckoning. Clearly, only one strategy will be selected but the Bayes criterion has the merit of highlighting the impact of the intermediate, less extreme payoffs of the various strategies. In this respect, the Bayes criterion has a lot to recommended it. However, this criterion suffers from the disadvantage that it is not clear what unknown possibilities are considered as equally probable. It may be possible to reclassify the various contingencies (states of nature) and thus change the probabilities, which in turn will affect the expected outcomes.

An alternative approach to the problem of risk and uncertainty is the use of the von Neumann and Morgenstern utility index and of mixed strategies. This may, indeed, provide a better yardstick for decision making than the maximin, and has also the merit that opponents cannot outguess the decision maker as to the mix of his strategies; thus some of the more lucrative payoffs are open for consideration. As this approach is fully explained in Chapter 10 on the section on Oligopolistic Interdependence, we do not pursue it here, but refer the reader to that discussion.

The foregoing analysis has illustrated that the various criteria can select different strategies, in fact all three have been selected, although strategy A has been preferred on most occasions. We are left with the awkward conclusion that no criterion can be considered as best or correct. All these criteria can do is to instil some consistency into decision making and make us think hard about the nature of our assumptions and premises for decision making. The decision maker will be guided by his firm's size, objectives and policies, his feelings or some other rational criterion. The Laplace or Bayes criterion is the only one which does not express any attitude other than the desire to be rational.

SUMMARY

This chapter has provided an introduction to the problems of risk and uncertainty and the decision rules that have been developed to cope with such problems. Thus, the concept of expected value, considered earlier in the book is also applicable in the present context. We have looked at how risk can be measured, at risk-earnings trade-offs and certainty equivalents, as well as decision trees. Subsequently, we have considered a number of criteria that have been proposed in the literature to dealing with risk, such as the Wald or maximin, the maximax, the Hurwich alpha, the Savage or minimax regret and the Laplace or Bayes criterion. In the appendix, we have provided a way of reducing uncertainty in financial markets.

PROBLEMS

1. A baker produces daily fresh cream cakes which he sells at a constant price of €50 per dozen. He has no fixed costs and the variable costs are €25 per dozen. However, any unsold cakes cannot be stored and have to be destroyed; thus the baker incurs a loss of €25 per dozen of unsold cakes. From past experience, he has determined the following probability distribution of the daily demand for his cakes:

Demand (in dozen)	Probability of occurrence
10	0.2
15	0.4
20	0.3
25	0.1

How many dozens of cakes does the baker produce daily to maximise his expected return? What is this return and how does it compare with alternative production plans?

2. A firm considers five alternative plant sizes for its operations, and the possibility of three different states of nature for the demand of its products, namely, a contracting, stable or expanding market. It has calculated the following matrix of payoffs, in euros, given in terms of net present values for its monthly sales:

Plant sizes	State of nature		
	Contracting	Stable	Expanding
A	−6 000	4 000	6 000
B	4 000	4 000	8 000
C	−2 000	5 000	14 000
D	2 000	6 000	12 000
E	4 000	6 000	6 000

What plant size would you choose on the basis of (a) maximin; (b) maximax; (c) Hurwicz (assuming a coefficient $\alpha = 0.6$); (d) minimax regret and (e) Laplace or Bayes criterion?

3. A cement company is considering expanding capacity and its engineers have produced four alternative plant sizes. However, the company is aware that the government is contemplating the introduction of strict regulations on pollution, and the cost of meeting such regulations depends on their severity, which is unknown at the moment. Nevertheless, three states of severity have been discussed, and the costs of meeting each of these for the alternative plant sizes have been estimated as in the following matrix of net present value payoffs, in euros.

Plant sizes	States of severity		
	Mild	Moderate	High
A	300 000	400 000	500 000
B	400 000	450 000	520 000
C	350 000	380 000	470 000
D	500 000	560 000	580 000

What plant size would you choose on the basis of (a) maximin; (b) maximax; (c) Hurwich (assuming a coefficient $\alpha = 0.7$); (d) minimax regret and (e) Laplace or Bayes criterion?

4. A firm is considering either buying an extra machine or placing its employees on overtime in order to meet the demand for its product. The management anticipates that in the next year there is a 2/3 chance that the demand will

increase and a 1/3 chance that it will drop. If demand increases, the firm expects that the net present values for the cash flows will be €700 000 in the case of the introduction of the new machine and €650 000 in the case of overtime. However, if there is a drop in demand, the anticipated net present values will be €400 000 for introducing the new machine and €560 000 for overtime. Set up a decision tree and advise the firm on the appropriate action.

APPENDIX: REDUCING FINANCIAL UNCERTAINTY THROUGH HEDGING (AN EXERCISE IN FUTURES CONTRACTS)

Hedging is a transaction aimed at reducing the risk of price fluctuations, and it is arranged by buying and selling a futures contract, which enables the participants to buy or sell a given quantity of a good at a fixed price. This contract represents a legal obligation of the parties to make the transaction at some time in the future at the agreed terms. Futures markets have existed for a long time for a number of agricultural products, various minerals and other commodities.

In the last 30 years or so, following the demise of the Bretton Woods Agreement on fixed exchange rates, the volatility of such rates, interest rates and asset prices has provided the opportunity to extend the futures contracts to the financial markets in order to reduce the risk of adverse movements of prices/interest rates. Starting with the Chicago Exchange in the 1970s, financial futures markets have been established in, practically, all parts of the developed world.

In the UK, futures contracts are arranged through the London International Financial Futures and Options Exchange (LIFFE). The financial instruments traded on LIFFE are 20-year gilt-edged stock, US Treasury bonds, the FT-SE 100 share index contracts, 3-month sterling deposits and 3-month Eurodollar deposits among others. The currency contracts are all expressed in US dollars.

Financial contracts are of standard size, for example, $1 million for a 3-month Eurodollar deposit, and transactions, therefore, are in multiples of $1 million. Also standardised are the maturity dates of such contracts, as the second Wednesdays of March, June, September and December. Such contracts enable firms and individuals to guarantee or 'lock in' a particular exchange rate or interest rate for a specific date. For example, if a firm intended depositing a sum of money in the Eurodollar market for a 3-month period but feared that interest rates might fall, it could offset this by buying financial futures contracts of an equivalent amount. In the event of a fall in interest rates, such contracts would guarantee that the interest rate on the deposit was close to the rate agreed in the financial futures contract. Contracts do not have to be held to maturity and holders can close a contract out by taking out an opposite contract. In our case this would mean that the firm would close out by selling futures contracts for the same amount and maturity date. Such opposing contracts cancel each other out and put an end to the firm's commitments in the futures market. Interest rate futures contracts are priced on an index basis. The index is equal to 100 less the annualised interest rate. Thus, if the annualised interest rate were 8%, the price would be $100 - 8 = 92$.

To illustrate the workings of a futures contract assume that a firm will require in mid-June $1 000 000 to meet certain obligations. Its treasurer arranges in March a loan with a bank. However, the firm fears that interest rates may rise above the current rate of 10% and to hedge against this possibility, it arranges to sell a June

3-month Eurodollar deposit futures contract at a price of 92, which implies an annualised interest rate of 8%. This ensures that if the interest rate did rise there will be a gain on futures trading. This gain is calculated by means of basis points or ticks. The tick is the smallest price movement accepted by LIFFE and, in terms of the index used in pricing futures, one tick is 0.01, or one per cent of one per cent. Each tick on Eurodollar futures has a value of $25 and if, for example, there were a change of 1% in interest rates this would be worth $25 \times 100 = $2500.

By mid-June the interest rate has risen to 12% and the firm's quarterly interest charge for its loan is calculated as $1\,000\,000 \times 0.12 \times 0.25 = $30\,000, which exceeds by $5000 what the firm expected to pay initially at a 10% interest rate, i.e., $1\,000\,000 \times 0.10 \times 0.25 = $25\,000. However, the increase in interest rates has also affected the 3-month Eurodollar futures rate which has risen to 10% per annum. As a result, the June futures price has fallen to $100 - 10 = 90$. This decline in futures prices means that the firm has gained $5000, i.e., $(92 - 90) \times 2500, as follows: Since the firm sold a futures contract for $1\,000\,000 in March, it can close out by buying a June Eurodollar contract at the new lower price of 90, thus gaining $5000. This gain leaves the firm paying a net interest charge of $25\,000, corresponding to an interest rate of 10%, as desired. In other words, the loss in the spot or cash market has been offset by the gain in the futures market.

In practice, this exact compensation between gains and losses may not be possible because of transaction costs, differences between the sizes of the standard futures contracts and the hedging required by firms and changes in the basis, i.e., the difference between the cash price of a financial instrument and the price of a particular futures contract relating to that investment. Whenever basis changes, the gain (or loss) from the futures market does not exactly match the loss (or gain) in the cash market. Nevertheless, the introduction of the futures and options has meant that firms can now reduce the risks associated with price changes in a variety of financial instruments, foreign trading and investments.

BIBLIOGRAPHY

Baumol, W.J. (1977), *Economic Theory and Operations Analysis*, 4th ed., Prentice-Hall.

Knight, F.H. (1921), *Risk, Uncertainty and Profit*, Houghton Miflin. Also reprinted by the London School of Economics, 1937.

Luce, R.D. and Raiffa, H. (1957), *Games and Decisions*, Wiley.

von Neumann, J. and Morgenstern, O. (1953), *The Theory of Games and Economic Behavior*, 3rd ed., John Wiley & Sons.

Redhead, K. and Hughes, S. (1988), *Financial Risk Management*, Gower.

Redhead, K. (1990), *Introduction to Financial Futures and Options*, Woodhead-Faulkner.

Seo, K.K. (1991), *Managerial Economics*, 7th ed., Irwin.

Shackle, G. (1952), *Expectations in Economics*, 2nd ed., Cambridge University Press.

Thierauf, R.J. and Grosse, R.A. (1970), *Decision Making through Operations Research*, Wiley.

Wagner, H.M. (1969), *Principles of Operations Research*, Prentice-Hall.

chapter thirteen

The Growth and Size of Firms and the Decision to become Multinational

Learning outcomes

After studying this chapter you should know about:

- Internal and external growth

- Horizontal and vertical integration

- Diversification/conglomeration

- Acquisitions and mergers

- The need to become multinational

- Modes of entry (joint ventures, greenfield investment, cross-border M&As)

- Alternative forms of internationalisation of business (licensing, franchising, strategic alliances, turnkey projects)

- Foreign direct investment (FDI)
  - The market power paradigm
  - The internalisation approach
  - Dunning's eclectic theory

13.1 INTRODUCTION

We have already touched upon the process of dynamic change and expansion of the firm in Chapter 3 under the theories of growth and also in Chapter 11 under the related issue of capital budgeting. Structural changes in many industries often force firms to adjust and adapt to new circumstances, for failure to do so may mean for some firms stagnation, decline and even extinction. Downie, who together with Penrose and Marris have been responsible for developing the theories of growth, has put it as follows: 'The most fundamental characteristic of a capitalist economy is growth and change ...(growth) is characterised by a restless urge to do better, to change the conditions lest, through inactivity, they are changed against you' (Downie 1958, p. 29). Accordingly, growth becomes a necessary condition for the survival of the firm over time. Our purpose in this chapter is to consider the sort of questions the process of growth raises for management, while in the following chapter we look at the corresponding problems for society.

Firms can change by growing within their existing industries, by extending their activities to different stages of their production process either towards the final consumer and/or towards their sources of raw materials, and by expanding their operations into other industries and fields. Two types of expansion are usually considered: internal or external. In the former case, the firm expands organically by engaging in investment that widens and deepens the range of its activities, a process that, necessarily, takes time. In the latter case, a firm can grow much faster simply by merging with or taking over other firms. The directions growth can take, i.e., horizontal integration, vertical integration and diversification are similar in nature, whether the firm expands internally or externally and, therefore, no separate analysis is necessary. However, the two types of growth have different implications on competition and create distinct public policy issues; thus, the question of external growth is the subject of separate treatment. Horizontal integration is the straightforward case of a firm expanding its activities either on its own or in combination with other similar firms, but remaining in the same stage of production and producing more of the same product or products. Consequently, it does not present any specific questions requiring special treatment.

13.2 VERTICAL INTEGRATION

One form of expansion is provided by vertical integration. This occurs when a firm decides to undertake successive stages in the productive process of a particular product. A firm may integrate backwards to produce intermediate products, or control raw materials it originally purchased from other suppliers. It can also integrate forwards, by extending the range of its operations towards the final consumer.

The major motives for vertical integration are provided by the firm's search for higher efficiency, in the form of cost minimisation; its need for security; and its desire for market power and the reduction of uncertainty through the restriction of competition. However, the degree of vertical integration will vary from one firm to another depending on the managerial ability and talent available and the firm's attitude to growth.

The theoretical justification for vertical integration, as a way towards cost minimisation, is provided by the original argument of Coase (1937) for establishing a firm, since '... the operation of a market costs something and by forming an organisation (a firm) ... certain marketing costs are saved'. As we saw in Chapter 3, these are transaction, contracting and coordinating costs of using the market, which can be avoided by vertical integration within the firm. Coase considers four main types of costs: the cost of discovering the correct price; the cost of arranging the contractual obligations of the parties in an exchange transaction; the risk of scheduling of goods or inputs and the taxes paid on exchange transactions. The entrepreneur sidesteps these costs by using administrative or internal prices, and controls the production and marketing of an intermediate product through vertically integrated operations.

When the various activities related to the production of a product are undertaken by a single firm, not only can such a firm economise on transaction costs, according to the Coasian argument by cutting out the 'middleman', it can also organise its production processes in a continuous manner to save other significant costs. This, for example, occurs in the production of steel, when the whole process is integrated from blast furnaces to rolling mills and the firm can save on costs of reheating. For many years, British Steel, now Corus, had suffered a cost disadvantage, as compared with other major international competitors, from the lack of properly integrated production processes, since the various activities of the production of steel were undertaken by various different, often small uncompetitive units, and despite nationalisation the same set-up had been allowed to continue. That meant excessive costs, before the restructuring effort of the early 1980s, prior to its privatisation, described in the Appendix to Chapter 7, brought such costs down.

Also, vertical integration and internalisation can help bring down costs associated with monitoring quality of supplies. Where exact specifications have to be met, quality control is best achieved under vertically integrated operations rather than relying upon outside sources. In addition, the firm can avoid uncertainty, caused by possible opportunistic behaviour of suppliers, who may wish to exploit particular market advantages, for example, a monopoly position on components.

The point just touched raises also the aspect of security. If the firm wishes to limit or sever its dependence on unreliable or dominant suppliers, it may decide to integrate backwards and produce intermediate products itself. However, such a decision, depending on the circumstances, may mean that the firm could be incurring some increased costs. For example, because of large technical economies of scale in the production of various intermediate products, such as components, a firm engaged in a forward stage of production that decided to integrate backwards, may be producing these components, for reasons of demand conditions for the final product, at sub-optimal plants. Whether the firm decided to accept the higher costs that go with the increased security of vertical backward integration, or carry on with its reliance on currently cheaper outside supplies but live with the danger of possible exploitation and, generally, opportunistic behaviour on behalf of its suppliers, is a question that management has to answer, as analysed in Chapter 3. The point that the present discussion tries to make is that, on occasions, vertical integration may very well result in higher costs, although the costs of uncertainty and insecurity could outweigh such considerations.

This discussion is connected with the concentration or competitiveness of the market for intermediate products. The underlying assumption of the earlier analysis has been that the market is dominated by a few large producers. If this is not the case and the market is reasonably competitive, much of the urge for vertical integration may not be present. Also, the same may be said about forward integration. In addition, it seems that the phase of the trade cycle does affect the direction of integration. Firms try to integrate backwards in periods of buoyant demand in order to secure uninterrupted supplies, and, thus, exploit the favourable demand conditions; on the other hand, in periods of low demand, the tendency is for the firm to integrate forwards, towards the final consumer.

13.3 DIVERSIFICATION/CONGLOMERATION

The theories of growth of the firm, as explained in Chapter 3, consider the firm as a multi-product organisation, capable of entering any area of economic activity. Penrose finds diversification to be the normal way firms choose to expand. Accordingly, diversification occurs

> ... whenever, without entirely abandoning its old lines of product, (the firm) embarks upon the production of new products, including intermediate products, which are sufficiently different from the other products it produces to imply some significant difference in the firm's production or distribution programmes. Diversification thus includes increases in the variety of final products produced, increases in vertical integration, and increases in the number of 'basic areas' of production in which a firm operates. (Penrose 1959, pp. 108–109)

Penrose emphasises the areas of specialisation of the firms and distinguishes them in terms of technological or production bases and market areas, and she argues that when opportunities occur for diversification, such opportunities will be related to those technological bases and market areas. Therefore, diversification may involve new products in any of the following combinations: same technological base and market area; same technological base and new market area; new technological base and same market area and new technological base and market area.

The main motives for diversification are provided by the firm's search for: (1) security; (2) profitability and (3) growth. In so far as security is concerned, diversification allows the firm to mitigate the risks and uncertainties associated with single product production. Changes in demand conditions, caused by changes in consumer tastes or by cyclical instability, can affect a single product firm much more drastically, than a diversified firm. The latter, by producing different products that may be at different stages of their life cycle, is able to 'hedge' against such risky changes. Essentially, this is a demonstration of the old adage of not keeping all of one's eggs in one basket.

Regarding the profitability motive, the main argument is that a firm diversifies in order to earn profits higher than it currently earns in its existing industry. Diversification presupposes some spare capacity of resources and/or services, that can be profitably directed towards activities in other industries. This is best achieved where there are already certain linkages between the existing and new activities, arising from similarities on the supply and demand. It is these similarities of the production processes and markets on the one hand, and the technological and managerial skills needed in the existing and new industries on the other, which provide the firm with the competitive advantages and allow it to earn higher profits through diversification.

Finally, the desire for growth provides the firm with an additional motive for diversification. If a firm wants to grow faster than the rate of growth of its existing industry, it will have to seek other activities in other industries to do so. This argument is quite general and encompasses both the case of declining existing industries, and also the case where the firm believes that its bundle of resources (managerial and technological) are capable of earning higher rates of return than are currently possible in its existing industry. Growth by diversification may also be strengthened by the antimonopoly policy, which, typically, operates against horizontal expansion but is less restrictive towards diversification, as is discussed in the following chapter.

Therefore, the desire for growth as well as the existence of spare capacity and competitive advantages provide powerful stimuli for diversification. In this respect, the role of R&D becomes crucial in the argument, since the technological advantages derived from the firm's R&D effort provide it with its new ideas and products. From the managerial point of view, two relationships involving diversification are worth examining further. The one is between diversification and competition; the other between diversification and the firm's R&D activities.

As regards the first relationship, it appears that competition encourages diversification and sets a limit to it. At the same time, since the relationship can best be seen in a simultaneous equations context, diversification may increase competition or reduce it. Where advertising and selling effort form an important aspect of competition, diversification will be encouraged because of the market advantages the firm has in producing and marketing a range of products. However, competition also serves to limit expansion by diversification. The competitive constraint is stronger where economies of scale and a rapid rate of technical progress are required in an existing area of production. If diversification necessitates the setting up of a new plant or establishment, this implies an increase in capacity and competition. Even in the case of acquisition of an existing firm, competition may be encouraged if the new management is more dynamic than the former one, puts the existing resources to better and more profitable uses, and plans future expansion at a greater rate, despite the fact that there is no increase in capacity. However, diversification can also increase market power – and usually does – and create barriers to entry, thus, limiting competition.

Regarding the relationship between R&D and diversification, Penrose observes that industrial innovation affects the quality of existing resources that determine, in turn, the internal opportunities for growth. Commenting on the firm's innovation policy, Penrose argues that

> . . . Even if the primary purpose is to develop ways of reducing the costs and improving the quality of existing products, the exploration and research involved will certainly speed up the production of new knowledge and the creation of new productive services within the firm. The new knowledge and services . . . may . . . still provide a foundation which will give the firm an advantage in some entirely new area. A firm's opportunities are necessarily widened when it develops a specialised knowledge of a technology which is not in itself very specific to any particular kind of product, for example, knowledge of different types of engineering or industrial chemistry. (Penrose 1959, pp. 114–115)

We have already commented upon the significance of R&D effort on the firm's operations elsewhere in this book so we need not repeat it here, but we need to discuss a little further the relationship between innovation and size. Research and development is an expensive process and hence larger firms are in a better position to finance such operations. Also, firms in oligopolistic and, generally, concentrated industries are more likely to undertake R&D, since in such industries R&D is used as a competitive weapon having replaced price competition. The theoretical justification of this is provided by the Schumpeterian thesis that a degree of monopoly power is required to produce technical change on which economic progress depends, and its echo in the Galbraithian statement that

> ... a benign Providence ... has made the modern industry of a few large firms an excellent instrument for inducing technical change and that technical development has long since become the preserve of the scientist and the engineer. Most of the cheap and simple inventions ... have been made ... Because development is costly, it follows that it can be carried on only by a firm that has the resources which are associated with considerable size. (Galbraith 1963, pp. 100–101)

However, this does not necessarily mean that the higher the size of the firm the greater the number of inventions. On the contrary, it has been established through a number of studies that among firms engaged in R&D, smaller firms tend to have a disproportionate higher percentage of inventions to their size, which could be turned into innovations; thus, pointing to higher efficiency of their R&D expenditure, as compared to that of larger firms. There is also evidence that a significant number of inventions in the first part of the twentieth century originated with small firms. Nevertheless, whilst it could be argued that major inventions have not been the product of the R&D effort of large oligopolistic firms, it is the case that the latter are often responsible for turning such inventions, through subsequent development, into successful innovations. This discussion has implications about antimonopoly policy, which is discussed below.

Having established the relationship between innovation and size, it is not surprising to find that successful innovations will be accompanied by higher profits for the innovating firm. Under competitive conditions, on the other hand, such rewards, assuming they were possible, may have to be shared out and this provides a disincentive for R&D spending in competitive industries. Other factors affecting R&D are the type of product; the size of the market, because the larger the market, the greater the benefits from successful innovation; the rate of growth of the market, since R&D is more common in rapidly expanding industries and, finally, oligopolistic rivalry. Where there are important economies of scale in research, it may seem that duplicated research can be wasteful. Nevertheless, different firms may have different ways of tackling problems that may result in a wider field of research and greater flexibility; application of R&D to industrial production will be quicker, the higher the oligopolistic rivalry, and even when a firm takes a lead with a new development, another firm may follow with a different one.

13.4   EXTERNAL GROWTH: ACQUISITIONS AND MERGERS

External expansion through acquisition and merger allows firms to grow much faster than internal expansion and it has, increasingly, become the preferred way of management to growth. It has been estimated that this form of corporate expansion accounts for a considerable increase in concentration in the UK manufacturing sector over time, varying from about 50% in the inter-war period to almost 100% in more recent periods. In the last 35 years we have witnessed major waves of merger activity in 1967–73 and 1984–90 when, on the average, annual spending on mergers as a percentage of gross domestic capital formation exceeded 40%.

By acquisition we mean the taking over or buying of one company by another; by merger the fusion of two or more companies into one. In either case the result is the same: a firm can acquire the plant, the products and markets of an already existing firm, rather than build new plant and expand existing or create new markets, as under internal growth. For this reason we do not differentiate between acquisition and merger, since the analysis is essentially the same. Following the earlier discussion we can distinguish horizontal mergers, where the firms involved are engaged in the same stage of production; vertical mergers, either backward or forward, where the firms involved operate at different stages of production and diversifying or conglomerate mergers, where the companies involved are in unrelated productive activities. Finally, reverse mergers or takeovers, though rarer, occur when the smaller of the two firms makes a successful bid for the larger. An example of a successful reverse merger in the British banking industry has been the taking over of the National Westminster Bank by the smaller Royal Bank of Scotland in the late 1990s. The empirical evidence regarding mergers in the UK, as recorded in the works by Singh (1971), Utton (1979), Newbould (1970), Kuehn (1975), as well as the Mergers Panel of the Monopolies and Mergers Commission, shows that horizontal mergers have predominated, accounting for almost three-quarters of all mergers in the post-war period, but with diversifying or conglomerate mergers increasing in importance in recent years. By contrast, in the US, the emphasis has been on conglomerate mergers, possibly as a result of antimonopoly legislation which, based on a *per se* approach, tends to condemn monopoly, whereas the pragmatic British and European approaches, of which more later, tend to tolerate it, but outlaw its abuse.

Given the choice between internal and external expansion, a firm will choose to expand by acquisition only if the latter is considered to be cheaper than internal expansion. If, however, the firm wishes to acquire monopoly position or control over existing assets, such as patents, trade marks, monopolised supplies of raw materials, retail outlets and the like, acquisition may be the only way of achieving these goals (Penrose 1959, pp. 156–157). For an acquisition or merger to take place, firms must be prepared to sell their assets, including their 'good-will', at a price equal to or lower than their value to the buyer. This implies that there must be a divergence in the valuation of the acquired firm placed by the buyer and seller. In this connection, the discussion of Chapter 3 on the theory of valuation, developed by Marris, is very pertinent. If, for any reason, there is an under-valuation of a firm's shares below their book value, and indeed below the replacement values of the firm's assets, this is likely to attract predators, since the firm is ripe for a takeover and even asset stripping. In addition, there are also other reasons causing divergence between the valuation placed by sellers and buyers. There are always personal characteristics and special circumstances of owners, particularly, of small firms who want to sell out. These may have to do with different perceptions about risk regarding the present value of the future stream of income; special pressures on the owner to sell of one kind or another; differential tax treatment of capital gains than income; managerial constraint on small firms, which means that, after a particular size has been reached, a crucial decision must be taken on whether the whole managerial and organisational structure of the firm must change to accommodate further growth, or simply for the owner-entrepreneur to sell out. However, such special considerations and circumstances, which may be present in most mergers and takeovers of small and medium firms, do not provide us with any general relationship between acquired and acquiring firms. In fact, no general theory of acquisitions and mergers has been put forward. Rather, what we have is a number of motives which have been proposed as partial explanations to this activity and, which, we discuss, briefly, as follows.

It has been argued that, because of synergy, the profits of the merged firm could be higher than the sum of the profits of the two separate firms, since the merger is expected to lead to increased market power, cost savings resulting from plant and firm economies and/or the exploitation of complementarities existing between the merged firms. A merger could provide greater competitiveness in export markets, and indeed this was one of the major arguments justifying the setting up by the British Government of the Industrial Re-organisation Corporation, a sort of marriage broker, in the 1960s to promote mergers in British industry. Also, as we saw earlier, a vertical merger safeguards essential raw material supplies and or retail outlets, while a diversifying merger allows a firm to make a quick entry into a different field of economic activity. Some of these explanations are of course explanations of growth as such, rather than expanding, specifically, by means of acquisition and merger.

Both horizontal and vertical mergers could increase market power over consumers and suppliers and reap economies of scale; however, the evidence regarding monopoly power and economies of scale is inconclusive and as far as post-merger profitability and efficiency are concerned rather disappointing (Meeks 1977, Cowling et al. 1980). The explanation for this development may be found in a combination of influences. First, the increased market power may lull management into a false sense of security and make it complacent, as a result of which X-inefficiency develops. Second, unless there is some restructuring in the merged firms, so that productive activity is concentrated in efficient plants and sub-optimal ones are closed down, plant economies and, thus, cost savings are unlikely to result. Examples of the former, in the context of British industry, had included the successful merger of the GEC in the 1960s that, following the necessary restructuring, resulted in a very profitable company, which remained at the forefront of its industry for decades. However, a change in management brought about a change in both its name (to Marconi) and direction of its activities, and also in the late 1990s its demise, as a result of a disastrous acquisition of an American telecommunications company. Examples of the former included the setting up of British Leyland (BL) again in the 1960s, through the merging of various British car manufacturers, to provide an effective rival to the large American car manufacturers Ford and General Motors, operating in Britain, and the European ones. The absence of any restructuring and bad industrial relations meant that the merger failed to achieve its aims. The company, having received substantial assistance from the state in the 1970s, was brought under public ownership, was downsized and part of it, eventually, was passed under a new name (Rover) into private hands. The GEC was an example of a successful merger, whilst the BL a lesson of how not to undertake a merger.

Gort (1969) has rejected the monopoly power and economies of scale explanation of mergers and has developed further the original Penrosian theme of divergences in the valuation of firms. He argued that the reason why non-owners are valuing the firm higher than owners is to be found in the different expectations about the future income stream generated by the firm's assets and the different perception of risks associated with the future stream of income. The divergences in valuation, in turn, are due to various economic disturbances, such as technical change, high levels of security prices and industry growth. Newbould (1970) has considered changes in the nature of the environment of the firm as a determining factor of mergers. Such changes, which may involve, among others, mergers between competitors of the firm, result in increased uncertainty for the firm and force its management to react defensively to reduce such uncertainty by undertaking merger activity themselves. This is an oligopolistic reaction hypothesis implying that uncertainty feeds on uncertainty, since the higher the uncertainty the greater the pressure to mergers, and the larger the number of actual mergers, the higher the uncertainty. However, there is also a self-correcting mechanism, since the higher the uncertainty, the more hesitant the management may become in getting involved in a merger.

Other authors too have considered the role of changes in the environment of the firm and argued that mergers take place when there are disturbances in that environment. Aaronovitch and Sawyer (1975) emphasise the costs of oligopolistic rivalry as the crucial factor to understand merger activity. The 'costs of rivalry' are R&D expenditure, marketing, promotion and costs connected with excess capacity. In the context of increased uncertainty, such rivalry costs tend to increase and the firms react by trying to reduce them. Depending on the nature of the market, the attempt to reduce such costs may take the form of price agreements and cartels in periods of depression and stagnation, but in periods of growth, the attempt may very well be merger.

Finally, another explanation of acquisitions and mergers is provided by the existence of a market for corporate control. This contends that rival management teams are vying with each other for the right to manage assets efficiently and if, for whatever reason, a firm fails to achieve satisfactory profits for its shareholders and maintain its share price, there is a danger of a takeover bid. This threat acts in most cases as a catalyst for improved performance, otherwise, the firm is taken over by another management, who can ensure a more efficient utilisation of its assets; therefore, the market for corporate control, so the argument goes, is the best guarantor that resources are used efficiently.

To the extent that the market for corporate control forces management to cut down on discretionary expenditure of any kind, it is said to be beneficial to shareholders. However, for the market for corporate control to operate properly, it requires an efficient stock market that, systematically and continuously, discounts and evaluates the expected future streams of income potential of the various companies, and reflects this evaluation in their share prices. Given that in the life of any firm dynamic changes can cause temporary short-term deviations of share prices from their long-term income potential, this can put the firm under threat of a takeover. This means that the market for corporate control, with its emphasis on current profits for the shareholders, encourages short-termism at the expense of necessary long-term investment in rationalisation, modernisation of plant and equipment and R&D. Nevertheless, to the extent that a firm is even temporarily undervalued, its chances of becoming the target of a hostile takeover bid are increased.

Finally, in a note of caution we should mention that while some dangers of mergers and acquisitions (M&A.), for example, those connected with reduction in competition and possibly social costs that do not show up in the balance sheet, are dealt with by public policy, there may be others, such as diseconomies of management scale, i.e., top management may become less efficient after the merger. The reason is that mergers, particularly clumsy and hasty ones, tend to destroy focus and motivation, and after a while they lead to strong pressures to demerge. Also, even where the growth in size is organic, it may still raise similar pressures, if such growth leads away from the core activities of the firm, because of the loss of focus. Thus, in the 1990s, in Britain there have been many cases of demergers, such as the ICI demerger of its bioscience business to create Zeneca Group, and the demergers of the various privatised utilities, for example the telecoms giant BT demerged its mobile phone unit BT Cellnet to establish mmO_2, and others that only serve to highlight this potential danger of size.

More importantly, in the same context, a recent survey by the accounting firm Deloitte & Touche has found that corporate demergers create significant value for shareholders for both the parent company and the demerged, within a year of the demerger. The survey looked at the analysis of the 118 biggest demergers worldwide between 1990 and 1999. Its main finding was that while demerger announcements were followed, initially, by up to 10% drops in the share price, there was a dramatic change within a year of the demerger. Accordingly, the share price of most parent companies increased from 12% to more than 52%, while the share price of the demerged units (companies) increased by between 13% and 46%. The initial drop is explained by investor fears of the loss of scale economies, but in reality these fears for both separating entities are far outweighed by the clarity of purpose entailed by the demerger. Thus, the managerial teams are able to focus on the core business, decision making becomes easier, and motivation rises with greater sense of ownership of the smaller business and clearer and shared sense of direction. The opposite was found to be true of mergers, with acquiring firms that are greeted with share price rises of 3% or more following the merger announcement failing to increase value in year one, while those greeted with a share price drop under-performing even further, because of the habit of destroying focus and motivation (*The Independent*, 22 July 2002).

13.5 WHY FIRMS BECOME MULTINATIONAL

So far the analysis has been conducted in terms of the national firm, i.e., one that conducts most of its operations in the country of its registration or domicile. National firms can still undertake certain activities involving international transactions such as, for example, exporting, licensing and the like without becoming multinational. The earlier analysis in terms of price discrimination, under monopoly, can easily be applied in the case of a foreign market, and indeed, we suggested so at the time. However, in the present context of expansion, any national firm may find in its life the need to expand its operations abroad by becoming multinational. A multinational enterprise (MNE) is simply defined as one that owns and manages productive facilities (such as plants) located in at least two countries (Caves 1996, p. 1).

13.5.1 Entry modes

An important question faced by firms wishing to expand abroad is the choice of entry mode, once they have decided which markets to enter. The basic modes by which firms can enter foreign markets are: (1) exporting; (2) turnkey projects; (3) licensing; (4) franchising; (5) strategic alliances; (6) joint ventures and (7) wholly owned subsidiaries. The last two modes are, potentially, more important as they refer to FDI. Strategic alliances and cross-border M&As represent new patterns of industrial globalisation, as compared with the traditional greenfield investments of FDI. However, each of these modes has associated advantages and disadvantages, implying that firms face various trade-offs, and we now turn to consider these modes of entry briefly.

Exporting can be the first stage of a domestic firm expanding internationally. It has the advantage of testing the host market, learning about the elasticities of demand and, generally, deriving valuable information about the specific market, before investing in expensive plant in the host country, while producing in a central manufacturing plant that realises economies of scale and serves several export markets simultaneously. The disadvantages include the failure of the firm to exploit lower-cost locations for producing abroad, if such locations exist. Where they do, and the mix of locational factors allows the firm to produce at lower unit costs, this location can become the preferred production point not only to serve host country's needs, but also those of the rest of the world, including the firm's home country. For example, in recent years many European and American firms have switched production to the Far East, mainly China, and use such plants to meet world needs. This, then is an argument not against exporting as such, but against exporting from the firm's home country. Other disadvantages of exporting include transport costs, particularly for bulky products, and tariff barriers by importing countries. While such barriers have decreased significantly, both as a result of bilateral and also multilateral agreements, chiefly through the work of World Trade Organisation (WTO) and its predecessor GATT, they are still important for certain products and markets and they may be forcing producers to consider setting up plants in host countries to overcome them. For example, Japanese car manufacturers have set up production units in various countries of the European Union to supply the whole of the union with cars produced locally, thus, avoiding tariffs and other non-tariff barriers. They have done likewise in the US too. Also, exporting firms may be facing marketing problems in export markets, where they have delegated authority to local agents, because of reasons of divided loyalties or expertise. Again the solution may be to set up a wholly owned subsidiary in the export market to handle marketing, provided it is justified by market size considerations.

Turnkey projects refer to the design, construction, training of personnel and start-up of particular plants involving the export of process technology in, for example, the chemical, oil refining, telecommunications or metal refining industries, by a contractor firm for a foreign client for a fee. Upon completion of the project, the contractor hands in the 'key' to a plant that is ready for operation – hence the name turnkey projects. Often the turnkey strategy provides firms possessing process technology and know-how with the only means of earning significant rents from that technology, when FDI into foreign markets may be restricted. This is the case, for example, in the oil extraction and refining industry, where host governments are keen to develop their own oil industry and are prepared to pay for the necessary technology and know-how, while at the same time keeping foreign investors out. This points also to the potential disadvantages of this method, since firms possessing the process technology may be afraid that the product of that turnkey project may develop into a lucrative market in the future from which the firm is excluded. The answer may very well involve some minority holding in the operation. Whether this can be achieved is a matter of hard bargaining between the host government and the small number of competitor firms having the required know-how and process technology and being prepared to provide it. Also, the same consideration may temper the eagerness of firms to provide their know-how and technology for fear of creating a powerful future competitor. In particular, if this know-how and technology is the source of competitive advantage to the firm, by selling it through a turnkey project, the firm is also selling such competitive advantage to potential competitors.

Licensing refers to various agreements between two parties, the licensor and the licensee, specifying the terms under which the former allows the latter to use certain intangible property rights belonging to the licensor. The terms will usually include the period for which such right is granted, confidentiality clauses and the royalty fees that must be paid to the licensor. Examples of such property rights include patents, trademarks, copyrights, blueprints, processes and formulas. Licensing represents a form of technology transfer, but certain obstacles connected chiefly with the need of the owner of the technology to maintain control over business secrets, patents and trademark rights, mean that its use may be somewhat limited. Reasons for which a firm may wish to license its intangible property rights abroad include both external factors (e.g., prohibition of FDI by host governments) and internal factors (e.g., unwillingness to invest directly abroad, shortage of sufficient resources and desire to receive a return on a sunk cost asset, technology or product approaching obsolescence). The above discussion also illustrates some of the disadvantages of licensing. The major one is the risk that by licensing intangible property rights, which could represent the competitive advantage of the firm, the latter runs the danger of losing control of such property rights to a potential foreign competitor. This happened, for example, in the case of the American RCA Corporation that had licensed its technology on colour TV to Japanese firms, only for the latter to absorb and improve it and use it to penetrate the American market (Hill 2001, p. 437). Also, licensing does not allow the licensor firm the ability to realise experience curve and location economies in the host economy, since the licensor has no tight control over manufacturing, marketing and overall strategy.

Experience curve economies are defined as production cost reductions over the lifetime of the product's life, while location economies are those obtained by performing an economic activity in the optimal location, in terms of inputs mix. These are powerful reasons for not undertaking licensing lightly, but preferring instead to engage in FDI. However, if FDI cannot take place, the transfer of technology can be accomplished through a technical assistance agreement and it can also include trademark rights and even the commitment by the seller of technology (typically a large corporation) to purchase part of the product of the recipient firm. These had been among the vehicles adopted for the transfer of Western technology to the countries of Eastern Europe in the 1960s and 1970s.

Franchising is a special form of licensing, where the firm granting the franchise (normally the use of a trademark) insists on and helps the franchisee firm to adhere to specific rules of running the business, so as to ensure as far as possible similarity of the product/service offered across borders. Again the franchiser receives royalty payments for allowing their intangible property right to be used by others, but the firm also takes a keen interest in the way the business is run by offering training of local personnel and management and, possibly, financial assistance. For example, McDonald's have grown by using franchising as the method to penetrate foreign markets. The idea is that no matter where the franchisee is located in the world, customers should receive, as far as possible, the same product/service. The advantages of franchising are similar to those of licensing, i.e., the franchiser avoids the risks and costs of opening its own subsidiaries in foreign markets, which are passed on to the local franchisee. The main disadvantage of franchising is maintaining the quality control necessary to attract customers in various parts of the world, who are accustomed to specific standards as those of the parent firm having the original trademark, otherwise quality will be compromised, which, ultimately, may have repercussions on the franchiser.

Strategic alliances is another mode of industrial globalisation and can take various forms, ranging from arm's length contract to joint venture, discussed below. The essence of a strategic alliance is the cooperation of the participating firms that enhances the effectiveness of their competitive strategies. This is achieved through the trading of mutually beneficial resources, including technologies, skills and the like. Yoshino (1995) suggests that strategic alliances have the following characteristics:

1. The firms entering a strategic alliance to pursue a set of agreed goals retain their independence following the formation of the alliance.

2. The firms entering a strategic alliance share its benefits and control of the performance of assigned tasks.

3. The firms entering a strategic alliance contribute on a continuing basis in one or more key strategic areas, for example, technology, products, and the like.

Strategic alliances take a wide range of inter-firm linkages, including joint R&D, joint manufacturing, joint marketing, minority equity holdings, equity swaps, shared distribution/services, long-term sourcing contracts, standard setting and joint ventures. The main advantage of strategic alliances is their flexibility, allowing partner firms to respond to changing market conditions effectively, without changes in the ownership structure of the participating firms. However, the disadvantages are the much higher transaction costs over other modes of foreign cooperation/entry.

13.5.2 Establishing an international joint venture – motives

From the point of view of the decision to invest abroad, however, only the last two modes of entry are relevant, namely entry by an international joint venture (IJV), or by a wholly owned subsidiary (WOS). In particular, the pressure to establish a joint venture, whilst not a new phenomenon, assumed significance in FDI in the late 1970s and 1980s. Essentially, a joint venture means establishing a company that is jointly owned by two or more independent companies. IJVs link companies across frontiers, bring together large and small firms and span most industrial and commercial sectors. They help in bridging the gap between technologically mature organisations and those with lower technological competencies; between firms possessing financial power, entrepreneurship, marketing resources and the innovators, on the one hand, and those firms requiring inputs to rationalise and bring order to their markets, on the other. An early commentator described joint ventures as 'symbiotic marketing' (Adler, 1966), drawing attention to the fact that such a venture aims at the harmonious co-habitation of different firms and the marketing idea; it focuses on the deliberate alliance of resources between two independent companies in order to improve their market growth potential by creating a third entity – the joint venture, which acquires its own momentum and which puts 'the multiplier into individual companies' (Adler 1966).

Generally, an IJV is a means by which different enterprises in different countries collaborate both as producers or as transactors. The reason is that a degree of cooperation is likely to prove beneficial to the two parties, since an IJV tries to exploit the various *complementarities* arising from the *comparative strengths* of the separate firms that have formed it. Other important attractions include the *clarity of purpose* that is a precondition for its existence, and also the *inherent flexibility*. The latter aspect includes, among others, cases where the equity share in the IJV varies from 5% to 95% for either participating firm; IJVs where a foreign firm improves a local company that retains its own indigenous management and identity; or IJVs where the local ownership may be widely distributed and/or have little direct say in the management process. Turning now to consider the various motives for establishing an IJV, it is useful to examine them under the classification suggested by the literature: (1) financial; (2) strategic and (3) country-specific motives.

13.5.2a *Financial motives to joint venture formation*

In considering the financial motives, the starting point is that in investment theory we have a trade-off between risk and return. Thus, the financial advantages from joint venture formation can be linked to the portfolio theory. According to the latter, a number of assets is held in such a way that risk and return from these assets is balanced. Similarly, when a firm decides to form a joint venture, it has to commit a certain level of financial capital. However, this capital is smaller as compared to the one that would be required for setting up a WOS. Consequently, the firm has the ability to invest in other activities as well, and, thus, it can create a diversified portfolio to maximise its return (Contractor and Lorange, 1988). Further, the same authors suggest that '... ventures can reduce partner's risk by ... enabling faster entry and ... a quicker payback'.

13.5.2b *Strategic motives to joint venture formation*

It was suggested earlier that one of the major aspects of joint ventures concerns the question of complementarity. The local partner may be able to contribute inputs in the form, for example, of raw materials, or cheaper labour, or a distribution network that can complement the other inputs offered by the foreign partner, such as technology, capital, organisational methods, marketing and so on. Thus,

Contractor and Lorange (1988) remark that '... joint ventures ... can also be in a form of vertical quasi integration, with each partner contributing one or more different elements in the production and distribution chains. The inputs of the partners are, in this case, complementary'. In addition, certain resources, such as technology and distribution networks, are not always available through the market and may only be acquired through a joint venture (Gullander 1976). Exploring this issue further, it could be argued that this may have strategic implications since it could represent a barrier to entry. A barrier can be created by the new entrant's need to secure distribution for his product. Since the logical distribution channels for the product have already been served by established firms, the new firm must persuade the channels to accept the product, through perhaps lower price, which tends to reduce profits. It follows that the more limited the wholesale and retail channels for a product are, the more difficult entry into the industry becomes (Porter 1980).

Turning to another strategic motive, as a source of cost minimisation, it is observed that '... in many industries advantages connected with the size of operations exist... Economies of scale pertain not only to manufacturing but to some other functions as well, notably R&D and sales. A joint venture ... allows a company to benefit from these economies in a way not possible if it remained completely independent' (Gullander 1976). Similarly, other researchers in the field suggest that ' ... joint ventures ... can achieve ... economies of scale and/or rationalisation' (Contractor and Lorange 1988). Thus, the exploitation of economies of scale and/or scope has been found to be a major motive of American, European and Japanese firms in their attempts to collaborate and establish joint ventures. Also, reminiscent of Knickerbocker's (1973) oligopolistic reaction thesis, the hypothesis has been put forward that IJV occur as a strategic reaction by simply following a domestic rival in a foreign market, by mimicking the latter's earlier entry into that market by an IJV.

More importantly, another set of strategic motives for the formation of IJVs has to do with risk reduction in a potentially unstable environment. Thus, Gullander (1976) remarks that '... nationalistic feelings have led many countries to ... impose formal or informal restrictions on foreigners ... To deal with such restrictions firms may enter a joint venture with a local company'. In the same context, Contractor and Lorange (1988) point out that ' ... another dimension of risk reduction has to do with containing some of the political risk by linking up with a local partner. Such a partner may have sufficient political clout to steer the joint venture clear of local government action or interference. It may also be that the joint venture has come about as a result of the host government's policy. In such a case added political risk reduction can be achieved; the government endorses the joint venture as being beneficial to its economic policy agenda'. Of course, knowledge of the local market, society, customs and the like has long been recognised as a very useful tool for a firm operating in a foreign market. Under these circumstances, a local partner may add to profitability through his 'know-how'. Thus, Beamish (1985) finds that '... the primary skill required by the MNE partner of the local firm was its knowledge of the local economy, politics and culture'. Furthermore, Gullander (1976) adds that ' ... through a JV firms can also benefit from the 'experience curve' effect... The reason for this is to be found in the successive improvements in efficiency that normally take place in companies as they gain more experience in the production of a particular good'.

13.5.2c   Country-specific motives to joint venture formation

The last set of motives to forming an IJV have to do with specific aspects of the host country and again they are related to risk reduction. An IJV may be the only option to enter a market if the government of that country raises barriers to WOS or, *in extremis*, prohibits this form of entry outright. On the other hand, the JV may, in fact, be sought by the MNE partner as a way of increasing his bargaining power with the local government, particularly, in connection with obtaining lucrative contracts. Thus, Raveed and Renforth (1983) in explaining the increasing number of IJVs put forward the view that it is the pressure from LDCs that is responsible for this trend, since ' . . . many economists from developing countries argue that a strong host country partner must be involved in any major investment project to protect the interests of the local population'. The implication here is that any possible barriers may be imposed by the host government on a *de facto* rather than on a *de jure* basis. However, there may be cases where the law prohibits the WOS option, since ' . . . host governments have sometimes enacted legislation and administered investment codes that permit foreign investment in selected industries only if co-operative ventures of foreign and local partners can be arranged' (Kofi 1988). However, while this is an argument from the point of view of developing countries, the option of IJV has been employed by first world countries as well, as a way of controlling a specific strategic project, which can better be accomplished through the expertise of a foreign partner. Actually, sometimes the government itself may be the local partner, in a public–private partnership arrangement, as has been the case during the 1990s with the construction of major infrastructure projects not only in a number of EU Cohesion countries, but elsewhere too.

13.5.3   Determinants of foreign direct investment

13.5.3a   Introduction

Turning now to the final form of entry mode, it is observed that since the early 1980s global FDI flows have been rising at a fast nominal rate, exceeding by far the rate of growth of merchandise exports and global nominal GDP growth. Thus, from an annual average of US $77.1 billion in the period 1983–87, to an annual average of $173.5 billion in the period 1987–92, FDI flows have reached $644.4 billion in 1998 and a record of $1271 billion in 2000, at current prices (UNCTAD 1996, 1998, 1999, 2001), although they declined in 2001. Whilst the bulk of these flows, (65%), was directed to developed countries, developing countries too have been consolidating their share to 32%, with the remainder accounted for by Central and Eastern European countries.

Foreign investors can enter a market through either Greenfield investments or M&As. The greenfield investment is a traditional form of entry and it establishes new productive facilities in the host country. Clearly, this mode of entry is riskier and more time consuming than acquiring existing firms in the host country (M&As), but it can be designed and implemented to incorporate the parent company's overall strategy and, therefore, it avoids the problems of integration of different companies involved with M&As. Also, from the point of view of host country, FDI policies favour greenfield investments, because they have more immediate positive effects on capital, output and employment over the alternative M&A

mode, where an increase in output, *ceteris paribus*, can occur only through a more efficient management, an assumption that must be tested in each particular case.

The method of M&A is the same as discussed earlier in this chapter. Thus, we have a merger or a fusion when two or more independent firms merge or fuse together to form a new company, and a takeover or an acquisition when one company takes over or acquires control of part or the whole of the business of other companies. Extending this analysis across frontiers, we define cross-border M&As to be the ones undertaken between companies of different national origin or home countries. Thus, a merger is the fusion of two or more companies from different countries into a new company, in order to achieve common objectives. In this case all companies involved in the merger cease to exist and their shareholders become shareholders of the new company (consolidation). When the business is taken over, the acquired company may cease to exist, with the acquiring firm assuming the assets and liabilities of the acquired firm (statutory merger), or the acquired company may become a 100% subsidiary of the acquiring firm (subsidiary merger). In other instances, the acquiring firm may buy a part of the shares or assets of the target company, in order to combine it with its own business. Cross-border M&As allow firms quick entry into specific foreign markets, through the acquisition of production facilities and intangible assets, which in some cases might have taken a very long time to accomplish. For example, Electricite de France (EDF) has entered the British electricity market by acquiring a number of British electricity distribution firms, including London Electricity, and a number of German utilities have bought British utility firms in the electricity and water industries. In these cases, without M&As it would have been very difficult, if not impossible for the French and German firms to enter the British markets. On the other hand, Japanese car manufacturers have entered the British market through greenfield investments, but the French firm Peugeot have entered the same market through the acquisition of a British car firm.

Given these developments and the fact that FDI flows represent significant injections into the economies of host countries it is pertinent to look, briefly, at the determining factors of FDI. The MNEs, which are responsible for such FDI flows are seen as vehicles of growth not only by developing but by developed countries too. Indeed, the bulk of FDI flows takes place among the world's developed countries and, in particular, those of the Triad, i.e., the EU, Japan and the US.

The positive effects of FDI on output, employment, technology and its diffusion, training, productivity, inter-industry linkages and trade have been documented in the literature, and explain why countries are eager to attract such investment. They also show that multinational firms help significantly in the process of integration of the recipient countries in the world economy.

13.5.3b　*Types of foreign direct investment and the role of subsidiaries*

Considering the explanations for the growth of FDI we must bear in mind that we can distinguish various types of such investment, such as resource-seeking, import-substituting, export-promoting or globally integrated. Also, FDI can be seen as: (1) horizontal investment, involving the production abroad of the same line of products as at home; (2) vertical investment, by moving abroad either backwards one or more stages in the firm's production processes towards the sources of raw materials (known also as resource-based), or forwards nearer the consumer, through the acquiring of outlets, and (3) diversification. The last type of FDI, which in the last 30 years has been in the ascendancy, allows for more specialised and/or rationalised operations with the emphasis on product and process specialisation. Thus, far from replicating abroad the products and processes produced at home, associated with a hierarchical structure, a more creative heterogeneity is encouraged among subsidiaries of multinationals; the latter approach has been termed heterarchy (Hedlund and Rolander 1990), or transnational (Bartlett and Ghoshal 1989). Empirical work tends to provide strong support for the view that MNE can be seen as a network of subsidiaries with evolving strategic priorities and roles (Young *et al.* 1988; Hood *et al.* 1994; Birkinshaw and Morrison 1995).

Consequently, the following roles of the subsidiaries can be identified: (1) truncated miniature replica (TMR), in which case the subsidiary merely reproduces part of the parent firm's product line and all its operations are directed by the centre; (2) rationalised product subsidiary (RPS), where the subsidiary is producing intermediate goods (inputs), and, thus, supplying the rest of the network of subsidiaries of the multinational firm. While its vital operations may still be dictated by the centre, the emphasis on producing technologically sophisticated inputs that help secure the quality of the final product, allows it an element of initiative, which means that there is a process of creative transition in the production orientation of some RPSs and (3) world or regional product mandate (WPM/RPM), in which case the subsidiary has a creative role within the group's network of subsidiaries, in the sense of introducing new products generated from the subsidiary's own resources. Such WPMs or RPMs contribute to the 'heterarchical' structures of organisation of the multinational group, by making extensive use of local resources and local talent, in contrast to the TMRs and RPSs, and help blur the distinction between centre and the periphery, as regards activities and roles.

13.5.3c   Theories of foreign direct investment

The above discussion on the types and diversity of FDI may help to illustrate that any single theory purporting to explain FDI can only provide partial answers and fail to account fully for the phenomenon of FDI.

The main factors affecting FDI can be conveniently classified as macro, micro and strategic. The macro factors, following closely the theories of corporate investment behaviour, emphasise the importance of the size of the host market (as given by the level of GDP), the growth of the host market, factor availability and their prices, productivity, profitability and the protection offered to investing firms by tariffs, quotas and/or other measures. Therefore, such factors represent locational characteristics of the host economy. The micro determinants, emanating from industrial organisation considerations, encompass those firm-specific and industry-specific characteristics, which have been found to confer advantages on multinational firms over most of their local rivals. These are monopoly (or market) power, product differentiation, technological advantages including intangible proprietary rights due to their R&D expenditure and marketing and advertising effects. The third category refers to a set of strategic and long-term factors, such as the desire of foreign investors to defend existing foreign markets and investments against encroachment by competitors; the desire to gain and maintain a foothold in a protected market or to gain and maintain a source of supply that in the long run may prove useful; the need to develop and sustain parent–subsidiary relations; the desire to induce the host country into a long-term commitment to a particular type of technology and know-how; the advantage of complementing another type of investment; the economies of new product development; competition for market shares among oligopolists and the concern for the strengthening of bargaining positions (Reuber 1973, pp. 47–49). In addition, political stability in the host country is often considered as another important determinant of FDI.

From the above motives and the development of the subject over the last 40–45 years, there have emerged a plethora of theoretical explanations of FDI. At the heart of most of the explanations lies the idea of market failure (Casson 1987), be it structural or transactional (Dunning and Rugman 1985), which makes it difficult if not impossible for the neoclassical model of factor endowments to explain completely, or even partially, international production (Dunning 1988). For our purposes we may find it convenient to group the various theories of FDI under the following distinct approaches, the first three of which have almost assumed the aura of schools of thought.

Market power approach

The first one is the market power hypothesis, stemming from the seminal work of Hymer (1960, published in 1976). The essence of this hypothesis is that multinational firms are usually found in industries noted for their high levels of concentration and product differentiation. Such firms have established through their R&D activities a proprietary right, for example, a patented invention or a differentiated product, and have found that its further profitable exploitation in foreign markets requires the establishment of a local subsidiary. However, given the high fixed costs of information and search associated with FDI, and also the minimum efficient scale of the investment itself, it becomes clear that only large firms that can generate sufficient internal funds and/or have a much wider credit basis find FDI an attractive option. Therefore, the postulated hypothesis is that differentiated oligopoly is associated positively with FDI. Early empirical evidence coming from the US has tended to support the view that the size of the firm in the US, as measured by sales, significantly influenced the propensity of a firm in any industry to invest abroad.

Similar considerations hold for the other two firm- or industry-specific characteristics, namely, technological effort and advertising outlays. It has been argued that technology and the multinational firm are often inextricably bound together, because firms often become multinational in order to exploit their technological superiority on a wider scale and also because such firms are an important vehicle in the production and diffusion of technology. Caves (1971) reported that R&D expenditures on new products were related to the outflow of new direct investment from the US, whereas Johnson (1970) argued that any advantage embodied in technology, information or technique that proved profitable in one market could do so in other markets, without incurring again the fixed costs of the initial discovery. Consequently, firms with such advantages have an incentive to exploit them fully through FDI, which offers them a better chance to do so than alternative ways, such as, for example, licensing agreements. Similar positive correlations were established between advertising expenditures and FDI expenditures, leading to the hypothesis that the two were positively related. However, simple correlation between technological activity and FDI on the one hand and advertising expenditure and FDI outlays on the other is not sufficient, since what is clearly required is the unequivocal establishment of causality, which in this case is rather tenuous, as the relation may not be free of circularity. Therefore, since both technological effort and advertising expenditures help in the creation and promotion of a differentiated oligopoly, it is better to consider the latter as the major determinant of FDI.

In the context of the industrial organisation theory, Knickerbocker (1973) considered FDI as a function of oligopolistic reaction. Accordingly, firms undertook such investment in order to cancel out the advantages that the original firm that invested abroad may have acquired from its foreign investment. Knickerbocker constructed an entry concentration index showing that the entry of American firms in foreign markets was bunched in time, a phenomenon consistent with the hypothesis that oligopolistic firms were following their rivals into the foreign markets in order to restore and maintain equilibrium. However, the oligopolistic reaction hypothesis fails to explain why the leading firm decided to invest abroad in the first place and, therefore, in common with other theories of FDI it provides only a partial explanation of what determines international production. To summarise, the market power hypothesis argues that the structural failure of oligopolistic competition at home provides the uninational firm with the motive to exploit its proprietary advantages abroad by engaging in international production and, thus, becoming multinational (Caves 1971, 1974, 1996; Cowling and Sudgen 1987; Dunning 1974, 1981, 1993; Kindleberger 1969, 1970).

The internalisation approach

The second approach extended the original work of Coase (1937) on the nature of the firm, considered in Chapter 3, and argued that, in much the same way that we need firms to save on transaction costs, firms become multinational to increase efficiency by replacing external markets through the internalisation of various functions. Buckley and Casson (1976) suggested that according to the internalisation hypothesis, firms try to maximise profits in an a world of imperfect markets. If markets in intermediate products are imperfect, firms have an incentive to bypass them by creating internal markets, which means that the activities linked by the market are brought under common ownership and control. In a final stage, when firms internalise such markets across frontiers, this process leads to FDI. Buckley and Casson argued that the markets for certain key intermediate products, for example, knowledge, marketing, managerial expertise and human capital are imperfect so that the linking of interdependent activities through these markets may involve considerable time lags and transaction costs. Thus, firms are encouraged to avoid these costs by replacing the external imperfect markets with their own internal markets for such products. The benefits accruing from internalising include the avoidance of time lags and of bargaining and buyer uncertainty, the ability to use price discrimination to achieve the most efficient exploitation of market power, and the minimisation of the impact of government intervention in international markets, through transfer pricing. However, the internalisation approach involves costs too, such as communication and administrative expenses, resource costs of fragmenting the market and costs of political discrimination against foreign-owned firms. For profit maximisation to occur, the internalisation process must proceed to the point where the benefits and costs associated with internalisation are equalised at the margin.

The main spur to internalisation is the presence of externalities. It is claimed that any type of externality in the goods or factor markets will provide the firm with an incentive to internalise these markets, and internalisation of various distortions in a worldwide setting will lead to the development of FDI (Rugman 1980). The multinational firm can respond to both government induced distortions, e.g., tariffs, quotas and the like, and also market failures, particularly, as regards research, information and knowledge. For it is in this area, mainly, that the lack of appropriate markets allows the multinational firm to organise an internal market of its own, so as to overcome the failure of an external market for the sale of information. Internalisation solves the problem by assigning property rights in knowledge to the multinational organisation. Such an internal market enables the firm to transform an intangible piece of research into a valuable asset to the firm. It pays the firm to exploit fully this advantage in various foreign markets, through production by WOSs, instead of licensing and joint ventures, since the latter arrangements cannot benefit from the internal market of the firm and are likely to dissipate the information monopoly of the firm (Rugman 1980).

It is claimed that the internalisation hypothesis, as applied to the multinational firms, represents a general theory of FDI, while the previously considered theories are subsets of the general theory of internalisation (Rugman 1980). It is clear that multinational firms do bypass the market in intermediate products through FDI. However, it is not certain that the motive for internalisation is the external market's inefficiency in terms of high transaction costs and longer time lags or anything else. It would appear that the argument by Dunning (1977) that firms want to retain the exclusive right of using the innovations generated by their R&D efforts is stronger, since the monopoly profits earned by them are greater. However, in the case of innovations there are no external markets, so the choice between inefficient external markets and efficient internal ones does not arise. The innovating firm will have the choice of either creating a market for its innovation or keeping it for its exclusive use, and it is more than likely that it will choose the latter option that offers the prospect of higher rewards. The empirical evidence regarding the internalisation hypothesis is not very strong. Buckley and Casson have shown that the process of internalisation is concentrated in industries with relatively high incidence of R&D expenditure, but this is a conclusion reached by many other studies (Agarwal 1980).

Dunning's eclectic theory

The internalisation hypothesis discussed above was strengthened with the development by Dunning (1977, 1979) of his eclectic theory, or OLI (Ownership, Location, Internalisation), which synthesises various strands of economic thinking, and claims that the propensity of firms to engage in FDI is a function of Ownership specific advantages, Locational advantages and Internalisation opportunities. According to this, a firm will engage in FDI provided the following conditions are satisfied:

(1)   The firm possesses certain ownership advantages over firms of other nationalities, which are exclusive or firm-specific proprietary rights, such as patents.

(2) It is more beneficial to the firm to use these advantages itself rather than sell or lease them to foreign firms, i.e., it pays the firm to internalise its advantages through an extension of its own activities.

(3) Assuming that (1) and (2) are satisfied, it must be profitable for the firm to utilise these advantages in conjunction with at least some factor inputs (including natural resources) outside its home country, otherwise foreign markets can be served by exports and domestic markets by domestic production.

It is clear that the eclectic approach draws heavily from different branches of economics, such as industrial organisation, trade and location theories. Industrial organisation explains the nature of the firm's advantages, some of which may be firm-specific and some may be due to multinationality; the theory of property rights and vertical integration explains under what conditions will the firm internalise these advantages and, finally, the theories of trade and location explain the factors determining the location of production. The eclectic theory suggests that all forms of FDI can be explained by reference to its conditions. However, the OLI approach also recognises that advantages due to ownership, internalisation and location may change over time and accepts that, if country-specific characteristics are important determinants of FDI, it may be invalid to generalise from one country's experience to another.

The competitive international industry and the macroeconomic development approaches

Cantwell (1991) in a survey of theories of international production, in addition to the aforementioned approaches, has also identified another two: the competitive international industry approach and the macroeconomic development approach. The former, echoing Knickerbocker's oligopolistic reaction thesis discussed earlier, stresses that international production tends to be associated with rivalry amongst multinationals, which helps sustain the process of technological competition amongst them (Graham 1978). This argument follows from the earlier discussion of Chapter 10 on oligopoly, where it was found that since oligopolists avoid price rivalry because of the fear of price wars and the impact on profitability they need alternative ways. Therefore, this rivalry is provided, not only by product differentiation, but also through technological competition for new methods, techniques and products and, generally, innovations (Cantwell 1989). Once these are achieved through their R&D expenditures, there is an incentive to exploit them in foreign markets through FDI.

The macroeconomic development approach emphasises macroeconomic considerations, for example, foreign trade and tariffs, as in the case of the Product Cycle Model; balance of payments; and the investment development cycle. We discuss here, briefly, the product cycle model and the investment development cycle.

The product cycle model was suggested by Vernon in an effort to explain US FDI in manufacturing products characterised by advanced technology and high income elasticity of demand. As discussed in Chapter 9, products go through a cycle of initiation, exponential growth, slowdown and decline, corresponding to the process of introduction, spread, maturation and senescence. Vernon (1966) argued that US firms, using the results of their R&D effort, introduce, originally into the American market and subsequently abroad, innovations that go through the following stages: (1) the American producer is initially an exporter with monopoly power for these novelties; (2) foreign production (made possible by either domestic or foreign – including American – investment) begins to displace such American exports in some markets abroad; (3) foreign goods become competitive in third markets, further reducing American exports and (4) finally, foreign goods become competitive in the American market. According to this model, the time period required for the completion of the stages and shape of the cycle will be determined by the appeal of the product to different income groups, the economies of scale available, as well as the importance of transportation costs and tariffs. Also, the model contends that the size of the foreign market depends on the income elasticity of demand for the product. On the other hand, costs are a function of plant size so that economies of scale become important. Therefore, the product cycle model considers income elasticity of demand and through it market size, economies of scale, transportation costs and tariffs as the variables likely to influence the decision to invest abroad.

The model provided an adequate explanation of the interaction between American production, exports and FDI in the 1950s and 1960s. However, the original hypothesis has been extended and generalised to apply to FDI of all developed countries. Accordingly, the reformulation of the model means that the rigid sequential relation between innovations, exports and, finally, FDI, discussed above, is no longer essential for its validity. The conditions that will influence a firm's decision to invest, rather than to serve a foreign market by exports, can be summarised as follows: foreign investment is undertaken if the relevant market can be supplied more cheaply by production on location than by imports from the investor's home country, and the foreign investor is more efficient than an actual or potential domestic investor. These conditions have been extended to cover FDI in developing countries too, and this generalisation has contributed to a gradual weakening of the predictive power of the model. Also, in a restatement of the product cycle hypothesis, Vernon (1979) considered the problem of entropy facing the multinational firm. The latter can belong to an innovating, or a mature or a senescent oligopoly, but in order to avoid the danger of entropy eroding its competitive advantages, the firm must generate new advantages. However, the widespread network of the innovating multinationals and the environmental changes that have been occurring over the years, that is the decline in the differences in incomes, technology and factor costs between the US and the rest of the industrialised world, have weakened the original assumptions of the product cycle hypothesis and have shortened the life of the cycle, which have limited its predictive power.

The investment development cycle or path has been proposed in a number of works by Dunning (1981, 1986, 1988) as an application of his OLI paradigm, discussed earlier. The basic idea of the hypothesis is that the level of inward and outward direct investment of countries depends on their national level of development. Thus, as a country develops, the configuration of the OLI advantages it offers to foreign investors, who might wish to invest in that country, and also to its own firms that might invest abroad changes, and that one can identify the conditions conducive to the change and its effects on the trajectory of development. Accordingly, the first stage is that of pre-industrialisation, in which a country neither attracts inward nor engages in outward direct investment, because it has no specific locational (L) advantages to offer to would-be foreign investors and its own firms have inadequate ownership (O) advantages. As the country moves to the next stage of its development, and succeeds in upgrading its capabilities and resources and in enlarging its markets, i.e., its (L) attractions, the OLI configuration changes making it possible for the country to start attracting inward direct investment in particular sectors. Governmental policies of the country can be instrumental in this respect, not only in terms of basic infrastructure projects, but also in terms of education, training and, in particular, whether the country has a closed-or an open-door policy towards FDI. Dunning offers Japan as an example of a country adopting the former, and Germany as adopting the latter policies in the 1960s. The improvement of the (L) advantages of a country may also help its own indigenous firms to develop their ownership (O) advantages. Also, the inward FDI the country receives can play the role of a catalyst for energising its own firms, through an emulation effect, to meet the challenge and compete against their foreign rivals, in order to maintain and improve their market shares, by developing their own technological and other advantages. This has been the case in a number of developing countries (Petrochilos 1989). At a later stage, the improvement in the (O) advantages causes a reconfiguration of the OLI advantages and enables the indigenous firms of that country to engage in outward FDI (Petrochilos and Salavrakos 2001, Salavrakos and Petrochilos 2003). However, this reconfiguration of the OLI advantages is a dynamic process, and in view of the fact that newly industrialised or industrialising economies are now engaged in outward FDI much earlier in their development that it was the case earlier, Dunning's proposition may need to be qualified by other aspects as well.

The New International Division of Labour (NIDL) Theory

Finally, the NIDL theory contends that as a response to the recession of the economies of the advanced countries in the 1980s, '... production moved offshore primarily in search of low-cost, relative docile labour in the periphery' (Schoenberger 1988). However, multinationals did so having retained at home control of technology and know-how, and having diffused high-level skilled production activities in various developed countries, on the basis of market opportunities, local labour market conditions and so on. However, while certain multinational enterprises behave in the way that NIDL asserts, such behaviour is not the dominant one since FDI flows in the advanced countries represent 2/3 of such flows, and the NIDL theory cannot provide a general explanation of FDI, thus, sharing a common characteristic with most other explanations of FDI, as we have seen. Also, the NIDL theory takes a narrow view of the direction of technological change, location and competition in various markets, which further restricts its applicability.

SUMMARY

In this chapter we have looked at the question of growth, particularly, the ways and direction of the growth of firms. Growth can be internal or external. The former involves the organic growth, discussed in the previous chapter on capital budgeting, whilst the latter is concerned with M&As or takeovers. Growth, whether internal or external, can be horizontal or vertical or it can take, instead, the form of diversification/conglomeration. At some stage in its development, a firm may decide to grow outside its national market by internationalising its activities and entering foreign markets. We have examined, briefly, various modes of entry into foreign markets, including foreign trade, licensing, franchising, turnkey projects, joint ventures and their motives, greenfield investments, cross-border M&As and WOSs. In addition, we have provided a short discussion of the main approaches explaining FDI, e.g. the market power paradigm, the internalisation approach, Dunning's eclectic theory, the competitive international industry approach, and the macroeconomic development approach. Under the latter we have examined the product cycle model and the investment development cycle and have concluded with the NIDL theory.

APPENDIX: CROSS-BORDER M&AS AND STRATEGIC ALLIANCES SHAPE THE NEW PATTERN OF GLOBALISATION

1.A.1   The VodafoneAirTouch–Mannesmann takeover

Between 1991 and 2000 we witnessed an unprecedented increase in the number and value of deals of M&As as a method of growing, both domestically and across borders. Thus, while in 1991 the value of global (both domestic and cross-border) M&As was $328.5 billion, by 2000 it had risen to $3459.1 billion, although in 2001, for a number of reasons to be discussed later, it fell to $1744.6 billion. The proportion of cross-border M&As varied between 22.9% and 35.3% of the total value. These figures illustrate that growing externally, i.e., through M&As or takeovers, has become the dominant mode of entry in foreign markets. In addition, during the same period the number of strategic alliances between firms has also grown dramatically, both domestically and across borders. Such alliances have varied from simple arm's length transactions between independent firms cooperating for specific projects to full-equity and non-equity alliances and joint ventures.

Concentrating on cross-border M&As we observe that cross-border activity has increased from $153 billion in 1991 to almost a trillion dollars in 2000. Such activity encompassed a broad spectrum of sectors, manufacturing industries – both high technology and mature manufacturing industries and services. Telecommunications, steel, automobiles, petroleum, chemicals, pharmaceuticals as well as financial and various business services are examples of industries that have attracted considerable cross-border merger activity.

The main motive for cross-border M&As is often provided by economies of scale and scope. By merging their decision-making structures, firms can exploit various synergies between their tangible and intangible assets. Also, firms can quickly enter foreign markets and establish a critical mass in such markets. In addition, cross-border mergers can eliminate actual or potential competition, in much the same way that domestic mergers do. Clearly, this raises questions both for national competition authorities and EU ones, as we shall see in the next chapter.

Strategic alliances, as we have seen above, are more flexible than M&As and offer firms a wider choice of partners in looser cooperations for various business activities. However, they are more difficult to accomplish, they involve a loss of control and more risks. Consequently, they have less investment spending but higher transaction costs than a merger. Both M&As and strategic alliances can result in higher efficiency gains in research, production and marketing, when firms combine their resources, human and non-human. They can also be expected to create wealth and employment through the integration of firms into global knowledge networks and value-added chains. There may also be spillover effects through various linkages with other firms and technology transfer, and taking into account learning effects and related efficiencies may help to raise social welfare.

However, given the earlier discussion and performance on domestic mergers and the actual performance of some of the cross-border M&As of the last 10 years, one should approach this subject with an element of scepticism. Not only is there a danger of overpaying for mediocre assets, but the problems of combining in a coherent whole the different cultures of the merging or acquired firms are often underplayed by management, particularly a complacent one. The major headaches arise once a merger or an acquisition has taken place, since following one there is normally a transition period during which management must act decisively to rationalise the various duplicate activities of the different companies in the areas of research, production and marketing. Synergy effects cannot arise without proper integration of the various assets of the new firm, under a coherent managerial plan. Only when management resolves efficiently these internal aspects, can it be said to have achieved a successful merger or acquisition, and can reasonably expect benefits to arise. Also, so far we have implicitly assumed that internal funds, generated through retained profits, were readily available to finance these M&As. If a large part of a M&A is financed through issuing debt, then the leveraged company becomes very vulnerable to changes in the capital market and the discussion of Chapter 12 acquires special significance. Also, one must remember that cash-rich companies, as GEC (Marconi) was before it embarked on its acquisition trail in the late 1990s, do not have to spend it! It is not always the right decision to spend accumulated profits. The earlier discussion on the opportunity cost is very pertinent here.

In addition, there may also be external aspects that need to be taken into consideration. For example, both the state of the industry within which the merger takes place, and the general global external environment can affect the speed of the consolidation process involved in M&As, and may be responsible for putting a brake on new deals. This external environment seemed to have played a crucial role in explaining the considerable slowdown of global M&As activity during 2001, referred to earlier. The reduction in this activity between 2000 and 2001 reached almost 50%. Even before the events of 11th September 2001 that seemed to destabilise the global economy, the global market for M&As was not buoyant.

Perhaps the debt financing of the merger activity was overextending the finances of most companies and putting a brake on further expansion. Taken in conjunction with a slowdown of the global economy, it was putting pressure on profitability, and, normally, docile shareholders started complaining about the poor value they were receiving from their investments. This forced management to be more careful, lest they followed the fate of other sacked colleagues elsewhere. Then came the collapse of Enron, the American energy giant that put the accounting practices of companies with high debt under the spotlight, only to be followed, immediately, by the scandal of the accounting/auditing firm Andersons, who as auditors of Enron's books felt obliged to shred crucial evidence. Inevitably, these unethical practices and the other scandals that followed in 2002 affected the global capital markets significantly, forcing the chairman of the Federal Reserve Bank of the USA, Allan Greenspan, to talk of the 'infectious greed' of top executives, and put on hold possible M&As plans.

We now turn to discuss the mega-merger between VodafoneAirTouch PLC and Mannesmann AG. During the 1990s, the British mobile telephone operator Vodafone Group PLC grew rapidly, both as a result of internal growth and external acquisitions. In 1999, Vodafone Group PLC bought the American firm AirTouch Communications Inc. for $60.3 billion and was renamed VodafoneAirTouch PLC, to reflect this change. In 2000, this new company also acquired the Spanish mobile telephone operator Airtel SA for $14.8 billion.

Mannesmann AG, on the other hand, was a major German conglomerate, which had grown in the last 40 years or so to occupy a significant position in German industry, particularly, engineering. As part of its diversification strategy, the firm decided to refocus on telecommunications, without however giving up its positions in other areas of strength. Thus, in the early 1990s it established a mobile telephony operation that soon acquired a significant share in the German market. In early 2000, Mannesmann AG bought the British mobile telephone firm Orange PLC for $32.6 billion and, thus, it acquired a foothold in the British mobile telephony market.

In 2000, VodafoneAirTouch PLC, as part of its drive to enter foreign markets, initiated a hostile takeover bid for the German giant Mannesmann AG. Actually, they were only interested in the mobile telephony operation, but as the Germans were not prepared to sell it, VodafoneAirTouch PLC had to bid for the whole of the Mannesmann group. The original bid valued the German conglomerate for $106 billion. This was rejected by the Mannesmann Board of Directors, while raising major concerns in Germany, that an icon of German industry was under a threat of a takeover. VodafoneAirTouch PLC insisted and, after revising upwards its bid a number of times, it succeeded in acquiring the whole of Mannesmann AG for $202.8 billion, including a $45 billion in net debt outstanding. The transaction was financed by stock swaps, which is a typical financing mode in mega-mergers. Thus, shareholders of VodafoneAirTouch and Mannesmann hold 50.5% and 49.5% of the shares of the combined group, respectively, while the final bid price evaluated one Mannesmann AG share as equal to 58.96 VodafoneAirTouch PLC shares.

Following the completion of the takeover, the new British management of the combined group started disposing of various assets of Mannesmann in order to recoup part of the money paid for the acquisition. First to go was the Orange PLC–Mannesmann AG operation, which was sold to France Telecom for $46 billion. What however irked Germans was the speed with which Vodafone sold anything that could be turned into cash quickly. Among the first to go was Mannesmann's fine art collection, including paintings by Picasso, watercolours by the expressionist Emil Nolde and sculptures by Eduardo Chillida. Also sold were the century-old wood panels in the board of directors' dinning room. Whilst a number of Germans complain that this reflects the lack of history, tradition and culture of Vodafone, as compared to the social traditions of Mannesmann, this can be indicative of the different approaches of management. On the one hand, the Anglo-American model decrees that management knows best and must be free to hire and fire and get rich quickly. On the other, we have the continental, almost paternalistic approach, with the strong social traditions based on the social market model, emphasising cooperation to resolve problems through social dialogue. We return to this theme in the last chapter on Business Ethics.

BIBLIOGRAPHY

Aaronovitch, S. and Sawyer, M. (1975), *Big Business*, Macmillan.

Adler, L. (1966), 'Symbiotic Marketing', *Harvard Business Review*, November/December.

Agarwal, J.P. (1980), 'Determinants of Foreign Direct Investment: A Survey', *Weltwirtschaftliches Archiv*, **116**, 739–773.

Bartlett, C.A. and Ghoshal, S. (1989), *Managing Across Borders – The Transnational Solution*, Hutchinson Business Books.

Beamish, P. (1985), 'The Characteristics of Joint Ventures in Developed and Developing Countries', *Columbia Journal of World Business*, **20**(3), 13–19.

Birkinshaw, J. and Morrison, A. (1995), 'Configurations of Strategy and Structure in Subsidiaries of Multinational Corporations', *Journal of International Business Studies*, **26**(4), 729–753.

Buckley, P.J. and Casson, M. (1976), *The Future of the Multinational Enterprise*, Macmillan.

Cantwell, J. (1989), *Technological Innovation and Multinational Corporations*, Blackwell.

Cantwell, J. (1991), 'A Survey of Theories of International Production', in Pitelis C.N. and Sudgen R. (eds), *The Nature of the Transnational Firm*, Routledge.

Casson, M.C. (1987), *The Firm and the Market*, Blackwell.

Caves, R.E. (1971), 'International Corporations: The Industrial Economics of Foreign Investment', *Economica*, **38**, 1–27.

Caves, R.E. (1974), 'Industrial Organisation', in Dunning J.H. (ed.), *Economic Analysis and the Multinational Enterprise*, Allen & Unwin.

Caves, R.E. (1996), *Multinational Enterprise and Economic Analysis*, 2nd edn, Cambridge University Press.

Coase, R.H. (1937), 'The Nature of the Firm', *Economica*, N.S., **4**, 396–405.

Contractor, F. and Lorange P. (1988), 'Why should firms co-operate? The Strategy and Economic Basis for Co-operative Ventures', in Contractor F. and Lorange P. (eds), *Co-operative Strategies in International Business*, Lexington Books.

Cowling, K. *et al.* (1980), *Mergers and Economic Performance*, Cambridge University Press.

Cowling, K. and Sudgen, R. (1987), *Transnational Monopoly Capital*, Wheatsheaf.

Downie, J. (1958), *The Competitive Process*, Duckworth.

Dunning, J.H. (1974), *Economic Analysis and the Multinational Enterprise*, Allen & Unwin.

Dunning, J.H. (1977), 'Trade, Location of Economic Activity and the Multinational Enterprise: A Search for an Eclectic Approach', in Ohlin, B. *et al.* (eds), *The International Allocation of Economic Activity*, Macmillan.

Dunning, J.H. (1979), 'Explaining Patterns of International Production: In Defence of the Eclectic Theory', *Oxford Bulletin of Economics and Statistics*, **41**, 269–295.

Dunning, J.H. (1981), *International Production and the Multinational Enterprise*, Allen & Unwin.

Dunning, J.H. (1986), 'The Investment Cycle Revisited', *Weltwirtschaftliches Archiv*, **122**, 667–677.

Dunning, J.H. (1988), *Explaining International Production*, Unwin Hyman.

Dunning, J.H. (1993), *The Multinational Enterprise and the Global Economy*, Addison Wesley.

Dunning, J.H. and Rugman A. (1985), 'The Influence of Hymer's Dissertation on Theory of Foreign Direct Investment', *American Economic Review*, **75**, 228–232.

Galbraith, J.K. (1963), *American Capitalism*, Pelican.

Gort, M. (1969), 'An Economic Disturbance Theory of Merger', *Quarterly Journal of Economics*, **93**, 624–642.

Graham, E. (1978), 'Transatlantic Investment by Multinational Firms: A Rivalistic Phenomenon', *Journal of Post-Keynesian Economics*, **1**, 82–99.

Graham, E. (1985), 'Intra-Industry Direct Investment, Market Structure, Firm Rivalry and Technological Performance', in Erdilek A. (ed.), *Multinationals as Mutual Invaders: Intra-Industry Direct Foreign Investment*, Croom-Helm.

Gullander, S. (1976), 'Joint Ventures and Corporate Strategy', *Columbia Journal of World Business*, **11**(1), 104–114.

Hedlund, G. and Rolander, D. (1990), 'Actions in Heterarchies: New Approaches to Managing the MNE', in Bartlett C.A., Doz, T. and Hedlund, G. (eds), *Managing the Global Firm*, Routledge.

Hill, C.W.L. (2001), *International Business. Competing in the Global Marketplace: Postscript 2001*, 3rd edn, McGraw-Hill.

Hood, N., Young, S. and Lall, S. (1994), 'Strategic Evolution within Japanese Manufacturing plants in Europe: UK Evidence', *International Business Review*, **3**(2), 97–122.

Hymer, S. (1960), *The International Operations of National Firm: A Study of Foreign Direct Investment*, PhD thesis, published in 1976 by MIT Press.

Johnson, H. (1970), 'The Efficiency and Welfare Implications of the International Corporations', in Kindleberger C.P. (ed.), *The International Corporation*, MIT Press.

Kindleberger, C. P. (1969), *American Business Abroad*, Yale University Press.

Kindleberger, C. P. (ed.) (1970), *The International Corporation*, MIT Press.

Knickerbocker, F.T. (1973), *Oligopolistic Reaction and the Multinational Enterprise*, Harvard University Press.

Kofi, A. (1988), 'Factor Choice Characteristics and Industrial Impact of Joint Ventures: Lessons from a Developing Economy', *Columbia Journal of World Business*, **23**(3), 51–62.

Kuehn, D. (1975), *Takeovers and the Theory of the Firm*, Macmillan.

Marris, R. (1964), *The Economic Theory of Capitalism*, Macmillan.

Meeks, G. (1977), *Disappointing Marriage: A Study of the Gains from Merger*, Cambridge University Press.

Newbould, G. (1970), *Management and Merger Activity*, Liverpool, Guthstead.

OECD (2001), *New Patterns of Industrial Globalisation – Cross-Border Mergers and Acquisitions and Strategic Alliances*, Paris, OECD.

Penrose, E. (1959), *The Theory of the Growth of the Firm*, Oxford University Press.

Petrochilos, G.A. (1989), *Foreign Direct Investment and the Development Process: The Case of Greece*, Avebury.

Petrochilos, G.A. and Salavrakos, I.D. (2001), 'An Analysis of the Mode of Entry of Greek Outward Foreign Investment in the Balkans and the Black Sea Economic Co-operation Area (BSECA)', in Kantarelis D. (ed.), *Global Business & Economics Review – Anthology 2001*, Selected Papers of the 2001 Business & Economics Society International Conference, B&ESI.

Porter, M.E., (1980), *The Competitive Advantage: Creating and Sustaining Superior Performance*, The Free Press, Collier Macmillan Publishers.

Raveed, S. and Renforth, W. (1983), 'State Enterprise-Multinational Corporation-Joint Ventures: How Well Do They Meet Both Partners' Needs?', *Management International Review*, part 5, 47–57.

Reuber, G.L. (1973), *Private Foreign Investment in Development*, Clarendon Press.

Rugman, A.M. (1980), 'Internalisation as a General Theory of Foreign Direct Investment: A Re-Appraisal of the Literature', *Weltwirtschaftliches Archiv*, **116**(2), 105–119.

Saigol, L. (2002), 'Dealmakers Prepare for Long and Slow Year', Global Investment Banking, *Financial Times*, 22 February 2002.

Salavrakos, I.D. and Petrochilos, G.A. (2003), 'An Assessment of the Greek Entrepreneurial Activity in the Black Sea Area (1989–1999): Causes and Prospects', *Journal of Socio-Economics*, **32**(3), 331–349.

Schoenberger, E., (1988) 'Multinational Corporations and the New International Division of Labour: A Critical Appraisal', *International Regional Science Review*, **11**(2), 105–119.

Singh, A. (1971), *Take-overs*, University of Cambridge, Dept. of Applied Economics, Monograph 19, Cambridge University Press.

UNCTAD (1996), *World Investment Report 1996: Investment, Trade and International Policy Arrangements*, Geneva, UNCTAD.

UNCTAD (1998), *World Investment Report 1998: Trade and Determinants*, Geneva, UNCTAD.

UNCTAD (1999), *World Investment Report 1999: Foreign Direct Investment and the Challenge of Development*, Geneva, UNCTAD.

UNCTAD (2001), *World Investment Report 2001: Promoting Linkages*, Geneva, UNCTAD.

Utton, M.A. (1979), *Diversification and Competition*, Cambridge University Press.

Vaughan-Adams, L. (2002), 'Demergers Get No Respect but Study finds they Boost Value', *The Independent*, 2nd July.

Vernon, R. (1966), 'International Investment and International Trade in the Product Cycle', *Quarterly Journal of Economics*, **80**, 190–207.

Vernon, R. (1979), 'The Product Cycle Hypothesis in a New International Environment', *Oxford Bulletin of Economics and Statistics*, **41**, 255–267.

Yoshino, M.Y. (1995), *Strategic Alliances: An Entrepreneurial Approach to Globalisation*, Harvard University Press.

Young, S., Hood, N. and Dunlop, S. (1988), 'Global Strategies, Multinational Subsidiary Roles and Economic Impact in Scotland', *Regional Studies*, **26**(6), 487–497.

chapter fourteen

The Government Sector and Public Regulation

14.1 INTRODUCTION

In most developed countries governments play a significant role in the economy, both in terms of influencing it through the budgetary activities of taxing and spending, which at the turn of the millennium exceeded on the average 40% of GDP, and also through running a significant number of government agencies and non-profit organisations, if not various nationalised industries still, despite the process of privatisation that has been going on in most countries for the last 20 years. In addition, governments affect the economic activities of households and firms through legislation. It follows that governments are regulators of economic activity and through their procurement policies a major customer of the output of business enterprises. They are also significant producers of goods and services, most of which is non-marketed.

In this chapter we look briefly at the role of the government sector in the provision of goods and services and focus on the differences with the private sector, and second, at the role of the state as a regulator, mostly in the form of competition policy and the regulation of utilities. The first aspect of government intervention is related to the question of redistribution. On the other hand, the *raison d' être* of public regulation is to be found in the failure of the free enterprise system, in certain forms of industrial organisation, to provide an efficient regulatory mechanism of the economy, and the need, therefore, to improve the working of the market.

14.2 THE RATIONALE FOR THE GOVERNMENT SECTOR

The reasons explaining government intervention in the economic system arise from two major aspects of economic life, namely, income redistribution and market failure. Income is earned by factors of production and, therefore, the original income of households or individuals depends on the amount of labour, capital and land they supply and the wage rates, salaries, interest, profit levels and dividends and rentals they receive in return. Since ownership of factors of production among households or individuals is unequal, original incomes earned by them display a great deal of inequality. For example, in the UK there is considerable inequality in the distribution of income and, correspondingly, wealth, with the poorest 20% of households earning less than a half of 1% of the original income, while the richest 20% of households earning more than 50% of original income (Central Statistical Office, *Economic Trends*, various issues). Thus, in the interests of equity, governments redistribute income from the rich to the poor mainly through transfer payments and income tax. In the UK, income is redistributed through state retirement pensions, widows' pensions, unemployment benefit, child benefit, sickness benefit, income support, family credits, housing benefit and student grants, among others, with some of these programmes targeting support to needy groups of people more directly than others. Market failure, on the other hand, provides a different explanation of government intervention.

14.2.1 Market failure

Market failure is said to exist when the unfettered market mechanism fails to achieve allocative efficiency, i.e., when the productive resources of the country are not used efficiently to produce the maximum output possible under the given state of technology and other constraints. Sometimes market failure is the result of imperfect information possessed by producers and/or consumers. However, to the extent that we have been assuming that producers try to maximise their profits (and thus, minimise their costs) and consumers try to maximise their utility, any market failure problems arising from imperfect information can be corrected or minimised, given that there is an incentive for producers to be efficient in production and consumers to be efficient in consumption. There are, however, three major sources of market failure under: (1) public goods; (2) externalities; and (3) monopolistic and/or oligopolistic restriction of output that are more serious and require special attention and treatment.

14.2.1a   Public and merit goods

A public good is one which is provided free of charge at the point of contact and whose opportunity cost of providing an extra unit is zero, thus, its price is zero. Examples of public goods include street lighting, lighthouses and security provided by a defence system. The chief characteristics of public goods are *non-rivalry* and *non-excludability*. The first has to do with the fact that such goods are *non-exhausted*. The consumption of an extra unit of street lighting by one consumer does not exhaust this good for other consumers, in the way that happens with private goods, which are characterised, instead, by *rivalry* and *excludability*. Of course, the cost of providing public goods is not zero, but it is borne by the state, municipality and the like, as appropriate from, say, general taxation. In this way one also avoids the *'free rider'* problem that arises when people have no incentive to pay for a product, if payment makes no difference to the quantity consumed of that product. If a public good were to be provided privately, there would be a tendency for too little to be produced, because of the *'free rider'* problem. If you knew that your neighbours were prepared to pay for street lighting, you would probably try to avoid payment, knowing that you could not be excluded from this product. Consequently, types of market failure connected with the *'free rider'* problem are dealt with by public provision of the good or service in question. Allied to this aspect are also merit goods that add to the quality of life, for example, education, health and the like. Their opportunity cost, however, is not zero, but in some societies it has been decided to provide them free of charge at the point of contact, as is the case of medical services in the UK under the NHS, and similar schemes in other European countries, and fund their provision through general taxation, in order to allow all people to benefit from improved health. Similar consideration apply to the education services.

14.2.1b   Externalities

Other forms of market failure involve externalities, under which the economic activity has an effect but it bypasses the market, as in the case of pollution, where, for example, a chemical plant discharges effluence into a river that pollutes it and affects negatively all those living and working downstream. In such cases there is a divergence between private benefit and social benefit on the one hand, and private cost and social cost on the other, and a system of subsidies and taxes can be devised by the government to encourage positive externalities and discourage negative ones.

14.2.1c Monopolistic and/or oligopolistic restriction of output

However, of greater significance are questions of market failure connected with oligopolistic/monopolistic market structures. The discussion of the previous chapter looked at the issue of growth of the firm, both internal and external, and also at the related issue of the national firm deciding to internationalise its activities by various ways and, ultimately, by engaging in foreign direct investment (FDI). However, as firms grow, their size tends to create problems within their respective markets or even the economy as a whole. Markets tend to become more concentrated over time, with questions of monopoly power, barriers to entry, restrictive practices and so on, acquiring special significance and requiring attention. It follows then that these issues become legitimate targets of public concern. The easy way of leaving it to the market to sort itself out, as some suggest, is not really, in most instances, an adequate solution, because of the observed failure of the free enterprise system to correct this type of anomaly. This then raises the need for some kind of government regulation. Such government concern can manifest itself with special legislation to outlaw certain activities injurious to the public interest and control and regulate others, and we pursue this question below.

14.3 PUBLIC UTILITIES

There is also the case that some economic activities, for example, gas or water distribution, can best be undertaken by a single firm that can supply the whole market at a lower price than two or more firms can. This is the case of the *natural monopoly*, where economies of scale are so strong that in the interest of efficiency it is best that such activities are carried out by a single firm, known as a utility. In some countries, governments had made in the past, for a number of reasons, such utilities public by nationalising them, although in the last 20 years we have seen the reverse process of privatisation. In others they had subjected them to close regulation. The major difference between a private enterprise and a public utility is that while the objective of the first is to serve the private interest of its shareholders or stakeholders, the objective of the latter is to serve the public interest. Whilst, a private firm need only concern itself with the private costs and benefits arising from its economic activities, a public utility, in serving the public interest, must take, in addition, into account the social costs and benefits of its activities. In the case of public utilities, a number of problems do arise, for example, with regard to pricing, investment and rates of return, which because of the different objectives of such utilities require somewhat a different treatment to what has been discussed before. The same analysis can also be extended to various government agencies and non-profit organisations. Therefore, we turn now to consider some of these questions.

14.3.1 Pricing policies

Given the monopolistic nature of public utilities, we can start by asking how far should profit be a constituent element of price and, insofar as that price is set to reflect cost, should that be average or marginal cost? The question of profit has to do with the rate of return that public utilities are expected to earn. This rate of return must be linked to the need to provide also for reserves for future investment, which in terms, for example, of the electricity industry are very large indeed. Thus, serving the public interest does not mean that publicly produced goods and services should be offered at very low prices irrespective of cost, in the interests of achieving certain other objectives, for example, keeping inflation down. This approach had been taken by a number of European governments in the past, including that of the UK, with deplorable consequences for the finances of the public utilities, which tended to sell cheap to the private sector and buy dear from the private sector of their economies. Since self-financing was limited and the size of the funds required for investment in the public utilities was vast, utilities had to rely to a very large extent on the budgets of their respective countries to finance such investment.

14.3.1a   Marginal cost pricing

In the UK two important White Papers published in 1961 and 1967 provided policy recommendations on the financial obligations and objectives of the nationalised industries and sought to link pricing policies and investment criteria through the target rate of return. From these target rates of return, the rate or rates of discount could be derived to be used for the appraisal of individual programmes of investment in the nationalised industries. In terms of prices, the recommendation was that prices had to be related to costs and in particular long-run marginal cost. Thus, following from the French *'green tariff'* for electricity, theoretical discussion and actual practice in the British electricity industry, which had produced a bulk supply tariff based on marginal principles in the mid-1960s, led to the idea of marginal cost pricing. In essence this means that the output produced should be such that the price people are prepared to pay for it equals the marginal cost associated with its production. In addition, this leads to an important investment rule. Thus, so long as the demand curve is above the marginal cost curve, we have an incentive to go on increasing output, since the valuation consumers put on that extra output exceeds the marginal cost of producing that extra output. Similarly, if at a given output marginal cost exceeds price, output should be reduced. However, if in the short run the marginal cost of producing an extra unit of output from an existing plant is the cost of additional labour and material, this concept of marginal cost needs to be redefined in the long run, when increases in demand require the installation of new plant and equipment. Thus, marginal cost must now include the cost of the additional plant required to produce the additional unit. Assuming for a moment that capacity or plant is divisible and can be adapted to changes in demand, it can be shown that any output can be produced at least cost – by building a plant appropriately adjusted to that level of output, so that the short-run marginal cost is equal to long-run marginal cost. This makes use of the discussion in Chapter 7 and it can be recapitulated in Figure 14.1. In Figure 14.1, we construct pairs of short-run average and marginal cost curves for three different outputs q_1, q_2 and q_3 per annum and the corresponding long-run average cost LAC envelope curve and its LMC curve. Clearly, if the firm always builds a plant to produce any given output optimally, i.e., at minimum cost, then price can be made simultaneously equal to both SMC and LMC. In Figure 14.1, this occurs at points A, B and C. Clearly, setting a price equal to marginal cost, according to our rule, would only cover total costs at output level q_2. For levels of output below q_2 marginal cost pricing would result in losses, while for output levels higher than q_2

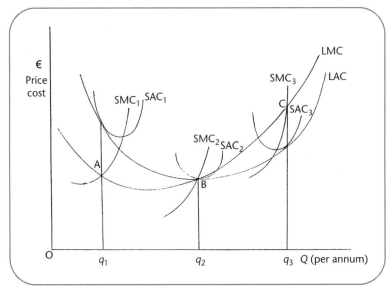

Figure 14.1 Short- and long-run cost curves under flexible plants

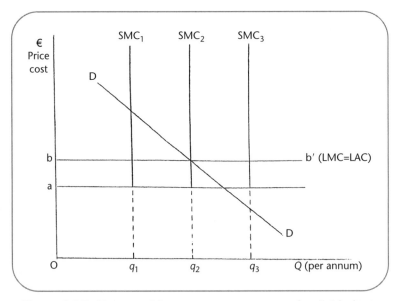

Figure 14.2 Short- and long-run cost curves under rigid plants

it would result in supernatural profits. Incorporating the demand curve DD in the case where capacity is perfectly divisible, but there are capacity limitations because of rigid plants, results in Figure 14.2, where we have three capacity sizes of outputs q_1, q_2 and q_3 per annum. The short-run marginal cost curves for the three plant sizes are given by: $OaSMC_1$, $OaSMC_2$ and $OaSMC_3$ showing that for each capacity size the SMC is constant at the level Oa (the running cost) up to the output limit and then becomes infinite, because of the need to add to capacity. Since we have assumed that capacity is perfectly divisible, the long-run marginal cost and also the long-run average cost is shown by the line bb', thus, LMC = LAC. Distance ab in the diagram represents the annual equivalent capital cost associated with that capacity. The diagram shows that at output level q_1 demand exceeds both SMC (Oa) and LMC (Ob) and, therefore, the investment rule, discussed above, indicates an expansion of output. On the other hand, at output level q_3 the demand curve is below both the SMC and LMC and so a contraction of capacity (i.e., disinvestments) is indicated. It is only at plant size q_2 that demand, and so price, is simultaneously equal to both SMC and LMC, consequently, size q_2 is the optimal one. However, here we need to explain how a price Ob, which is equal to LMC is also equal to SMC. Clearly, it is not equal to the running cost of that capacity, which is Oa. The running cost of plant q_2 is exceeded by distance ab, which is the annual equivalent cost of building a plant of capacity q_2. Here the relevant marginal cost concept is the marginal user opportunity cost. While for the horizontal part of the SMC curve, the conventional concept of the opportunity cost as referring to the next best use of the resources adequately explains marginal cost, in the vertical part of the SMC curve we need to replace the concept of the opportunity cost by the concept of the value of the resources in their current use to the marginally excluded consumer. The valuation of the resources by the marginal consumer of output q_2 exceeds Oa but falls just short of Ob. This valuation is called the marginal user opportunity cost, and it is the relevant marginal cost concept for the vertical part of the SMC curve (Webb 1973). To recapitulate, by adjusting capacity it is possible to make price equal to both SMC and LMC, as is the case with output level q_2.

We pointed out earlier that in the case of decreasing costs, the application of marginal cost pricing could result in losses. However, in practice, this problem is easily resolved when one does not charge a single price for all units of output sold, as is the case, for example, of the electricity and gas industries, where a fixed charge can also be, and usually is charged to ensure that the utility is covering its costs and achieves its target rate of return. Thus, optimum allocation of resources requires that price be made equal to the marginal cost of the last unit of output sold. Earlier units can be charged at different prices or, typically, a fixed charge can be levied independent of the number of units of output consumed. What has to be remembered is that marginal cost pricing is not an end in itself, but a means of getting the most out of given resources. 'And getting the most out of a given set of resources is only one of the ends to the attainment of which a public authority's pricing policy ought properly to be directed' (Meek 1967). Whilst efficiency in resource allocation is important in economics, and marginal cost pricing may be under certain circumstances appropriate, it is only one of a number of different and possibly conflicting economic objectives of public authority pricing policy. To other objectives some other different pricing policy may be appropriate, and the problem is to resolve the conflict in a rational manner, remembering that in economics we are usually faced with various trade-offs.

14.3.1b Peak load pricing

A related problem in public utilities arises when the demands for the goods/services of such utilities are not constant over time but exhibit considerable variation. For example, the demand for electricity varies both during the day and the seasons, thus, it tends to be higher at 6 p.m. than at 2 a.m. and it is higher during the winter than during the summer. The same can be said about the demands for gas, transport services and the like. In other words, the demand for such services are subject to periodicity, which creates peaks and troughs and raises questions about the pricing policy to be pursued. In such circumstances, one needs to identify the marginal costs to be used for efficient pricing.

Since, in these industries it is not practicable to store outputs and meet the peak demand out of stocks, the peak demand can only be met by the available capacity. This means that the size of the available capacity cannot be less than the size of the peak demand, if the latter is to be satisfied. Clearly, at off-peak periods, the existing capacity will be much higher and only part of it will be required. These considerations imply that all the capacity costs must be borne by the consumers responsible for generating the peak demand, because it is this demand that determines the size of capacity required, and also changes in peak demand determining, in turn, changes in capacity. Consumers of off-peak demand need only be charged a price equal to running costs, since they make use of existing capacity. Clearly, the problem at hand is one of, first, determining the optimal capacity required and, second, allocating the capacity costs. Such capacity costs are joint costs to the different demands of the various sub-periods considered, for example, electricity for day-time and night-time and so on. We can distinguish two cases: (1) the firm peak case, where only the demand of one sub-period creates the need for additional capacity, thus, the differential prices charged do not eliminate the peak; and (2) the shifting peak case, in which the demands of both sub-periods are causing capacity changes, and where the differential prices charged can cause the previous off-peak demand to become the new peak demand.

Firm peak case

We present the firm peak case in Figures 14.3 and 14.4 as follows: In Figure 14.3 we have split the 24 hours into two 12-hour segments for day-time and night-time demand and assume that while there is a variation in the demand, for example, for electricity between the two segments there is no variation within the segments themselves. Therefore, the demand for night-time is given by $D_nD'_n$ and the demand for day-time is $D_dD'_d$. The running costs are given as Ob, and the capacity of the plant is fixed at output q_d in each 12-hour segment, meaning that the plant is 'rigid'. The diagram illustrates the case where capacity has already been adjusted to meet the demand, and thus, it might be called the long-run equilibrium solution. Thus, the SMC curve is bAB, i.e., it becomes vertical at the maximum output of the fixed capacity. The prices that optimise social benefit are p_n and p_d for night and day, respectively, since at these prices the social benefit is given as: $bp_nD_n + bAp_dD_d$ and it is the maximum obtainable. At these prices the outputs for night and day are found as q_n and q_d, respectively. The price p_d is inclusive of the running or energy cost Ob and the capacity cost Ap_d. The capacity cost is part of the marginal cost in the peak period, because capacity must be added to satisfy this demand, and the concept of the SMC appropriate for peak demand is the user opportunity cost, mentioned earlier. The price p_d acts as a rationing mechanism to allocate the fixed output q_d to the customers of the peak demand.

However, at first capacity may be either short or in excess of the equilibrium found in Figure 14.3 and we need to discuss how optimum capacity is determined. On the basis of the earlier discussion, this must be related to the equality of

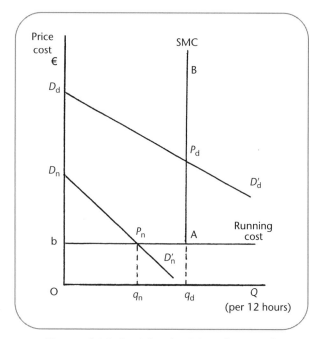

Figure 14.3 Peak load pricing, firm peak

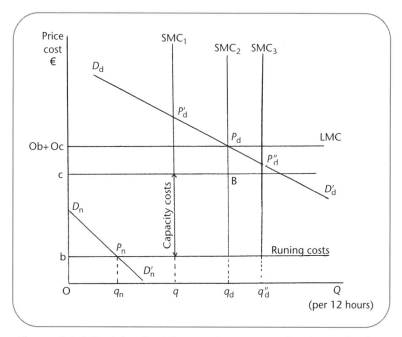

Figure 14.4 Peak load pricing, optimum capacity determination

short- and long-run marginal costs. Assume constant demands for night and day given by D_nD_n' and D_dD_d' and constant running cost Ob and capacity cost Oc per unit, respectively.

Therefore, up to the capacity limit short-run marginal cost is Ob, and long-run marginal cost is Ob + Oc, as shown in Figure 14.4. In the same diagram we present three possible plants to produce outputs q, q_d and q_d'', whose short-run marginal cost curves are given by SMC_1, SMC_2 and SMC_3, respectively. If the first plant were built to produce output q, the night price would be set at p_n for output q_n and the day price would be p_d' for output q. The off-peak price is set equal to the running cost Ob, but the peak (day) price p_d' is above the long-run marginal cost given by the line Ob + Oc. Clearly this indicates that the capacity of the first plant is not optimal (it is in fact deficient), since the last unit consumed is charged a price in excess of the marginal cost of producing it, and this is a signal for capacity to be expanded. If instead, the third plant were constructed to produce output q_d'', again the night price would be set at p_n for output q_n but the day or peak price would be p_d'', which is clearly below the long-run marginal cost of Ob + Oc. Since this price does not cover the marginal cost of producing the last unit consumed, capacity is not optimal indicating that we should disinvest. It is only with plant two, with SMC_2 that we have optimal capacity. Here again off-peak (night) output is q_n and it is charged a price of p_n, equal to running cost Ob, as before. The day (peak) output is q_d and it is charged a price of p_d, which is exactly equal to the long-run cost, given by Ob + Oc, of producing the last unit of output. In the firm peak case all capacity charges, given by the rectangle $OcBq_d$ are borne by the consumers of the peak demand, who are responsible for generating such demand. Here, charging a much lower price for the night output does not cause the off-peak demand to exceed the peak demand, and requiring extra capacity to be added. Since capacity is determined solely by reference to the peak demand, this capacity is of the nature of 'free good' to the off-peak consumers (Webb 1973, p. 111).

Shifting peak case

Applying the previous analysis to the situation depicted in Figure 14.5, we observe the following. Again we have rigid plants and the demands are given as D_nD_n' for night and D_dD_d' for day. However, now setting the price for the night demand at Ob, the required output becomes q_n, while charging a price Ob + Oc for day demand, the output becomes q_d, which is less than q_n. In other words, the application of our previous pricing rule results in the off-peak demand becoming the peak demand, thus, we have the shifting peak case, and requiring increased capacity to satisfy it! Clearly, this is an unsatisfactory turnaround and we need to examine the efficient pricing policy for this shifting peak case. Whereas in the firm peak case capacity costs were separable, now capacity costs are joint to both periods, night and day. Therefore, in Figure 14.5 we have also drawn the combined demand for day and night D_cKD_d', which is derived by adding vertically the two separate demands, because a unit of capacity can be justified by either the demand in one period alone or by the combined demand in the different periods. These demands are complementary, with the capacity costs being joint to both periods. In this case the joint LMC curve shows the cost of satisfying a unit increase in demand during the whole 24 hours and, therefore, it is derived by adding the unit running costs Ob in each period, i.e., 2Ob, plus the cost of getting an additional unit of capacity

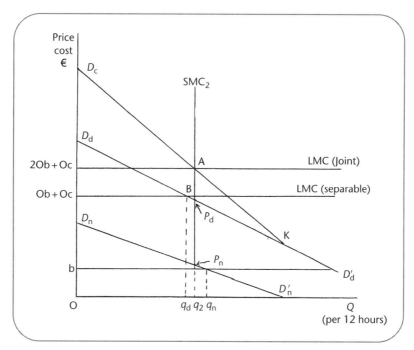

Figure 14.5 Peak load pricing, shifting peak

throughout the 24 hours, which is Oc. Consequently, the joint LMC curve is drawn at the height of 2Ob + Oc. This contrasts with the firm peak case, where the cost of providing for a unit increase in output within either of the two periods (day or night) when capacity increases are required is given by Ob + Oc, which is drawn as LMC (separable). Optimal capacity is, thus, obtained at the point of intersection of the combined demand curve D_c and the LMC (joint) curve, point A, resulting in the optimal output q_2. Once this optimal capacity has been found, the efficient pricing policy should sought to encourage consumers in both periods to use this capacity, provided the running costs of its period are covered. This means that with the optimum output set at q_2 for both periods, night and day, the optimum prices are $p_n q_2$ for the night output, and $p_d q_2$ for day output. These two prices sum up to $A q_2$, which is the joint long-run marginal cost of providing an additional unit of output in both periods. It is clear from the diagram that in this case the output in the two periods is the same, q_2, but is sold at different prices. As compared with the firm peak case, now consumers in both sub-periods share in the capacity costs.

As an extension to the foregone analysis one can relax the assumption of rigid capacity and consider the appropriate pricing policy under flexible plants, and also the assumption of demands of equal duration in favour of individual demands weighted so as to relate to the whole 24 hour demand cycle. However, as this goes beyond the confines of this text, interested readers are advised to consult the relevant literature, given in the bibliography.

14.3.2 Investment policies

During the course of the preceding discussion, we had cause to refer to the investment rule, which should underlie public authority decisions. Thus, it was shown that when, for a given level of capacity, demand exceeded the long-run cost of production, expansion was indicated; conversely, if for a given level of capacity, demand was below the long-run marginal cost, contraction was the optimal decision to take. When it comes to considering the investment decisions of public authorities, the discussion of the earlier Chapter 11 is very pertinent. However, that discussion referred essentially to the private sector and, consequently, the costs and benefits of particular investment proposals entering the calculations for the derivation of the net present values were private costs and private benefits. In the present context, however, we need to consider the social costs and social benefits. Thus, in what follows we shall look at: (1) cost–benefit analysis; and (2) the choice of rate of discount, as applied to public authorities' investment decisions.

14.3.2a   Cost–benefit analysis (social costs, social benefits)

Cost–benefit analysis is a practical method of evaluating the desirability of projects, where it is necessary because of various external effects to consider the overall repercussions of the activity, both for the short and long term and also for the side-effects on people, industries, regions and the like (Prest and Turvey 1965). This means that, because of the existence of important external effects associated with the project, the latter cannot be evaluated adequately simply by looking at the effects it has on the cost and revenue flows of the agency (or utility) undertaking the project. The main difference between the cost–benefit analysis and the investment appraisal criteria we considered in Chapter 11 lies in the definition of the costs and benefits that must be considered and quantified (Webb 1973).

The objective of cost–benefit analysis is the maximisation of the present value of all benefits minus that of all costs, subject to any relevant constraints. To accomplish this, one needs to identify which costs and benefits to include; how are they to be valued; what is the interest rate to be used in the discounting process and what are the relevant constraints. We deal, briefly, with the first two issues here and the latter two in the next section. Thus, in their influential survey, Prest and Turvey (1965) suggest that under the enumeration of costs and benefits we need to consider: (1) how a project is defined; (2) externalities; (3) secondary benefits and (4) the project's life, whereas in terms of the valuation of the costs and benefits important questions arise in terms of: (1) relevant prices; (2) non-marginal changes; (3) market imperfections; (4) taxes and controls; (5) unemployment; (6) collective goods and (7) intangibles.

In terms of project definition it is important that all feasible methods of performing a particular activity are considered as alternatives. Also, where the project has important effects, as for example, with the building of a motorway that can relieve congestion along it but increase congestion on feeder roads, allowances must be made for such effects in estimating costs and benefits. A project often has effects on bodies or individuals other than the agency (or utility) undertaking it. These are externalities, or spillover effects and, usually, they are split into technological and pecuniary. Technological externalities affect the physical production possibilities of other producers or the utility enjoyed by consumers and should be taken into account. Pecuniary externalities, on the other hand, affect prices of goods and/or resources and should not be considered, unless the distributional consequences of a project are assessed. The reason is that we need to avoid double-counting, and so 'we have to eliminate the purely transfer or distributional items from a cost–benefit evaluation: we are concerned with the value of the increment of output arising from a given investment and not with the increment in value of existing assets' (Prest and Turvey 1965). This is easily said but the distinction is not always simple and easy in practice.

The notion of including some pecuniary spillovers in the benefits is linked with the so-called secondary benefits. For example, if as a result of an irrigation project we have an increase in the production of wheat, the primary benefit of the project is the value of the increased wheat production minus the corresponding increased costs of production. However, the increased wheat production will affect others associated with wheat, namely wheat merchants, transport firms, milling firms, bakers and so on, whose profits are likely to rise, as a result of the irrigation project. These are referred to as 'stemming' or secondary benefits. Also, we can have 'induced' secondary benefits, which are extra profits from activities that sell to the farmers. Can we impute values for these secondary benefits? The answer is that, provided the price mechanism works properly, the prices of wheat and of farming inputs are adequate to produce an estimate of the benefits of the increased output of wheat, because such prices will reflect marginal social costs and benefits. Only where such prices do not reflect marginal social costs and benefits need we worry about secondary benefits, which means that this problem is one of second-best allocation. Estimation of the project's length of life can be a subjective process, influenced by assessments of the physical length of life, technological developments, shifts in demand and so on. Also, we need to be aware that the effect of any errors can be mitigated or pronounced by the rate of discount adopted for the discounting process. For example, the higher the rate of discount, the lower the effect of errors of estimation becomes. In this context, we must remember that the length of life contemplated for these types of projects is likely to be very long and, therefore, the estimates of the streams of costs and benefits are likely to be based on considerable guesswork. For example, waterways in England are centuries old and are still in operation producing benefits and associated costs.

Having identified the costs and benefits, we turn to consider their valuation. As suggested earlier, provided the optimum Pareto conditions are met, market prices are the relevant ones to use. If such Pareto conditions are not satisfied, then the market prices must be adjusted to arrive at social valuations. Thus, if prices are set above marginal costs, for example, because of market imperfections, they should be adjusted towards the marginal cost. Again, if the discrepancy between price and marginal cost is due to taxes, a correction will be required, unless the tax was imposed in the first place to make market prices equal to marginal social opportunity cost (SOC), as it may be in the case of pollution and, generally, of 'bads'. In the case of non-marginal changes in the final output, resulting from the project, benefits can be obtained by multiplying price with quantity and adding any consumers' surplus, the latter given by the area under the demand curve. We can simplify matters by assuming that the demand curve is linear, and so the relevant price would be the arithmetic average of the before and after the change prices. Similarly, for non-marginal changes in inputs, having corrected input prices so as to reflect transfer payments (by eliminating any rental payments), again on the linearity assumption the relevant price to use would be the arithmetic mean of the before and after the change prices (Webb 1973, p. 123).

Taxes and government controls also cause a divergence between market prices and social costs or benefits. Normally, taxed inputs should be evaluated at their factor cost rather than at their market value, although the latter can be the relevant price to use in instances where the 'total supply of the input in question has a zero elasticity of supply, *e.g.*, an important item subject to a strict quota' (Prest and Turvey 1965). In the case of income tax, public investment decisions can differ from private investment decisions in the sense that while the latter should allow for income and profits tax payments, the former (i.e., the public sector ones) should not. The major concern here is the evaluation of cost that reflects the use of real resources excluding transfer payments. This means that profits or income taxes on the income derived by a public utility from its investment projects are irrelevant.

In the case where there are unemployed resources, which can be utilised by the investment project, corrections to the market prices are again required, because under excess supply at the market price of any input that price overstates the social costs of using the specific input. This is more so in the case of general unemployment, when spending on an investment project creates additional incomes to the rest of the economy, through the multiplier. In such a case, the use of market prices to evaluate costs and benefits of a project overstates its social costs and understates its social benefits.

Also, market prices cannot be used in the evaluation of benefits that are not capable of being marketed, as for example in the case of collective or public goods, mentioned earlier. Here all members of the community benefit equally, for example, from defence expenditure, or all ships in its vicinity benefit equally from the availability of a lighthouse, thus, the quantity of the public (collective) good supplied to any one member of the relevant population cannot be varied. In the case of marketable goods, to obtain the aggregate demand we add the individual demands horizontally; however, in the case of the (non-marketed) collective goods, the aggregate demand is obtained by vertical summation of the individual demands, to reflect the fact that each unit of the good is consumed by all consumers. This means that in the case of collective goods, or any such similar case where the government has decided to supply a range of goods and services free or at nominal prices, which have no relationship to consumer preferences, we cannot arrive at investment decisions by computing the present value of sales.

Finally, some costs and benefits of particular projects (such as the amenities of a public park, or the scenic effect of building overhead electricity transmission lines) can neither be quantified nor evaluated. Others, although they can be quantified cannot be evaluated, for example, a reduction in deaths occurring as a result of an improvement in a road network. Such costs and benefits have been called intangibles and they are characterised by the fact that there are no markets for them, thus, prices cannot be established, which could be considered in our calculations. Nevertheless, they are very important in the present discussion, they tend to complicate matters and must not be left out of consideration. The decision maker must be aware of their presence, and it is the task of the person(s) preparing the computations for the effects of a project, which can be expressed in money terms to do so, and also identify the relevant intangibles associated with the project that have a positive or negative influence. The presentation could also indicate what values society is likely to place on such intangibles, rather than the decision maker. Alternatively, imputed or shadow prices could be used to show the different outcomes of the cost–benefit analysis.

14.3.2b   The choice of the rate of discount

The analysis of Chapter 11 on capital budgeting made clear the importance of the rate of discount for the estimation of the present value of the net benefits of investment projects in the private sector. In the present context, the question is: of the great variety of interest rates available, which is the most appropriate to choose, for the purposes of discounting to their present values the streams of future income of investment projects undertaken by public utilities? Additionally, the choice of the rate of discount is related to the total amount of investment to be undertaken within a country in each year; how this investment could be allocated between the private and the public sector and how funds could be allocated between competing agencies existing within the private and public sectors. The solution to the last two problems will be the same, provided we assume the objective of maximisation of the excess of social benefits over social costs, the absence of capital rationing and also that satisfactory money values can be placed on the inputs and outputs of the public sector, in the manner indicated above.

Following the analysis of Chapter 11, we can start by considering that the undertaking of public investment implies that society abstains from consumption today for more consumption tomorrow and, thus, we can define the rate of discount to be used for our discounting purposes as the society's marginal rate of substitution of consumption tomorrow for consumption today minus one. This rate is called the marginal social time preference (STP) rate. The STP rate reflects the government's judgement about the relative value which society as a whole assigns, or ought to assign, to present as opposed to future consumption at the margin (Henderson 1965). According to various writers, the STP rate attaches more importance to the future than private time preference rate, and so it should be the former that is the relevant rate to be used for determining the allocation of present resources between investment and consumption. This is based on Pigou's argument that individuals are short-sighted about the future and that without government intervention not enough investment would be forthcoming to meet the needs of future generations. This implies that the STP rate is lower than the private one. However, the difficulty with this approach is the determination of the social rate of time preference and that, under non-optimal conditions that are likely to be the norm, different rates would be used in the private and public sectors, which will lead to inefficiency in the allocation of funds for investment purposes. This would be less of a problem if the government took steps to reduce market rates down to the social rate, so that all investment decisions could be made on the same basis. However, while this principle may be fine it is not easy to accomplish in practice, where we still have to deal with sub-optimisation problems, and thus choices of the rate of discount.

As an alternative to STP rate, one may consider the SOC rate of interest associated with the relevant project. The opportunity cost of any public investment project is the value to society of the best alternative use that the resources financing the public investment project would have been put instead. In other words, it is the value of the best foregone alternative. This value (opportunity cost) can then be divided by the resources (initial capital of the project) and multiplied by 100 to give us a rate in percentage terms, the SOC rate that can be used for discounting purposes (Henderson 1968). The underlying assumption here is that one allocates scarce resources between the private and public sectors, rather than determining the total amount to be invested in an economy. However, because of company taxation and of risk in undertaking private investment projects, market rates of return are likely to diverge from an SOC rate (Baumol 1968). In addition, it may be argued that public investment does not displace at the margin private investment. Private consumption or public consumption on goods and services may be equal candidates. Earlier suggestions that one may use the government's borrowing rate as an appropriate rate of discount are not without problems either, despite the fact that such a rate may be considered as a risk-free rate of interest. First, it is not always the case that public funds invested are only raised through selling long-term debt, i.e., bonds, since the state can use funds raised through taxation to finance investment projects too. Second, the long-term bond rate fluctuates in accordance with the government's monetary policy and, therefore, it has very little, if any, relevance to be used either as an SOC or as an STP rate of discount.

Given this disquiet regarding the earlier approaches, a number of writers have suggested a method that takes into account both the STP rate and a calculation of the SOC. This approach rejects the assumption that public investment displaces at the margin an equivalent amount of private investment. It can displace, instead, any kind of expenditure. The idea here is that one discounts a public investment project at a predetermined STP rate. At the next stage we need to examine the stream of net benefits of the best alternative project that is displaced by the public investment project in social terms (i.e., the SOC) and then evaluate its present value at the same STP rate used earlier. Clearly, the public investment project is accepted only if its present value discounted at the STP rate exceeds the present value of the SOC discounted at the STP rate. Thus, denoting by PV the present value, r the STP rate, NB the net benefits (returns) of the public investment project and SOC the social value of the net benefits of the best foregone alternative (i.e., the social opportunity cost) of the public investment project, we have:

$$PV_r(NB) - PV_r(SOC) > 0$$

The above method suffers from the difficulty of determining the SOC of a project and the need to find out exactly what kind (or kinds) of final expenditure it displaces. Particularly, if a public investment project is thought to have displaced public consumption, private investment and private consumption in some given proportions, one needs to find the present values of the displaced categories of expenditure, expressed in social terms, to arrive at the present value of the SOC of the initial capital cost of the public investment project.

The previous discussion has demonstrated that no clear and unequivocal instruction exists as regards the choice of a discount rate for the purposes of public investment projects. Prest and Turvey (1965) conclude their section on the choice of interest rate as 'whatever one does, one tries to unscramble an omelette, and no one has yet invented a uniquely superior way of doing this'. And one way of unscrambling this problem may lie at the hands of governments. We conclude, therefore, by noting at this juncture that the UK had introduced a test rate of discount of 8% in 1967, raised to 10% in 1969, for the purposes of the evaluation of investment projects of nationalised industries. That rate had been justified on the grounds that it ought be sufficient to ensure that resources were used efficiently and that it represented the minimum rate of return to be expected on a marginal low-risk investment undertaken in the private sector in the UK at the time, as explained in the White Paper, *Nationalized Industries: A Review of Economic and Financial Objectives* (1967). The derivation of that rate was based, partly, on opportunity cost considerations, as described above, and partly on promoting growth and did not allow for inflation.

14.4   REGULATION OF INDUSTRY

Over the years governments have expanded drastically their involvement in the running of the economy and have sought to regulate industry for a number of reasons aiming, among others, at the support of business, the protection of consumers, workers and the environment. According to the economic theory of regulation, the latter is the result of the action of various pressure groups, such as business and professional associations, trades unions, environmentalists and the like lobbying their governments for legislation protecting their interests. Thus, governments operate a system of licences, which are necessary for entering into particular industries, such as operating a radio or a TV station, or occupations, be they professions (e.g., law, medicine, pharmacy), or certain trades (train drivers, lorry drivers). Whilst this is done for the protection of the public, it does confer an element of monopoly power to powerful associations or trades unions through their ability to enforce a strict system of admissions into their occupations. This restriction of entry and competition is clearly translated into higher incomes for the licence holders, be they doctors or train drivers. The pharmaceutical industry is also subject to controls and licencing of new medicines. Also, governments intervene by granting patents to inventors, which provide the right to the latter for the exclusive use of their inventions for a number of years. Whilst this results in a form of monopoly power for the patent holder, it is done in order to encourage inventions and technological development and change. Other government legislation aims at the protection of workers at the workplace, and this has become also part of the EU's social policy. In the past, other restrictions were aimed at the free flow of international trade, in the form of tariffs or quotas, in order to support domestic producers. This form of intervention has now become illegal certainly for intra-EU trade, and through the work of the World Trade Organisation (WTO) has declined in importance, but in certain industries, for example, the automotive industry it is still present. In this chapter, we look very briefly at the work of a number of bodies that have been set up in recent years for the regulation, primarily, of the privatised utilities and more extensively at competition policy in the UK and the EU.

14.4.1   Regulation of privatised utilities and other industries

In the UK, the privatisations of the public utilities in the 1980s and 1990s have enabled the government to introduce new forms of regulation by establishing a number of independent regulators. Thus, utilities, whether public or private, are regulated by appropriate authorities, or bodies, such as Office of Gas Supply (OFGAS) in the case of the British Gas distribution and supply industry, Office of Telecommunications (OFTEL) in the case of the telecommunications industry, Office of Electricity Regulation (OFFER) for electricity generation, supply and distribution, Office of Water Services (OFWAT) for water supply and disposal, Civil Aviation Authority (CAA) for the major British airports operated by the British Airports Authority, the Office of the Rail Regulator for the railways and so on. These bodies are headed by a Director General and their main aim is to licence the various operators and administer the industry in a way to obtain the best deal for consumers in quality, choice and value for money. This aim is best achieved through the promotion of effective competition in their particular industries and, consequently, such regulatory bodies are in close collaboration with the Competition Commission (formerly MMC), of which more below.

Regulation by these bodies may focus on specific aspects of the utilities' policies and/or operations, for example, pricing. The government afraid that the newly privatised utilities would exercise their considerable monopoly power to make monopoly profits sought to regulate price increases in the utilities by means of a general formula having the form: $(RPI - X + Y)$. In the formula, RPI stands for the retail price index taken to be an index of inflation, the X element represents a percentage increase in productivity gains for the industry in question that are likely to reduce its costs of production and, finally, element Y stands for a percentage increase in costs that lie outside the control of the regulated firm. For example, with $X = 5\%$, price increases given by the $(RPI - X)$ part of the formula are limited to 5% below the RPI, meaning that real prices should fall by 5% for that part. However, the overall price change must take into account the Y element, which in the case, for example, of British Gas may be high, illustrating the fact that supplies from North Sea can only be secured at additional cost. Such increased costs would be allowed to be passed on to final consumers to ensure the industry's viability. The Y element would depend on the industry's forecasts, and any errors in such forecasts – and thus the Y element – and ultimately in prices would have to be adjusted accordingly in future. Clearly the X and Y elements are set differently for the different industries to reflect their underlying conditions, and the Y element may take the value of zero. These price formulas apply for a period of 4–5 years and then they are renegotiated.

As an example we consider the case of telecommunications where, on account of the dominant position of British Telecom (BT) in fixed telephony, price controls have been used by OFTEL since 1984 to restrict BT from excessive pricing and to protect consumers. These controls have required BT to lower prices because there has been insufficient competition in the retail market to exert downward pressure on prices. Since price controls were introduced, BT's residential calls prices have fallen by over 50% in real terms. However, at the same time the controls have also been used to encourage BT to increase its efficiency. This was done by offering BT incentives to increase its efficiency and keep the benefits of cost reductions until the end of the price control period, if these cost reductions are higher than those that had been anticipated when the controls were set in. These controls have, generally, been set for four years. More specifically BT has been subject to the current price controls since 1 August 1997. In terms of our earlier formula these controls were set at $(RPI - 4.5\%)$, thus Y was set at a value of zero, and limited BT's ability to increase prices for a basket of services provided to the bottom 80% of residential customers. The services controlled have included: connection of a new service; takeover of a service already installed; line rental; local geographic call; national geographic call; international calls; and operator assisted calls. The controls excluded the top 20% of residential customers because OFTEL believed that this highest spending residential segment together with business customers would get a better deal by competition than it would be delivered by the price controls. These controls were extended for a further year to 31 July 2002. In addition, OFTEL has also controlled BT's retention for calls to BTCellnet and Vodafone since 1 April 1999. These controls were introduced because competition in calls to mobiles was not strong enough to protect consumers. They were set at (RPI − 7%) for three years, and were extended for four months to align them with controls for the other retail services referred to above. Looking now at the case of fixed telephony, provided BT manages to achieve cost reductions in excess of 4.5% in the period of the price controls it can keep such efficiency gains. However, if at the next renegotiation OFTEL decides to increase the X element, because of publicity regarding the 'excessive' profits, then this amounts not so much to price controls as profit regulation, which may have adverse effects on future investment by BT.

These price controls are expected to be removed once competition in the industry is judged to have increased sufficiently to achieve the same result. OFTEL cannot create investment in infrastructure. Instead it sets the rules consistent with its overall strategy and in response to the needs of new entrants and overall impact on the market. OFTEL's objectives are: effective competition – benefiting consumers; well informed consumers; adequately protected consumers; and prevention of anti-competitive practice. The general principle underlying these objectives is to regulate only where it is likely to bring a net benefit to the consumers and keep regulation to a minimum necessary to obtain appropriate outcomes. In pursuing these objectives, OFTEL's policies helped during the 1990s in the establishment of infrastructure competition in both the fixed and mobile sectors by the creation of alternative networks, so that currently over half of the UK households are covered by cable networks; there are four UK-wide mobile networks; for business customers, key business areas of major cities are covered by one or more alternative metropolitan networks; and there is significant capacity in trunk networks between major cities. These developments were the result of significant investment in UK telecoms networks of all types, which reached around €8 billion in both 2000 and 2001 and was on top of substantial investment in the 1990s by cable, BT, mobile and other operators of around €50 billion (OFTEL 2002a, 2002b). At the time of writing, a new body is proposed to be established, OFCOM, which will be a super-regulatory authority replacing a number of other bodies, including OFTEL, for the communications industry as a whole.

14.4.2 Competition policy

We now turn to consider another very important area of industry regulation, namely, competition policy. Competition policy or antitrust (or antimonopoly) legislation is the main form of industry regulation and has been in existence for many years in most industrially advanced countries. For example, antitrust legislation in the US has been present for over hundred years, with the Sherman Act having been enacted in 1890; although in the UK the experience has been shorter, since the first antimonopoly legislation was passed in 1948, and in most other European countries such experience has been shorter still. In the context of the EU competition policy was an explicit part of the Treaty of Rome. In what follows we shall be reviewing the American, British and European experiences of competition policy and trying to establish what conclusions management can draw from the application of such policies.

The reasons for such policy have to do with concerns regarding the persistent divergence, in some markets, of price from marginal cost and, thus, the failure of the system to achieve a more efficient allocation of resources in those markets. In addition, a number of other impediments may be obstructing competition, consequently, antimonopoly, or antitrust, or competition policy is proposed in order to curb certain excesses of the market and improve its allocative efficiency. This shows that an essential element of competition policy is agreement on its objectives. It is the role of economic theory to provide such objectives, but there does not seem to be a consensus among economists on this issue. Indeed, there is disagreement on the desirability of even having an antimonopoly policy at all. Nevertheless, in a decentralised economy, most people would agree that there is a need for a means to checking the excesses of the system and strengthening the 'unseen hand' to perform its job better. The objectives and rules of antitrust policy are controversial, and an attempted resolution of the controversy is outside the confines of this book. Nevertheless, a proper understanding of antimonopoly legislation requires a brief discussion of economic and legal factors.

14.5 THE ECONOMIC BASIS OF ANTIMONOPOLY POLICY

Antimonopoly policy is usually cast in terms of promoting or protecting the competitive process, for the purpose of the more efficient working of the markets. By encouraging efficiency, competition also contributes to the international competitiveness of the country. Not unnaturally, a precise definition of the kind of competition the policy seeks to preserve or achieve is usually omitted. The difficulty is that only perfect competition can produce beneficial results to society, in terms of the optimum allocation of resources, usually associated with 'competition'. This concept of competition, however, is unrealistic for the purposes of antitrust policy, since it is not desirable to change drastically the structural organisation of various markets. In addition, in a competitive market, the incentive for research and innovation in new products and new methods of production may be missing. Technical progress may require some element of monopoly, as Schumpeter suggested. In this context, one needs to examine also the movement towards the establishment of a more concentrated industrial structure through mergers and takeovers. Whether mergers are or are not in the public interest requires the analysis of a set of diverse factors; reliable data on which to base such analysis may, in many cases, be unavailable to management of merging firms, let alone be at the disposal of any commission charged with antimonopoly policy enforcement. Since the degree of confidence with which one can pronounce upon the desirability of mergers is limited, how can economic theory help?

In neoclassical economics monopoly is condemned, *per se*, on the familiar grounds of misallocation of resources. The case is presented in Figure 14.6 where we assume a perfectly competitive industry, with constant average costs in a long-run state. In this case, equilibrium occurs at point B, where AR = AC and, therefore, the competitive price and output configuration is given by P_C and Q_C. In this state, the industry is earning only normal profits and the consumers enjoy a consumers' surplus given by the triangle AP_CB. If this industry is monopolised, with everything else remaining the same, the monopolist in his attempt to maximize profits equates his marginal revenue to marginal cost and, thus, equilibrium occurs at point C, implying an output and price configuration of Q_M and P_M. Clearly, in this case there is a lower output and a higher price, as compared with the competitive

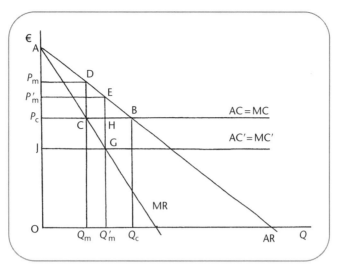

Figure 14.6 The cost of monopoly

equilibrium. In addition, the monopolist appropriates for himself the area $P_C P_M DC$ that becomes his supernormal profit. This is a straight transfer from consumers' surplus to the producer. The new consumers' surplus is restricted to the area $AP_M D$ and the triangle DCB, which was part of the competitive consumers' surplus, vanishes into thin air, as a result of the monopolisation of the industry. This area DCB is known as the dead-weight welfare loss of monopoly, and represents the grounds on which monopoly is condemned a priori. By considering the effect of a merger we see that by increasing monopoly power, a merger might help bring about higher prices and consequently allocative inefficiency. Early estimates of such welfare losses of monopoly in the US, had suggested that they came to represent less than 0.1 per cent of GNP (Harberger 1954; Schwartzman 1960). However, other researchers have argued that the costs of monopoly cannot be ignored, and have estimated such costs to be as high as 7% of national income (Cowling and Mueller 1978).

A problem with the preceding analysis is that it is essentially static in nature and assumes that the monopolist's costs remain the same as under the competitive industry. The opposite argument suggests that the monopolisation of a competitive industry, by concentrating production in optimal plants and shutting down sub-optimal ones, can result in significant cost reductions. Therefore, it should be possible to trade-off such cost savings against the social costs of monopoly, in the form of dead-weight welfare losses, and if such cost savings exceeded the welfare losses for the monopolisation (or the merger for that matter) to be permitted to proceed. In Figure 14.6 we assume that after the monopolisation of the competitive industry, the monopolist's average costs are given by $AC' = MC'$. The new equilibrium occurs at point G, corresponding to an output and price configuration of Q'_M and P'_M. As compared with the earlier competitive equilibrium, in this case price is higher and output is lower. The reduction in output releases resources given by the rectangle $Q_C BHQ'_M$, which, we assume, can be used elsewhere in the economy and produce an output equal to their opportunity cost. The new dead-weight welfare loss is given by the triangle EHB. But the new monopoly output Q'_M is produced by using fewer resources, given by the rectangle $OJGQ'_M$, than the competitive output, thus, resulting in cost savings given by the rectangle JP_CHG. The social welfare function, W, to be maximised by society is given by the difference between total social benefit, TSB, and total social cost, TSC, i.e., $W = TSB - TSC = TR + CS - TC = CS + (TR - TC) = CS + PS$, where CS and PS are consumers' surplus and producers' surplus, respectively. Since social welfare, whose maximisation is sought, is given by the sum of consumers' and producers' surpluses, it is possible for the benefits of mergers in the form of cost reductions (accruing to producers) to outweigh the social costs of mergers, i.e., for area JP_CHG to be larger than EHB, and, thus, for mergers to be beneficial to public interest. Therefore, in a case where through an increase of market power, a merger leads to both allocative inefficiency and economies, it is proposed that a test be conducted to decide on whether the merger should be allowed. Mergers passing this test, should, subject to certain qualifications, be permitted to proceed (Williamson 1966). This argument, of course, leaves the question of distribution unanswered. It is assumed that to deal with the problem of the redistribution of income from consumers to producers, entailed by the merger, the authorities have at their disposal means other than antimonopoly policy, such as, for example, taxation policy.

However, the preceding discussion fails to take account of the fact that, apart from worsening allocative efficiency through the increase in price-cost margins, the increased monopoly power, likely to be entailed by a merger, influences what Leibenstein has termed 'X-inefficiency'. Since by a merger the forces of competition are diminished, there is less incentive for the firm to pursue policies of cost minimisation. It is likely, therefore, according to this argument, that X-inefficiency increases, as a result of an increase in market power. It has, in fact, been estimated that the welfare loss due to X-inefficiency is likely to be much larger than the welfare loss due to misallocation of resources (Leibenstein 1966; Comanor and Leibenstein 1969). Scherer, in the first edition of his book, calculates total losses, due to market power, for the American economy in 1966 to be 6.2% of GNP, but he also points out that because such estimates are subject to wide errors '. . .it seems improbable that the "true" combined social cost of monopoly, if it could be ascertained, would prove to be less than half or more than twice the estimated total of 6.2%' (Scherer 1970, p. 408). Further evidence of X-inefficiency in oligopolistic markets is provided by the managerial and behavioural theories of the firm, where 'management slack' or 'organisational slack' are recognised as important elements in shaping business objectives.

14.5.1 Workable competition

The preceding discussion has shown that the definition of competition provided by welfare theory is not particularly useful to guide us in shaping policy towards monopoly. We recall that under 'perfect' conditions, the tendency is for resources to be efficiently allocated, for prices to reflect the true opportunity cost of the resources used and, in the long run, for only the internally efficient firms to remain in operation, each producing at the lowest average cost (under the given technological conditions) and to full capacity. However, in industries characterised by significant economies of scale, only a few producers can remain effectively in the industry. In such cases, perfect competition may not be the best solution for society or the industry in question, and one may be forced to choose between a large number of competing firms, each unable to reach the required economies of scale for drastic cost reductions and consequent price reductions, or a few large firms, each able to achieve the full economies of scale but opposed to price competition. In other words, the choice may be between an industry conducive to maximising allocative efficiency and one that best serves the interests of technical efficiency. Therefore, since the preoccupation of perfect competition with price rivalry makes it unsuitable as a basis for antitrust policy, what kind of competition is acceptable as a guide to the formulation of such policy?

A number of authors had suggested in the past that a more appropriate definition to use is 'workable competition' originally coined by J.M. Clark (1940). The concept of workable competition is dynamic in nature, because its main concern are the elements stimulating economic rivalry, which are subject to change. Thus, the theory tries to evaluate different forms of industrial organisation and entrepreneurial policies by reference to the extent that they promote or hamper such rivalry. The main prerequisite for the existence of workable competition is an *adequate* number of choices of action open to both buyers and sellers. That is, there must be enough competition to provide reasonable alternatives. Workable competition could describe a market in which there were sufficient pressures to reward the enterprising and penalise the laggards and so promote progress. Consequently, workable competition might be a general condition of economic efficiency and progress and a handy tool of analysis (Allen 1968, p. 24). This view was supported by both academic economists and the American authorities in their treatment of antitrust laws (Oppenheim 1952; Berki 1966; Hunter 1969), and was reinforced by Schumpeter's thesis of *creative destruction* at the heart of which lies the idea that a degree of monopoly is necessary if an economy is to be progressive, discussed in Chapter 3.

However, while the apparent simplicity of workable competition can make the concept attractive, nevertheless the latter is not precise and leaves the 'adequate' to be determined in each case. In addition, the mere existence of opportunities does not necessarily mean that they will be grasped and exploited by 'budding' entrepreneurs, unless there is a desire for active behaviour or 'animal' spirits in the industry (Allen 1968, p. 23). Critics of the workable competition concept are opposed to its use on the grounds that it does not provide a clear, definite or measurable standard and its vagueness makes it unsuitable both as a basis on which to build an antitrust policy or as something that antitrust policy should aim to serve. According to these critics, the concept fails to outline how much competition must exist before an industry can be called 'workably competitive', or put it differently how much monopoly must be shown before antitrust action is justified. Proponents of the workable competition thesis had failed to cite examples of an American industry that was too monopolistic to be considered workably competitive. If anything, workable competition assumes that if predatory practices and monopolistic abuses can be controlled, an industry's market structure is of secondary importance, thus, ignoring Professor Stigler's dictum that 'an industry that does not have a competitive structure will not have competitive behaviour' (as quoted by Adams 1953). One has to remember that because of the very large size of the American market, which allows many competitors to achieve the full economies of scale, one can have the best of both worlds, namely, competition and technological development. Consequently, the dilemma posed by the pragmatism of workable competition that for efficiency and progress one needs very concentrated industries need not arise. After all competition policies and, in the context of American industry, the Sherman Act requires the promotion of more competition rather than the supervision of the policies and practices of monopoly (Adams 1953).

14.5.2 The structure–conduct–performance approach

The preceding discussion serves to illustrate that the issues under consideration are of an empirical nature and that the information required for formulating public policy should be obtained by empirical evidence, since knowledge of an a priori nature is often uncertain. Also, for countries where market size is a crucial consideration, a pragmatic approach, akin to workable competition, may be the only option available to inform policy-makers on the questions of monopoly and competition. The part of economic theory best suited for an analysis of this kind is the one dealing with market structure, conduct and economic performance. To the extent that it provides a better understanding of the workings of the various markets, the structure–conduct–performance approach enables economists to evaluate the contribution made by different market structures, according to a number of criteria of performance, and, therefore, it offers a firmer basis for an antitrust policy.

The structure–conduct–performance approach recognises that there is a functional relationship between structure, or rather the various elements of market structure, and performance through the conduct or behaviour of firms (i.e., through their pricing, investment and product policies). This then could allow us to set up certain non-controversial objectives of antitrust policy, which can be used, in turn, to assess performance. Basic elements of market structure likely to influence the conduct of firms strongly are seller concentration, barriers to entry of new firms and product differentiation. The precise way in which these elements (structure) interact and help form a firm's behaviour pattern, which in turn influences the firm's performance, may not be quite known and have to be established empirically in each case. Much more research is required in this area so that one could have

> ... fairly conclusive tests of the theoretically predicted associations of the seller concentration of industries to their price-cost margins or profit rates (measuring allocative efficiency); of their conditions of entry to the same and related aspects of performance; and of the degree of differentiation of their products to the size of their selling costs and possibly to other dimensions of performance (Bain 1968, p. 432).

Although the exact form of this functional relationship is not given, economic analysis and empirical work on the subject provide useful information with which the economist can attempt to formulate specific objectives of antitrust policy. One may begin by stressing that the main aim of legislation should be to foster a competitive system characterised by progressiveness and efficiency. This may sound like broad platitudes, but it has the merit of highlighting some of the crucial issues involved. By concentrating on the aspects of efficiency and progressiveness, one can evaluate the workings of different market structures and use the policy to bridge the gap between actual and potential performance.

Therefore, it should be possible to set up certain non-controversial goals that can be used as a means of testing and appraising market performance, by establishing the extent to which actual performance in specific markets deviates from potential performance, and then utilise public policy to correct certain deficiencies

(Bain 1968, p. 498; Caves 1972, p. 94). In discussing the industry's performance we are confronted with some issues best dealt with under macroeconomic theory. However, given that the industrial sector contributes, in most industrial countries, in excess of 25% of their GDP, the market performance of industries becomes the litmus test of how well they satisfy their social function of enhancing welfare within the economy as a whole, and so we are justified in setting down these goals. In doing so we are concerned with how the economy should perform in order to improve the living standards of its citizens. Thus, the overall goals that should be attained can be listed as follows:

1. *Efficiency*: The economy should be efficient utilising its scarce resources in ways that yield the greatest possible return.

2. *Full employment*: The economy should operate at or near its full employment level, otherwise we waste resources by keeping them idle and fail to provide for more income. In addition, one cannot ignore the personal hardships of the unemployed.

3. *Price stability*: If possible we must try to achieve price stability. There may be a conflict between this goal and the previous one, but we should try to achieve the second goal without undue inflation in the general price level.

4. *Growth–Technical progress–Innovations*: The economy should be progressive. It should improve and add to its stock of factors of production, raise the quality and variety of products it produces and also improve the techniques with which it arranges and organises production.

5. *Equitable distribution*: The economy should be equitable, distributing its output among its citizens in order to provide for their essential needs and reasonable expectations, and also rewarding their productive efforts.

We can define market performance as the appraisal of how much the economic results of an industry's market conduct deviate from the best possible contribution it could make towards achieving the above goals. Clearly, these are not the goals and objectives of individual firms. However, they are set exactly in order to test the firm's or industry's contribution to the goals of the economy as a whole. By finding out how much actual market performance deviates from potential market performance, we could establish reasons for these deviations and suggest ways of eliminating them.

It has been the case that competition policies following the '*rule of reason*' approach, which is discussed below, have relied on some kind of market appraisal along the lines referred to above. As suggested earlier, the explanation is to be found in the size of the national market and the related issue of economies of scale argument, which was and still is underlying most of European competition policies, but this argument has been much weakened by the establishment of the Single Market in the EU.

14.6 LEGAL RULES, METHODS AND MACHINERY

If antimonopoly policy is to be successful, appropriate legal rules need to be formulated and the machinery for the implementation of such policy needs to be set up (Berki 1966). Generally speaking, the choice is between a set of rules charac-terised either by flexibility or by rigidity. Fixed rules, often denounced because of their rigidity, nonetheless provide firms with sufficient assurance as to where they stand *vis-à-vis* the law. The predictability of fixed rules ensures businessmen know whether their actions and decisions are 'legal' or 'illegal'. In this respect fixed rules tend to minimise uncertainty as regards certain actions of management, and there may be some merit in recommending them. On the other hand, it is agreed that fixed rules do impose a straightjacket on business. Accordingly, one looks at the alternative of flexible rules. The adoption of general principles guiding antimono-poly policy, with the advantage of greater flexibility, would result in an element of uncertainty, and also in unavoidable delays in antimonopoly litigation.

Flexible rules, therefore, suffer in two respects; they increase uncertainty for firms, and tend to render the antimonopoly legislation ineffective. In the American antitrust literature, fixed and flexible rules have come to be known as the *'per se'* versus the *'rule of reason'* doctrines, respectively. Under the *'per se'* doctrine if certain company agreements, decisions or actions, which themselves are illegal, are shown to have taken place then this means that an offence has been committed and the necessary penalties have to be imposed; while the latter exercises 'reasonableness' as the means to establish whether or not illegal conduct exists. The *'rule of reason'* doctrine considers, for example, that the loss in competition may be outweighed by other advantages. However, the role of these legal rules is to facilitate judicial enquiries and to help in the interpretation of the law in particular cases. This means that discussion of the main lines of thought regarding legislation for the promotion of competition must precede the examination of such legal rules. By and large, antimonopoly policy has sought to promote and to protect competition by any of the following methods, either singly or in combination:

1. By the outright prohibition of certain agreements, decisions or actions by two or more firms; for example, the fixing of prices, the sharing of markets and so on.

2. By allowing such agreements, decisions or actions but retaining the right to refer such agreements to an appropriate body, which would be vested with the authority to proscribe such practices, on the grounds that they are 'socially unacceptable'.

3. By requiring prior notification and registration of such agreements, decisions and actions. An appropriate body would then be called upon to recommend whether or not the said agreements should be put on the register.

It should be emphasised that these methods deal with the problem of restrictive practices only, leaving the problem of monopoly to be tackled in a different man-ner, if at all. However, the legal rules mentioned above seem to apply to both issues; the treatment of monopoly power and that of restrictive practices. The first and third methods constitute a more appropriate preventative approach to antitrust, while the second is more applicable if a curative approach is favoured or is necessary.

The first method proves 'illegality' simply by showing that certain agreements have indeed taken place. Conviction depends, however, upon the court's inter-pretation of the law. This method is obviously rigid and, within the framework of the free enterprise system, can be considered a significant constraint on the freedom of businessmen. Under the second method, firms are, in principle, free to enter into certain agreements, but face the possibility of having such agreements investigated by authorised bodies, which can declare them either lawful and retainable or unlawful and, thus, unenforceable. Therefore, particular agreements or decisions harmful to society can be perpetuated until such time as the rather slow investigative machinery catches up with the culprits. In the interim, however, markets may have been injured and consumers exploited. The judicial decisions cannot hope to remedy fully the damage done in the interim period, because such decisions tend to be made tardily and acted upon half-heartedly. The third method relies on prior notification of such agreements to a competent authority, which must rule on whether or not the agreements are within the law. Those agreements, which pass the test of acceptability, are then placed on a special register and are allowed to be implemented. This method may go some way towards meeting criticisms levelled at the other two.

It would appear that the first method is more likely to give rise to conflict between the *rule of reason* and the *per se* doctrines. The rigidity of approach of this first method contrasts with the flexibility inherent in the other two. Legislation, which reflects a *pragmatic* approach to problems of monopoly and of restrictive practices tends to be based upon either the second or third methods, or upon a combination of the two. On the other hand, a *per se* or *structural* approach is based upon the first method.

It has been suggested that if the first method is used, the existence of any prohibited action proves guilt. However, as regards the second and third methods, the distinction between a firm's lawful or unlawful behaviour is based upon consideration of all the relevant factors. Each case, in other words, is examined solely on its own merits. To facilitate examination along these lines, it is useful to compare the results of each case against some kind of abstract criterion, namely, that which purports to promote the public interest. However, 'public interest' is by no means easy to define. Indeed, even legislation explicitly stated to be for the purpose of protecting the public interest contains no such definition. The most that one can expect is perhaps to obtain a list of various guidelines which, in the opinion of the legislators, can be considered conducive to protecting the public interest. What these specific guidelines are, and how they are arrived at, is the product of a weighing up of economic, social, political and other factors. In this respect, political will to arrive at, and to enforce an effective policy, is an important factor, not only in shaping such guidelines, but in making antimonopoly policy successful.

The last element in an antitrust legislation is the establishment of an appropriate mechanism, i.e., of the various procedures and of competent authority, the latter being empowered to implement and to enforce the legislation. For example, the tasks of initiating searches and of bringing to light legislative violations, of instituting proceedings for ascertaining and remedying such violations, of preparing and presenting the case against the culprits in a court, and of ensuring that the recommendations of the court are enforced, must be covered and established by the legislation.

However, the mere existence of such legislation does not necessarily ensure the promotion and protection of competitive forces in an economy. This depends upon the way in which the policy is enforced. As is the case in the entire field of public policy, applicability may be circumscribed by a number of factors. Prominent amongst these factors are the political will, i.e., the degree of political commitment to its aims, and the compatibility/incompatibility between the aims of the legislation and those of general public policy, notably economic policy. It is unlikely that the promotion and protection of competition will feature highly in the list of priorities of any government. Usually, whenever there are economic difficulties, the first victim is competition. These considerations, as well as the 'pragmatic' approach, may well lead to a less than eager enforcement of such policy (Petrochilos 1979, 1981).

14.7 ANTITRUST POLICY IN THE US

It is customary to start discussion of antimonopoly policy with the American experience, since the Americans were the first to tackle this problem. The first American antitrust legislation, the Sherman Act of 1890, had its origins in radical opposition to the excesses of the free enterprise system. It was a reaction to the growth of trusts and of restrictive practices of business. The Act contained two types of prohibition: one proscribed various restrictive practices (contracts, combinations, conspiracies), while the other made it illegal for a person to 'monopolise' or 'attempt to monopolise'. Further legislation was enacted in 1914 with the Federal Trade Commission Act, in 1915 with the Clayton Act, in 1936 with the Robinson–Patman Amendment to the Clayton Act, in 1938 with the Wheeler–Lee Amendment to the Federal Trade Commission Act, in 1950 with the Celler–Kefauver Anti-merger Amendment of the Clayton Act (Section 7) and, finally, in 1952 with the Federal Fair Trade Act.

One would have expected then that such huge panoply of antitrust legislation should have precluded monopoly and monopolistic practices in the American economy. However, that has not quite been the case. It was mainly in the area of anti-competitive conduct that the attention of the authorities was directed. The early vigorous application of the Sherman Act resulted in the formulation of the fixed rules, discussed above, with two stringent standards, which made illegal restrictive practices of trade and mergers between previously competing firms. Price fixing, in particular, was declared illegal, *per se*, a declaration reaffirmed on a number of occasions and under which, in 1961, seven executives were given prison sentences.

American antitrust legislation is almost unique in that it places such importance on competition that it, i.e., competition, becomes not the means towards certain ends but the end itself. Yet, the Sherman Act has been powerless to deal with concentration of power; no significant case seeking to reduce or limit concentration having been filed for at least 20 years prior to 1972 (Boyle 1972, p. 159). On the monopoly front, Blair summarises the history of the Sherman Act as follows: 'Broadly speaking, enforcement of the Sherman Act's proscription of monopoly began with a little more than a decade of quiet neglect, followed by vigorous application up to 1911, only to be followed by nearly a half century of quiet judicial interment, then by a little-noted rebirth in the late 1940s and early 1950s, and finally a second interment – this time at the hands of the enforcing agency' (Blair 1972, p. 555). To an extent, this may be due to the original *'per se'* rule having been changed in 1911 and the *'rule of reason'* doctrine having been introduced into judicial thinking. This, according to a number of critics, led to the emasculation of the antitrust policy.

Before 1945, the attitude both of the Antitrust agencies and of the courts was that the mere size of a firm did not constitute an offence and that a firm had to exert monopoly power, through restrictive conduct, before it could be prosecuted. However, in the Alcoa case in 1945 there was a change in judicial thinking, which condemned monopoly *per se* and put an end to the 'good-trust v. bad-trust' criterion, which had dominated judicial decisions for the previous quarter of a century.

On the merger front, there had virtually been a free run up to 1950, with all types of merger activity continuing almost unchecked. This was due to the fact that: (1) Section 7 of the Clayton Act prohibited only the acquisition of a competing firm's stock not its assets, and (2) a decision of the Supreme Court in 1926 made prosecution under the Clayton Act almost impossible. However, following the amendment of this Act in 1950, the American Antitrust agencies, i.e., the Federal Trade Commission and the Antitrust Division of the Department of Justice, have pursued a different policy, have filed many merger complaints and have managed almost to eliminate horizontal mergers. During the period 1926–30, horizontal mergers accounted for 64.3% of total merger activity; between 1951 and 1969, during which time such activity accelerated from 235 manufacturing and mining acquisitions to 2407, horizontal mergers declined from 35% to 9% of the total. 'In summary, it appears that it is only in the area of horizontal merger activity, and even there only since 1950, that the government has made any progress in halting or slowing the pace of increasing concentration' (Boyle 1972, p. 161). But the pace of the conglomerate mergers continued unabated, reaching 82% of the total in the period 1966–69 and persuading even businessmen of the need for stronger legislation (Blair 1972, pp. 597–599). However, the operation of the amended Section 7 of the Clayton Act, with its restrictive effect on merger activity, drew the wrath of the defenders of mergers, who argued that, far from impeding competition, mergers may be actually enhancing it – provided monopoly and oligopoly are attained through efficiency and are characterised by freedom of entry, and asked for the repeal of Section 7 of the Clayton Act (Peterson 1961).

The best case of vertical restrictions on trade is given by resale price maintenance (RPM), i.e., the practice of manufacturers combining to set a retail price and force retailers to accept it, and it provides us with an example of frequent changes in direction of official US policy. While collective RPM is proscribed by the Sherman Act, individual RPM had a rather uneven path. In the early years individual RPM had been declared to be a *'per se'* violation of the Sherman Act and, thus, illegal, but this ruling was challenged on the grounds of fair trading and legislative action established its legality. In fact, the Federal Fair Trade Act of 1952 not only established the right of manufacturers and retailers to agree to RPM, but could also force other retailers who were not party to such agreement to charge the same price. However, in the mid-1970s the fair trade legislation was repealed and the *'per se'* ruling was again adopted. Nevertheless, changes in attitude were such that in 1982 the Department of Justice itself tried unsuccessfully to remove the *per se* approach to RPM! And despite the fact that the courts have retained the *'per se'* doctrine, the scope on the proscription of RPM has narrowed, and over the last ten years vertical restrictions have remained practically unchallenged.

The vacillations of American antitrust policy may be due to the fact that in spite of the professed devotion to the competitive ideals, few people in Congress, the courts and in business seem prepared to see antitrust policy becoming an effective means of checking economic power and restrictive practices. Businessmen have an incentive to avoid competition and instead try to build up monopolistic defences against the uncertainties and insecurities associated with competitive markets. For example, the ability to manipulate the market, and make price decisions independently of its competitive forces, is one of the characteristics of oligopoly attractive to businessmen. In this, they may be prepared to evade or even violate the law, particularly where the 'rewards' of such actions are large. In these attempts they have inadvertently been helped by a confusion between Congress and the courts as regards the objectives of antitrust. Other factors contributing to this situation have been the shortage of funds and of personnel in the antitrust agencies. This shortage has, naturally, hindered the agencies' ability to deal effectively with laborious and time-consuming cases. Even where companies have been found guilty of breaches of antitrust, the penalty has often been small and, consequently, could not have a strong deterrent effect upon other companies contemplating similar actions. As a result, the overall effect of American antitrust policy in shaping the industrial organisation of the American economy has, at best, been minimal.

14.8   COMPETITION POLICY IN THE UK

The British experience of monopoly and restrictive practices has varied over time. Before the enactment of special antimonopoly legislation these aspects were treated under the common law. In certain cases contracts tending to create monopoly by eliminating competition, restricting output and regulating prices and wages, have been declared to be an illegal restraint of trade and, thus, void. But the courts have been reluctant to declare contracts void on account of reasons of public policy and few agreements were, therefore, upset on this ground (Stevens and Borrie 1973, p. 517). The British antimonopoly legislation was the product of a social, legal and political environment different to the American, and it followed in the wake of the full employment policy of the government, envisaged in the White Paper of 1944, being almost a by-product of that policy.

14.8.1   The original legislation

The first antitrust legislation in Britain was enacted in 1948 with the Monopolies and Restrictive Practices Act. The Act established the Monopolies and Restrictive Practices Commission, an independent administrative tribunal with a minimum of four and a maximum of ten members that was empowered to examine: (1) if a monopoly did exist and (2) if the monopoly worked against the 'public interest'. Monopoly was held to exist if a firm had one-third or more of a particular market, though it was not the existence but the abuse of monopoly power that was contrary to public interest. The Commission would act on cases referred to it by the Minister of the Board of Trade. After investigation, the Commission would report its findings to the Minister, who would then decide on appropriate action.

The Act did not define 'public interest' but it gave the Commission certain guidelines according to which the public interest would best be served. Within these guidelines came any firm with monopoly power, which ensured: the most efficient production and distribution for home and overseas markets; the reflection of such efficiency in quality, volume and prices; the encouragement of new enterprise; the optimum allocation of the country's resources; significant technological advance; the expansion of existing markets and the development of new ones. This guidance, however, proved of little use to the members of the Commission, who were left to use their common sense in dealing with these problems (Allen 1968, p. 66).

The policy introduced a pragmatic approach to tackling the problems of monopoly and restrictive practices, but it suffered from the lack of clear objectives and criteria; pragmatism being insufficient to ensure the policy's effectiveness. To meet criticisms of the way in which the legislation worked, the Monopolies and Restrictive Practices Commission Act was passed in 1953. This Act increased the size of the Commission and, in order to expedite matters, allowed it to subdivide and to process several enquiries simultaneously.

Following a general report by the Commission on the incidence and possible harmful effects of widespread restrictive practices in the UK industry, the Restrictive Trade Practices Act was enacted in 1956. The Act separated the control of restrictive practices from that of monopoly and established both: a Registrar of Restrictive Trading Agreements and a Restrictive Practices Court to deal with the former. It also set up a new Monopolies Commission, abolishing at the same time the old one, to deal with the question of monopoly. The Act, however, reduced the size of the Commission and prevented it from subdividing for the purpose of pursuing simultaneous investigations. It also prohibited the collective enforcement of resale price maintenance (RPM), whereas the 1964 Resale Prices Act prohibited the enforcement of minimum resale prices by individual manufacturers, except under certain conditions.

However, dissatisfaction with the monopolies legislation continued. Existing monopolies could be dealt with by the legislation but there was no preventative means of dealing with takeovers and mergers, which threatened to create new monopolies or to strengthen existing ones. Moreover, the legislation applied only to suppliers and processors of goods, thus, excluding the service industries. The small size of the Commission was also an obstacle in that it slowed down the pace of investigations. As a result, the Monopolies and Mergers Act was passed in 1965. It envisaged that proposed and actual mergers, with certain qualifications, could be referred to the Monopolies Commission for investigation of possible harmful effects on public interest. This particularly applied where mergers involved assets in excess of €5 million. The Act increased the size of the Commission and empowered them to subdivide again. It also brought the service industries within the ambit of the law. In 1968, the Restrictive Practices Act amended the 1956 Restrictive Trade Practices Act in three minor ways.

14.8.2   The changing nature of competition policy

Nevertheless, the vagueness both of the legislative objectives and criteria were such that uncertainty persisted. The reference of mergers to the Commission was characterised by an element of arbitrariness and inconsistency, which was due, in some measure, to the pragmatic way in which merger policy applied. Also responsible for this inconsistency was the overall economic policy of the government.

Thus, in 1966, the government established the Industrial Reorganisation Corporation (IRC), as a marriage broker, which sought to promote rationalisation schemes that would yield substantial benefits to the national economy. This involved the IRC in the promotion of some 50 mergers; it even involved the acceptance of one merger that the Commission had previously declared to be against the public interest.

To correct the above deficiencies, the Fair Trading Act was promulgated in 1973. The Act introduced new administrative machinery for the implementation of the legislation, as well as two important points of substance. It repealed the 1946 and 1965 Acts and amended others. It set up the Office of Fair Trading (OFT) and the Consumer Protection Advisory Committee and appointed a Director General of the Office of Fair Trading (DGFT). The Director General, among other functions, took over the duties of the Registrar of the Restrictive Trading Agreements; he was also empowered to initiate references to a reconstituted Monopolies and Mergers Commission (MMC). The Secretary of State, however, could overrule the Director General and the former retained also the right of reference.

Apart from these essentially administrative changes, the Act was significant in other ways. For example, the extent of market share necessary to constitute a monopoly was reduced from one-third to one-quarter. The guidance as to what constitutes public interest was also altered and for the first time it emphasised the maintenance and promotion of competition. This was the clearest indication yet that competition was recognised as desirable and in the public interest. However, this did not change the basic favourable attitude of government towards mergers. For example, of a total of 353 acquisitions in 1976 there were only four references.

In 1976, the Restrictive Trade Practices Act was promulgated, consolidating earlier provisions of a restrictive practices nature, followed also by the Restrictive Practices Act of 1977. Similarly, in 1976 the Resale Prices Act was passed, bringing together part II of the 1956 Act proscribing collective RPM, and the prohibition of the 1964 Act of individual RPM, except for certain conditions. Finally, in 1980, the Competition Act was enacted to enable the DGFT to investigate anti-competitive practices of firms and refer them to the MMC, and also refer monopolies to the same body.

To recapitulate and see who did what in UK competition policy until the end of the 1990s we provide the following summary. In the area of mergers, the powers involved the DGFT, who as head of the OFT would advise the Secretary of State on merger activity, and the latter, helped by the services of the Department of Trade and Industry (DTI), would decide on whether to refer the merger to the MMC for a report.

Mergers were referred only if the assets involved exceeded €30 million, or a 25% share of the market was created or increased. Mergers could only be blocked if the MMC found them to be against the public interest, although the Secretary of State might decide to let them proceed, subject to conditions. In the area of monopoly and anti-competitive practices, i.e., conduct distorting the market, again the DGFT, helped by the OFT, would investigate anti-competitive practices and could refer them to the MMC for a report. He could also refer to the MMC monopolies, if he suspected unfair behaviour. The MMC would have to assess whether anti-competitive practices or a monopoly were against the public interest. The Secretary of State was empowered to stop practices, which the MMC had found to be against the public interest. In the area of restrictive practices, the DGFT would register restrictive agreements and would refer them to the Restrictive Practices Court for a ruling. The latter could ban restrictions found to be against the public interest.

Finally, in addition to the functions already mentioned, the MMC could be asked to investigate on general issues and restrictive labour practices, on nationalised industries and other public bodies and on utilities.

In a survey of attitudes of industry towards the competition policy and authorities, undertaken by Coopers & Lybrand Deloitte, almost 600 senior executives of UK companies in the Times top 500 list were questioned on the following areas of merger policy: independence of the various bodies responsible for competition policy; European issues; effectiveness, efficiency and consistency of the authorities and decisions; dissemination of information and staffing (Aaronson *et al.* 1991). The main results of this survey of business opinion were as follows:

1. There is strong support from UK companies and their advisers for the principle of merger control in the public interest.

2. A majority is in favour of the authorities considering broader aspects of the public interest, in addition to maintenance of competition.

3. There is strong support for the independence of the MMC and some concern about the way the European Commission will operate.

4. There is also support for the existing structure of institutions in the UK.

5. There is pressure for further shortening of the merger investigation process, especially between the time of an MMC recommendation and the Secretary of State's final decision.

6. Those respondents previously involved with a merger reference tend to see greater value in devoting time and resources to key merger investigations.

7. A suggestion which we have made previously that mergers in very small markets do not need to be investigated received substantial support.

8. Opinion is divided on the consistency of the authorities' decisions and the degree to which their ground rules are understood; further guidance from the authorities would be welcomed but a flexible approach needs to be maintained. (Aaronson *et al.*, 1991).

14.8.3   The current policy

However, since 1973, when the UK joined the EU (then EEC), the Community competition legislation enshrined in Art. 85 and 86 of the Treaty of Rome 1957 (now renumbered as Art. 81 and 82 of the Treaty of Amsterdam 1997 – Treaty of the EU and used hereafter) was also applicable, causing some confusion. Thus, to meet concerns regarding the effectiveness of the policy and also align UK law with EU competition legislation, the Competition Act 1998 was passed. This Act introduced significant reforms to UK competition law, provided new substantive rules and changed enforcement mechanisms. The Act repealed the Restrictive Trade Practices legislation (i.e., the Restrictive Trade Practices Act 1976, the Resale Prices Act 1976, the Restrictive Practices Court Act 1976, the Restrictive Trade Practices Act 1977 and the provisions on anti-competitive practices contained in the Competition Act 1980). In their place, a new set of competition rules have been provided in the form of two prohibitions, based on Art. 81 and 82 of the Treaty of Amsterdam 1997 – Treaty of the EU, which has amended the Treaty of Rome 1957. Also provision is made for the investigation and enforcement of the legislation, and also for the newly constituted Competition Commission (CC) that replaces the MMC of the earlier legislation.

More specifically, the Act introduced the Chapter I prohibition, according to which anti-competitive agreements, business practices and conduct that damage competition in the UK are outlawed, such as those that:

1. directly or indirectly fix purchase or selling prices or any other trading conditions;

2. limit or control production, markets, technical development or investment;

3. share markets or sources or supply;

4. apply dissimilar conditions to equivalent transactions with other trading partners, thereby placing them at a competitive disadvantage;

5. make the conclusion of contracts subject to acceptance by the other parties of supplementary obligations which, by their nature or according to commercial usage, have no connection with the subjects of such contracts.

However, agreements will only be caught by the Act if they have an appreciable effect on competition. The guidelines on Chapter I suggest that an agreement is unlikely to be considered as having an appreciable effect on competition if the combined market share of the parties involved does not exceed 25%. Nevertheless, agreements to fix prices, impose minimum resale prices or share markets will, generally, be seen as capable of having an appreciable effect, even where the parties' combined market share falls below 25%.

Similarly, an agreement between two or more parties may be exempted from the Act if it satisfies certain criteria. There are three main types of exemption as follows:

1. individual exemptions, which may be granted for individual agreements – and which must be applied for;

2. block exemptions, which apply automatically to certain categories of agreements; and

3. parallel exemptions, which apply where an agreement is covered by an EU individual or block exemption under Art. 81(3) of the EU Treaty, or would be covered by an EU block exemption if the agreement had an effect on trade between member states of the European Union.

On the other hand, the Chapter II prohibition deals with the abuse by one or more parties of a dominant position in a market within the UK. In particular, conduct may constitute such an abuse if it consists in:

1. directly or indirectly imposing unfair purchase or selling prices or other unfair trading conditions;

2. limiting production, markets or technical development to the prejudice of consumers;

3. applying dissimilar conditions to equivalent transactions with other trading parties, thereby placing them at a competitive disadvantage;

4. making the conclusion of contracts subject to acceptance by the other parties of supplementary obligations which, by their nature or according to commercial usage, have no connection with the subject matter of the contracts.

In determining whether or not a business is in a dominant position, the OFT will look first at its market share. A firm is unlikely to be considered as dominant if its market share is less than 40%. However, there may be cases where a firm with a market share less than 40% may very well exercise dominance, if the market structure allows the firm to act independently of its competitors. Therefore, the OFT must consider not only the market share of the firm but also the market structure, in terms of the number and size distribution of existing rivals, as well as the potential for new entrants into the market. Clearly, of crucial importance in this respect is how the relevant market is defined. There have been examples, as in the case of Continental Can discussed below, where failure to define the market precisely has resulted in the Courts finding for the defendants, rather than the prosecuting antimonopoly authorities.

Certain agreements are excluded from the prohibitions of Chapter I and Chapter II, for example, those of mergers and acquisitions dealt with under the Fair Trading Act 1973, as we saw above, and other exclusions as a result of other enactments. Chapter III of the Act confers on the Director of the OFT powers to investigate and enforce the legislation and impose fines up to 10% of the firm's UK turnover. In addition, third parties may also claim for damages.

Chapter IV of the Act establishes the CC superseding the MMC of the earlier legislation, which is dissolved. Thus, the functions and powers of the MMC are transferred to the CC and in any enactment, instrument or document, any reference to the MMC that has continuing effect is to be read as reference to the CC. The CC will have two important and distinct roles. It will hear appeals against decisions made by the DGFT or the industry sector regulators (i.e., OFTEL, OFGEM etc.) under the Chapter I and Chapter II prohibitions. Also, it will take over the functions of the MMC, including enquiries into mergers and monopolies under the 1973 Act and regulatory enquiries involving appeals by utilities against licence amendments to the respective licence.

The CC has three panels of members, namely, the appeals panel, the reporting panel and the specialist panel. A tribunal drawn from members of the appeals panel will hear each appeal. The reporting panel will deal with functions, which under the earlier legislation were carried out by the MMC. The merging of the MMC into the new Competition Commission (bringing into existence an appeals panel and a reporting panel) reflects a close, yet distinct, relationship between the Chapter II prohibition and the Fair Trading Act 1973. The Competition Act 1998 is concerned with types of conduct or agreements, which are anti-competitive and undesirable, and thus made illegal. By contrast, the 1973 Act deals mainly with structural issues, for example, market concentration. The dual approach recognises that it is necessary to analyse mergers under a system that does not seek to prohibit any structural re-arrangement in advance without due consideration. In terms of the earlier discussion, it considers each case on its merits by following a *pragmatic* approach.

The reporting panel of the CC will investigate and report on issues referred to it by the Secretary of State, the Director General and the industry sector regulators. By contrast, the appeals tribunals of the CC will have no investigative functions and will decide on matters such as whether the Director General or the industry sector regulators have erred in fact or law (Current Law Statutes 1998).

14.8.4 Postscript – The Enterprise Act 2002

This chapter had been written when in November 2002 the Enterprise Act 2002 received Royal Assent and it will gradually come into force in 2003. The provisions of the Act will work alongside the Competition Act 1998 and various pieces of consumer legislation, largely replacing the Fair Trading Act 1973 (FTA73). The Enterprise Act establishes the OFT as a legal entity in its own right, abolishing the former statutory office of the Director General of Fair Trading. The Act establishes too the Competition Appeal Tribunal as a new independent body, which will take on the functions of the Appeals Tribunals of the CC. The board of OFT will consist of a Chairman and no fewer than four members, appointed by the Secretary of State. The OFT will appoint other staff as required and existing staff will transfer to the new OFT to provide continuity. It is expected that the OFT board will be largely concerned with strategic decisions and will not usually be involved in specific cases.

The functions of the OFT include the investigations of markets that are not working well for consumers by the Markets and Policy Initiatives Division, which are distinct from investigation references to the CC.

On the mergers front the Act replaces the acquisitions and mergers provisions of the FTA73 by introducing two significant changes, as follows:

- Decisions on merger control will, in general, be taken by the OFT and the CC as specialist, independent competition authorities and not by the Secretary of State.

- Excepting certain special cases, mergers will be assessed against a pure competition test, rather than the hitherto applied wider public interest test. Generally, mergers will be prohibited, or remedies required, if they would result in a substantial lessening of competition.

The OFT must investigate acquisitions and mergers that meet either the 'turnover test' or the 'share of supply test'. The turnover test is met if the target company has a UK turnover of €70 million or more when an investigation is triggered. The share of the market test is met if the merging companies will together supply at least 25% of goods or services of a particular description, either in the UK as a whole or in a substantial part of it. If a merger meets the tests for assessment by the EU, the OFT will not investigate and cannot refer the merger, since the EC will do that. If the OFT believes that the merger is expected to result in a substantial lessening of competition, then it must either refer the merger to the CC or, if appropriate, seek undertakings in lieu of reference from the merging parties.

The Act provides for a system of market investigations by the CC where it appears that the market structure or the conduct of suppliers is harming competition. These market investigations replace the existing FTA73 monopoly enquiries, and the Act will repeal the parts of the FTA73 relating to those enquiries. In addition to the OFT, the sectoral or industry regulators may also make market investigation references to the CC for their respective industries.

Finally, the Act introduces a criminal offence for individuals who dishonestly engage in cartel agreements such as price-fixing, limitation of supply or production, market-sharing and bid-rigging.

14.9 COMPETITION POLICY IN THE EU

The importance of competition in the context of the EU cannot be understated. It was understood early on that the best way to achieve the aims of the Treaty of Rome 1957 that established the then EEC was through competition and competitive markets. This was reiterated in the Single European Act 1986 establishing the Single Market, and became a key principle of the Treaty of Amsterdam 1997 that advocated an open market with free competition. The EU's competition policy is based on Art. 81 and 82 of the Treaty of Amsterdam (formerly Art. 85 and 86 of the Treaty of Rome). Art. 83 to 89 of the Treaty (formerly Art. 87 to 94) regulate aspects of antitrust machinery and cover the problems of dumping and of aid granted by member states, where such aid is compatible with the aims of the Single Market. The European competition policy only applies where trade between member states is affected. Where the violations are confined within a national market, the competent competition authorities of that member state are wholly responsible for enforcing national law. In addition, the Merger Control Regulation 4064/1989, revised in 1997, completes the provisions regarding the treatment of the behaviour of private firms.

Art. 81 prohibits all agreements between and restrictive practices by firms, such as the fixing of selling or of buying prices; control of production, distribution, technological development or investment; sharing of markets or of sources of supply; applying dissimilar conditions to equivalent transactions with other parties, thereby placing them at a disadvantage. However, certain agreements and decisions, which contribute to efficiency, distribution and so on and which do not impose undue restrictions or eliminate competition are exempted.

Art. 82 prohibits a firm from abusing its position of dominance within the Community. Such abuse may consist of: direct or indirect compulsion to fix prices or other unfair trading conditions; limiting production, consumption or technological development to the detriment of the consumers; applying dissimilar conditions to equivalent transactions with other parties, thereby placing them at a disadvantage and making the conclusion of contracts subject to the acceptance by other parties of additional obligations unconnected with the subject of such contracts.

The Community's antitrust policy was initially focused on ending restrictive practices and also on defining the areas and the fixing of limits of cooperation among enterprises. Art. 81 (85) was used to put an end to restrictive practices and to impose fines on culprits. In addition, it was employed as a means of granting negative clearance to agreements and decisions, the object of which was not detrimental to competition. The Community, thus, proceeded warily in its attempt to develop rules and criteria for future use and at the same time to lay down decisions, which could protect and promote competition in the Community.

To an extent the pursuance of this policy against restrictive practice may have been dictated by the total lack of any merger or monopoly policy at the time. If anything, cross-frontier mergers had been encouraged in an attempt to expedite economic integration. Before the enactment of special legislation to control merger activity in the Community, Art. 82(86) was used to regulate the conduct of enterprises that exercise a dominant position within their respective industries. The criteria that need to be satisfied if an act is to be prohibited were largely established as a result of the first three cases brought in connection with violation of Art. 82(86). They are: (1) the undertaking charged with the act must occupy a dominant position in a particular product market and in a certain geographical area; (2) the act must be deemed to be an improper exploitation of that position; and (3) there must be the possibility that trade between member states will be affected. In one of these cases, the Continental Can case, the company was found by the Commission to had abused its dominant position as a result of merger activity, having eliminated the remaining competitors from three sub-sectors of the packaging industry. The significance of that case lay in the fact that, although the Court of Justice annulled the Commission's decision to take action to dissolve the mergers (because the Commission failed to adequately define the market concerned), the court's ruling was hailed as a landmark for future cases, because it confirmed the soundness of the interpretation of Art. 82(86), which the Commission had developed in its decision. The interpretation was that 'the merger of an enterprise in a dominant position with a competing enterprise is an abuse within the meaning of Art. 86, if it restricts the freedom of choice of consumers in such a manner as to be incompatible with the competitive system laid down in the Treaty' (EEC 1972, p. 79).

In dealing with violations of Art. 81(85) and 82(86), the policy has been flexible, and both the Commission and the Court of Justice have accepted the *'rule of reason'* approach, although it has also been suggested that in dealing with certain cases, the Continental Can case included, the Commission and the Court of Justice accepted instead the *'per se'* approach, thus, moving towards a more rigid policy. Whether those cases were decided by application of the *'per se'* or the *'rule of reason'* is debatable, since the Court consistently followed the previously established criteria regarding abuse of dominant position, and in those cases the criteria were clearly satisfied and so action was justified. More importantly, the problem seems to be one of underlying economic theory rather than of legality. As if to confirm that there had been no shift in judicial thinking, in a different case it was made clear that the investigation of the company's entire marketing policy was undertaken 'not so much as to attack its commercial dynamism and economic performance, since this is not the purpose of Art. 81(85), but because a dominant firm has an obligation not to indulge in business practices which are at variance with the goal of integrated markets and undistorted competition in the common Market' (EEC 1976, p. 59).

In 1989 after a long gestation period lasting almost 20 years, the European Community adopted the Merger Control Regulation 4064/89, which came into effect in September 1990, to deal explicitly with mergers or, in the Community language, concentrations. Only those mergers with a Community dimension come under the Community Regulation.

For the purposes of this Regulation, a concentration has a Community dimension where the:

1. combined aggregate worldwide turnover of all the undertakings concerned is more than €5 billion; and

2. aggregate Community-wide turnover of each of at least two of the undertakings concerned is more than €250 million, unless each of the undertakings concerned achieves more than two-thirds of its aggregate Community-wide turnover within one and the same member state.

Thus, only those mergers meeting the above conditions would be subject to examination by the EC. In the context of this Regulation, the concept of concentration is broader than the concept of merger and it must be distinguished from a cooperation agreement in which Art. 81(85) applies. Concentrations include both the case of the fusion of two or more independent companies into one legal entity, but also cases where the control of one or more independent companies is obtained through the purchase of the shares or assets by another company. It also includes hostile takeovers and joint ventures, provided they are 'concentrative' in nature than 'cooperative'.

However, in the light of experience and also in order to bring more mergers under the Community legislation not covered by the thresholds, particularly in view of the anticipated wave of mergers as a result of the introduction of the single currency – euro, the EU lowered, in 1997, the thresholds by amending the Community Regulation 4064/1989 through the Council Regulation 1310/97.

Accordingly, for the purposes of this Regulation, a concentration that does not meet the earlier thresholds of 4064/89 has a Community dimension where:

1. the combined aggregate worldwide turnover of all the undertakings concerned is more than €2.5 billion;

2. in each of at least three Member States, the combined aggregate turnover of all the undertakings concerned is more than €100 million;

3. in each of at least three Member States included for the purposes of point (2), the aggregate turnover of each of at least two of the undertakings concerned is more than €25 million; and

4. the aggregate Community-wide turnover of each of at least two of the undertakings concerned is more than €100 million;

unless each of the undertakings concerned achieves more than two-thirds of its aggregate Community-wide turnover within one and the same Member State.

It is interesting to note, in passing, that other member states of the EU, as the UK, have based or aligned their competition policies on Art. 81 and 82 of the Treaty of Amsterdam (formerly Art. 85 and 86 of the Treaty of Rome). For example, Greece's competition policy is based on Law 703/1977, which not only follows closely the relevant Community legislation, but its Art. 1 and 2 – that are the essence of the whole legislation, are *verbatim* translations of Art. 85 and 86 of the Treaty of Rome (Petrochilos 1979, 1981). Following the passing of the Merger Control Regulation 4064/89, Greece extended its legislation, through Law 1934/91, to include the control of concentrations and require the prior notification to the competent bodies of all concentrations where: (1) the market share of all firms involved in the concentration in the national market, or a significant part of it, represents at least 35% of the total turnover; and (2) the total turnover of all firms involved in the concentration in the national market exceeds €75 millions. Similarly, the Netherlands, Ireland and Italy have introduced competition legislation based on the Community model.

More significantly, this has helped the EC to propose in 1999 a radical decentralisation of the enforcement of competition policy. Accordingly, national competition bodies and courts are now competent to enforce Art. 81 and 82, with the EC only getting involved when uniformity of Community law would be undermined (Pelkmans 2001, p. 226). In addition this decentralisation is in line with one of the key principles underlying European integration, namely, *subsidiarity*, according to which collective solutions within the EU are required only where such solutions cannot be provided at the national level.

SUMMARY

In the present chapter we have reviewed, briefly, the rationale for the government sector with the provision of public and/or merit goods and also considered some important questions regarding utilities, public or private. These have to do with pricing and investment policies, under which we have looked at marginal cost pricing, peak load pricing (firm and shifting peak cases), cost–benefit analysis with emphasis on social costs and benefits, and the choice of the rate of discount. In addition, we have looked at the problem of regulation and considered the role of industry regulators, such as OFTEL, OFGAS and the like, and in some detail the role of competition policy. Under the latter we have examined the economic basis of antimonopoly policy in terms of the neoclassical model, and the concepts of workable competition and the structure–conduct–performance approach. Further, we have looked at legal rules and examined the antitrust policy in the US, competition policy in the UK, and in the EU.

APPENDIX A: WHO DOES WHAT IN BRITISH AND EUROPEAN COMPETITION POLICY

In this appendix we provide a summary of the actual procedures followed in British and European competition policy. We start first with monopolies and anti-competitive practices in the British context and consider the role of the various institutions involved with the protection of the public interest, namely, the Director General of Fair Trading (DGFT), the Secretary of State (SoS), Office of Fair Trading (OFT) and the Competition Commission (CC – formerly the MMC). The DGFT receives complaint or other evidence of suspected abuse concerning: (1) the existence of monopoly and (2) anti-competitive practice. In the first case (that of monopoly), the DGFT conducts preliminary inquiries in order to find out whether there is possible abuse. If the inquiries reveal no abuse, no further action is taken. However, if the inquiries reveal possible abuse of monopoly power, the DGFT makes a monopoly reference to the CC. The latter hear evidence and weigh up the public interest, produce a report and send it to the SoS and the DGFT. If the report finds that the monopoly does not act against the public interest, no further action is taken and the SoS publishes the report. If the report finds that the monopoly acts against the public interest, the SoS has to decide on the appropriate action to take and can make an order. In this respect, the DGFT advises the SoS on the action to be taken on the CC's report. The SoS can ask the DGFT to obtain suitable undertakings by the firm concerned to end the acts harming the public interest and to monitor such undertakings. An undertaking is a promise by someone (such as a firm) to take action, or to stop doing something, following an adverse CC report. Firms may give an undertaking as an alternative to being made subject to an order. If undertakings are not given by the firm, the SoS can make an order for the firm to comply with, which can be enforced by the courts, and publishes the report. Breach of the court's order may be contempt of court, and can result in fines. If undertakings are given, the DGFT has to monitor such undertakings.

A similar procedure is followed in the case of suspected anti-competitive practices. These are defined as any behaviour that restricts or distorts competition. Initially, the DGFT has to decide on whether or not further inquiries are justified, following a complaint or other evidence pointing to an anti-competitive practice. If not, then no action is taken. In the opposite case, the DGFT conducts an inquiry and produces a report to reveal whether anti-competitive practices exist. If there are no anti-competitive practices, no further action is taken. However, if the report reveals such practices, the DGFT can demand undertakings by the firm to seize such practices and in the case where the firm does give such undertakings to monitor them, and also monitor any order issued by the SoS in this matter. If the firm refuses to give such undertakings, the DGFT refers the case to the CC. The latter hear evidence and weigh up the public interest, produce a report and send it to the SoS and the DGFT. As in the case of monopoly above, the SoS follows a similar procedure. If the CC's report finds no injury to the public interest by the anti-competitive practices, the SoS takes no further action and publishes the report. In the opposite case, and on the advice of the DGFT, the SoS has to decide on the appropriate action to take and publishes the report. The SoS can make an order for the anti-competitive practices to be terminated and ask the DGFT to monitor the order and the courts to enforce it. Alternatively, he can ask the DGFT to obtain suitable undertakings by the firm to seize the anti-competitive practices. If such undertakings are given, the DGFT has to monitor them. If no undertakings are given, the SoS can make and order for the anti-competitive practices to be stopped and ask the DGFT to monitor and enforce such order through the courts.

In terms of mergers, the actual procedure followed by the British institutions can be summarised as follows: The DGFT learns about the merger and considers whether the merger qualifies for reference on the basis of the two criteria, namely: (1) that assets involved in the merger exceed €30 millions or (2) the merger is likely to lead to a 25% marker share and above. If neither criterion applies, then the DGFT takes no further action and the merger proceeds. If either criterion applies, the DGFT has to consider the impact of the merger on competition and to advise the SoS on whether to recommend the merger for reference to the CC. If the DGFT advises against reference, the SoS has to decide on whether to refer the merger to the CC or not. If the SoS decides against reference, no further action is required and the merger proceeds. However, if the DGFT recommends to the SoS reference to the CC, the SoS may consider divestment in lieu of reference and seek to obtain undertakings by the parties involved in the proposed merger. If such undertakings regarding divestments are obtained, no further action is needed and the merger proceeds. However, if such undertakings are not given by the parties, or if the SoS does not wish to consider divestment in lieu of reference, he may decide to refer the proposed merger to the CC or not. Clearly, if he decides against reference, the procedure stops and the merger proceeds. In the opposite case, the merger is referred to the CC, which hears evidence and weighs up the public interest and sends the report to the SoS and the DGFT. If the report shows that the merger is not against the public interest, the SoS publishes the report and allows the merger to proceed. If the report shows that the merger is against the public interest, the DGFT also advises the SoS on what action to take on the CC's report. The SoS has to decide on whether to block the merger, in which case (s)he publishes the report, or to impose conditions, and in the latter case can ask the DGFT to seek suitable undertakings by the parties involved in the merger. If such undertakings are not given to the DGFT, the SoS can make an order, stop the merger and publish the report. If undertakings are given, the SoS accepts the undertakings and allows the merger to proceed.

Turning now to the European case it is observed that the competent authorities for the enforcement of competition policy are the Directorate General for Competition of the EC (hereafter Commission) and the European Court of First Instance (hereafter Court) helped by the member states. In so far as restrictive practices (Art. 81) and abuse of dominant position (Art. 82) are concerned, the Commission receives complaint or request for the clearance or exemption of a particular agreement. The Commission notifies member states and starts investigating the complaint or request for clearance/exemption and seeking the views of the firms concerned. Having received these views, the Commission subsequently sets out its preliminary views on the matter, which can be in favour or against the issue at hand and prepares a hearing. At the hearing the Commission hears the views of those concerned, including the firms and third parties. The member states are represented in the so-called Advisory Committees, which submit their own opinions to the Commission in all formal proceedings. In addition, the member states may submit comments on individual cases to the Commission at any time. More generally, there is close liaison between the national authorities and the Commission, which is reflected in regular exchanges of information and staff. Consequently, in each particular case considered, the Advisory Committee is consulted on the matter and gives its views. The Commission having heard the views of those concerned has to weigh the arguments and arrive at a final decision for or against the firm(s) involved.

If the decision is for the firm(s), third parties can appeal to the European Court of First Instance against the Commission's decision. If the Commission finds against the firm(s), it puts a stop to the restrictive practice and can impose a fine on the firm(s). The latter can accept the Commission's decision, rectify the situation and the matter ends. However, they can appeal to the European Court of

First Instance and submit their views to the court. The Court hears the appeal(s) and it either upholds the Commission's decision or overturns it.

Similar procedure is followed in the case of mergers.

APPENDIX B: MERGER CONTROL OF GERMAN COMPANIES BY THE BUNDESKARTELLAMT AND THE EU COMMISSION[1]

The Bundeskartellamt (BKA – Federal Cartel Office) is a German independent higher Federal authority responsible for applying the Act against Restraint of Competition (ARC), which was enacted for the protection of competition and came into force on 1 January 1958.

The ARC protects competition in the Federal Republic of Germany against all forms of restrictions, irrespective of whether the restriction results from actions taken within or outside Germany. The ARC applies to the German economy as a whole, but there are certain exemptions to this rule concerning agriculture, banking and insurance. In addition, exemptions to the transport and forestry sectors are provided for in special laws. Since the word *cartel* is used in this appendix, it is recalled that cartels are arrangements involving price fixing, output controls, bid-rigging, sharing of markets, allocation of sales by product or area, establishment of trade practices or combinations of these, and, generally, they represent restrictions on competition.

Decisions on mergers, cartels and abusive practices are made by the Decision Divisions of the BKA, which are organised according to sectors of the economy. A collegiate body consisting of a chairman and two other members decides upon each case, by majority decision. The Decision Divisions do not receive instructions from other bodies and make their decisions independently. The BKA has extensive investigatory powers to enforce the ban on cartels. It may request information from enterprises, inspect business documents and, after obtaining a relevant order from a local court, search enterprises and seize evidence. If an illegal cartel is detected, the BKA may impose fines on the enterprises involved. Authorised cartels are subject to abuse supervision. The competition authorities may revoke an exemption or, in the event of an abuse, order the enterprises concerned to discontinue it.

As examples of authorised cartels, in 1997, the BKA allowed a cartel of small- and medium-sized firms consisting of eight small shipyards. The aim of the cartel was to make these shipyards competitive through joint R&D and also, in the case of large orders, through cooperating in their production. In 1983, the BKA authorised a *crisis cartel* formed by manufacturers of welded steel mesh. Over a period of 5 years, the companies involved reduced their total capacities by about 40% and, thus, they adjusted them to the decreased demand. Owing to this planned capacity reduction, a number of efficient small- and medium-sized firms were saved from closure. Since the ARC came into effect in 1958, around 780 applications for the authorisation of the above-mentioned types of cartels have been filed with the BKA. At present, around 340 of the authorised cartels are still in operation, approximately 110 of which come under the responsibility of the *Lander* (regional governments) cartel authorities.

The German law does not prohibit external growth but merely controls mergers of companies above a certain size. In terms of the preceding discussion, it tends to follow a '*rule of reason*' approach. Even this control was not part of the original legislation, but was added in 1973. Perhaps this was not surprising in view of the figures in the table, giving the development of merger activity in Germany since 1973, which shows clearly that starting from a very low position the number of mergers increased steadily, thus making their control inevitable.

Number of mergers in Germany

Year	Mergers not subject to control	Mergers subject to control	Total	Year	Mergers not subject to control	Mergers subject to control	Total
1973			34	1986	121	681	802
1974			294	1987	183	704	887
1975			445	1988	247	912	1159
1976			453	1989	269	1145	1414
1977			554	1990	221	1327	1548
1978			558	1991	199	1808	2007
1979			602	1992	154	1589	1743
1980			635	1993	154	1360	1514
1981			618	1994	147	1417	1564
1982			603	1995	161	1369	1530
1983			506	1996	148	1286	1434
1984	118	457	575	1997	178	1573	1751
1985	172	537	709	1998	197	1691	1888

The law requires announcement of proposed mergers if the firms participating in the merger recorded a combined aggregate worldwide turnover of more than €500 million, or if at least one of the firms participating in the merger recorded a domestic turnover of more than €25 million. The turnover figures refer to the last completed business year preceding the merger. Also, registration of the merger is compulsory if the participating firms have a combined turnover exceeding €2 billion, or two companies have turnovers in excess of €1 billion each. In such cases, the BKA scrutinises the proposals to find out whether the merger will result in market dominance, or will intensify the existing situation. Mergers subject to control have to be notified, before they are put into effect. Mergers involving firms with combined annual turnovers of less than €500 million are not subject to merger control in Germany.

The following transactions are deemed to be mergers within the meaning of the legislation:

1. acquisition of all or of a substantial part of the assets of another firm;

2. acquisition of direct or indirect control by one or several undertakings of the whole or parts of one or more undertakings;

3. acquisition of shares in another enterprise if the shares, either separately or together with other shares already held by the acquirer, reach 50% of the capital or 25% of the voting rights of the other undertaking;

4. any other combination of undertakings enabling one or several undertakings to directly or indirectly exert a competitively significant influence on another undertaking.

Once a proposed merger has been notified to the BKA, the competent Decision Division has a maximum of 4 months to decide on the proposal. However, this 4-month period is available only if the Division sends the so-called 'one-month letter' within 1 month of receiving the notification. This letter informs the participating firms that the Division has initiated an examination of the concentration (main examination proceedings). The main examination proceedings are initiated if a further examination of the concentration (merger) is necessary. At this stage, the BKA decides by way of a formal decision whether the concentration is cleared or prohibited. The clearance may be subject to conditions and obligations.

Before prohibiting a merger, the BKA has to give the firm an opportunity to comment. The Decision Division fully informs them of the arguments in support of prohibition, so that the firms are still able to put forward counter arguments. There is a right of appeal to the Higher Regional Court in Düsseldorf against prohibitory decisions of the BKA. Appeals on points of law can be lodged with the Federal Supreme Court against decisions of the Higher Regional Court.

During the period 1973–94 of actual decision-making practice, the BKA prohibited 108 merger requests, some of which resulted in court decisions. When in doubt firms approach the BKA to discuss projects before they ever reach the stage of notification. Firms abandon many projects raising competition concerns at this early stage, after BKA officials have signalled that prohibition is likely. These cases are known as the BKA's pre-notification stage cases. In 1997, 6 of the 1751 concentrations were turned down, while 10 projects were abandoned in view of the competition concerns voiced by the BKA. In 1998, six of the 1888 mergers examined were prohibited and there were also fourteen pre-notification stage cases.

The BKA may impose fines for infringement of the ARC or decisions of the BKA; prohibit concentrations; prohibit practices that are forbidden under the ARC, and skim off the additional proceeds obtained; and grant exemptions in respect of certain agreements and decisions. The BKA may impose administrative fines of up to €500 000 for violations of the prohibitions contained in the ARC. It may also impose fines of up to three times the additional proceeds obtained as a result of the infringement.

Since 1990, German companies are also subject to the European Merger Control Regulation 4064/89 discussed earlier, as well as the national merger control. The competences are clear cut. The EC has to approve any merger with a Europe-wide dimension and turnover in excess of €5 billion. Excluded are companies earning 2/3 of their turnover in one member state. The BKA controls all those mergers of companies with the features outlined above. In case of announcement, the control can happen after the merger has taken place. However, whenever registration with the BKA is necessary, because of the company size, the control has to be done before the merger can be carried out. The intention of merging with another company is sufficient reason for the BKA to investigate whether the merger will result in a market-dominating position first. After this matter has been decided, the BKA can make an overall decision in that particular case. This is a much more complicated procedure than the one followed by the EU Commission, and creates what in Germany is called 'Zwei-klassen-recht' (die kleinen hängt man, die

Grossen läßt laufen), freely translated as 'Two-class-law' (the small are caught, the big get away). Collective companies (GU) are created under German law when a mutual subsidiary is formed following a merger because this is seen as sharing the parent company between each other. But only the concentrative GUs (those created for a long-term operating period) are subject to EU law. The cooperative GUs, that might only exist for one period, are solely dealt with by German law. The former type of GUs can create a clash between German and European legislation, because such GUs might not be permitted under the stricter German law but are allowed under European law. That explains the tendency of German companies to register any such intentions in Brussels, where such mergers are less likely to be rejected, than in Bonn (the new home of BKA). This had also forced the German government to seek changes in the European merger legislation towards lowering the limits of turnover, in a way that has been achieved by the amendment brought about by the Council Regulation 1310/97, as discussed above.

Note

1. This Appendix was prepared by Professor Dr. Helga Grote, formerly of Fachbereich Wirtschaft, Fachhochschule Aachen, Germany and Mr. E. Stoll. I am grateful to both.

BIBLIOGRAPHY

Aaronson, R., Murphy, M. and Shopland, J. (1991), *Competition Policy Briefing*, Issue No 6, Coopers & Lybrand Deloitte.

Adams, W. (1953), 'The "Rule of Reason": Workable Competition or Workable Monopoly?', *The Yale Law Journal*, **63**(3), 348–370, reprinted in Berki, S.E. (ed.), *Antitrust Policy: Economics and Law*, Heath, 1966, which also contains a selection of interesting articles on the subject.

Allen, G.C. (1968), *Monopoly and Restrictive Practices*, George Allen & Unwin.

Bain, J.S. (1968), *Industrial Organisation*, 2nd edn, J. Wiley & Sons.

Baumol, W.J. (1968), 'On the Social Rate of Discount', *American Economic Review*, **58**, 788–802.

Berki, S.E. (ed.) (1966), *Antitrust Policy – Economics and the Law*, Heath.

Blair, J.M. (1972), *Economic Concentration – Structure, Behaviour and Public Policy*, Harcourt Brace Jovanovich.

Boyle, S.E. (1972), *Industrial Organisation – An Empirical Approach*, Holt Rinehart & Wilson.

Caves, R. (1972), *American Industry: Structure–Conduct–Performance*, 3rd edn, Prentice-Hall.

Clark, J. (1940), 'Towards a concept of Workable Competition', *American Economic Review*, **30**.

Comanor, W.S. and Leibenstein, H. (1969), 'Allocative Efficiency, X-Efficiency and the Measurement of Welfare Losses', *Economica*, N.S., **36**, 304–309.

Cowling, K. and Mueller, D.C. (1978), 'The Social Costs of Monopoly Power', *Economic Journal*, **88**, 727–748.

The European Communities Commission (1972), *First Report on Competition Policy*, April.

——(1973), *Second Report on Competition Policy*, April.

——(1974), *Third Report on Competition Policy*, April.

——(1976), *Fifth Report on Competition Policy*, April.

Harberger, A. (1954), 'Monopoly and Resource Allocation', *American Economic Review*, **44**, 77–92.

Henderson, P.D. (1965), 'Investment Criteria for Public Enterprises', *Bulletin of the Oxford University Institute of Economics and Statistics*, **27**, 55–89. Revised and reprinted in Turvey, R. (ed.), *Public enterprise*, Penguin, 1968, pp. 86–169, and used here.

Hirshleifer, J., (1958), 'Peak Loads and Efficient Pricing: Comment', *Quarterly Journal of Economics*, **72**, 451–468.

HMSO (1961), *The Financial and Economic Obligations of Nationalised Industries*, Cmnd 1337, White Paper.

HMSO (1967), *Nationalised Industries: A Review of Economic and Financial Objectives*, Cmnd 3437, White Paper.

HMSO (1979), *A Review of Monopolies and Mergers Policy, A Consultative Document*, Cmnd 7199, Green Paper.

Hunter, A. (ed.) (1969), *Monopoly and Competition*, Penguin.

Leibenstein, H. (1966), 'Allocative Efficiency v. X–Efficiency', American *Economic Review*, **56**, 392–415.

Mansfield, E. (ed.) (1968), *Monopoly Power and Economic Performance*, revised edn., Norton.

Meek, R. (1967), *'Public Authority Pricing'*, Paper read at the British Association, Leeds, 4/9/1967.

_____ (1968), 'The New Bulk Supply Tariff for Electricity', *Economic Journal*, **78**, 43–66.

Mishan, E.J. (1971), *Cost–Benefit Analysis*, George Allen & Unwin.

Office of Fair Trading (2002), *Overview of the Enterprise Act 2002*, Product code OFT508, edn 11/02.

OFTEL (2002a), 'Oftel Management Plan 2002/3: Statement', 18/4/2002.

OFTEL (2002b), 'Protecting Consumers by Promoting Competition: Oftel's Conclusions', 20/6/2002.

Oppenheim, S.C. (1952), 'Federal Antitrust Legislation: Guideposts to a Revised National Antitrust Policy', *Michigan Law Review*, **50**, 1139–1244, reprinted in Berki, S.E. (ed). *Antitrust Policy: Economics and Law*, Heath, 1966.

Pearce, D.W. (1971), *Cost–Benefit Analysis*, Macmillan Studies in Economics.

Pelkmans, J. (2001), *European Integration : Methods and Economic Analysis*, 2nd edn, Financial Times–Prentice Hall.

Peterson, W.H. (1961), 'The Case against Anti-merger Policy', *Business Horizons*, **4**, 111–120.

Petrochilos, G.A. (1979), 'Greek Antitrust Policy: An Analysis', *Antitrust Bulletin*, **24**, 595–619.

—— (1981), 'The Effectiveness of Greek Antitrust Policy: Comparative Study', *Greek Review of Social Research*, **41**, 26–40.

Prest, A.R. and Turvey, R. (1965), 'Cost–Benefit Analysis: A Survey', *Economic Journal*, **75**, December, reprinted in *Surveys of Economic Theory*, American Economic Association and Royal Economic Society, Vol. III, Macmillan, 1966.

Rowley, C.K. (1973), *Antitrust and Economic Efficiency*, Macmillan Studies in Economics.

Scherer, F.M. (1970), *Industrial Market Structure and Economic Performance*, Rand McNally.

Schumpeter, J.A. (1952), *Capitalism, Socialism and Democracy*, 5th edn, Unwin.

Schwartzman, D. (1960), 'The Burden of Monopoly', *Journal of Political Economy*, **66**, 627–630.

Steiner, P., 'Peak Loads and Efficient Pricing', *Quarterly Journal of Economics*, **71**, 585–610.

Stevens, T.M. and Borrie, G.J. (1973), *Mercantile Law*, 16th edn, Butterworths.

Turvey, R. (ed.) (1968), *Public Enterprise*, Penguin.

Webb, M.A. (1973), *The Economics of Nationalized Industries*, Nelson.

Williamson, O.E. (1966a), 'Economies as Anti-Trust Defense', *American Economic Review*, **56**, 16–36, reprinted in Rowley, C.K. (ed.) *Readings in Industrial Economics*, Vol. 2, Macmillan, 1972, pp. 136–149.

_____ (1966b), 'Peak-load pricing and optimal capacity under indivisibility constraints', *American Economic Review*, **56**, 810–827, reprinted in Turvey, R. (ed.), *Public enterprise*, Penguin, 1968, pp. 64–85.

chapter fifteen

Ethics in Business

Learning outcomes

When you finish studying this chapter you should know:

- The nature of ethics

- The classical value system *(kalokagathia, justice, honesty)*

- The golden rule

- Other approaches to ethics
  - ☐ Utilitarianism
  - ☐ Deontology
  - ☐ Rights-based

- Corporate governance and ethics
  - ☐ The OECD code
  - ☐ The UK practice

- Social responsibilities and social partnerships

- The stakeholder approach

15.1   INTRODUCTION

The purpose of this chapter is to consider Ethics in Business, a subject that has mushroomed in the past 30–35 years almost as a separate discipline. This is an unusual theme, particularly for a book on Managerial Economics, for the simple reason that most of managerial economics is couched in terms of the neoclassical model and many economists have argued in the past for a separation of ethics and economics on the grounds that 'Economics deals with ascertainable facts, ethics with valuations' (Robbins 1935). However, despite the fact that the rationalist, technocratic approach to economics championed by Robbins seemed to had won the day, there is also the alternative ethical approach to economics that originated with the ancient Greeks in the classical period and in our days promoted by, among others, Sen (1987).

The recent spate of scandals involving Enron, Tyco, WorldCom, and accounting/auditing firms, which should have been the guardians of the public interest and of the various kinds of stakeholders, illustrates in the starkest possible manner the need for such an ethical approach and appropriate policies to underlie business behaviour. Also, ironically, the same scandals make a mockery of Friedman's dictum that 'there is only one social responsibility of business...to increase its profits so long as it stays within the rules of the game' (Friedman 1970), since the major losers in the above scandals have been, primarily, the shareholders. The same can be said about other business crises, such as Union Carbide's leak at its chemical plant in Bhopal, India, resulting in 2000 deaths and in excess of 200 000 injuries, the Exxon Valdez and Prestige oil spills resulting in ecological disasters and the like. More importantly, these scandals and crises point to the urgent need of formulating and/or strengthening regulatory mechanisms with a clout to punish culprits. The question of ethics in business behaviour has acquired recently such urgency that in January 2003 the World Economic Forum at Davos, Switzerland, an annual meeting of world business and political leaders, had as its main theme, the fight against corporate corruption and the restoration of trust and confidence in companies and financial reporting and auditing. In addition, the OECD has been considering strengthening its voluntary code of ethical conduct for business, of which more below.

Thus, in this chapter we look briefly at the nature of ethics and the classical heritage as bequeathed to us by the ancient Greeks; its influence on the development of social theory, ethics and economics in the West; other approaches to ethics, corporate governance and ethics; social responsibilities and social partnerships and the stakeholder approach to ethics.

15.2   THE NATURE OF ETHICS

Ethics or the philosophy of morals is concerned with the question of what is morally good or bad, right or wrong. In other words, the main focus is on what is proper, right or obligatory to do or not to do. The main concern of ethics is: (1) the analysis of the meaning and nature of the normative moral elements in man's actions, thought and language and of the methods supporting moral judgements; and (2) normative ethics as such, i.e., of evaluating these elements and methods by developing criteria to justify rules and judgements of good and right and presenting analysing and appraising them. Typically, ethics has strong links with religion, particularly Christianity. However, Greek ethics discussed here is free of religion, as it was developed before the appearance of Christianity. It can be said, therefore, that Greek ethics is secular and universal. Nevertheless, as we shall see below later writers, notably Ruskin, have sought to combine Christian teaching with the Greek concept of justice.

In the last 30–35 years we have witnessed a new awareness and need for firms to assume social responsibilities, in addition to their other objectives and goals. Consequently, we have seen a proliferation of writings on business ethics (Dean 1997), or on the morals as applied to business enterprises, with specialist chairs established in universities, specialised publications devoted to the subject and firms busy in setting out, and pursuing (?), ethical policies. Multilateral organisations, in particular the UN and OECD, are creating blueprints and policies on the social responsibility of transnational corporations.

While the newly found awareness for firms to assume social responsibilities is long overdue and it is to be applauded, it raises the question as to whether we can really distinguish between ethics and business ethics. It has to be remembered that ethics has existed as a separate and recognised discipline since the days of Plato and Aristotle for over 2400 years. Business ethics, by contrast, is a relatively new phenomenon. While other disciplines, notably medicine, have long established an ethical code of conduct and accept the Hippocratic oath, business, particularly in the Anglo-American world, has remained unmoved and untouched by calls for a similar code and only recently it has been dragged, reluctantly in most cases, to adopt an ethical policy. So what explains this considerable delay and reluctance, and what are, if any, the differences in approach between the Anglo-American and continental Europe?

This question acquires more pertinence when it is recalled that the Greeks discussed economic and business questions in the context of ethics and politics rather than as a separate discipline. Their political economy was part of their wider ethical and political enquiries, whose sole purpose was the best social organisation of the *polis* (city-state). Thus, their contributions on atomistic behaviour, private property, division of labour, exchange, value, money and interest, free foreign trade and so on were discussed in the context of the quest for the establishment of the best constitution, by which to govern the city-state, so as to achieve worthier social and ethical ends. Society and the social *sumpheron* (benefit), rather than private riches, were uppermost in the minds of the Greek philosophers and acted as a guiding light (Petrochilos 1999, 2002a, 2002b).

15.3   THE GREEK VALUE SYSTEM – *KALOKAGATHIA*

Of the pre-Socratic philosophers and sophists, the first to enquire on social matters and morals were the latter. Socrates took a keen interest in what the sophists had to say on these issues, and his discourse with the most famous of the sophists Protagoras, is described by Plato in the dialogue of the same name. Protagoras taught that laws and moral codes ought to be observed because the state of nature where there are no laws is a terrible one. He observed that there is a difference between savages and civilised men and that the state of nature was an evil one;

men could achieve a good life only by living in a community under laws and conventions of behaviour handed down from one generation to another. Therefore, all laws and moral codes were civilising and improving influences, and it was right for each man to obey the laws of his own community (Huby 1967, p. 12). But as moral codes or laws differ from one another, the wise man would be able to appreciate the differences and teach them to others. Protagoras felt that as a wise man himself, he could instruct others and claimed to be able to teach them how to improve their *arete* (virtue or excellence), and to make them better citizens. In his encounter with Socrates in the *Protagoras*, he starts by considering *dike* (justice) and *aidos* (respect for others, shame) as the two most important and 'divinely instilled elements in mankind which make civil society possible' (Lowry 1987, p. 33). Lowry states that 'if one accepts these concepts as meaning "a sense of order and mutual sympathy", one gets a clearer picture of Protagoras's social philosophy', which may be considered as a forerunner to Adam Smith's concept of fellow feeling or human sympathy, developed in his *Theory of Moral Sentiments* (Lowry 1987, p. 33).

Sophists apart, Socrates was the first to consider the philosophy of man and for the first time we have discussion on social, ethical, political and economic issues. Plato, in book 2 of the *Republic*, has Socrates arguing with his pupils on the origins and composition of a *polis* (city-state) and claiming that this depends on the needs of life. Accordingly, people associate for mutual support, because different people have different abilities, thus, there are two basic principles underlying any society: (1) mutual need and (2) differences in aptitude. The first is the result of the fact that man is not self-sufficient; so, in order to survive, people have to live together by forming societies. The second, which is at the heart of the principle of the division of labour, means that different people are good at different things, so it would be best for all if each concentrated on developing their particular skills and aptitudes. Society flourishes because it is efficient.

In the Socratic viewpoint, economic relationships, as well as social and political ones, are essentially ethical issues, following from Socrates's major ethical concern which is 'how should one live'. Xenophon in his *Memorabilia* sets out to provide a detailed discussion of the Socratic teachings to his disciples focusing around the concepts of justice, virtue, temperance and goodness and, generally, he argues that Socrates's aim is to lead his disciples to a life of *kalokagathia*, by teaching them how to become *kaloi kagathoi*. So, what exactly is *kalokagathia*?

15.3.1 *Kalokagathia*

The concepts of *kalokagathia* and of *kalos kagathos*, or as an epithetic form *kalokagathos*, play an important role in classical Hellenic ethics, politics and economics. The latter cannot be properly understood without a thorough knowledge of the ethical basis provided by justice and *kalokagathia* (Petrochilos 2002a, 2002b). The word *kalokagathia* means the character and conduct of *kalos kagathos*, i.e., of the perfect and just man, thus, it could mean kindness, uprightness, honesty, attributes that, finally, lead to happiness. In classical Greek, the meaning of the word *kalos* is linked with the form than the character, thus, *kalos* has to do with the beauty, the harmony of the body, attained through physical exercise. The word *agathos* meant the good and virtuous man, who is wise, brave and just. Clearly, in the present context, the emphasis is on *agathos*.

The term *agathos* has been part of the Greek system of ethical values regarding commendation and moral responsibility since Homeric times. According to Adkins (1960) and Gouldner (1965), in Homer's time the most powerful words of commendation were *agathos* and *arete* (virtue). In men, *arete* is identified with military prowess, Homer after all lauds the heroes; in women the qualities demanded of *arete* are beauty, skill in weaving and housekeeping, chastity and faithfulness. These Homeric values are suited to a community organised on the basis of scattered individual households, which to be defended against enemies will require individual prowess. In addition, in Homeric times society is a 'shame-culture'. The chief sanction is presumably 'what people will say'. As this persists into classical times, it becomes Socrates's mission to redirect and oppose this inclination telling the Greeks, in effect, 'let them mock' (Adkins 1960, chapter 8; Gouldner 1965, chapter 3). But as society is changing, Hesiod, the creator of the didactic epic as distinct from the Homeric heroic epic, sings a different tune and considers the origin of civilisation and the problem of justice. The new societies prefer the praiser of peace (Hesiod) to the praiser of war (Homer), and they are ready to accept what Adkins calls the quieter values of *sophron* (prudent, moderate) and *dikaios* (just). Justice is important and may become part (or even the whole) of *arete*. Different skills are required for people to survive in the new societies, like farming and, thus, a good farmer is *agathos* too (Adkins 1960 p. 72). As people move on to form cities, Adkins's 'quiet' virtues become cooperativeness, temperance, civic service, justice and wisdom because of the need of the *polis* to defend itself against enemies and to wage war, if need be. Gouldner too, produces a similar list of Greek values for his contest system centring on fame, competitive achievement and envy. Thus, the citizens must have both sets of traits (values). In addition, cities require *eunomia* (good order) which will restore civic calm, prevent unjust government and subdue *hubris* (arrogance, insolence). While in Homeric times, *hubris*, typically, will be punished by the gods, in democratic Athens, the mechanisms of franchise and ostracism empower poor citizens to inflict cost on the proudest families. There is an egalitarian streak in the Greek belief system, and the threat of punishment for *hubris* is a threat to anyone regardless of status (Gouldner 1965, p. 89).

By the fifth century BC, the cooperative virtues or quieter values have infiltrated the system of competitive values and the agathos-standard is changing. Now, *agathos* is *ennomos* (upright), *dikaios* (just), *hosios* (pious), helpful. However, lineage (noble birth), wealth, poverty and the like are no guide to *agathos*. *Agathos* is open to all. 'Judge a man's nobility by the company he keeps and how he behaves to others' (Euripides, *Electra*). So morality has infiltrated the Greek value system. In addition, *agathoi* administer well both their own households and their cities. Such ability lies in man's nature and in his excellence of spirit. Justice and self-control are important for the prosperity of cities.

Nevertheless, the concept of *sumpheron* (advantageous benefit) is considered to be *agathon* for the state and becomes the cornerstone of Athens' relations with its allies, whether it is just or unjust. So, the aspect of *sumpheron* emphasises that this is a system of values based on calculation (Adkins 1960, p. 223). Given that justice is a quiet cooperative virtue and that the achievement of prosperity for the city, *sumpheron*, may require *adikia* (injustice), the question arises when does injustice become a better means to the desired end of stability and prosperity than justice? Indeed, this aspect of *sumpheron* becomes also important for individuals. Since this *sumpheron* can bring prosperity to an individual and his family it is surely an *agathon*, even if it may be unjust. The controversy arises that at the level of the individual an *adikia*, which leads to someone being better off, may be considered as an *arete* (virtue). This is a question that was put to Plato by his pupils, and in a number of his works he tried to deal with it, not entirely satisfactorily. Perhaps the historical times he was living and writing and his upbringing were preventing him from doing so. This may also be linked to Plato's tripartite anatomy of personality involving: reason, passion and *thymos* (soul). Euripides shows human passion and emotion to be as real as reason, and often more powerful; and cautions those who do not allow it room to live within themselves. But through the experience of taking the role of the other (through the theatre), some Greeks came in time to abandon the rules of retaliation and reciprocity, by accepting Isocrates's Golden Rule 'Do not do to others that which angers you when they do it to you' (Gouldner 1965, p. 114).

Justice must be linked with *arete* to lead to *eudaimonia* (happiness, prosperity). Plato must show that internal *agatha* (things that are good to a man psychologically) are much more important and conducive to the stability and efficiency of both man and state than any external *agatha* (Adkins 1960, p. 283). If this were achieved, Plato would have fulfilled the general expectation of this system of values, which can become generally acceptable. In the *Republic* he sets out to demonstrate that justice is a 'good thing' (*agathon*) for its possessor and he starts with the state, which is split into three classes: the Guardians, who are *sophoi* (wise) and govern it; the military (defenders), who have *andreia* (courage) and the rest of the population, who specialise in all the other functions required in a city and who also have their *arete*, which is *sophrosune* (prudence, moderation, self-restraint). If everybody minds their own business, efficiency and political harmony are achieved. Plato argues that there are four *aretai* of the soul: justice, prudence, courage and wisdom, of which every citizen must possess justice and prudence. In the *Laws* Plato ranks these as justice, wisdom, prudence and courage. A state possessing these will have stability and efficiency, which will lead to a satisfactory concept of moral responsibility (Adkins 1960, p. 294). In Plato's terms the stability and efficiency, that is the efficient administration of the state will be provided mainly by the philosopher-king and his guardian class, who are *kaloi kagathoi* and have all the necessary ethical attributes to rule in the best interest of the community (Petrochilos 2002a, 2002b). This shows that Plato had a more value-oriented notion of a society structured to support an 'ethical elite', and his notion of efficiency was oriented towards a narrower value-loaded goal.

Originally, the phrases *kalos kagathos, kaloi kagathoi* were said of the noble and famous men, although, as mentioned above, the terms were extended later to cover everyone who was behaving accordingly. Thus, *kalos kagathos* was the just and perfect man, he who had all the attributes of the truly noble and well raised man, and the term *kalos kagathos* could also be used to describe properties and actions. Xenophon, in his *Memorabilia* (book C, chapter IV), describes the *kalos kagathos* as the just and perfect man who manages his private economic affairs well and enriches himself justly, who manages public affairs as if they were his private ones and serves his country loyally. And again the role of the *kalos kagathos* leader is not to look after himself, but to contribute to the welfare of those who have elected him (*Memorabilia*, book C, chapter II). Similarly, in *Oikonomikos*, Xenophon presents Ischomachos, another *kalos kagathos*, who offers practical advice on how to be an effective and good administrator, and how to manage and motivate foremen, workers and slaves to improve productivity and raise production (Petrochilos 1999). Thus, in Xenophon, the ethical aspects of efficient administration are couched in terms of natural and material efficiency and human capital. In this respect, Aristotle too tends to reflect Xenophon's more open perspective than Plato's. Returning to the concept of *kalokagathia* we find that well-off Greeks in the classical era do not use their fortunes to glorify themselves through the building of sumptuous private mansions, but rather use their wealth for the general good, such as to construct agorai, gymnasia, temples, theatres and the like for all. In addition, they are under a moral obligation to provide *choregiai* (grants) for the benefit of the city-state, for example, to build, equip and maintain military ships, and also for their friends. So the concept of *filia* (friendship) is linked with that of *kalokagathia* (Petrochilos 2002a, 2002b).

The quest for virtue, goodness and perfection reach their highest point with Plato and his pupil Aristotle. Plato claims that there is an absolute standard against which human conduct and its ethical quality must be assessed, and in his *Republic* and the *Laws* he sets out to provide this ideal standard of human behaviour. Aristotle, is equally concerned about the 'good' and thinks that knowledge of the good is a great advantage to us in the conduct of our lives. Aristotle opposes the *kalon* (good) to the *sumpheron* (benefit), and feels confident that his pupils will choose the *kalon*. However, he has his doubts, as to whether it is possible to articulate an ideal, an absolute standard of behaviour from your inner consciousness and then force people to follow it. Before you can tell people how to behave, you must find out how they behave, thus, Aristotle in the *Nicomachean Ethics* (NE) is interested in the practice than the theory of morals. He lays stress on the individuals who need to possess *arete* and be *agathoi* and display it in government, if the latter is to operate efficiently. The *agathos* must know what he is doing. This requires *phronesis* (practical wisdom), for they do not have a philosopher-king to do their thinking for them. According to Aristotle, the *agathos* must have all these excellences, intellectual, moral, social and economic. The *agathos* acts 'for the sake of the *kalon* (good)'. *Kalon* commends all the manifestations of all the *aretai,* which make up the complete *arete* of the citizen (Adkins 1960, chapter 16). To become a good man you must behave like a good man, and then you will know what goodness is.

In terms of the link between ethics, politics and economics, Aristotle argues that the end of politics is the good, and in its pursuit politics can utilise the other sciences such as ethics, economics, oratory and the like. Ethics and economics, thus, become subservient to the 'master science' of politics in the pursuit of a noble objective: the good of the community. 'And that end in politics, as well as in ethics, can only be the good for man. For even if the good of the community coincides with that of the individual, the good of the community is clearly a greater and more perfect good both to get and to keep. This is not to deny that the good of the individual is worthwhile. But what is good for a nation or a city has a higher, diviner quality' (NE, book I, chapter 2). In the same context, Sen states that when ethical considerations affect human behaviour, we have 'the ethics-related view of motivation', and when we are concerned about the good of the society than that of the individual, we have a judgement of social achievement. He finds that these are important issues for modern economics, particularly, modern welfare economics (Sen 1987, pp. 3–4).

Both Plato and Aristotle are prepared to sacrifice the individual pursuit of wealth and riches, as well as economic and market relations in general, to the political community and civic virtue. They are concerned about the social fabric of the society and want to avoid the possible conflict that could emerge from the unfettered pursuit of riches and wealth. Consequently, in the aftermath of the catastrophic Peloponnesian war, Plato in his *Republic* goes as far as to propose public ownership of property and of women and children for his Guardian class. However, Aristotle disagrees and argues instead in favour of private property and the monogamic system, but expects people to use their wealth with an element of friendship and moral responsibility (Petrochilos 1999). In the *Laws*, Plato's most mature work, he shows his total disapproval of wealth. In that work, Plato seeks, again, the ideal political system and emphasises the highest value that justice and law and order must have for the development of society. In book 8 of the *Laws*, he considers sports and military training, the sexes, the economy and commerce and finds that the reason why people do not engage in military training is that they are occupied with their insatiable thirst for wealth and profit; thus, Plato proposes a harsh political system, which is unlikely to make people fond of money. This disdain may have had to do with the earlier experiences of Greek city-states, which were witnessing a weakening of the moral and social fabric. For example, in response to social conflict between the landed aristocracy and peasantry, Solon's economic reforms, known as *seisachthia* (the shifting of burdens), cancelled debts, freed enslaved debtors and forbade borrowing on the security of the person. Therefore, as Gordon (1975, p. 23) suggests, 'economic analysis in the hands of the philosophers is not a tool to be developed for use in the pursuit of transitory national strength as the Athenian proved to be. Instead, it is an intellectual activity required for an understanding of the nature of the just society and the application of that understanding to the preservation of a certain quality of life.'

The Platonic and Aristotelian viewpoint wants man to be a political animal and to take a keen interest in public affairs. This finds its application in democratic Athens, where the citizen has the right and the duty to speak freely in the assembly. Free speech is guaranteed to every (free) citizen, in contrast to the oligarchic city-states, to the earlier Homeric times and to the later experiences of Rome (Stone 1989, pp. 225–230). The same viewpoint is echoed later in the Graeco-Roman era by the Stoics. Stoicism as a philosophy stressed, among others, the moral code of duty, and in contrast to Epicureanism, views man as a world citizen, who is obliged to play an active role in civic affairs. The influence of Greek literature in the development of German social theory, in general, and in providing a strong ethical underpinning in Marxist thought, in particular, is discussed in the next section. However, it has to be remembered that Adam Smith was also influenced by the ancient Greek writers (Scott 1947) and that he was a Professor of morals. Sen finds that the Stoic influence on Smith '. . . also make it clear why both sympathy and self-discipline played such an important part in Smith's conception of good behaviour' (Sen 1987, p. 22). This at first sight is unusual, since the proponents of the 'engineering' or technocratic approach to economics look to Smith as the man foremost associated with the rationality of the self-interest and the efficiency argument rather than the neoclassical economists. Sen finds that many advocates of self-interest have ignored 'parts of Smith's writings on economics and society, dealing with observations of misery, the need for sympathy, and the role of ethical considerations in human behaviour ... as these considerations have themselves become unfashionable in economics' (Sen 1987, p. 28).

15.4 THE INFLUENCE ON MODERN SOCIAL THEORY, ETHICS AND ECONOMICS

The influence of Greek philosophy on Western thinking originated in the twelfth century AD when, through the Arab conquest of the Iberian peninsula, the Arabian philosopher Averroes introduced the work of Aristotle to the West and initiated the so-called scholastic interpretations of the Aristotelian philosophy. In the next century or so, six commentaries of Aristotle's *Nicomachean Ethics* were formulated by the scholastic thinkers on such matters as context, labour and expenses, human wants, aggregation and scarcity, effective demand and synthesis (Langholm 1979). The most prominent among the scholastics was Thomas Aquinas, whose work left an indelible mark, not only during medieval times but even in modern ones, on Catholic thinking about value and the just price. It is this Latinised Aristotle, with the ethical underpinning, that came to dominate scholastic economic thinking, who was introduced and taught in the great Western universities in mediaeval times, and who was preferred to Plato, and was simply known as the philosopher.

Also, during the same period and later on, the constant contact between the West, primarily through Italy, and the Byzantine Empire, brought to the attention of Westerners the rich classical Hellenic cultural heritage, retained and cultivated by the Byzantines, and affected significantly the rise of Western European renaissance, enlightenment and humanism. This heritage included, among others, elements of ancient Greek philosophy, mostly that of Plato's, through the work of the Byzantine neoplatonist philosopher George Gemistos Plethon and other Byzantine thinkers, such as, for example, Cardinal Bessarion, and of Aristotelianisn, through the work of Georgios Trapezuntios. The latter, a Byzantine humanist, scholar and Aristotelian follower, taught Greek at Vicenza and at Venice and argued of the superiority of Aristotle's Realism over Plato's Idealist theory of knowledge. Thus, the great dispute, raging in the Byzantine intellectual circles, between the aristotelians and the platonists, as to the preeminence of their respective teachings, became known to the West. The Platonists Gemistos Plethon and Cardinal Bessarion attacked Georgios Trapezuntios fervid Aristotelianism, and Bessarion's attempts to reconcile the two philosophies influenced Italian philosophy, which assimilated the Byzantine philosophical tradition after 1453 (Woodhouse 1986). It is interesting to note in this context the ethical basis of Plethon's teaching. Among others, Plethon, following Plato, advocated the lifting of property rights on land, by claiming that everyone has a right on so much land that he can cultivate; thus, the property right of one person ends where the other person's cultivation begins (Tzermias 1995, p. 181).

It is through these original links that the Western enlightenment and thinking is affected by ancient Greek philosophy. In fact, it is mostly continental social thought and, in particular, German social theory that has been influenced by Hellenic classical literature, particularly by Aristotle and Epicurus. Kant (1724–1804) in his writings, of which more below, is reminiscent of Platonic philosophy and the general Greek value system, discussed earlier. Also, Marx was influenced both directly, through his dissertation on the theories of Democritus and Epicurus and his reading of Aristotle, whom he admired and called him Alexander the Great of Greek philosophy, and indirectly through the teachings of Hegel. Marx's distinctive theory of historical materialism, with its dialectic of thesis, antithesis and synthesis, is based on Hegelianism and, indirectly, on Hellenic classical thought. Marx's view that societies are formed solely for the purpose of providing, collectively, the means of existence, is reminiscent of Plato's view, discussed in his *Republic* that society flourishes because it is efficient. For it enables each person to devote himself to the task he is best fitted for and saves him from dispersing his energies in other tasks he is not fitted for at all. The influence of Aristotle on Marx, and later writers, is also shown by Aristotle's treatment of wealth acquisition. His concern regarding the ethical aspects of wealth getting leads him to distinguish between what is natural acquisition by those in charge of the household or the city. It is their duty to ensure such supplies and in this case trade can be used to supply what is required, so we have the C–M–C' (Commodity–Money–Commodity) exchange. In this case, wealth is only sought as a basis for livelihood, not for its own sake. But, contrary to what Solon thought, there is a natural limit to this wealth, which nevertheless will give households financial autarky for a good life. This is the 'natural limit' theory where, in community trade, natural needs provide a limit on commercial activity, and Aristotle bestows his approval on that. This is contrasted to the other kind of wealth acquisition, which is not considered natural and on which there is no limit to riches. Here money is the object of trade among merchants, and there is no natural restraint to create an ethically stabilising market process in the community. This, Aristotle calls money-getting (*chrematistike*) and it provides the familiar M–C–M' (Money–Commodity–Money) exchange. On ethical grounds, Aristotle disapproves of this kind of trade (*Politics*, Bk. 1, chapter 8). The strong ethical underpinning of ancient Greek economics, which is not value free, is echoed not only in the writings of Marx, but also in the German Historical school of economic thought. In our days the same influence still survives in the form of the social market model, as distinct from the Anglo-American approach of the belief in the free and unfettered market (Petrochilos 2002a, 2002b).

In Britain the reception of Aristotle was mixed. In the first translation of *Nicomachean Ethics* in 1797, J. Gillies refers to Aristotelian 'discoveries of science, unjustly claimed by the vanity of modern writers' and compares the quotation in *Nicomachean Ethics* V, 5 favourably with 'the works of modern oeconomists, not excepting those of Hume and Smith', as quoted in Langholm (1979, p. 21). However, Gillies was probably an exception as by that time economics and ethics were becoming incompatible, and thus, Aristotle's ethical basis was unacceptable to the 'rationalists' and to the market-oriented society. Also, it appears that Aristotle's association with the Catholic Church, through the schoolmen, made him an easy target for anglophone writers, originally Hobbes and later on Hume, who either did not understand or simply disliked immensely his metaphysics and found it expedient to dispense with it. For example, Hobbes calls the Greek philosophy vain and finds 'the Schoole of the Graecians unprofitable', 'their Morall Philosophy is but a description of their own Passions', and he concludes 'And I believe that scarce any thing can be more absurdly said in natural Philosophy, than that which now is called *Aristotles Metaphysiques;* nor more repugnant to Government, than much of that hee hath said in his *Politiques;* nor more ignorantly, than a great part of his *Ethiques*' (Hobbes, Part IV, chapter 46, pp. 686–687). This however, in terms of the development of philosophical enquiry, may have amounted to throwing out the baby with the bathwater. For, what these anglophone writers meant by metaphysics was a science trying to prove the existence of things in the supernatural world, which is how the term was understood during the Enlightenment period, rather than the abstract forces and concepts, in which the term is normally understood, and how Aristotle was using it. 'Neither side distinguished between this sense of the term, and the primary sense in which metaphysics, together with logic, is the most fundamental area of philosophical inquiry, and one which informs all other areas of thought, since thought of any kind works to one metaphysics or another. When Hume and others "eliminated" metaphysics, they eliminated it in both senses at once. Logic and metaphysics largely disappeared from native anglophone philosophy for the best part of 300 years' (Meikle 1995, pp. 181–182).

However, in Britain there was a significant exception. John Ruskin (1819–1900), the English writer, critic and artist did also much to inspire opposition to a *laissez-faire* philosophy, as contravening the ethical and religious thinking. He disagreed with J.S. Mill, who could not conceive economics with aesthetics. Ruskin was imbued with the 'Platonic ideal of justice, harmony ... and truth' (Henderson 2000, p. 22). Thus, he turned his attention towards political economy and the improvement of the working class through satisfaction in work. In a series of publications, prominent amongst which were, in particular, four essays, originally published separately in 1862 in the *Cornhill*, he expounded his ideas on the first principles of political economy. These essays were: (1) The Roots of Honour; (2) The Veins of Wealth; (3) Qui Judicatis Terram and (4) Ad Valorem and appeared later as a book under the general title: *Unto This Last*. It is the strong ethical approach of these essays, which proved very controversial at the time, that shows a considerable influence by the Greeks, particularly Xenophon and Plato. In the first essay he attacked as dangerous the assumptions of the science of political economy, whose atomistic competition, instead of producing the rich, harmonious society, proved very divisive by setting men against men and giving the successful an excuse to neglect the welfare of those less fortunate. Businessmen refused to accept their social responsibilities, as other traditional professions, and they behaved dishonourably by the pursuit of profit. In the second, by following probably Aristotle, he distinguished between 'mercantile economy', (Aristotle's *chrematistike*), in which the pursuit of profit was uppermost, and 'true political economy' in which, following the Greek classical tradition, the economy of the state or the household has as its objective 'the production, preservation and distribution at fittest time and place, of useful and pleasurable things' (par. 28). In the third essay, Ruskin seeks true economic leadership and he argues that the essential principle in the relations between employer and worker is not supply and demand but justice. He argues for a more equitable distribution of income and prosperity and does not think that this is socialism, which as a true Tory he abhorred, but merely Christian teaching, which the capitalist rich professed on Sunday and carefully ignored during the rest of the week. In his last essay, he went beyond J.S. Mill's definition of value as the cost of production, and defined value as 'to avail towards life' and declared that it was an intrinsic quality of things. That is, he incorporated elements of demand as a determining factor and argued about subjective judgements, which were important in establishing what was valuable or wealth, thus, anticipating the modern theories of value (Ruskin 1994).

Ruskin, following the ethical tradition of Xenophon's *Oikonomikos* and the implications for the betterment of the working class of wealth generation through manual labour, wondered how his work was admired by ancients and in Middle Ages but neglected in England. Thus, he had *Oikonomikos* translated by two of his students to which he contributed an introduction/commentary and had it published under the title: *The Economist of Xenophon* (1876) (Hilton 2000). Later he translated Plato's *Laws*. Ruskin himself is explicit about Xenophon's influence: 'the philosophy I teach is Plato's…the economy Xenophon's'. And 'my political economy is all in Xenophon', as quoted by Henderson (2000, p. 65). Henderson, in discussing Ruskin's ethical values notes that 'Ruskin's primary image involves a balance between the production of necessities and luxuries, a balance he did not feel had been achieved given the economic consequence of an unequal distribution of wealth. His conception of stewardship is an amalgamation of Christian and Greek sources' (Henderson 2000, p. 78). Ruskin finds that in Xenophon's *Oikonomikos* there is a sophisticated theory of management, and claims in his preface to its translation that he found there: 'a faultless definition of wealth', 'the most perfect ideal of kingly character and kingly government' (an idea related to his notion of personal ethics and responsibility) and 'the ideal of domestic life' (Henderson 2000, p. 77).

Henderson (2000, chapter 5) finds interesting parallels between the lives and works of Plato and Ruskin. They both shocked their contemporary societies with the *Republic* and *Unto This Last*. The administrative element is an essential part of Greek ideas in the nature of economic activity. So, in much the same way that in the *Laws* Plato sets out to legislate the proper conduct of economic life, Ruskin too looks for the development of self-regulation and for a legislative framework for a number of problems. Plato's attack on conventional notions of justice and his attempts to reconstruct it are echoed in Ruskin's concern about economic justice and his calls for a reconstruction of social relationships and institutions. Cooperation than competition is Ruskin's social ideal, within which justice can be realised. For the most efficient functioning of the city, Plato advocates in the *Republic* specialisation, which is based on cooperation and not competition, and Ruskin is interested, as is Plato, in how such cooperation can be secured. Ruskin frames his economic agent in terms of duty to society rather than duty to making money. This is a Platonic idea found in the *Republic* and the *Laws*, where trade is to place goods in the appropriate hands, while profit maximisation would suggest money-making (Henderson 2000, p. 96). In much the same way that Plato argues in the *Republic* for selecting and educating his Guardian class, Ruskin is concerned with finding the fittest to lead as a basis for working-class self-help. 'Plato makes explicit a link between achieving and sustaining social reform and education. Ruskin, also accepts a link between social reform and education' (Henderson 2000, p. 98). His attempts to create an ethical economics, are like Plato's justice, utopian. But beyond his attack on the principles of *laissez-faire*, his theories have practical policy and behavioural implications. He is looking forward for a new type of economic analysis, which grows out of concern for worldwide poverty, which is akin to the 'structuralist' approach aiming to marginalise the market and putting emphasis on coordinated administrative action, because of market failures and externalities. Therefore, Ruskin, although drawing on Greek sources, may be considered to have developed ideas similar to the 'structuralist' economic argument, which was not fully developed until almost one hundred years after the first publication of *Unto This Last*.

Also, among modern economists who were influenced by the ethical teachings of the Greeks were N. Senior and P.H. Wicksteed. The former had used Aristotle's *Logic, Nicomachean Ethics* and *Politics* in the original Greek in his *Industrial Efficiency and Social Economy (1928)*; while Wicksteed, in discussing the marginal analysis, brings out the connection between economics and ethics as follows:

> Now I conceive that the application of this differential method to economics must tend to enlarge and to harmonise our conception of the scope of the study, and to keep it in constant touch with the wider ethical, social and sociological problems and aspirations from which it must always draw its inspiration and derive its interest; for if we really understand and accept the principle of differential significances we shall realise, as already pointed out, that Aristotle's system of ethics and our reconstructed system of economics are twin applications of one identical principle or law, and that our conduct in business is but a phase or part of our conduct in life, both being determined by our sense, such as it is, of differential significances and their changing weights as the integrals of which they are the differences expand or contract. (Wicksteed 1914)

However, despite this strong recommendation, the rise of neoclassical economics, with the sole behavioural assumption of rationality sweeping everything else in its way, meant the complete demise of any ethical considerations, in the development of economics. Modern economic analysis is value free. Ethics and economics must be kept separate and this is championed by Robbins in his influential *Essay on the Nature and Significance of Economic Science*, where we find that 'Economics deals with ascertainable facts; ethics with valuations and obligations' (Robbins 1935, p. 148), and where also other, interventionist, approaches to economics, such as Institutionalism or the German Historical School are clearly disapproved.

15.5 OTHER APPROACHES TO ETHICS

In the last two sections we have presented and emphasized in a summary form the basics of the Greek ethical value system as was developed over time and bequeathed to us. It is upon this system that subsequent writers, both of the distant and not so distant past but also the present return for inspiration when expanding on ethical questions. Clearly, not everyone has accepted the Greek terms of reference and as it is natural alternative approaches to ethics have been put forward. We have already touched upon some of the proponents of these other approaches in the earlier discussion, notably the rationalist utilitarians and Kant. In what follows, we present, very briefly, some of these alternatives, and endeavour to illustrate their relevance for the business community.

15.5.1 Utilitarianism

Utilitarianism is a school of thought in early economics founded around the principle of rationality and promoted chiefly by D. Hume (1711–76), J. Bentham (1748–1832) and J.S. Mill (1806–73), and provides the philosophical underpinning of marginalism and neoclassical economics. Hume argued that moral decisions depend on moral sentiments and that qualities are valued either for their utility or their agreeableness. Hume's moral system aims both at the happiness of others and of self, although his emphasis is on regard for others. Altruism informs most of Hume's moral system, since of the moral sentiments that he claims to find in man, he traces them to a sentiment for and sympathy for one's fellow beings. The major propositions of utilitarianism as formulated by Bentham and continue to be accepted today are that: (1) individual well-being ought to be the end of moral actions; (2) each individual is to 'count for one and no more than one'; and (3) the object of the social action should be to maximise general utility, or in Bentham's terms, to promote the greatest happiness of the greatest number. Bentham had equated utility with pleasure, something that most modern utilitarians would reject. Utilitarianism left an indelible mark on one of the moral sciences, namely, economics, particularly in the area of welfare economics, where the need to determine a 'welfare function' is utilitarian in nature, since it seeks to measure individual want-satisfaction and also to establish utility indices. Utilitarianism is not based on ethical principles but on goals (Singer 1993, p. 3). People act to satisfy their own interests and they are the best judges of those interests. For example, producers try to maximise their profits, consumers aim at the maximisation of their utility and so on. In our context, utilitarianism is the moral theory stating that right conduct should be determined solely by the usefulness of its consequences.

Therefore, it is argued that any action is right if it produces the maximum possible happiness for all those affected by it, as compared with any alternative action. According to J.S. Mill 'the utility or the greatest happiness principle holds that actions are right . . . if they tend to promote happiness, wrong if they intend to produce the reverse of happiness. By happiness I mean pleasure, by unhappiness pain and the privation of pleasure' (1861, p. 5). Consequently, when confronted with a choice, utilitarianism dictates that the correct approach is that course of action that results in the best possible outcome for as many people as possible, provided that the minority does not suffer disproportionally; nothing is wrong that allows this, and nothing is right that fails to do so. In the same context J.S. Mill, following Bentham's quantitative rationality and subjective individualism (referred to as hedonic calculus), argues that 'pleasure and freedom from pain are the only desirable ends' (Mill 1861, p. 6). Mill's case for the moral worth of happiness rests with the 'fact' that people desire it, since '. . . No reason can be given why the general happiness is desirable except that each person, so far as he believes it to be attainable, desires his own happiness' (Mill 1861, p. 44). Mill was troubled by the suggestion that the basic psychological theory, underlying utilitarianism, that one is only motivated to obtain their own good implied: (1) a narrow materialistic view of pleasure; and (2) egoistic hedonism (i.e., that each person ought to maximise his own pleasure). In answer to the first point, Mill argued for qualitative differences in pleasure, but this argument affected negatively utilitarianism, since if there are lower and higher pleasures, a different standard other than pleasure is implied as the criterion of judgement between them. To answer the second point, Mill stated that utilitarianism is a system of ethical hedonism, i.e., that the criterion applied to individual moral action is general happiness not individual interest. The problem, however, is defining what constitutes happiness and on this issue there was no agreement even among the utilitarians. While to Bentham happiness was the avoidance of pain, Mill tried to identify different degrees of happiness, leading to weakening of the internal consistency of utilitarianism.

15.5.2 Deontology

This approach to ethics has its origins also in the Greek and Roman classic writers, particularly the Stoics, and defends 'duty for duty's sake'. According to deontology (from the Greek *deon* = proper, right, duty and *logos* = word, thought, reason, science), an action is ethically right because of some characteristic of the action itself, rather than the goodness of its outcomes. That is, one acts ethically because it is one's duty to do so irrespective of the consequences. Therefore, deontological ethics holds the opposite of teleological ethics, which emphasise that the basic standard of morality is the value of what an action brings about. Since the central principle of deontological ethics is the conformity of the action to some rule or law, they have also been called formalist. The Stoics, and particularly Epictetus, held that ethical wisdom consists in living 'according to nature', and so did the Roman Emperor Marcus Aurelius. Nature provides a rational world order with which man can live in harmony, provided he distinguishes between things within his power and those beyond it. Of the religions, Judaism and Christianity can be considered as espousing a formalist ethic, because they require of their followers a duty of obedience to God.

The German critical philosopher I. Kant (1724–1804) was the chief proponent of modern deontology. His ethical views were influenced by Christianity and the Rationalism of the Enlightenment. Kant held that people should act not only according to the moral law, but also out of respect for that law, rather than out of natural inclinations. Thus, people must make the right decisions for the right reasons; for example, they must behave honestly because honesty is the proper thing to do, if people are honest because honesty pays, then honesty itself is cheapened. Equally, firms acting ethically out of fear of prosecution are not really behaving ethically at all. To Kant moral law is a categorical imperative and its content could be established by reason alone. He argued that reason begins with the principle, 'Act only on that maxim whereby thou canst at the same time will that it should become a universal law'. However, this view, that all duties can be derived from this formal principle, has been challenged by critics who have argued that Kant, in his preoccupation with rational consistency, ignored the concrete content of moral obligations.

The British philosopher and foremost twentieth century deontologist W.D. Ross argued that there are various '*prima facie* duties', rather than a single formal principle for obtaining them. Such *prima facie* duties are promise keeping, reparation, gratitude and justice, and these must be distinguished from actual duties. This is so because each act has many sides to it, and all these sides contribute to its rightness or wrongness; therefore, these must all be weighed before forming a judgement as an actual obligation in the given circumstances.

In the end, deontology relies heavily on a system of rules, which tends to make it inflexible. Any ethical uncertainties and ambiguities can only be resolved by constructing even more complicated or specific rules, and ranking such rules in a hierarchical manner, so that any conflict between them is avoided (Singer 1993, p. 3). Whether firms approach ethical decision making from the standpoint of what is *proper*, i.e., a deontological starting point remains open to question.

15.5.3　Rights-based approach

The gist of this approach is that people have certain inalienable rights that must be upheld and that these rights are common to all mankind. The rights-based approach emanates from the Declaration of the Rights of Man and of the Citizen of 1789, which was the basic charter of human liberties that inspired the French Revolution. The main principle of the Declaration was that 'all men are born free and equal in rights', which were specified as the rights of liberty, private property, the inviolability of the person, and resistance to oppression. All citizens were equal before the law and had the right to participate, directly or indirectly, in legislation; no one was to be arrested without a judicial order, and freedom of religion and of speech were guaranteed, within the bounds of 'public order' and 'law'. This sometimes can be referred to as 'natural law' taken to refer to a system of right or justice held to be common to all mankind. 'Natural law' as a system of recognised principles of right conduct is contrasted with 'positive law', representing the legal rules promulgated by the state and enforced by appropriate sanctions.

However, there was a reaction to both 'natural law' and the French Declaration of Rights. For example, Bentham appalled at the excesses of the French revolution, known as Terror, claimed that: (1) rights are not anterior to political society but are created by law; thus an inalienable or non-legal right is a self-contradictory notion; and (2) a philosophy of natural rights provides no way to adjudicate the competing claims of such rights to priority; a non-legal moral right is a 'criterionless notion' (Welch 1998, vol. 4, p. 771). Not surprisingly then that the utilitarians do not take rights or their violation into consideration.

In this respect, significant is the Universal Declaration of Human Rights, developed and adopted by the UN in 1948. The Declaration (Art. 22) proclaims that 'Everyone, as a member of society, . . . is entitled to the realisation, through national effort and international cooperation and in accordance with the organisation and resources of each State, of the economic, social and cultural rights indispensable for his dignity and the free development of his personality'. The Declaration also recognises that everyone has the right to a standard of living adequate for the health and well-being of himself and his family; the right to work; to just and favourable remuneration and working conditions; to rest and reasonable limits on working hours; to social security; and to education. It is interesting to note that these rights have been incorporated into the EU's Social Charter, discussed below. In connection with the realisation of these rights, Cassel (2001) argues that in the post–Cold War era and in the face of rapid globalisation of the economy, global political institutions are too weak to regulate global corporate power and national governments no longer have the reach to control large multinationals, whilst corporate self-regulation is mostly ineffective. Nevertheless, the world must not succumb to a 'radical capitalist ideology', which 'blindly entrusts' social problems to market forces, but rather consider the business responsibilities towards solving such problems. For 'if our incipient global economy is not for the well-being of the people of the word, then what is it for?' Clearly, this is a concern reminiscent of the Greeks, discussed earlier. Whether the solution will come from pressure exerted on the multinationals by their customers at home to mend their business practices abroad, remains to be seen.

In the present context what is required is a recognition of such rights and the need to minimise their violation. Also, it must be made clear that while such rights may be inviolable, they extend up to the point where the rights of others begin. Thus, the rights of others provide effective constraints on action. Attempts in the corporate world to establish and agree certain such rights that would replace the utilitarianism's total happiness, include the EU's social charter. The latter provides, among others, for the right to freedom of movement, right to social protection, right to freedom and collective bargaining, right of all to equal treatment, right to health protection and safety at the workplace and, significantly, right to information, consultation and worker participation in the running of a business. While that proved too much for the then UK Prime Minister Mrs Thatcher, who refused to sign up to the Social Charter by obtaining an opt-out on the grounds that 'the UK had not rolled back the frontiers of the state only to have then re-imposed by the EU', ironically, it was a rights-based approach though, admittedly, a minimalist one that both Mrs Thatcher in the UK and President Reagan in the US were championing in their policies of the 1980s. It is recalled that those policies reduced significantly the collective rights of trade unions, while increasing the rights of individual employees, particularly, those prepared to stand up to the power of trade unions (Mellahi and Wood 2003, p. 16).

Given the above discussion on the theoretical underpinnings of ethical behaviour, we turn now to consider reasons for such corporate behaviour and what firms are doing in practice to implement ethical policies.

15.6　CORPORATE GOVERNANCE AND ETHICS

By corporate governance we mean the system, and more specifically, the set of rules and arrangements by which an organisation is directed and controlled. However, this is a narrow definition of the term failing to take account of the accountability and responsibilities, particularly, of the top executives not only towards their shareholders, but more generally the firm's various stakeholders. Therefore, a much broader definition is provided by the OECD (1999) as follows:

> The corporate governance structure specifies the distribution of rights and responsibilities among different participants in the corporation, such as, the board, managers, shareholders and other stakeholders, and spells out the rules and procedures for making decisions on corporate affairs.

The observed keen interest in how modern corporations are governed and decisions are arrived at by their boards of directors is explained chiefly by a number of important factors, some of which are long standing and others are relatively current, as follows:

1. *The separation of ownership from control:* As discussed in Chapter 3, in the context of the theories of the firm, the divorce of ownership from control in the large corporation creates additional requirements for the firm to consider the interests of groups other than the shareholders of the traditional neoclassical theory. In particular, as the behavioural theory of the firm suggests, various other stakeholders, such as managers, workers, suppliers and the like have more than a passing interest in the fortunes of the firm, and their concerns must also be taken into account, when policies are formulated by the board of directors. This is more so when it is recognised that there may very

well be conflict between some of these group interests requiring resolution, for the smooth running of the enterprise. In addition, in most industrially advanced societies, the role of the stock exchange and of the financial institutions (e.g., pension funds) means that not only they help in the growth of the firms by providing finance, but also that shareholding is much more dispersed now than in the past. Therefore, this means that what happens in boardrooms is of crucial importance not only to people holding shares directly, but also to all those holding them indirectly, through their pension funds.

2. *The growth of the transnational enterprise:* As discussed in Chapter 13, on the growth of the multinationals, in the last 50 years we have seen an unprecedented increase in the importance of the transnational firms. Such firms control productive assets in many countries, producing thousands of products and employing hundreds of thousands of employees around the world. The turnover of some of these firms far exceeds the GDP of most countries in which such firms operate. This provides transnational enterprises with considerable power, which their boards are prepared to exploit in furtherance of their objectives, which may not be always in accord with the objectives of host governments and peoples. Decisions by multinationals affect the livelihood of individuals in the host countries in ways not envisaged originally, and for which the firm, typically, has no social responsibility. For many years, concern about the role and the policies of the multinationals has been voiced not only by less developed countries (LDCs) but by many developed countries too, and has led to the development of codes of conduct by international organisations to regulate the activities of such corporations, in the teeth of considerable opposition by the neo-liberal proponents of the virtues of the unfettered market.

3. *Corporate failure and crisis:* Corporate failure and bankruptcy is part and parcel of business activity and the accepted penalty for inefficiency and laggard and incompetent management, and a way in which productive resources, in the long run, may be reallocated to alternative uses. However, in recent years there has been an increase in reported corporate failings of very large firms, due mostly to management incompetence, abuse of power and also fraudulent behaviour. The failures of the American energy giant Enron, of the telecom firm WorldCom and of others have highlighted significant flaws in the US accounting and auditing practices, as a result of which investors lost faith in corporate statements and annual reports and accentuated the collapse in equity markets. Also, sharp corporate practices including, among others, inside trading and golden good byes to failed executive officers increased disquiet among not only shareholders but other stakeholders too and contributed to a demand for change. This, clearly, was at variance with how the 'invisible hand' of the free market was supposed to guide in the proper running of enterprises. And it brought demands for a more ethical approach to corporate governance, again at the protestations of the neo-liberals.

However, the difficulty is that there is not a single best governance model. The governance of an enterprise depends largely on the ownership structure, the business sector and, for internationally trading companies, the national corporate governance systems and cultural values and norms. Thus, Japanese companies, for example, are subject to a different set of national norms and values from American, or continental European or English firms. In terms of ownership structure, for a publicly traded firm with dispersed shareholding, the main problem is how the outsiders (shareholders) can control the performance of the insiders (professional managers), given the information gap that exists between the two groups. Outsiders can perhaps influence the governance by setting rules for selecting directors and monitoring and controlling the latter's performance through annual general meetings, in which however, the role of the powerful institutional investors would be crucial. In the case of a tightly held company with a major shareholder exercising a controlling interest and a minority of outside shareholders, the managers are under the scrutiny and control of the major shareholder, and the challenge is how the company can develop appropriate governance mechanisms to protect the interests of the minority shareholders and limit the power of the major shareholder to extract self-benefits from the company (Mellahi and Wood 2003, p. 25).

The increase in the importance of corporate governance in recent years is explained by the realisation that the common elements of most failed firms are management incompetence, fraudulent behaviour and arrogance and abuse of power. If this is also combined with weak monitoring and control systems, as in the Anglo-American business world, because of ideological reasons that 'management knows best', it tends to produce poorer performance as compared with countries, such as Germany, in which the social market model encourages a corporate governance structure of cooperation with the various stakeholders, rather than confrontation.

15.6.1   The OECD corporate governance code

In 1999, the Paris-based Organisation for Economic Co-operation and Development (OECD) of 29 leading industrialised countries in the word, in the wake of the financial crises in Asia, Russia and developing countries, introduced a corporate governance code to help rebuild investor confidence. The code was hailed as an 'astonishing achievement' in arriving at a broad consensus among countries with widely different management cultures from the US and UK to continental Europe and Japan. The code set a number of principles and standards, which could be used as benchmarks for internationally accepted standards of management behaviour and offered a solid basis for analysis and practices in various countries, subject to country-specific characteristics, such as cultural traditions and legal rules. The main points of the OECD corporate governance code are:

> *Rights of shareholders:* The rights of shareholders must be protected. Such rights include the right to participate in the running of the company; to have relevant information about the company's state of affairs; to participate in decisions concerning fundamental corporate changes; to have the necessary information on the rules and voting procedures governing general shareholders meetings and to have the opportunity to participate effectively and to vote in general shareholder meetings.
>
> *Equitable treatment of shareholders:* The governance of the company should ensure that all shareholders are treated equally, irrespective of whether they are

majority, minority or foreign shareholders. In addition all shareholders should have the opportunity to obtain redress for violation of their rights. In particular, all shareholders of the same class should be treated equally and insider trading and abusive self-dealing should be prohibited.

Role of other stakeholders in corporate governance: This provides explicit recognition of the rights of other stakeholders in general in the company, as established by law, and the encouragement of the active cooperation of the corporation and its stakeholders in the creation of wealth, jobs and a financially sound enterprise. The business code should provide assurance that the rights of the stakeholders that are protected by law are respected, that stakeholders have the opportunity to obtain redress for violation of their rights and that there are available the appropriate mechanisms for stakeholder participation.

Disclosure and transparency: This aspect has to do with the timely and accurate disclosure of all information as regards the corporation, particularly, with reference to its financial position, performance, ownership and the rules of its governance.

The board of directors responsibilities: The corporate governance code must ensure that the board of directors provides strategic guidance to the company and effective monitoring of the activities of the managers, but also of how the board is accountable to the company and its shareholders. The board of directors should act on the fullest of information, in good faith, with due diligence and faith in the best interest of the company and its shareholders. In cases where board decisions affect various groups of shareholders differently, the board should treat all shareholders fairly, in accordance with the requirement for the equitable treatment of shareholders, mentioned above.

The board of directors should be able to exercise objective judgement on corporate affairs independently from management: To achieve this there is a need for the board to assign an appropriate number of expert non-executive board members capable of exercising independent judgement to tasks where there is potential for conflict of interest. Critical areas requiring attention include financial reporting, nomination of board members as well as executive and board members' remuneration.

Towards the end of 2002, and as a result of the collapse in investor confidence in the financial markets in the major Western countries, there were moves to strengthen the OECD code of corporate governance. This is treated in the appendix to this chapter.

15.6.2   The UK experience: corporate governance at BG Group PLC

In the UK concern about standards of corporate governance, particularly, regarding accountability and responsibility led to the publication of the Cadbury Report in 1992 (*Report of the Committee on the Financial Aspects of Corporate Governance 1992*). The report required that all UK listed companies in the Stock Exchange include a statement on corporate governance, i.e., the system by which the company is directed and controlled, in their annual reports to their shareholders. The report also emphasized the need for a clear division of responsibilities at the top of the company, to achieve a balance of power and responsibility, with separate persons as chairman of the board of directors and as chief executive, so that no one person had unlimited powers of decision making. The chairman of the board deals with external aspects of the company's operations, such as communications with major shareholders (institutional investors) and government departments and acts as the spokesman of the company to the outside world. The chief executive, on the other hand, deals with internal matters, such as operational and executive aspects and coordinates the work of the other executive managers (i.e., financial, production, marketing and the like) This separation of responsibilities in the UK contrasts with the US practice, where one, usually, powerful personality tends to combine the two positions.

The Combined Code, as the official guide on corporate governance in the UK is known, recommends that there should be more non-executive directors on a board than executives, but many companies ignore the advice. In January 2003, the Higgs report on the review of boardrooms recommended the strengthening of the role of the non-executive directors in order to stamp out cosy relationships in many boards, by advising the government to amend the code to require that at least half the board should be independent. In addition, not only should the majority be non-executives, but they should meet new criteria of being 'independent', which are defined as having no financial ties or other types of relationships with executives. Also, a change in the code is proposed to stipulate that executives should only be allowed to hold one other non-executive post at another company. In order to attract more talented non-executives, Higgs also addressed the issue of non-executives' pay, saying the post should attract more than the current average salary of €37 000 that a FTSE100 non-executive receives. Currently, there are a number of companies falling foul of the Higgs proposals, since there are people with more than one chairmanship of listed companies; companies that effectively combine chief executive/chairman and; chairmen who are former executives of the same company. This has caused some disquiet among business leaders who fear that shareholders may push for changes soon after 1 July 2003, when the new amended governance code in the UK comes into effect. Higgs expected that many of the review's recommendations would take 'some years' to be adopted and that the code should be 'sensibly' applied to people falling foul of it, by taking the approach of either 'complying' with the code or 'explaining' the reasons for non-compliance. The National Association of Pension Funds, major institutional investors, said it would encourage compliance from 1 July 2003.

As an example of the UK experience, we consider the corporate governance at the BG group PLC. BG, which derives from the former British Gas, is an integrated major gas explorer and producer in the UK and other parts of the world, and also deals with liquefied natural gas (LNG), the development and operation of transmission and distribution networks and the supply of gas through these to the end customers and, finally, with electric power generation through natural gas-fired power generation plants.

In accordance with the requirement that UK listed companies provide a statement of their governance in their annual reports, particularly, on whether the company has complied or not with the provisions of the Combined Code, appended to the Listing Rules of the UK Listing Authority, the BG group Annual

Report and Accounts 2002 gives the following information:

The Company is committed to achieving and maintaining high standards of corporate governance throughout the Group and to integrity and high ethical standards in all its business dealings. The board continually reviews developments in corporate governance... The Directors consider that the Company has complied throughout the financial period with the provisions set out in Section 1 of the Combined Code.

The Board of Directors:

The Board leads and maintains full and effective control over all wholly-owned companies and all activities where BG has a controlling shareholding. Where it has a minority interest, BG encourages and helps its partners to establish such controls... BG Group plc has separate posts of Chairman and Chief Executive. The Board consists of three Executive Directors (the Chief Executive, the Deputy Chief Executive and the Chief Financial Officer) and ten non-executive Directors, including the Chairman and the Deputy Chairman. The Deputy Chairman acts also as the Senior Independent Director. All Directors are subject to election by shareholders at the first opportunity after their appointment by the Board and to re-election by shareholders every three years... The Board is supplied with high quality and timely information to enable it to discharge its duties... The Board has a schedule of matters specifically reserved to it for decision, including matters of key strategic importance, financial policy and material acquisitions and disposals.... All Directors have access to the advice and services of the Company Secretary, and Directors, if necessary, are free to take independent professional advice as to Board decisions at BG's expense.... The Board considers that all Directors bring an independent judgement to the Board's deliberations in respect of strategy, performance, resources, key appointments and standards of conduct. All non-executive Directors are considered by the Board to be independent of management and free from any business or other relationship which could interfere with the exercise of their independent judgement.

Committees:

The Board has delegated authority to the following committees on specific matters. All of the committees have formal terms of reference or, in the case of the Audit Committee, a written charter, approved by the Board.

- The Group Executive Committee manages BG's day-to-day business within limits set by the Board, focuses on strategy, Group performance, people and organisation and has delegated authority to six sub-committees (investment; exploration; business development; health, safety, security and environment; policy and risk; and energy trading risk management).

- The Chairman's Committee advises and assists the Chairman in the preparation of Board meetings.

- The Audit Committee oversees the Company's financial reporting process, monitors the adequacy of internal control and risk management processes and reviews the external and internal auditors' independence and performance. The Audit Committee meets the membership requirements of the Combined Code in the UK and the Blue Ribbon Report in the US. The Blue Ribbon Report is a New York

Stock Exchange publication, which makes recommendations on improving the effectiveness of corporate audit committees.

- The Finance Committee considers financing and treasury decisions concerning the Group.

- The Nominations Committee recommends appointments to the Board.

- The Remuneration Committee consists exclusively of non-executive Directors. It has responsibility for setting, reviewing and recommending to the Board the Company's overall remuneration policy and strategy and for setting, reviewing and approving the remuneration of the Executive Directors.

Relationship with shareholders and AGM:
The Company recognises the importance of maintaining a purposeful relationship with its shareholders and uses the Annual General Meeting (AGM) as an opportunity to communicate with its shareholders ... BG has an annual Investor Relations Programme and maintains a dialogue with its institutional shareholders in this country and overseas. In order to facilitate this dialogue regular meetings are held with institutional shareholders.

Internal control:
The Board has overall responsibility for our system of internal control and for reviewing the effectiveness, whilst the role of management is to implement Board policies on risk and control. The system of internal control is designed to manage, rather than eliminate, the risk of failure to achieve business objectives. In pursuing these objectives, internal controls can provide only reasonable and not absolute assurance against material misstatement or loss. The Board has established key policies and has carried out a specific assessment of the Group's system of internal control. The Company, as required by the Listing Rules, has complied with the Combined Code provisions on internal control by establishing the procedures necessary to implement the guidance issued by the Internal Control working party of the Institute of Chartered Accountants in England and Wales in September 1999 (the Turnbull Committee Report) and by reporting in accordance with that guidance. The processes used by the Board to review the effectiveness of the system of internal control include the following:

- The Audit Committee reviews the effectiveness of internal financial, operational, compliance and risk management controls. Significant issues are referred to the Board for consideration.

- The Company has an Internal Audit department and its scope of work, authority and resources are reviewed annually by the Audit Committee.

- The Finance Committee considers financing decisions concerning the Group, including the giving of guarantees and indemnities, and monitors policy and control mechanisms for managing treasury risk.

Disclosure Controls and Procedures:
As a listed company in the UK and USA the BG Group is obliged to make statements with regard to its disclosure controls and procedures. In accordance with these obligations the Chief Executive and the Chief Financial Officer have evaluated the effectiveness of

the Group's disclosure controls.... and have concluded that...such controls and procedures were effective to ensure that material information relating to the Group would be made known to them by others within the Group. There were no significant changes (including corrective actions with regard to significant deficiencies and material weaknesses) in the Group's internal controls or in other factors that could materially affect these controls after the date the Chief Executive and Chief Financial Officer completed their evaluation.

Risk management:
The process for identifying, evaluating and managing the significant risks faced by the Company is embedded in our business activities. Risk management is a core part of our strategy and business planning, investment appraisal, performance management and health, safety, security and environmental management processes. The effectiveness of this process is regularly reviewed by the Audit Committee on behalf of the Board.

In addition, the Annual Report includes the Audit Committee Charter, which provides detailed information on the purpose, composition and meetings and authority and responsibilities of the said Committee, as well as guidance on the way it exercises its auditing activities.

15.7   SOCIAL RESPONSIBILITIES AND SOCIAL PARTNERSHIPS

The preceding discussion has highlighted a number of reasons of why corporate directors have certain 'social responsibilities' that go beyond looking after the interest of their shareholders. However, according to a proponent of neo-liberalism, this is a fundamental misconception of the character and nature of the free economy because, he argues

in such an economy there is one and only one social responsibility of business – to use its resources and engage in activities designed to increase its profits so long as it stays within the rules of the game, which is to say, engages in open and free competition, without deception or fraud. Similarly, the 'social responsibility' of labor leaders is to serve the interests of the members of their unions. It is the responsibility of the rest of us to establish a framework of law such that an individual in pursuing his own interest is, to quote Adam Smith..., 'led by an invisible hand to promote an end which was no part of his intention. Nor is it always the worse for the society that it was no part of it. By pursuing his own interest, he frequently promotes that of society more effectually than when he really intends to promote it. I have never known much good done by those who affected to trade for the public good.' (Friedman 1962, p. 133)

We have seen in Chapter 10 that in order for the 'invisible hand' to promote also a best end for society as a whole a number of strict conditions have to be satisfied. Indeed, the conditions alluded to in the above quotation by Smith were conditions of competition and in particular perfect competition. While in the days of Adam Smith, at the beginning of the industrial revolution in England, conditions among producers were not far removed from the competitive model, the industrial structure in most industrialised countries has changed appreciably between 1776 when Adam Smith's *Wealth of Nations* appeared and today. The industrial structure has become much more concentrated with considerable power found in the hands of very few. Even Friedman accepts that the monopolist is visible and has power and, consequently, it would be easy to argue that the latter should discharge his power not exclusively to further his own interests but to advance socially desirable ends. One cannot ignore the fact that the hand of the market today is not particularly 'invisible'. Yet, Friedman fears that the widespread application of such a doctrine would destroy a free society. This is the libertarian view expressed by a number of authors who, for ideological reasons, do not accept any interference with the market arguing that the market itself is capable of sorting out any problems that may arise. The difficulty with this argument is that you cannot both accept that society can set the rules of the game and at the same time suggest that these rules are destroying a free society. This is a very tendentious view. Suggesting that European governments today, prepared to regulate their markets, are helping in destroying the very fabric of their free societies is mere scare-mongering.

In fact, the notion of 'social responsibility' has been accepted by most of the listed companies in the London Stock Exchange and, particularly, in continental Europe, where the 'social market model' or the 'Rhineland model' has been in existence for much longer and where the so-called 'social partnerships' were developed. What we mean by 'social responsibility' is that businesses take account of the social environment in which they operate, so that their activities tend to enhance the positive effects while limiting the negative effects on society. In other words, it is an attempt to incorporate elements of social benefits and costs to the private benefits and costs recognised by the traditional theory of the firm. This may mean that some part of its profits may be diverted to 'worthy causes', for example, to improving working conditions and the quality life of its workers or helping the local community, by adopting policies that benefit the environment. Even where most of these policies are on the firm's own terms, and thus can be considered as a 'free gift' that can be bestowed or revoked at will, their revocation is not 'costless' to the firm, since it harms its 'reputation' and 'good will' of its employees, suppliers, customers and the community in general. It follows that ethical policies and a sense of 'social responsibility' make perfect business sense and many firms pursuing such policies use them also as major marketing means.

For example, in Britain we have already examined the case of the major retailing firm Marks & Spencer in the Appendix to Chapter 9. Here we provide some information regarding the banking group Abbey National, which includes, according to its Annual Report 2002, social, ethical and environmental responsibilities in their management standards across the business at every level. They are committed to adopting policies and procedures across the Group that benefit the environment, for example, in the design and management of their buildings and in the material resources used, such as paper, water, energy and furnishings. Abbey National's ethical principles are set out in their policy 'How We Do Business', covering their responsibilities to their regulators, customers, employees, the community and suppliers. It also includes a commitment to incorporating ethical concerns in investment decisions on a case-by-case basis. Thus, when investing they take human rights issues into consideration and exercise special care before making investments in a number of areas, including the defence sector and organisations or activities that could have an adverse impact on public health or the environment. They believe there are real business benefits of being a good corporate citizen, and feel that their long-term financial success is closely linked to the way they manage their wider responsibilities. Abbey National is also a member of the FORGE Group, a consortium of UK banks and insurance companies, which developed management and reporting guidance on corporate social responsibility. It is expected that these guidelines will provide the foundation on which to build future environmental and social management and help achieve a higher level of commitment and consistency across the sector.

Society-linked social partnerships recognise the limits of initiatives of social responsibility by firms and consider the views of the major social partners (or stakeholders) explicitly, thus, achieving greater stability and success of their outcomes. Such arrangements can be based on social dialogue between the partners to achieve desirable objectives and can involve the company, its major stakeholders and the local community or, at a different level, employers federations, trade unions and the state. A very successful partnership of the latter type was formed in the early 1990s in the Irish Republic involving employers, trade unions and the government to achieve industrial peace and, through reforms, to accelerate economic growth. Taken together with investment policies, the social partnership resulted in the Irish economy growing at an average annual real rate in excess of 10%, which transformed the Irish economy in less than a decade from a cohesion country to one of the richest among the 15 member states of the EU.

The best example of a social partnership at a supra-national level is the Social Charter of the EU, referred to earlier. The launch of the Single Market programme in 1986 eventually led to the Social Charter, signed in October 1989 by 11 states out of the then EU12 except the UK. The latter also signed it after the election of the Labour government in 1997, by which time the three newcomers (Austria, Finland and Sweden) had already accepted it. The Social Charter consists of 29 articles under the headings of: improvement of living and working conditions; right of freedom of movement; right to social protection; employment and remuneration; right to freedom and collective bargaining; right to vocational training; right of all to equal treatment; right to information, consultation and worker participation; right to health protection and safety at the workplace; protection of children and adolescents and elderly and disabled persons. The rationale of the Social Charter is provided by the realisation that economic growth requires the consensus of all participants, and thus the EC sees the dialogue between management and labour as a crucial element. These consultations between management and labour can result in recommendations to be put to the European Council and may be adopted as Council decisions, having legal binding. In this respect there was a divergence of opinion, particularly regarding worker participation in company boards, stretching from the Anglo-American approach of 'allowing management to manage' or the 'right to hire and fire' without interference, to the German or Franco-Belgian models of different degrees of workers' representation on management boards (Petrochilos 1991). The Anglo-American model is based on the 'engineering' approach to economics, while the continental European model of the social market derives from the Greek 'ethics-related view of economics', which is not value-free but has a strong ethical foundation, based on the concept of *kalokagathia*, discussed at the beginning of this chapter.

15.8   A STAKEHOLDER APPROACH TO BUSINESS ETHICS

Intimately related to the preceding discussion is the stakeholder approach, that has been developed in response to disquiet felt with the neoclassical theory of the firm and the latter's sole objective of the maximisation of profits to its owners, i.e., its shareholders. The stakeholder approach follows the development of the theory of the firm, as discussed in Chapter 3. It is recalled that while the managerial theories of the firm have introduced explicitly managers' aspirations as an objective of the firm, the behavioural and organizational theories have expanded this by considering the firm as a coalition of, often, conflicting interests of various groups, such as owners, managers, employees, suppliers and the like, and have sought to illustrate how conflict can be resolved.

The stakeholder approach simply asserts that the firm is required to take account of the interests of all groups affected by the firm. Freeman has defined stakeholder as 'any individual or group who can affect or is affected by the actions, decisions, policies, practices, or goals of the organisation' (Freeman 1984, p. 25). In other words, there are various groups of people that have certain 'stakes' or interests in a business, that the latter needs to address. In the development of the concept we can now distinguish 'primary stakeholders', i.e., those having an official or contractual relationship with the business, which include shareholders (investors), managers, employees, suppliers and customers, as well as its board of directors and 'secondary' or 'public stakeholders', i.e., those having a looser contractual relationship with the firm, such as the government and local authorities (municipalities) offering infrastructure to the firm and receiving taxes or rates from it, though other authors may add trade associations, competitors, environmental groups and many more to the second list. It is interesting to note at this stage the importance of various organisational stakeholders to managers of American corporations. Posner and Schmidt (1984) have asked executive, middle and supervisory managers to rank various stakeholders in a scale from 1 to 7 (1 = lowest, 7 = highest). The executive managers produced the following list: customers (6.40), myself (6.28), subordinates (6.14), employees (6.01), bosses (5.82), co-workers (5.81), colleagues (5.75), managers (5.75), owners (5.30), general public (4.52), stockholders (4.51), elected public officials (3.79), government bureaucrats (2.90). What is interesting is that both supervisory and middle managers are equally narcissistic about their own importance having put 'myself' first and second, respectively in their rankings, but they have also ranked 'customers' seventh and fourth, thus, confirming Gandhi's quotation that: 'The customer is the most important person in our business', given at the beginning of this book.

It is the recognition of this 'plurality of values' of the stakeholder approach that provides the link with business ethics and, thus, it is relevant in the present context. Underlying the stakeholder approach is the ethical imperative that firms are mandated in their relationship to their shareholders and stakeholders to act in the best interests and for the benefit of their shareholders, employees, suppliers and customers and to respect and fulfil their rights. Respect and justice towards these rights act as a constraint to profit maximisation. Whereas a 'stockholder' approach focuses on financial and economic aspects, a 'stakeholder' approach encompasses wider interests of an ethical, ecological, political and human welfare nature, in addition to economic interests. It follows that the stakeholder approach is 'a means of studying managers' social and moral responsibility strategies, actions, and outcomes toward other stakeholders. The stakeholder approach is a pragmatic way of understanding multiple, competing political, economic, and moral claims of a host of constituencies' (Weiss 1994, p. 29).

At a practical level, for the stakeholder approach to be an effective tool at management's hands what is required is a framework to map and, subsequently, manage present and future corporate relationships with individuals or groups who affect or are affected by the corporation's actions and policies. This is referred to as a stakeholder analysis and it can be anticipated, rather than result from a crisis situation. It follows that stakeholder analysis is akin to the cost–benefit analysis, discussed above.

For the purposes of this introductory chapter on ethics in business, this is as far as we need to take this discussion. For those interested in the stakeholder approach or any of the other aspects referred to above consulting, the references can be a starting point for further study.

15.9 EPILOGUE

The preceding discussion has considered some of the basic approaches underlying business ethics. It has delved at some length on the teachings of the ancient Greeks, on which much of the subsequent developments on ethics are based. Among others, the discussion has shown that Classical Hellenic economics is not value free, but has a strong ethical foundation, which is crystallized in the concept of *kalokagathia*, therefore, as we understand the term today, it is akin to political economy. Ancient Greeks were not interested in economics *per se*, but in what economics could do for the well being of their community and how it could cement social cohesion. It is for this reason that they subordinated economics to the greater good of society. Thus, Hellenic economics is judgmental and interventionist. In this respect, it is similar to other approaches to economics, which also are not value free, but interventionist.

So what is the relevance of the foregone discussion for our present issue, that of business ethics? Xenophon, among the ancient writers is much more pragmatic, but his insistence on *kalokagathia* means that in order to have a demarcation between greed and sound business ethics, money-making must be achieved by honourable means (Baeck 1994, p. 57). In other words, the Socratic ideal of 'how one should live' in this context becomes 'how one should behave'. Thus, if people, and in particular top management, were following the fundamental ethical principles of the ancients of honesty, justice and uprightness in their business dealings, we would not have witnessed the recent scandals, business crises and upheavals in the capital markets. Ruskin too, reminiscent of Plato, frames his economic agent in terms of duty to society rather than duty to making money and advocates coordinated action to deal with market failures and externalities. Wicksteed, in turn, sees no difference between what we do in business and what we do in the rest of our time, since 'our conduct in business is but a phase or part of our conduct in life'. Ruskin, Senior and Wicksteed find no difficulty in accommodating the ethical principles of the ancients to the behaviour of the businessmen of their day. On the contrary they expect them to behave in an honourable way. This shows that there is really no difference between ethics and business ethics.

Naturally, similar arguments can be advanced with reference to the other approaches to ethics we have considered, briefly, above. All these approaches have in common one element, namely, the need for business to assume wider social responsibilities. We have already seen that Marxist thought was influenced considerably by ancient Greek literature. The same can be said today about the social market model of continental Europe, Keynesianism or post-Keynesianism. There too we have a strong ethical foundation (Keynes 1931, p. 329) and a concern for society, reminiscent of the Greeks. Nowadays perhaps nothing exemplifies the dilemma in starker terms than the difference in approach to dealing with industrial relations. On the one hand, the Anglo-American model decrees that management knows best and must be free to hire and fire, and on the other hand, the continental social market model promotes cooperation between the social partners to resolve problems through social dialogue. It is interesting that Mrs. Thatcher as Prime Minister had expressed her disdain at the EU's social policy and refused to accept the Social Charter, advocating social dialogue and cooperation, by suggesting that they (the Conservative government) had not rolled back the boundaries of the state only to have them re-imposed by Europe. This is merely another manifestation of the clash of the two approaches to economics, mentioned earlier. The 'engineering' approach, on the one hand, and the 'ethics'-based approach emanating from the Greeks, on the other. And it is not too simplistic to say that the Anglo-American model promotes the first, whilst the continental model is based on the second. And if this sounds harsh one has to remember Mrs. Thatcher's saying 'There is no such thing as society'. The Greeks would have abhorred such an idea.

SUMMARY

In this chapter we have examined the nature of ethics and how ethical questions are intimately related to everyday business life. We have sought to provide a detailed description and analysis of the classical value system of the ancient Greeks centred on the concept of *kalokagathia*, which itself is based on the concepts of justice and honesty. This provides the basis of understanding not only the alternative approaches to ethics, such as utilitarianism, deontology and the rights-based approach, which we have briefly, examined but also much of the ongoing discussion on business ethics. Thus, the discussion on corporate governance and ethics, social responsibility and social partnerships and the stakeholder approach are manifestations of the basic view that businesses have wider social responsibilities that go beyond the mere confines of profit maximization of the neoclassical theory of the firm.

APPENDIX: THE STRENGTHENING OF THE OECD CORPORATE GOVERNANCE CODE[1]

It is recalled that in the discussion of Chapter 15 we had cause to consider the OECD corporate governance code and to refer to efforts undertaken currently to strengthening this code, in order to rebuild investor confidence in financial markets, that had been seriously affected negatively in recent years. The OECD is already consulting a number of international corporate governance experts, in an attempt to revise and expand the code, which was approved in 1999.

In addition, the OECD is to consult businesses, trade unions, non-governmental organisations and others, and also to survey its member states in order to find out what scope there is for consensus on a revised and tougher code, to be approved by ministers in the spring of 2004.

While the original code was brought in as an international response to the financial crises in Asia, Russia and the developing countries in the 1990s, the current crisis had its roots within the developed countries of the OECD. The reason was that the recent corporate scandals in the US and Europe went a long way to undermine investor confidence, which exacerbated a natural correction in the financial markets after the almost continuous rise they experienced during the 1990s. These scandals had to do with misleading financial reporting and negligent and misleading auditing.

While the headline cases in the US included Enron, Tyco, WorldCom and the accounting/auditing firm Anderson, other cases of fraud involved rogue trading in the Allied Irish Bank in which one of their traders was sentenced to seven and a half years for concealing trading losses of $700 million. Indeed, research by the accounting firm Ernst & Young reveals that newly promoted managers are more likely to commit the largest frauds. Managers are seen as more potentially corrupt than employees. According to the Ernst & Young survey in global fraud, instances of fraud are forecast to rise, as economic pressures mount and managers come under increasing pressure to perform. The reason is that companies are setting ambitious targets that are unattainable, leaving no room for managers but perform accounting gymnastics.

Similar research by another accountancy firm, KPMG, also shows that the cost of fraud in the UK is increasing. Thus, UK fraud cases in 2002 increased to €717 million as compared with €244 million in 2001. Also, cases involving public sector fraud rose from €20 million in 2001 to €318 million in 2002. The research by KPMG endorses the view that management is increasingly resorting to fraud.

Given the above developments it is no wonder that OECD looks at the toughening of its business code as a way of dealing with the problem of fraud. The Financial Stability Forum, established in Basle, Switzerland in the wake of the Asian crisis, concluded recently that restoring confidence in the quality and integrity of external audits was the 'single most critical' element in re-establishing trust in financial reporting.

According to the OECD, there was now a need to establish independent oversight bodies for auditing companies, because self-regulation was not sufficient.

The revised OECD corporate governance code is likely to include detailed recommendations covering the role of lawyers, financial analysts and rating agencies; greater protection for shareholders; urging institutional investors to take a more active role, and requiring them to disclose what they do with their voting rights; greater transparency in corporate structures involving cross-shareholdings and pyramids of holding companies, as well as the use of shell companies to disguise ownership; and a definition of independence in the context of boards, audit committees and other oversight bodies. Also, the intention is that business ethics should be part of the new code.

The OECD emphasised that the corporate governance code should be extended not only to listed companies but also to cover state-owned enterprises and how governments managed corporate assets. There is a need for the role of the state as a minority or majority shareholder to be subject to the same rules as for the private sector.

However, while it was relatively easy to agree to the general principles of the 1999 corporate code, as given earlier in the chapter, experts believe that agreeing to more specific rules, as envisaged, may prove much more difficult.

Note

1. The above discussion is based on: Ashworth J., 'Managers "turning to fraud to hit targets" ', *The Times*, 3/2/2003 and Betts P., 'OECD may toughen its business code', *Financial Times*, 15/11/2002.

BIBLIOGRAPHY

Adkins, A.W.H. (1960), *A study in Greek Values: Merit and Responsibility*, Oxford University Press.

Aristotle (1953), *Nicomachean Ethics,* translated by J.A.K. Thomson, Penguin.

_____ (1962), *Politics*, translated by T.A. Sinclair, Penguin.

Baeck, L. (1994), *The Mediterranean Tradition in Economic Thought*, Routledge.

Cassel, D. (2001), 'Human Rights and Business Responsibilities in the Global Marketplace', *Business Ethics Quarterly*, **11**(2), 261–274.

Dean, P.J. (1997), 'Examining the Profession and the Practice of Business Ethics', *Journal of Business Ethics*, **16**, 1637–1649.

Donaldson, T. (1996), 'Values in Tension: Ethics Away from Home', *Harvard Business Review*, September–October, 48–62.

Euripides (1998), *Electra*, translated by J. Davie, Penguin.

Freeman, R.E. (1984), *Strategic Management: A Stakeholder Approach*, Pitman.

Friedman, M. (1962), *Capitalism and Freedom*, Chicago University Press.

_____ (1970), 'The Social Responsibility of Business is to Increase Its Profits', *New York Times Magazine*, 13 September, 33.

Gouldner, A.W. (1965), *Enter Plato: Classical Greece and the Origins of Social Theory*, Basic Books.

Gordon, B. (1975), *Economic Analysis Before Adam Smith: Hesiod to Lessius*, Macmillan.

Griffiths, M.R. and Lucas, J.R. (1996), *Ethical Economics*, Macmillan.

Henderson, W. (2000), *John Ruskin's Political Economy*, Routledge.

Hilton, T. (2000), *John Ruskin The Later Years*, Yale University Press, New Haven and London.

Hobbes, T. (1651), *Leviathan*, C.B. MacPherson (ed.), Penguin, 1985.

Huby, P. (1967), *Greek Ethics*, Macmillan.

Keynes, J.M. (1931), *Essays in Persuasion, The Collected Writings of J.M. Keynes*, Vol. IX, Macmillan.

Langholm, O. (1979), *Price and Value in the Aristotelian Tradition*, Universitetsforlaget.

Lowry, S.T. (1987), *The Archaeology of Economic Ideas: The Classical Greek Tradition*, Duke University Press.

Meikle, S. (1995), *Aristotle's Economic Thought*, Clarendon.

Mellahi, K. and Wood, G. (2003), *The Ethical Business: Challenges and Controversies*, Palgrave.

Mill, S.J. (1861), *Utilitarianism: Liberty and Representative Government*, London, Everyman, 1964.

OECD (1999), *OECD Principles of Corporate Governance*, Paris, OECD.

Petrochilos, G.A. (1991), 'The Economic and Social Dimensions of the Single European Market: The Issues', *British Review of Economic Issues*, **13**(31), October.

_____ (1999), 'The Hellenic Contribution to Economic Thought', *Global Business and Economic Review*, **1**(2).

_____ (2002a), '*Kalokagathia*: The Ethical Basis of Hellenic Political Economy and its Influence from Plato to Ruskin and Sen', *History of Political Economy*, **34**(3), 599–631.

_____ (2002b), '(Business) Ethics: The Hellenic Heritage from Plato to the Present', in Kantarelis D. (ed.) *Global Business & Economics Review – Anthology 2002*, Selected Papers 2002 Business & Economics Society International Conference, pp. 6–18.

Plato (1955), *Republic*, translated by H.D.P. Lee, Penguin.

_____ (1993), *Nomoi (The Laws)*, Kaktos, Athens (in Greek).

Posner, B.Z. and Schmidt, W.H. (1984), 'Values and the American Manager: An Update', *California Management Review*, **26**(3), Spring, 80–94.

Robbins, L. (1935), *An Essay on the Nature and Significance of Economic Science*, 2nd edn, Macmillan.

Ruskin, J. (1994), *Unto this Last: Four Essays on the First Principles of Economics*, George Allen 1906, new edition with a new introduction by P. Cain, Routledge/Thoemmes Press.

Scott, W. (1947), 'The Greek Influence on Adam Smith', *Archive of Economic and Social Sciences*, **27–29**, 81–108 (in Greek).

Sen, A. (1987), *On Ethics and Economics*, Blackwell.

Senior, N. (1928), *Industrial Efficiency and Social Economy*, **I** and **II**, P.S. King & Son, (original manuscripts arranged and edited by S. Leon Levy).

Singer, P. (1993), *Practical Ethics*, 2nd edn, Cambridge, Cambridge University Press.

Sorel, T. and Hendry, J. (1994), *Business Ethics*, Butterworth-Heineman Ltd.

Stone, I.F. (1989), *The Trial of Socrates*, Picador.

Tzermias, P. (1995), *The Other Byzantium: The Contribution of Constantinople to Europe*, 2nd edn., Elliniki Euroekdotiki (in Greek).

UNCTAD (1999), 'The Social Responsibility of Transnational Corporations', Chapter XII, *World Investment Report: Foreign Direct Investment and the Challenge of Development*, UNCTAD, New York, Geneva.

Weiss, J.W. (1994), *Business Ethics: A Managerial, Stakeholder Approach*, Wadsworth Publishing Company.

Welch, C. (1998), 'Utilitarianism', in Eatwell, J., Milgate, M. and Newman, P. (eds), *The New Palgrave Dictionary of Economics*, Palgrave.

Wicksteed, P.H. (1914), 'The Scope and Method of Political Economy in the Light of the "Marginal" Theory of Value and Distribution', *Economic Journal*, **XXIV**(93), March, 1–23, reprinted in *The Common Sense of Political Economy* (edited with an introduction by L. Robbins), Vol. II, Routledge, 1938.

Wilson, R. (1997), *Economics, Ethics and Religion: Jewish, Christian and Muslim Economic Thought*, Macmillan.

Woodhouse, C.M. (1986), *George Gemistos Plethon: The Last of the Hellenes*, Oxford: Clarendon.

Xenophon (1939), *Oikonomikos*, translated by E. Moros (in Greek) Zacharopoulos, Athens.

_____ (1939), *Apomnimoneumata (Memorabilia)*, translated by K. Varnalis (in Greek) Zacharopoulos.

_____ (1939), *Poroi (Revenues)*, translated by E. Moros (in Greek) Zacharopoulos, Athens.

Authors' Index

Subject Index